READINGS IN

The Philosophy
of Religion

READINGS IN
The Philosophy
of Religion

JOHN A. MOURANT

Professor of Philosophy
The Pennsylvania State University

New York
THOMAS Y. CROWELL COMPANY

For

MARGARET

PREFACE

WITH THE DEEPENING UNREST of our times there has appeared an ever-increasing interest in the perennial problems of religion. Many of these problems, being equally the concern of the philosopher, have their place in what has traditionally been termed the philosophy of religion. This book has been planned to present at first hand the more significant answers that have been given both in the past and in the present to some of the basic questions that fall within the philosophy of religion. Without attempting to resolve all the unsolved problems and issues in the philosophy of religion, we have presented a diversity of viewpoints, designed to stimulate the interest of the student and to give him a clearer understanding of some of the basic problems.

The selections have been drawn from a wide range of philosophical traditions, such as scepticism, scholasticism, rationalism, and idealism. Similarly, adequate representation has been given to different religious traditions. As would be expected, Western thought and Christian tradition have been favored because these have a background that is familiar to the student. At all times every attempt has been made to avoid overemphasizing any one point of view, so that both the student and the instructor may have greater freedom to choose and to study the selections of their own interests.

Since one of our principal objectives is to stimulate the interest of the student in the basic problems of the philosophy of religion, we feel that this can best be accomplished by directing the student to the original sources. By examining and reflecting upon the contrasting contributions of the great religious and philosophical thinkers of the past and present, the student should achieve not only a deeper appreciation of philosophical and religious thought but also a quickening of any latent dialectical skill he may possess.

The diversity and the number of selections, in combination with the general introductions and the headnotes preceding each selection, make this book suitable for use in place of the conventional type of text. With the guidance of the instructor it provides greater flexibility in use in addition to all the other advantages of the conventional text. The instructor can organize the material and direct the study of the students and find sufficiently representative points of view to make the course rewarding to all regardless of their particular religious faith or lack of any religious faith.

Some readers will be disappointed, perhaps, by the exclusion of humanism, and others may be provoked that nothing is included on the relation of religion to social problems. But there are limits to what can be encompassed within a course of readings of this type, and we have gone beyond what could possibly be covered in the usual course. At least we have assured instructor and student of a wide latitude of choice by providing an abundance of material.

In conclusion we wish to acknowledge our indebtedness to our colleagues John M. Anderson, Henry A. Finch, and Ernest H. Freund in the Department of Philosophy, and Joseph Dahmus in the Department of History, at The Pennsylvania State University for their many good suggestions and wise counsel. Our debt is even greater to Margaret E. Mourant for her constant encouragement and her very able assistance in the task of reading proof and in the preparation of the manuscript.

JOHN A. MOURANT

State College, Pennsylvania
December 22, 1953

CONTENTS

Part One

GOD

WHAT MEN HAVE WRITTEN on the subject of God is so vast in scope and so detailed in treatment, that anyone attempting to classify these writings is forced from the beginning to set limits for his work. Even so, any limitation of the subject still leaves the compiler with an extensive amount of material and almost as great a difficulty in making his selections as if he had the whole of the material to classify. In keeping with the purposes noted in our Preface our task was partially simplified with the limitation of our selections primarily to philosophers. But there are many philosophers and so again we had to choose, at times almost arbitrarily but always with the hope that our selections will answer some need on the part of the reader. We have endeavored to choose as nearly as possible the more outstanding philosophers and those representative of different points of view. Hence we have selected from sceptics as well as believers, from atheists as well as theists and pantheists. Finally, we have had to limit the subject of God to two main types of problems: *first,* the arguments or proofs for the existence of God; *second,* the nature of God and more particularly here, the problem of the method by which we come to have a knowledge of God. And as a kind of epilogue to the entire discussion we have included some contemporary perspectives on the problem of God, this time from three philosophers representative of the major religious faiths of the Western world.

For the guidance of our readers we now add a few introductory comments concerning each of the selections in the order in which they appear in the book.

The selections from Calvin, Anselm, Aquinas, Pascal, and Feuerbach all deal primarily with the question of God's existence. The order they follow is chronological, with the exception of Calvin, whom we have placed first because his statement is very brief and serves

1

to introduce the topic. Although Calvin is not primarily a philosopher, he expresses well what some philosophers have urged, namely, that the belief in God is universal; he then adds, as a theologian might, that even the contumacy of the wicked cannot escape the sense of God's presence. The argument of Anselm exhibits the greatest dialectical skill and originality and it is as challenging today as it was to Gaunilon in the eleventh century or to Kant in the eighteenth century. It has been expressed in somewhat different ways by Descartes and Leibniz, and our selection from Spinoza includes his version of this argument. The famous "five ways" of Aquinas are quite the opposite in character. Here the proofs of God's existence proceed not from an idea in the mind,—and let it be noted that Aquinas vigorously rejects the argument of Anselm,—but always from some aspect of experience. Aquinas' proofs for the existence of God do not have the same originality as Anselm's ontological argument, for Aquinas was indebted to many of his predecessors for earlier formulations of these arguments. The argument from design (Aquinas' fifth way), e.g., dates back at least as far as Plato. The contribution of Aquinas consisted in the revisions and the more adequate formulations he gave to each of these arguments.

At this point in the books, assuming that all these arguments have been studied, some of our readers may have decided that Anselm was right; some, that there was really no need to read beyond the selection from Calvin; and others that Aquinas has said the last word on the subject of the existence of God. Still others may be completely unpersuaded, the more rebellious already looking forward to Feuerbach and the remainder ready perhaps to be charmed by Pascal's eloquence and alliance with the "reasons of the heart." There is little doubt that Pascal is persuasive, for he appeals powerfully to one part of our nature—to our feelings and emotions, to our instinct for gain. We may not like his Jansenism,* nor be inclined to accept his deprecation of reason and his despairing attitude toward human nature, but we cannot question his fervor and sincerity. To many his appeal is as irresistible as his wager is delightful.

Feuerbach contradicts all that has gone before and therefore his work does not make for easy reading at this point. For many he will be difficult to approach objectively because he represents the viewpoint of atheism. Atheists are no longer rare, but usually they are content to state their belief in atheism rather than give a systematic

---

* The doctrine of Cornelius Jansen (Jansenius), 1581-1638, Bishop of Ypres, which virtually denied the freedom of the will and the possibility of resisting divine grace.

defense of that position. Some of them (especially the young) use a kind of pretended atheism as a way of asserting their independence or of frightening others and attracting attention to themselves. Feuerbach attracted attention in his day, not because he was interested in frightening people or asserting his independence, but rather because he was deadly serious about the whole subject of the existence of God and completely convinced in his own mind that God could be identified with the mind, attributes, feelings, and emotions of man. And it was because he was so deadly serious in his convictions that he argued in such a systematic way for his position. Nietzsche did little more than state that "God was dead"; Feuerbach tried to prove that religion was only a dream. And one of his disciples was to say that religion was an opiate.

We hope that our readers will not be convinced by Feuerbach, for the selections which follow, on the assumption that God *does* exist, have to do with the nature of God and the knowledge that men can obtain of Him. The selections from Dionysius, Maimonides, Cajetan, and Hume all center around one particular problem and for that reason have been placed together and should be read together. The problem concerns the knowledge that we can have of God: not, primarily, *what* attributes we can ascribe to God, as *how we can ascribe* such attributes to Him. The possible answers which these four selections propose seem to be limited to the unknowability of God, to positive and negative affirmations, to an analogical knowledge of God, and to the conception of anthropomorphism and a finite deity.

The *Divine Names* of Dionysius the Areopagite (Pseudo-Dionysius) stands out as the classical treatise in early Christian thought on the nature of our knowledge of God; it is, in addition, the source of much of the mysticism in Christian thought. Dionysius was frequently quoted and commented on by mystics, theologians, and philosophers throughout the Middle Ages; Aquinas, for example, was definitely influenced by his *via negativa*. The conception that many philosophers and theologians have of the incomprehensibility of God and that mystics have of the "darkness of unknowing" finds its source in the *Divine Names*. Hence, although the selection is difficult and often quite obscure, it deserves a place in a study of this nature if only because of its extraordinary influence on so many religious thinkers.

Whereas Dionysius accepts both the positive and the negative ways of approaching a knowledge of God, Maimonides is interested primarily in the *via negativa* and states emphatically that the only true attributes of God are the negative attributes. His analysis of the possible relation between God and man leads him to the notion of

the *Deus Absconditus* and the denial of the possibility of any analogical knowledge of God. Cajetan, on the contrary, accepts the possibility of analogical knowledge of God and endeavors to establish it
on the firm foundation of an analogy of proportionality—an effort
which many regard as his original contribution to the problem. At
the same time he does not deny the validity of the *via negativa.*

The selection from Hume is a bit more extensive than the three
preceding it, and admits of several different interpretations. If we
consider the dialogue from the point of view of Cleanthes, we can
maintain that the principal viewpoint presented is that of anthropomorphism and a finite deity. Hume's use of analogy here contrasts sharply with the function of analogy in the selection from
Cajetan; as applied by Hume, analogy leads to anthropomorphism
and a denial of all rationalistic conceptions of deity. Some modern
philosophers of religion have been strongly influenced by the conclusions of Hume and have revived with some degree of success the
idea of a finite deity. In general, philosophers within the Judaeo-
Christian tradition have tended to accept either the *via negativa*
or some form of the analogical principle, whereas Eastern philosophers have been almost wholly inclined toward a position of atheism
or the incomprehensibility of deity.

The positions outlined in the selections by Spinoza and Sankara
make an interesting contrast. Each presents us with a philosophy of
pantheism, Spinoza representing the best Western religious thought
on this topic, and Sankara representing the best Eastern religious
thought. Both selections demand close reading, although Spinoza's is
undoubtedly the more difficult and the more exhaustive in nature.
What is merely set forth in brilliant intuitions by Sankara is made
the subject of elaborate reasoning by Spinoza. Sankara's approach and
his entire argument are far more mystical in character than is
Spinoza's, which attempts to set down in mathematical and logical
order a pantheism based on substance, attributes, and modes. Sankara
is interested in the relation of the self to Brahman; Spinoza gives
attention to the relation of the universe to God and argues vigorously
for a deterministic universe.

The selection from Alexander's *Space, Time, and Deity* we have
permitted to stand more or less by itself because of the difficulty
of placing it in any particular category. The author is not concerned
with any proof for the existence of God, declaring that all such proofs
are invalid. Neither, according to Alexander, can God be defined,
nor is any attempt made to answer the historic questions of our
knowledge of God. Paradoxically, the author does assert more than

once that deity is a quality which is beyond all our knowledge. Still (to continue his argument), deity somehow is a quality and it would seem that it does exist in some potential way in the universe. God exists, but always potentially, as the universe at any particular point in its development strives toward deity; thus deity, or what may be said to be the full actuality of God, lies in the future. Despite the obscurities and even the inconsistencies of Alexander's view here, he does make a sincere attempt to found an original cosmology upon physical and biological categories.

Now that he has some knowledge of the history of this attempt to solve the problem of God in His existence and nature, the reader may well be curious concerning the views of his contemporaries within the great religious traditions of the West. To satisfy this curiosity, at least partially, the last three selections in Part One are representative of the thought of some of the more prominent modern philosophers within the traditions of Protestanism, Judaism, and Catholicism. The selection by Schweitzer is intent upon emphasizing the *ethical* character of Christianity in contrast to the logical nature of the religions of the East. Even the mysticism of Christianity, he insists, is ethical in character, whereas Eastern mysticism is logical in nature. In thus stressing the ethical, he reaffirms what has always been an important element in the religious and philosophical thought of Protestanism. It is not enough, according to Schweitzer, to know God; the individual must be united with God ethically, for this is the highest type of spirituality. It is the living God, revealed to man in Ethical Personality or Ethical Will, that is significant for man today.

This emphasis on a living God—an ethical union with God, rather than intellectual contemplation and understanding—receives a somewhat different, but nevertheless pronounced, emphasis in the selection by Martin Buber. Here we have the leading Jewish existentialist contending that the philosophical way of abstraction and knowledge will not lead man to God, but rather that any such "meeting" with God must be established through an existential relationship, through faith and what he calls the I-Thou relationship. By this means alone, according to Buber, can man be brought into a more concrete and intimate relation with God. Philosophy with its abstractions has led more often than not to the abandonment of God.

The selection from Maritain (the final selection in Part One) reveals something of this same trend, of the search for a more living and concrete relation between the individual and his God. Although Maritain emphasizes here, as he does so often in his other writings, the need for and value of reason and the importance of metaphysics, he has not been left untouched by the existentialist revolt of modern times. His notion of our intuition of Being-with-nothingness—which at least verbally, approaches the existentialist position—and of our intuition of Being in itself is significant. Although he does connect such intuitions with human reason, he accepts and adds these intuitions of existence to his traditionally Thomistic position to establish what he calls the "naturality of our knowledge of God."

THE EXISTENCE OF GOD

1

JOHN CALVIN

The Innateness of God *

CALVIN HAS little regard for those who would deny the existence of God or who would contend that religion is merely an invention of the mind of man. With a fervent faith, Calvin argues for the innateness of the idea of God, declaring that the existence of God is a matter of universal belief and one which "nature permits none to forget."

WE LAY IT DOWN as a position not to be controverted, that the human mind, even by natural instinct, possesses some sense of a Deity. For that no man might shelter himself under the pretext of ignorance, God hath given to all some apprehension of his existence, the memory of which he frequently and insensibly renews; so that, as men universally know that there is a God, and that he is their Maker, they must be condemned by their own testimony, for not having worshipped

---

* From *The Institutes of the Christian Religion* by John Calvin as translated by John Allen. Published by the Presbyterian Board of Education, 1936, pp. 21-24.

John Calvin (1509-64) studied law for a time, then turned to humanism. Finally, with his "conversion" in 1533, he broke with humanism, revolted from the Catholic Church, and devoted himself to what he termed the preaching of the "pure doctrine." He moved to Switzerland in 1536, published his famous *Institutes,* and then became the religious leader and ruler of Geneva in 1538. He remained there until his death and made Geneva a great world-wide center of Protestantism.

him and consecrated their lives to his service. If we seek for ignorance of a Deity, it is nowhere more likely to be found, than among tribes the most stupid and furthest from civilization. But, as the celebrated Cicero observes, there is no nation so barbarous, no race so savage; as not to be firmly persuaded of the being of a God. Even those who in other respects appear to differ but little from brutes, always retain some sense of religion; so fully are the minds of men possessed with this common principle, which is closely interwoven with their original composition. Now, since there has never been a country or family, from the beginning of the world, totally destitute of religion, it is a tacit confession, that some sense of the Divinity is inscribed on every heart. Of this opinion, idolatry itself furnishes ample proof. For we know how reluctantly man would degrade himself to exalt other creatures above him. His preference of worshipping a piece of wood or stone, to being thought to have no god, evinces the impression of a Deity on the human mind to be very strong, the obliteration of which is more difficult than a total change of the natural disposition; and this is certainly changed, whenever man leaves his natural pride, and voluntarily descends to such meannesses under the notion of worshipping God.

It is most absurd, then, to pretend, as is asserted by some, that religion was the contrivance of a few subtle and designing men, a political machine to confine the simple multitude to their duty, while those who inculcated the worship of God in others, were themselves far from believing that any god existed. I confess, indeed, that artful men have introduced many inventions into religion, to fill the vulgar with reverence, and strike them with terror, in order to obtain the greater command over their minds. But this they never could have accomplished, if the minds of men had not previously been possessed of a firm persuasion of the existence of God, from which the propensity to religion proceeds. And that they who cunningly imposed on the illiterate, under the pretext of religion, were themselves wholly destitute of any knowledge of God, is quite incredible. For though there were some in ancient times, and many arise in the present age, who deny the existence of God, yet, in spite of their reluctance, they are continually receiving proofs of what they desire to disbelieve. We read of no one guilty of more audacious or unbridled contempt of the Deity than Caligula; yet no man ever trembled with greater distress at any instance of Divine wrath, so that he was constrained to dread the Divinity whom he professed to despise. This you may always see exemplified in persons of similar character. For the most audacious contemners of God are most alarmed, even at the noise of a falling leaf. Whence arises this, but from the vengeance of the Divine Majesty, smiting their consciences the more powerfully in proportion to their efforts to fly from it? They try every refuge to hide themselves from the Lord's presence, and to efface it from their minds; but their attempts to elude it are all in vain. Though it may seem to disappear for a moment, it presently returns with increased violence; so that, if they have any remission of the anguish of conscience, it resembles the sleep of persons intoxicated, or subject to frenzy, who enjoy no placid rest while sleeping, being continually harassed with horrible and tremendous dreams. The impious themselves, therefore, exemplify the observation, that the idea of a God is never lost in the human mind.

It will always be evident to persons of correct judgment, that the idea of a Deity impressed on the mind of man is indelible. That all have by nature an innate persuasion of the Divine existence, a persuasion inseparable from their very constitution, we have abundant evidence in the contumacy of the wicked, whose furious struggles to extricate themselves from the fear of God are unavailing. Though Diagoras, and others like him, turn to ridicule what all ages have believed of religion; though Dionysius scoff at the judgment of Heaven —it is but a forced laughter, for the worm of a guilty conscience torments them within, worse than if they were seared with hot irons. I agree not with Cicero, that errors in process of time become obsolete, and that religion is increased and ameliorated daily. For the world, as will shortly be observed, uses its utmost endeavors to banish all knowledge of God, and tries every method of corrupting his worship. I only maintain, that while the stupid insensibility which the wicked wish to acquire, to promote their contempt of God, preys upon their minds, yet the sense of a Deity, which they ardently desire to extinguish is still strong, and frequently discovers itself. Whence we infer, that this is a doctrine, not first to be learned in the schools, but which every man from his birth is self-taught, and which, though many strain every nerve to banish it from them, yet nature itself permits none to forget. Now, if the end for which all men are born and live, be to know God,—and unless the knowledge of God have reached this point, it is uncertain and vain,—it is evident, that all who direct not every thought and action of life to this end, are degenerated from the law of their creation. Of this the heathen philosophers themselves were not ignorant. This was Plato's meaning, when he taught that the chief good of the soul consists in similitude to God, when the soul, having a clear knowledge of him, is wholly transformed into his likeness. The reasoning also of Gryllus, in Plutarch, is very accurate, when he affirms, that men entirely destitute of religion, not only do not excel the brutes, but are in many respects far more wretched, being obnoxious to evil under so many forms, and always dragging on a tumultuous and restless life. The worship of God is therefore the only thing which renders men superior to brutes, and makes them aspire to immortality.

2

ST. ANSELM

The Ontological Argument *

St. Anselm is the originator of the famous ontological argument for the existence of God, an argument that for centuries has found both defenders and critics within the history of philosophy. Decartes and Leibniz both accepted and modified the argument; on the other hand, St. Thomas Aquinas and Immanuel Kant were among its more severe critics. In this selection from the *Proslogium,* St. Anselm argues from the idea of God as absolute perfection to the necessary existence of God in reality. And he insists that we cannot even conceive the nonexistence of such a Being. The argument by St. Anselm is followed by a criticism of it by Gaunilon, taken from the Appendix, which argues (as did the later criticisms of St. Anselm) that his proof makes an unwarranted transition from the conceptual order to the real order. St. Anselm's Apologetic refutes the argument of Gaunilon and questions the validity of his example of the lost island.

. . . I began to ask myself whether there might be found a single argument which would require no other for its proof than itself alone; and alone would suffice to demonstrate that God truly exists, and that there is a supreme good requiring nothing else, which all other things require for their existence and well-being; and whatever we believe regarding the divine Being.

* From the *Proslogium,* translated by Sidney Norton Deane (Open Court, 1903), pp. 1-2, 6-9, 149-51, 158-59.

St. Anselm (1033-1109) studied at Avranches in Burgundy. He entered the Benedictine Order and became abbot at Bec in Normandy. He was named Archbishop of Canterbury in 1093 and retained that position until his death.

Although I often and earnestly directed my thought to this end, and at some times that which I sought seemed to be just within my reach, while again it wholly evaded my mental vision, at last in despair I was about to cease, as if from the search for a thing which could not be found. But when I wished to exclude this thought altogether, lest, by busying my mind to no purpose, it should keep me from other thoughts, in which I might be successful; then more and more, though I was unwilling and shunned it, it began to force itself upon me, with a kind of importunity. So, one day, when I was exceedingly wearied with resisting its importunity, in the very conflict of my thoughts, the proof of which I had despaired offered itself, so that I eagerly embraced the thoughts which I was strenuously repelling.

. . . . .

. . . I do not endeavor, O Lord, to penetrate thy sublimity, for in no wise do I compare my understanding with that; but I long to understand in some degree thy truth, which my heart believes and loves. For I do not seek to understand that I may believe, but I believe in order to understand. For this also I believe,—that unless I believed, I should not understand.

. . . . .

And so Lord, do thou, who dost give understanding to faith, give me, so far as thou knowest it to be profitable, to understand that thou art as we believe; and that thou art that which we believe. And, indeed, we believe that thou art a being than which nothing greater can be conceived. Or is there no such nature, since the fool hath said in his heart, there is no God? But, at any rate, this very fool, when he hears of this being of which I speak—a being than which nothing greater can be conceived—understands what he hears, and what he understands is in his understanding; although he does not understand it to exist.

For, it is one thing for an object to be in the understanding, and another to understand that the object exists. When a painter first conceives of what he will afterwards perform, he has it in his understanding, but he does not yet understand it to be, because he has not yet performed it. But after he has made the painting, he both has it in his understanding, and he understands that it exists, because he has made it.

Hence, even the fool is convinced that something exists in the understanding, at least, than which nothing greater can be conceived. For, when he hears of this, he understands it. And whatever is understood, exists in the understanding. And assuredly that, than which nothing greater can be conceived, cannot exist in the understanding alone. For, suppose it exists in the understanding alone: then it can be conceived to exist in reality; which is greater.

Therefore, if that, than which nothing greater can be conceived, exists in the understanding alone, the very being, than which nothing greater can be conceived, is one, than which a greater can be conceived. But obviously this is impossible. Hence, there is no doubt that there exists a being, than which nothing greater can be conceived, and it exists both in the understanding and in reality.

.　.　.　.　.

And it assuredly exists so truly, that it cannot be conceived not to exist. For, it is possible to conceive of a being which cannot be conceived not to exist, and this is greater than one which can be conceived not to exist. Hence, if that, than which nothing greater can be conceived, can be conceived not to exist, it is not that, than which nothing greater can be conceived. But this is an irreconcilable contradiction. There is, then, so truly a being than which nothing greater can be conceived to exist, that it cannot even be conceived not to exist; and this being thou art, O Lord, our God.

So truly, therefore, dost thou exist, O Lord, my God, that thou canst not be conceived not to exist; and rightly. For if a mind could conceive of a being better than thee, the creature would rise above the Creator; and this is most absurd. And, indeed, whatever else there is, except thee alone, can be conceived not to exist. To thee alone, therefore, it belongs to exist more truly than all other beings, and hence in a higher degree than all others. For, whatever else exists does not exist so truly, and hence in a less degree it belongs to it to exist. Why, then, has the fool said in his heart, there is no God, since it is so evident, to a rational mind, that thou dost exist in the highest degree of all? Why, except that he is dull and a fool?

.　.　.　.　.

IN BEHALF OF THE FOOL

AN ANSWER TO THE ARGUMENT OF ANSELM IN THE PROSLOGIUM
BY GAUNILON, A MONK OF MARMOUTIER

5. . . . if it should be said that a being which cannot be even conceived in terms of any fact, is in the understanding, I do not deny that this being is, accordingly, in my understanding. But since through

this fact it can in no wise attain to real existence also, I do not yet concede to it that existence at all, until some certain proof of it shall be given.

For he who says that this being exists, because otherwise the being which is greater than all will not be greater than all, does not attend strictly to what he is saying. For I do not yet say, no, I even deny or doubt that this being is greater than any real object. Nor do I concede to it any other existence than this (if it should be called existence) which it has when the mind, according to a word merely heard, tries to form the image of an object absolutely unknown to it.

How, then, is the veritable existence of that being proved to me from the assumption, by hypothesis, that it is greater than all other beings? For I should still deny this, or doubt your demonstration of it, to this extent, that I should not admit that this being is in my understanding and concept even in the way in which many objects whose real existence is uncertain and doubtful, are in my understanding and concept. For it should be proved first that this being itself really exists somewhere; and then, from the fact that it is greater than all, we shall not hesitate to infer that it also subsists in itself.

6. For example: it is said that somewhere in the ocean is an island, which, because of the difficulty, or rather the impossibility, of discovering what does not exist, is called the lost island. And they say that this island has an inestimable wealth of all manner of riches and delicacies in greater abundance than is told of the Islands of the Blest; and that having no owner or inhabitant, it is more excellent than all other countries, which are inhabited by mankind, in the abundance with which it is stored.

Now if someone should tell me that there is such an island, I should easily understand his words, in which there is no difficulty. But suppose that he went on to say, as if by a logical inference: "You can no longer doubt that this island which is more excellent than all lands exists somewhere, since you have no doubt that it is in your understanding. And since it is more excellent not to be in the understanding alone, but to exist both in the understanding and in reality, for this reason it must exist. For if it does not exist, any land which really exists will be more excellent than it; and so the island already understood by you to be more excellent will not be more excellent."

If a man should try to prove to me by such reasoning that this island truly exists, and that its existence should no longer be doubted, either I should believe that he was jesting, or I know not which I ought to regard as the greater fool: myself, supposing that I should allow this proof; or him, if he should suppose that he had established with any certainty the existence of this island. For he ought to show first that the hypothetical excellence of this island exists as a real and indubitable fact, and in no wise as any unreal object, or one whose existence is uncertain, in my understanding.

ANSELM'S APOLOGETIC
IN REPLY TO GAUNILON'S ANSWER IN BEHALF OF THE FOOL

But, you say, it is as if one should suppose an island in the ocean, which surpasses all lands in its fertility, and which, because of the difficulty, or rather the impossibility, of discovering what does not exist, is called a lost island; and should say that there can be no doubt that this island truly exists in reality, for this reason, that one who hears it described easily understands what he hears.

Now I promise confidently that if any man shall devise anything existing either in reality or in concept alone (except that than which a greater cannot be conceived) to which he can adapt the sequence of my reasoning, I will discover that thing, and will give him his lost island, not to be lost again.

But it now appears that this being than which a greater is inconceivable cannot be conceived not to be, because it exists on so assured a ground of truth; for otherwise it would not exist at all.

Hence, if any one says that he conceives this being not to exist, I say that at the time when he conceives of this either he conceives of a being than which a greater is inconceivable, or he does not conceive at all. If he does not conceive, he does not conceive of the nonexistence of that of which he does not conceive. But if he does conceive, he certainly conceives of a being which cannot be even conceived not to exist. For if it could be conceived not to exist, it could be conceived to have a beginning and an end. But this is impossible.

He, then, who conceives of this being conceives of a being which cannot be even conceived not to exist; but he who conceives of this being does not conceive that it does not exist; else he conceives what is inconceivable. The nonexistence, then, of that than which a greater cannot be conceived is inconceivable.

3

ST. THOMAS AQUINAS

The Five Ways *

ST. THOMAS' celebrated "five ways" need little introduction. After distinguishing between the two types of demonstration, he argues that the existence of God can be demonstrated from His effects which are known to us, assuming of course the principle that every effect has a cause. Hence each argument basically is a causal one and it is this which gives a unity to the five proofs. Yet each one is also distinct in that each takes as a starting point different observable effects in the natural order, namely, motion, efficient cause, possibility, grades of perfection, and order. It should be noted that in all of the proofs the possibility of an infinite regress is denied, and that the eternity of the world is assumed.

WHETHER IT CAN BE DEMONSTRATED THAT GOD EXISTS **

Objection 1. It seems that the existence of God cannot be demonstrated. For it is an article of faith that God exists. But what is of faith cannot be demonstrated, because a demonstration produces scientific knowledge, whereas faith is of the unseen, as is clear from the Apostle (*Heb*. xi. 1). Therefore it cannot be demonstrated that God exists.

Obj. 2. Further, essence is the middle term of demonstration. But we cannot know in what God's essence consists, but solely in what it does not consist, as Damascene says. Therefore we cannot demonstrate that God exists.

Obj. 3. Further, if the existence of God were demonstrated, this could only be from His effects. But His effects are not proportioned to Him, since He is infinite and His effects are finite, and between

* Reprinted from the *Summa Theologica* with the permission of Benziger Brothers, Inc., publishers, Question 2, Articles 2 and 3.

St. Thomas Aquinas (1225-74) was born at Rocca Secca near the Abbey of Monte Cassino in Italy. He attended the University of Naples and in 1244 entered the Dominican Order. His education was continued under Albert the Great at Cologne. He received his license to teach at the University of Paris in 1256 and taught there intermittently until 1272. He died in 1274 while on his way to the Council of Lyons. He was canonized in 1323, named Angelic Doctor in 1567, and declared by Pope Leo XIII in 1880 to be Patron of Catholic Schools.

** Question 2, Article 2.

the finite and infinite there is no proportion. Therefore, since a cause cannot be demonstrated by an effect not proportioned to it, it seems that the existence of God cannot be demonstrated.

On the contrary, the Apostle says: *The invisible things of Him are clearly seen, being understood by the things that are made* (Rom. i. 20). But this would not be unless the existence of God could be demonstrated through the things that are made; for the first thing we must know of anything is, whether it exists.

I answer that, Demonstration can be made in two ways: One is through the cause, and is called *propter quid,* and this is to argue from what is prior absolutely. The other is through the effect, and is called a demonstration *quia;* this is to argue from what is prior relatively only to us. When an effect is better known to us than its cause, from the effect we proceed to the knowledge of the cause. And from every effect the existence of its proper cause can be demonstrated, so long as its effects are better known to us; because, since every effect depends upon its cause, if the effect exists, the cause must pre-exist. Hence the existence of God, in so far as it is not self-evident to us, can be demonstrated from those of His effects which are known to us.

Reply Obj. 1. The existence of God and other like truths about God, which can be known by natural reason, are not articles of faith, but are preambles to the articles, for faith presupposes natural knowledge, even as grace presupposes nature and perfection the perfectible. Nevertheless, there is nothing to prevent a man, who cannot grasp a proof, from accepting, as a matter of faith, something which in itself is capable of being scientifically known and demonstrated.

Reply Obj. 2. When the existence of a cause is demonstrated from an effect, this effect takes the place of the definition of the cause in proving the cause's existence. This is especially the case in regard to God, because, in order to prove the existence of anything, it is necessary to accept as a middle term the meaning of the name, and not its essence, for the question of its essence follows on the question of its existence. Now the names given to God are derived from His effects, as will be later shown. Consequently, in demonstrating the existence of God from His effects, we may take for the middle term the meaning of the name *God.*

Reply Obj. 3. From effects not proportioned to the cause no perfect knowledge of that cause can be obtained. Yet from every effect the existence of the cause can be clearly demonstrated, and so we can demonstrate the existence of God from His effects; though from them we cannot know God perfectly as He is in His essence.

WHETHER GOD EXISTS *

. . . . .

On the contrary, It is said in the person of God: *I am Who am* (*Exod.* iii. 14).

I answer that, The existence of God can be proved in five ways.

The first and more manifest way is the argument from motion. It is certain, and evident to our senses, that in the world some things are in motion. Now whatever is moved is moved by another, for nothing can be moved except it is in potentiality to that towards which it is moved whereas a thing moves inasmuch as it is in act. For motion is nothing else than the reduction of something from potentiality to actuality. But nothing can be reduced from potentiality to actuality, except by something in a state of actuality. Thus that which is actually hot, as fire, makes wood, which is potentially hot, to be actually hot, and thereby moves and changes it. Now it is not possible that the same thing should be at once in actuality and potentiality in the same respect, but only in different respects. For what is actually hot cannot simultaneously be potentially hot; but it is simultaneously potentially cold. It is therefore impossible that in the same respect and in the same way a thing should be both mover and moved, i.e., that it should move itself. Therefore, whatever is moved must be moved by another. If that by which it is moved be itself moved, then this also must needs be moved by another, and that by another again. But this cannot go on to infinity, because then there would be no first mover, and, consequently, no other mover, seeing that subsequent movers move only inasmuch as they are moved by the the first mover; as the staff moves only because it is moved by the hand. Therefore, it is necessary to arrive at a first mover, moved by no other; and this everyone understands to be God.**

* Question 2, Article 3.

** Note here the following remarks of St. Thomas from the *Summa Contra Gentiles:*

"Now two things would seem to weaken the above arguments. The *first* of these is that they proceed from the supposition of the eternity of movement, and among Catholics this is supposed to be false. To this we reply that the most effective way to prove God's existence is from the supposition of the eternity of the world, which being supposed, it seems less manifest that God exists. For if the world and movement had a beginning, it is clear that we must suppose some cause to have produced the world and movement, because whatever becomes anew must take its origin from some cause of its becoming, since nothing evolves itself from potentiality to act, or from non-being to being.

The second way is from the nature of efficient cause. In the world of sensible things we find there is an order of efficient causes. There is no case known (neither is it, indeed, possible) in which a thing is found to be the efficient cause of itself; for so it would be prior to itself, which is impossible. Now in efficient causes it is not possible to go on to infinity, because in all efficient causes following in order, the first is the cause of the intermediate cause, and the intermediate is the cause of the ultimate cause, whether the intermediate cause be several, or one only. Now to take away the cause is to take away the effect. Therefore, if there be no first cause among efficient causes, there will be no ultimate, nor any intermediate, cause. But if in efficient causes it is possible to go on to infinity, there will be no first efficient cause, neither will there be an ultimate effect, nor any intermediate efficient causes; all of which is plainly false. Therefore it is necessary to admit a first efficient cause, to which everyone gives the name of God.*

The third way is taken from possibility and necessity, and runs thus. We find in nature things that are possible to be and not to be, since they are found to be generated, and to be corrupted, and consequently, it is possible for them to be and not to be. But it is im-

---

The *second*, is that the aforesaid arguments suppose that the first moved thing, namely the heavenly body, has its motive principle in itself, whence it follows that it is animated: and by many this is not granted.

To this we reply that if the first mover is not supposed to have its motive principle in itself, it follows that it is immediately moved by something altogether immovable. Hence also Aristotle draws this conclusion with an alternative, namely that either we must come at once to a first mover immovable and separate, or to a self-mover from which again we come to a first mover immovable and separate." (I, 13.)

* In connection with this argument the following statement from the *Summa Theologica* should be studied: "In efficient causes it is impossible to proceed to infinity *per se*. Thus, there cannot be an infinite number of causes that are *per se* required for a certain effect; for instance, that a stone be moved by a stick, the stick by the hand, and so on to infinity. But it is not impossible to proceed to infinity *accidentally* as regards efficient causes; for instance, if all the causes thus infinitely multiplied should have the order of only one cause, while their multiplication is accidental: e.g., as an artificer acts by means of many hammers accidentally, because one after the other is broken. It is accidental, therefore, that one particular hammer should act after the action of another, and it is likewise accidental to this particular man as generator to be generated by another man; for he generates as a man, and not as the son of another man. For all men generating hold one grade in the order of efficient causes—viz., the grade of a particular generator. Hence it is not impossible for man to be generated by man to infinity; but such a thing would be impossible if the generation of this man depended upon this man, and on an elementary body, and on the sun, and so on to infinity." (Question 46, Article 2, Reply to Objection 7.)

possible for these always to exist, for that which can not-be at some time is not. Therefore, if everything can not-be, then at one time there was nothing in existence. Now if this were true, even now there would be nothing in existence, because that which does not exist begins to exist only through something already existing. Therefore, if at one time nothing was in existence, it would have been impossible for anything to have begun to exist; and thus even now nothing would be in existence—which is absurd. Therefore, not all beings are merely possible, but there must exist something the existence of which is necessary. But every necessary thing either has its necessity caused by another, or not. Now it is impossible to go on to infinity in necessary things which have their necessity caused by another, as has been already proved in regard to efficient causes. Therefore we cannot but admit the existence of some being having of itself its own necessity, and not receiving it from another, but rather causing in others their necessity. This all men speak of as God.

The fourth way is taken from the gradation to be found in things. Among beings there are some more and some less good, true, noble, and the like. But *more* and *less* are predicated of different things according as they resemble in their different ways something which is the maximum, as a thing is said to be hotter according as it more nearly resembles that which is hottest; so that there is something which is truest, something best, something noblest, and, consequently, something which is most being, for those things that are greatest in truth are greatest in being, as it is written in *Metaph.* II (*Metaph.* Ia, 1 993b30). Now the maximum in any genus is the cause of all in that genus, as fire, which is the maximum of heat, is the cause of all hot things, as is said in the same book. (993b25). Therefore there must also be something which is to all beings the cause of their being, goodness, and every other perfection; and this we call God.

The fifth way is taken from the governance of the world. We see that things which lack knowledge, such as natural bodies, act for an end, and this is evident from their acting always, or nearly always in the same way, so as to obtain the best result. Hence it is plain that they achieve their end, not fortuitously, but designedly. Now whatever lacks knowledge cannot move towards an end, unless it be directed by some being endowed with knowledge and intelligence; as the arrow is directed by the archer. Therefore some intelligent being exists by whom all natural things are directed to their end; and this being we call God.

4

BLAISE PASCAL

The Heart Has Its Reasons *

PASCAL REJECTS the metaphysical proofs for God's existence and declares that only through faith, through reasons of the heart, can we come to know God. With high eloquence he pictures the position of man in the universe—between two infinites—vainly striving for certainty, but through the weakness of reason being constantly deceived. Even his nature, as both a spiritual and material being, adds to the difficulty of man's comprehension. Yet man cannot remain in a state of doubt; indeed, it is a great evil, says Pascal, to be in doubt and it is our duty to free ourselves of doubt. Pascal has no regard for the sceptics; they cannot be our friends and they cannot be trusted. Their great insensibility to the truth of religion astounds him and he questions their sincerity and sees only a strange confusion in their attitude. Resorting to dialectic, he offers his famous wager: that if a person wagers *for* the existence of God (and he must wager, as Pascal shows) and God exists, then the individual achieves infinite gain (heaven); if God does not exist, there is no loss. On the other hand, if a person wagers *against* the existence of God and God does exist, then there is no loss and no gain; however, if God does exist, then there is infinite loss (damnation). Hence by wagering for God's existence we have everything to gain and nothing to lose; by wagering against His existece we have everything to lose and nothing to gain.

THE METAPHYSICAL PROOFS of God are so remote from the reasoning of men, and so complicated, that they make little impression; and if they should be of service to some, it would be only during the moment

---

* From the book *Pensées* by Pascal, translated by W. F. Trotter, published by Everyman's Library, E. P. Dutton and Co., Inc. The selections follow the numbering of the original text but have been arranged in the following order by the editor: 542, 277, 257, 72, 434, 194, 233.

Blaise Pascal (1623-62) was educated by his father with noteworthy results. At the age of twelve Pascal had composed a treatise on sound, and at sixteen one on conic sections. At the age of nineteen he had constructed an arithmetic machine and by the age of twenty-six had completed most of his works on mathematics. He is noted for his contributions to probability theory. In 1646 he was converted to Jansenism and in 1654 had his famous mystical experience. The remainder of his life was devoted to an extremely ascetic discipline and to his religious writings.

that they see such demonstration; but an hour afterwards they fear they have been mistaken. . . .

The heart has its reasons, which reason does not know. . . . It is the heart which experiences God, and not the reason. This, then is faith: God felt by the heart, not by the reason. . . .

There are only three kinds of persons: those who serve God, having found Him; others who are occupied in seeking Him, not having found Him; while the remainder live without seeking Him, and without having found Him. The first are reasonable and happy, the last are foolish and unhappy; those between are unhappy and reasonable.

* * * * *

MAN'S DISPROPORTION

. . . Let man then contemplate the whole of nature in her full and grand majesty, and turn his vision from the low objects which surround him. . . . The whole visible world is only an imperceptible atom in the ample bosom of nature. No idea approaches it. . . . It is an infinite sphere, the centre of which is everywhere, the circumference nowhere. In short it is the greatest sensible mark of the almighty power of God, that imagination loses itself in that thought.

Returning to himself, let man consider what he is in comparison with all existence; let him regard himself as lost in this remote corner of nature; and from the little cell in which he finds himself lodged, I mean the universe, let him estimate at their true value the earth, kingdoms, cities and himself. What is a man in the Infinite?

But to show him another prodigy equally astonishing, let him examine the most delicate things he knows. Let a mite be given him, with its minute body and parts incomparably more minute, limbs with their joints, veins in the limbs, blood in the veins, humours in the blood, drops in the humours, vapours in the drops. Dividing these last things again, let him exhaust his powers of conception, and let the last object at which he can arrive be now that of our discourse. Perhaps he will think that here is the smallest point in nature. I will let him see therein a new abyss. I will paint for him not only the visible universe, but all that he can conceive of nature's immensity in the womb of this abridged atom. Let him see therein an infinity of universes, each of which has its firmament, its planets, its earth, in the same proportion as in the visible world; in each earth animals, and in the last mites, in which he will find again all that the first had, finding still in these others the same thing without end and without cessation. Let him lose himself in wonders as amazing in their littleness as the others in their vastness. For who will not be astounded at the fact that our body, which a little while ago was imperceptible in the universe, itself imperceptible in the bosom of the whole, is now a colossus, a world, or rather a whole, in respect of the nothingness which we cannot reach? He who regards himself in this light will be afraid of himself, and observing himself sustained in the body given him by nature between those two abysses of the Infinite and Nothing, will tremble at the sight of these marvels; and I think that, as his curiosity changes into admiration, he will be more disposed to contemplate them in silence than to examine them with presumption.

For in fact what is man in nature? A Nothing in comparison with the Infinite, an All in comparison with the Nothing, a mean between nothing and everything. Since he is infinitely removed from comprehending the extremes, the end of things and their beginning are hopelessly hidden from him in an impenetrable secret; he is equally incapable of seeing the Nothing from which he was made, and the Infinite in which he is swallowed up.

.   .   .   .   .

Let us then take our compass; we are something, and we are not everything. The nature of our existence hides from us the knowledge of first beginnings which are born of the Nothing; and the littleness of our being conceals from us the sight of the Infinite.

Our intellect holds the same position in the world of thought as our body occupies in the expanse of nature.

Limited as we are in every way, this state which holds the mean between two extremes is present in all our impotence. Our senses perceive no extreme. Too much sound deafens us; too much light dazzles us; too great distance or proximity hinders our view. . . . First principles are too self-evident for us; too much pleasure disagrees with us. . . . We feel neither extreme heat nor extreme cold. Excessive qualities are prejudicial to us and not perceptible by the senses; we do not feel but suffer them. Extreme youth and extreme age hinder the mind, as also too much and too little education. In short, extremes are for us as though they were not, and we are not within their notice. They escape us, or we them.

This is our true state; this is what makes us incapable of certain knowledge and of absolute ignorance. We sail within a vast sphere, ever drifting in uncertainty, driven from end to end. When we think to attach ourselves to any point and to fasten to it, it wavers and leaves us; and if we follow it, it eludes our grasp, slips past us, and vanishes for ever. Nothing stays for us. . . .

Let us therefore not look for certainty and stability. Our reason is always deceived by fickle shadows; nothing can fix the finite between the two Infinites, which both enclose and fly from it.

．　．　．　．　．

And what completes our incapability of knowing things, is the fact that they are simple, and that we are composed of two opposite natures, different in kind, soul and body. For it is impossible that our rational part should be other than spiritual; and if any one maintain that we are simply corporeal, this would far more exclude us from the knowledge of things, there being nothing so inconceivable as to say that matter knows itself. It is impossible to imagine how it should know itself.

So if we are simply material, we can know nothing at all; and if we are composed of mind and matter, we cannot know perfectly things which are simple, whether spiritual or corporeal. Hence it comes that almost all philosophers have confused ideas of things, and speak of material things in spiritual terms, and of spiritual things in material terms. For they say boldly that bodies have a tendency to fall, that they seek after their centre, that they fly from destruction, that they fear the void, that they have inclinations, sympathies, antipathies, all of which attributes pertain only to mind. And in speaking of minds, they consider them as in a place, and attribute to them movement from one place to another; and these are qualities which belong only to bodies.

．　．　．　．　．

What then shall man do in this state? Shall he doubt everything? Shall he doubt whether he is awake, whether he is being pinched, or whether he is being burned? Shall he doubt whether he doubts? Shall he doubt whether he exists? We cannot go so far as that; and I lay it down as a fact that there never has been a real complete sceptic. Nature sustains our feeble reason, and prevents it raving to this extent.

Shall he then say, on the contraray, that he certainly possessed truth —he who, when pressed ever so little, can show no title to it, and is forced to let go his hold?

What a chimera then is man! What a novelty! What a monster, what a chaos, what a contradiction, what a prodigy! Judge of all

things, imbecile worm of the earth; depositary of truth, a sink of
uncertainty and error; the pride and refuse of the universe!

Who will unravel this tangle? Nature confutes the sceptics, and
reason confutes the dogmatists. What then will you become, O men!
who try to find out by your natural reason what is your true condition?
You cannot avoid one of these sects, nor adhere to one of them.

Know then, proud man, what a paradox you are to yourself. Humble
yourself, weak reason; be silent, foolish nature; learn that man infinitely transcends man, and learn from your Master your true condition, of which you are ignorant. Hear God.

For in fact, if man had never been corrupt, he would enjoy in his
innocence both truth and happiness with assurance; and if man had
always been corrupt, he would have no idea of truth or bliss. But,
wretched as we are, and more so than if there were no greatness in
our condition, we have an idea of happiness, and cannot reach it.
We perceive an image of truth, and possess only a lie. Incapable of
absolute ignorance and of certain knowledge, we have thus been
manifestly in a degree of perfection from which we have unhappily
fallen.

·   ·   ·   ·   ·

Surely then it is a great evil thus to be in doubt, but it is at least an
indispensable duty to seek when we are in such doubt; and thus the
doubter who does not seek is altogether completely unhappy and
completely wrong. And if besides this he is easy and content, professes
to be so, and indeed boasts of it; if it is this state itself which is the
subject of his joy and vanity, I have no words to describe so silly
a creature.

How can people hold these opinions? What joy can we find in the
expectation of nothing but hopeless misery? What reason for boasting
that we are in impenetrable darkness? And how can it happen that
the following argument occur to a reasonable man?

"I know not who put me into the world, nor what the world is, nor
what I myself am. I am in terrible ignorance of everything. I know
not what my body is, nor my senses, nor my soul, not even that part
of me which thinks what I say, which reflects on all and on itself,
and knows itself no more than the rest. I see those frightful spaces
of the universe which surround me, and I find myself tied to one
corner of this vast expanse, without knowing why I am put in this
place rather than in another, nor why the short time which is given
to me to live is assigned to me at this point rather than at another
of the whole eternity which was before me or which shall come after

me. I see nothing but infinites on all sides, which surround me as an atom, and as a shadow which endures only for an instant and returns no more. All I know is that I must soon die, but what I know least is this very death which I cannot escape.

"As I know not whence I come, so I know not whither I go. I know only that in leaving this world, I fall for ever either into annihilation or into the hands of an angry God, without knowing to which of these two states I shall be for ever assigned. Such is my state, full of weakness and uncertainty. And from all this I conclude that I ought to spend all the days of my life without caring to inquire into what must happen to me. Perhaps I might find some solution to my doubts, but I will not take the trouble, nor take a step to seek it; and after treating with scorn those who are concerned with this care, I will go without foresight and without fear to try the great event, and let myself be led carelessly to death, uncertain of the eternity of my future state."

Who would desire to have for a friend a man who talks in this fashion? Who would choose him out from others to tell him of his affairs? Who would have recourse to him in affiliction? And indeed to what use in life could one put him?

In truth, it is the glory of religion to have for enemies men so unreasonable; and their opposition to it is so little dangerous that it serves on the contrary to establish its truths. For the Christian faith goes mainly to establish these two facts; the corruption of nature, and redemption by Jesus Christ. Now I contend that if these men do not serve to prove the truth of the redemption by the holiness of their behavior, they at least serve admirably to show the corruption of nature by sentiments so unnatural.

Nothing is so important to man as his own state, nothing is so formidable to him as eternity; and thus it is not natural that there should be men indifferent to the loss of their existence, and to the perils of everlasting suffering. They are quite different with regard to all other things. They are afraid of mere trifles; they foresee them; they feel them. And this same man who spends so many days and nights in rage and despair for the loss of office or for some imaginary insult to his honor, is the very one who knows without anxiety and without emotion that he will lose all by death. It is a monstrous thing to see in the same heart and at the same time this sensibility to trifles and this strange insensibility to the greatest objects. It is an incomprehensible enchantment, and a supernatural slumber, which indicates as its cause an all-powerful force.

There must be a strange confusion in the nature of man, that he should boast of being in that state in which it seems incredible that a single individual should be. However, experience has shown me so great a number of such persons that the fact would be surprising, if we did not know that the greater part of those who trouble themselves about the matter are disingenuous, and not in fact what they say. They are people who have heard it said that it is the fashion to be thus daring. It is what they call shaking off the yoke, and they try to imitate this. But it would not be difficult to make them understand how greatly they deceive themselves in thus seeking esteem. This is not the way to gain it, even I say among those men of the world who take a healthy view of things, and who know that the only way to succeed in this life is to make ourselves appear honorable, faithful, judicious, and capable of useful service to a friend; because naturally men love only what may be useful to them. Now what do we gain by hearing it said of a man that he has now thrown off the yoke, that he does not believe there is a God who watches our actions, that he considers himself the sole master of his conduct, and that he thinks he is accountable for it only to himself? Does he think that he has thus brought us to have henceforth complete confidence in him, and to look to him for consolation, advice, and help in every need of life? Do they profess to have delighted us by telling us that they hold our soul to be only a little wind and smoke, especially by telling us this in a haughty and self-satisfied tone of voice? Is this a thing to say gaily? Is it not, on the contrary, a thing to say sadly, as the saddest thing in the world. . . .

Thus those who only feign these opinions would be very unhappy, if they restrained their natural feelings in order to make themselves the most conceited of men. If, at the bottom of their heart, they are troubled at not having more light, let them not disguise the fact; this avowal will not be shameful. The only shame is to have none. Nothing reveals more an extreme weakness of mind than not to know the misery of a godless man. Nothing is more indicative of a bad disposition of heart than not to desire the truth of eternal promises. Nothing is more dastardly than to act with bravado before God. Let them then leave these impieties to those who are sufficiently illbred to be really capable of them. Let them at least be honest men, if they cannot be Christians. Finally, let them recognize that there are two kinds of people one can call reasonable; those who serve God with all their heart because they know Him, and those who seek Him with all their heart because they do not know Him.

THE WAGER

Let us now speak according to natural lights.

If there is a God, He is infinitely incomprehensible, since, having neither parts nor limits, He has no affinity to us. We are then incapable of knowing either what He is or if He is. This being so, who will dare to undertake the decision of the question? Not we, who have no affinity to Him.

Who then will blame Christians for not being able to give a reason for their belief, since they profess a religion for which they cannot give a reason? They declare, in expounding it to the world, that it is a foolishness, *stultitiam*: and then you complain that they do not prove it! If they proved it, they would not keep their word; it is in lacking proofs that they are not lacking in sense. "Yes, but although this excuses those who offer it as such, and takes away from them the blame of putting it forward without reason, it does not excuse those who receive." Let us then examine this point, and say, "God is, or He is not." But to which side shall we incline? Reason can decide nothing here. There is an infinite chaos which separates us. A game is being played at the extremity of this infinite distance where heads or tails will turn up. What will you wager? According to reason, you can do neither the one thing nor the other; according to reason, you can defend neither of the propositions.

Do not then reprove for error those who have made a choice; for you know nothing about it. "No, but I blame them for having made, not this choice, but a choice, for again both he who chooses heads and he who chooses tails are equally at fault, they are both in the wrong. The true course is not to wager at all."

Yes; but you must wager. It is not optional. You are embarked. Which will you choose then? Let us see. Since you must choose, let us see which interests you least. You have two things to lose, the true and the good; and two things to stake, your reason and your will, your knowledge and your happiness; and your nature has two things to shun, error and misery. Your reason is no more shocked in choosing one rather than the other, since you must of necessity choose. This is one point settled. But your happiness? Let us weigh the gain and the loss in wagering that God is. Let us estimate these two chances. If you gain, you gain all; if you lose, you lose nothing. Wager, then, without hestitation that He is.—"That is very fine. Yes, I must wager; but I may perhaps wager too much."—Let us see. Since there is an equal risk of gain and of loss, if you had only to gain two lives, instead of one, you might still wager. But if there were three lives to gain, you would have to play (since you are under the necessity of playing), and you would be imprudent, when you are forced to play, not to chance your life to gain three at a game where there is an equal risk of loss and gain. But there is an eternity of life and happiness. And this being so, if there were an infinity of chances, of which one only would be for you, you would still be right in wagering one to win two, and you would act stupidly, being obliged to play, by refusing to stake one life against three at a game in which out of an infinity of chances there is one for you, if there were an infinity of an infinitely happy life to gain. But there is here an infinity of an infinitely happy life to gain, a chance of gain against a finite number of chances of loss, and what you stake is finite. It is all divided; wherever the infinite is and there is not an infinity of chances of loss against that of gain, there is no time to hesitate, you must give all. And thus, when one is forced to play, he must renounce reason to preserve his life, rather than risk it for infinite gain, as likely to happen as the loss of nothingness.

For it is no use to say it is uncertain if we will gain, and it is certain that we risk, and that the infinite distance between the *certainty* of what is staked and the *uncertainty* of what will be gained, equals the finite good which is certainly staked against the uncertain infinite. It is not so, as every player stakes a certainty to gain an uncertainty, and yet he stakes a finite certainty to gain a finite uncertainty, without transgressing against reason. There is not an infinite distance between the certainty staked and the uncertainty of the gain; that is untrue. In truth, there is an infinity between the certainty of gain and the certainty of loss. But the uncertainty of the gain is proportioned to the certainty of the stake according to the proportion of the chances of gain and loss. Hence it comes that, if there are as many risks on one side as on the other, the course is to play even; and then the certainty of the stake is equal to the uncertainty of the gain, so far is it from fact that there is an infinite distance between them. And so our proposition is of infinite force, when there is the finite to stake in a game where there are equal risks of gain and of loss, and the infinite to gain. This is demonstrable; and if men are capable of any truths, this is one.

"I confess it, I admit it. But, still, is there no means of seeing the faces of the cards?"—Yes, Scripture and the rest, etc. "Yes, but I have my hands tied and my mouth closed; I am forced to wager, and am not free. I am not released, and am so made that I cannot believe. What, then would you have me do?"

True. But at least learn your inability to believe, since reason brings you to this, and yet you cannot believe. Endeavor then to convince yourself, not by increase of proofs of God, but by the abatement of your passions. You would like to attain faith, and do not know the way; you would like to cure yourself of unbelief, and ask the remedy for it. Learn of those who have been bound like you, and who now stake all their possessions. These are people who know the way which you would follow, and who are cured of an ill of which you would be cured. Follow the way by which they began; by acting as if they believed, taking the holy water, having masses said, etc. Even this will naturally make you believe, and deaden your acuteness.—"But this is what I am afraid of."—And why? What have you to lose?

.   .   .   .   .

. . . Now, what harm will befall you in taking this side? You will be faithful, honest, humble, grateful, generous, a sincere friend, truthful. Certainly you will not have those poisonous pleasures, glory and luxury; but will you have not others? I will tell you that you will thereby gain in this life, and that, at each step you take on this road, you will see so great certainty of gain, so much nothingness in what you risk, that you will at last recognize that you have wagered for something certain and infinite, for which you have given nothing.

If this discourse pleases you and seems impressive, know that it is made by a man who has knelt, both before and after it, in prayer to that Being, infinite and without parts, before whom he lays all he has, for you also to lay before Him all you have for your own good and for His glory, that so strength may be given to lowliness.

5

LUDWIG FEUERBACH

Atheism *

FEUERBACH'S POSITION is admittedly materialistic, naturalistic, and anti-Hegelian. Declaring that atheism is the true answer of religion, he proceeds to show that religion is the dream of the human mind, that self-consciousness and the consciousness we have of God are one—that the knowledge of God is only self-knowledge. On this basis he traces the historical development of religion, and concludes that the antithesis of the divine and human is illusory and that "the object and contents of the Christian religion are altogether human."

Next he develops the notion of this identity of God and man with reference to the attributes of God. He protests against an agnostic view of the nature of God and declares that a being without qualities or attributes is virtually nonexistent. This he says, is but a disguised atheism. He rejects any possible analogy between the human attributes and the divine on the grounds that man cannot take a point of view above himself. God is no more than the attributes we find in ourselves and predicate of him. Hence we cannot deny the attributes without denying the existence of God and the true atheist is not he who denies God, the subject, but he who denies the predicates or attributes of the divine being. Once we have established that God is his attributes, that the subject is identified with the predicates, then we have also established that if such predicates are merely attributes of human nature, God is no more than man.

After further reflections on the implications of this identity, Feuerbach develops in the Appendix the notion that God is the objectification of human feelings, that he reflects our emotions.

* From *The Essence of Christianity*, translated from the second German edition by Marian Evans (Kegan Paul, Trench, Trübner and Co., Ltd., 1893), pp. viii-xvi, 12-30, 282-83.

Ludwig Feuerbach (1804-72) was born at Landshut in Bavaria. He studied theology at Heidelberg and Berlin. Hegel exerted a considerable influence upon him, and he turned to the study of philosophy and received his doctorate in that subject. He was a correspondent of Karl Marx and sympathized with the Socialist movement but took no active part in it. He devoted his life to the study of philosophy and religion.

PREFACE TO SECOND EDITION

. . . I AM NOTHING but a *natural philosopher in the domain of mind;* and the natural philosopher can do nothing without instruments, without material means. In this character I have written the present work, which consequently contains nothing else than the principle of a new philosophy verified practically, i.e. *in concreto,* in application to a special object, but an object which has a universal significance: namely, to religion, in which this principle is exhibited, developed, and thoroughly carried out. This philosophy is essentially distinguished from the systems hitherto prevalent, in that it corresponds to the real complete nature of man; but for that very reason it is antagonistic to minds perverted and crippled by a superhuman, i.e., anti-human, antinatural religion and speculation. . . .

This philosophy has for its principle, not the Substance of Spinoza, not the *ego* of Kant and Fichte, not the Absolute Identity of Schelling, not the Absolute Mind of Hegel, in short, no abstract, merely conceptional being, but a *real* being, the true *Ens realissimum*—man; its principle, therefore, is in the highest degree positive and real. It generates thought from the *opposite* of thought, from Matter, from existence, from the senses; it has relation to its object first through the senses, i.e. passively, before defining it in thought. Hence my work, as a specimen of this philosophy, so far from being a production to be placed in the category of Speculation,—although in another point of view it is the true, the incarnate result of prior philosophical systems,—is the direct opposite of speculation, nay, puts an end to it by explaining it. Speculation makes religion say only what it has itself thought, and expressed far better than religion; it assigns a meaning to religion without any reference to the *actual* meaning of religion; it does not look beyond itself. I, on the contrary, let religion itself speak; I constitute myself only its listener and interpreter, not its prompter. Not to invent, but to discover, "to unveil existence," has been my sole object; to *see* correctly, my sole endeavor. It is not I, but religion that worships man, although religion, or rather theology, denies this; it is not I, an insignificant individual, but religion itself that says: God is man, man is God; it is not I, but religion that denies the God who is *not* man, but only an *ens rationis*,—since it makes God become man, and then constitutes this God, not distinguished from man, having a human form, human feelings, and human thoughts, the object of its worship and veneration. I have only found the key to the cipher of the Christian religion, only extricated its true meaning from the web of contradictions and delusions called theology;

—but in doing so I have certainly committed a sacrilege. If therefore my work is negative, irreligious, atheistic, let it be remembered that atheism—at least in the sense of this work—is the secret of religion itself; that religion itself, not indeed on the surface, but fundamentally, not in intention or according to its own supposition, but in its heart, in its essence, believes in nothing else than the truth and divinity of human nature. Or let it be *proved* that the historical as well as the rational arguments of my work are false; let them be refuted—not, however, I entreat, by judicial denunciations, or theological jeremiads, by the trite phrases of speculation, or other pitiful expedients for which I have no name, but by *reasons,* and such reasons as I have not already thoroughly answered.

· · · · ·

Religion is the dream of the human mind. But even in dreams we do not find ourselves in emptiness or in heaven, but on earth, in the realm of reality; we only see real things in the entrancing splendour of imagination and caprice, instead of in the simple daylight of reality and necessity. Hence I do nothing more to religion—and to speculative philosophy and theology also—than to open its eyes, or rather to turn its gaze from the internal towards the external, i.e., I change the object as it is in the imagination into the object as it is in reality.

But certainly for the present age, which prefers the sign to the thing signified, the copy to the original, fancy to reality, the appearance to the essence, this change, inasmuch as it does away with illusion, is an absolute annihilation, or at least a reckless profanation; for in these days *illusion* only is *sacred, truth profane.*

· · · · ·

My principal theme is Christianity, is Religion, as it is the *immediate object,* the *immediate nature,* of man. Erudition and philosophy are to me only the means by which I bring to light the treasure hid in man.

· · · · ·

INTRODUCTION
THE ESSENCE OF RELIGION CONSIDERED GENERALLY

In the perceptions of the senses consciousness of the object is distinguishable from consciousness of self; but in religion, conscious-

ness of the object and self-consciousness coincide. The object of the
senses is out of man, the religious object is within him, and therefore
as little forsakes him as his self-consciousness or his conscience; it is
the intimate, the closest object. "God," says Augustine, for example,
"is nearer, more related to us, and therefore more easily known by
us, than sensible, corporeal things" (*De Genesi ad litteram*, l. v. c.
16). The object of the senses is in itself indifferent—independent of
the disposition or of the judgment; but the object of religion is a
selected object; the most excellent, the first, the supreme being; it
essentially presupposes a critical judgment, a discrimination between
the divine and the non-divine, between that which is worthy of
adoration and that which is not worthy. And here may be applied,
without any limitation, the proposition: the object of any subject is
nothing else than the subject's own nature taken objectively. Such
as are a man's thoughts and dispositions, such is his God; so much
worth as a man has, so much and no more has his God. Consciousness of God is self-consciousness, knowledge of God is self-knowledge.
By his God thou knowest the man, and by the man, his God; the two
are identical. Whatever is God to a man, that is his heart and soul;
and conversely, God is the manifested inward nature, the expressed
self of a man,—religion the solemn unveiling of a man's hidden treasures, the revelation of his intimate thoughts, the open confession of
his lovesecrets.

But when religion—consciousness of God—is designated as the self-
consciousness of man, this is not to be understood as affirming that
the religious man is directly aware of this identity; for, on the contrary,
ignorance of it is fundamental to the peculiar nature of religion. To
preclude this misconception, it is better to say, religion is man's
earliest and also indirect form of self-knowledge. Hence, religion
everywhere precedes philosophy, as in the history of the race, so also
in that of the individual. Man first of all sees his nature as if *out of*
himself, before he finds it in himself. His own nature is in the first
instance contemplated by him as that of another being. Religion is
the childlike condition of humanity; but the child sees his nature—
man—out of himself; in childhood a man is an object to himself, under
the form of another man. Hence the historical progress of religion
consists in this; that what by an earlier religion was regarded as
objective, is now recognized as subjective; that is, what was formerly
contemplated and worshipped as God is now perceived to be something *human*. What was at first religion becomes at a later period
idolatry; man is seen to have adored his own nature. Man has given
objectivity to himself, but has not recognized the object as his own

nature: a later religion takes this forward step; every advance in religion is therefore a deeper self-knowledge. But every particular religion, while it pronounces its predecessors idolatrous, excepts itself —and necessarily so, otherwise it would no longer be religion—from the fate, the common nature of all religions: it imputes only to other religions what is the fault, if fault it be, of religion in general. Because it has a different object, a different tenor, because it has transcended the ideas of preceding religions, it erroneously supposes itself exalted above the necessary eternal laws which constitute the essence of religion—it fancies its objects, its ideas, to be superhuman. But the essence of religion, thus hidden from the religious, is evident to the thinker, by whom religion is viewed objectively, which it cannot be by its votaries. And it is our task to show that the antithesis of divine and human is altogether illusory, that it is nothing else than the antithesis between the human nature in general and the human individual; that, consequently, the object and contents of the Christian religion are altogether human.

Religion, at least the Christian, is the relation of man to himself, or more correctly to his own nature (i.e., his subjective nature); but a relation to it, viewed as a nature apart from his own. The divine being is nothing else than the human being, or, rather, the human nature purified, freed from the limits of the individual man, made objective— i.e., contemplated and revered as another, a distinct being. All the attributes of the divine nature are, therefore, attributes of the human nature.

In relation to the attributes, the predicates of the Divine Being, this is admitted without hesitation, but by no means in relation to the subject of these predicates. The negation of the subject is held to be irreligion, nay, atheism; though not so the negation of the predicates. But that which has no predicates or qualities, has no effect upon me; that which has no effect upon me has no existence for me. To deny all the qualities of a being is equivalent to denying the being himself. A being without qualities is one which cannot become an object to the mind, and such a being is virtually non-existent. Where man deprives God of all qualities, God is no longer anything more to him than a negative being. To the truly religious man, God is not a being without qualities, because to him he is a positive, real being. The theory that God cannot be defined, and consequently cannot be known by man, is therefore the offspring of recent times, a product of modern unbelief. . . . On the ground that God is unknowable, man excuses himself to what is yet remaining of his religious conscience for his forgetfulness of God, his absorption in the world: he denies God practically by his conduct,—the world has possession of all his thoughts and inclinations,—but he does not deny him theoretically, he does not attack his existence; he lets that rest. But this existence does not affect or incommode him; it is merely negative existence, an existence without existence, a self-contradictory existence,—a state of being which, as to its effects, is not distinguishable from non-being. The denial of determinate, positive predicates concerning the divine nature is nothing else than a denial of religion, with, however, an appearance of religion in its favor, so that it is not recognized as a denial; it is simply a subtle, disguised atheism. The alleged religious horror of limiting God by positive predicates is only the irreligious wish to know nothing more of God, to banish God from the mind. Dread of limitation is dread of existence.

.   .   .   .   .

There is, however, a still milder way of denying the divine predicates than the direct one just described. It is admitted that the predicates of the divine nature are finite, and more particularly, human qualities, but their rejection is rejected; they are even taken under protection, because it is necessary to man to have a definite conception of God, and since he is man he can form no other than a human conception of him. In relation to God, it is said, these predicates are certainly without any objective validity; but to me, if he is to exist for me, he cannot appear otherwise than as he does appear to me, namely, as a being with attributes analogous to the human. But this distinction between what God is in himself, and what he is for me destroys the peace of religion, and is besides in itself an unfounded and untenable distinction. I cannot know whether God is something else in himself or for himself than he is for me; what he is to me is to me all that he is. . . . In the distinction above stated, man takes a point of view above himself, i.e., above his nature, the absolute measure of his being; but this transcendentalism is only an illusion; for I can make the distinction between the object as it is in itself, and the object as it is for me, only where an object can really appear otherwise to me, not where it appears to me such as the absolute measure of my nature determines it to appear—such as it must appear to me.

.   .   .   .   .

Scepticism is the arch-enemy of religion; but the distinction between object and conception—between God as he is in himself, and God as he is for me—is a sceptical distinction, and therefore an irreligious one.

.   .   .   .   .

Wherever, therefore, this idea, that the religious predicates are only anthropomorphisms, has taken possession of a man, there has doubt, has unbelief, obtained the mastery of faith. And it is only the inconsequence of faint-heartedness and intellectual imbecility which does not proceed from this idea to the formal negation of the predicates, and from thence to the negation of the subject to which they relate. If thou doubtest the objective truth of the predicates, thou must also doubt the objective truth of the subject whose predicates they are. If thy predicates are anthropomorphisms, the subject of them is an anthropomorphism, too. If love, goodness, personality, etc., are human attributes, so also is the subject which thou presupposest, the existence of God, the belief that there is a God, an anthropomorphism—a presupposition purely human. Whence knowest thou that the belief in a God at all is not a limitation of man's mode of conception? . . .

Thou believest in love as a divine attribute because thou thyself lovest; thou believest that God is a wise, benevolent being because thou knowest nothing better in thyself than benevolence and wisdom; and thou believest that God exists, that therefore he is a subject—whatever exists is a subject, whether it be defined as substance, person, essence, or otherwise—because thou thyself existed, art thyself a subject. Thou knowest no higher human good than to love, than to be good and wise; and even so thou knowest no higher happiness than to exist, to be a subject; for the consciousness of all reality, of all bliss, is for thee bound up in the consciousness of being a subject, of existing. God is an existence, a subject to thee, for the same reason that he is to thee a wise, a blessed, a personal being. The distinction between the divine predicates and the divine subject is only this, that to thee the subject, the existence, does not appear an anthropomorphism, because the conception of it is necessarily involved in thy own existence as a subject, whereas the predicates do appear anthropomorphisms, because their necessity—the necessity that God should be conscious, wise, good, etc.,—is not an immediate necessity, identical with the being of man, but is evolved by his self-consciousness, by the activity of his thought. I am a subject, I exist, whether I be wise or unwise, good or bad. To exist is to man the first datum; it constitutes the very idea of the subject; it is presupposed by the predicates. Hence man relinquishes the predicates, but the existence of God is to him a settled, irrefragable, absolutely certain, objective truth. But, nevertheless, this distinction is merely an apparent one. The necessity of the subject lies only in the necessity of the predicate. Thou art a subject only in so far as thou art a human subject; the certainty and reality of thy existence lie only in the certainty and reality of thy human attributes. What the subject is lies only in the predicate; the predicate is the *truth* of the subject—the subject only the personified, existing predicate, the predicate conceived as existing. Subject and predicate are distinguished only as existence and essence. The negation of the predicates is therefore the negation of the subject. What remains of the human subject when abstracted from the human attributes? Even in the language of common life the divine predicates—Providence, Omniscience, Omnipotence—are put for the divine subject. . . .

.   .   .   .   .

Religion is that conception of the nature of the world and of man which is essential to, i.e., identical with, a man's nature. But man does not stand above this his necessary conception; on the contrary, it stands above him; it animates, determines, governs him. The necessity of a proof, of a middle term to unite qualities with existence, the possibility of a doubt, is abolished. Only that which is apart from my own being is capable of being doubted by me. How then can I doubt of God, who is my being? To doubt of God is to doubt of myself. Only when God is thought of abstractly, when his predicates are the result of philosophic abstraction, arises the distinction or separation between subject and predicate, existence and nature—arises the fiction that the existence of the subject is something else than the predicate, something immediate, indubitable, in distinction from the predicate, which is held to be doubtful. But this is only a fiction. A God who has abstract predicates has also an abstract existence. Existence, being, varies with varying qualities.

.   .   .   .   .

Thus what theology and philosophy have held to be God, the Absolute, the Infinite, is not God; but that which they have held not to be God is God: namely, the attribute, the quality, whatever has reality. Hence he alone is the true atheist to whom the predicates of the Divine Being,—for example, love, wisdom, justice,—are nothing; not he to whom merely the subject of these predicates is nothing. And in no wise is the negation of the subject necessarily also a negation of the predicates considered in themselves. These have an intrinsic, independent reality; they force their recognition upon man by their very nature; they are self-evident truths to him; they prove, they attest themselves. It does not follow that goodness, justice, wisdom, are chimeras because the existence of God is a chimera, nor truths because this is a truth. The idea of God is dependent on the idea of justice, of benevolence; a God who is not benevolent, not just, not wise, is no God; but the converse does not hold. The fact is not that a quality is divine because God has it, but that God has it because it is in itself divine; because without it God would be a defective being. Justice, wisdom, in general every quality which constitutes the divinity of God, is determined and known by itself independently, but the idea of God is determined by the qualities which have thus been previously judged to be worthy of the divine nature; only in the case in which I identify God and justice, in which I think of God immediately as the reality of the idea of justice, is the idea of God self-determined. But if God as a subject is the determined, while the quality, the predicate, is the determining, then in truth the rank of the godhead is due not to the subject, but to the predicate.

·   ·   ·   ·   ·

Now, when it is shown that what the subject is lies entirely in the attributes of the subject; that is, that the predicate is the true subject; it is also proved that if the divine predicates are attributes of the human nature, the subject of those predicates is also of the human nature. But the divine predicates are partly general, partly personal. The general predicates are the metaphysical, but these serve only as external points of support to religion; they are not the characteristic definitions of religion. It is the personal predicates alone which constitute the essence of religion—in which the Divine Being is the object of religion. Such are, for example, that God is a Person, that he is the moral Lawgiver, the Father of mankind, the Holy One, the Just, the Good, the Merciful. It is, however, at once, clear, or it will at least be clear in the sequel, with regard to these and other definitions, that, especially as applied to a personality, they are purely human definitions, and that consequently man in religion—in his relation to God—is in relation to his own nature; for to the religious sentiment these predicates are not mere conceptions, mere images, which man forms of God, to be distinguished from that which God is in himself, but truths, facts, realities. Religion knows nothing of anthropomorphisms; to it they are not anthropomorphisms. It is the very essence of religion, that to it these definitions express the nature of God. They are pronounced to be images only by the understanding, which reflects on religion, and which while defending them yet before its own tribunal denies them. But to the religious sentiment God is a real Father, real Love and Mercy; for to it he is a real, living, personal being, and therefore his attributes are also living and personal. Nay, the definitions which are the most sufficing to the religious sentiment are precisely those which give the most offence to the understanding, and which in the process of reflection on religion it denies. Religion is essentially emotion; hence, objectively also, emotion is to it necessarily of a divine nature. Even anger appears to it an emotion not unworthy of God, provided only there be a religious motive at the foundation of this anger.

But here it is also essential to observe, and this phenomenon is an extremely remarkable one, characterizing the very core of religion, that in proportion as the divine subject is in reality human, the greater is the apparent difference between God and man; that is, the more, by reflection on religion, by theology, is the identity of the divine and human denied, and the human, considered as such, is depreciated. The reason of this is, that as what is positive in the conception of the divine being can only be human, the conception of man, as an object of consciousness, can only be negative. To enrich God, man must become poor; that God may be all, man must be nothing. But he desires to be nothing in himself, because what he takes from himself is not lost to him, since it is preserved in God. Man has his being in God; why then should he have it in himself? Where is the necessity of positing the same thing twice, of having it twice? What man withdraws from himself, what he renounces in himself, he only enjoys in an incomparably higher and fuller measure in God. . . .

. . . . .

In brief, man in relation to God denies his own knowledge, his own thoughts, that he may place them in God. Man gives up his personality; but in return, God, the Almighty, infinite, unlimited being, is a person; he denies human dignity, the human *ego;* but in return God is to him a selfish, egotistical being, who in all things seeks only himself, his own honor, his own ends, he represents God as simply seeking the satisfaction of his own selfishness, while yet he frowns on that of every other being; his God is the very luxury of egoism. Religion further denies goodness as a quality of human nature; man is wicked, corrupt, incapable of good; but, on the other hand, God is only good—the Good Being. Man's nature demands as an object goodness, personified as God; but is it not hereby declared that goodness is an essential tendency of man? If my heart is wicked, my understanding perverted, how can I perceive and feel the holy to be holy, the good to be good? . . .   Either goodness does not exist at all for man, or, if it does exist, therein is revealed to the individual man the holiness and goodness of human nature.

. . . . .

Man—this is the mystery of religion—projects his being into objectivity, and then again makes himself an object to this projected image of himself thus converted into a subject; he thinks of himself as an object to himself, but as the object of an object, of another being than himself. Thus here. Man is an object to God. That man is good or evil is not indifferent to God; no! He has a lively, profound interest in man's being good; he wills that man should be good, happy —for without goodness there is no happiness. Thus the religious man virtually retracts the nothingness of human activity, by making his dispositions and actions an object to God, by making man the end of God—for that which is an object to the mind is an end in action; by making the divine activity a means of human salvation. God acts, that man may be good and happy. Thus man, while he is apparently humiliated to the lowest degree, is in truth exalted to the highest. Thus, in and through God, man has in view himself alone. It is true that man places the aim of his action in God, but God has no other aim of action than the moral and eternal salvation of man; thus man has in fact no other aim than himself. The divine activity is not distinct from the human.

·   ·   ·   ·   ·

APPENDIX

Man has his highest being, his God, in himself; not in himself as an individual, but in his essential nature, his species. No individual is an adequate representation of his species, but only the human individual is conscious of the distinction between the species and the individual; in the sense of this distinction lies the root of religion. The yearning of man after something above himself is nothing else than the longing after the perfect type of his nature, the yearning to be free from himself, i.e., from the limits and defects of his individuality. Individuality is the self-conditionating, the self-limitation of the species. Thus man has cognizance of nothing above himself, of nothing beyond the nature of humanity; but to the individual man this nature presents itself under the form of an individual man. Thus, for example, the child sees the nature of man *above itself* in the form of its parents, the pupil in the form of his tutor. But all feelings which man experiences toward a superior man, nay, in general, all moral feelings which man has towards man, are of a religious nature. *Man feels nothing towards God which he does not also feel toward man. Homo homini deus est.* Want teaches prayer; but in misfortune, in sorrow, man kneels to entreat help of man also. Feeling makes God a man, but for the same reason it makes man a God. How often in deep emotion, which alone speaks genuine truth, man exclaims to man: Thou art, thou hast been my redeemer, my saviour, my protecting spirit, my God! We feel awe, reverence, humility, devout admiration, in thinking of a truly great, noble man; we feel ourselves worthless, we sink into nothing, even in the presence of human greatness. The purely, truly human emotions are religious; but for that reason the religious emotions are purely human; the only difference is that the religious emotions are vague, indefinite; but even this is only the case when the object of them is indefinite. Where God is positively defined, is the object of positive religion, there God is also the object of positive, definite human feelings, the object of fear and love, and therefore he is a positively human being; for there is nothing more in God than what lies in feeling. If in the heart there is fear and terror, in God there is anger; if in the heart there is joy, hope, confidence, in God there is love. . . . Thus even in religion man bows before the nature of man under the form of a personal human being; religion itself expressly declares—and all anthropomorphisms declare this in opposition to Pantheism,—*quod supra nos nihil ad nos;* that is, a God who inspires us with no human emotions, who does not reflect our own emotions, in a word, who is not a man,—such a God is nothing to us, has no interest for us, does not concern us.

. . . . .

It is clear from what has been said, that only where in truth, if not according to the subjective conception, the distinction between the divine and human being is abolished, is the objective existence of God, the existence of God as an objective, distinct being abolished— only there, I say, is religion made a mere matter of feeling or conversely, feeling the chief point in religion. The last refuge of theology therefore is feeling. God is renounced by the understanding; he has no longer the dignity of a real object, of a reality which imposes itself on the understanding; hence he is transferred to feeling: in feeling his existence is thought to be secure. And doubtless this is the safest refuge; for to make feeling the essence of religion is nothing else than to make feeling the essence of God. And as certainly as I exist, so certainly does my God exist. The certainty of God is here nothing else than the self-certainty of human-feeling, the yearning after God is the yearning after unlimited, uninterrupted, pure feeling. In life the feelings are interrupted; they collapse; they are followed by a state of void, of insensibility. The religious problem, therefore, is to give fixity to feeling in spite of the vicissitudes of life, and to separate it from repugnant disturbances and limitations: God himself is nothing else than undisturbed, uninterrupted feeling, feeling for which there exists no limits, no opposite. If God were a being distinct from thy feeling, he would be known to thee in some other way than simply in feeling; but just because thou perceivest him only by feeling, he exists only in feeling—he is himself only feeling.

THE NATURE OF GOD

6

DIONYSIUS THE AREOPAGITE

Our Knowledge of God *

PERHAPS WE CAN TRACE, through the maze of terminology and obscurity of thought that characterizes the *Divine Names,* at least the main lines of the author's approach to a recondite subject. We are told that man has at best an inadequate knowledge of God and that he is dependent at all times upon the guidance of Divine Scripture. The Affirmative method of ascribing to God perfections that are found in creatures is used throughout the text. But even the names we ascribe to Him are insufficient and we must speak of Him in such superlatives as "super-essential Essence," "super-essential Goodness," which, though positive affirmations indicate His complete transcendence. The nature of God is said to be un-differentiated, but in Its manifestations or emanations is said to be differentiated into those attributes by which we know Him. The transcendent unity of God is described with the aid of the meta-

* From *On the Divine Names and the Mystical Theology,* translated and edited by C. E. Rolt (The Society for the Promotion of Christian Knowledge, 1920), pp. 51-56, 60-61, 69-75, 131-32, 135-36, 142-43, 149-51, 185-89, 191-98. Reprinted with the permission of the publisher.

Dionysius the Areopagite, or more accurately the Pseudo-Dionysius, lived circa the fifth century A.D. For several centuries these writings of the Pseudo-Dionysius were falsely ascribed to Dionysius the Areopagite, an illustrious convert of St. Paul. The actual author is unknown but definitely reveals the influence of the Greek philosopher Proclus.

phor of light and the author analyzes with questionable orthodoxy the nature and relation of the Trinity to the Godhead. In what sense we can speak of the knowledge of God and how we can apply the titles of "Perfect" and "One" to Him are other subjects discussed. The author concludes by stating his preference for the Negative method of describing God. The brief selections from the *Mystical Theology* present his conception of this method.

DIONYSIUS THE PRESBYTER, TO HIS FELLOW-PRESBYTER TIMOTHY. WHAT IS THE PURPOSE OF THE DISCOURSE, AND WHAT THE TRADITION CONCERNING THE DIVINE NAMES

1. Now Blessed Timothy, the *Outlines of Divinity* ° being ended, I will proceed, so far as in me lies, to an Exposition of the Divine Names. And here also let us set before our minds the scriptural rule that in speaking about God we should declare the Truth, not with enticing words of man's wisdom, but in demonstration of the power which the Spirit stirred up in the Sacred Writers, whereby, in a manner surpassing speech and knowledge, we embrace those truths which, in like manner, surpass them, in that Union which exceeds our faculty, and exercise of discursive, and of intuitive reason. We must not then dare to speak, or indeed to form any conception of the hidden super-essential Godhead, except those things that are revealed to us from the Holy Scriptures.°° For a super-essential understanding of It is proper to Unknowing, which lieth in the Super-Essence Thereof surpassing Discourse, Intuition and Being; acknowledging which truth let us lift up our eyes towards the steep height, so far as the effluent light of the Divine Scriptures grants its aid, and, as we strive to ascend unto those Supernal Rays, let us gird ourselves for the task with holiness and the reverent fear of God. For, if we may safely trust the wise and infallible Scriptures, Divine things are revealed unto each created spirit in proportion to its powers, and in this measure is perception granted through the workings of the Divine goodness, the which in just care for our preservation divinely tempereth unto finite measure the infinitude of things which pass man's understanding. For even as things which are intellectually discerned cannot be comprehended or perceived by means of those things which belong to the senses, nor simple and imageless things by means of types and images, nor the formless and intangible essence of

° [This work is lost.—*Ed.*]

°° [The Affirmative path of knowing is here contrasted with the Negative path of knowing. The former has value as leading up to the latter; but it is only safe so far as we keep within the bounds of Scripture.—*Ed.*]

unembodied things by means of those which have bodily form, by the same law of truth the boundless Super-Essence surpasses Essences, the Super-Intellectual Unity surpasses Intelligences, the One which is beyond thought surpasses the apprehension of thought, and the Good which is beyond utterance surpasses the reach of words. Yea, it is an Unity which is the unifying Source of all unity and a Super-Essential Essence, a Mind beyond the reach of mind and a Word beyond utterance, eluding Discourse, Intuition, Name, and every kind of being. It is the Universal Cause of existence while Itself existing not, for It is beyond all Being and such that It alone could give, with proper understanding thereof, a revelation of Itself.

2. Now concerning this hidden Super-Essential Godhead we must not dare, as I have said, to speak, or even to form any conception Thereof, except those things which are divinely revealed to us from the Holy Scriptures. For as It hath lovingly taught us in the Scriptures concerning Itself the understanding and contemplation of Its actual nature is not accessible to any being: for such knowledge is super-essentially exalted above them all. And many of the Sacred Writers thou wilt find who have declared that It is not only invisible and past incomprehensible, but also unsearchable and past finding out, since there is no trace of any that have penetrated the hidden depths of Its infinitude. . . .

3. In obedience to these divine behests which guide all the holy dispositions of the heavenly hosts, we worship with reverent silence the unutterable Truths and with the unfathomable and holy veneration of our minds, approach that Mystery of Godhead which exceeds all Mind and Being. . . . Thus we do learn that It is the Cause and Origin and Being and Life of all creation. . . . Yea, in a super-essential manner, above the category of origin, It is the Origin of all origin, and the good and bounteous Communication of hidden mysteries; nay, in a word, It is the life of all things that live and the Being of all that are, the Origin and Cause of all life and being through Its bounty which both brings them into existence and maintains them.

.   .   .   .   .   .

5. Thus, as for the Super-Essence of the Supreme Godhead (if we would define the Transcendence of its Transcendent Goodness) it is not lawful to any lover of that Truth which is above all truth to celebrate It as Reason or Power or Mind or Life or Being, but rather as most utterly surpassing all condition, movement, life, imagination, conjecture, name, discourse, thought, conception, being, rest, dwelling,

union, limit, infinity, everything that exists. . . . Conscious of this, the Sacred Writers celebrate It by every Name while yet they call it Nameless. . . .

CONCERNING THE UNDIFFERENCING AND THE DIFFERENTIATION IN DIVINITY, AND THE NATURE OF DIVINE UNIFICATION AND DIFFERENTIATION

. . . . .

4. But needs must we, methinks, go deeper into the matter and thoroughly explain the difference between Undifference and Differentiation as concerning God, in order that our whole Discourse may be made clear. . . . For, as I said elsewhere, the Initiates of our Divine Tradition designate the Undifferenced Attributes of the Transcendently Ineffable and Unknowable Permanence as hidden, incommunicable Ultimates, but the beneficent Differentiations of the Supreme Godhead, they call Emanations and Manifestations; and following the Holy Scripture they declare that some Attributes belong especially to Undifference, and some, on the other hand, to Differentiation. For instance, they say concerning the Divine Unity, or Super-Essence, that the undivided Trinity holds in a common Unity without distinction Its Subsistence beyond Being, Its Godhead beyond Deity, Its Goodness beyond Excellence; the Identity, surpassing all things, of Its transcendently Individual Nature; Its Oneness above Unity; Its Namelessness and Multiplicity of Names; Its Unknowableness and perfect intelligibility; Its universal Affirmation and universal Negation in a state above all Affirmation and Negation, and that It possesses the mutual Abiding and Indwelling (as it were) of its indivisibly supreme Persons in an utterly Undifferentiated and Transcendent Unity, and yet without any confusion even as the lights of lamps (to use visible and homely similes) being in one house and wholly interpenetrating one another, severally possess a clear and absolute distinction each from each, and are by their distinctions united into one, and in their unity are kept distinct. Even so do we see, when there are many lamps in a house, how that the lights of them all are unified into one undifferentiated light, so that there shineth forth from them one indivisible brightness; and no one, methinks, could separate the light of one particular lamp from the others, in isolation from the air which embraces them all, nor could he see one light without another, inasmuch as, without confusion, they yet are wholly commingled.

Yea, if any one takes out of the dwelling one of the burning lamps, all its own particular light will therewith depart from the place without either carrying off in itself aught of the other lights or bequeathing any of its own brightness to the rest. For, as I said, the entire and complete union of the lights one with another brought no confusion or commixture in any parts—and that though the light is literally embodied in the air and streams from the material substance of fire. The Super-Essential Unity of God, however, exceedeth not only the unions of material bodies, but even those of Souls and of Intelligences, which these Godlike and celestial Luminaries in perfect mutual interpenetration supernaturally and without confusion possess, through a participation corresponding to their individual powers of participating in the All-Transcendent Unity.

5. There is, on the other hand, a Differentiation made in the Super-Essential Doctrine of God—not merely such as I have just mentioned (viz. that in the very Unity, Each of the Divine Persons possesses without confusion its own distinct existence), but also that the Attributes of the Super-Essential Divine Generation are not interchangeable. The Father alone is the Source of the Super-Essential Godhead, and the Father is not a Son, nor is the Son a Father; for the Divine Persons all preserve, Each without alloy, His own partticular Attributes of praise. Such, then, are the instances of Undifference and of Differentiation in the Ineffable Unity and Subsistence of God. And if the term "Differentiation" be also applied to the bounteous act of Emanation whereby the Divine Unity, brimming Itself with goodness in the excess of Its Undifferenced Unity thus enters into Multiplicity, yet an undifferenced unity worketh even in those differentiated acts whereby, in ceaseless communications, It bestows Being, Life, and Wisdom, and those other gifts of the all-creative Goodness in respect of which (as we behold the communications and the participants thereof) we celebrate those things wherein the creatures supernaturally participate. Yea, 'tis a common and undifferenced activity of the whole Godhead that It is wholly and entirely communicated unto each of them that share It and unto none merely in part; even as the centre of a circle is shared by all the radii which surround it in a circle; and as there are many impressions of a seal all sharing in the seal which is their archetype while yet this is entire, nor is it only a part thereof that belongeth unto any of them. But the Incommunicable All-creative Godhead transcends all such symbols in that It is beyond Apprehension nor hath It any other mode of communion such as to join It unto the participants.

Perhaps, however, some one will say: "The seal is not entire and the same in all the printed copies." I answer that this is not due to the seal itself (for it gives itself wholly and identically to each), but the difference of the substances which share it makes the impressions of the one, entire, identical archetype to be different. . . .

6. Again, it is by a Differentiated act of God's benevolence that the Super-Essential Word should wholly and completely take Human Substance of human flesh and do and suffer all those things which, in a special and particular manner, belonging to the action of His Divine Humanity. In these acts the Father and the Spirit have no share in the loving generosity of the Divine counsels and in all that transcendent Divine working of unutterable mysteries which were performed in Human Nature by Him Who as God and as the Word of God is Immutable. So do we strive to differentiate the Divine Attributes, according as these Attributes are Undifferenced or Differentiated.°

7. Now all the grounds of these Unifications, and Differentiations in the Divine Nature which the Scriptures have revealed to us, we have explained in the Outlines of Divinity, to the best of our abilities, treating separately of each. The latter class we have philosophically unravelled and unfolded, and so have sought to guide the holy and unspotted mind to contemplate the shining truths of Scripture, while the former class we have endeavored (in accordance with Divine Tradition) to apprehend as Mysteries in a manner beyond the activities of our minds. For all Divine things, even those that are revealed to us, are only known by their Communications. Their ultimate nature, which they possess in their own original being, is beyond Mind and beyond all Being and Knowledge. . . .

.   .   .   .   .

8. . . . For there is no exact similitude between the creatures and the Creative Originals; °° for the creatures possess only such images of the Creative Originals as are possible to them, while the Originals Themselves transcend and exceed the creatures by the very nature of Their own Originality. To employ human examples, we say that pleasant or painful conditions produce in us feelings of pleasure or pain while yet they possess not these feelings themselves; and we do not say that the fire which warms and burns is itself burnt or warmed. Even so if any one says that Very Life lives, or that Very Light is enlightened, he will be wrong (according to my view) unless,

---

° Undifference belongs to the ultimate Godhead, Differentiation to the distinction between the Three Persons of the Trinity. The former is the sphere of Mystical Theology, the latter is that of Dogmatic Theology. The former implies the *Via Negativa* the latter the *Via Affirmativa*.

°° The Persons of the Godhead.

perchance, he were to use these terms in a different sense from the ordinary one to mean that the qualities of created things pre-exist, after a superlative manner as touching their true Being in the Creative Originals.

. . . . .

CONCERNING "EXISTENCE" AND ALSO CONCERNING "EXEMPLARS"

1. Now must we proceed to the Name of "Being" which is truly applied by the Divine Science to Him that truly Is. But this much we must say, that it is not the purpose of our discourse to reveal the Super-Essential Being in its Super-Essential Nature * (for this is unutterable, nor can we know It, or in anywise express It, and It is beyond even the Unity), but only to celebrate the Emanation of the Absolute Divine Essence into the universe of things. For the Name of "Good" revealing all the emanations of the universal Cause, extends both to the things which are, and to the things which are not, and is beyond both categories. And the title of "Existent" extends to all existent things and is beyond them. And the title "Life" extends to all living things and is beyond them. And the title of "Wisdom" extends to the whole realm of Intuition, Reason, and Sense-Perception, and is beyond them all.

. . . . .

4. . . . . . For God is not Existent in any ordinary sense, but in a simple and undefinable manner embracing and anticipating all existence in Himself. Hence He is called "King of the Ages," because in Him and around Him all Being is and subsists, and He neither was, nor will be, nor hath entered the life-process, nor is doing so, nor ever will, or rather He doth not even exist, but is the Essence of existence in things that exist; and not only the things that exist but also their very existence comes from Him that Is before the ages. For He Himself is the Eternity of the ages and subsists before the ages.

5. Let us, then, repeat that all things and all ages derive their existence from the Pre-Existent. All Eternity and Time are from Him and He who is Pre-Existent is the Beginning and the Cause of all Eternity and Time and of anything that hath any kind of being. All things participate in Him, nor doth He depart from anything that exists; He is before all things, and all things have their maintenance in Him; and,

* The ultimate Godhead is reached only by the Negative Path, and known only by unknowing. The Affirmative Path of philosophical knowledge leads only to the differentiated manifestations of the Godhead: e.g. the Trinity.

in short, if anything exists under any form whatever, 'tis in the Pre-Existent that it exists and is perceived and preserves its being. . . .

.   .   .   .   .

10. Thus the Pre-Existent is the Beginning and the End of all things: the Beginning as their Cause, the End as their Final Purpose. He bounds all things and yet is their boundless Infinitude, in a manner that transcends all the opposition between the Finite and the Infinite. For, as hath been often said, He contains beforehand and did create all things in One Act, being present unto all and everywhere, both in the particular individual and in the Universal Whole, and going out unto all things while yet remaining in Himself. He is both at rest and in motion, and yet is in neither state, nor hath He beginning, middle, or end; He neither inheres in any individual thing, nor is He any individual thing. We cannot apply to Him any attribute of eternal things nor of temporal things. He transcends both Time and Eternity, and all things that are in either of them; inasmuch as Very Eternity and the world with its standard of measurement and the things which are measured by those standards have their being through Him and from Him. But concerning these matters let that suffice which hath been spoken more properly elsewhere.

.   .   .   .   .

CONCERNING "WISDOM," "MIND," "REASON," "TRUTH," "FAITH"

.   .   .   .   .

2. . . . . We must now ask in what sense God, Who is Supra-Sapient, can be spoken of as Wisdom, Mind, Reason, and Knowledge? How can He have an intellectual intuition of intelligible things when He possesses no intellectual activities? Or how can He know the things perceived by sense when His existence transcends all sense-perception? And yet the Scripture says that He knoweth all things and that nothing escapes the Divine Knowledge. But, as I have often said, we must interpret Divine Things in a manner suitable to their nature. For the lack of Mind and Sensation must be predicated of God by excess and not by defect. And in the same way we attribute lack of Reason to Him that is above Reason, and Imperfectibility to Him that is above and before Perfection; and Intangible and Invisible Darkness we attribute to that Light which is Unapproachable because It so far exceeds the visible light. And thus the Mind of God embraces all things in an utterly transcendent knowledge and, in Its causal relation to all

things, anticipates within Itself the knowledge of them all—knowing and creating angels before the angels were, and knowing all other things inwardly and from the very beginning, and thus bringing them into existence. . . . And It doth not perceive each class specifically, but in one embracing causality It knows and maintains all things —even as Light possesses beforehand in itself a causal knowledge of the darkness, not knowing the darkness in any other way than from the Light. Thus the Divine Wisdom in knowing Itself will know all things; will in that very Oneness know and produce material things immaterially, divisible things indivisibly, manifold things under the form of Unity. For if God, in the act of causation, imparts Existence to all things, in the same single act of causation He will support all these His creatures the which are derived from Him and have in Him their forebeing, and He will not gain His knowledge of things from the things themselves, but He will bestow upon each kind the knowledge of itself and the knowledge of the others. And hence God doth not possess a private knowledge of Himself and as distinct therefrom a knowledge embracing all the creatures in common; for the Universal Cause, in knowing Itself, can scarcely help knowing the things that proceed from it and whereof It is the Cause. With this knowledge, then, God knoweth all things, not through a mere understanding of the things but through an understanding of Himself. . . .

.   .   .   .   .

CONCERNING "PERFECT" AND "ONE"

1. . . . Now let us, if thou art willing, proceed to the most important Title of all. For the Divine Science attributes all qualities to the Creator of all things and attributes them all together, and speaks of Him as One. Now such a Being is Perfect: not only in the sense that It is Absolute Perfection and possesseth in Itself and from Itself a distinctive Uniformity of Its Existence, and that It is wholly perfect in Its whole Essence, but also in the sense that, in Its transcendence It is *beyond* Perfection; and that, while giving definite form or limit to all that is indefinite, It is yet in Its simple Unity raised above all limitation, and is not contained or comprehended by anything, but penetrates to all things at once and beyond them in Its unfailing bounties and never-ending activities. Moreover the Title "Perfect" means that It cannot be increased (being *always* Perfect) and cannot be diminished, and that It contains all things beforehand in Itself and overflows in one ceaseless, identical, abundant and inexhaustible sup-

ply, whereby It perfects all perfect things and fills them with Its own
Perfection.

2. And the title "One" implies that It is all things under the form
of Unity through the Transcendence of Its Oneness, and is the Cause
of all things without departing from that Unity. For there is nothing
in the world without a share in the One; and, just as all number participates in unity (and we speak of *one* couple, *one* dozen, *one* half,
one third, or *one* tenth) even so everything and each part of everything participates in the One, and on the existence of the One all other
existences are based, and the One Cause of all things is not one of the
many things in the world, but is before all Unity and Multiplicity and
gives to all Unity and Multiplicity their definite bounds. For no
multiplicity can exist except by some participation in the One. . . .

3. Moreover, we must bear this in mind: that when we attribute a
common unity to things we do so in accordance with the preconceived
law of their kind belonging to each one, and that the One is thus
the elementary basis of all things. And if you take away the One there
will remain neither whole nor part nor anything else in the world; for
all things are contained beforehand and embraced by the One as an
Unity in Itself. . . .   And you will not find anything in the world
but derives from the One (which, in a super-essential sense, is the
name of the whole Godhead) both its individual existence and the
process that perfects and preserves it. . . .   For Unity, as found in
the creatures, is numerical; and number participates in Essence: but
the Super-Essential Unity gives definite shape to existent unity and to
every number, and is Itself the Beginning, the Cause, the Numerical
Principal and the Law of Unity, number and every creature. And
hence, when we speak of the All-Transcendent Godhead as an Unity
and a Trinity, It is not an Unity or a Trinity such as can be know by
us or any other creature, though to express the truth of Its utter Self-
Union and Its Divine Fecundity we apply the titles of "Trinity" and
"Unity" to That Which is beyond all titles, expressing under the form
of Being That Which is beyond Being. But no Unity or Trinity or
Number or Oneness or Fecundity or any other thing that either is a
creature or can be known to any creature, is able to utter the mystery,
beyond all mind and reason, of that Transcendent Godhead which
super-essentially surpasses all things. It hath no name, nor can It be
grasped by the reason; It dwells in a region beyond us, where our feet
cannot tread. Even the title of "Goodness" we do not ascribe to It
because we think such a name suitable; but desiring to frame some
conception and language about this Its ineffable Nature, we consecrate
as primarily belonging to It the Name we most revere. And in this too

we shall be in agreement with the Sacred Writers; nevertheless the actual truth must still be far beyond us. Hence we have given our preference to the Negative method, because this lifts the soul above all things cognate with its finite nature, and, guiding it onward through all the conceptions of God's Being which are transcended by that Being exceeding all Name, Reason, and Knowledge, reaches beyond the farthest limits of the world and there joins us unto God Himself, in so far as the power of union with Him is possessed even by us men.

．　　．　　．　　．　　．

THE MYSTICAL THEOLOGY

Trinity, which exceedeth all Being, Deity, and Goodness! . . . Guide us to that topmost height of mystic lore which exceedeth light and more than exceedeth knowledge, where the simple, absolute, and unchangeable mysteries of heavenly Truth lie hidden in the dazzling obscurity of the secret Silence, outshining all brilliance with the intensity of their darkness, and surcharging our blinded intellects with the utterly impalpable and invisible fairness of glories which exceed all beauty! Such be my prayer; and thee, dear Timothy, I counsel that, in the earnest exercise of mystic contemplation, thou leave the senses and the activities of the intellect . . . and that thine understanding being laid to rest, thou strain . . . towards an union with Him whom neither being nor understanding can contain. For, by the unceasing and absolute renunciation of thyself and all things, thou shalt in pureness cast all things aside, and be released from all, and so shalt be led upwards to the Ray of that divine Darkness which exceedeth all existence.

These things thou must not disclose to any of the unitiated, by whom I mean those who cling to the objects of human thought. . . . And, if the Divine Initiation is beyond such men as these, what can be said of others yet more incapable thereof, who describe the Transcendent Cause of all things by qualities drawn from the lowest order of being, while they deny that it is in any way superior to the various ungodly delusions which they fondly invent in ignorance of this truth? That while it possesses all the positive attributes of the universe (being the universal Cause), yet in a stricter sense It does not possess them, since It transcends them all, wherefore there is no contradiction between affirming and denying that It has them inasmuch as It precedes and surpasses all deprivation, being beyond all positive and negative distinctions?

．　　．　　．　　．　　．

Unto this Darkness which is beyond Light we pray that we may come, and may attain unto vision through the loss of sight and knowledge, and that in ceasing thus to see or to know we may learn to know that which is beyond all perception and understanding (for this emptying of our faculties is true sight and knowledge), and that we may offer Him that transcends all things the praises of a transcendent hymnody, which we shall do by denying or removing all things that are—like as men, who, carving a statue out of marble, remove all the impediments that hinder the clear perceptive of the latent image and by this mere removal display the hidden statue itself in its hidden beauty. Now we must wholly distinguish this negative method from that of positive statements. For when we were making positive statements we began with the most universal statements, and then through intermediate terms we came at last to particular titles, but now ascending upwards from particular to universal conceptions we strip off all qualities in order that we may attain a naked knowledge of that Unknowing which in all existent things is enwrapped by all objects of knowledge, and that we may begin to see that super-essential Darkness which is hidden by all the light that is in existent things.

·   ·   ·   ·   ·

. . . But why is it, you will ask, that after beginning from the highest category when one method was affirmative we begin from the lowest category where it is negative? Because, when affirming the existence of that which transcends all affirmation, we were obliged to start from that which is most akin to It, and then make the affirmation on which the rest depended; but when pursuing the negative method, to reach that which is beyond all negation, we must start by applying our negations to those qualities which differ most from the ultimate goal. Surely it is truer to affirm that God is life and goodness than that He is air or stone, and truer to deny that drunkenness or fury can be attributed to Him than to deny that we may apply to Him the categories of human thought.

7

MOSES MAIMONIDES

The Attributes of God *

ON THE QUESTION of the knowledge man has of the nature of God,
Maimonides argues vigorously and effectively for the conception
of the *via negative*. He asserts that we cannot predicate any positive
attributes of God except in the nominal sense. An analysis of the
nature of attributes reveals that they are superadded to the essence
of their objects. Attributes therefore cannot be positively predicated of God, for they would be accidental to His being and, as
accidents, would destroy his essential unity. Furthermore, there
can be no relation between God and creatures, for they have
nothing in common and even existence is applied to them homony-
mously. In God existence and essence are identical, whereas in
creatures existence is accidental. Finally, the negative attributes
are said to be the only true attributes. They give us an indirect
knowledge of God, for by denying, e.g., existence (as an attribute),
plurality, and imperfection of God, we know that He is, is One,
and Perfect.

IF . . . you have a desire to rise to a higher state, viz., that of
reflection, and truly to hold the conviction that God is One and
possesses true unity, without admitting plurality or divisibility in any
sense whatever, you must understand that God has no essential attribute in any form or in any sense whatever, and that the rejection
of corporeality implies the rejection of essential attributes. Those who
believe that God is One, and that He has many attributes, declare the
unity with their lips, and assume plurality in their thoughts. This is
like the doctrine of the Christians, who say that He is one and He is
three, and that the three are one. Of the same character is the doctrine
of those who say that God is One, but that He has many attributes,
and that He with His attributes are One. . . .

. . . . .

* From the *Guide of the Perplexed,* translated by M. Friedländer (Trübner
and Co., 1885), pp. 171-212.

Moses Maimonides (1135-1204), was educated in Spain and became one of
the leading physicians and philosophers of that country. He exerted a strong
influence on both Moslem and Christian philosophers and theologians. With the
Moslem persecution of the Jews he was forced to leave Spain. He took up residence in Cairo, where he remained until his death.

. . . For it is a self-evident truth that the attribute is not inherent in the object to which it is ascribed, but it is superadded to its essence, and is consequently an *accident*; if the attribute denoted the essence of the object, it would be either mere tautology, as if, e.g., one would say "man is man," or the explanation of a name, as, e.g., "man is a speaking animal"; for the words "speaking animal" include the true essence of man, and there is no third element besides life and speech that constitutes man; when he, therefore, is described by the attributes of life and speech, these are nothing but an explanation of the name "man," that is to say, that the thing which is called man, consists of life and speech. It will now be clear that the attribute must be one of two things, either the essence of the object described—in that case it is a mere explanation of a name, and on that account we might admit the attribute in reference to God, but we reject it from another cause as will be shown—or the attribute is something different from the object described, some extraneous superadded element; in that case the attribute would be an accident, and he who merely rejects the appellation "accidents" in reference to the attributes of God, does not thereby alter their character; for everything superadded to the essence of an object joins it without forming part of its essential properties, and that constitutes an accident. Add to this the logical consequences of admitting many attributes, viz., the existence of many eternal beings. There cannot be any belief in the unity of God except by admitting that He is one simple substance, without any composition or plurality of elements; one from whatever side you view it, and by whatever test you examine it; not divisible into two parts in any way and by any cause, nor capable of any form of plurality either objectively or subjectively. . . .

.   .   .   .   .   .

. . . A thing is described by its relation to another thing, e.g., to time, to space, or to a different individual; thus we say, Zaid, the father of A, or the partner of B, or who dwells at a certain place, or who lived at a stated time. This kind of attribute does not necessarily imply plurality or change in the essence of the object described; for the same Zaid, to whom reference is made, is the partner of Amru, the father of Becr, the master of Khalid, the friend of Zaid, dwells in a certain house, and was born in a certain year. Such relations are not the essence of a thing, nor are they so intimately connected with it as qualities. At first thought, it would seem that they may be employed in reference to God, but after careful and thorough consideration we are convinced of their inadmissibility. It is quite clear that there is no relation between God and time or space. For time is an accident connected with motion . . .; and since motion is one of the conditions to which only material bodies are subject, and God is immaterial, there can be no relation between Him and time. Similarly there is no relation between Him and space.* But what we have to investigate and to examine is this: whether some real relation exists between God and any of the substances created by Him, by which He could be described? That there is no correlation between Him and any of His creatures can easily be seen; for the characteristic of two objects correlative to each other is the equality of their reciprocal relation. Now, as God has absolute existence, while all other beings have only possible existence, as we shall show, there consequently cannot be any correlation between God and His creatures. That a certain kind of relation does exist between them is by some considered possible, but wrongly. It is impossible to imagine a relation between intellect and sight, although, as we believe, the same kind of existence is common to both; how, then, could a relation be imagined between any creature and God, who has nothing in common with any other being; for even the term existence is applied to Him, and other things, according to our opinion, only by way of pure homonymity. Consequently there is no relation whatever between Him and any other being. For whenever we speak of a relation between two things, these belong to the same species; but when two things belong to different species though of the same class, there is no relation between them. We therefore do not say, this red compared with that green, is more, or less, or equally intense, although both belong to the same class—color; when they belong to two different classes, there does not appear to exist any relation between them, not even to a man of ordinary intellect, although the two things belong to the same category; e.g., between a hundred cubits and the heat of pepper there is no relation, the one being a quality, the other a quantity; or between wisdom and sweetness, between meekness and bitterness, although all these come under the head of quality in its more general signification. How, then, could there be any relation between God and His creatures, considering the important difference between them in respect to true existence, the greatest of all differences. Besides, if any relation existed between them, God would be subject to the accident of relation; and although that would not be an accident to the essence of God, it would still be, to some extent, a kind of accident. You would, therefore, be wrong if you applied affirmative attributes in their literal sense to God, though they contained only relations; these, however, are the most

---

* That is, space is an accident connected with bodies . . . .

appropriate of all attributes, to be employed, in a less strict sense, in reference to God, because they do not imply that a plurality of eternal things exists, or that any change takes place in the essence of God, when those things change to which God is in relation.

．　　．　　．　　．　　．　　．

The circumstance which caused men to believe in the existence of divine attributes is similar to that which caused others to believe in the corporeality of God. The latter have not arrived at that belief by speculation, but by following the literal sense of certain passages in the Bible. The same is the case with the attributes; when in the books of the Prophets and of the Law, God is described by attributes, such passages are taken in their literal sense, and it is then believed that God possesses attributes. . . . We apply to all such passages the principle, "The Torah speaketh in the language of man," and say that the object of all these terms is to describe God as the most perfect being, not as possessing those qualities which are only perfections in relation to created living beings. . . .

It is known that existence is an accident appertaining to all things, and therefore an element superadded to their essence. This must evidently be the case as regards everything the existence of which is due to some cause; its existence is an element superadded to its essence. But as regards a being whose existence is not due to any cause—God alone is that being, for His existence . . . is absolute—existence and essence are perfectly identical; He is not a substance to which existence is joined as an accident, as an additional element. . . . Consequently God exists without possessing the attribute of existence.° Similarly He lives without possessing the attribute of life; knows, without possessing the attribute of knowledge; is omnipotent without possessing the attribute of omnipotence; is wise, without possessing the attribute of wisdom; all this reduces itself to one and the same entity; there is no plurality in Him. . . .

Know that the negative attributes of God are the true attributes: they do not include any incorrect notions or any deficiency whatever in reference to God, while positive attributes imply polytheism, and are inadequate, as we have already shown. . . .

. . . The negative attributes have this in common with the positive, that they necessarily circumscribe the object to some extent, although such circumscription consists only in the exclusion of what otherwise would not be excluded. In the following point, however,

° The term "existence" is applied to God in the sense of denying His non-existence.

the negative attributes are distinguished from the positive. The positive attributes, although not peculiar to one thing, describe a portion of what we desire to know, either some part of its essence or some of its accidents; the negative attributes, on the other hand, do not, as regards the essence of the thing which we desire to know, in any way tell us what it is, except it be indirectly. . . .

. . . The negative attributes, however, are those which are necessary to direct the mind to the truths which we must believe concerning God; for, on the one hand, they do not imply any plurality, and, on the other, they convey to man the highest possible knowledge of God; e.g., it has been established by proof that some being must exist besides those things which can be perceived by the senses, or apprehended by the mind; when we say of this being, that it exists, we mean that its non-existence is impossible. We thus perceive that such a being is not, for instance, like the four elements, which are inanimate, and we therefore say it is living, expressing thereby that it is not dead. We call such a being incorporeal, because we notice that it is unlike the heavens, which are living, but material. Seeing that it is also different from the intellect, which, though incorporeal and living, owes its existence to some cause, we say it is the first, expressing thereby that its existence is not due to any cause. We further notice, that the existence, that is, the essence, of this being is not limited to its own existence; many existences emanate from it, and its influence is not like that of the fire in producing heat, or that of the sun in sending forth light, but consists in constantly giving them stability and order by well-established rule, . . . we say, on that account, it has power, wisdom, and will, i.e., it is not feeble or ignorant, or hasty, and does not abandon its creatures; when we say that it is not feeble, we mean that its existence is capable of producing the existence of many other things; by saying it is not ignorant, we mean "it perceives" or "it lives"—for everything that perceives is alive—by saying "it is not hasty, and does not abandon its creatures," we mean that all these creatures preserve a certain order and arrangement; they are not left to themselves, or produced aimlessly, but whatever condition they receive from that being is given them with design and intention. We thus learn that there is no other being like unto God, and we say that He is One, i.e., there are not more Gods than one.

It has thus been shown that every attribute predicated of God either denotes the quality of an action, or—when the attribute is intended to convey some idea of the Divine Being itself, and not of His actions—the negation of the opposite. . . . What, then, can be the result of our efforts, when we try to obtain a knowledge of a Being that is free from substance, that is most simple, whose existence is absolute, and not due to any cause, to whose perfect essence nothing can be superadded, and whose perfection consists, as we have shown, in the absence of all defects. All we understand, is the fact that He exists, that He is a Being to whom none of all His creatures is similar, who has nothing in common with them, who does not include plurality, who is never too feeble to produce other beings, and whose relation to the universe is that of a steersman to a boat; and even this is not a real relation, a real simile, but serves only to convey to us the idea that God rules the universe; that is, that He gives it duration, and preserves its necessary arrangement. . . . In the contemplation of His essence, our comprehension and knowledge prove insufficient; in the examination of His works, how they necessarily result from His will, our knowledge proves to be ignorance, and in the endeavor to extol Him in words, all our efforts in speech are mere weakness and failure.

8

CAJETAN

Analogy of Proportionality *

THE FOLLOWING DOCTRINE of analogy is an attempt to define and explicate the meaning of analogy of proportionality, as distinct from analogy of attribution, and to show how we may reason on the basis of this type of analogy to a knowledge of the nature of God. The author indicates that this type of analogy has its source in the writing of St. Thomas, and he emphasizes the significance of analogy for metaphysics. He explains how analogy is a mean between equivocation and univocation. In conclusion, he criticizes

* From *The Analogy of Names*, translated by Edward A. Bushinski and Henry J. Koren (Duquesne University Press, Philosophical Series 4, 1953), pp. 24-31, 68-72. Reprinted with the permission of the publisher.

Thomas de Vio (1468-1534), commonly known as Cajetan, entered the Dominican Order at the age of sixteen. He studied at Naples, Bologna, and Padua. Later he lectured at Pavia and Padua and in 1508 was elected Master-General of his order. He was made a cardinal in 1517. He wrote many commentaries on St. Thomas and Aristotle and is generally recognized as one of the greatest of the commentators on St. Thomas. His contribution to the doctrine of analogy has had a considerable influence on Thomists.

an argument of Scotus and then cites an example of syllogistic reasoning which he believes illustrates the applicability and validity of his principle of analogy of proportionality.

PASSING OVER from what is called incorrectly analogous to analogy in the proper sense, we say that analogous by proportionality are called those things which have a common name, and the notion expressed by this name is proportionally the same. . . . For instance, to see by corporeal vision and by intellectual vision are indicated by the common term *to see*, because just as *to understand* presents something to the mind, so *to see* presents something to the animated body.

The name *proportion* is given to a definite relation of one quantity to another; e.g. we say that four is twice as much in proportion to two. The name *proportionality* is given to a similitude of two proportions; e.g. we say that eight is to four as six is to three, because both are twice as much in proportion, etc. However, philosophers have transferred the term proportion from the sphere of mathematics and use it to express any relationship of conformity, commensuration, capacity, etc. As a result they have extended the use of the term proportionality to every similitude of relationships. . . .

Analogy of proportionality can occur in two ways—namely, metaphorically and properly. It is *metaphorical* when the common term has absolutely one formal meaning which is realized in one of the analogates and predicated of the other by metaphor. For example, *to smile* has one meaning in itself, but is metaphorically analogous with respect to a true smile and a blooming meadow or good fortune; for thus we indicate that these things are just like a man smiling. Sacred Scripture is full of examples of this sort of analogy wherever it teaches us about God by means of metaphors.

Analogy of proportionality occurs in the *proper* sense when the common name is predicated of both analogates without the use of metaphors. For instance, *principle* can be predicated of the heart with respect to an animal and of a foundation with respect to a house. . . .

By means of analogy of proportionality we know indeed the intrinsic entity, goodness, truth, etc. of things. . . . For this reason, metaphysical speculations without knowledge of this analogy must be said to be unskilled. . . . The situation has perhaps never been so dangerous since the time of Aristotle as it is in our day—one is almost held guilty of blasphemy if one says that metaphysical terms are analogous and explains them as common by proportionality. . . .

This analogy is referred to by St. Thomas in *I. Sentent.* as analogy *"according to 'to be' and according to intention."* The reason is that the analogates are not considered equal in the perfection expressed by the common name, nor in the "to be" of this perfection, yet they agree proportionally both in the perfection expressed by that name and in its "to be."

Since analogy is a mean between pure equivocation and univocation, its nature should be explained by means of the extremes. . . .

. . . By an *equivocal* name diverse things are so signified that, as such, they are united only by the external word. By a *univocal* name diverse things are so signified that, as such, they are united into some thing which in itself is absolutely one, and which is abstracted and separated from them in the cognitive order. By an analogous name, however, diverse things are so signified that, as such, they are united to diverse things according to one proportion. . . .

Hence the difference between univocation and analogy is the following. Things which give rise to *univocation* are similar to one another in the sense that the foundation of similitude in one has exactly the same nature as the foundation of similitude in the other. Thus the notion of one contains in itself nothing which the notion of the other does not contain. . . . On the other hand, things which give rise to analogy are similar in the sense that the foundation of similitude in one is absolutely different in nature from the foundation of similitude in the other. Thus the notion of one thing does not contain in itself what the notion of the other contains. For this reason the foundation of analogous similitude in either of the extremes is not to be abstracted from the extremes themselves but the foundations of similitude remain distinct, although they are similar according to proportion, and because of this they are said to be the same proportionally or analogically.°

REASONING AND ANALOGOUS NAMES

Some have the impression that the analogon cannot be known except in the way equivocals are known because it implies several, though similar, notions. More than that, for the same reason they argue that a fallacy of equivocation is committed in syllogisms in which an analogon is taken as the middle term and a definite analogate is used in the minor, although perhaps the process could be valid materially.

° [Thus animality is essentially the same in man and in animals, whereas being, wisdom, etc. have only a proportional similitude in man and God. The first instance exemplifies *univocal* predication, the second *analogical* (proportional) predication.—*Ed.*]

They also assert that from the notion of one analogate, as expressed by the name of the analogon, one cannot conclude that the other analogate formally realizes the same notion, but that for the same reason one will always fall in the above mentioned fallacy.

For example, if we assert that wisdom is analogically common to God and man in virtue of the fact that wisdom as found in man, taken precisely according to its formal concept, indicates a simple perfection, we cannot conclude that therefore God is formally wise, by arguing in the following manner:

> Every simple perfection is in God.
> Wisdom is a simple perfection.
> Therefore, wisdom is in God.

For the minor must be distinguished. If the word *wisdom* stands for character of wisdom as it is in man, the argument has four terms; for in the conclusion wisdom stands for the character of wisdom as it is found in God when we conclude that there is wisdom in God. On the other hand, if in the minor wisdom represents the character of wisdom as it is in God, then the conclusion that God is wise is not drawn from the perfection of created wisdom; yet all philosophers and theologians assert the opposite. This is the argument given by Scotus.

Those who follow Scotus in this argument are deceived. While paying attention to the diversity of notions in the analogon, they fail to consider whatever unity and identity lies hidden in it. For, as was explained, the notions of the analogon can be taken in two ways.

In one way, *in themselves*, insofar as they are distinguished from one another and according to what pertains to them as such, i.e. insofar as they are distinct.

In another way, insofar as they are *the same proportionally*. Used in the first way, it is obvious that they would lead to the error of equivocation. By using them in the second way, however, one does not commit any fault, because whatever belongs to one belongs also to the other proportionally, and whatever is denied of the one is also denied of the other proportionally. The reason is that whatever pertains to a similar object as such pertains also to that to which it is similar, proportionality of course being always duly observed.

Therefore, if from the immateriality of the soul one concludes that it is intellectual, from immateriality proportionally posited in God one could very well conclude that God is proportionally intellectual, i.e. to the degree that his immateriality exceeds that of man, His intellectuality exceeds that of man, etc. . . .

This analogy does not prevent a formal process of reasoning leading to the conclusion that God and creatures have some predicate in common. One can take the notion of wisdom and separate from it by means of the intellect whatever is imperfect. From the fact that what is proper to wisdom, taken formally, implies perfection without any imperfection, the conclusion can be drawn that the character of wisdom in God is not entirely diverse nor entirely the same, but the same proportionally, because the similitude between God and creature is not univocal but analogous.

On the other hand, we cannot conclude by a similar argument that God is a stone proportionally. For formally considered the character of a stone, no matter how purified, includes some imperfection, which prevents that character, whether in an absolute sense or proportionally, from being in God, except metaphorically, in the sense in which it is said that: "The rock was Christ."

Consequently, in a process of reasoning like the following:

> Every simple perfection is in God
> Wisdom is a simple perfection
> Therefore, wisdom is in God,

the word *wisdom* in the minor does not stand for this or that notion of wisdom, but for wisdom which is proportionally one, i.e. for both notions of wisdom, not taken in conjunction nor in disjunction, but insofar as they are undivided proportionally, insofar as one is the other proportionally, and insofar as both constitute a notion which is proportionally one.

Both are signified by the analogous term insofar as they are the same. Hence it is not necessary to distinguish the analogon in order to make it serve as the basis of a contradiction and become the subject or predicate of a proposition. Of its very nature it can do this, in virtue of the proportional identity which is included in it and which it principally expresses.

For contradiction is said to consist in the affirmation and negation of one and the same predicate of one and the same subject, etc., and not in the affirmation and negation of a univocal predicate of one and the same univocal subject. For, as was repeated so often, identity, both of things and of their notions, extends also to proportional identity.

9

DAVID HUME

Analogy and Anthropomorphism *

IN PART I of the *Dialogues* Hume sets forth the limits and extent
of the sceptical position. The selection here begins with Part II,
which opens with Cleanthes' argument for the existence of God.
His argument is based upon an appeal to experience and an analogy
between the works of man and the works of nature which leads
him to the conclusion that the author of nature bears a resemblance
to the mind of man in contriving its works and carrying out its
purposes. Philo is willing to accept the empirical basis of Cleanthes'
position but he argues vigorously against the validity of any analogical argument and questions the teleological view of nature which
has been presented. Cleanthes, in reply, appeals to the self-evi-
dence of design in nature and declares that the analogical argument
affords us the only valid knowledge we have concerning the nature
of Deity. He rejects the views of the mystics and the notion of the
incomprehensibility of God as being tantamount to atheism, but
Demea retorts in like vein that the view of Cleanthes is no better
than an anthropomorphism. The selection concludes with Philo
joining Demea in an attack upon the position of Cleanthes, and
enumerating in detail all the inconveniences and difficulties of
anthropomorphism.

NOT TO LOSE any time in circumlocutions, said Cleanthes, addressing
himself to Demea, much less in replying to the pious declamations
of Philo, I shall briefly explain how I conceive this matter. Look
around the world, contemplate the whole and every part of it: you
will find it to be nothing but one great machine, subdivided into
an infinite number of lesser machines, which again admit of sub-
divisions to a degree beyond what human senses and faculties can
trace and explain. All these various machines, and even their most
minute parts, are adjusted to each other with an accuracy which

* From *Dialogues Concerning Natural Religion* in his *Philosophical Works*
(Little, Brown and Co., 1854), II, 411-15, 417-23, 431-45.

David Hume (1711-76) was born at Edinburgh. He studied law but turned
against it and the business world in favor of a literary and philosophical career.
He wrote extensively on history, economics, and politics, as well as on philosophy.
For several years he held the position of librarian at Edinburgh and retired after
a brief career in the diplomatic service.

ravishes into admiration all men who have ever contemplated them. The curious adapting of means to ends, throughout all nature, resembles exactly, though it much exceeds, the productions of human contrivance—of human design, thought, wisdom, and intelligence. Since therefore the effects resemble each other, we are led to infer, by all the rules of analogy, that the causes also resemble, and that the Author of nature is somewhat similar to the mind of man, though possessed of much larger faculties, proportioned to the grandeur of the work which he has executed. By this argument *a posteriori*, and by this argument alone, do we prove at once the existence of a Deity and his similarity to human mind and intelligence.

I shall be so free, Cleanthes, said Demea, as to tell you that from the beginning I could not approve of your conclusion concerning the similarity of the Deity to men, still less can I approve of the mediums by which you endeavor to establish it. What! No demonstration of the Being of God! No abstract argument! No proofs *a priori*! Are these which have hitherto been so much insisted on by philosophers all fallacy, all sophism? Can we reach no farther in this subject than experience and probability? I will not say that this is betraying the cause of a Deity; but surely, by this affected candor, you give advantages to atheists which they never could obtain by the mere dint of argument and reasoning.

What I chiefly scruple in this subject, said Philo, is not so much that all religious arguments are by Cleanthes reduced to experience, as that they appear not to be even the most certain and irrefragable of that inferior kind. That a stone will fall, that fire will burn, that the earth has solidity, we have observed a thousand and a thousand times; and when any new instance of this nature is presented, we draw without hesitation the accustomed inference. The exact similarity of the cases gives us a perfect assurance of a similar event, and a stronger evidence is never desired nor sought after. But wherever you depart, in the least, from the similarity of the cases, you diminish proportionably the evidence, and may at last bring it to a very weak *analogy*, which is confessedly liable to error and uncertainty. After having experienced the circulation of the blood in human creatures, we make no doubt that it takes place in Titius and Maevius; but from its circulation in frogs and fishes it is only a presumption, though a strong one, from analogy that it takes place in men and other animals. The analogical reasoning is much weaker when we infer the circulation of the sap in vegetables from our experience that the blood circulates in animals; and those who hastily followed that imperfect analogy are found, by more accurate experiments, to have been mistaken.

If we see a house, Cleanthes, we conclude, with the greatest certainty, that it had an architect or builder because this is precisely that species of effect which we have experienced to proceed from that species of cause. But surely you will not affirm that the universe bears such a resemblance to a house that we can with the same certainty infer a similar cause, or that the analogy is here entire and perfect. The dissimilitude is so striking that the utmost you can here pretend to is a guess, a conjecture, a presumption concerning a similar cause; and how that pretension will be received in the world, I leave you to consider.

．　．　．　．　．

Now, according to this method of reasoning, Demea, it follows (and is, indeed, tacitly allowed by Cleanthes himself) that order, arrangement, or the adjustment of final causes, is not of itself any proof of design, but only so far as it has been experienced to proceed from that principle. For aught we can know *a priori*, matter may contain the source or spring of order originally within itself, as well as mind does; and there is no more difficulty in conceiving that the several elements, from an internal unknown cause, may fall into the most exquisite arrangement, than to conceive that their ideas, in the great universal mind, from a like internal unknown cause, fall into that arrangement. The equal possibility of both these suppositions is allowed. But, by experience, we find (according to Cleanthes) that there is a difference between them. Throw several pieces of steel together, without shape or form, they will never arrange themselves so as to compose a watch. Stone and mortar and wood, without an architect, never erect a house. But the ideas in a human mind, we see, by an unknown, inexplicable economy, arrange themselves so as to form the plan of a watch or house. Experience, therefore, proves that there is an original principle of order in mind, not in matter. From similar effects we infer similar causes. The adjustment of means to ends is alike in the universe, as in a machine of human contrivance. The causes, therefore, must be resembling. . . .

That all inferences, Cleanthes, concerning fact are founded on experience, and that all experimental reasonings are founded on the supposition that similar causes prove similar effects, and similar effects similar causes, I shall not at present much dispute with you. But observe, I entreat you, with what extreme caution all just reasoners proceed in the transferring of experiments to similar cases. Unless the cases be exactly similar, they repose no perfect confidence in applying their past observation to any particular phenomenon. Every alteration of circumstances occasions a doubt concerning the event; and it requires new experiments to prove certainly that the new circumstances are of no moment or importance. . . .

But can you think, Cleanthes, that your usual phlegm and philosophy have been preserved in so wide a step as you have taken when you compared to the universe houses, ships, furniture, machines, and, from their similarity in some circumstances, inferred a similarity in their causes? Thought, design, intelligence, such as we discover in men and other animals, is no more than one of the springs and principles of the universe, as well as heat or cold, attraction or repulsion, and a hundred others which fall under daily observation. It is an active cause by which some particular parts of nature, we find, produce alterations on other parts. But can a conclusion, with any propriety, be transferred from parts to the whole? Does not the great disproportion bar all comparison and inference? From observing the gowth of a hair, can we learn anything concerning the generation of a man? Would the manner of a leaf's blowing, even though perfectly known, afford us any instruction concerning the vegetation of a tree?

But allowing that we were to take the *operations* of one part of nature upon another for the foundation of our judgment concerning the *origin* of the whole (which never can be admitted), yet why select so minute, so weak, so bounded a principle as the reason and design of animals is found to be upon this planet? What peculiar privilege has this little agitation of the brain which we call *thought*, that we must thus make it the model of the whole universe? Our partiality in our own favor does indeed present it on all occasions, but sound philosophy ought carefully to guard against so natural an illusion.

So far from admitting, continued Philo, that the operations of a part can afford us any just conclusion concerning the origin of the whole, I will not allow any one part to form a rule for another part if the latter be very remote from the former. Is there any reasonable ground to conclude that the inhabitants of other planets possess thought, intelligence, reason, or anything similar to these faculties in men? When nature has so extremely diversified her manner of operation in this small globe, can we imagine that she incessantly copies herself throughout so immense a universe? And if thought, as we may well suppose, be confined merely to this narrow corner and has even there so limited a sphere of action, with what propriety can we assign it for the original cause of all things? The narrow views of a peasant who makes his domestic economy the rule for the government of kingdoms is in comparison a pardonable sophism. . . .

A very small part of this great system, during a very short time, is very imperfectly discovered to us; and do we thence pronounce decisively concerning the origin of the whole?

Admirable conclusion? Stone, wood, brick, iron, brass, have not, at this time, in this minute globe of earth, an order or arrangement without human art and contrivance; therefore, the universe could not originally attain its order and arrangement without something similar to human art. But is a part of nature a rule for another part very wide of the former? Is it a rule for the whole? Is a very small part a rule for the universe? Is nature in one situation a certain rule for nature in another situation vastly different from the former?

. . . And will any man tell me with a serious countenance that an orderly universe must arise from some thought and art like the human because we have experience of it? To ascertain this reasoning it were requisite that we had experience of the origin of worlds; and it is not sufficient, surely, that we have seen ships and cities arise from human art and contrivance. . . . Can you pretend to show any such similarity between the fabric of a house and the generation of a universe. Have you ever seen nature in any such situation as resembles the first arrangement of the elements? Have worlds ever been formed under your eye, and have you had leisure to observe the whole progress of the phenomenon, from the first appearance of order to its final consummation? If you have, then cite your experience and deliver your theory.

.   .   .   .   .

How the most absurd argument, replied Cleanthes, in the hands of a man of ingenuity and invention, may acquire an air of probability! Are you not aware, Philo, that it became necessary for Copernicus and his first disciples to prove the similarity of the terrestrial and celestial matter because several philosophers, blinded by old systems and supported by some sensible appearances, had denied this similarity? But that it is by no means necessary that theists should prove the similarity of the works of *nature* to those of *art* because this similarity is self-evident and undeniable? . . .

Let me here observe, too, continued Cleanthes, that this religious argument, instead of being weakened by that scepticism so much affected by you, rather acquires force from it and becomes more firm and undisputed. To exclude all argument or reasoning of every kind is either affectation or madness. The declared profession of every reasonable sceptic is only to reject abstruse, remote, and refined arguments; to adhere to common sense and the plain instincts of nature; and to assent, wherever any reasons strike him with so full a force that he cannot, without the greatest violence, prevent it. Now the arguments for natural religion are plainly of this kind; and nothing but the most perverse, obstinate metaphysics can reject them. Consider, anatomize the eye, survey its structure and contrivance, and tell me, from your own feeling, if the idea of a contriver does not immediately flow in upon you with a force like that of sensation. The most obvious conclusion, surely, is in favor of design; and it requires time, reflection, and study, to summon up those frivolous though abstruse objections which can support infidelity. Who can behold the male and female of each species, the correspondence of their parts and instincts, their passions and whole course of life before and after generation, but must be sensible that the propagation of the species is intended by nature? Millions and millions of such instances present themselves through every part of the universe, and no language can convey a more intelligible irresistible meaning than the curious adjustment of final causes. To what degree, therefore, of blind dogmatism must one have attained to reject such natural and such convincing arguments? . . .

. . . And if the argument for theism be, as you pretend, contradictory to the principles of logic, its universal, its irresistible influence proves clearly that there may be arguments of a like irregular nature. Whatever cavils may be urged, an orderly world, as well as a coherent, articulate speech, will still be received as an incontestable proof of design and intention.

.   .   .   .   .

[*Demea speaking*] The ancient Platonists, you know, were the most religious and devout of all the pagan philosophers, yet many of them, particularly Plotinus, expressly declare that intellect or understanding is not to be ascribed to the Deity, and that our most perfect worship of him consists, not in acts of veneration, reverence, gratitude, or love, but in a certain mysterious self-annihilation or total extinction of all our faculties. These ideas are, perhaps, too far stretched, but still it must be acknowledged that, by representing the Deity as so intelligible and comprehensible, and so similar to a human mind, we are guilty of the grossest and most narrow partiality, and make ourselves the model of the whole universe.

All the *sentiments* of the human mind, gratitude, resentment, love, friendship, approbation, blame, pity, emulation, envy, have a plain reference to the state and situation of man, and are calculated for preserving the existence and promoting the activity of such a being in such circumstances. It seems, therefore, unreasonable to transfer such sentiments to a supreme existence or to suppose him actuated by them; and the phenomena, besides, of the universe will not support us in such a theory. All our *ideas* derived from the senses are confessedly false and illusive, and cannot therefore be supposed to have place in a supreme intelligence. And as the ideas of internal sentiment, added to those of the external senses, compose the whole furniture of human understanding, we may conclude that none of the *materials* of thought are in any respect similar in the human and in the divine intelligence. Now, as to the *manner* of thinking, how can we make any comparison between them or suppose them anywise resembling? Our thought is fluctuating, uncertain, fleeting, successive, and compounded; and were we to remove these circumstances, we absolutely annihilate its essence, and it would in such a case be an abuse of terms to apply to it the name of thought or reason. At least, if it appear more pious and respectful (as it really is) still to retain these terms when we mention the Supreme Being, we ought to acknowledge that their meaning, in that case, is totally incomprehensible, and that the infirmities of our nature do not permit us to reach any ideas which in the least correspond to the ineffable sublimity of the Divine attributes.

It seems strange to me, said Cleanthes, that you Demea, who are so sincere in the cause of religion, should still maintain the mysterious, incomprehensible nature of the Deity, and should insist so strenuously that he has no manner of likeness or resemblance to human creatures. The Deity, I can readily allow, possesses many powers and attributes of which we can have no comprehension; but, if our ideas, so far as they go, be not just and adequate and correspondent to his real nature, I know not what there is in this subject worth insisting on. Is the name, without any meaning, of such mighty importance? Or how do you mystics, who maintain the absolute incomprehensibility of the Deity, differ from sceptics or atheists, who assert that the first cause of all is unknown and unintelligible? Their temerity must be very great if, after rejecting the production by a mind—I mean a mind resembling the human (for I know of no other)—they pretend to assign, with certainty, any other specific intelligible cause; and their conscience must be very scrupulous, indeed, if they refuse to call the universal unknown cause a God or Deity, and to bestow on him as many sublime eulogies and unmeaning epithets as you shall please to require of them.

Who could imagine, replied Demea, that Cleanthes, the calm philosophical Cleanthes, would attempt to refute his antagonists by affixing a nickname to them, and, like the common bigots and inquisitors of the age, have recourse to invective and declamation instead of reasoning? Or does he not perceive that these topics are easily retorted, and that *anthropomorphite* is an appelation as invidious, and implies as dangerous consequences, as the epithet of *mystic* with which he has honored us? In reality, Cleanthes, consider what it is you assert when you represent the Deity as similar to a human mind and understanding. What is the soul of man? A composition of various faculties, passions, sentiments, ideas—united, indeed, into one self or person, but still distinct from each other. When it reasons, the ideas which are the parts of its discourse arrange themselves in a certain form or order which is not preserved entire for a moment, but immediately gives place to another arrangement. New opinions, new passions, new affections, new feelings arise which continually diversify the mental scene and produce in it the greatest variety and most rapid succession imaginable. How is this compatible with that perfect immutability and simplicity which all true theists ascribe to the Deity? By the same act, say they, he sees past, present, and future; his love and hatred, his mercy and justice, are one individual operation; he is entire in every point of space, and complete in every instant of duration. No succession, no change, no acquisition, no diminution. What he is implies not in it any shadow of distinction or diversity. And what he is this moment he ever has been and ever will be, without any new judgment, sentiment, or operation. He stands fixed in one simple, perfect state; nor can you ever say, with any propriety, that this act of his is different from that other, or that this judgment or idea has been lately formed and will give place, by succession, to any different judgment or idea.

I can readily allow, said Cleanthes, that those who maintain the perfect simplicity of the Supreme Being, to the extent in which you have explained it, are complete mystics, and chargeable with all the consequences which I have drawn from their opinion. They are, in a word, atheists, without knowing it. For though it be allowed that the Deity possesses attributes of which we have no comprehension, yet ought we never to ascribe to him any attributes which are absolutely incompatible with that intelligent nature essential to him. A mind whose acts and sentiments and ideas are not distinct and successive, one that is wholly simple and totally immutable, is a mind which has no thought, no reason, no will, no sentiment, no love, no hatred; or in a word, is no mind at all. It is an abuse of terms to give it that appellation, and we may as well speak of limited extension without figure, or of number without composition.

Pray consider, said Philo, whom you are at present inveighing against. You are honoring with the appelation of *atheist* all the sound, orthodox divines, almost, who have treated of this subject; and you will at last be, yourself, found, according to your reckoning, the only sound theist in the world. But if idolaters be atheists, as, I think, may justly be asserted, and Christian theologians the same, what becomes of the argument, so much celebrated, derived from the universal consent of mankind?

But, because I know you are not much swayed by names and authorities, I shall endeavor to show you, a little more distinctly, the inconveniences of that anthropomorphism which you have embraced, and shall prove that there is no ground to suppose a plan of the world to be formed in the Divine mind, consisting of distinct ideas, differently arranged, in the same manner as an architect forms in his head the plan of a house which he intends to execute. . . .

How, therefore, shall we satisfy ourselves concerning the cause of that Being whom you suppose the Author of nature, or, according to your system of anthropomorphism, the ideal world into which you trace the material? Have we not the same reason to trace that ideal world into another ideal world or new intelligent principle? But if we stop and go no farther, why go so far? why not stop at the material world? How can we satisfy ourselves without going on *in infinitum*? And, after all, what satisfaction is there in that infinite progression? Let us remember the story of the Indian philosopher and his elephant. It was never more applicable than to the present subject. If the material world rests upon a similar ideal world, this ideal world must rest upon some other, and so on without end. It were better, therefore, never to look beyond the present material world. By supposing it to contain the principle of its order within itself, we really assert it to be God; and the sooner we arrive at that Divine Being, so much the better. When you go one step beyond the mundane system, you only excite an inquisitive humor which it is impossible ever to satisfy. . . .

But to show you still more inconveniences, continued Philo, in your anthropomorphism, please to take a new survey of your principles. *Like effects prove like causes.* This is the experimental argument; and this, you say too, is the sole theological argument. . . .

Now, Cleanthes, said Philo, with an air of alacrity and triumph, mark the consequences. *First,* by this method of reasoning you renounce all claim to infinity in any of the attributes of the Deity. For, as the cause ought only to be proportioned to the effect, and the effect, so far as it falls under our cognizance, is not infinite, what pretensions have we, upon your suppositions, to ascribe that attribute to the Divine Being? You will still insist that, by removing him so much from all similarity to human creatures, we give in to the most arbitrary hypothesis, and at the same time weaken all proofs of his existence.

Secondly, you have no reason, on your theory, for ascribing perfection to the Deity, even in his finite capacity, or for supposing him free from every error, mistake, or incoherence, in his undertakings. There are many inexplicable difficulties in the works of nature which, if we allow a perfect author to be proved *a priori,* are easily solved, and become only seeming difficulties from the narrow capacity of man, who cannot trace infinite relations. But according to your method of reasoning, these difficulties become all real, and, perhaps, will be insisted on as new instances of likeness to human art and contrivance. At least, you must acknowledge that it is impossible for us to tell, from our limited views, whether this system contains any great faults or deserves any considerable praise if compared to other possible and even real systems. Could a peasant, if the *Aeneid* were read to him, pronounce that poem to be absolutely faultless, or even assign to it its proper rank among the productions of human wit, he who had never seen any other production?

But were this world ever so perfect a production, it must still remain uncertain whether all the excellences of the work can justly be ascribed to the workman. If we survey a ship, what an exalted idea must we form of the ingenuity of the carpenter who framed so complicated, useful, and beautiful a machine? And what surprise must we feel when we find him a stupid mechanic who imitated others, and copied an art which, through a long succession of ages, after multiplied trials, mistakes, corrections, deliberations, and controversies, had been gradually improving? Many worlds might have been botched and bungled, throughout an eternity, ere this system was struck out; much labor lost, many fruitless trials made, and a slow but continued improvement carried on during infinite ages in the art of world-making. In such subjects, who can determine where the truth, nay, who can conjecture where the probability lies, amidst a great number of hypotheses which may be proposed, and a still greater which may be imagined?

And what shadow of an argument, continued Philo, can you produce from your hypothesis to prove the unity of the Deity? A great number of men join in building a house or ship, in rearing a city, in framing a commonwealth; why may not several deities combine in contriving and framing a world? This is only so much greater similarity to human affairs. By sharing the work among several, we may so much further limit the attributes of each, and get rid of that extensive power and knowledge which must be supposed in one deity, and which, according to you, can only serve to weaken the proof of his existence. And if such foolish, such vicious creatures as man can yet often unite in framing and executing one plan, how much more those deities or demons, whom we may suppose several degrees more perfect!

To multiply causes without necessity is indeed contrary to true philosophy, but this principle applies not to the present case. Were one deity antecedently proved by your theory who were possessed of every attribute requisite to the production of the universe, it would be needless, I own, (though not absurd) to suppose any other deity existent. But while it is still a question whether all these attributes are united in one subject or dispersed among several independent beings, by what phenomena in nature can we pretend to decide the controversy? Where we see a body raised in a scale, we are sure that there is in the opposite scale, however concealed from sight, some counterpoising weight equal to it; but it is still allowed to doubt whether that weight be an aggregate of several distinct bodies or one uniform united mass. And if the weight requisite very much exceeds anything which we have ever seen conjoined in any single body, the former supposition becomes still more probable and natural. An intelligent being of such vast power and capacity as is necessary to produce the universe, or, to speak in the language of ancient philosophy, so prodigious an animal exceeds all analogy and even comprehension.

But further, Cleanthes: Men are mortal, and renew their species by generation; and this is common to all living creatures. The two great sexes of male and female, says Milton, animate the world. Why must this circumstance, so universal, so essential, be excluded from those numerous and limited deities? Behold, then, the theogeny of ancient times brought back upon us.

And why not become a perfect anthropomorphite? Why not assert the deity or deities to be corporeal, and to have eyes, a nose, mouth, ears, etc.? Epicurus maintained that no man had ever seen reason but in a human figure; therefore, the gods must have a human figure. And this argument, which is deservedly so much ridiculed by Cicero, becomes, according to you, solid and philosophical.

In a word, Cleanthes, a man who follows your hypothesis is able, perhaps, to assert or conjecture that the universe sometimes arose from something like design; but beyond that position he cannot ascertain one single circumstance, and is left afterwards to fix every point of his theology by the utmost license of fancy and hypothesis. This world, for aught he knows, is very faulty and imperfect, compared to a superior standard, and was only the first rude essay of some infant deity who afterwards abandoned it, ashamed of his lame performance; it is the work only of some dependent, inferior deity, and is the object of derision to his superiors; it is the production of old age and dotage in some superannuated deity, and ever since his death has run on at adventures, from the first impulse and active force which it received from him. You justly give signs of horror, Demea, at these strange suppositions; but these, and a thousand more of the same kind, are Cleanthes' suppositions, not mine. From the moment the attributes of the Deity are supposed finite, all these have place. And I cannot, for my part, think that so wild and unsettled a system of theology is, in any respect, preferable to none at all.

These suppositions I absolutely disown, cried Cleanthes: they strike me, however, with no horror, especially when proposed in that rambling way in which they drop from you. On the contrary, they give me pleasure when I see that, by the utmost indulgence of your imagination, you never get rid of the hypothesis of design in the universe, but are obliged at every turn to have recourse to it. To this concession I adhere steadily; and this I regard as a sufficient foundation for religion.

10

BENEDICT DE SPINOZA

Of God *

INFLUENCED BY Descartes and the remarkable development that took place in mathematics in his time, Spinoza was led to formulate his discussions in the *Ethic* according to a geometric method. Such a method does not lend itself to easy reading but it does

° From the *Ethic,* translated by William Hale White (Trubner and Co., 1883), pp. 1-37.

Benedict de Spinoza (1632-77) was born in The Netherlands. At the age of twenty-four he was expelled from the synagogue on the grounds of heresy and enable Spinoza to set forth clearly and precisely at the beginning of his work the basic definitions and axioms from which he proceeds to deduce in succeeding propositions the principal features of his pantheism. Thus he establishes successively the nature of substance, its unity and simplicity, its infinitude, and its necessary existence. Substance is identified with God and Spinoza offers several proofs for God's existence, including his version of the famous ontological argument. The world is conceived as participating in the existence of God through the divine attributes and modes, and God is considered as the immanent or internal cause of all things. The world has no separate existence from God but is intimately bound to Him both causally and substantially. In the concluding propositions, Spinoza is concerned to emphasize further that God alone is a free cause, that there is nothing of a contingent nature in the world but that all things flow from the necessity of the divine nature. Thus a rigorous determinism is upheld and the implications of this position for the problem of good and evil are briefly drawn.

DEFINITIONS

I. By CAUSE OF ITSELF, I understand that, whose essence involves existence; or that, whose nature cannot be conceived unless existing.

II. That thing is called finite in its kind which can be limited by another thing of the same nature.

III. By substance, I understand that which is in itself and through itself; in other words, that the conception of which does not need the conception of another thing from which it must be formed.

IV. By attribute, I understand that which the intellect perceives of substance, as if constituting its essence.

V. By mode, I understand the affections of substance, or that which is in another thing through which also it is conceived.

VI. By God, I understand Being absolutely infinite, that is to say, substance consisting of infinite attributes, each one of which expresses eternal and infinite essence.

Explanation.—I say absolutely infinite but not infinite in its own kind; for of whatever is infinite only in its own kind, we can deny infinite attributes; but to the essence of that which is absolutely infinite pertains whatever expresses essence and involves no negation.

· · · · ·

was banished from Amsterdam. He lived for many years in a nearby village and earned his living by polishing lenses. Later he lived in modest retirement in The Hague, and continued to devote his time to the study of philosophy and to his correspondence with the great scholars, mathematicians, and philosophers of the day.

AXIOMS

I. Everything which is, is either in itself or in another.

II. That which cannot be conceived through another must be conceived through itself.

III. From a given determinate cause an effect necessarily follows; and, on the other hand, if no determinate cause be given, it is impossible that an effect can follow.

IV. The knowledge of an effect, depends upon and involves the knowledge of the cause.

V. Those things which have nothing mutually in common with one another cannot through one another be mutually understood, that is to say, the conception of the one does not involve the conception of the other.

VI. A true idea must agree with that of which it is the idea.

VII. The essence of that thing which can be conceived as not existing does not involve existence.

Proposition I.—*Substance is by its nature prior to its affections.*
Demonstration.—This is evident from Definitions 3 and 5.

Proposition II.—*Two substances having different attributes have nothing in common with one another.*
Demonstration.—This is also evident from Definition 3. For each substance must be in itself and must be conceived through itself, that is to say, the conception of one does not involve the conception of the other.

Proposition III.—*If two things have nothing in common with one another, one cannot be the cause of the other.*
Demonstration.—If they have nothing mutually in common with one another, they cannot (Ax. 5) through one another be mutually understood, and therefore (Ax. 4) one cannot be the cause of the other.

Proposition IV.—*Two or more distinct things are distinguished from one another, either by the difference of the attributes of the substances, or by the difference of their affections.*
Demonstration.—Everything which is, is either in itself or in another (Ax. 1), that is to say (Definitions 3 and 5), outside the intellect there is nothing but substances and their modifications. There is nothing therefore outside the intellect by which a number of things can be distinguished from one another, but substances or (which is the same thing by Definition 4) their attributes and their affections.

Proposition V.—*In nature there cannot be two or more substances of the same nature or attribute.*

Demonstration.—If there were two or more distinct substances, they must be distinguished one from the other by difference of attributes or difference of affections (Proposition 4). If they are distinguished by difference of attributes, it will be granted that there is but one substance of the same attribute. But if they are distinguished by difference of affections, since substance is prior by nature to its affections (Proposition 1), the affections therefore being placed on one side, and the substance being considered in itself, or, in other words (Definition 3 and Ax. 6), truly considered, it cannot be conceived as distinguished from another substance, that is to say (Proposition 4), there cannot be two or more substances, but only one possessing the same nature or attribute.

Proposition VI.—*One substance cannot be produced by another substance.*

Demonstration.—There cannot in nature be two substances of the same attribute (Proposition 5), that is to say (Proposition 2), two which have anything in common with one another. And therefore (Proposition 3) one cannot be the cause of the other, that is to say, one cannot be produced by the other.

Corollary.—Hence it follows that there is nothing by which substance can be produced, for in nature there is nothing but substances and their affections (Ax. 1 and Definitions 3 and 5). But substance cannot be produced by substance (Proposition 6). Therefore absolutely there is nothing by which substance can be produced.

Proposition VII.—*It pertains to the nature of substance to exist.*

Demonstration—There is nothing by which substance can be produced (Corollary Proposition 6). It will therefore be the cause of itself, that is to say (Definition 1), its essence necessarily involves existence, or in other words, it pertains to its nature to exist.

Proposition VIII.—*Every substance is necessarily infinite.*

Demonstration.—Substance which has only one attribute cannot exist except as one substance (Proposition 5), and to the nature of this one substance it pertains to exist (Proposition 7). It must therefore from its nature exist as finite or infinite. But it cannot exist as finite substance, for (Definition 2) it must (if finite) be limited by another substance of the same nature, which also must necessarily exist (Proposition 7), and therefore there would be two substances of the same attribute, which is absurd (Proposition 5). It exists therefore as infinite substance.

•　•　•　•　•　•

Scholium 2.— . . . a demonstration by a different method is possible, showing that there are not two substances possessing the same nature. But in order to prove this methodically it is to be noted: 1. That the true definition of any one thing neither involves nor expresses anything except the nature of the thing defined. From which it follows, 2. That a definition does not involve or express any certain number of individuals, since it expresses nothing but the nature of the thing defined. For example, the definition of a triangle expresses nothing but the simple nature of a triangle, and not any certain number of triangles. 3. It is to be observed that of every existing thing there is some certain cause by reason of which it exists. 4. Finally, it is to be observed that this cause by reason of which a thing exists, must either be contained in the nature itself and definition of the existing thing (simply because it pertains to the nature of the thing to exist), or it must exist outside the thing. This being granted, it follows that if a certain number of individuals exist in nature, there must necessarily be a cause why those individuals, and neither more nor fewer, exist. If, for example, there are twenty men in existence (whom, for the sake of greater clearness, I suppose existing at the same time, and that no others existed before them), it will not be sufficient, in order that we may give a reason why twenty men exist, to give a cause for human nature generally; but it will be necessary, in addition, to give a reason why neither more nor fewer than twenty exist, since as we have already observed under the third head, there must necessarily be a cause why each exists. But this cause (as we have shown under the second and third heads) cannot be contained in human nature itself, since the true definition of a man does not involve the number twenty, and therefore (by the fourth head) the cause why these twenty men exist, and consequently the cause why each exists, must necessarily lie outside each one; and therefore we must conclude that everything whose nature involves the existence of a certain number of individuals must of necessity have, since they exist, an external cause.

Since now it pertains to the nature of substance to exist (as we have shown in this scholium), its definition must involve necessary existence, and consequently from its definition alone its existence must be concluded. But from its definition (as we have already shown under the second and third heads) the existence of more substances than one cannot be deduced. It follows, therefore, from this definition necessarily that there cannot be two substances possessing the same nature.

. . . .

Proposition XI.—*God, or substance, consisting of infinite attributes, each one of which expresses eternal and infinite essence, necessarily exists.*

Demonstration.—If this be denied, conceive, if it be possible, that God does not exist. Then it follows (Ax. 7) that His essence does not involve existence. But this (Proposition 7) is absurd. Therefore God necessarily exists.

Another proof.—For the existence or non-existence of everything there must be a reason or cause. For example, if a triangle exists, there must be a reason or cause why it exists; and if it does not exist, there must be a reason or cause which hinders its existence or which negates it. For example, the nature of the thing itself shows the reason why a square circle does not exist, the reason being that a square circle involves a contradiction. . . . But the reason why a circle or triangle exists or does not exist is not drawn from their nature, but from the order of corporeal nature generally; for from that it must follow, either that a triangle necessarily exists, or that it is impossible for it to exist. But this is self-evident. Therefore it follows that if there be no cause nor reason which hinders a thing from existing, it exists necessarily. If, therefore, there be no reason nor cause which hinders God from existing, or which negates His existence, we must conclude absolutely that He necessarily exists. But if there be such a reason or cause, it must be either in the nature itself of God or must lie outside it, that is to say, in another substance of another nature. For if the reason lay in a substance of the same nature, the existence of God would be by this very fact admitted. But substance possessing another nature could have nothing in common with God (Proposition 2), and therefore could not give Him existence nor negate it. Since, therefore, the reason or cause which could negate the divine existence cannot be outside the divine nature, it will necessarily, supposing that the divine nature does not exist, be in His nature itself, which would therefore involve a contradiction. But to affirm this of the Being absolutely infinite and consummately perfect is absurd. Therefore neither in God nor outside God is there any cause or reason which can negate His existence, and therefore God necessarily exists.

. . . . . .

Proposition XIV.—*Besides God, no substance can be nor can be conceived.*

Demonstration.—Since God is Being absolutely infinite, of whom no attribute can be denied, which expresses the essence of substance (Definition 6), and since He necessarily exists (Proposition 11), it follows that if there were any substance besides God, it would have to be explained by some attribute of God, and thus two substances would exist possessing the same attribute which (Proposition 5) is absurd; and therefore there cannot be any substance excepting God, and consequently none other can be conceived. For if any other could be conceived, it would necessarily be conceived as existing, and this (by the first part of this demonstration) is absurd. Therefore besides God no substance can be, nor can be conceived.

Proposition XV.—*Whatever is, is in God, and nothing can either be or be conceived without God.*

Demonstration.—Besides God there is no substance, nor can any be conceived (Proposition 14), that is to say (Definition 3), nothing which is in itself and is conceived through itself. But modes (Definition 5) can neither be nor be conceived without substance; therefore in the divine nature only can they be, and through it alone can they be conceived. But besides substances and modes nothing is assumed (Ax. 1). Therefore nothing can be or be conceived without God.

Scholium.—There are those who imagine God to be like a man, composed of body and soul and subject to passions; but it is clear enough from what has already been demonstrated how far off men who believe this are from the true knowledge of God. But these I dismiss, for all men who have in any way looked into the divine nature deny that God is corporeal. That He cannot be so they conclusively prove by showing that by "body" we understand a certain quantity possessing length, breadth, and depth, limited by some fixed form; and that to attribute these to God, a being absolutely infinite, is the greatest absurdity. But yet at the same time, from other arguments by which they endeavor to confirm their proof, they clearly show that they remove altogether from the divine nature substance itself corporeal or extended, affirming that it was created by God. By what divine power, however, it could have been created they are altogether ignorant, so that it is clear they do not understand what they themselves say. But I have demonstrated, at least in my own opinion, with sufficient clearness (see Corollary Proposition 6 and Scholium 2, Proposition 8), that no substance can be produced or created by another. Moreover (Proposition 14), we have shown that besides God no substance can be nor can be conceived; and hence we have concluded that extended substance is one of the infinite attributes of God. . . . All things, I say, are in God, and everything which takes place takes place by the laws alone of the infinite nature of God, and follows (as I shall presently show) from the necessity of His essence.

Therefore in no way whatever can it be asserted that God suffers from anything, or that substance extended, even if it be supposed divisible, is unworthy of the divine nature, provided only it be allowed that it is eternal and infinite. . . .

Proposition XVI. *From the necessity of the divine nature infinite numbers of things in infinite ways (that is to say, all things which can be conceived by the infinite intellect) must follow.*

Demonstration.—This proposition must be plain to everyone who considers that from the given definition of anything a number of properties necessarily following from it (that is to say, following from the essence of the thing itself) are inferred by the intellect, and just in proportion as the definition of the thing expresses a greater reality, that is to say, just in proportion as the essence of the thing defined involves a greater reality, will more properties be inferred. But the divine nature possesses absolutely infinite attributes (Definition 6), each one of which expresses infinite essence in its own kind, and therefore, from the necessity of the divine nature, infinite numbers of things in infinite ways (that is to say, all things which can be conceived by the infinite intellect) must necessarily follow.

Proposition XVII.—*God acts from the laws of His own nature only, and is compelled by no one.*

Demonstration.—We have just shown (Proposition 16) that from the necessity, or (which is the same thing) from the laws only of the divine nature, infinite numbers of things absolutely follow: and we have demonstrated (Proposition 15) that nothing can be, nor can be conceived, without God, but that all things are in God. Therefore, outside Himself, there can be nothing by which He may be determined or compelled to act; and therefore He acts from the laws of His own nature only, and is compelled by no one.

Corollary 1.—Hence it follows, firstly, that there is no cause either external to God or within Him, which can excite Him to act except the perfection of His own nature.

Corollary 2.—It follows, secondly, that God alone is a free cause; for God alone exists from the necessity alone of His own nature (Proposition 11, and Corollary 1, Proposition 14), and acts from the necessity alone of His own nature (Proposition 17).

Scholium.—There are some who think that God is a free cause because He can, as they think, bring about that those things which we have said follow from His nature—that is to say, those things which are in His power—should not be, or should not be produced by Him. But this is simply saying that God could bring about that it should not follow from the nature of a triangle that its three angles should be equal to two right angles, or that from a given cause an effect should not follow, which is absurd.

I know, indeed, that there are many who think themselves able to demonstrate that intellect of the highest order and freedom of will both pertain to the nature of God, for they say that they know nothing more perfect which they can attribute to Him than that which is the chief perfection in ourselves. But although they conceive God as actually possessing the highest intellect, they nevertheless do not believe that He can bring about that all those things should exist which are actually in His intellect, for they think that by such a supposition they would destroy His power. If He had created, they say, all things which are in His intellect, He could have created nothing more, and this, they believe, does not accord with God's omnipotence; so then they prefer to consider God as indifferent to all things, and creating nothing excepting that which He has decreed to create by a certain absolute will. But I think that I have shown with sufficient clearness (Proposition 16) that from the supreme power of God, or from His infinite nature, infinite things in infinite ways, that is to say, all things, have necessarily flowed, or continually follow by the same necessity, in the same way as it follows from the nature of a triangle, from eternity to eternity, that its three angles are equal to two right angles. The omnipotence of God has therefore been actual from eternity, and in the same actuality will remain to eternity. In this way the omnipotence of God, in my opinion, is far more firmly established. My adversaries seem . . . to deny the omnipotence of God, for they are forced to admit that He has in His mind an infinite number of things which might be created, but which, nevertheless, He will never be able to create, for if He were to create all things which He has in His mind, He would, according to them, exhaust His omnipotence and make Himself imperfect. Therefore, in order to make a perfect God, they are compelled to make Him incapable of doing all those things to which His power extends, and anything more absurd than this, or more opposed to God's omnipotence, I do not think can be imagined. . . .

.　.　.　.　.

Proposition XXIX.—*In nature there is nothing contingent, but all things are determined from the necessity of the divine nature to exist and act in a certain manner.*

Demonstration.—Whatever is, is in God (Proposition 15) but God cannot be called a contingent thing, for (Proposition 11) He exists necessarily and not contingently. Moreover, the modes of the divine nature have followed from it necessarily and not contingently (Proposition 16), and that, too, whether it be considered absolutely or as determined to action in a certain manner. But God is the cause of these modes, not only in so far as they simply exist but also in so far as they are considered as determined to any action. And if they are not determined by God, it is an impossibility and not a contingency that they should determine themselves; and on the other hand if they are determined by God, it is an impossibility and not a contingency that they should render themselves indeterminate. Wherefore all things are determined from the divine nature, not only to exist, but to exist and act in a certain manner, and there is nothing contingent.

Scholium.—Before I go any farther, I wish here to explain what we mean by *natura naturans* and what by *natura naturata.* For, from what has gone before, I think it is plain that by *natura naturans* we are to understand that which is in itself and is conceived through itself, or those attributes of substance which express eternal and infinite essence, that is to say God in so far as He is considered as a free cause. But by *natura naturata* I understand everything which follows from the necessity of the nature of God, or of any one of God's attributes, that is to say, all the modes of God's attributes in so far as they are considered as things which are in God, and which without God can neither be nor can be conceived.

. . . . .

Proposition XXXIII.—*Things could not have been produced by God in any other manner or order than that in which they were produced.*

Demonstration.—All things have necessarily followed from the given nature of God (Proposition 16), and from the necessity of His nature have been determined to existence and action in a certain manner (Proposition 29). If, therefore, things could have been of another nature, or could have been determined in another manner to action, so that the order of nature would have been different, the nature of God might then be different to that which it now is, and hence (Proposition 11) that different nature would necessarily exist, and there might consequently be two or more Gods, which (Corollary 1, Proposition 14), is absurd. Therefore, things could be produced by God in no other manner nor in any other order than that in which they have been produced.

. . . . .

Scholium 2.—It clearly follows that things have been produced by God in the highest degree of perfection, since they have necessarily followed from the existence of a most perfect nature. Nor does this doctrine accuse God of any imperfection, but on the contrary, His perfection has compelled us to affirm it. Indeed, from its contrary would clearly follow . . . that God is not absolutely perfect, since, if things had been produced in any other fashion, another nature would have had to be assigned to Him, different from that which the consideration of the most perfect Being compels us to assign to Him . . . although it be granted that will pertains to God's essence, it follows nevertheless from His perfection that things could be created in no other mode or order by Him. This it will be easy to show if we first consider that which my opponents themselves admit, that it depends upon the decree and will of God alone that each thing should be what it is, for otherwise God would not be the cause of all things. It is also admitted that all God's decrees were decreed by God Himself from all eternity, for otherwise imperfection and inconstancy would be proved against Him. But since in eternity there is no *when* nor *before* nor *after*, it follows from the perfection of God alone that He neither can decree nor could ever have decreed anything else than that which He has decreed; that is to say, God has not existed before His decrees, and can never exist without them. But it is said that although it be supposed that God had made the nature of things different from that which it is, or that from eternity He had decreed something else about nature and her order, it would not thence follow that any imperfection exists in God. But if this be said, it must at the same time be allowed that God can change His decrees. For if God had decreed something about nature and her order other than that which He has decreed—that is to say, if He had willed and conceived something else about nature—He would necessarily have had an intellect and a will different from those which He now has. And if it be allowed to assign to God another intellect and another will without any change of His essence and of His perfections, what is the reason why He cannot now change His decrees about creation and nevertheless remain equally perfect? For His intellect and will regarding created things and their order remain the same in relationship to His essence and perfection in whatever manner His intellect and will are conceived. Moreover, all the philosophers whom I have seen admit that there is no such thing as an intellect existing potentially in God, but only an intellect existing actually. But since His intellect and His will are not distinguishable from His essence, as all admit, it follows from this also that if God had had another intellect actually and another will, His essence would have been necessarily different, and hence, as I showed at the beginning, if things had been produced by God in a manner different from that in which they now exist, God's intellect and will, that is to say, His essence (as has been granted), must have been different, which is absurd.

Since, therefore, things could have been produced by God in no other manner or order, this being a truth which follows from His absolute perfection, there is no sound reasoning which can persuade us to believe that God was unwilling to create all things which are in His intellect with the same perfection as that in which they exist in His intellect. But we shall be told that there is no perfection nor imperfection in things, but that that which is in them by reason or which they are perfect or imperfect and are said to be good or evil depends upon the will of God alone, and therefore if God had willed He could have effected that that which is now perfection should have been the extreme of imperfection, and *vice versa*. But what else would this be than openly to affirm that God, who necessarily understands what He wills, is able by His will to understand things in a manner different from that in which He understands them, which, as I have just shown, is a great absurdity. I can therefore turn the argument on my opponents in this way. All things depend upon the power of God. In order that things may be differently constituted, it would be necessary that God's will should be differently constituted; but God's will cannot be other than it is, as we have lately most clearly deduced from His perfection. Things therefore cannot be differently constituted. I confess that this opinion, which subjects all things to a certain indifferent God's will, and affirms that all things depend upon God's good pleasure, is at a less distance from the truth than the opinion of those who affirm that God does everything for the sake of the Good. For these seem to place something outside of God which is independent of Him, to which He looks while He is at work as to a model, or at which He aims as if at a certain mark. This is indeed nothing else than to subject God to fate, the most absurd thing which can be affirmed of Him whom we have shown to be the first and only free cause of the essence of all those things as well as of their existence. Therefore it is not worth while that I should waste time in refuting this absurdity.

11

SANKARA

Brahman *

THE FOLLOWING SELECTION from the great Indian mystic and philosopher is illustrative of Oriental Pantheism. Brahman or the
Eternal Self is affirmed to exist and to be known by the individual
as the ground of the individual self. Concerning the nature of
Brahman, Sankara indicates what Brahman is not and then points
out that as eternal subject it can never be an object and that all
such distinctions as knowing, known, and knower are the result of
ignorance. Quoting the Upanishads, he states further that Brahman
is one, immanent, all-pervading, and without evil. Despite their
unity, there is an apparent difference between the individual (or
embodied self) and Brahman (the highest Self). But the difference
is one in name only, ignorance (nescience) makes them appear
different but perfect knowledge would reveal the identity of the
self and Brahman. Once we attain this knowledge we have attained
our highest end. The world around us has no existence apart from
Brahman and appears to have such existence only when we lack
perfect knowledge. Sankara concludes by noting that Brahman,
though unmoving, moves the universe and is the all-knowing first
cause of all.

BRAHMAN, which is all-knowing and endowed with all powers, whose
essential nature is eternal purity, intelligence, and freedom, exists.
For if we consider the derivation of the word "Brahman," from the
root *brih* "to be great," we at once understand that eternal purity, and
so on belong to Brahman. Moreover the existence of Brahman is
known on the ground of its being the Self of every one. For every one
is conscious of the existence of (his) Self, and never thinks "I am not."

* From the *Sacred Books of the East*, translated by George Thibaut, edited by
F. Max Müller (Clarendon Press, 1890), XXXIV, 14-15, 34, 61, 113-16, 155,
185-86, 251, 282-83, 286, 321, 324, 341, 349, 427. In the choice of selections
here, I was guided by the excellent judgment of Charles Hartshorne and William
L. Reese, editors of *Philosophers Speak of God* (University of Chicago Press,
1953), pp. 170-73, to whom I am deeply indebted.
    Sankara Acharya (c. 789-820) is said to have been born at the village of
Kaladi in Malabar. He is known as one of the greatest Hindu philosophers and
theologians, perhaps his greatest achievment being the perfecting of the Vedanta
philosophy. He has been regarded by some as the incarnation of the Hindu god
Siva.

If the existence of the Self were not known, every one would think "I am not." And this Self (of whose existence all are conscious) is Brahman. But if Brahman is generally known as the Self there is no room for an enquiry into it! Not so, we reply; for there is a conflict of opinions as to its special nature. Unlearned people . . . are of opinion that the mere body endowed with the quality of intelligence is the Self; others that the organs endowed with intelligence are the Self; others maintain that the internal organ is the Self; others, again, that it is the Void. Others, again (to proceed to the opinion of such as acknowledge the authority of the Veda), maintain that there is a transmigrating being different from the body, and so on, which is both agent and enjoyer (of the fruits of action); others teach that that being is enjoying only, not acting; others believe that in addition to the individual souls, there is an all-knowing, all-powerful Lord. Others, finally (i.e. the Vedântins), maintain that the Lord is the Self of the enjoyer (i.e., of the individual soul whose individual existence is apparent only, the product of Nescience).

. . . Brahman as the eternal subject (*pratyagâtman,* the inward Self) is never an object, and . . . the distinction of objects known, knowers, acts of knowledge, etc. . . . is fictitiously created by Nescience.

Of Brahman, . . . the two following passages declare that it is incapable of receiving any accretion and eternally pure, "He is the one God, hidden in all beings, all-pervading, the Self within all beings, watching over all works, dwelling in all beings, the witness, the perceiver, the only one; free from qualities" (Sv. Up. VI, 11); and "He pervaded all, bright, incorporeal, scatheless, without muscles, pure, untouched by evil" (Is. Up. 8).

. . . Brahman, whose nature is eternal cognition—as the sun's nature is eternal luminousness—can impossibly stand in need of any instruments of knowledge.

With regard to this (unreal limitation of the one Self) the distinction of objects of activity and of agents may be practically assumed, as long as we have not learned—from the passage, "That art thou"— that the Self is one only. As soon, however, as we grasp the truth that there is only one universal Self, there is an end to the whole practical view of the world with its distinction of bondage, final release, and the like.

. . . between the embodied Self and the highest Self, there is the difference that the former acts and enjoys, acquires merit and demerit, and is affected by pleasure, pain, and so on; while the latter is of the opposite nature, i.e. characterized by being free from all evil and the like. On account of this difference of the two, the fruition of the one does not extend to the other. To assume merely on the ground of the mutual proximity of the two, without considering their essentially different powers, that a connexion with effects exists (in Brahman's case also), would be no better than to suppose that space is on fire when something in space is on fire. The same objection and refutation apply to the case of those also who teach the existence of more than one omnipresent Self.

In spite of their unity, fruition on the part of the soul does not involve fruition on the part of Brahman; because there is a difference. For there is a difference between false knowledge and perfect knowledge, fruition being the figment of false knowledge while the unity (of the Self) is revealed by perfect knowledge. Now, as the substance revealed by perfect knowledge cannot be affected by fruition which is nothing but the figment of false knowledge, it is impossible to assume even a shadow of fruition on Brahman's part.

The Self is not to be known as manifold, qualified by the universe of effects; you are rather to dissolve by true knowledge the universe of effects, which is the mere product of Nescience, and to know that one Self, which is the general abode, as uniform.

BRAHMAN AND THE INDIVIDUAL SOUL

That same highest Brahman constitutes—as we know from passages such as "that art thou"—the real nature of the individual soul, while its second nature, i.e., that aspect of it which depends on fictitious limiting conditions, is not its real nature. For as long as the individual soul does not free itself from Nescience in the form of duality—which Nescience may be compared to the mistake of him who in the twilight mistakes a post for a man—and does not rise to the knowledge of the Self, whose nature is unchangeable, eternal Cognition—which expresses itself in the form "I am Brahman"—so long it remains the individual soul. But when, discarding the aggregate of body, sense-organs and mind, it arrives, by means of Scripture, at the knowledge that it is not itself that aggregate, that it does not form part of transmigratory existence, but is the True, the Real, the Self, whose nature is pure intelligence; then knowing itself to be of the nature of unchangeable, eternal Cognition, it lifts itself above the vain conceit of being one with this body, and itself becomes the Self, whose nature is unchanging, eternal Cognition. As is declared in such scriptural passages as "He who knows the highest Brahman becomes even Brahman" (Mu. Up. III, 2, 9). And this is the real nature of the individual soul by means of which it arises from the body and appears in its own form.

To the highest Self which is eternally pure, intelligent and free, which is never changing, one only, not in contact with anything, devoid of form, the opposite characteristics of the individual soul are erroneously ascribed; just as ignorant men ascribe blue color to the colorless ether.

A man may, in the dark, mistake a piece of rope lying on the ground for a snake, and run away from it, frightened and trembling; thereon another man may tell him, "Do not be afraid, it is only a rope, not a snake"; and he may then dismiss the fear caused by the imagined snake, and stop running. But all the while the presence and subsequent absence of his erroneous notion, as to the rope being a snake, make no difference whatever in the rope itself. Exactly analogous is the case of the individual soul which is in reality one with the highest soul, although Nescience makes it appear different.

As therefore the individual soul and the highest Self differ in name only, it being a settled matter that perfect knowledge has for its object the absolute oneness of the two; it is senseless to insist (as some do) on a plurality of Selfs, and to maintain that the individual soul is different from the highest Self, and the highest Self from the individual soul. For the Self is indeed called by many different names, but it is one only.

The Self is thus the operative cause, because there is no other ruling principle, and the material cause because there is no other substance from which the world could originate.

BRAHMAN AND THE WORLD

In the same way as those parts of ethereal space which are limited by jars and waterpots are not really different from the universal ethereal space, and as the water of a mirage is not really different from the surface of the salty steppe—for the nature of that water is that it is seen in one moment and has vanished in the next, and moreover, it is not to be perceived by its own nature (i.e., apart from the surface of the desert)—so this manifold world with its objects of enjoyment, enjoyers and so on has no existence apart from Brahman.

. . . the entire complex of phenomenal existence is considered as true as long as the knowledge of Brahman being the Self of all has not arisen; just as the phantoms of a dream are considered to be true until the sleeper wakes. For as long as a person has not reached the true knowledge of the unity of the Self, so long it does not enter his mind that the world of effects with its means and objects of right knowledge and its results of actions is untrue; he rather, in consequence of his ignorance, looks on mere effects (such as body, offspring, wealth, etc.) as forming part of and belonging to his Self, forgetful of Brahman being in reality the Self of all. Hence, as long as true knowledge does not present itself, there is no reason why the ordinary course of secular and religious activity should not hold on undisturbed. The case is analogous to that of a dreaming man who in his dream sees manifold things, and, up to the moment of waking, is convinced that his ideas are produced by real perception without suspecting the perception to be a merely apparent one.

We maintain, therefore, . . . that milk and other substances are called effects when they are in the state of curds and so on, and that it is impossible, even within hundreds of years, ever to bring about an effect which is different from its cause. The fundamental cause of all appears in the form of this and that effect, up to the last effect of all, just as an actor appears in various robes and costumes, and thereby becomes the basis for all the current notions and terms concerning the phenomenal world.

But—an objection will be raised—your Self even if joined to a body is incapable of exercising moving power, for motion cannot be effected by that the nature of which is pure intelligence.—A thing, we reply, which is itself devoid of motion may nevertheless move other things. The magnet is itself devoid of motion, and yet it moves iron; and colors and the other objects of sense, although themselves devoid of motion, produce movements in the eyes and the other organs of sense. So the Lord also who is all-present, the Self of all, all-knowing and all-powerful may, although himself unmoving, move the universe.— If it finally be objected that (on the Vedânta doctrine) there is no room for a moving power as in consequence of the oneness (aduality) of Brahman no motion can take place; we reply that such objections have repeatedly been refuted by our pointing to the fact of the Lord being fictitiously connected with Mâyâ, which consists of name and form presented by Nescience.—Hence motion can be reconciled with the doctrine of an all-knowing first cause.

For unless there exists one continuous principle equally connected with the past, the present, and the future, or an absolutely unchangeable (Self) which cognises everything, we are unable to account for remembrance, recognition, and so on, which are subject to mental impressions dependent on place, time, and cause.

12

S. ALEXANDER

Deity and God *

ALEXANDER ARGUES, in this selection, that religion and metaphysics are complementary in their approach to the meaning of God. The proofs for the existence of God are invalid, and, although the argument from design is persuasive, it makes an illegitimate use of analogy. But if we cannot prove God's existence or define him directly, perhaps we can discover the quality of deity in the world and verify the reality of the being possessing it. On the basis of his description of the nature of reality, Alexander next argues that within the stuff of Space-Time there is a nisus toward deity and that the quality of deity is always the next higher empirical quality on the different levels of finite existence. To us, deity is beyond mind and unknown. For other levels of existence it may be matter, or life, and equally unknown to the beings on those levels. Although God or the being possessing deity appears at each level in time, the quality of deity is always higher than that of each level at which it appears. It is natural for us, at the level of mind or spirit, to represent God as a greater spirit. God, however, is the world with its nisus toward deity; but deity actually seems to be unknown. The infinitude of God's deity is said to differentiate him from all other empirical beings, but in a sense our minds and all finite things are infinite as well. We are finitely infinite; deity is infinitely infinite. Following an explanation of this rather elusive formula, the author concludes by emphasizing that an infinite God is purely ideal or conceptual, but that as actual God is only the universe striving toward deity, and that there is no actual infinite being with the quality of deity, although there is an actual infinite, the whole universe, with a nisus to deity—the God of the religious consciousness.

IN A UNIVERSE so described, consisting of things which have developed within the one matrix of Space-Time; we ourselves being but the

---

* From *Space, Time, and Deity,* Macmillan and Co., Ltd., 1920), II, 341-65. Reprinted with the permission of St. Martin's Press, New York.

S. Alexander (1850-1938) is one of the founders of the doctrine known as *emergent evolution.* He was born in Australia but later moved to England and became a Fellow of the British Academy. In the years 1916-18 he was named as the Gifford Lecturer. He was a Professor of Philosophy at Victoria University of Manchester from 1893 to 1924.

highest finite existences known to us because the empirical quality which is distinctive of conscious beings is based on finites of a lower empirical quality; what room is there for, and what place can be assigned to, God?

Primarily God must be defined as the object of the religious emotion or of worship. He is correlative to that emotion or sentiment, as food is correlative to appetite. What we worship, that is God. This is the practical or religious approach to God. But it is insufficient for our theoretical needs. It labors under the defect that so far as religion itself is able to assure us, the object of religion, however vitally rooted in human nature, however responsive to its needs, may be disconnected with the rest of the world. God may be but an ennobling fancy, a being whom we project before us in our imagination, in whom to believe may sustain and inspire us and have its own sufficient justification in its effects on our happiness, but to whom no reality corresponds which can be co-ordinated with familiar realities of the world. The appetite for food arises from internal causes, but the food which satisfies it is external and independent of the organism, and it is known to us apart from the satisfaction which it gives to our hunger. The passion for God is no less a real appetite of our nature, but what if it creates the very object which satisfies it? Always, indeed, the religious emotion believes in the reality of its object, as something greater than man and independent of him, in whom the finite creature may even in some phases of feeling be submerged; and it would reject as preposterous the suggestion that God may be a fancy with which it plays, like a lover with a dream of perfection. But the religious sentiment itself can supply us with no such theoretical assurance of reality, and it needs to be supplemented with a metaphysical inquiry, what place if any the object of worship occupies in the general scheme of things.

On the other hand from the metaphysical approach, God must be defined as the being, if any, which possesses deity or the divine quality; or, if there are more Gods than one, the beings which possess deity. The defect of this definition (which is only apparently circular) is that the being which possesses deity need not necessarily, so far as the bare metaphysical description goes, be the object of religious sentiment. It has to be shown that the being which possesses deity coincides with the object of religious passion and is its food. Neither definition is therefore for theory complete in itself. The religious description wants authentic coherence with the system of things. The metaphysical one wants the touch of feeling which brings it within the circle of human interests. Were the passion towards God not

already lit, no speculative contemplation or proof of the existence
or attributes of a metaphysical God would make him worshipful. Even
the intellectual love of God which in Spinoza's system has the force
of religion can do so, not as a mere passion for truth in its fullest form,
but because it presupposes a religious passion. Were it not on the
other hand for the speculative or reflective justification, the God of
religious sentiment would have no sure root in things. Religion leans
on metaphysics for the justification of its indefeasible conviction of
the reality of its object; philosophy leans on religion to justify it in
calling the possessor of deity by the religious name of God. The two
methods of approach are therefore complementary.

But whichever method of approach be adopted, in either case God
is defined indirectly. Religion is not the sentiment which is directed
upon God; but God is that upon which the religious sentiment is
directed. The datum of experience is that sentiment, and what God
is is known only by examining its deliverances. In metaphysics, deity
is not so much the quality which belongs to God as God is the being
which possesses deity. The quality of deity is here the datum of
experience. It is idle to hope that by defining God in conceptual terms,
whether as the sum of reality, or the perfect being, or the first cause,
or by other device, we can establish the connection between such a
being and the rest of our experience. We do but start with an abstraction and we do but end with one. Proofs of God's existence and nature
there are none, if such a God is to be identified with the object of
worship. Granted that there is a sum of reality; in what respect does
it stir the religious passion? The answer must be: because of its deity,
and on what this deity is the conception of a sum of reality offers no
light. The same thing holds in different degrees of the conceptions
of a first cause or a supreme designer.

Nor can we even prove the existence of a being called God, whether
worshipful or not, except on the basis of experience. No one now is
convinced by the traditional arguments for God's existence. The
reason is that at some point or other they introduce conceptions which
are *a priori* in the bad sense of that phrase, in which it means not
something experienced which is pervasive of all things but something
supplied by the mind; or in other words they desert the scientific
interpretation of things, along the lines indicated by experience itself,
by a rigidly limited use of analogy. The only one of the three which
at all persuades is the argument from design which is based on the
wonderful adaptation of living forms to their surroundings . . .
by which the lower serves the purposes of the higher. Because such
adaptation implies in human products the operation of a designing

mind, the conception is extended from this particular case, by an illegitimate use of analogy, to experience as a whole. The easy conception of a designing mind was foisted upon nature as a whole, without considering whether it could be used under conditions which required it to be infinite and to create its own material. Subsequent knowledge has shown that the experience which was thought unintelligible without such a conception points in the opposite direction. For adaptation to the surroundings, or the internal teleology of forms, is the result of selection operating on variations; and the external teleology of ministration is not to be assigned to a force operating in the past but is an incident of passage to the future. Who does not see that sheep were not created for man, but that man survives because he is able to live on sheep? On the other hand, if for this external designer we substitute the notion of an immanent design, we do but name the fact that the world works out so as to produce a plan. We may call the world so conceived by the name of God, and forget or possibly explain the wastefulness and destruction involved in the process. But in what sense is such a God worshipful? He is worshipful only if we silently reintroduce into the notion of an immanent design, which in the end is a bare compendious description of certain facts, that of a designer, and fall back on the previous and invalid view.

What we can hope to do is something more modest, and more consistent with scientific procedure in other matters. Abandoning the attempt to define God directly, we may ask ourselves whether there is place in the world for the quality of deity; we may then verify the reality of the being which possesses it, that is of the Deity or God; and having done so, we may then consult the religious consciousness to see whether this being coincides with the object of worship. Where then, if at all, is deity in the scheme of things?

Within the all-embracing stuff of Space-Time, the universe exhibits an emergence in Time of successive levels of finite existences, each with its characteristic empirical quality. The highest of these empirical qualities known to us is mind or consciousness. Deity is the next higher empirical quality to the highest we know; and, as shall presently be observed, at any level of existence there is a next higher empirical quality which stands towards the lower quality as deity stands towards mind. Let us for the moment neglect this wider implication and confine our attention to ourselves. There is an empirical quality which is to succeed the distinctive empirical quality of our level; and that new empirical quality is deity. If Time were as some have thought a mere form of sense or understanding under which the mind envisages things, this conception would be meaningless and impossible. But Time is an element in the stuff of which the universe and all its parts are made, and has no special relation to mind, which is but the last complexity of Time that is known to us in finite existence. Bare Time in our hypothesis, . . . is the soul of its Space, or performs towards it the office of soul to its equivalent body or brain; and this elementary mind which is Time becomes in the course of time so complicated and refined in its internal grouping that there arise finite beings whose soul is materiality, or color, or life, or in the end what is familiar as mind. Now since Time is the principle of growth and Time is infinite, the internal development of the world, . . . cannot be regarded as ceasing with the emergence of those finite configurations of space-time which carry the empirical quality of mind. We have to think upon the lines already traced by experience of the emergence of higher qualities, also empirical. There is a nisus in Space-Time which, as it has borne its creatures forward through matter and life to mind, will bear them forward to some higher level of existence. There is nothing in mind which requires us to stop and say this is the highest empirical quality which Time can produce from now throughout the infinite Time to come. It is only the last empirical quality which we who are minds happen to know. Time itself compels us to think of a later birth of Time. For this reason it was legitimate for us to follow up the series of empirical qualities and imagine finite beings which we called angels, who would enjoy their own angelic being but would contemplate minds as minds themselves cannot do, in the same way as mind contemplates life and lower levels of existence. This device was adopted half-playfully as a pictorial embodiment of the conception forced upon us by the fact that there is this series of levels of existence. It was used illustratively to point the distinction of enjoyment and contemplation. But we now can see that it is a serious conception. For the angelic quality the possession of which enables such beings to contemplate minds is this next higher empirical quality of deity and our supposed angels are finite beings with this quality. We shall have to ask how such finite deities are related to the infinite God, for they themselves are finite gods.

Deity is thus the next higher empirical quality to mind, which the universe is engaged in bringing to birth. That the universe is pregnant with such a quality we are speculatively assured. What that quality is we cannot know; for we can neither enjoy nor still less contemplate it. Our human altars still are raised to the unknown Gods. If we could know what deity is, how it feels to be divine, we should first have to have become as gods. What we know of it is but its relation to the other empirical qualities which precede it in time. Its nature we cannot penetrate. We can represent it to ourselves only by analogy. It is fitly described in this analogical manner as the color of the universe. For color, we have seen, is a new quality which emerges in material things in attendance on motions of a certain sort. Deity in its turn is a quality which attends upon, or more strictly is equivalent to, previous or lower existences of the order of mind which itself rests on a still lower basis of qualities, and emerges when certain complexities and refinements of arrangement have been reached. . . .

We have not yet asked what the being is which possesses deity. But before attempting to raise the question we may still linger over the quality of deity itself. In the first place it is clear that, while for us men deity is the next higher empirical quality to mind, the description of deity is perfectly general. For any level of existence, deity is the next higher empirical quality. It is therefore a variable quality, and as the world grows in time, deity changes with it. On each new level a new quality looms ahead, awfully, which plays to it the part of deity. For us who live upon the level of mind deity is, we can but say, deity. To creatures upon the level of life, deity is still the quality in front, but to us who come later this quality has been revealed as mind. For creatures who possessed only the primary qualities,—mere empirical configurations of space-time—deity was what afterwards appeared as materiality, and their God was matter, for I am supposing that there is no level of existence nearer to the spatio-temporal than matter. On each level of finite creatures deity is for them some "unknown" (though not "unexperienced") quality in front, the real nature of which is enjoyed by the creatures of the next level. I do not mean that a material being would in some way think or forecast life; for there is no thinking in the proper sense till we reach mind. I do not even mean that matter forecasts deity in the sense in which it is sometimes said that to a dog his master is God. For the dog though he may not think, does feel and imagine, and his master is a finite being presented to his senses, for whom he feels attachment. I mean only that corresponding to the sense of a mysterious something which is more than we are and yet is felt in feeling and is conceived by speculation, there is some quality in the purview of material things which lies ahead of material quality. If we think ourselves back into material existence, we should feel ourselves, though matter would be the highest that we know, still swept on in the movement of Time. A merely material universe would not be exhausted by materiality and its lower empirical qualities; there would still be that restless movement of Time, which is not the mere turning of a squirrel in its cage, but the nisus towards a higher birth. That it is so, events show. How its being so would be 'experienced' in the material 'soul' may need for its description a greater capacity to strip off human privileges and sympathise with lower experience than most persons, and certainly I, possess.

Having thus realised that the relation of deity to mind is not peculiar to us but arises at each level between the next higher quality and the distinctive quality of that level, we can at once pass to another observation. We cannot tell what is the nature of deity, of our deity, but we can be certain that it is not mind, or if we use the term spirit as equivalent to mind or any quality of the order of mind, deity is not spirit, but something different from it in kind. God, the being which possesses deity, must be *also* spirit, for according to analogy, deity presupposes spirit, just as spirit or mind presupposes in its possessor life, and life physico-chemical material processes. But though God must be spiritual in the same way as he must be living and material and spatio-temporal, his deity is not spirit. To think so would be like thinking that mind is purely life, or life purely physico-chemical. The neural complexity which is equivalent to mind is not merely physiological, but a selected physiological constellation which is the bearer of mind, though it is also physiological, because it has physiological relations to what is purely physiological. That complexity and refinement of spirit which is equivalent to deity is something new, and while it is also spirit it is not merely spirit. Deity is therefore, according to the pattern of the growth of things in time, not a mere enlargement of mind or spirit, but something which mere spirit subserves, and to which accordingly the conception of spirit as such is totally inadequate. Spirit, personality, mind, all these human or mental characters belong to God but not to his deity. They belong as we must hold not to his deity but to his 'body.' Yet since it is through spirit that we become aware of God, whether in the practical shape of the object of religious feeling or philosophically as the possessor of deity, since what is beyond spirit is realised through spirit, and since more particularly spirit is the highest quality whose nature we know, and we are compelled to embody our conceptions in imaginative shapes, it is not strange that we should represent God in human terms. Instead of the shadowy quality of which we can only say that it is a higher quality than mind, God is made vivid to us as a greater spirit; and we conceal the difference in kind of the divine and the human nature under magnified representations of human attributes. These are the inevitable devices of our weakness and our pictorial craving. But, for philosophy, God's deity is not different from spirit in degree but in kind, as a novelty in the series of empirical qualities. . . .

In the religious emotion we have the direct experience of something higher than ourselves which we call God, which is not presented through the ways of sense but through this emotion. The emotion is our going out or endeavor or striving towards this object. Speculation enables us to say wherein the divine quality consists, and that it is an empirical quality the next in the series which the very nature of Time compels us to postulate, though we cannot tell what it is like. But besides assuring us of the place of the divine quality in the world, speculation has also to ask wherein this quality resides. What is the being which possesses deity? Our answer is to be a philosophical one; we are not concerned with the various forms which the conception of God has assumed in earlier or later religions. Ours is the modester (and let me add far less arduous) inquiry what conception of God is required if we think of the universe as Space-Time engendering within itself in the course of time the series of empirical qualities of which deity is the one next ahead of mind. God is the whole world as possessing the quality of deity. Of such a being the whole world is the 'body' and deity is the 'mind.' But this possessor of deity is not actual but ideal. As an actual existent, God is the infinite world with its nisus towards deity, or, to adapt a phrase of Leibniz, as big or in travail with deity.

Since Space-Time is already a whole and one, why, it may be urged, should we seek to go beyond it? Why not identify God with Space-Time? Now, no one could worship Space-Time. It may excite speculative or mathematical enthusiasm and fill our minds with intellectual admiration, but it lights no spark of religious emotion. Worship is not the response which Space-Time evokes in us, but intuition. Even Kant's starry heavens are material systems, and he added the moral law to them in describing the sources of our reverence. In one way this consideration is irrelevant; for if philosophy were forced to this conclusion that God is nothing but Space-Time, we should needs be content. But a philosophy which left one portion of human experience suspended without attachment to the world of truth is gravely open to suspicion; and its failure to make the religious emotion speculatively intelligible betrays a speculative weakness. For the religious emotion is one part of experience, and an empirical philosophy must include in one form or another the whole of experience. The speculative failure of the answer is patent. It neglects the development within Space-Time of the series of empirical qualities in their increasing grades of perfection. The universe, though it can be expressed without remainder in terms of Space and Time, is not merely spatio-temporal. It exhibits materiality and life and mind. It compels us to forecast the next empirical quality or deity. On the one hand we have the totality of the world, which in the end is spatio-temporal; on the other the quality of deity engendered, or rather being engendered, within that whole. These two features are united in the conception of the whole world as expressing itself in the character of deity, and it is this and not bare Space-Time which for speculation is the ideal conception of God.

Belief in God, though an act of experience, is not an act of sight, for neither deity nor even the world as tending to deity is revealed to sense, but of speculative and religious faith. . . . Any attempt, therefore, to conceive God in more definite maner must involve a large element of speculative or reflective imagination. Even the description of God as the whole universe, as possessing deity, or as in travail with deity, is full of figurative language. If we are to make our conception less abstract we must try to represent to ourselves some individual in whom deity is related to its basis in the lower levels of empirical quality as far down as the purely spatio-temporal; and a being of this kind is, as we shall see, rather an ideal of thought than something which can be realised in fact in the form of an individual. What we have to do is to be careful to conceive the ideal in conformity with the plan of what we know of things from experience.

The simplest way of doing so is to forget for a moment that God being the whole world possessing deity is infinite, and, transporting ourselves in thought to the next level of existence, that of deity, to imagine a finite being with that quality, a god of a polytheistic system, or what we have called an angel. We must conceive such a being on the analogy of ourselves. In us a living body has one portion of itself specialised and set apart to be the bearer of the quality of mind. That specialised constellation of living processes, endowed with the quality of mind, is the concrete thing called mind. The rest of the body in its physiological, material, and spatio-temporal characters, sustains the life of this mind-bearing portion, which in its turn is said in the physiological sense to represent the rest of the body, because there is a general correspondence between the affections of the body and the excitements of the mind-bearing portion which are enjoyed as mental processes. In virtue of some of these mental enjoyments the mind contemplates the things outside its body, in virtue of others it contemplates its own bodily conditions in the form of organic sensa or sensibles, or of other sensibles of movement, touch, and the rest. In the superior finite which has deity, we must conceive the immediate basis of deity to be something of the nature of mind, just as the immediate basis of our mind is life, and the mind of the finite deity will rest on a substructure of life as with us. One part of the god's mind will be of such complexity and refinement as mind, as to be fitted to carry the new quality of deity. Thus whereas with us, a piece of Space-Time, a substance, which is alive, is differentiated in a part of its life so as to be mind, here a substance or piece of Space-Time which is mental is differentiated in a portion of its mental body so as to be divine, and this deity is sustained by all the space-time to which it belongs, with all those qualities lower than deity itself which belong to that substance. Moreover, as our mind represents and gathers up into itself its whole body, so does the finite god represent or gather up into its divine part its whole body, only in its body is included mind as well as the other characters of a body which has mind. Now for such a being, what for us are organic sensibles would include not merely the affections of its physiological body, but those of its mental 'body,' its mental affections. To speak more accurately, its mental affections, the acts of its mind-body, would take the place of our organic or motor sensa, while sensa, like hunger and thirst, which are the affections of its life-body, would fall rather into the class of sensa which with us are, like the feel and visual look of our bodies, contemplated by special senses. For such a being its specially differentiated mind takes the place of the brain or central nervous system with us. The body which is equivalent with the deity of the finite god, that is to say, whose processes are not parallel to but identical with the 'deisings' or enjoyments of the god, is of the nature of mind.

Only this proviso must be added. The mental structure of which a portion more complex and subtle is the bearer of deity, must not be thought necessarily to be a human mind or aggregation of such, but only to be of the mental order. To assume it to be of the nature of human mind would be as if a race of seaweeds were to hold that mind when it comes (the quality of deity for seaweeds) must be founded on the life of seaweeds, and minds the offspring of seaweeds. What form the finite god would assume we cannot know, and it is idle to guess. The picture has been drawn merely in order to give some kind of definiteness to the vague idea of a higher quality of existence, deity as founded upon the highest order of existence we know. There is always a danger that such attempts at definiteness where precise knowledge from the nature of the case is out of the question may seem a little ridiculous. Fortunately when we leave the finite god and endeavor to form a conception of the infinite God in his relation to things, we may avail ourselves of what is useful in the picture and avoid the danger of seeming to affect a prevision of how things in the future will come to be. We use the picture merely in order to understand how the whole world can be thought of as possessing deity.

We have now to think, not as before of a limited portion of Space-Time, but of the whole infinite Space-Time, with all its engendered levels of existence possessing their distinctive empirical qualities, as sustaining the deity of God. But when we imagine such an individual, we discover two differences which mark him off from all finites, including finite gods. The first is this. Our experience is partly internal and partly external; that is, the stimuli which provoke our enjoyments and through them are contemplated by us (and the same account applies with the proper extension of the terms to all finites) partly arise within our bodies and partly from external ones. The objects which we contemplate are partly organic or motor sensa and partly special sensa, in which are included our bodies as seen or touched or similarly apprehended. Now the body of God is the whole universe and there is no body outside his. For him, therefore, all objects are internal, and the distinction of organic and special sensa disappears. Our minds, therefore, and everything else in the world are 'organic sensa' of God. All we are are the hunger and thirst, the heart-beats and sweat of God. This is what Rabbi ben Ezra says in Browning's poem, when he protests that he has never mistaken his end, to slake God's thirst. For God there is still the distinction of enjoyment or deising and contemplation, for God's deity is equivalent only to a portion of his body. But it is only for the finites which belong to God's body, all the finites up to finites with mind, that the objects of contemplation are some organic and some external.

The second difference, and ultimately it is a repetition of the first, is this. God's deity is lodged in a portion of his body, and represents that body. But since his body is infinite, his deity (I allow myself to turn deity from a quality into a concrete thing, just as I use mind sometimes for the mental quality, sometimes for the concrete thing, mental processes), which represents his body, is infinite. God includes the whole universe, but his deity, though infinite, belongs to, or is lodged in, only a portion of the universe. The importance of this for the problem of theism will appear later. I repeat that when God's deity is said to represent his body, that representation is physiological; like the representation on the brain of the different portions of the body which send nervous messages to the brain. Deity does not represent the universe in the mathematical sense, in which, for example, the odd numbers represent or are an image of the whole series of numbers. Such mathematical representation would require God's deity also to be represented in his deity; and it is not so represented in the same fashion as his body is represented.

The infinitude of God's deity marks the difference between him and all other empirical beings. Deity is an empirical quality, but though it is located in a portion only of the universe, which universe of Space-Time with all its finites of lower order is God's body, yet that portion is itself infinite in extent and duration. Not only is God infinite in extent and duration, but his deity is also infinite in both respects. God's body being the whole of Space-Time is omnipresent and eternal; but his deity, though not everywhere, is yet infinite in its extension, and though his time is a portion only of infinite Time his deity is, in virtue of what corresponds in deity to memory and expectation in ourselves, infinite in both directions. Thus empirical as deity is, the infinity of his distinctive character separates him from all finites. It is his deity which makes him continuous with the series of empirical characters of finites, but neither is his 'body' nor his 'mind' finite.

For clearness' sake I must linger a little over this important and difficult matter; for in one sense our minds and all finite things are infinite as well. We are, however, finitely infinite; while deity is infinitely infinite. We are finite because our minds, which are extended both in space and time, are limited pieces of Space-Time. We are infinite because we are in relation to all Space-Time and to all things in it. Our minds are infinite in so far as from our point of view, our place or date, we mirror the whole universe; we are compresent with everything in that universe. . . . Though only a limited range of distinct things comes within our view, they are fringed with their relations to what is beyond them, and are but islands rising out of an infinite circumambient ocean. The whole of which they are parts may shrink in our apprehension into a vague object of feeling or be conceived more definitely as infinite. Still it is there. But this infinite world of Space-Time with its finite things engendered within it finds access to our minds only through our bodies and thence to our brains, and is cognised through our neuromental processes and the combinations of them. Our minds consist of our mental processes, which are also neural ones. If we follow a dangerous method of language, or of thinking, and fancy that the objects we know are the 'content' of our minds we may be led into the belief that, since our minds contain representations of all things in the universe, our minds are infinite, in the same way as God's deity. If, however, we recollect that our minds are nothing but the processes of mind and have no contents but their process-characters we shall avoid this danger. We shall then understand how our minds can be finite in extent and duration and yet be compresent with and correspond to an infinite world.

We may distinguish two sorts of infinity, which I will call internal and external. An inch is internally infinite in respect of the number of its parts and corresponds to an infinite line of which it forms only a part. But it is itself finite in length. In the same way our minds, though finite in space-time, may be infinite in respect of their correspondence with the whole of things in Space-Time.

We said that our minds represented our bodies, because to speak generally the various parts of our body were connected neurally with their corresponding places in the cortex. External objects excite our minds through first impinging on our organs of sense. As such representations of our body, our mind is finite. But through that body it is brought into relation with the infinite world. Thus though finite in extent of space and time we are internally infinite. We are so as pieces of Space and Time. But also within the brain there is room for multitudinous combinations initiated from within and enjoyed as imaginations and thoughts, and, for all I know, these are infinitely numerous in their possibilities of combination. We have at least enough of them to comprehend the universe as a whole so far as such apprehension is open to our powers. It is sufficient for our purposes of argument that our minds as spatio-temporal substances are like all spatio-temporal extents internally infinite. Externally we are finite.

But there is nothing whatever outside the body of God, and his deity represents the whole of his body, and all the lower ranges of finites are for him 'organic sensa.' The spatio-temporal organ of his deity is not only internally but externally infinite. Deity, unlike mind, is infinitely infinite. . . .

We are now led to a qualification of the greatest importance. The picture which has been drawn of the infinite God is a concession to our figurative or mythological tendency and to the habit of the religious consciousness to embody its conception of God in an individual shape. Its sole value lies in its indication of the relation that must be understood upon the lines traced by experience to subsist between deity and mind. This is adequate for finite gods, supposing the stage of deity to have been reached. But the infinite God is purely ideal or conceptual. The individual so sketched is not asserted to exist; the sketch merely gives body and shape, by a sort of anticipation, to the

actual infinite God whom, on the basis of experience, speculation
declares to exist. As actual, God does not possess the quality of deity
but is the universe as tending to that quality. This nisus in the universe, though not present to sense, is yet present to reflection upon
experience. Only in this sense of straining towards deity can there
be an infinite actual God. For, again following the lines of experience,
we can see that if the quality of deity were actually attained in the
empirical development of the world in Time, we should have not one
infinite being possessing deity but many (at least potentially many
finite ones. Beyond these finite gods or angels there would be in
turn a new empirical quality looming into view, which for them would
be deity—that is, would be for them what deity is for us. Just as
when mind emerges it is the distinctive quality of many finite individuals with minds, so when deity actually emerges it would be the
distinctive quality of many finite individuals. If the possessor of deity
were an existent individual he must be finite and not infinite. Thus
there is no actual infinite being with the quality of deity; but there
is an actual infinite, the whole universe, with a nisus to deity; and
this is the God of the religious consciousness, though that consciousness habitually forecasts the divinity of its object as actually realised
in an individual form. . . .

Infinite deity then embodies the conception of the infinite world in
its straining after deity. But the attainment of deity makes deity
finite. Deity is an empirical quality like mind or life. Before there
was mind the universe was straining towards infinite mind. But there
is no existent infinite mind, but only many finite minds. Deity is subject
to the same law as other empirical qualities, and is but the next
member of the series. At first a presage, in the lapse of time the quality
comes to actual existence, animates a new race of creatures, and is
succeeded by a still higher quality. God as an actual existent is always
becoming deity but never attains it. He is the ideal God in embryo.
The ideal when fulfilled ceases to be God, and yet it gives shape and
character to our conception of the actual God, and always tends to
usurp its place in our fancy.

SOME CONTEMPORARY PERSPECTIVES
ON GOD

13

ALBERT SCHWEITZER

Christianity and God *

DR. SCHWEITZER's main thesis in the discussion that follows is his
conception of Christianity as an ethical religion. He shows how
all religions can be distinguished according to the following philosophical conceptions: (a) optimism and pessimism; (b) monism
and dualism; and (c) the extent to which ethical motives are
present. Next, he notes the relation of Christianity to these categories, but is most concerned to explain how Christianity is fundamentally an ethical religion in which God reveals Himself to the
individual as Ethical Will and Ethical Personality. He concludes
with a criticism of what he describes as the logical mysticism of
the East and affirms that Christianity alone is ethical mysticism and
can effect a union of the individual and God.

WHEN EXAMINING the fundamental ideas of the higher religions,
we notice three lines of distinction which are determinative for the
character of each religion. The first is that between optimistic and
pessimistic; the second that between monistic and dualistic; thirdly,
there is the greater or lesser extent to which ethical motives are
present.

A religion is optimistic if it represents the conviction that the forces
at work in the natural world have their origin in a perfect primal
force, which leads all things towards perfection through a natural
development.

The religious mind is said to hold a pessimistic view, if it cannot
conceive the forces at work in the world of sense as the expression of

* From *Christianity and the Religions of the World,* translated by Johanna
Powers (The Macmillan Co., Inc., 1923), pp. 35-37, 73-80, 84. Reprinted with
the permission of George Allen and Unwin, Ltd., original publishers.

Albert Schweitzer (1875–) was born and educated in Germany. He holds
degrees in theology, philosophy, music, and medicine. He has been serving as
a medical missionary in Africa since 1913. In 1953 he was awarded the Nobel
Prize.

divine goodness and perfection. It therefore does not rest its hopes on the possibilities of development within this physical world, but looks beyond into the world of pure, spiritual being.

A religion is monistic if it considers God to be the sum-total of all the forces at work in the universe, and, therefore, believes that in the knowledge of the universe we can attain to a perfect knowledge of God. Thus, in its very nature, monism is pantheistic.

A religion is dualistic if it does not make any attempt to arrive at a full knowledge of the nature of God by examining the forces which are active in the natural world, but seeks to realize Him in accordance with the ideal conception of Him that we carry within us. Of necessity this leads to the idea that this God stands to a certain extent in contrast with the forces of Nature, however great may be the difficulties which this involves for human reasoning. The God whom we have within us as an ideal is an ethical Personality; on the other hand, the happenings due to the forces at work in the universe bear no ethical character. Thus the dualistic religion is theistic.

The distinction we have so far touched upon concern more the philosophical conceptions on which a religion may be based. It is the ethical content, however, that determines its inner nature. The great question, therefore, which each religion must be asked is, how far it produces permanent and profound incentives to the inward perfecting of personality and to ethical activity. . . .

. . . . .

Every rational faith has to choose between two things: either to be an ethical religion or to be a religion that explains the world. We Christians choose the former, as that which is of higher value. We turn away from the logical self-contained religion. To the question, how a man can be in the world and in God at one and the same time, we find the answer in the Gospel of Jesus: "By living and working in this world as one who is not of the world."

Thus we no longer rely on the bridges formed by ordinary logical thought. Our path leads into the region of *naiveté* and of paradox. We tread it resolutely and with confidence. We hold to the absolutely and profoundly ethical religion as to the one thing needful, though philosophy may go to rack and ruin. That which appears to be *naiveté* in Christianity is in reality its profundity.

There are two kinds of *naiveté:* one which is not yet aware of all the problems and has not yet knocked at all the doors of knowledge; and another, a higher kind, which is the result of philosophy having looked into all problems, having sought counsel in all the spheres of knowledge, and then having come to see that we cannot explain anything but have to follow convictions whose inherent value appeals to us in an irresistible way.

Compared with the logical religions of the East, the Gospel of Jesus is illogical. It presupposes a God who is an Ethical Personality, and who is, therefore, so to speak, outside the world. When trying to answer questions as to the relation between this Ethical Personality and the forces at work in the world, Christianity cannot rise above the mist. It must hold fast the belief that God is the sum-total of the forces working in the world—that all that is, is in God. So far, therefore, Christianity, too is obliged to think on monistic and pantheistic lines. And yet it does not rest satisfied with conceiving God as the sum-total of the forces that are active in the world, for the God of monism and pantheism—the God of Nature philosophies—is impersonal and has no ethical character. For this reason, Christianity accepts all the difficulties of the dualistic view; it is ethical theism and apprehends God as a Will that is distinct from the world and compels us not to conform to the world.

Again and again, in the course of centuries, Christianity has sought to harmonize the philosophical and ethical conceptions of God, but it has never succeeded. It carries within itself, unresolved, the antinomy between monism and dualism, between logical and ethical religion.

Neither can Christianity definitely choose between pessimism and optimism. It is pessimistic, not only because, like Brahmanism and Buddhism, it realizes that imperfection, pain, and sorrow are essential features of the natural world, but for this additional and still more important reason, that in man it finds a will which does not answer tc the will of the ethical God and which, therefore, is evil.

Again, Christianity is optimistic, because it does not abandon the world, does not, as do Brahmanism and Buddhism, withdraw from it in negation of life and of the world, but assigns to man a place in this world and commands him to live in it and to work in it in the spirit of the ethical God. Further, Christianity gives him the assurance that thereby God's purpose for the world and for man is being fulfilled; it cannot, however, explain how. For what significance have the ethical character and the ethical activity of the religious individual in the infinite happenings of the Universe? What do they accomplish? We must admit that the only answer we have to this question is, that thereby the will of God is fulfilled.

All problems of religion, ultimately, go back to this one—the experience I have of God within myself differs from the knowledge concerning Him which I derive from the world. In the world He appears to me as the mysterious, marvellous creative Force; within me He reveals Himself as ethical Will. In the world He is impersonal Force, within me He reveals Himself as Personality. The God who is known through philosophy and the God whom I experience as ethical Will do not coincide. They are one; but how they are one I do not understand.

Now, which is the more vital knowledge of God? The knowledge derived from my experience of Him as ethical Will. The knowledge concerning God which is derived from nature is always imperfect and inadequate, because we perceive the things in the world from without only. I see the tree grow and I see it cover itself with leaves and blossoms; but I do not understand the forces which effect this; their generative power remains a mystery to me. In myself, on the other hand, I know things from within. The creative force which produces and sustains all that is, reveals itself in me in a way in which I do not get to know it elsewhere, namely, as ethical Will, as something which desires to be creative within me. . . . My life is completely and unmistakably determined by the experience of God revealing Himself within me as ethical Will and desiring to take hold of my life. . . .

Let me express it in a simile. There is an ocean—cold water without motion. In this ocean, however, is the Gulf Stream, hot water, flowing from the Equator towards the Pole. Inquire of all scientists how it is physically imaginable that a stream of hot water flows between the waters of the ocean, which, so to speak, form its banks, the moving within the motionless, the hot within the cold: no scientist can explain it. Similarly, there is the God of love within the God of the forces of the universe—one with Him, and yet so totally different. We let ourselves be seized and carried away by that vital stream.

It is true that Christianity, too, has always sought to explain as much as possible. The first Christians expected the solution of the problem to lie in a speedy transformation of this natural world into the perfect world of the Kingdom of God. With ardent longing they looked forward to seeing God and the world harmonized with each other in that way, and to a life in the world perfectly congruous with existence in God. The world continued in its old course; and as event followed event, God's voice could be heard to say: "My thoughts are not your thoughts."

Since then, Christians have tried again and again to make of Christianity a doctrine in which the activity of the ethical God and the course of events in the natural world are brought into harmony with each other. Never has the attempt been successful. Over and over again reality undermined the theories built up by faith, as an insidious flood saps the dike till it collapses and disappears.

Thus Christianity has had to give up one piece after another of what it still imagined it possessed in the way of explanation of the universe. In this development it grows more and more into an expression of what constitutes its real nature. In a remarkable process of spiritualization it advances further and further from naive *naiveté* into the region of profound *naiveté*. The greater the number of explanations that slip from its hands, the more is the first of the Beatitudes, which may indeed be regarded as a prophetic words concerning Christianity, fulfilled: "Blessed are the poor in spirit; for theirs is the Kingdom of Heaven."

When Christianity becomes conscious of its innermost nature, it realizes that it is godliness rising out of inward constraint. The highest knowledge is to know that we are surrounded by mystery. Neither knowledge nor hope for the future can be the pivot of our life or determine its direction. It is intended to be solely determined by our allowing ourselves to be gripped by the ethical God, who reveals Himself in us, and by our yielding our will to His.

All profound religion is mystical. To be freed from the world by being in God: that is the longing we have within us, so long as we do not numb ourselves in thoughtlessness. A union with God, however, which is realized through the intellectual act of "knowing," as conceived in the Eastern religions, must always remain a dead spirituality. It does not effect a re-birth, in God, into living spirituality. Living spirituality, real redemption from the world, cannot come but from that union with God which is ethically determined. The religions of the East are logical mysticism, Christianity alone is ethical mysticism.

. . . . .

Christianity must, clearly and definitely, put before men the necessity of a choice between logical religion and ethical religion, and it must insist on the fact that the ethical is the highest type of spirituality, and that it alone is living spirituality. Thus Christianity shows itself as the religion which, penetrating and transcending all knowledge, reaches forward to the ethical, living God, who cannot be found through contemplation of the world, but reveals Himself in man only. And it is thus that Christianity speaks with all the authority of its inherent truth.

14

MARTIN BUBER

The Eclipse of God *

BUBER BEGINS by stating that the eclipse of God is a phenomenon
of our time and more than mere philosophy is needed to restore
to man the transcendent reality of God. Philosophy is concerned
with the relation of subject and object; religion is concerned with
faith founded on the duality of the I and Thou relationship. The
former is concerned with thought and reflection; the latter, with
existential reality. The meaning of existence is to be found in life,
action, and suffering, rather than in reflection on the concrete
stuff of life. Religious faith begins with the "fear of God," with
the dread uncertainty we experience of our existence. Religious
expression is bound to the concrete situation. Philosophy begins
with the act of abstraction, but as Descartes discovered, cannot
attain the real "I" of existence. Religion is the act of holding fast
to God—to the existing God. Philosophy in its last stage has
reached the intellectual letting go of God. The historical development of this process is noted by the author, who then points out
that an analogous process takes place in religion when what the
author terms the I-It relationship is replaced by the I-Thou relationship. Returning to the notion of the eclipse of God we are told
that through faith one can establish an existential relationship with
God—an I-Thou relationship in which we can meet with God—
whereas the I-It relationship acquaints us objectively merely with
aspects of that Being. In our age the I-It relationship, and especially the nature of the I, has intruded to eclipse God. Selfhood, he
declares, has become omnipotent and "shuts off from us the light
of heaven."

ECLIPSE OF the light of heaven, eclipse of God—such indeed is the
character of the historic hour through which the world is passing.
But it is not a process which can be adequately accounted for by
instancing the changes that have taken place in man's spirit. An

* Abridged from *The Eclipse of God* by Martin Buber, pp. 34-36, 44, 46-48,
49-54, 58, 159-167. Copyright 1952 by Harper & Row, Publishers, Inc. Reprinted
by permission of the publishers.

Martin Buber (1878–) was born at Vienna and educated in Austria and
Germany. He was Professor of Comparative Religion at the University of Frankfurt
until 1938, when he left Germany. Since then he has been Professor of Social
Philosophy at the Hebrew University in Jerusalem.

eclipse of the sun is something that occurs between the sun and our eyes, not in the sun itself. Nor does philosophy consider us blind to God. Philosophy holds that we lack today only the spiritual orientation which can make possible a reappearance of "God and the gods," a new procession of sublime images. But when, as in this instance, something is taking place between heaven and earth, one misses everything when one insists on discovering within earthly thought the power that unveils the mystery. He who refuses to submit himself to the effective reality of the transcendence as such—our *vis-à-vis* —contributes to the human responsibility for the eclipse.

Assume that man has now fully brought about the "elimination of the self-subsisting suprasensual world," and that the principles and the ideals which have characterized man in any way, to any extent, no longer exist. His true *vis-à-vis*, lives intact behind the wall of darkness. Man may even do away with the name "god," which after all implies a possessive, and which, if the possessor rejects it, i.e., if there is no longer a "God of man," has lost its *raison d'etre*: yet He who is denoted by the name lives in the light of His eternity. But we, "the slayers," remain dwellers in darkness, consigned to death.

According to a Jewish legend, Adam and Eve, when they rejected God on the day of their creation and were driven out of the Garden, saw the sun set for the first time. They were terrified, for they could interpret this phenomenon only as a sign that the world was to sink back into chaos because of their guilt. Both of them wept, sitting face to face, the whole night through, and they underwent a change of heart. The morning dawned. Adam rose, caught a unicorn, and offered it as a sacrifice in place of himself.

RELIGION AND PHILOSOPHY

All great religiousness shows us that reality of faith means living in relationship to Being "believed," that is, unconditionally affirmed, absolute Being. All great philosophy, on the other hand, shows us that cogitative truth means making the absolute into an object from which all other objects must be derived. Even if the believer has in mind an unlimited and nameless absolute which cannot be conceived in a personal form, if he really thinks of it as existing Being which stands over against him, his belief has existential reality. Conversely, even if he thinks of the absolute as limited within personal form, if he reflects on it as on an object, he is philosophizing. Even when the "Unoriginated" is not addressed with voice or soul, religion is still founded on the duality of I and Thou. Even when the philosophical act culminates in a vision of unity, philosophy is founded on the duality of subject and object. The duality of I and Thou finds its fulfilment in the religious relationship; the duality of subject and object sustains philosophy while it is carried on. The first arises out of the original situation of the individual, his living before the face of Being, turned toward him as he is turned toward it. The second springs from the splitting apart of this togetherness into two entirely distinct modes of existence, one which is able to do nothing but observe and reflect and one which is able to do nothing but be observed and reflected upon. I and Thou exist in and by means of lived concreteness; subject and object, products of abstraction, last only as long as that power is at work. . . .

Philosophy errs in thinking of religion as founded in a noetical act, even if an inadequate one, and in therefore regarding the essence of religion as the knowledge of an object which is indifferent to being known. As a result, philosophy understands faith as an affirmation of truth lying somewhere between clear knowledge and confused opinion. Religion, on the other hand, insofar as it speaks of knowledge at all, does not understand it as a noetic relation of a thinking subject to a neutral object of thought, but rather as mutual contact, as the genuinely reciprocal meeting in the fullness of life between one active existence and another. Similarly, it understands faith as the entrance into this reciprocity, as binding oneself in relationship with an undemonstrable and unprovable, yet even so, in relationship, knowable Being, from whom all meaning comes.

.   .   .   .   .

When we look at the history of a historical religion, we see the reoccurrence in different periods and phases of an inner battle which remains essentially the same. It is the struggle of the religious elements against the non-religious elements which invade it from all sides—metaphysics, gnosis, magic, politics, etc. This medley seeks to take the place of the flowing life of faith which is renewed in the flux. It finds helpers in myth and cult, both of which originally served only as expression of the religious relationship. In order to preserve its purity the religious element must combat the tendency of this conglomerate to become autonomous and to make itself independent of the religious life of the person. This battle is consummated in prophetic protest, heretical revolt, reformational retrenchment, and a new founding which arises through the desire to return to the original religious element. It is a struggle for the protection of lived concreteness as the meeting place between the human and the divine. The actually lived concrete is the "moment" in its unforeseeableness and its irrecoverableness, in its undivertible character of happening but once, in its decisiveness, in its secret dialogue between that which happens and that which is willed, between fate and action, address and answer. This lived concreteness is threatened by the invasion of the extra-religious elements, and it is protected on all fronts by the religious in its unavoidable aloneness.

The religious essence in every religion can be found in its highest certainty. That is the certainty that the meaning of existence is open and accessible in the actual lived concrete, not above the struggle with reality but in it.

That meaning is open and accessible in the actual lived concrete does not mean it is to be won and possessed through any type of analytical or synthetic investigation or through any type of reflection upon the lived concrete. Meaning is to be experienced in living action and suffering itself, in the unreduced immediacy of the moment. . . .

Every religious utterance is a vain attempt to do justice to the meaning which has been attained. All religious expression is only an intimation of its attainment. The reply of the people of Israel on Sinai, "We will do it, we will hear it," expresses the decisive with naive and unsurpassable pregnancy. The meaning is found through the engagement of one's own person; it only reveals itself as one takes part in its revelation.

All religious reality begins with what Biblical religion calls the "fear of God." It comes when our existence between birth and death becomes incomprehensible and uncanny, when all security is shattered through the mystery. This is not the relative mystery of that which is inaccessible only to the present state of human knowledge and is hence in principle discoverable. It is the essential mystery, the inscrutableness of which belongs to its very nature; it is the unknowable. Through this dark gate (which is only a gate and not, as some theologians believe, a dwelling) the believing man steps forth into the everyday which is henceforth hallowed as the place in which he has to live with the mystery. He steps forth directed and assigned to the concrete, contextual situations of his existence. That he henceforth accepts the situation as given him by the Giver is what Biblical religion calls the "fear of God."

An important philosopher of our day, Whitehead, asks how the Old Testament saying that the fear of God is the beginning of wisdom is to be reconciled with the New Testament saying that God is love. Whitehead has not fully grasped the meaning of the word "beginning." He who begins with the love of God without having previously experienced the fear of God, loves an idol which he himself has made, a god whom it is easy enough to love. He does not love the real God who is, to begin with, dreadful and incomprehensible. Consequently, if he then perceives, as Job and Ivan Karamazov perceive, that God is dreadful and incomprehensible, he is terrified. He despairs of God and the world if God does not take pity on him, as He did on Job, and bring him to love Him Himself. This is presumably what Whitehead meant when he said that religion is the passage from God the void to God the enemy and from Him to God the companion. That the believing man who goes through the gate of dread is directed to the concrete contextual situations of his existence means just this: that he endures in the face of God the reality of lived life, dreadful and incomprehensible though it be. He loves it in the love of God, whom he has learned to love.

For this reason, every genuine religious expression has an open or a hidden personal character, for it is spoken out of a concrete situation in which the person takes part as a person. This is true also in those instances where, out of a noble modesty, the word "I" is in principle avoided. Confucius, who spoke of himself almost as unwillingly as of God, once said: "I do not murmur against God, and I bear no ill will toward men. I search here below, but I penetrate above. He who knows me is God." Religious expression is bound to the concrete situation. . . .

Philosophizing and philosophy, in contrast, begin ever anew with one's definitely looking away from his concrete situation, hence with the primary act of abstraction. . . . The decisivness of this abstraction, of this turning away, is sometimes hidden from sight when a philosopher acts as if he would and could philosophize within his concrete situation. Descartes offers us the clearest example. When we hear him talk in the first person, we feel as if we were hearing the voice of direct personal experience. But it is not so. The I in the Cartesian *ego cogito* is not the living, body-soul person whose corporality had just been disregarded by Descartes as being a matter of doubt. It is the subject of consciousness, supposedly the only function which belongs entirely to our nature. . . . *Ego cogito* means to Descartes, indeed, not simply "I have consciousness," but "It is I who have consciousness." *Ego cogito* is, therefore, the product of a triply abstracting reflexion. Reflexion, the "bending back" of a person on himself, begins by extracting from what is experienced in the concrete situation "consciousness" *(cogitatio)*, which is not as such experienced there at all. It then ascertains that a subject must belong to a consciousness and calls this subject "I." In the end, it identifies the person, this living body-soul person, with that "I" that is, with the abstract and abstractly-produced subject of consciousness. . . .

In this way Descartes sought through the method of abstraction to capture the concrete starting-point as knowledge, but in vain. Not through such a deduction but only through genuine intercourse with a Thou can the I of the living person be experienced as existing. The concrete, from which all philosophizing starts, cannot again be reached by way of philosophical abstraction; it is irrecoverable.

. . . .

Religion, however, is not allowed, even in the face of the most self-confident pride of philosophy, to remain blind to philosophy's great engagement. . . . Religion must know knowledge not only as a need but also as a duty of man. It must know that history moves along the way of this need and duty, that, Biblically speaking, the eating of the tree of knowledge leads out of Paradise but into the world.

GOD AND THE SPIRIT OF MAN

If philosophy is here set in contrast to religion, what is meant by religion is not the massive fulness of statements, concepts, and activities that one customarily describes by this name and that men sometimes long for more than for God. Religion is essentially the act of holding fast to God. And that does not mean holding fast to an image that one has made of God, nor even holding fast to the faith in God that one has conceived. It means holding fast to the existing God. The earth would not hold fast to its conception of the sun (if it had one) nor to its connection with it, but to the sun itself.

In contrast to religion so understood, philosophy is here regarded as the process, reaching from the early becoming independent of reflection to its more contemporary crisis, the last stage of which is the intellectual letting go of God.

This process begins with man's no longer contenting himself, as did the prephilosophical man, with picturing the living God, to whom one formerly only called—with a call of despair or rapture which occasionally became His first name—as a Something, a thing among things, a being among beings, an It.

The beginning of philosophizing means that this Something changes from an object of imagination, wishes, and feelings to one that is conceptually comprehensible, to an object of thought. It does not matter whether this object of thought is called "Speech" (Logos), because in all and each one hears it speak, answer, and directly address one, or "the Unlimited" *(Apeiron)*, because it has already leapt over every limit that one may try to set for it, or simply "Being," or whatever. If the living quality of the conception of God refuses to enter into this conceptual image, it is tolerated alongside of it, usually in an unprecise form, as in the end identical with it or at least essentially dependent on it. Or it is depreciated as an unsatisfactory surrogate for the help of men incapable of thought.

In the progress of its philosophizing the human spirit is ever more inclined to fuse characteristically this conception, of the Absolute as object of an adequate thought, with itself, the human spirit. In the course of this process, the idea which was at first noetically contemplated finally becomes the potentiality of the spirit itself that thinks it, and it attains on the way of the spirit its actuality. The subject, which appeared to be attached to being in order to perform for it the service of contemplation, asserts that it itself produced and produces being. Until, finally, all that is over against us, everything that accosts us and takes possession of us, all partnership of existence, is dissolved in free-floating subjectivity.

The next step already takes us to the stage familiar to us, the stage that understands itself as the final one and plays with its finality: the human spirit, which adjudges to itself mastery over its work, annihilates conceptually the absoluteness of the absolute. It may yet imagine that it, the spirit, still remains there as bearer of all things and coiner of all values; in truth, it has also destroyed its own absoluteness along with absoluteness in general. The spirit can now no longer exist as an independent essence. There now exists only a product of human individuals called spirit. . . .

In this stage there first takes place the conceptual letting go of God because only now philosophy cuts off its own hands, the hands with which it was able to grasp and hold Him.

But an analogous process takes place on the other side, in the development of religion itself (in the usual broad sense of the word).

From the earliest times the reality of the relation of faith, man's standing before the face of God, world-happening as dialogue, has been threatened by the impulse to control the power yonder. Instead of understanding events as calls which make demands on one, one wishes oneself to demand without having to hearken. "I have," says man, "power over the powers I conjure." And that continues, with sundry modifications, wherever one celebrates rites without being turned to the Thou and without really meaning its Presence.

The other pseudo-religious counterpart of the relation of faith, not so elementally active as conjuration but acting with the mature power of the intellect, is unveiling. Here one takes the position of raising the veil of the manifest, which divides the revealed from the hidden, and leading forth the divine mysteries. "I am," says man, "acquainted with the unknown, and I make it known." The supposedly divine It that the magician manipulates as the technician his dynamo, the Gnostic lays bare, the whole divine apparatus. His heirs are not "theosophies" and their neighbors alone; in many theologies also, unveiling gestures are to be discovered behind the interpreting ones.

We find this replacement of I-Thou by an I-It in manifold forms in that new philosophy of religion which seeks to "save" religion. In it the "I" of this relation steps ever more into the foreground as "subject" of "religious feeling," as profiter from a pragmatist decision to believe, and the like.

Much more important than all this, however, is an event penetrating to the innermost depth of the religious life, an event which may be described as the subjectivizing of the act of faith itself. Its essence can be grasped most clearly through the example of prayer.

We call prayer in the pregnant sense of the term that speech of man to God which, whatever else is asked, ultimately asks for the manifestation of the divine Presence, for this Presence's becoming dialogically perceivable. The single presupposition of a genuine state of prayer is thus the readiness of the whole man for this Presence, simple turned-towardness, unreserved spontaneity. This spontaneity, ascending from the roots, succeeds time and again in overcoming all that disturbs and diverts. But in this our stage of subjectivized reflection not only the concentration of the one who prays, but also his spontaneity is assailed. The assailant is consciousness, the over-consciousness of this man here that he is praying, that he is *praying*, that *he* is praying. And the assailant appears to be invincible. The subjective knowledge of the one turning-towards about his turning-towards, this holding back of an I which does not enter into the action with the rest of the person, an I to which the action is an object—all this depossesses the moment, takes away its spontaneity. The specifically modern man who has not yet let go of God knows what that means: he who is not present perceives no Presence.

One must understand this correctly: this is not a question of a special case of the known sickness of modern man, who must attend his own actions as a spectator. It is the confession of the Absolute into which he brings his unfaithfulness to the Absolute, and it is the relation between the Absolute and him upon which this unfaithfulness works, in the middle of the statement of trust. And now he too who is seemingly holding fast to God becomes aware of the eclipsed Transcendence.

What is it that we mean when we speak of an eclipse of God which is even now taking place? Through this metaphor we make the tremendous assumption that we can glance up to God with our "mind's eye," or rather being's eye, as with our bodily eye to the sun, and that something can step betwen our existence and His as between the earth and the sun. That this glance of the being exists, wholly unillusory, yielding no images yet first making possible all images, no other court in the world attests than that of faith. It is not to be proved; it is only to be experienced; man has experienced it. And that other, that which steps in between, one also experiences, today. . . .

The double nature of man, as the being that is both brought forth from "below" and sent from "above," results in the duality of his basic characteristics. These cannot be understood through the categories of the individual man existing-for-himself, but only through the categories of his existing as man-with-man. As a being who is sent, man exists over against the existing being before which he is placed. As a being who is brought forth, he finds himself beside all existing beings in the world, beside which he is set. The first of these categories has its living reality in the relation I-Thou, the second has its reality in the relation I-It. The second always brings us only to the aspects of an existing being, not to that being itself. . . . Only the first relation, that which establishes essential immediacy between me and an existing being, brings me just thereby not to an aspect of it but to that being itself. To be sure, it brings me only to the existential meeting with it; it does not somehow put me in a position to view it objectively in its being. As soon as an objective viewing is established, we are given only an aspect and ever again only an aspect. But it is also only the relation I-Thou in which we can meet God at all, because of Him, in absolute contrast to all other existing beings, no objective aspect can be attained. . . .

It is not the case, however, that the I in both relations, I-Thou and I-It, is the same. Rather where and when the beings around one are seen and treated as objects of observation, reflection, use, perhaps also of solicitude or help, there and then another I is spoken, another I manifested, another I exists than where and when one stands with the whole of one's being over against another being and steps into an essential relation with him. Everyone who knows both in himself . . . knows whereof I speak.

In our age the I-It relation, gigantically swollen, has usurped, practically uncontested, the mastery and the rule. The I of this relation, an I that possesses all, makes all, succeeds with all, this I that is unable to say Thou, unable to meet a being essentially is the lord of the hour. This selfhood that has become omnipotent, with all the It around it, can naturally acknowledge neither God nor any genuine absolute which manifests itself to men as of non-human origin. It steps in between and shuts off from us the light of heaven.

Such is the nature of this hour. But what of the next? It is a modern superstition that the character of an age acts as fate for the next. One lets it prescribe what is possible to do and hence what is permitted. One surely cannot swim against the stream, one says. But perhaps one can swim with a new stream whose source is still hidden? In another image, the I-Thou relation has gone into the catacombs—who can say with how much greater power it will step forth! Who can say when the I-It relation will be directed anew to its assisting place and activity!

The most important events in the history of that embodied possibility called man are the occasionally occurring beginnings of new epochs, determined by forces previously invisible or unregarded. Each age is, of course, a continuation of the preceding one, but a continuation can be confirmation and it can be refuation.

Something is taking place in the depths that as yet needs no name. Tomorrow even it may happen that it will be beckoned to from the heights, across the heads of earthly archons. The eclipse of the light of God is no extinction; even tomorrow what has stepped in between may give way.

15

JACQUES MARITAIN

A New Approach to God *

MARITAIN URGES that if our civilization is to survive, we need a renewal of metaphysics, a reconciliation of science and wisdom, and a rediscovery of God. This need for God, this desire to discover again the sense of being, is reflected in the popularity of the existential philosophies; however the author maintains that true existentialism must be the product of reason, not unreason. The rediscovery of God proceeds through three stages: my awareness of the independent existence of things, my intuition of my own existence and its possible nothingness, and the intuition of Being in itself. Reason reveals to the individual that this intuition of Being-with-nothingness (my being) implies for its existence, Being-without-nothingness—the existence of God. Maritain acknowledges that this is not a new approach to God but rather the "eternal approach of man's reason." What is new in this natural reasoning is the intuition of existence, of the specific naturality of our knowledge of God. This rediscovery of the value of existence means also the rediscovery of love, the intuition that God is self-subsisting Love activating all creatures. Finally, the author comments on a new approach to God in the cultural and historical life of man. The great need of the present age is a theocentric humanism. The fulfillment of this need entails a spiritual revolution and a rehabilitation of man in God; the way to achieve this theocentric humanism is briefly outlined. The author concludes with the observation that such a spiritual revolution depends primarily upon God's grace and His initiative.

IF CIVILIZATION is to survive . . . the coming age must be an age of spiritual as well as social integration.

Today the human mind is torn and divided between positivism and irrationalism. The endeavors of pragmatism succeeded in making

* From "A New Approach to God" by Jacques Maritain in *Our Emergent Civilization,* edited by Ruth Nanda Anshen (copyright 1947 by Harper & Row, Publishers), pp. 280-90. Reprinted with the permission of the publishers.

Jacques Maritain (1882–) was born in Paris and educated at Heidelberg and Paris. He is recognized as one of the outstanding leaders of Neo-Thomism. He has served as Lecturer in Philosophy at Harvard University, University of Chicago, and Princeton University.

important discoveries concerning a number of basic attitudes in thought and morality, and in what might be called the sociology of knowledge. As a universal system of knowledge and life, as a philosophy, however, pragmatism has been a failure.

What is essentially needed is a renewal of metaphysics. The conceptions of modern science—the unification of matter and energy, physical indeterminism, the notion of space-time—are invaluable means of deciphering material phenomena. A cosmos of electrons and stars in which the stars are the heavenly laboratories of elements, subjected everywhere to genesis and transmutation, a universe which is finite but whose limits cannot be attained because of the curvation of space, and which dynamically evolves in a definite direction, namely, toward the highest forms of individuation and concentration and toward a simultaneous degradation of the quality of its total energy—all this is external description and scientific imagery rather than ontological insight. Such knowledge can never directly serve the purpose of any philosophical or metaphysical extrapolations. Yet all this constitutes at the same time a basic representation of the world incomparably more favorable to the edification of a philosophy of nature and more open to the deepening labor of metaphysical reason than the old Newtonian physics. The opportunity is now given for that reconciliation between science and wisdom for which the human mind thirsts. What the emergent civilization is anticipating . . . is a rediscovery of Being, and by the same token a rediscovery of Love.

This means axiomatically a rediscovery of God. The *existential* philosophies which are today in fashion are but a sign of a certain deep want, an inability to find again the sense of Being. This want is now unfulfilled, for these philosophies are still enslaved by irrationalism and seek for the revelation of existence, for ontological ecstasy, in the breaking of reason, in the experience of Despair and Nothingness, of Anguish or Absurdity. True existentialism is the work of reason. The act by virtue of which I exist and things exist, transcends concepts and ideas; it is a mystery for the intellect. But the intellect lives on this mystery. In its most natural activity it is as ordinary, daily and vulgar as eating or drinking. The act of existing is indeed the very object of every achieved act of the intellect, that is, of judgment. It is perceived by that intellectual intuition, immersed in sense experience, which is the common treasure (all the more precious since it is natural and imbues the depths of our thought) of all our assertions, of all this mysterious activity by means of which we declare either *ita est* or *fiat!* in the face of the world or at the moment of making a decision. Now, when the intellect passes the threshold of philosophy, it does so by becoming aware of this intellectual intuition, freeing its genuine power, and making it the peculiar weapon of a knowledge whose subject matter is Being itself. I do not refer here to Platonic essences. I refer to the act of existing in so far as it establishes and centers the intelligible structure of reality, as it expands into activity in every being; and as, at its supreme plenitude, it activates and attracts to itself the entire dynamism of nature. At their ontological peak, in the transcendence of the Pure Act and the Absolute, Being, Reason and God are one and the same reality. In the created realm Reason confronts Being and labors to conquer it, both to transfer Being into its own immaterial life and immaterially to be or become Being. In perceiving Being Reason knows God, in an enigmatic but inescapable manner.

Yet my thesis does not deal only with philosophers and philosophy, but with the mental behavior of the common man. Werner Sombart used to say that the "bourgeois," the man of the "capitalistic" era, was *neither "ontological" nor "erotic,"* had lost the sense of Being and the sense of Love. Torture and death have made us aware of the meaning of ontology. Hate has awakened an awareness of the meaning of eros. Let us emerge from sleep, cease to live in the dream or magic of images and formulas, well-systematized words, practical symbols and world-festering kabbala! Once a man is awakened to the reality of existence and the true life of Reason, to the intelligible value of Being, once he has really perceived this tremendous fact, sometimes exhilarating, sometimes disgusting and maddening in the knowledge that *I exist,* he is henceforth taken hold of by the intuition of Being and the implications it involves.

Precisely speaking, this prime intuition is both the intuition of *my* existence and of the existence of things; but first and foremost of the existence of things. When it takes place, I suddenly realize that a given entity, man, mountain or tree, exists and exercises that sovereign activity *to be* in its own way, totally self-assertive and totally implacable, completely independent from *me.* And at the same time I realize that I also exist but as thrown back into my loneliness and frailty by such affirmation of existence in which I have positively no part, to which I am exactly as naught. So the prime intuition of Being is the intuition of the solidity and inexorability of existence; and secondly, of the death and nothingness to which *my* existence is liable. And thirdly, in the same flash of intuition, which is but my becoming aware of the intelligible value of Being, I realize that the solid and inexorable existence perceived in anything whatsoever implies—I don't know in what way, perhaps in things themselves, perhaps separately from them—some absolute, irrefragable existence, completely free from

nothingness and death. These three intellective leaps—to actual existence as asserting itself independently from me; from this sheer objective existence to my own threatened existence; and from my existence
spoiled with nothingness to absolute existence—are achieved within
that same and unique intuition which philosophers would explain as
the intuitive perception of the essentially analogical content of the
first concept, the concept of Being.

Then a quick, spontaneous reasoning, as natural as this intuition
(and, as a matter of fact, more or less involved in it) immediately
springs forth, as the necessary fruit of such primordial apperception
and as enforced by and under its light. I see that my Being, first, is
liable to death; and, second, that it depends on the totality of nature,
on the universal whole whose part I am; and that Being-with-nothingness, as my own being is, implies, in order to be, Being-without-
nothingness. It implies that absolute existence which I confusedly
perceived as involved in my primordial intuition of existence. The
universal whole, whose part I am, is Being-with-nothingness, from
the very fact that I am part of it; so that finally, since the universal
whole does not exist by itself, there is another, separate, whole, another Being, transcendent and self-sufficient and unknown in itself
and activating all beings, which is Being-without-nothingness, that is,
Being by itself.

Thus the inner dynamism of the intuition of existence, or of the
intelligible value of Being, causes me to see that absolute existence
or Being-without-nothingness transcends the totality of nature, and
compels me to face the existence of God.

This is not a new approach to God. It is the eternal approach of
man's reason to God. What is new is the manner in which the modern
mind has become aware of the simplicity and liberating power, the
natural and somehow intuitive characteristics of this eternal approach.
The science of the ancients was steeped in philosophy. Their scientific
imagery was a pseudo-ontological imagery. Consequently there was a
kind of continuum between their knowledge of the physical world and
their knowledge of God. The latter appeared as the summit of the
former, a summit which was to be climbed through the manifold
paths of the casual connections at play in the sublunar world and the
celestial spheres. The sense of Being that ruled their universal thought
was for them a too usual atmosphere to be felt as a surprising gift.
At the same time the natural intuition of existence was so strong in
them that their proofs of God could take the form of the most conceptualized and rationalized scientific demonstrations, and be offered
as an unrolling of logical necessities, without losing the inner energy

of that intuition. Such logical machinery was quickened instinctively by the basic intuition of Being.

We are in a quite different position now. In order to solve the enigma of physical reality and to conquer the world of phenomena, our science has become a kind of Maya—a maya which succeeds and makes us masters of nature. But the sense of Being is absent from it. Thus when we happen to experience the impact of Being upon the mind it appears to us as a kind of intellectual revelation, and we realize clearly both its liberating and its awakening power and the fact that it involves a knowledge which is separated from that sphere of knowledge peculiar to our science. At the same time we realize that the knowledge of God, before being developed into logical and perfectly conceptualized demonstrations, is first and foremost a natural fruit of the intuition of existence, and forces itself upon our mind in the imperative virtue of this intuition.

In other words, we have become aware of the fact that human reason's approach to God, in its primordial vitality, is neither a mere intuition, which would be suprahuman, nor is it that artlike philosophical reasoning by which it is expressed in its achieved form, each step of which is pregnant with involved issues and problems. Human reason's approach to God in its primordial vitality is a *natural* reasoning, that is, intuitive-like or irresistibly vitalized by and maintained within the intellectual flash of the intuition of existence. Then the intuition of existence, grasping in some existing reality Being-with-nothingness, makes the mind grasp by the same stroke the necessity of Being-without-nothingness. And nowhere is there any problem involved, because the illumining power of this intuition takes hold of the mind and obliges it to see. Thus it naturally proceeds, in a primary intuitive flash, from imperative certainty to imperative certainty. I believe that from Descartes to Kierkegaard, the effort of modern thought—to the extent that it has not completely repudiated metaphysics, and if it is cleansed of the irrationalism which has gradually corrupted it—tends to such an awareness of the specific *naturality* of man's knowledge of God, definitely deeper than any logical process scientifically developed. It tends to the awareness of man's knowledge of God, and of the primordial and simple intuitivity in which it originates. Availing itself of any true progress achieved by the critique of knowledge, and realizing its own existential requirements, philosophy must enforce this new awareness and make clear in this way the manner in which the eternal approach of man, of the common man, to God proceeds.

.   .   .   .   .

Finally, the rediscovery of the value of existence not only means the rediscovery of God. It also means the rediscovery of Love. For when the intuition of Being and Existence takes place in me, it normally carries along with itself another intuition, the intuition of my own existence or my Self, the intuition of Subjectivity as subjectivity. Now Subjectivity, in so far as it is subjectivity, is not an object presented to thought but rather the very wellspring of thought—a deep, unknown and living center which superabounds in knowledge and superabounds in love, attaining only through love its supreme level of existence, existence as giving itself.

This is what I mean: Self-knowledge as a mere psychological analysis of phenomena more or less superficial, a wandering through images and memories, is but an egotistic awareness, however valuable it may be. But when it becomes ontological, then Knowledge of the Self is transfigured, implying intuition of Being and the discovery of the actual abyss of subjectivity. At the same time it is the discovery of the basic generosity of existence. Subjectivity, this essentially dynamic, living and open center, both receives and gives. It receives through the intellect, by superexisting in knowledge. It gives through the will, by superexisting in love; that is, by having within itself other beings as inner attractions directed toward them and giving oneself to them, and by spiritually existing in the manner of a gift. And "it is better to give than to receive." The spiritual existence of love is the supreme revelation of existence for the Self. The Self, being not only a material individual but also a spiritual personality, possesses itself and holds itself in hand in so far as it is spiritual and in so far as it is free. And to what purpose does it possess itself and dispose of itself, if not for what *is better*, in actual existence and absolutely speaking, or to give of itself? Thus it is that when a man has been really awakened to the sense of being or existence, and grasps intuitively the obscure, living depth of the Self and subjectively, he discovers by the same token the basic generosity of existence and realizes, by virtue of the inner dynamism of this intuition, that love is not passing pleasure or emotion, but the very meaning of his being alive. He becomes both an "ontological" and an "erotic" man, he is a man renewed.

And not only does he know, by virtue of his primordial intellectual grasping of existence, that God exists and is absolute Being, is self-subsisting *Esse*. He also knows that because of this very fact God is absolute ontological generosity, self-subsisting Love; and that such transcendent Love inherently causes, permeates and activates every creature, which in answer loves God more than itself. Thus love for

God, the natural and universal eros, is the very virtue and innermost vitality in which all beings desire and love, act and strive.

In the preceding pages I have emphasized our new awareness of the eternal approach to God. Summing up what I have often tried to point out, I should like now to outline what may be called, properly speaking, a new approach to God, not in the field of knowledge but in the field of culture and in the historical life of man.

Every great age of culture receives its deepest meaning and direction from a particular constellation of spiritual factors or dominating ideas; let us say, from a particular historical heaven. And the most significant factor to be considered in such moving appearances of the Zodiac of history is the peculiar approach to God characterizing a given period of culture. What are, from this point of view, the main characteristics of the human approach to God, or of the human attitude toward God, in the new age of civilization that is emerging?

The Medieval Age was a humble and magnanimous period of history. I would say that at the end of the *sacral* era man experienced not humility but humiliation. Whereas new forces awakened in history, he felt distressed and crushed by the old structures of a civilization which had considered itself as God's stronghold built upon earth. From the Renaissance on, he endeavored to become aware of and establish his own dignity by the sole effort of his own reason liberating itself both from the old structures of the world and from all sorts of disciplines and authorities which were in the name of God the keystone of these structures. He isolated himself progressively from God. God, the heavenly God of Christianity, or the immanent and evolving God of pantheism, was but the supreme assurance of his own greatness and power. He expected progress and happiness from the effort of man centered upon himself and set apart from God. He realized his dignity; he became the master of nature. But he was alone. The age was an age of anthropocentric humanism. It ended in human devastation.

If civilization is to be saved, the new age must be an age of theocentric humanism. Today human dignity is everywhere trampled down. Still more, it crumbles from within, for in the mere perspective of science and technology we are at a loss to discover the rational foundations of the dignity of the human person and to believe in it. The task of the emergent civilization consists in refinding and refounding the sense of that dignity, in rehabilitating man in God and through God, not apart from God. This means a complete spiritual revolution. Then all the conquests of the preceding epoch will be both purified and saved, redeemed from the errors of this epoch and transfigured, brought to a new flowering. The age will be an age of dignification of the creature, in its living relation with the Creator; as vivified by Him, and as having in Him the justification of its very existence, its labor on earth, its essential claims and its trend toward freedom. It will be again, at least for those capable of understanding, an age of humility and magnanimity, but with a new awareness of human potentialities and of the depth, magnitude and universality of human problems. The new approach to God will be a new approach to the true God of the Judaeo-Christian tradition, the true God of the gospel, whose grace perfects nature and does not destroy it, transcending reason in order to strengthen, not to blind or annihilate it; making moral conscience progress in the course of time and leading human history, that is, the ceaseless and ceaselessly thwarted effort of mankind toward emancipation, in the direction of its supratemporal accomplishment. This new approach will proceed neither in the adoration of creatures, which was the foolishness of our time, nor in that bitter contempt which too many Christians mistake for the divine madness of the saints. It will manifest itself in a deeper respect and an understanding of the creature and a greater attention will be given to the discovery in man of every vestige of God.

Hence there are a number of consequences which I should like merely to enumerate. Doubtless metaphysical anguish, the great anguish of Augustine and Pascal, will always play its part in the human search for God. Yet it seems that in the present situation of mankind it is rather through the practical effort to rediscover man, through the actual experience of the basic conditions of personality, justice, freedom, respect and love for our fellow men, that we shall be led to the rediscovery of God. On the other hand, it appears that the controversial emphasis of religious thought has now shifted from humbling to promoting reason. Religious thought will have to defend itself not so much against philosophical (critical) reason, as at the time of the Enlightenment, as it will have to defend philosophical (ontological) reason against sheer irrationalism and a metaphysics of despair and also against such ultimate fruits of rationalism as old pseudo-scientific positivism and dialectical materialism. It will have to defend the existence of supernatural reality less against naturalistic exaltation than against naturalistic destruction of nature. In the structure of human knowledge theology occupies and will always occupy the highest position. Yet with regard to the role played by it, in fact, in the inner stimulations of culture, it is through Christian philosophy, in addition to the irrefragable ontological truth promulgated by every great religion, that the new civilization will be spurred, at least to the extent that it will be inspired by the spirit of Truth. The momentous question will be more than ever: What is man? I mean man not only essentially, but existentially. In the very perspectives of religious thought there must be developed a philosophical ethic, as distinguished from moral theology and as encompassing anthropology as well as sociology. The notion of natural law . . . will be re-examined and restored. Whereas for centuries the most crucial issues for religious thought were the great theological controversies centered on the dogmas of faith, these most crucial issues will now deal with political theology and political philosophy.

Yet, since the preaching of the gospel, what has had, in the supreme regions of knowledge, and will always have, a characteristic and all-pervading significance for a given period of civilization, is the peculiar way in which the human mind is able to grasp the mystery of human freedom and divine grace. I think that the emergent civilization will not fail to have it say in the matter. At the same time the reverse mystery, which displays the power of refusal and nothingness, the problem of evil, will be scrutinized anew in its metaphysical and psychological recesses and implications.

Finally, we are searching for the deepest characterization, from the spiritual point of view, of the new age we are considering. It is necessary to make clear that the spiritual dynamism at work in human culture implies a twofold movement. First, there is the movement of descent, the movement by which the divine plenitude, the prime source of existence, descends into human reality to permeate and vivify it. For God infuses in every creature goodness and lovability together with being and has the *first* initiative in every good activity. Then there is the movement of ascent, which is the answer of man, by which human reality takes the *second* initiative, activates itself toward the unfolding of its energies and toward God. From the point of view of the Absolute, the first movement is obviously what matters most; to receive from God is of greater moment for man than to give to God, and man can only give what he has received.

Thus we shall observe that the great error of modern times, from the Renaissance on, has been to believe that the second movement matters more than the first, or to expect from man the *first* initiative; let us say to forget that the word of God precedes man's answer, and perversely to consider the answer to be the first utterance.

And we shall conclude that the emergent civilization will realize again that the descent of divine plenitude into man matters more than the ascent of man toward self-perfection. In this new age the movement by which the human being answers God's movement of effusion will not take place, as in the Middle Ages, in a childlike, ignorant-of-itself humanity. Its new simplicity will be a mature and experienced, self-awakened simplicity, enlightened by what might be called a free and evangelical introspection.

Such will be the new approach to God peculiar to this age, the age of the spiritual revolution. Man will understand that he ascends toward his own fullness and toward God all the better because he himself espouses the movement of descent of the uncreated Love and in so doing reveals all that he is and possesses. He will understand that he must edify himself in order to receive such an effusion. Gospel generosity, by accustoming human life to divine ways, appears at the same time as a manifestation of the "philanthropy of our God," as St. Paul puts it, and corresponds to that rehabilitation and dignification of the creature in God of which I spoke above. Man will find anew his internal unity by definitely preferring the evangelical loss of himself which is produced by love—that readiness to give everything, the mantle and the tunic and the skin—to the rationalist self-achievement which is the conquest of illusion and delusion, and to the irrationalist self-achievement which is dissolution in the sea of despair and absurdity.

Part Two

MYSTICISM

MYSTICISM OFFERS another approach, and for some the only solution, to the problem of the existence of God.* The mystics' approach to God is grounded completely in the personal experience of the individual—an experience at times so awesome and overpowering that a description of it may be written down and preserved with all the solicitude that Pascal gave to his famous "memorial." The significance of the mystical experience lies essentially in the fact that it is the very nature of the religious experience itself in its most intense form. It is partly for this reason that Rufus Jones, in so many of his writings on mysticism, insists that it is a universal phenomenon in the religious life. This viewpoint may be accepted if we identify the religious experience at all times with the mystical experience. Another view is that the mystical experience is to be identified only with the *highest moments* of the religious experience. Thus through prayer, study, and worship, we may feel close to God, but the experience in any instance is usually not the overpowering intimacy and sense of union that the mystics feel. The mystic's actual experience of God in this way may be something very transitory, and clearly it is not of continuous occurrence even with the greatest of the mystics. It is, nonetheless, very real—so much so, that the mystic is led to devote his life to the religious calling and to the expectation of union with God. Thus the mystic orders his life and sets it apart from ordinary concerns; he dedicates his life to God and all else becomes secondary to this. But the average individual who has a religious experience—which Jones would identify with mysticism—makes such an experience secondary to the concerns of everyday living. In effect, then, mystics constitute a class apart.

* Particularly pertinent to this subject are the remarks of Henri Bergson in his *Two Sources of Morality and Religion,* translated by Audra and Brereton (Henry Holt, 1935), pp. 229 ff.

The experience of the mystics affords us a further claim (in addition to those discovered by reason) to a knowledge of God as certain and vivid as any we can claim for ordinary sense experience. The mystics state that they have a direct and immediate knowledge of God, rather than an inferred knowledge. Whether the experience of the mystic is a true one and whether his claim is valid, constitutes a serious problem for the philosopher. For the experience of the mystic is essentially ineffable and incommunicable and as such may lead to conflicting and varied interpretations. The tough-minded may scoff at the claims of the mystic, the sceptics may be inclined to dismiss them all as mad, and even the religiously minded may differ on the sincerity of the mystic's report. Indeed, it often becomes difficult to determine whether the mystic's report of his experience is a sincere and accurate statement, or whether it is merely an abnormal state of mind. The mystic may claim to hear voices, have visions, experience raptures and ecstasies—but many who are sick in mind have what seem to be identical experiences and forms of behavior. This problem of differentiation is not an easy one, but it has been done; and we may decide that because such phenomena occur in those who are mentally sick, it would certainly be a *non sequitur* to say that all who have such experiences are mentally ill.

Accepting as true the reports of the great mystics, or at least assuming the validity of the mystical experience, we are concerned in the selections that follow with the nature of that experience, the relation of the individual mystic with God, and the discipline or rule of life that he imposes upon himself in order to attain in this life even a transitory union with God.

Our examination of the problems of mysticism is begun with Pascal's testament to his mystical experience, "The Memorial." The selection from Underhill on the characteristics of mysticism serves as a general introduction to the subject. Drawing upon an extraordinarily extensive acquaintance with the whole history and literature of mysticism, Underhill brings out, even in this brief selection, an abundance of detailed information on the nature of the mystical experience. It is the best general introduction to a difficult subject of which the editor is aware, and it develops particularly well the relation between the aesthetic and the mystical experience. Above all the approach to the subject is sympathetic, without which attitude the mystics can hardly be enjoyed, much less understood.

With this background of a general nature, we may now proceed to an examination of selections from the individual mystics. The contribution from Plotinus is the first in this book, because of his posi-

tion as the progenitor of much of the intellectual background of
the mystical movement in the West. Even a superficial study of
many of the mystics of the West clearly reveals the great influence
of the Neo-Platonic philosophy and particularly of the contributions
of Plotinus. His mysticism is highly contemplative and intellectual
in nature; it is based entirely upon philosophical considerations rather
than religious revelation or inspiration. We would maintain that he
is a true mystic even though Bergson, for example, would limit the
term solely to those mystics who would continue what he calls the
"divine action." He argues that the true mystical experience must
always result in some form of practical activity exemplifying the
religious wisdom one has acquired, such as preaching, crusading,
building monasteries, and so forth.

The introduction of Yoga within the topic mysticism may strike
some as rather odd, for perhaps we have thought of Yoga as some
esoteric doctrine or rite involving magic, theosophy, and clairvoyance.
It is none of these; rather, it has a long and respected tradition—
even though some of its followers may become a little too zealous
or extravagant in their practice of its discipline. Again, certain
physical aspects of Hatha Yoga may seem rather strange to the
average reader's conception of mysticism, yet it should be remembered that mysticism definitely has its physical side, and the counterpart of the Yoga physical discipline is found in the ascetic discipline
of the West. The practise, for instance, of postures by the Yogi may
seem alien to the Western mind, until we remember St. Simeon
Stylites and his pillar. And the observances and abstinences of Yoga
discipline are clearly duplicated in various ways in the monastic
rules of the West. A more fundamental characteristic distinguishing
Yoga as mysticism is what Rudolph Otto calls its soul-mysticism in
contrast to the God-mysticism of the Western world. The mysticism
of Yoga, Otto contends, aims not at a union with God, but rather
at the freedom of the soul and what he terms the sense of the holy.

The mysticism of Eckhart moves on a high intellectual and religious
plane, combining elements of Neo-Platonic and Scholastic philosophy
with a deep and abiding faith in the religious truth of Christianity.
Here we have far more than the simple piety, of let us say, a St.
Francis of Assisi or a George Fox. Religious piety here is combined
with a profundity that stamps Eckhart as one of the greatest of the
speculative mystics. His emphasis on the intellectual side of mysticism
is apparent in the priority he gives to understanding as a higher perfection than being in God, and in the analysis he makes of the
soul and the nature of its relation to the Godhead. The reading of

the selection from Eckhart will be difficult, but it will be highly rewarding.

The *Theologia Germanica* is much less speculative in nature than Eckhart's writing, although it stems indirectly from Eckhart as its source. The emphasis of the *Theologia* is religious rather than philosophical, and the author is more concerned with man as a sinful creature than he is with any analysis of the soul or the Godhead. The need for a union of the soul with God is stressed; this, the selection has in common with other examples of mysticism. But perhaps more than the others it concentrates on the necessity for the individual's putting off his own will and making his will and his love one with God. Perfect union with God, it is reiterated often, will be achieved only with the death of self-will. This selection may also be distinguished as being more a set of exercises in piety and devotion than a treatise in mystical theology.

St. John of the Cross has often been called the "mystic's mystic" and the title is well deserved, yet he also claims a large following from those who are not proficient in mysticism. Few mystics have received the attention that he has in recent years, and in the opinion of many he achieves in many ways the highest attainments of mystical thought and feeling. At the same time he seems more able than many of the mystics to give a clear reporting of his own experience and to set that experience down in the form of a well-organized and well-thought-out discipline which will enable others to follow in his path. By dividing the mystical experience into the active and passive nights of sense and spirit, he provides an easier guide for the prospective mystic, and at the same time fills in more completely for the uninitiated the full nature of the mystical way.

The selection from Ruysbroeck has been chosen, primarily, in order to set forth his excellent, though at times rather difficult, account of the nature of the Spiritual Marriage. All the mystics—with the exception of the followers of Yoga if we accept the qualification made by Otto—emphasize the importance of the union of the soul with God. This union has long been spoken of as a spiritual marriage of the soul with God or Christ, and even Luther who is not essentially a mystic speaks of the third function of faith as effecting such a spiritual marriage. The nature of this marriage has been well described by many mystics, but we favor the account of Jan Van Ruysbroeck. We are of the opinion that what he has to say about the other stages in the progress of the soul toward God has been better said by St. John of the Cross, and that the philosophical aspects of mysticism are developed better by Meister Eckhart, but that the

Spiritual Espousals of Ruysbroeck is the best summary presentation of this rather difficult and, in the nature of the case rather obscure mystical state.

The *Spiritual Guide* of Molinos takes an aspect of the mysticism of St. John of the Cross, the passive character of the night of spirit, and by overemphasizing this aspect, becomes the source of that religious phenomenon of the seventeenth century known as Quietism. Though somewhat dreary, the meditations of Molinos are not uninspiring or without value, but his originality appears most in the latter part of his work where he deals with the mystical states of prayer. His overemphasis of the part that God plays by means of His grace in the progress of the mystic toward union with God easily leads, however, to the dangerous position in which everything is left to God and nothing to the individual will. "Laissez-faire Dieu" is the outcome of the Quietism of Molinos.

Quite removed from the interior passivity that characterizes the teachings of Molinos, are the writings and the life of George Fox. If, as some would say, the active life rather than the contemplative life is the true mark of the mystic, then certainly George Fox would come up to that qualification, for his life was one of constant travelling and preaching. He is far from being a philosopher or a theologian, and has little interest in any ascetic discipline, but he is intensely and actively concerned to preach and to live the gospel of Christ as it was revealed to him. And just as Luther claimed that his interpretation of the doctrine of faith made every man a priest, so Fox might have contended that his "openings" and his doctrine of the inner light make every man a mystic. Our primary reason for choosing the material from the life of George Fox was to give an example of one who, in the opinion of those who believe that the religious experience and the mystical experience are one and that, consequently, mysticism is a common or universal phenomenon in the life of man, would best illustrate their position.

16

BLAISE PASCAL

The Memorial *

The year of grace 1654, Monday 23 November, day of St. Clement, pope and martyr, and others of the martyrologium . . . from about ten at night to half past twelve.

FIRE

God of Abraham, God of Isaac, God of Jacob,
Not of the philosophers and the learned.
Certitude. Joy. Certitude. Emotion. Peace. Joy.
The world has not known Thee, but I have known Thee.
Joy! Joy! Joy! Tears of joy.
My God, wilt thou leave me?
Let me not be separated from Thee in all eternity
This is life eternal that they may know thee.
The only true God and him whom thou has sent, Jesus Christ.

* "The Memorial" is the record of an ecstatic mystical experience left by Pascal. It was written on parchment and found sewn in the lining of his doublet after his death. The version that appears here has been slightly abbreviated and adapted from Brémond's *Histoire littéraire du sentiment réligieux en France,* IV, 368.

For a brief biographical sketch of Pascal, see selection 4 on page 19.

17

EVELYN UNDERHILL

The Characteristics of Mysticism *

AFTER SKETCHING the sharp contrast that exists between the "way of magic" and the "way of mysticism," our author emphasizes the importance and the need of setting up the true characteristics of mysticism. Mysticism is defined as the "science of union with the Absolute," and the relationship of mysticism to the arts is commented upon at some length. Here the contrast between the mystical experience and the esthetic experience and the place of symbolism and imagery in the communication of the mystical experience is brought out with considerable skill and with particular attention to historical sources. The author then proceeds to reject William James' four marks of the mystic state and elaborates upon her own contribution of the characteristics of the mystic state as practical, as a spiritual activity, as love, and as a psychological experience. In conclusion we are given a corollary to these four characteristics or rules in which it is contended that "mysticism is never self-seeking."

THE SPIRITUAL HISTORY of man reveals two distinct and fundamental attitudes towards the unseen; and two methods whereby he has sought to get in touch with it. For our present purpose I will call these methods "the way of magic" and the "way of mysticism." Having said this, we must at once add that although in their extreme forms these methods are sharply contrasted, their frontiers are far from being clearly defined: that, starting from the same point, they often confuse the inquirer by using the same language, instruments and methods. Hence, much which is really magic is loosely and popularly described as mysticism. They represent as a matter of fact the opposite poles of the same thing: the transcendental consciousness of humanity. Between them lie the great religions, which might be described under this metaphor as representing the ordinarily habitable

* From the book *Mysticism* by Evelyn Underhill. Copyright, 1914, by E. P. Dutton and Co., Inc., renewal, 1942, by Evelyn Underhill, pp. 70-94.

Evelyn Underhill (Mrs. Stuart Moore) (1875-1941) was born and educated in England. She became a Fellow of King's College, London and was named Upton Lecturer on Religion at Manchester College, Oxford, 1921-22. Her hobbies were said to be gardening and talking to cats.

regions of that consciousness. Thus, at one end of the scale, pure mysticism "shades off" into religion—from some points of view seems to grow out of it. No deeply religious man is without a touch of mysticism; and no mystic can be other than religious, in the psychological if not in the theological sense of the word. At the other end of the scale religion, no less surely, shades off into magic.

The fundamental difference between the two is this: magic wants to get, mysticism wants to give. . . . In mysticism the will is united with the emotions in an impassioned desire to transcend the sense-world, in order that the self may be joined by love to the one eternal and ultimate Object of love. . . . In magic, the will unites with the intellect in an impassioned desire for supersensible knowledge. This is the intellectual, aggressive, and scientific temperament trying to extend its field of consciousness, until it includes the supersensual world: obviously the antithesis of mysticism, though often adopting its title and style.

Mysticism . . . is non-individualistic. It implies, indeed, the abolition of individuality; of that hard separateness, that "I, Me, Mine" which makes of man a finite isolated thing. It is essentially a movement of the heart, seeking to transcend the limitations of the individual standpoint and to surrender itself to ultimate Reality; for no personal gain, to satisfy no transcendental curiosity, to obtain no other-worldly joys, but purely from an instinct of love. . . . The mystic is "in love with the Absolute" not in any idle or sentimental manner, but in that vital sense which presses at all costs and through all dangers towards union with the object beloved. . . .

What then do we really mean by mysticism? A word which is impartially applied to the performances of mediums and the ecstasies of the saints, to "menticulture" and sorcery, dreamy poetry and mediaeval art, to prayer and palmistry, the doctrinal excesses of Gnosticism, and the tepid speculations of the Cambridge Platonists even, according to William James, to the higher branches of intoxication—soon ceases to have any useful meaning. Its employment merely confuses the inexperienced student, who ends with a vague idea that every kind of supersensual theory and practice is somehow "mystical." Hence the need of fixing, if possible, its true characteristics: and restating the fact that Mysticism, in its pure form, is the science of ultimates, the science of union with the Absolute, and nothing else, and that the mystic is the person who attains to this union, not the person who talks about it. Not to *know about,* but to Be, is the mark of the real initiate.

Now we have said that the end which the mystic sets before him is conscious union with a living Absolute. That Divine Dark, that Abyss of the Godhead, of which he sometimes speaks as the goal of his quest, is just this Absolute, the Uncreated Light in which the Universe is bathed, and which—transcending, as it does, all human powers of expression—he can only describe to us as *dark*. In the mystic this union is conscious, personal, and complete. "He enjoys," says St. John of the Cross, "a certain contact of the soul with the Divinity; and it is God Himself who is then felt and tasted." . . .

As genius in any of the arts is—humanly speaking—the final term of a power of which each individual possesses the rudiments, so mysticism may be looked upon as the final term, the active expression, of a power latent in the whole race: the power, that is to say, of so perceiving transcendent reality. Few people pass through life without knowing what it is to be at least touched by this mystical feeling. He who falls in love with a woman and perceives—as the lover really does perceive—that the categorical term "girl" veils a wondrous and unspeakable reality: he who, falling in love with nature, sees the landscape "touched with light divine," he who falls in love with the Holy, or as we say "undergoes conversion"; all these have truly known for an instant something of the secret of the world. . . .

This intuition of the Real lying at the root of the visible world and sustaining its life, is present in a modified form in the arts. . . . It is this which gives to them that peculiar vitality, that strange power of communicating a poignant emotion, half torment and half joy, which baffle their more rational interpreters. We know that the picture which is "like a photograph," the building which is at once handsome and commodious, the novel which is a perfect transcript of life, fail to satisfy us. It is difficult to say why this should be so, unless it were because these things have neglected their true business; which was not to reproduce the illusions of ordinary men but to catch and translate for us something of that "secret plan," that reality which the artistic consciousness is able, in a measure, to perceive. "Painting as well as music and poetry exists and exults in immortal thoughts," says Blake. . . .

The mystic may say—is indeed bound to say—with St. Bernard, "My secret to myself." Try how he will, his stammering and awestruck reports can hardly be understood but by those who are already in the way. But the artist cannot act thus. On him has been laid the duty of expressing something of that which he perceives. He is bound to tell his love. In his worship of Perfect Beauty faith must be balanced by works. By means of veils and symbols he must interpret his free vision, his glimpse of the burning bush, to other men. He is the mediator between his brethren and the divine, for art is the link betwen appearance and reality.

But we do not call every one who has these partial and artistic intuitions of reality a mystic, any more than we call every one a musician who has learnt to play the piano. The true mystic is the person in whom such powers transcend the merely artistic and visionary stage, and are exalted to the point of genius. . . . As artists stand in a peculiar relation to the phenomenal world, receiving rhythms and discovering truths and beauties which are hidden from other men, so this true mystic stands in a peculiar relation to the transcendental world; there experiencing actual, but to us unimaginable tension and delight. . . . Hence his mysticism is no isolated vision, no fugitive glimpse of reality, but a complete system of life carrying its own guarantees and obligations. As other men are immersed in and react to natural or intellectual life, so the mystic is immersed in and reacts to spiritual life. He moves towards that utter identification with its interests which he calls "Union with God."

The earthly artist, because perception brings with it the imperative longing for expression, tries to give us in color, sound or words a hint of his ecstasy, his glimpse of truth. Only those who have tried, know how small a fraction of his vision he can, under the most favorable circumstance, contrive to represent. The mystic, too, tries very hard to tell an unwilling world his secret. But in his case, the difficulties are enormously increased. First, there is the huge disparity between his unspeakable experience and the language which will most nearly suggest it. Next, there is the great gulf fixed between his mind and the mind of the world. His audience must be bewitched as well as addressed, caught up to something of his state, before they can be made to understand.

Were he a musician, it is probable that the mystic could give his message to other musicians in the terms of that art, far more accurately than language will allow him to do . . . of all the arts music alone shares with great mystical literature the power of waking in us a response to the life-movement of the universe: brings us—we know not how—news of its exultant passions and its incomparable peace.

One contemplative at least, Richard Rolle of Hampole, "the father of English mysticism," was acutely aware of this music of the soul, discerning in it a correspondence with the measured harmonies of the spiritual universe. In those enraptured descriptions of his inward experience which are among the jewels of mystical literature, nothing is more remarkable than his constant and deliberate employment of musical imagery. . . . He does not "see" the spiritual world: he "hears" it. For him, as for St. Francis of Assisi, it is a "heavenly melody, intolerably sweet."

"Song I call," he says, "when in a plenteous soul the sweetness of eternal love with burning is taken, and thought into song is turned, and the mind into full sweet sound is changed." He who experiences this joyous exaltation "says not his prayers like other righteous men" but "is taken into marvellous mirth: and, goodly sound being descended into him, as it were with notes his prayers he sings." . . .

The song, however, is a mystic melody having little in common with its clumsy image, earthly music. Bodily song "lets it"; and "noise of janglers makes it turn again to thought," "for sweet ghostly song accords not with outward song, the which in churches and elsewhere is used. It discords much: for all that is man's voice is formed with bodily ears to be heard; but among angels' tunes it has an acceptable melody, and with marvel it is commended of them that have known it." To others it is incommunicable. "Worldly lovers soothly words or ditties of our song may know, for the words they read: but the tone and sweetness of that song they may not learn."

Such symbolism as this . . . seems almost essential to mystical expression. The mind must employ some device of the kind if its transcendental perceptions . . . are ever to be grasped by the surface consciousness. Sometimes the symbol and the perception which it represents become fused in that consciousness; and the mystic's experience then presents itself to him as "visions" or "voices" which we must look upon as the garment he has himself provided to veil that Reality upon which no man may look and live. The nature of this garment will be largely conditioned by his temperament—as in Rolle's evident bias towards music, St. Catherine of Genoa's leaning towards the abstract conceptions of fire and light—and also by his theological education and environment. Cases in point are the highly dogmatic visions and auditions of St. Gertrude, Suso, St. Catherine of Siena, the Blessed Angela of Foligno; above all of St. Teresa, whose marvellous self-analyses provide the classic account of these attempts of the mind to translate transcendental intuitions into concepts with which it can deal.

The greatest mystics, however—Ruysbroeck, St. John of the Cross, and St. Teresa herself in her later stages—distinguish clearly between the ineffable Reality which they perceive and the image under which they describe it. Again and again they tell us with Dionysius and Eckhart, that the Object of their contemplation "hath no image"; or with St. John of the Cross that "the soul can never attain to the height of the divine union, so far as it is possible in this life, through the medium of any forms or figures." Therefore the attempt which has sometimes been made to identify mysticism with such forms and figures—with visions, voices, "supernatural favors" and other abnormal phenomena—is clearly wrong.

"The highest and most divine things which it is given us to see and to know," says Dionysius the Areopagite plainly, "are but the symbolic language of things subordinate to Him who Himself transcendeth them all: through which things His incomprehensible Presence is shown, walking on those heights of His Holy Places which are perceived by the mind."

The mystic, as a rule, cannot wholly do without symbol and image, inadequate to his vision though they must always be: for his experience must be expressed if it is to be communicated, and its actuality is inexpressible except in some side-long way, some hint or parallel which will stimulate the dormant intuition of the reader, and convey, as all poetic language does, something beyond its surface sense. Hence the large part which is played in all mystical writings by symbolism and imagery. . . .

. . . . Symbol—the clothing which the spiritual borrows from the material plane—is a form of artistic expression. That is to say, it is not literal but suggestive: though the artist who uses it may sometimes lose sight of this distinction. Hence the persons who imagine that the "Spiritual Marriage" of St. Catherine or St. Teresa veils a perverted sexuality, that the vision of the Sacred Heart involved an incredible anatomical experience, or that the divine inebriation of the Sufis is the apotheosis of drunkenness, do but advertise their ignorance of the mechanism of the arts: like the lady who thought that Blake must be *mad* because he said that he had touched the sky with his finger.

Now returning to our original undertaking, that of defining if we can the characteristics of true mysticism, I think that we have already reached a point at which William James's celebrated "four marks" of the mystic state, Ineffability, Noetic Quality, Transiency, and Passivity, will fail to satisfy us. In their place I propose to set out, illustrate and, I hope, justify four other rules or notes which may be applied as tests to any given case which claims to take rank among the mystics.

(1) *Mysticism is practical, not theoretical.* . . . Mysticism, like revelation, is final and personal. It is not merely a beautiful and suggestive diagram but experience in its most intense form. That

experience, in the words of Plotinus, is the soul's solitary adventure: "the flight of the Alone to the Alone." It provides the material, the substance, upon which mystical philosophy cogitates; as theologians cogitate upon the revelation which forms the basis of faith. Hence those whom we are to accept as mystics must have received, and acted upon, intuitions of a Truth which is for them absolute. If we are to acknowledge that they "knew the doctrine" they must have "lived the life"; submitted to the interior travail of the Mystic Way, not merely have reasoned about the mystic experiences of others. . . .

Over and over again the great mystics tell us, not how they speculated, but how they acted. To them, the transition from the life of sense to the life of spirit is a formidable undertaking, which demands effort and constancy. The paradoxical "quiet" of the contemplative is but the outward stillness essential to inward work. . . .

(2) *Mysticism is an entirely Spiritual Activity.* . . . The mystic never . . . tries to combine the advantages of two worlds. At the term of his development he knows God by communion, and this direct intuition of the Absolute kills all lesser cravings. He possesses God, and needs nothing more. . . . Having his eyes set on eternity, his consciousness steeped in it, he can well afford to tolerate the entanglements of time. "His spirit," says Tauler, "is as it were sunk and lost in the Abyss of the Deity, and loses the consciousness of all creature-distinctions. All things are gathered together in one with the divine sweetness, and the man's being is so penetrated with the divine substance that he loses himself therein, as a drop of water is lost in a cask of strong wine. And thus the man's spirit is so sunk in God in divine union, that he loses all sense of distinction . . . and there remains a secret, still union, without cloud or color." "I wish not," said St. Catherine of Genoa, "for anything that comes forth from Thee, but only for Thee, oh sweetest Love!" . . .

(3) *The business and method of Mysticism is Love.* Here is one of the distinctive notes of true mysticism; marking it off from every other kind of transcendental theory and practice. . . . It is the eager, outgoing activity whose driving power is generous love, not the absorbent, indrawing activity which strives only for new knowledge, that is fruitful in the spiritual as well as in the physical world.

Having said this, however, we must add—as we did when speaking of the "heart"—that the word Love as applied to the mystics is to be understood in its deepest, fullest sense; as the ultimate expression of the self's most vital tendencies, not as the superficial affection or emotion often dignified by this name. Mystic Love is a total dedication of the will; the deep-seated desire and tendency of the soul toward its Source. It is a condition of humble access, a life-movement of the self: more direct in its methods, more valid in its results— even in the hands of the least lettered of its adepts—than the most piercing intellectual vision of the greatest philosophic mind. Again and again the mystics insist upon this. "For silence is not God, nor speaking is not God; fasting is not God nor eating is not God; onliness is not God nor company is not God; nor yet any of all the other two such quantities. He is hid between them, and may not be found by any work of thy soul, but all only by love of thine heart. He may not be known by reason, He may not be gotten by thought, nor concluded by understanding; but he may be loved and chosen with the true lovely will of thine heart. . . . Such a blind shot with the sharp dart of longing love may never fail of the prick, the which is God."

Volumes of extracts might be compiled from the works of the mystics illustrative of this rule, which is indeed their central principle. "Some there are," says Plotinus, "that for all their effort have not attained the Vision; the soul in them has come to no sense of the splendor there. It has not taken warmth it has not felt burning within itself the flame of love for what is there to know." "Love," says Rolle, "truly suffers not a loving soul to bide in itself, but ravishes it out to the Lover, that the soul is more there where it loves, than where the body is that lives and feels it." . . .

Love to the mystic, then, is (a) the active, conative, expression of his will and desire for the Absolute : (b) his innate tendency to that Absolute, his spiritual weight. He is only thoroughly natural, thoroughly alive, when he is obeying its voice. For him it is the source of joy, the secret of the universe, the vivifying principle of things. In the words of Récéjac, "Mysticism claims to be able to know the Unknowable without any help from dialectics; and believes that, by the way of love and will, it reaches a point to which thought alone is unable to attain." Again, "It is the heart and never the reason which leads us to the Absolute." Hence in St. Catherine of Siena's exquisite allegory it is the feet of the soul's affection which brings it first to the Bridge, "for the feet carry the body as affection carries the soul." . . . The mystic's outlook, indeed, is the lover's outlook. It has the same element of wildness, the same quality of selfless and quixotic devotion, the same combination of rapture and humility. This parallel is more than a pretty fancy: for mystic and lover, upon different planes, are alike responding to the call of the Spirit of Life. The language of human passion is tepid and insignificant beside the language in which the mystics try to tell the splendors of their love. They

force upon the unprejudiced reader the conviction that they are dealing with an ardor far more burning for an Object far more real.

"This monk can give lessons to lovers!" exclaimed Arthur Symons in
astonishment of St. John of the Cross. It would be strange if he could
not; since their finite passions are but the feeble images of his infinite
one, their beloved the imperfect symbol of his First and only
Fair. . . .

(4) *Mysticism entails a definite Psychological Experience.* . . .
there are two distinct sides to the full mystical experience. (A) The
vision or consciousness of Absolute Perfection. (B) The inward transmutation to which that Vision compels the mystic, in order that he
may be to some extent worthy of that which he has beheld: may take
his place within the order of Reality. He has seen the Perfect; he
wants to be perfect too. The "third term," the necessary bridge between the Absolute and the Self, can only, he feels, be moral and
spiritual transcendence—in a word, *Sanctity*—for "the only means of
attaining the Absolute lies in adapting ourselves to It." The moral
virtues are for him, then, the obligatory "ornaments of the Spiritual
Marriage" as Ruysbroeck called them: though far more than their
presence is needed to bring that marriage about. Unless this impulse
for moral perfection be born in him, this travail of the inner life begun,
he is no mystic: though he may well be a visionary, a prophet, a
"mystical" poet.

Moreover, this process of transmutation, this rebuilding of the self
on higher levels, will involve the establishment within the field of
consciousness, the making "central for life," of those sub-conscious
spiritual perceptions which are the primary material of mystical experience. The end and object of this "inward alchemy" will be the raising
of the whole self to the condition in which conscious and permanent
union with the Absolute takes place; and man, ascending to the
summit of his manhood, enters into that greater life for which he was
made. In its journey towards this union, the subject commonly passes
through certain well-marked phases, which constitute what is known
as the "Mystic Way." This statement rules out from the true mystic
kingdom all merely sentimental and affective piety and visionary
poetry, no less than mystical philosophy. . . .

More than the apprehension of God, then, more than the passion for
the Absolute, is needed to make a mystic. These must be combined
with an appropriate make-up, with a nature of extraordinary concentration, an exalted moral emotion, a nervous organization of the
artistic type. All these are necessary to the successful development
of the mystic life process. In the experience of those mystics who have

left us the records of their own lives, the successive stages of this life process are always traceable. . . . Rolle, Suso, St. Teresa, and many others have left us valuable self-analyses for comparison: and from them we see how arduous, how definite, and how far removed from mere emotional or intellectual activity, is that educational discipline by which "the eye which looks upon Eternity" is able to come to its own. . . .

It is one of the many indirect testimonies to the objective reality of mysticism that the stages of this road, the psychology of the spiritual ascent, as described to us by different schools of contemplatives, always present practically the same sequence of states. The "school for saints" has never found it necessary to bring its curriculum up to date. The psychologist finds little difficulty, for instance, in reconciling the "Degrees of Orison" described by St. Teresa—Recollection, Quiet, Union, Ectasy, Rapt, the "Pain of God," and the Spiritual Marriage of the soul—with the four forms of contemplation enumerated by Hugh of St. Victor, or the Sufi's "Seven Stages" of the soul's ascent to God, which begin in adoration and end in spiritual marriage. Though each wayfarer may choose different landmarks, it is clear from their comparison that the road is one.

(5) As a corollary to these four rules, it is perhaps well to reiterate the statement already made, that *True Mysticism is never self-seeking.* It is not, as many think, the pursuit of supernatural joys; the satisfaction of a high ambition. The mystic does not enter on his quest because he desires the happiness of the Beatific Vision, the ecstasy of union with the Absolute, or any other personal reward. That noblest of all passions, the passion for perfection for Love's sake, far outweighs the desire for transcendental satisfaction. "O Love," said St. Catherine of Genoa, "I do not wish to follow thee for sake of these delights, but solely from the motive of true love." Those who do otherwise are only, in the plain words of St. John of the Cross, "spiritual gluttons." . . . The true mystic claims no promises and makes no demands. He goes because he must, as Galahad went towards the Grail: knowing that for those who can live it, this alone is life. He never rests in that search for God which he holds to be the fulfilment of his highest duty; yet he seeks without any certainty of success. He holds with St. Bernard that "He alone is God who can never be sought in vain: not even when He cannot be found." . . .

Like his type, the "devout lover" of romance, then, the mystic serves without hope of reward. By one of the many paradoxes of the spiritual life, he obtains satisfaction because he does not seek it; completes his personality because he gives it up. "Attainment," says

Dionysius the Areopagite in words which are writ large on the annals of Christian ecstasy, "comes only by means of this sincere, spontaneous, and entire surrender of yourself and all things." Only with the annihilation of selfhood comes the fulfilment of love. Were the mystic asked the cause of his often extraordinary behavior, his austere and steadfast quest, it is unlikely that his reply would contain any reference to sublime illumination or unspeakable delights. It is more probable that he would answer in some such words as those of Jacob Boehme, "I am not come to this meaning, or to this work and knowledge through my own reason or through my own will and purpose; neither have I sought this knowledge, nor so much as to know anything concerning it. I sought only for the heart of God, therein to hide myself."

"Whether we live or whether we die," said St. Paul, "we are the Lord's." The mystic is a realist, to whom these words convey not a dogma but an invitation: an invitation to the soul to attain that fullness of life for which she was made, to "lose herself in That which can be neither seen nor touched; giving herself entirely to this sovereign Object without belonging either to herself or to others; united to the Unknown by the most noble part of herself and because of her renouncement of knowledge; finally drawing from this absolute ignorance a knowledge which the understanding knows not how to attain." Mysticism, then, is seen as the "one way out" for the awakened spirit of man; healing that human incompleteness which is the origin of our divine unrest. "I am sure," says Eckhart, "that if a soul knew the very least of all that Being means, it would never turn away from it."

18

PLOTINUS

The Flight of the Alone *

PLOTINUS IS sometimes described as the father of Western mysticism, and certainly his influence on the Christian mystics has been
unquestionably great. His mysticism centers around his conception
of the One (designated by some of his interpreters as the Absolute,
or God), and is but an aspect of a profound and complex metaphysical system. All things, he tells us, have emanated from the
One which manifests itself in the successive appearance of Mind
and Soul. The individual soul of man descends out of Soul and the
problem then is to explain the ways in which the individual or
particular soul may ascend once more to its ultimate source in the
One. The passages that follow sketch only briefly some aspects of
this ascent of the soul, emphasizing the importance of love in the
union of the soul with the One, the problem of maintaining the
existence of the soul in such a union with the One, the felicity of
the soul and the difficulty of explaining its vision of the One.

. . . THE PRINCIPLE of all things, therefore, not having any difference, is always present; but we are present with it when we have
no difference. And it indeed does not aspire after us, in order that
it may be conversant with us; but we aspire after it, in order that we
may revolve about it. We indeed perpetually revolve about it, but
we do not always behold it. As a band of singers, however, though
it moves about the coryphaeus, may be diverted to the survey of
something foreign to the choir [and thus become discordant], but
when it converts itself to him, sings well, and truly subsists about
him;—thus also we perpetually revolve about the principle of all
things, even when we are perfectly loosened from it, and have no
longer a knowledge of it. Nor do we always look to it; but when we
behold it, then we obtain the end of our wishes, and rest from our

* From the *Select Works of Plotinus,* translated by Thomas Taylor (London:
G. Bell and Sons, Ltd., 1929), pp. 315-22. Reprinted with the permission of the
publisher.

Plotinus (204-70 A.D.) studied under Ammonius in Egypt. He came to Rome
in 245 A.D., where he wrote and taught until his death. His writings were compiled by his disciple Porphyry who tells us that Plotinus achieved the mystic state
on four different occasions in a period of six years.

search after felicity. Then also we are no longer discordant, but form a truly divine dance about it.

In this dance, however, the soul beholds the fountain of life, the fountain of intellect, the principle of being, the cause of good, and the root of the soul. And these are not poured forth from this fountain, so as to produce in it any diminution. For it is not a corporeal mass; since if it were, its progeny would be corruptible. But now they are perpetual, because the principle of them abides with invariable sameness; not being distributed into them, but remaining whole and entire. Hence, they likewise remain, just as if the sun being permanent, light also should be permanent. For we are not cut off from this fountain, nor are we separated from it, though the nature of body intervening, draws us to itself. But we are animated and preserved by an infusion from thence, this principle not imparting, and afterwards withdrawing itself from us; since it always supplies us with being, and always will as long as it continues to be that which it is. Or rather, we are what we are by verging to it. Our well-being also consists in this tendency. And to be distant from it is nothing else than a diminution of existence. Here, likewise, the soul rests, and becomes out of the reach of evils, running back to that place which is free from ill. And here also, she energizes intellectually, is liberated from perturbations, and lives in reality. For the present life, and which is without God, is a vestige of life, and an imitation of that life which is real. But the life in the intelligible world consists in the energy of the intellect. Energy also generates Gods, through a tranquil and quiet contact with the principle of all things. It likewise generates beauty, justice, and virtue. For the soul being filled with deity, brings forth these. And this is both the beginning and end to the soul. It is the beginning indeed, because she originates from thence; but it is the end, because *the good* is there, and because when the soul is situated there, she becomes what she was before. For the good which is here, and in sensible concerns, is a lapse, a flight, and a defluxion of the wings of the soul. But that *the good* is there, is indicated by the love which is connascent with the soul; conformably to which Love is conjoined in marriage with souls, both in writings and in fables. For since the soul is different from God, but is derived from him, she necessarily loves him, and when she is there she has a celestial love; but the love which she here possesses is common and vulgar. For in the intelligible world the celestial Venus reigns; but here the popular Venus, who is as it were meretricious.* Every soul also is a Venus. And this the nativity

---

* Plotinus says this, looking to the illegitimate participations of this Venus by mankind.

of Venus, and Love who was born at the same time with her, obscurely signify. The soul, therefore, when in a condition conformable to nature, loves God, wishing to be united to him, being as it were the desire of a beautiful virgin to be conjoined with a beautiful Love. When, however, the soul descends into generation, then being as it were deceived by spurious nuptials, and associating herself with another other and a mortal Love, she becomes petulant and insolent through being absent from her father. But when she again hates terrene wantonness and injustice, and becomes purified from the defilements which are here, and again returns to her father, then she is affected in the most felicitous manner. And those indeed who are ignorant of this affection, may from terrene love form some conjecture of divine love, by considering how great a felicity the possession of a most beloved object is conceived to be; and also by considering that these earthly objects of love are mortal and noxious, that the love of them is nothing more than the love of images, and that they lose their attractive power because they are not truly desirable, nor our real good, nor that which we investigate. In the intelligible world, however, the true object of love is to be found, with which we may be conjoined, which we may participate, and truly possess, and which is not externally enveloped with flesh. *He however who knows this, will know what I say,* and will be convinced that the soul has then another life. The soul also proceeding to, and having now arrived at the desired end, and participating of deity, will know that the supplier of true life is then present. She will likewise then require nothing farther; for on the contrary, it will be requisite to lay aside other things, to stop in this alone, and to become this alone, amputating every thing else with which she is surrounded. Hence, it is necessary to hasten our departure from hence, and to be indignant that we are bound in one part of our nature, in order that with the whole of our true selves, we may fold ourselves about divinity, and have no part void of contact with him. When this takes place therefore, the soul will both see divinity and herself, as far as it is lawful for her to see him. And she will see herself indeed illuminated, and full of intelligible light; or rather she will perceive herself to be a pure light, unburthened, agile, and becoming to be a God, or rather being a God, and then shining forth as such to the view.* But if she again becomes heavy, she then as it were wastes away.

* Hence Aristotle in his "Politics" also says, that he who surpasses beyond all comparison the rest of his fellow-citizens in virtue, ought to be considered as a God among men . . . . Observe, too, that when Plotinus calls the man who is able in this life to see divinity a God, he means that he is a God

How does it happen, therefore, that the soul does not abide there? Is it not because she has not yet wholly migrated from hence? But she will then, when her vision of deity possesses an uninterrupted continuity, and she is no longer impeded or disturbed in her intuition by the body. That however which sees divinity, is not the thing which is disturbed, but something else; when that which perceives him is at rest from the vision. But it is not then at rest according to a scientific energy, which consists in demonstrations, in credibilities, and a discursive process of the soul. For here vision, and that which sees, are no longer reason, but greater than and prior to reason. And in reason, indeed, they are as that is which is perceived. He therefore who sees himself, will then, when he sees, behold himself to be such a thing as this, or rather he will be present with himself thus disposed, and becoming simple, will perceive himself to be a thing of this kind. Perhaps, however, neither must it be said that he sees, but that he is the thing seen; if it is necessary to call these two things, i.e. the perceiver and the thing perceived. But both are one; though it is bold to assert this. Then, indeed, the soul neither sees, nor distinguishes by seeing, nor imagines that there are two things; but becomes as it were another thing, and not itself. Nor does that which pertains to itself contribute anything there. But becoming wholly absorbed in deity, she is one, conjoining as it were centre with centre. For here concurring, they are one; but they are then two when they are separate. For thus also we now denominate that which is another. Hence this spectacle is a thing difficult to explain by words. For how can any one narrate that as something different from himself, which when he sees he does not behold as different, but as one with himself?

This, therefore, is manifested by the mandate of the mysteries, which orders that they shall not be divulged to those who are uninitiated. For as that which is divine cannot be unfolded to the multitude, this mandate forbids the attempt to elucidate it to any one but him who is fortunately able to perceive it. Since, therefore, in this conjunction with deity there were not two things, but the perceiver was one with the thing perceived, as not being properly speaking vision but union; whoever becomes one by mingling with deity, and afterwards recollects this union, will have with himself an image of it. But he was also himself one, having with respect to himself no difference, nor with respect to other things. For then there was not any thing excited with him who had ascended thither; neither

---

only according to *similitude*; for in this way, men transcendently wise and good are called by Plato, Gods and divine.

anger, nor the desire of anything else, nor reason, nor a certain intellectual perception, nor, in short, was even he himself moved, if it be requisite also to assert this; but being as it were in an ecstasy, or energizing enthusiastically, he became established in quiet and solitary union, not at all deviating from his own essence, nor revolving about himself, but being entirely stable, and becoming as it were stability itself. Neither was he then excited by any thing, beautiful; but running above the beautiful, he passed beyond even the choir of the virtues. Just as if some one having entered into the interior of the shrine should leave behind all the statues in the temple, which on his departure from the shrine will first present themselves to his view, after the inward spectacle, and the association that was there, which was not with a statue or an image, but with the thing itself which the images represent, and which necessarily become the second objects of his perception. Perhaps, however, this was not a spectacle, but there was another mode of vision, viz. ecstasy, and an expansion and accession of himself, a desire of contact, rest, and a striving after conjunction, in order to behold what the shrine contains. But nothing will be present with him who beholds in any other way. The wise prophets, therefore, obscurely signified by these imitations how this highest God is seen. But the wise priest understanding the enigma, and having entered into the shrine, obtains a true vision of what is there. If, however, he has not entered, he will conceive this shrine to be a certain invisible thing, and will have a *knowledge* of the fountain and principle, as the principle of things. But when situated there, he will *see* the principle, and will be conjoined with it, by a union of like with like, neglecting nothing divine which the soul is able to possess. Prior to the vision also it requires that which remains from the vision. But that which remains to him who passes beyond all things, is that which is prior to all things. For the nature of the soul will never accede to that which is entirely non-being. But proceeding indeed downwards it will fall into evil; and thus into non-being, yet not into that which is perfect nonentity. Running, however, in a contrary direction, it will arrive not at another thing, but at itself. And thus not being in another thing, it is not on that account in nothing, but is in itself. *To be in itself alone, however, and not in being, is to be in God.* For God also is something which is not essence, but beyond essence. Hence the soul when in this condition associates with Him. He, therefore, who perceives himself to associate with God, will have himself the similitude of him. And if he passes from himself as an image to the archetype, he will then have the end of his progression. But when he falls from the vision of God, if he again excites the virtue which is in himself, and perceives himself to be perfectly adorned; he will again be elevated through virtue, proceeding to intellect and wisdom, and afterwards to the principle of all things. *This, therefore, is the life of the Gods, and of divine and happy men, a liberation from all terrene concerns, a life unaccompanied with human pleasures, and a flight of the alone to the alone.*

19

PATANJALI

Yoga *

YOGA, as a form of Eastern mysticism, is of great antiquity. Some authorities date the Yoga Sutras of Patanjali between 800 B.C. and 300 B.C. As a discipline and as a philosophy of religion it appears not merely in this early source, but also in the Hindu scriptures, in the numerous commentaries on those scriptures, and in the more highly specialized Sanscrit treatises which are devoted exclusively to Yoga. As will be seen it appears in several different forms, but we have selected for study the more common forms of Hatha yoga and Raja yoga, with more emphasis on the former for the following reasons: first, because, as our author indicates, it is a necessary and preparatory step to Raja yoga, which bears a close resemblance to the best examples of Western mysticism; and second, because it emphasizes to a higher degree and in more detail than is ordinarily found in Western mysticism, a very thorough physical discipline,—which make it appear at times as much a matter of medicine as of mysticism.

THE MEANING AND FORMS OF YOGA

ACCORDING TO the grammarians the word "yoga" comes from the sanskrit root "yuj" "to link, unite," to which is added the suffix "ghan"

---

* From *Yoga, The Method of Re-Integration* by Alain Daniélou (London: Christopher Johnson, 1949), pp. 6, 12-13, 17-22, 25-31, 57-58, 67, 70-82. Reprinted with the permission of the publisher.

Nothing is known of the life of Patanjali. Some authorities date him from the second century B.C., others much earlier. He is said to have been the incarnation of the serpent king Sesa, who surrounds and supports the universe in the form of the Cosmic Ocean.

indicating completion. (cf. the English "to yoke" which is from the same root).

The universe is throughout pervaded by the Supreme Being. There is, therefore, no aspect of the universe which cannot be used as a means for attaining realization of the divine, and, consequently, there are innumerable forms of the method of yoga.

The chief of these forms are variously classified: one of the common classifications is that found in the Bhagavad Gîtâ namely: Re-integration through action, or Karma yoga, Re-integration through knowledge, or Jnâna yoga, Re-integration through Love or Bhakti yoga. . . .

Technically, yoga makes use of five main methods, each of which has eight steps or stages. These five main methods are known as:

(1) Hatha yoga, Re-integration through strength. . . .
(2) Râja yoga, the Royal way of re-integration
(3) Mantra yoga, Re-integration by means of hermetic utterances.
(4) Laya yoga, Re-integration by mergence.
(5) Shiva yoga, Re-integration into the metaphysical principle. . . .

HATHA YOGA
"THE SELF IS NOT WITHIN THE REACH OF THE WEAK"

Hatha Yoga is the name given to the technical practices and disciplines by which the body and the vital energies can be brought under control. Although but one of the means of yoga, it is the first preparation towards the way of re-integration, essential for further realization. Only exceptional beings of surpassing development, which in itself implies the possession of all the "attainments" of Hatha yoga, can dispense with its rules and practices.

.   .   .   .   .

The eight steps of Hatha yoga are divided into two stages: (a) the "Outer stage" which comprises abstinences, observances, sitting postures and breath control, and (b) the "Inner stage," which comprises withdrawal, concentration, contemplation and identification. . . .

THE FIVE ABSTINENCES

According to Patanjali:

"The abstinences are non-violence, truth, non-stealing, chastity and non-possession." (Yoga Darshana 2, 30)

(1) *Non-violence:* "To abstain from causing pain at any time, in any way however small, in mind, word, or body, to any living thing including oneself, is non-violence." All other abstinences and observ-

ances lead up to it . . . it is said that they exist only for the sake of non-violence. . . .

(2) *Truth:* "According to the testimony of the inner senses and faculties, to show things as they are with the aim and doing good, in friendly words and without deceit is truth."

(3) *Non-stealing:* "Not to steal, take away or appropriate the possessions of another, in any way, by mind, word or body, is non-stealing." . . .

(4) *Chastity:* "The complete absence of erotic perturbation or emotion, in mind, senses or body is chastity." . . .

(5) *Non-possession:* "To abstain from accumulating in any way the means for enjoyment, whether they pertain to the field of word, touch, form, taste or smell, is non-possession."

THE FIVE OBSERVANCES

The aim of the observances is to counteract such laws (dharma) of our nature as lead us towards attachments, while developing those which lead us to detachment and thus are the cause of liberation.

"The observances are purity, contentment, austerity, self-development and the constant thought of Divinity." (Yoga Darshana 2, 32.)

(1) *Purity* is of two kinds, outward and inward. To cleanse one's body, to eat pure food and to observe all rules of right-living, and even to act selflessly is outward purity. . . . *Inward purity* is gained through the possession of the heavenly treasures which are: control over the senses, absence of fear, contentment of mind, charity, ritual sacrifices, reading of the "Scripture of Eternal Wisdom" (the Veda). . . .

(2) *Contentment:* "To maintain a joyful and satisfied mind whether one meets with pleasure or pain, profit or loss, fame or contempt, success or failure, sympathy or hatred, is contentment."

(3) *Austerity:* "Forbearance, the practice of fasts and other forms of abstinence, and the bearing of pain for the sake of controlling the mind and senses and of performing one's duty, is austerity." . . .

(4) *Self-development:* "Self-development consists in the study of the revealed Scriptures, which are the source of human progress and happiness. Together with the practice of bead-telling or repetition of the name of that aspect of Divinity chosen for worship. It includes also the learning and the teaching of divine praise and commenting upon the divine qualities." To witness the Supreme Self is the aim of self-development. It is reached by study, teaching, listening, pondering and meditating.

(5) *The Constant Thought of Divinity:* "The constant thought of Divinity is devotion, it is a tendency of our whole being to act in mind, word and body in such a way as will lead us to God." This surrender of our being to Divinity by offering up all our actions and their results, and thus becoming without desire, is the most important of the five observances.

THE BODILY POSTURES OR ÂSANAS

The bodily postures help to strengthen the body and stabilize the mind. That posture in which a man can remain longest without effort is for him the best. The very word "âsana" means "easy, comfortable," and so the postures should be to have their full effect.

"To remain motionless for a long time without effort is an âsana." (Yoga Darshana 2, 46.)

The aim of the bodily postures is secured when "the physical reactions of the body are eliminated and the mind dissolves into the Infinite" (Yoga Darshana 2, 47).

To feel its effect it is necessary to remain in one posture motionless for one watch (of three hours). Even adepts need usually no less than eight hours to reach the state of identification (Samâdhi).

Different âsanas are described in detail in different books of yoga. . . . All however agree that the number of the chief postures is 84, although there exist some technical differences in defining them. Four only of the âsanas are very generally practised. They are the Posture of Attainment, the Lotus posture, the Auspicious posture and the Lion posture.*

---

* [A rather lengthy description is given by the author of the main postures, and in the appendix to his book he lists all eighty-four of the known postures. It should be sufficient in this abridgement of the author's account if we note his description of two of the postures:

"(1) The Lotus Posture is considered by some schools to be the best posture It has two forms: free and bound.

In the Bound Lotus posture, the right foot should be placed on the left thigh and the left foot on the right thigh. The arms should go round the back and catch hold of the toes. Press the chin against the chest, the focus the eyes on the tip of the nose. This posture cures illnesses and disorders. . . .

. . . in the Free Lotus posture, the arms do not go round the back, but rest, palms up on the knees.

(2) The Auspicious Posture: "In the auspicious posture the soles of both the feet are said to be placed upon the knees one after the other." (Trishikhi Brahmana Upanishad 35.)

The left foot should be underneath, the right foot on the top. When other postures are not advisable on account of a state of weak health, this posture is recommended."—*Ed.*]

BREATH CONTROL OR PRÂNÂYÂMA

"The voluntary interruption of the movement of breathing in and out is prânâyâma." (Yoga Darshana 2, 49.)

"The soul purified by prânâyâma realizes the Supreme Spirit, the Para Brahman, hence, according to the scripture of Principial Revelation, the Shruti, there is nothing higher than prânâyâma." (Shankarâchârya Com, on 2, 7 of Shvetâshvatara Up.)

"To keep still without breathing in, nor breathing out, nor move any limb, such are the characteristics of the Chalice." (Amrita Nâda Up. 15.)

Holding the breath or "Chalice" is of two kinds:

(a) *The outward Chalice* consists in breathing out and then stopping the breath. The method usually adopted is to breathe in for the time it takes to repeat four times the sacred Syllable of Obeisance AUM, breathe out for the time it takes to repeat the syllable eight times, and stop breathing for the time it takes to repeat AUM sixteen times.

(b) *The inward Chalice* consists in breathing in, then holding the breath before breathing out. The method usually adopted is to breathe in for four AUM-s, hold for sixteen AUM-s, and breathe out for eight AUM-s.

The Absolute Chalice, or Stupified Breathing consists in stopping the breath without effort at any point of in- or out-breathing. To do this, breathe regularly for some time, in-breathing for four AUM-s, and breathing out for eight AUM-s; then stop wherever convenient, and hold the breath for sixteen AUM-s.

"He who is successful in the absolute chalice, without breathing in or out, finds nothing in the three worlds beyond his reach" (Vasishtha samhitâ). . . .

Ancient authors enjoined the practice of breath-control four times a day: at dawn, midday, sunset and midnight. The Yoga Kundali Upanishad says that beginning with ten breathings at a time and increasing daily by five breathings, by the end of a fortnight's practice eighty breathings at a time should be attained, that is three hundred and twenty a day. . . . For most people, however, it is best to practice breath control only twice a day. . . .

THE WITHDRAWAL OF THE SENSES FROM EXTERNAL OBJECTS

"When the senses have withdrawn from their objects and transmuted themselves into the modes of consciousness, this is called 'the Withdrawal'." (Yoga Darshana 2, 54.)

The process of withdrawal consists in disentangling the senses, sight, hearing, etc., from the objects of their natural perception always linked with the opposing tendencies of attachment and aversion. . . .

It is through "Withdrawal" that complete control over the senses is gained. It purifies the mind, increases austerity, gives self-confidence, freedom from illness and the mental qualification for final identification (samâdhi).

"Let him hold all the senses under control and, concentrating the mind, surrender to me, for he who has his senses under his sway has knowledge abidingly set." (Bhagavad Gîtâ 2, 61.)

The chief methods used for "Withdrawal" are:

(1) To take the Lotus posture and, stopping all motion of the breath, to remain in the "absolute" chalice.

(2) To take the posture of Attainment, fix the sight, without blinking, on the forehead or on the tip of the nose.

(3) To repeat twelve thousand times, with a quiet mind, the Syllable of Obeisance AUM. . . .

CONCENTRATION

Having gone through the outer stage, i.e. the process by which the body and all the physical and mental obstacles are controlled, the yogi is now ready for the "inner stage," the inner journey towards re-integration.

"To maintain the mind fixed on one spot is called concentration." (Yoga Darshana 3, 1.)

The object of the concentration may be anything . . . although it is said that a worthy object is to be preferred to whichever world it pertains. . . .

It is through concentration that the movements of the mind are stilled. Preparation for concentration is through practice and detachment. . . .

CONTEMPLATION

"To keep the mind solely on one object is contemplation." (Yoga Darshana 3, 2.)

Contemplation is of three kinds: material, luminous and subtle.

(a) In "material contemplation," the image of a deity or one's guru is thought of.

(b) In "luminous contemplation," the radiance of Divinity or of Nature is pondered.

(c) In "subtle contemplation," the mind is concentrated on the point-limit where the unmanifest becomes manifest. . . .

. . . "Contemplation without a perceptible form is beyond the grasp of words and mind, it belongs to the unmanifest, is all-pervading and cannot be pointed to as 'this' or 'that'. It is only through a long process of identification that yogis can cognize it. I explain material contemplation to you to this end alone, that the seeker in his desire for subtle contemplation may practice it, concentrating his mind to attain the object of his desire." (Mahânirvâna tantra.)

IDENTIFICATION

"When alone the object of contemplation remains and one's own form is annihilated, this is known as 'identification'." (Yoga Darshana 3, 3.)

In contemplation three elements are present: he who contemplates, the fact of contemplating and the object of contemplation. In identification, these three elements cease to be distinct.

The practice of the method of identification with a material object or with a subtle entity gives superhuman powers, but these powers are hindrances on the path of spiritual realization. Identification with the Supreme Reality alone leads to liberation.

"That which we call experience, is but a limited experience subject to error and delusion. The only genuine experience is the mystical experience which gives total knowledge of subtle causes and is beyond the limitations of space and time." (Yoga-trayânanda, Shiva archana tattva, p. 33.)

"The light of knowledge, which shines when the impurity of ignorance is dissolved by practice of the steps of yoga, is called the radiance of discernment." (Yoga Darshana 2, 28.)

Then only can supreme reality be witnessed.

There are two degrees in this supreme identification: it can take place with or without the maintenance of individual consciousness. . . .

Identification with individual consciousness is also called "with thought". . . . In this form the faculties dissolve into the shape of the non-dual principle and there remains no perceived difference between knower and known, although the notion of an individual existence and of the fact of knowing clearly remain.

The second degree of identification is . . . also called without thought. At this stage there remains no place for either an individualized knower or for a particularized knowledge. As salt in water becomes part of the water so the movements of the mind dissolve into the non-dual Principle, the Brahman, and nothing but the Brahman remains to be perceived. . . . At this stage there remains no individual support and all mental movements are stilled. This is the "motionless" state, to be reached through transcendent detachment. . . . This stage is also called the "witnessing of the Self"; it is the ultimate aim of existence and its fulfilment.

RÂJA YOGA OR THE ROYAL WAY TO RE-INTEGRATION

The movements of the mind are the causes of man's bondage, the action of his intellect is the instrument of his freedom. That particular mode of action by which the intellect stills the movements of the mind is known as The Royal Way to re-integration. This is the highest form of yoga, all other forms being preparatory.

The only purpose of Hatha yoga is to render Râja yoga possible and, except in very exceptional cases, Râja yoga cannot be successfully achieved without the preliminary training of Hatha yoga, by which alone the subtle machinery of our subconscious instincts can be controlled.

"For the sake of Râja yoga alone is Hatha yoga taught." (Hatha yoga Pradipikâ.)

Like the method of Hatha yoga, that of Râja yoga comprises eight main steps which bear the same names as those of Hatha yoga, but, although they are their equivalents, they are very different, being on another plane. These eight steps are sometimes further sub-divided to make fifteen.

THE FIFTEEN STEPS OF RÂJA YOGA

(1) *Abstinence:* "Abstinence is the bringing of the senses under control through the knowledge that 'all is the Brahma.' This abstinence should be constantly practised." (Tejo-bindu Upanishad 1, 17.)

(2) *Observance:* "To direct the mental current towards the basic unity of all things and to divert it from the observation of differences is 'Observance'; therein lies transcendent bliss. It should be practised regularly by the wise. (Tejo-bindu Upanishad 1, 18.)

(3) *Renunciation:* "Renunciation of all manifest forms through the contemplating of the Self which is Existence and Bliss is the mode of worship of the great. It smoothly leads them towards liberation." (Tejo-bindu Upanishad 1, 19.)

(4) *Silence:* "That Silence which ever dwells in inanimate things and whence words and mind fall back having no grasp, should be sought by the yogis. Who can express that which words cannot seize? How can the world be told about that for which there is no word? The Principle, the Brahman, is ever spoken of as 'Silence' because all things are known through their inherent qualities. Not to speak is the

silence of children. Other is that of the Knowers of Supreme Reality."
(Tejo-bindu Upanishad 1, 20-22.)

From the negative description, "neither this nor that" (neti neti),
given of him by the scriptures, we see that nothing different from the
Self-of-all has reality. It is the complete assurance of this in the
mind which is called Silence.

(5) *Solitude:* "That place which is everywhere at all times present
(being the basis of all that evolves) and in which, in the beginning,
at the end, or in the middle, there is no living creature, that place
which is their own Self, the yogis call 'Solitude'." (Tejo-Bindu
Upanished 1, 23.)

(6) *Time:* "By the word Time is meant the succession of instants
through which the Creator Brahmâ and all other beings are conceived
within the non-dual indivisible Supreme bliss." (Tejo-bindu Upanishad 1, 24.)

(7) *Posture:* "That (state) in which, without effort, constant meditation on the Principle of all, the Brahman, is possible is called 'âsana';
any change in it destroys the experience of joy." (Tejo-bindu Upanishad 1, 25.)

"The feeling of indifference towards all things is said to be the
highest âsana." (Trishikhi Brâhmana Upanishad 29.)

(8) *The Root Contraction:* ° "That (Self) which is the root of all
worlds and which is the root of the control of the mind should always
be sought by yogis, seekers of the Principle. This is called the Root
contraction." (Tejo-bindu Upanishad 1, 27.)

(9) *The Straightening of the Body:* "Looking upon all the steps of
yoga as equal, dissolve them equally in the Brahma. Without this, to
try to straighten the waist or limbs is as (useless as) if they were
(the branches of) a dead tree." (Tejo-bindu Upanishad 1, 28.)

(10) *Sight:* "When seen with the sight of knowledge, the Universe
appears filled with the Principle, the Brahman. It is that sight which
uplifts, not the looking at the tip of one's nose." °° (Tejo-bindu
Upanishad 1, 29.)

(11) *Breath-Control:* "When in the mind and in all perceptions, the
single notion of the Principle, the Brahman, persists and all movements
are stilled, this is called 'breath-control'." (Tejo-bindu Upanishad 1,
31.)

"Certainty of the unreality of the world is called breathing out. The
constantly recurrent notion 'I am the Principle, the Brahman,' is

° [In Hatha yoga a muscular contraction supplementing the postures.—*Ed.*]

°° [In Hatha yoga corresponds to the "gestures" which like the muscular con-
tractions supplement the postures.—*Ed.*]

called 'breath-in.' This notion, become rigidly fixed in the mind is the chalice or holding of the breath. Such is the breath-control of the enlightened, controlling the breath by pressing the nostrils is that of the ignorant." (Tejo-bindu Upanishad 1, 32-33.)

(12) *Withdrawal:* "Seeing Divinity in all perceptible forms brings delight to the mind and its faculties." (Tejo-bindu Upanishad 1, 34.)

"To direct the mental faculties inwards is the withdrawal, O best of men!" (Trishikhi Brahmana Upanishad 30.)

(13) *Concentration:* "Wherever the mind goes, it sees only the Brahman. This attitude of mind is considered the transcendent concentration." (Tejo-bindu Upanishad 1, 35.)

"To hold the mind motionless is known as concentration." (Trishikhi Brâhmana Up. 31.)

(14) *Contemplation:* "The one changeless thought 'I am the Principle, the Brahman,' with no other notion, is known under the name of 'contemplation' and is the giver of supreme bliss." (Tejo-bindu Up. 1, 36.)

There are three stages of contemplation, according to the degree of development of the seeker. They are the religious, mystical and abstract stages. Religious contemplation is contemplation of Divinity manifest. Mystical contemplation is contemplation of Causal or Ruling Divinity. Abstract contemplation is contemplation of the Unmanifest Principle beyond cause and effect.

(15) *Identification:* "When the very notion of contemplation is forgotten, this is known as 'identification'." (Trishikhi Brâhmana Up. 32.)

According to the object with which the consciousness identifies itself, there are four degrees of identification, namely: Where the object is the principle of material existence the identification is said to be 'of the reasoning faculty'; Where the object is the principle of subtle existence the identification is said to be 'of the thinking faculty'; Where the object is the principle of sensorial perception identification is with the 'experience of joy'; Where the object is the principle of individual existence, i.e. the Supreme Person, identification is said to be with the I, or with the notion of existence (asmitâ).

(d) *Asmitâ:* ° "Having thus gone through the different stages . . . the seeker attains, in the very same object of his meditation the changeless all-pervading pure consciousness and through it the very nature of the Self. This is known as identification with the notion of Existence (Asmitâ), so named because it appears in the form of the

° [The three earlier stages are omitted.—*Ed.*]

perception "I am distinct from all bodies, etc." Since, after cognizing the Self, nothing remains to be cognized, identification with Existence is the final stage." . . .

20

MEISTER ECKHART

God and the Soul *

Outstanding among Christian mystics is Meister Eckhart, of whom it was said:

> "This is Meister Eckhart
> From whom God kept nothing hid."

What Eckhart has to say is often difficult and profound. His mysticism is not just a simple and detailed account of the itinerary of the soul to God, but is more often concerned with the mysteries of the Godhead and the Trinity and the attempt to comprehend the supernatural life of the soul in the depths of the divine understanding. Virtually all his writing is mystical, so the few selections we have chosen will reveal but in a small way his intuitive wisdom and the moving quality of his prose. The first selection on "Detachment" argues for the priority of detachment over all other virtues, for the "aloneness" of the soul in the presence of the "Alone." The "Tractate" emphasizes a common theme of Eckhart's mysticism— the nothingness of the soul and its need for God. "The Flow into the Father" points up the place of the Trinity in the mysticism of Eckhart, notes the powers of the soul and what the soul must do to plunge into the divine nothingness until she "knows that she is but not what she is." The last selection, "The Soul's Rage," describes in highly colorful and moving language the frustrations of the soul in its quest for union with the divine essence.

* From Franz Pfeiffer's edition of the *Works of Meister Eckhart*, translated by C. de B. Evans (London: John M. Watkins, 1924), pp. 340-48, 362-63, 371-76, 389-90. Reprinted with the permission of the translator and publisher.

Meister Eckhart (1260-1327) was born at Hochheim near Gotha. He entered the Dominican Order and later became Provincial of Saxony and then Vicar-General of the Order. He lectured at Paris between 1311 and 1314 and then moved to Cologne where he remained until his death in 1327. There his teachings were investigated by the Archbishop and, despite Eckhart's appeal, several propositions from his later writings were condemned by Pope John XXII in 1329.

DETACHMENT

I HAVE READ many writings of heathen philosophers and sages, of the old covenant and of the new, and have sought earnestly and with all diligence which is the best and highest virtue whereby a man may knit himself most narrowly to God, and wherein he is most like to his exemplar, as he was in God, wherein was no difference between himself and God, ere God created creature. And having approfounded all these scriptures to the best of my ability, I find it is none other than absolute detachment from all creatures. . . .

Our doctors sing love's praises, as did St. Paul, who said, "Whatsoever things I do and have not charity I am nothing." But I extol detachment above any love. First, because it is far better my constraining God to me than for me to be constrained to God. My eternal happiness depends on God and me becoming one; but God is apter to adapt himself to me and can easier communicate with me than I can communicate with God. Detachment forces God to come to me, and this is shown as follows. Everything is fain to be in its own natural state. But God's own natural state is unity and purity and these come from detachment. Hence God is bound to give himself to a heart detached.—Secondly, I rank detachment above love because love constrains me to suffer all things for God's sake: detachment constrains me to admit nothing but God. Now it is far better to tolerate nothing but God than to suffer all things for God's sake. For in suffering one has regard to creatures, whence the suffering comes, but detachment is immune from creature. Further, that detachment admits of none but God I demonstrate in this wise: anything received must be received in aught. But detachment is so nearly naught that there is nothing rare enough to stay in this detachment, except God. He is so simple, so ethereal, that he can sojourn in the solitary heart. Detachment then admits of God alone. . . .

And humility the masters laud beyond most other virtues. I rank detachment before any meekness and for the following reasons. Meekness can be without detachment, but complete detachment is impossible without humility. Perfect humility is a matter of self-naughting; but detachment so narrowly approximates to naught that no room remains for aught betwixt zero and absolute detachment. Wherefore without humility is no complete detachment. Withal two virtues are always better than one.—Another reason why I put detachment higher than humility is this: humility means abasing self before all creatures and in that same abasement one goes out of oneself to

creatures. But detachment abideth in itself. Now no going out however excellent, but staying in is better still.

.　　.　　.　　.　　.

Perfect detachment is without regard, without either lowliness or
loftiness to creatures: it has no mind to be below nor yet to be above;
it is minded to be master of itself, loving none and hating none, having neither likeness nor unlikeness, neither this nor that, to any creature; the only thing it fain would be is *same*. But to be either this or
that it does not want at all. He who is this or that is aught; but detachment is altogether naught. It leaves things unmolested. . . .

I prize detachment more than mercy too, for mercy means naught
else but a man's going forth of self by reason of his fellow-creatures'
lack, whereby his heart is wrung. Detachment is exempt from this;
it stays within itself permitting nothing to disturb it. In short, when
I reflect on all the virtues I find not one so wholly free from fault, so
unitive to God as is detachment.

It was Avicenna the philosopher who said, "The mind detached is
of such nobility that what it sees is true, what it desires befalls and
its behests must be obeyed." For you must know that when the free
mind is quite detached it constrains God to itself and could it remain
formless and free from adventitiousness it would take on the nature
of God. But God grants this to none beside himself; so God can do
no more for the solitary soul than make it a present of himself. The
man who is in absolute detachment is rapt away into eternity where
nothing temporal affects him nor is he in the least aware of any
mortal thing; he has the world well dead, he having no relish for
aught earthly. St. Paul meant this when he declared, "I live and yet
not I: Christ liveth in me."

.　　.　　.　　.　　.

. . . True detachment means a mind as little moved by what
befalls, by joy and sorrow, honor and disgrace, as a broad mountain
by a gentle breeze. Such motionless detachment makes a man super-
latively Godlike. For that God is God is due to his motionless detachment, and it is from his detachment that he gets his purity and
his simplicity and his immutability. If then a man is going to be
like God, so far as any creature can resemble God, it will be by detachment. This leads to purity and from purity to simplicity and from
simplicity to immovability; and it is these three which constitute the
likeness between man and God, which likeness is in grace, for it is

grace which draws a man away from mortal things and purges him from things corruptible. I would have you know that to be empty of creatures is to be full of God and to be full of creatures is to be empty of God.

What then, I ask, is the object of absolute detachment? I answer, that the object of absolute detachment is neither this nor that. It is absolutely nothing, for it is the culminating point where God can do precisely as he will. God cannot have his way in every heart, for though God is almighty yet he cannot work except where he finds readiness or makes it. I add, or makes it, by reason of St. Paul in whom he found no readiness but whom he did make ready by infusion of his grace; wherefore I affirm, God works according to the aptitude he finds. He works differently in man and in a stone, and for this we have a natural analogy. If you heat a baker's oven and place in it the dough, some made of barley, some of oats and some of wheat and some of rye, then albeit in the oven the heat is all the same it does not tell alike on all the doughs, but one yields a fine bread, another one more coarse and a third a coarser still. The heat is not to blame: it is the material which differs. Nor does God tell alike on every heart but according to the readiness and the capacity he finds. In any heart containing this or that there is something to hinder God's highest operation. For a heart to be perfectly ready it has to be perfectly empty, this being its condition of maximum capacity. . . .

Then again I ask, What is the prayer of the solitary heart? I answer, that detachment and emptiness cannot pray at all, for whoso prays desires of God something: something added to him or something taken from him. But the heart detached has no desire for anything nor has it anything to be delivered from. So it has no prayers at all; its only prayer consists in being uniform with God. . . . Attaining this the soul loses her name; God absorbs her in himself so that as self she comes to naught, just as the sunlight swallows up the dawn and naughts it. To this pass nothing brings the soul but absolute detachment. And here it is germane to quote St. Augustine's dictum: "The soul has a private door into divine nature at the point where for her things all come to naught." This door on earth is none other than absolute detachment. At the height of her detachment she is ignorant with knowing, loveless with loving, dark with enlightment. . . .

That God would sooner be in a solitary heart than any other, I argue in this fashion. Starting from thy question, What does God seek in all things? I answer in his words out of the Book of Wisdom, "In all things I seek rest." Now there is nowhere perfect rest save in

a heart detached. Ergo, God is happier there than in any other thing
or virtue. Know that the more we are disposed to receive the inflowing God, the more happy we shall be; perfect receptivity gives perfect
felicity. . . .

List ye, good people all: there is none happier than he who stands
in uttermost detachment. No temporal, carnal pleasure but brings
some ghostly mischief in its train, for the flesh lusts after things that
run counter to the spirit and spirit lusts for things that are repugnant
to the flesh. He who sows the tares of love in flesh reaps death but
he who sows good love-seed in the spirit reaps of the spirit eternal
life. . . . Detachment is the best of all, for it cleanses the soul,
clarifies the mind, kindles the heart and wakes the spirit; it quickens
desire and enhances virtue giving intuition of God; it detaches creature and makes her one with God. . . . He who would attain
unto the highest life while here in time, let him take in a few words
culled out of all the scriptures the summary philosophy which I will
now set down.

Keep thyself detached from all mankind; keep thyself devoid of
all incoming images; emancipate thyself from everything which
entails addition, attachment or encumbrance, and address thy mind
at all times to a saving contemplation wherein thou bearest God fixed
within thy heart as the object from which its eyes do never waver;
any other discipline, fasts, vigils, prayers, or whatever it may be,
subordinate to this as to its end, using thereof no more than shall
answer for this purpose, so shalt thou win the goal of all perfections.

Here someone may object, But who can persist in unwavering contemplation of the divine object? I answer, no one living here in time.
This is told thee merely so that thou mayst know the highest, that
whereon thy aspirations and desires should be set. . . .

·   ·   ·   ·   ·

TRACTATE XI

·   ·   ·   ·   ·

Nothing is without beginning, and since nothing is without beginning God could make us from nothing better than nothing, like himself. Alone God's power did make the soul, so she like him is free
from matter. And soul could have no homelier road into divinity
than by way of nothing to nothing, for nothing unites like natural
affinity. . . .

The naught we were before we were created was indigent of naught. Moreover of itself it could do absolutely naught and naught withstood creatures: all but the power of God; it was this caused naught to stir when God made all things from naught. Now we have got to be more motionless than naught.—"But how?" Mark how. God gat the soul the mistress of herself . . . so whatever in this body she elects of her free will she is free to carry through. Say she chooses to need nothing and to be more motionless than naught. . . . To reach this point of needing naught and being more immutable than naught, soul must be sunk so deep in the bottomless well of the divine naught that nothing can draw her thereout to spend herself on mortal things, but there she steadfastly abides. . . .

. . . . .

. . . Up, noble Soul! Out of thyself so far thou never comest in again and enter into God so deep thou never comest out again: there stay nor ever deign to stoop to creature; and burden not thyself with things made clear to thee, nor wander among objects presented to thy mind, nor be not hindered from achievement by any service. Steadfastly pursue thy simple nature and the unnecessitous nothingness, seeking no other place than this unnecessitous naught. God who made thee out of nothing, he in his unnecessitous nothingness and immovableness shall himself be thy place. There thou shall be more immovable than nothing.

. . . . .

THE FLOW INTO THE FATHER

Concerning the flow into the Father, note as follows.

The Godhead is contained in the Father as nature, wherefore he is omnipotent and receives naught from aught that he is not himself in his divine potentiality, seeing that he has it in him in essence, as his own. Nevertheless, speaking of the Father we mean the Person of the Father, and speaking of the Godhead we mean his nature, his impartible substance, that is to say. Now since this nature stays brooding in settled immoveable stillness, moving all things which have proceeded in eternity in the word of his power (or potential Word), it follows that, as power, it has ever been flowing into the Father making him able to beget a Son like unto himself. . . .

Now mark. The soul has received two powers by nature. The first of these powers is understanding. This comprehends the Trinity, although it is incomprehensible, and all its works. . . . The soul in her understanding is the image of the Son and the Son is the Father's understanding. So when the soul is empty of her own understanding, and only the Son is her understanding, she understands with the Son the Son and the Father and their common Spirit. That is how the soul comprehends the Trinity and all its works.

Her other power is will. It is its nature to cast itself into the unknown which is God. God is said to be unknown because no creature knows him as he knows himself; as known to himself he is unknowing to all creatures. Hence we call God agnosia. Now the chief power of the soul is too fastidious to dally with temporal, known things, so free will boldly disregards the known and cleaves to what it knows not. As St. Paul says, "I know not; God knoweth."

With the powers received from the Trinity the soul knows the ordering of all things ordained by God in such exalted fashion. But those that turn away their eyes from God relapse into the self-same naught wherein they were before they had received the likeness of the Trinity, this likeness of the Trinity aye informing them of the dark nothing back to which they wend. In this darkness gather all the pangs of hell. The dark enwraps them and hides the sight of God; it burns them past soothing by their created aught. This is better to their conscience which damns them to all time. In this pit of nothingness they sink for evermore, powerless to grasp the naught they were before they had the likeness of the Trinity.

The fastidious soul can rest her understanding on nothing that has name. She escapes from every name into the nameless nothingness. Escaping her own nature she falls clear of her own aught. The naught she falls into is the unknowing, which is called the dark. . . . To approfound the naught wherein they drown they are as helpless as they were when they were not. All sense and knowledge end in the darkness of their naught. For this darkness is the incomprehensible nature of God. She sinks for evermore in the depths of this naught. She sinks and drowns; she drowns to her own aught. . . . But the naught that sinks can never comprehend the naught it sinks in. Every virtue mastered and transcended, the soul cries; "Even so I cannot glorify and love God to the full. I die then to the virtues casting me into the naught of the Godhead to sink eternally from naught to aught." The highest meed of love and praise the soul can lavish on the sovran good is given in the knowledge that all her love and praise fall short of God. So down she goes through the little she can call her own and dying to her virtues is cast into the naught of her own self.

.   .   .   .   .

Further, God absorbs the soul leaving no trace. This means that the soul ravished by God into the peace and quiet of his secret self makes little show save to her kind. There the soul knows no separation, for he who has absorbed her has merged her in himself. She well knows that she is but knows not what she is. . . .

．　．　．　．　．

Behold the soul divorced from every aught. For he who stoops to aught that is not God can never be received into God's unity. This unity is causeless: it is self-caused. Of bottomless depth the floor, of endless height the roof, of boundless space the rim. I refer to the Trinity of Persons: the unity underlies it, holding it together; it overtops it, energising it; it surrounds it, ending its distinctions. Thus the Trinity is in the unity and the unity in the Trinity. As saith the psalm *Quicumque vult*.

That we should know ourselves and God so far as we are able, that is God's will. If we would know ourselves we have to recognize that we are nothing but the raw material of God for the blessed Trinity to work in. It behooves us therefore to be vastly careful not to hamper in any way the work which the exalted workman designs to carry out in us to his glory, but so to maintain ourselves that the material is always ready for the workman to do his work in us. . . .

God's will is our welfare, and our welfare consists in knowing God and doing accordingly. Here timorousness mutters in the soul, both she will and she will not. And hard on this comes rage of soul. . . .

．　．　．　．　．

THE SOUL'S RAGE

The soul is furious for self-knowledge. Her face is lit with passion, red with rage for the arrears withheld from her in God, because she is not all God by nature, because she has not all God has by nature.

The masters say there is no fiercer appetite than a friend's desire to possess his friend and all that he possesses. The soul proclaims her rage so boundless she cannot be appeased by him. The bonds of love are all too cruel for her. Alas! she cries, who shall console me? My misery is too deep. Were I the one creator, beginningless and endless, and had I made creatures and were the soul like me, then I would go straight out of my estate and let her enter in and be God while I was creature; and if it were an obstacle to God to get his being from me, he would be welcome to efface me for I would perish sooner than be a hindrance to him. But seeing it is common to everything created to have somewhat of the eternal in man's nature ever present in it, therefore I know not where to turn to find a place. So I take refuge in myself and there I find the lowest place, aye, one more base than hell for even thence do my shortcomings hound me. It seems I cannot then escape myself. Here I sit me down and herein will I stay. And I beseech thee, Lord, that thou never callest me to mind and forbiddest any creature ever to console me and deniest to my powers that ever any one of them should come before thy face, lest I offend thee. So I go out and let the soul go in.

The third rage of the soul is that she should be God and that there should not be a single creature, like when God was in his eternity ere he created creature, so that she may enjoy God-nature in its simplicity as he did before. But then his love were lacking to him, for it is the nature of good things to communicate themselves.

Fourthly, she rages to be absolutely nothing but the naked essence, there being neither God nor creature. She asks, What is the good of the three persons in the Godhead and what is the use of creatures? But hold, she cries, except for them there would be no creatures. That must be the reason why there are three Persons in the Godhead: they are the cause of creatures. God is God-exalted; the creatures he has made cannot exalt him. All that creatures do to God is themselves: such glory as they can give to God is the same as they are.

21

"Put off thine own will . . ." *

THE *Theologica Germanica,* an anonymous devotional classic, was composed about 1350 A.D. It exerted a considerable influence on Martin Luther, who published an edition of it in 1516. Its author refers to himself as a priest and warden of the Order of Teutonic Knights and he is also said to have been a member of a group of religious and mystics who called themselves the Friends of God. In the *Theologica* he emphasizes the finite and sinful nature of man in contrast to the infinite and transcendent goodness of God, and the

---

* From the *Theologica Germanica,* translated by Susanna Winkworth (Macmillan and Co., 1893). Author unknown, pp. 46-227.

necessity for man's uniting himself to God if he is to achieve "true love, true peace, true rest." With the grace of God man can achieve such a union if he will purify himself of all sin, put off his own will, and make the created will wholly one with the Eternal Will, so that it is "swallowed up and lost therein." To partake in this way of the divine nature it is not enough that the soul be enlightened with knowledge, it must also love God alone and above all things and be united with Him in love.

Now BE ASSURED that no one can be enlightened unless he be first cleansed or purified and stripped. So also, no one can be united with God unless he be first enlightened. Thus there are three stages: first the purification; secondly, the enlightening; thirdly, the union. The purification concerneth those who are beginning or repenting, and is brought to pass in a threefold wise; by contrition and sorrow for sin, by full confession, by hearty amendment. The enlightening belongeth to such as are growing, and also taketh place in three ways: to wit, by the eschewal of sin, by the practice of virtue and good works, and by the willing endurance of all manner of temptation and trials. The union belongeth to such as are perfect, and also is brought to pass in three ways: to wit by pureness and singleness of heart, by love, and by the contemplation of God, the Creator of all things.

.   .   .   .   .

Man is created for true obedience, and is bound of right to render it to God. And this obedience fell and died in Adam, and rose again and lived in Christ.   .   .   .

Again, when we read of the old man and the new man we must mark what that meaneth. The old man is Adam and disobedience, the Self, the Me, and so forth. But the new man is Christ and true obedience.   .   .   .

If then it were possible for a man to renounce himself and all things, and to live as wholly and purely in true obedience, as Christ did in his human nature, such a man were quite without sin, and were one thing with Christ, and the same by grace which Christ was by nature. So also it is said: "there is none without sin." But be that as it may, this much is certain; that the nearer we are to perfect obedience, the less we sin, and the farther from it we are, the more we sin. In brief: whether a man be good, better, or best of all; bad, worse, or worst of all; sinful or saved before God; it all lieth in this matter of obedience. Therefore it hath been said: the more of Self and Me, the more of sin and wickedness. So likewise it hath been said: the more the Self, the I, the Me, the Mine, that is, self-seeking and selfishness abate in a man, the more doth God's I, that is God Himself increase in him.

Of a truth we ought to know and believe that there is no life so noble and good and well pleasing to God, as the life of Christ, and yet it is to nature and selfishness the bitterest life. A life of carelessness and freedom is to nature and the Self and the Me, the sweetest and pleasantest life, but it is not the best; and in some men may become the worst. But though Christ's life be the most bitter of all, yet it is to be preferred above all. Hereby shall ye mark this: There is an inward sight which hath power to perceive the One true Good, and that it is neither this nor that, but that of which St. Paul saith; "when that which is perfect is come, then that which is in part shall be done away." By this he meaneth, that the Whole and Perfect excelleth all the fragments, and that all which is in part and imperfect, is as nought compared to the Perfect. Thus likewise all knowledge of the parts is swallowed up when the Whole is known; and where that Good is known, it cannot but be longed for and loved so greatly, that all other love wherewith the man hath loved himself and other things, fadeth away. And that inward sight likewise perceiveth what is best and noblest in all things, and loveth it in the one true Good, and only for the sake of that true Good.

Behold! where there is this inward sight, the man perceiveth of a truth, that Christ's life is the best and noblest life. . . . And he who vainly thinketh otherwise is deceived, and he who saith otherwise, lieth, and in what man the life of Christ is not, of him the true Good and eternal Truth will never more be known.

Now, after that a man hath walked in all the ways that lead him unto the truth, . . . behold! the Devil cometh and soweth his seed in the man's heart. From this seed spring two fruits; the one is spiritual fullness or pride, the other is false, lawless freedom. These are two sisters who love to be together. Now, it beginneth on this wise: the Devil puffeth up the man, till he thinketh himself to have climbed the topmost pinnacle, and to have come so near to heaven, that he no longer needeth Scripture, nor teaching, nor this nor that, but is altogether raised above any need. Whereupon there ariseth a false peace and satisfaction with himself, and then it followeth that he saith or thinketh: "Yea, now I am above all other men, and know and understand more than any one in the world; therefore it is certainly just and reasonable that I should be the lord and commander of all creatures, and that all creatures, and especially all men, should serve me and be subject unto me." . . . And seeing that this proud and puffed-up spirit thinketh that she needeth neither Scripture, nor instruction, nor anything of the kind, therefore she giveth no heed to the admonitions, order, laws and precepts of the holy Christian Church, nor to the Sacraments, but mocketh at them and at all men who walk according to these ordinances and hold them in reverence. Hereby we may plainly see that those two sisters dwell together.

But it is quite otherwise where there is poorness of spirit, and true humility; and it is so because it is found and known of a truth that a man, of himself and his own power, is nothing, hath nothing, can do and is capable of nothing, but only infirmity and evil. . . .

Moreover, when a man hath this poor and humble spirit, he cometh to see and understand aright, how that all men are bent upon themselves, and inclined to evil and sin, and that on this account it is needful and profitable that there be order, customs, law and precepts, to the end that the blindness and foolishness of men may be corrected, and that vice and wickedness may be kept under, and constrained to seemliness. . . .

So order, laws, precepts and the like are merely an admonition to men who understand nothing better and know and perceive not wherefore all law and order is ordained. . . . For those who are perfect are under no law. . . . And the perfect accept the law along with such ignorant men as understand and know nothing better, and practise it with them, to the intent that they may be restrained thereby, and kept from evil ways, or if it be possible, brought to something higher. . . .

 . . . we are to understand . . . that the union with God standeth not in any man's powers, in his working or abstaining, perceiving or knowing, nor in that of all the creatures taken together.

Now what is this union? It is that we should be of a truth purely, simply, and wholly at one with the One Eternal Will of God, or altogether without will, so that the created will should flow out into the Eternal Will, and be swallowed up and lost therein, so that the Eternal Will alone should do and leave undone in us. Now mark what may help or further us towards this end. Behold, neither exercises, nor words, nor works, nor any creature nor creature's work, can do this. In this wise therefore must we renounce and forsake all things, that we must not imagine or suppose that any words, works, or exercises, any skill or cunning or any created thing can help or serve us thereto. Therefore we must suffer these things to be what they are, and enter into the union with God. . . .

. . . To God, as Godhead, appertain neither will, nor knowledge, nor manifestation, nor anything that we can name, or say, or conceive. But to God as God,* it belongeth to express Himself, and know and love Himself and to reveal Himself to Himself; and all this without any creature. . . .

. . . I would have you to understand, that God (in so far as He is good) is goodness as goodness, and not this or that good. But here mark one thing. Behold! what is sometimes here and sometimes there is not everywhere, and above all things and places; so also, what is today, or tomorrow, is not always at all times, and above all time; and what is some Thing, this or that, is not all things and above all things. Now, behold, if God were something, this or that, he would not be all in all, and above all, as he is; and so also, He would not be true Perfection. Therefore God is, and yet he is neither this nor that which the creature, as creature, can perceive, name, conceive, or express. Therefore if God (in so far as He is good) were this or that good, He would not be all good, and therefore he would not be the One Perfect Good, which He is.

Some may say: "Now since God willeth and desireth and doth the best that may be to everyone, He ought so to help each man and order things for him, that they should fall out according to his will and fulfil his desires, so that one might be a Pope, another a Bishop, and so forth." Be assured, he who helpeth a man to his own will, helpeth him to the worst that he can. For the more a man followeth after his own self-will, and self-will groweth in him, the farther off is he from God, the true Good, for nothing burneth in hell but self-will. Therefore it hath been said, "Put off thine own will, and there will be no hell." . . . For a man's highest good would be and truly is, that he should not seek himself nor his own things, nor be his own end in any respect, either in things spiritual or things natural, but should seek only the praise and glory of God and His holy will. This doth God teach and admonish us.

But what then is there which is contrary to God and hateful to Him? Nothing but Sin. But what is Sin? Mark this: Sin is nothing else than that the creature willeth otherwise than God willeth, and contrary to Him. . . . And this contradiction to God's will is what we call, and is, disobedience. And therefore Adam, the I, the Self, Self-will, Sin, or the Old Man, the turning aside or departing from God, do all mean one and the same thing.

Now mark, the True Light is God or divine, but the False light is Nature or natural. Now it belongeth to God, that He is neither this

* As a Person.

nor that, neither willeth nor desireth, nor seeketh anything in the man whom he hath made a partaker of the divine nature, save goodness as Goodness, and for the sake of Goodness. This is the token of the True Light. But to the Creature and Nature it belongeth to be somewhat, this or that, and to intend and seek some thing, this or that, and not simply what is good without any Wherefore. And as God and the True Light are without all self-will, selfishness, and self-seeking, so do the I, the Me, the Mine, and the like, belong unto the natural and false Light; for in all things it seeketh itself and its own ends, rather than Goodness for the sake of Goodness. . . .

Some may ask, "What is it to be 'a partaker of the divine nature,' or a godlike man?" Answer: he who is imbued with or illuminated by the Eternal or divine Light, and inflamed or consumed with Eternal or divine love, he is a godlike man and a partaker of the divine nature; and of the nature of this True Light we have said something already.

But ye must know that this Light or knowledge is worth nothing without Love. This ye may see if ye call to mind, that though a man may know very well what is virtue or wickedness, yet if he doth not love virtue, he is not virtuous, for he obeyeth vice. But if he loveth virtue he followeth after it, and his love maketh him an enemy to wickedness. . . . And to him virtue is its own reward, and he is content therewith, and would take no treasure or riches in exchange for it.

It is the same with justice. Many a man knoweth full well what is just or unjust, and yet neither is nor ever will become a just man. . . .

Thus we may perceive that knowledge and light profit nothing without Love. We see this in the Evil Spirit; he perceiveth and knoweth good and evil, right and wrong, and the like; but since he hath no love for the good that he seeth, he becometh not good. . . . It is indeed true that Love must be guided and taught of Knowledge, but if Knowledge be not followed by Love, it will avail nothing. It is the same with God and divine things. Let a man know much about God and divine things, nay, dream that he seeth and understandeth what God himself is, if he have not Love, he will never become like unto God, or a "partaker of the divine nature."

And this love so maketh a man one with God, that he can never more be separated from Him. . . .

Now, he who shall or will love God, loveth all things in One as One and All, and One in All as All in One; and he who loveth somewhat, this or that, otherwise than in the One, and for the sake of the One, loveth not God, for he loveth somewhat which is not God. Therefore he loveth it more than God. Now he who loveth somewhat more than God or along with God, loveth not God, for He must be and will be alone loved, and verily nothing ought to be loved but God alone. And when the true divine Light and Love dwell in a man, he loveth nothing else but God alone, for he loveth God as Goodness, and for the sake of Goodness, and all Goodness as One, and One as All; for, in truth, All is One and One is All in God.

.   .   .   .   .

Christ said, "He that believeth not," or will not or cannot believe, "shall be damned." It is so of a truth; for a man, while he is in this present time, hath not knowledge; and he cannot attain unto it, unless he first believe. And he who would know before he believeth, cometh never to true knowledge. We speak not here of the articles of the Christian faith, for every one believeth them, and they are common to every Christian man, whether he be sinful or saved, good or wicked, and they must be believed in the first place, for without that, one cannot come to know them. But we are speaking of a certain Truth which it is possible to know by experience, but which ye must believe in, before that ye know it by experience, else ye will never come to know it truly. This is the faith of which Christ speaketh in that saying of His.

Now some may ask: "since this tree, to wit, Self-will, is so contrary to God and the Eternal Will, wherefore hath God created it, and set it in Paradise?"

Answer: whatever man or creature desireth to dive into or understand the secret counsel and will of God . . . desireth the same as Adam and the Devil. For this desire is seldom from aught else than that the man taketh delight in knowing, and glorieth therein, and this is sheer pride. And so long as this desire lasteth, the truth will never be known. . . .

However, there is yet another answer to this question, for we may say: the most noble and delightful gift that is bestowed on any creature is that of perceiving, or Reason, and Will. . . . And if it were not for these two gifts, there would be no reasonable creatures, but only brutes and brutishness; and that were a great loss, for God would never have His due, and behold Himself and his attributes manifested in deeds and works; the which ought to be, and is necessary to perfection. . . .

But here ye must consider more particularly, somewhat touching the Will. There is an Eternal Will, which is in God a first principle and substance, apart from all works and effects, and the same will is in Man, or the creature, willing certain things, and bringing them to pass. . . . For it were in vain, unless it had some work to do, and this it cannot have without the creature. Therefore there must be creatures, and God will have them, to the end that the Will may be put in exercise by their means, and work, which in God is and must be without work. Therefore the will in the creature, which we call a created will, is as truly God's as the Eternal Will, and is not of the creature.

And now, since God cannot bring His will into exercise, working and causing changes, without the creature, therefore it pleaseth Him to do so in and with the creature. Therefore the will is not given to be exerted by the creature, but only by God, who hath a right to work out His own will by means of the will which is in man, and yet is God's. And in whatever man or creature it should be purely and wholly thus, the will would be exerted not by the man but by God, and thus it would not be self-will, and the man would not will otherwise than as God willeth; for God Himself would move the will and not man. And thus the will would be one with the Eternal Will. . . .

Now cometh the Devil or Adam, that is to say, false nature, and taketh this will unto itself and maketh the same its own, and useth it for itself and its own ends. And this is the mischief and wrong, and the bite that Adam made in the apple, which is forbidden, because it is contrary to God. And therefore, so long as there is any self-will, there will never be true love, true peace, true rest. . . . And there will never be true blessedness either in time or eternity, where this self-will is working. . . . If there were no reason or will in the creatures, God were, and must remain for ever, unknown, unloved, unpraised and unhonored, and all the creatures would be worth nothing, and were of no avail to God. Behold thus the question which was put to us is answered.*

That which is free, none may call his own, and he who maketh it his own, committeth a wrong. Now, in the whole realm of freedom, nothing is so free as the will, and he who maketh it his own, and suffereth it not to remain in its excellent freedom, and free nobility . . . doth a grievous wrong. . . . Wherever there is a man in whom the will is not enslaved, but continueth noble and free, there is a true freeman not in bondage to any, one of those to whom Christ said: "the truth shall make you free"; and immediately after, he saith: "if the Son shall make you free, ye shall be free indeed."

* [Why God had created the will.—*Ed.*]

Furthermore, mark ye that where the will enjoyeth its freedom, it hath its proper work, that is, willing. And where it chooseth whatever it will unhindered, it always chooseth in all things what is noblest and best. . . . And the more free and unhindered the will is, the more it is pained by evil, injustice, iniquity, and in short all manner of wickedness and sin, and the more do they grieve and afflict it. . . . But when men claim freedom for their own, so as to feel no sorrow or indignation at sin . . . this is no true and divine freedom springing from the true divine Light, but a natural, unrighteous, false, and deceitful freedom, springing from a natural false and deluded light.

Were there no self-will, there would be also no ownership. In heaven there is no ownership; hence there are found content, true peace and all blessedness. If any one there took upon him to call anything his own, he would straightway be thrust into hell, and would become an evil spirit. But in hell every one will have self-will, therefore there is all manner of misery and wretchedness. So is it also here on earth. But if there were one in hell who should get quit of his self-will and call nothing his own, he would come out of hell into heaven. Now, in this present time, man is set betwen heaven and hell, and may turn himself towards which he will. For the more he hath of ownership, the more he hath of hell and misery; and the less of self-will, the less of hell, and the nearer he is to the Kingdom of Heaven. . . . He who hath something, or seeketh or longeth to have something of his own, is himself a slave, and he who hath nothing of his own, nor seeketh nor longeth thereafter, is free and at large, and in bondage to none. . . .

That we may thus deny ourselves, and forsake and renounce all things for God's sake, and give up our own wills, and die unto ourselves, and live unto God alone and to His will, may He help us, who gave up His Will to His Heavenly Father—Jesus Christ our Lord to whom be blessing for ever and ever. Amen.

22

ST. JOHN OF THE CROSS

The Purgation of the Soul *

ONE OF the greatest poets, as well as one of the greatest mystics, of Spain, St. John of the Cross summarized his mystical doctrine in poetry and expounded it in prose. The objective of the discipline set down by this writer is the unitive life, the spiritual marriage of the soul with God. To achieve this end the soul must purge itself (active night) of its sensual and spiritual parts. Then the soul must be purged solely through the action and the grace of God (passive night, in which the soul waits upon God) of all sensible and spiritual desires and affections. The mystical discipline is divided in this way into four distinct stages: (1) the active night of the sense, (2) the active night of the spirit, (3) the passive night of the sense, (4) the passive night of the spirit. The difficulties encountered by the soul, the nature of the discipline in each stage, and the continuing progress of the soul are all described by the author in considerable detail. Then, when the soul has been purged of all sense desire—of all pleasures and feelings—when memory, understanding, and will have been annihilated, and the soul completely emptied of all intelligible forms and images, then it is ready for the inflowing of God, for that infused contemplation which alone can lead to the unitive life with God.

PROLOGUE

SO GREAT ARE the trials, and so profound the darkness, spiritual as well as corporal, through which souls must pass, if they will attain to perfection, that no human learning can explain them, nor experience describe them. He only who has passed through them can know them, but even he cannot explain them.

* The selections that follow are taken from *The Collected Works*, translated by David Lewis (Thomas Baker, 1889). Since the passages have been abbreviated considerably in many instances and occasionally re-arranged, page references to the text would be of negligible value. The verse summary of St. John's mysticism has been retained in the form of an appendix.

St. John of the Cross (1542-1601) was born near Avila in Spain. In 1563 he entered the Carmelite Order and in the following year was sent to the University of Salamanca for his studies. In 1568 he began his task of reforming the Carmelite Order in Spain. The succeeding years were given over to this reform work, to the establishment of monasteries, and to his writings. He was canonized in 1726.

I am treating here of a solid and substantial doctrine suited to all, if they seek to advance to that detachment of spirit which is here described. My principal object, however, is not to address myself to all, but only to certain persons of our holy order of Mount Carmel. . . .

THE ACTIVE NIGHT OF THE SENSES

THE DARK NIGHT OF SENSE AND DESIRE

In order to reach perfection, the soul has to pass, ordinarily through two kinds of night, which spiritual writers call purgations, or purifications, of the soul, and which I have called night, because in the one as well as in the other the soul travels, as it were by night, in darkness.

The first night is the night, or purgation of the sensual part of the soul, which is the privation of all desire, wrought by God. . . . The second night is the night of the spiritual part, which is for those who are more advanced, when God wishes to bring them into union with Himself.

The night is divided into three parts. The first . . . may be likened to the commencement of night when material objects begin to be invisible. The second . . . may be compared to midnight, which is utter darkness. The third resembles the close of night, which is God, when the dawn of day is at hand.

There is no detachment, if desire remains . . . detachment consists in suppressing desire, and avoiding pleasure; it is this that sets the soul free, even though possession may be still retained. It is not the things of this world that occupy or injure the soul, for they do not enter within, but rather the wish for, and desire of them, which abide within it.

Even one unruly desire, though not a mortal sin, sullies and deforms the soul, and indisposes it for the perfect union with God, until it be cast away. . . . The reason is this: the state of divine union consists in the total transformation of the will into the will of God, in such a way that every movement of the will shall be always the movement of the will of God only. . . . If the soul knowingly cleaves to any imperfection, contrary to the will of God, His will is not done, for the soul wills that which God wills not. . . .

ENTRY INTO THE NIGHT OF THE SENSES

Ordinarily, the soul enters this night in two ways; one is the active way, the other is the passive. The active way is that by which the soul is able to make, and does make, efforts of its own to enter in, assisted by divine grace. Of this I shall speak in the instructions that follow. The passive way is that in which the soul does nothing as of itself, neither does it make therein any efforts of its own; but it is God who works in it, giving special aids, and the soul is, as it were, patient, freely consenting thereto.

COUNSELS FOR ENTERING

1. Be continually careful and earnest in imitating Christ in everything, conforming thyself to His life: for this end thou must meditate thereon, that thou mayest know how to imitate it, and conduct thyself in all things as He would have done Himself.

2. To do this well, every satisfaction offered to the senses, which is not for God's honor and glory, must be renounced and rejected for the love of Jesus Christ. . . . For instance, if the pleasure of listening to anything which tends not to the service of God presents itself, seek not that pleasure, neither give ear to what is said. . . . Practise the same mortification with respect to the other senses, as far as possible; and if it be not possible, it will be enough not to seek the pleasure that is offered. . . .

In order to mortify and calm the four natural passions of joy, hope, fear and grief . . . the following instructions are a perfect means of great merit and the source of great virtues:—

Strive always, not after that which is most easy, but after that which is most difficult.

Not after that which is most pleasant, but after that which is most unpleasant.

Not after that which giveth pleasure, but after that which giveth none.

Not after that which is consoling, but after that which is afflictive.

Not after that which ministers repose, but after that which ministers labor.

Not after great things, but after little things.

Not after that which is higher and precious, but after that which is lower and despised.

Strive not to desire anything, but rather nothing.

Speak disparagingly of thyself, and contrive that others may do so too.

Think humbly and contemptuously of thyself, and desire that others may do so also.

THE ACTIVE NIGHT OF THE SPIRIT

There is no means of union with God except faith. After traversing
the night of sense, the soul should perfect its faith by the first mortification of the spirit, that of the understanding. . . . In the night
of sense, there remains still some light, because the understanding
remains, and the reason also, which are not blind. But in this spiritual
night, the night of faith, all is darkness, both in the understanding
and the sense. . . . The soul, to be rightly guided by faith
towards union, must be in darkness, not only as to that part thereof—
the sensual and the inferior, of which I have already spoken—which
regards temporal and created things, but also as to that part thereof,
the rational and the superior, of which I am now speaking, which
regards God and spiritual things.

Inasmuch as this union and transformation are not cognisable by
sense or any human power, the soul must be completely and voluntarily empty of all that can enter into it, of every affection and inclination, so far as it concerns itself. Who shall hinder God from doing
His own will in a soul that is resigned, detached, and self-annihilated?
The soul must be emptied of all that its own powers are capable of;
and however great may be its supernatural endowments, it must be
as it were detached from them, in darkness like a blind man, leaning
on the obscure faith, and taking it for its light and guide; not trusting
to anything it understands, tastes, feels, or imagines—for all this is
darkness, which will lead it astray, or keep it back; and faith is above
all understanding, taste, and sense.

If the soul be not blind herein, and in total darkness as to all such
things, it will never reach to those higher things which faith teaches.
A blind man, if he be not totally blind, will not commit himself wholly
to his guide, but because he sees a little he thinks a certain road
secure, not seeing another which is better. . . . He that will attain to the union of God must not rely on his own understanding, nor
lean upon his own imagination, sense, or feeling, but must believe
in the perfection of the divine essence, which is not cognisable by
the understanding, desire, imagination, nor any sense of man.

On this road, therefore, to abandon one's own way is to enter on
the true way, or, to speak more correctly, to pass onwards to the
goal; and to forsake one's own way is to enter on that which has none,
namely God. . . . The soul has need, therefore, to be detached
from . . . its own understanding, liking, and feeling and all that
is unlike to, and not in conformity with, God, so that He, Who communicates Himself to it naturally, in the order of nature, may also
communicate Himself supernaturally, in the order of grace. . . .

He communicates His own supernatural being in such a way that the soul seems to be God Himself and to possess the things of God. Such a union is then wrought when God bestows on the soul that supreme grace which makes the things of God and the soul one by the transformation which renders the one a partaker of the other. The soul seems to be God rather than itself, and indeed is God by participation, though in reality preserving its own natural substance as distinct from God as it did before, although transformed in Him, as the window preserves its own substance distinct from that of the rays of the sun shining through it and making it light. . . .

Hence it is that contemplation, by which God enlightens the understanding, is called mystical theology, that is, the secret wisdom of God, because it is a secret even to the understanding which receives it. St. Dionysius calls it a ray of darkness. . . . It is therefore clear that the understanding must be blind, as to every path along which it has to travel, in order to be united with God.

The two powers of imagination and fancy serve for meditation, which is a discursive act by means of imagery, forms and figures, wrought and fashioned in the senses. We picture to ourselves Christ on the cross, or bound to the pillar, or God sitting on His throne in great majesty. . . . All these imaginations and apprehensions are to be emptied out of the soul, in order that we may attain to the divine union, because they bear no proportion to the proximate means of union with God; as neither do bodily things, the objects of the five exterior senses.

Great, therefore, is the mistake of those spiritual persons who, having labored to draw near unto God by means of imagery, forms and meditations, such as become beginners—while God would attract them to the more spiritual, interior, and unseen good, by depriving them of the joy and sweetness of discursive meditation—do not accept the guidance, neither venture nor know how to detach themselves from these sensible methods to which they have been accustomed.

To these my counsel is—learn to abide with attention in loving waiting upon God in the state of quiet; give no heed to your imagination, nor to its operations, for now, as I have said, the powers of the soul are at rest and are not exercised, except in the sweet and pure waiting of love. . . .

SIGNS FOR LEAVING MEDITATION

It is necessary to explain when the spiritual man should abstain from the meditation which rests on imaginary forms and mental representations, in order that he may abstain from it neither sooner nor later than when the Spirit calls him. . . .

First Sign: When he finds he cannot meditate nor exert his imagination, nor derive any satisfaction from it—then the time is come.

Second Sign: When he sees that he has no inclination to fix the imagination or the senses on particular objects, exterior or interior. . . .

Third Sign: The third sign is the most certain of the three, namely, when the soul delights to be alone, waiting lovingly on God, without any particular considerations, in interior peace, quiet, and repose, when the acts and exercises of the understanding, memory, and will, at least discursively—which is the going from one subject to another—have ceased. . . .

The spiritual man must have observed these three signs together, at least, before he can venture with safety to abandon the state of meditation for that of the way of spiritual contemplation.

It appears, then, from all this that the soul, when it shall have purified and emptied itself from all intelligible forms and images, will then dwell in this pure and simple light, transformed thereto in the state of perfection. This light is ever ready to be communicated to the soul, but does not flow in, because of the forms and veils of the creature which infold and embarrass the soul. Take away these hindrances and coverings, as I shall hereafter explain, and the soul in detachment and poverty of spirit will then, being pure and simple, be transformed in the pure and sincere divine Wisdom who is the Son of God. For then that which is natural having failed, that which is divine flows supernaturally into the enamored soul; for God leaves it not empty without filling it.

THE PURGATION OF MEMORY AND WILL

When the reader observes that I teach the annihilation of the understanding, the memory and the will in the matter of their operations, he will perhaps imagine that I am destroying, and not building up, the spiritual edifice. This objection would be valid, if my purpose here was to instruct only beginners. . . . But as I am teaching how to advance by contemplation to the divine union . . . it is necessary to release the faculties and to empty them . . . in order that the supernatural may fill and enlighten them.

The natural knowledge of the memory is all that knowledge it can form about the objects of the five bodily senses: hearing, seeing, smelling, tasting and touching, and all else of the like kind. The memory must be stripped and emptied of all this knowledge and of these forms; it must labor to destroy all sense of them, so that no impression whatever of them shall be left behind. . . . Nothing less than the annihilation of the memory as to all these forms will serve, if it is to be united with God. For that union can never take place without a total separation from these forms which are not God, for God is without form; neither is He the object of any distinct knowledge whatever.

As God is without form or image, on which the memory may dwell, so when the memory is united with God . . . it remains without form or figure, with the imagination suppressed, and itself absorbed in supreme felicity, in profound oblivion, remembering nothing. The divine union expels every fancy, and shuts out all forms and knowledge; it raises the memory to that which is supernatural, leaving it in such deep forgetfulness that it must do violence to itself, if it will remember anything at all. . . . In the beginning, when this is going on, great forgetfulness ensues, for these forms and knowledge fall into oblivion, men neglect themselves in outward things, forgetting to eat or drink. . . .

But he who has attained to the habit of union does not forget, in this way, that which relates to moral and natural reason; he performs in much greater perfection all necessary and befitting actions, though by the ministry of forms and knowledge, in the memory, supplied in a special manner by God. In the state of union, which is a supernatural state, the memory and the other faculties fail as to their natural functions, and rise beyond their natural objects upwards unto God.

God must raise the soul up into this supernatural state; but the soul, so far as it can, must also be in good dispositions, which it may acquire by the help which God supplies. And so when the soul rejects these forms and empties itself of them, God causes it to enter into the enjoyment of this union. When God does this, the soul is passive, as I shall explain in speaking of the passive night; and He will then bestow upon it the habit of perfect union, proportional to its good dispositions, when it shall seem to Him good to do so.

What we have to do, then, in order to live in the simple and perfect hope of God, whenever these forms knowledge and distinct images occur, is not to fix our minds upon them, but to turn immediately to God, emptying the memory of all such matters in loving affection.

We have done nothing . . . if we have not purified the will in the order of charity, which is the third theological virtue.

I. *Temporal Goods:* By these I mean riches, rank, office . . . ; children, relations. . . .

II. *Natural Goods:* By natural goods I mean beauty, grace, comeliness, and all other physical endowments, and also good understanding, discretion, and other rational qualities. He who is thus endowed, ought to be very cautious, and watchful in his conduct, lest he should furnish another with the opportunity of withdrawing his heart from God even for a moment. . . .

III. *Sensible Goods:* By sensible goods I mean all that is cognisable by the senses . . . and of the interior working of the imaginative powers. . . . Whenever, in hearing music, or other agreeable sounds, in smelling sweet odors, in tasting what is delicious, in touching what is soothing, the affections of the will rise consciously in an instant unto God, and that movement gives us more pleasure than the sensible occasion of it, and when we have no pleasure in that cause, but because of its effects, that is a sign of profit, and shows that the objects of sense minister unto the spirit. In this way we may use them, for now they subserve that end for which God hath made them; namely, that He may be the better known and loved on their account. . . .

IV. *Moral Goods:* . . . By these I mean virtues, the moral habits of them, works of mercy, keeping the law of God and of the state, good dispositions and temper.

A Christian ought to rejoice, not because of his good works and virtuous life, but because his life and acts are such solely for the love of God, and for no other reason whatever. God will not reward them for their good works, because they seek it here in this world, in the joy, or the comfort, or the honorable advantages of their good works; of them Our Savior saith, "Amen. I say to you, they have received their reward."

V. *Supernatural Goods:* By these I mean all those gifts and graces of God, which surpass our natural powers and capacities . . . such as the gifts of "wisdom and understanding" given to Solomon, and those mentioned by St. Paul, namely, "faith, the grace of healing, working of miracles, prophecy. . . ."

He who is supernaturally endowed ought, therefore, to cleanse himself from all desire of, and from all joy in, the exercise of his supernatural gifts; and God, Who gives them supernaturally for the edification of the Church in general, or of its members in particular, will also supernaturally direct him in the use of them, in the right way and at the right time. . . .

When men attach much importance to miracles, they depart from the substantial exercise of faith, which is an obscure habit; and thus where signs and miracles abound, there is the less merit in believing. "Faith has no merit," saith S. Gregory the Great, "where human reason supplies proof." For this reason did God work many signs, before He showed Himself to His disciples; that they might believe without seeing, and so not lose the merit of faith in His resurrection, which they would have done had they seen Him first.

As God is exalted when our joy is grounded on our detachment from all things, much more is He exalted when we refrain from joy in His most marvellous works to place it in Him alone; for these graces are of a higher nature by reason of their supernatural character, and therefore to detach ourselves from them to rejoice in God alone is to give greater honor and glory to God than to them. . . .

THE PASSIVE NIGHT OF SENSE

Souls begin to enter the dark night when God is drawing them out of the state of beginners, which is that of those who meditate on the spiritual road, and is leading them into that of proficients, the state of contemplatives, that, having passed through it, they may arrive at the state of the perfect, which is that of the divine union with God.

SPIRITUAL IMPERFECTIONS OF BEGINNERS

I. Pride

When beginners become aware of their own fervor and diligence in their spiritual works and devotional exercises, this prosperity of theirs give rise to secret pride—though holy things tend of their own nature to humility—because of their imperfections; and the issue is that they conceive a certain satisfaction in the contemplation of their works and of themselves. . . .

Some of them go so far as to desire none should be thought good but themselves, and so, at all times both in word and deed fall into condemnation and detraction of others. They are occasionally desirous that others should perceive their spirituality and devotion, and for that end they give outward tokens by movements, sighs, and divers ceremonies; sometimes, too, they fall into certain trances in public rather than in private—whereto Satan contributes—and are pleased when others are witnesses of them.

They are ashamed to confess their sins plainly, lest their confessors should think less of them, so they go about palliating them, that they may not seem so bad; which is excusing rather than accusing themselves. Sometimes they go to a stranger to confess their sins that their usual confessor may think they are not sinners, but good people.

II. Spiritual Avarice

Many a beginner also falls at times into great spiritual avarice. Scarcely anyone is contented with that measure of the spirit which

God gives; they are very disconsolate and querulous because they do not find the comfort they desire in spiritual things. Many are never satisfied with listening to spiritual counsels and precepts, with reading books which treat of their state and they spend more time in this than in doing their duty, having no regard to that mortification, and perfection of interior poverty of spirit to which they ought to apply themselves. Besides, they load themselves with images, rosaries, and crucifixes, curious and costly.

.   .   .   .   .

IV. Anger

When spiritual things give beginners no more sweetness and delight, they naturally become peevish, and in that bitterness of spirit prove a burden to themselves in all they do; trifles make them angry, and they are at times intolerable to all about them. This happens generally after great sweetness in prayer; and so, when that sensible sweetness is past, their natural temper is soured and rendered morose. . . .

There are other spiritual persons, too, among these who fall into another kind of spiritual anger. They are angry with other people for their faults, with a sort of unquiet zeal, and watch them; they are occasionally moved to blame them, and even do so in anger, constituting themselves guardians of virtue. All this is contrary to spiritual meekness.

Others, again, seeing their own imperfections, become angry with themselves with an impatience that is not humble. They are so impatient with their shortcomings as if they would be saints in one day. . . . There is no perfect remedy for this but in the dark night. There are, however, some people who are so patient, and who advance so slowly in their spiritual progress, that God wishes they were not so patient.

V. Spiritual Gluttony

There is scarcely one among beginners, however good his progress, who, in the matter of this sin, does not fall into some of the many imperfections to which beginners are liable, because of that sweetness which in the beginning they find in spiritual exercises.

For, allured by the delights they then experience, some of them kill themselves with penances, and others weaken themselves by fasting. They take upon themselves more than they can bear, without rule or advice; they try to conceal their austerities from those whom they are bound to obey, and some even venture to practise them though commanded to abstain. . . .

The perfection and value of things consist not in the multitude thereof, but in our knowing how to deny ourselves in them.

VI. Envy and Sloth

Many are often vexed because of other men's goodness. They are sensibly afflicted when others outstrip them on the spiritual road, and will not endure to hear them praised. They become fretful over other men's virtues, and are sometimes unable to refrain from contradiction when they are commended; they depreciate them as much as they can, looking on them with an evil eye.

As to spiritual sloth, beginners are wont to find their most spiritual occupations irksome, and avoid them as repugnant to their taste.

THREE SIGNS OF THE PASSIVE NIGHT OF THE SENSES

The first is this: when we find no comfort in the things of God, and none also in created things. . . .

The second test and condition of this purgation is that the memory dwells ordinarily upon God with a painful anxiety and carefulness, the soul thinks it is not serving God, but going backwards, because it is no longer conscious of any sweetness in the things of God. . . . The cause of this dryness is that God is transferring to the spirit the goods and energies of the senses, which, being now unable to assimilate them, become dry, parched up, and empty; for the sensual nature of man is helpless in those things which belong to the spirit simply. Thus the spirit having tasted, the flesh shrinks and fails. . . . God is now working in the soul, in the state of contemplation, that is, when it advances from meditation to the state of proficients, in such a way as to seem to have bound up all the interior faculties, leaving no help in the understanding, no sweetness in the will, no reflections in the memory. Therefore, at this time, all that the soul can do of itself ends . . . in disturbing the peace and the work of God in the spirit amid the dryness of sense.

The third sign we have for ascertaining whether this dryness be the purgation of sense, is inability to meditate and make reflections, and to excite the imagination, as before, notwithstanding all the efforts we may make; for God begins now to communicate Himself no longer through the channel of sense . . . but in pure spirit . . . and in the act of pure contemplation, to which neither the interior nor the exterior senses of our lower nature can ascend.

The conduct to be observed in the night of sense is this: in nowise have recourse to meditations, for, as I have said, the time is now past, let the soul be quiet and at rest, though they may think they are doing nothing, that they are losing time, and that their lukewarmness is the reason of their unwillingness to employ their thoughts. They will do enough if they keep patience, and persevere in prayer; all they have to do is keep their soul free, unembarrassed, and at rest from all thoughts and all knowledge, not anxious about their meditation, contenting themselves simply with directing their attention lovingly and calmly towards God; and all this without anxiety or effort, or desire to feel and taste His presence. For all such efforts disquiet the soul, and distract it from the calm repose and sweet tranquillity of contemplation to which they are now admitted.

When the house of sensuality is at rest, that is, when the passions are mortified and concupiscence is quenched, the soul begins to set out on the way of the spirit, the way of those who progress and of proficients, which is also called the illuminative way.

THE PASSIVE NIGHT OF THE SPIRIT

The soul, which God is leading onwards, enters not into the night of the spirit at once . . . rather it must spend some time, perhaps years, after quitting the state of beginners, in exercising itself in the state of proficients.

In this state—as one released from a rigorous imprisonment—it occupies itself in divine things with much greater freedom and satisfaction, and its joy is more abundant and interior than it was in the beginning before it entered the night of sense; its imagination and faculties are not held, as hitherto, in the bonds of meditation and spiritual reflections; it now rises at once to most tranquil and loving contemplation, and finds spiritual sweetness without the fatigue of meditation.

It is in this way that God purifies some souls who are not to rise to so high a degree of love as others. He admits them at intervals into the night of contemplation or spiritual purgation. . . . These morsels of dim contemplation are, however, never so intense as is that awful night of contemplation of which I am speaking, and in which God purposely places the soul, that He may raise it to the divine union.

God now denudes the faculties, the affections, and feelings, spiritual and sensual, interior and exterior, leaving the understanding in darkness, the will dry, the memory empty, the affections of the soul in the deepest affliction, bitterness, and distress. . . . All this our Lord effects in the soul by means of contemplation, pure and dark.

The dark night is a certain inflowing of God into the soul which cleanses it of its ignorances and imperfections, habitual, natural, and spiritual. Contemplatives call it infused contemplation, or mystical theology, whereby God secretly teaches the soul and instructs it in the perfection of love, without efforts on its own part beyond a loving attention to God, listening to His voice and admitting the light He sends, but without understanding how this is infused contemplation. . . .

The divine wisdom is, for two reasons, not night and darkness only, but pain and torment also to the soul. The first is, the divine wisdom is so high that it transcends the capacity of the soul, and therefore is, in that respect, darkness. The second reason is based on the meanness and impurity of the soul, and in that respect the divine wisdom is painful to it, afflictive and dark also.

The divine touches the soul to renew it and to ripen it, in order to make it divine, to detach it from the habitual affections and qualities of the old man to which it clings and conforms itself. The divine extreme so breaks and bruises the spiritual substance, that the soul, at the sight of its own wretchedness, seems to perish and waste away. . . .

But the greatest affliction of the sorrowful soul in this state is the thought that God has abandoned it, of which it has no doubt; that He has cast it away into darkness as an abominable thing.

The soul is conscious of a profound emptiness, and destitution of the three kinds of goods, natural, temporal, and spiritual. The sensual part is purified in aridities, the faculties in the emptiness of their powers, and the spirit in the thick darkness.

All this God brings about by means of this dim contemplation, in which the soul is made to suffer from the failure and withdrawal of its natural powers, which is a most distressing pain. It is like that of a person being suffocated, or hindered from breathing. But this contemplation is also purifying the soul, undoing or emptying it, or consuming in it, as fire consumes the rust and mouldiness of metal, all the affections and habits of imperfection which it had contracted in the whole course of its life.

They are occasionally felt so acutely that the soul seems literally to suffer the pains of hell . . . and to have its purgatory in this life; for this is the purgation which would have been endured there. Thus the soul which passes through this state in the present life, either enters not into purgatory, or is detained there but a moment, for one hour here is of greater profit than many there.

But if this purgation is to be real it will last, notwithstanding its vehemence, for some years, but admitting of intermissions and relief, during which, by the dispensation of God, the dim contemplation divested of its purgative form and character assumes that of the illuminative and of love.

As the dark night hinders the exercise of the faculties and affections, it cannot lift up the heart and mind to God as before, nor pray to Him. . . . And, in truth, this is not the time for the soul to speak to God, but . . . to put its "mouth in the dust," suffering in patience this purgation.

It is God Himself Who is now working in the soul, and the soul is therefore powerless. Hence it comes that it cannot pray or give much attention to divine things. Neither can it attend to temporal matters, for it falls into frequent distractions, and the memory is so profoundly weakened, that many hours pass by without its knowing what it has done or thought, what it is doing or is about to do; nor can it give much heed to what it is occupied with, notwithstanding all its efforts.

Without this purgation it is altogether impossible to taste of the abundance of these spiritual delights. For one single affection remaining in the soul, or any one matter to which the mind clings either habitually or actually, is sufficient to prevent all perception and all communication of the tender and interior sweetness of the spirit of love. . . .

This darkness must continue so long as it is necessary to destroy the habit, long ago contracted, of understanding things in a natural way, and until the divine enlightening shall have taken its place. For this night is drawing the spirit away from its ordinary and common sense of things, that it may draw it towards the divine sense, which is a stranger and an alien to all human ways; so much so that the soul seems to be carried out of itself. . . .

By correcting and drying up all affections of sense and spirit, by weakening and wasting the natural attachment of the soul to inferior things, God makes the soul to die to all that is not God, that, being denuded and stripped, it may clothe itself anew. This is nothing else but the supernatural light giving light to the understanding, so that the human understanding becomes divine, made one with the divine.

God, being the sovereign Lord, dwells substantially in the soul, and neither angel nor devil can discover what is going on there, nor penetrate the profound and secret communications which take place between Him and the soul. These communications, because the work of our Lord Himself, are wholly divine and supreme, and, as it were, substantial touches of the divine union between Himself and the soul; in one of these, because it is the highest possible degree of prayer, the soul receives greater good than in all the rest. Then indeed the evil spirit would not venture to assail the soul, because he could not succeed, neither can he know of those divine touches in the substance of the soul with the loving substance of God. No man can arrive at this blessed condition but by the most perfect purgation and detachment, by being spiritually hidden from all created things.

Darkness has deprived it of all things—yet love and faith, now burning within it, drawing the heart towards the Beloved, influence and guide it, and make it fly upwards to God along the road of solitude, while it knows neither how nor by what means that is done.

STANZAS OF THE SOUL [*]

In a dark night,
With anxious love inflamed,
O happy lot
Forth unobserved I went,
My house being now at rest.

In darkness and in safety,
By the secret ladder, disguised
O happy lot!
In darkness and concealment,
My house being now at rest.

In that happy night
In secret, seen of none,
Seeing nought myself,
Without other light or guide
Save that which in my heart was burning.

That light guided me
More surely than the noon day sun
To the place where He was waiting for me,
Whom I knew well,
And where none appeared.

[*] [St. John of the Cross summarized his doctrine in the form of the above stanzas and then noted his intention to comment upon each of the stanzas. Apparently, however, he wrote no commentary on the last five stanzas and his commentary on the first three is very uneven. For an excellent discussion of the whole problem see the general introduction to E. Allison Peers' translation and edition of *The Complete Works of Saint John of the Cross* (Newman Press, 1952), pp. xxxi-lxxvii.—*Ed.*]

O guiding night;
O night more lovely than the dawn;
O night that hast united
The lover with His beloved
And changed her into her love

On my flowery bosom
Kept whole for Him alone,
There He reposed and slept;
And I caressed Him, and the waving
Of the cedars fanned Him.

As I scattered His hair in the breeze
That blew from the turret,
He struck me on the neck
With His gentle hand,
And all sensation left me.

I continued in oblivion lost,
My head was resting on my love;
Lost to all things and myself,
And, amid the lillies forgotten,
Threw all my cares away.

23

JAN VAN RUYSBROEK

The Life of Contemplation of God *

THE DRAMA of the Christian faith—the original innocence and
happiness of man, his fall, his redemption, and his reunion with
God—is told briefly in the Prologue through an explication of

* From *The Spiritual Espousals,* translated by Eric Colledge, copyright 1953 by
Faber and Faber, pp. 43-44, 179-90. Distributed in the United States by Harper
and Brothers and reprinted with the permission of that publisher.

Jan van Ruysbroek (1293-1381) was born at Brabant in the Low Countries.
He was ordained a priest in 1317. He first became prominent in 1344 when he
attacked the heretical doctrine of Bloemardinne on "seraphic love." He entered

Matt. xxv:6. The treatise that follows is a commentary on this passage, and develops the theme of the three lives which are possible for man: the active life, the life of yearning for God, and the supernatural life of the contemplation of God. Few can attain to this life of contemplation that is beyond all contemplation. Only the person who is illumined by God can attain to this state which is a life with God and an understanding of God. The incomprehensible light of God is given to the contemplative and he becomes in a way that very light itself, "and so with God is God comprehended and seen, wherein lies our blessedness." The selection continues with a description of our life in God; how we have been created in the image of the Holy Trinity, and how by going beyond reason and created nature contemplative men can attain to the image in which they were created, contemplate God in the Divine light, and emulate Him in the out-going and in-flowing of His love. When the contemplative man is illumined in this way with the divine truth there occurs that incomprehensible union with God which is beatitude. The author then expresses this action in terms of the Trinity, around which much of his mysticism is centered. This final union is a matter of delectable blessedness, unfathomable joy—"this is the dark silence in which all lovers are lost."

CONCERNING A SPIRITUAL ESPOUSAL BETWEEN GOD AND OUR HUMANITY

"SEE, THE BRIDEGROOM comes: go out to meet Him." St. Matthew the Evangelist writes these words for us, and Christ spoke them to His disciples, and to all men, as we may read in the parable of the virgins. This Bridegroom is Christ, and man's nature is the bride, whom God has made in the image and the likeness of Himself. And in the beginning he had set her in the highest place, and in the fairest and richest and most splendid of dwellings, that was in paradise. And to her He had subjected all creatures, and He had adorned her with graces, and to her He had given a commandment: and had she showed obedience, she would have deserved to live steadfast and secure in everlasting wedlock with her Bridegroom and never to fall into any distress or sin.

Then there came a knave, the fiend from hell, cunningly in the guise of a serpent, and he was envious of this and he deceived the woman, and the two of them deceived the man, in whom humanity first existed. And by false counsel he seduced her, Nature, the bride of

---

the Augustinian Order in 1351 and later became Prior of the Augustinian convent of Groenendael near Brussels.

God. And she was driven out into a strange land, poor and wretched, and was made prisoner and oppressed and enslaved by her foes, as if she should never return to her native land or have pardon.

But when God thought it time, and when He had pity on this anguish of His subjects, then He sent His only-begotten Son on earth, into a splendid court and into a glorious temple, which was the body of the glorious maiden Mary. There He espoused this bride, our nature, and united her with His Person by the noble virgin's most pure blood. The priest who blessed the bride, that was the Holy Ghost. The angel Gabriel brought the command. The glorious maiden gave the consent.

Thus has Christ, our plighted Bridegroom, united our nature with Him, and has visited us in a strange land, and has taught us with heavenly laws and with the uttermost faith. And He has labored and striven as a champion against our foes, and He has broken open the prison and has won the battle, and by His death has dealt death to our death, and has ransomed us with His blood and has set us free with the waters of His baptism, and has enriched us with His sacraments and His gifts, so that we may go out clad in all virtues, as He says, and meet Him in the court of glories, and enjoy Him without end and evermore.

Now Christ, the master teaching truth, says: 'See, the Bridegroom comes, go out to meet Him.' In these words Christ our true love teaches us four things. First, He gives us a command in that He says 'See.' Those who shut their eyes and neglect this command, they are all condemned. In the next words He shows us what we shall see, that is the coming of the Bridegroom. Then thirdly He teaches us and commands what we should do, in that He says 'Go out.' Fourthly, when He says 'To meet Him,' He makes plain to us the profit and use of all our labor and all our life, that is, a loving meeting with the Bridegroom.

Let us expound and make plain these words in three manners. First, according to common usage, as they concern the life of the beginner, which is called active life, needful to all men who wish to be saved. Next let us make plain the same words as they concern the interior, exalted, yearning life which many men achieve by virtues and the grace of God. Thirdly,° let us illumine them as they concern the supernatural life of the contemplation of God, which a few men can achieve in this manner or can savor, by way of their exalted and excellent form of living.

.   .   .   .   .

° [The material that follows is concerned entirely with this third point.—*Ed.*]

THE LIFE OF CONTEMPLATION OF GOD

. . . This contemplation establishes us in a purity which is above all our understanding, for it is a peculiar adornment and a heavenly crown and in addition an everlasting reward for all virtue and all life. And no-one can attain to this through knowledge or skill, nor with any exercise, but only he whom God will unite with Him in spirit, and will illumine with Himself, is able to contemplate God, and no-one else.

The secret nature of the Divinity, as it has the manner of the Persons, is everlastingly active in contemplation and love, and is everlastingly in delectation in the uniting of the Persons in the unity of Their essence. In this uniting in the essential unity of God all inward spirits are one with God in a loving flowing-out, and they are one in themselves, that same oneness that the Divine essence itself is, as they have the manner of blessedness. And in this high unity of the Divine natures, the heavenly Father is a source and a beginning of all the works that are worked in heaven and in earth. And He says in the hidden depths of our spirit: "See, the Bridegroom comes, go out towards Him."

Let us now make plain and expound these words as they concern a superessential contemplation, which is the foundation of all holiness and of all the life that men can live.

There are few who can attain to this Divine contemplation, because of men's own ineptitude and inability, and because the light by which men contemplate is a hidden light. And therefore no-one shall utterly understand the depths of what we now expound by means of any instruction or of any narrow observation of his own. For all words and everything which a man of his natural powers is able to learn and understand, all this is far beneath the truth which I mean, and foreign to it. But the man who is united with God and illumined by this truth, he is able, through the truth, to understand it. For to comprehend and understand God, above all use of image and analogy, as He is in Himself, that is to be God, with God, without mean or any inequality which could hinder us or make means. And therefore I desire that every man who does not in the delectable unity of his spirit understand or feel this, that he remain unperturbed and leave matters as they are. For what I wish to say is true, and Christ the everlasting Truth has Himself said it in His teachings in many places, if it were so that we could well reveal and show it. And therefore he who shall understand this must have died to himself and live in God, and he must turn his face to the eternal light in the depths of his spirit, where the secret truth reveals itself without mean.

"SEE." THE CONDITIONS FOR SEEING (CAP. I)

For the heavenly Father wishes that we should see, because He is a Father of light. And therefore He speaks eternally, without mean and without ceasing, in the secret places of our spirit, one single unfathomable word and nothing more. And in this word He enunciates Himself and all things. And this word is nothing else than 'See'; and this is the going-out and the birth of the Son of everlasting light, in Whom men recognize and see all blessedness.

A. *The Necessary Ability (cap. ii)*

If the spirit is now with God to contemplate God without means in this Divine light, there are three things which are necessary to man. The first is that he must be well ordered in all virtues from without, and that within he be unhindered, and that he be empty of all outward works, just as though he performed nothing. For if within he is preoccupied with any work of virtue, so he is distracted by images. As long as this lasts in him, he is unable to contemplate. Secondly, he must within depend upon God with compelling intention and love, just as a kindled and glowing fire that never again can be put out. And when he feels himself to be thus, then he is able to contemplate. Thirdly, he must have lost himself in a lack of manner, and in a darkness in which all contemplative men fare in delectation, and can never again find themselves in any way natural to the creature.

B. *The Illumining Word (cap. iii)*

In the depths of this darkness, in which the loving spirit has died to itself, begins the revelation of God and the eternal life. For in this darkness there shines and there is born an incomprehensible light, which is the Son of God, in Whom we contemplate eternal life. And in this light we see. And this Divine light is given in the simple being of the spirit, where the spirit receives the clarity which is God Himself. . . . And the spirit becomes immediately the very clarity which it receives.

Behold how this secret clarity in which man contemplates all that he has desired, in the manner of the emptiness of the spirit, this clarity is so great that the loving contemplative sees and feels in his depths where he rests nothing except an incomprehensible light. And according to the manner of this single nakedness which embraces all things, he finds himself and feels himself to be that very light by which he sees, and nothing else.

And in this you have the first point of how one sees in the Divine light. Blessed are the eyes that see thus, for they possess the eternal life.

"THE BRIDEGROOM COMES." THE ILLUMINATION, AND ITS EFFECT (CAP. IV)

After we have thus come to see, we may joyfully contemplate the eternal coming of our Bridegroom, and this is the second matter, of which we will now speak.

What is then this coming of our Bridegroom which is eternal? That is the new birth and a new illumination without cease. For the depths from which the clarity shines forth, and which are the clarity itself, are living and fruitful. And therefore the revelation of the eternal light is ceaselessly renewed in the hidden places of the spirit. Behold, all works of the creature and all exercises of virtue may here pass away, for here God alone is His only work in the highest excellence of the spirit. And here there is nothing else than an eternal contemplation and beholding of the light, with the light and in the light. And the coming of the Bridegroom is so swift that He is always come and is always dwelling within us with all His riches; and ceaselessly and ever and again He is coming in His own Person with new clarity, just as if He never were come before. For to be come consists in an eternal now, without time, which is constantly received in new joy and new delight.

Behold how the gladness and the joy which this Bridegroom brings in His coming are unfathomable and immeasurable, for so is He Himself. And therefore the eyes of the spirit, with which it contemplates and gazes upon its Bridegroom, are opened so wide that they never may be closed again. For this beholding and contemplating of the spirit remains eternally in the secret revelation of God, and the understanding of the spirit is opened so wide against the coming of the Bridegroom that the spirit itself becomes the wideness which it comprehends.

And so with God is God comprehended and seen, wherein lies all our blessedness. . . .

"GO OUT": OUR LIFE WITH GOD, REMAINING IN HIM AND FLOWING OUT FROM HIM, WHEN WE HAVE ATTAINED TO HIM, OUR FIRST IMAGE (CAP. V)

Now the Spirit of God says within the secret out-flowing of our spirit: 'Go out in an eternal contemplation and delectation, according to the manner of God.'

A. *The Reasons making possible this co-existence*

a. *That which God by His Nature possesses is possessed by us through love (cap. vi).* All the riches which are natural in God we possess through love in God, and God possesses them in us, through the immeasurable love which is the Holy Ghost. For in this love men savor everything for which they can yearn. And therefore through this love we die to ourselves and go forth in a loving flowing-out, in darkness, and lacking all manner. There the spirit is embraced in the Holy Trinity, eternally remaining in the superessential unity in rest and in delectation. And in this same unity, according to the manner of fruitfulness, the Father is in the Son and the Son in the Father, and all creatures are in Them both. And this is above any differentiation of Persons, for here, so far as reason is concerned, we understand the nature of Fatherhood and Sonhood in a living fruitfulness of the Divine natures.

b. *Our flowing-out in God, our first image, is cause of our being (cap. vii).* Out of this there springs and begins an everlasting going-out and an everlasting work without begining. For here is a beginning that has no beginning. For since the Almighty Father in the depths of His fruitfulness has perfectly comprehended Himself, the Son is the everlasting Word of the Father, proceeding forth as a Second Person in the Divinity. And through the everlasting birth, all creatures proceed forth everlastingly, before ever they have been created in time. So they have seen and acknowledged God in themselves, discreetly according to the *ratio vivens,* and with that difference which is His, not, however, a difference in every respect, for everything which is in God is God.

This everlasting going-out and this eternal life which we evermore have in God, and which we are without ourselves, this is a cause of our created being in time. . . . And this everlasting being and life which we have and are in the eternal wisdom of God, that is like to God. For it remains eternally without differentiation in the Divine Being, and it flows out eternally, through the birth of the Son, with difference and with differentiation according to the *ratio vivens.* And through these two points our being and life are so like to God that they ceaselessly acknowledge and imagine Him in this likeness as He is in Being and in Person. For even though, as the reason is concerned, all is here discretion and difference, this likeness is still one with that same image of the Holy Trinity which is the wisdom of God, in which God contemplates Himself and all things in an eternal instant before which nothing came, after which nothing goes. With a single glance He contemplates Himself and all things; and this is the image and likeness of God, and our image and likeness, for in this God makes the image of Himself and of all things. In this image like to God, all creatures have an everlasting life, outside themselves, as it were in their everlasting exemplar. And the Holy Trinity made us in this everlasting image and in this likeness.

B. How We Attain to God, our First Image, and how in Contemplation and Delectation with Him We remain in Him and Flow out from Him (cap. viii)

And therefore God would have us go forth from ourselves in this Divine light, and supernaturally attain to this image, which is our own life, and possess it with Him, operatively and in delectation, in everlasting blessedness. . . .

And therefore men who are inward and contemplative must go out, according to the maner of contemplation, beyond reason and beyond discretion; and beyond their created nature, with an everlasting beholding in this inborn light, and so they shall become transformed, and one with this same light by which they see, and which they are. And so contemplative men attain to that everlasting image in which they are made, and they contemplate God and all things without any discretion in a single act of beholding in Divine clarity. And this is the most excellent and the most profitable contemplation to which a man can attain in this life. For in this contemplation best of all does man remain free and master of himself, and he can increase in every meritorious form of living, each time that with love he turns inward, beyond all that men can understand. For he remains free and master of himself in inwardness and in virtue. And that beholding in the Divine light preserves him above all inwardness and above all virtue and above all merit, for it is the crown and the prize for which we strive, and which in this manner we now have and possess, for the life of contemplation is the light of heaven. . . .

This going-out of the contemplative man is also loving. For through delectable love he passes beyond his created nature, and finds and savors the riches and the joy which are God Himself, and which cause the secret places of the spirit to be immediately transfused, when now he stands made like to the high excellence of God.

"TO MEET HIM": THE LOVING ASCENT, THROUGH THE HOLY GHOST, TO
THE DELECTATION OF THE GODHEAD (CAP. IX)

When the inward contemplative man has thus attained his everlasting image, and in this purity, by means of the Son, possesses the bosom of the Father, he is illumined with Divine truth. And each hour he receives afresh the everlasting birth, and he goes out, according to the manner of the light, in a Divine contemplation. And from this there springs the fourth point and the last, which is a loving meeting, in which above all else our highest blessedness consists.

You shall know that the heavenly Father, as He is a living depth, has gone operatively with all that lives in Him into His Son, as into the everlasting wisdom which is He; and this same wisdom, and all that lives in it, is operatively returned again into the Father, that is into the same depths whence it proceeds. And from this meeting springs the third Person, between the Father and the Son, that is the Holy Ghost, the love of Them both, Who is one with both of Them in the same nature. And the Holy Ghost embraces and transfuses, operatively and in delectation, the Father and the Son and all that lives in Them, with so great riches and joy that concerning this all creatures must evermore be silent. For the incomprehensible miracle that lies in this love everlastingly exceeds the comprehension of all creatures. But in the spirit, above himself and one with the Spirit of God, man understands and savors this wonder without wonderment, and tastes and sees without measure as God does, the riches which are God, in the unity of the living depths where man possesses Him according to the manner of His uncreated being.

Then this most blessed meeting in us according to God's manner is ceaselessly renewed operatively. . . . For just as the Father ceaselessly contemplates all things anew in the birth of His Son, so all things are loved anew by the Father and by the Son in the flowing-out of the Holy Ghost.

And this is the operative meeting of the Father and of the Son in which we are lovingly embraced through the Holy Ghost in eternal love.

Now this operative meeting and this loving embrace are in their depths delectable and without manner. For God's impenetrable lack of manner is so dark and so without manner that in itself it comprehends all the Divine manners, and the work and the attributes of the Persons in the rich embrace of Their essential unity; and in the abyss of God's namelessness it makes a Divine delectation. And in this there is a delectable passing-over and a flowing-away and a sinking-down into the essential nakedness, with all the Divine names and all manners and all living reason which has its image in the mirror of Divine truth: all these fall away into this simple nakedness, wanting manner and without reason. For in this unfathomable joy of simplicity, all things are embraced in a delectable blessedness, and the depths

themselves remain uncomprehended, except it be in our essential
unity with God. Before this all created personality must fail, and all
that lives in God, for here there is nothing but an eternal resting in
a delectable embrace of the flowing-out of love.

And this is in the being without manner which all inward spirits
have chosen above all things. This is the dark silence in which all
lovers are lost. But could we thus, as I have told, so prepare ourselves in virtues, we should then hasten to divest ourselves of this
our mortal flesh, and we should launch ourselves on the waves of
this blessedness, and no creature could ever call us back again.

That we in delectation may possess this essential unity, and that
we may clearly contemplate Unity in Trinity, grant to us that Love
which denies no prayer addressed to its Divinity.

Amen. Amen.

24

MICHAEL DE MOLINOS

The Prayer of the Soul *

THE ADMONITIONS in the Preface form an admirable introduction to
the author's work. We are told that there are two ways of approaching God: meditation and contemplation. The first is for beginners;
the second, for proficients. Meditation and contemplation are defined and Molinos notes the signs of the transition from meditation
to contemplation. Perfect contemplation is explained here by a
lengthy and approving quotation from St. Theresa. The first part
of Book I adds little that is original to material already covered by

° From *The Spiritual Guide,* edited by Kathleen Lyttelton (Methuen and Co.,
Ltd., 1907), pp. 55, 58-66, 69, 73, 78-79, 85, 91-94, 97-101, 103-4, 116-17,
121-22, 139, 143-44, 152, 156, 168-69, 175, 177, 180, 185, 195-96, 198. Reprinted
with the permission of the publisher.

Michael de Molinos (1628-96) was born in Aragon. He was ordained a priest
in 1652 and in 1663 took up residence in Rome where he became a popular
preacher and writer. His *Spiritual Guide* exerted an enormous influence and became the source for the whole Quietist movement. The Quietism of Molinos
developed out of certain exaggerations in his doctrine of passive contemplation
and the Prayer of Quiet. The Inquisition condemned sixty-eight of his propositions
in 1685. He was imprisoned but later released and remained in Rome until his
death.

other mystics. But in the latter half of this book the author develops
with originality the notions of Internal Recollection, the Prayer of
Quiet, and Mystical Silence. After a brief comment on Obedience,
he returns again to the distinction between meditation and contemplation and classifies spiritual persons on this basis. He is particularly concerned here with the state of Infused Contemplation,
which is the inner way and for the very few. The sufferings of the
state of contemplation are described—a little too frighteningly at
times—and after noting the steps of Infused Contemplation
Molinos concludes with some comments on the final state of perfection to be attained by the soul in which it will be "overwhelmed
with nothingness."

PREFACE

FIRST ADMONITION

THERE ARE two ways of approaching God, the one by Consideration
and discursive thought, and the other by Pure Faith, an indistinct,
general and confused knowledge. The first is called Meditation, the
second Internal Recollection, or Acquired Contemplation. The first
is the way of Beginners, the second of Proficients. The first is sensible,
and material, the second detached, pure and interior.

SECOND ADMONITION

St. John Damascene and other Saints say, that Prayer is an ascent
or elevation of the mind to God. God is above all Creatures, and the
Soul cannot see Him, nor converse with Him, if she raise not herself above them all. This friendly conversation, which the Soul hath
with God, that is to say, Prayer, is divided into Meditation and Contemplation.

When the Mind, in order to move the affections of the will, considers the Mysteries of our holy Faith with attention, so as to know
their truth, reasoning upon the details, and weighing the circumstances, such mental Discourse and pious Act is properly called Meditation.

When the Soul already knows the truth and fixes the eyes of the
mind on the demonstrated truth, beholding it sincerely in quietness
and silence, without requiring considerations, reasonings or other
proofs in order to be convinced, and when the will loves the truth,
admiring and delighting itself therein, then this properly is called the
Prayer of Faith, the Prayer of Rest, Internal Recollection or Contemplation. . . . So if the Soul after she hath wearied herself

by means of Meditation, shall arrive at the stillness, tranquillity, and rest of Contemplation, she ought then to put an end to all discursive thought, and repose in the loving Contemplation and simple Vision of God . . . calming the Mind in that Divine Presence, collecting the Memory and fixing it wholly on God, contenting herself with the general and vague knowledge, which she has of God by means of Faith, with all the force of the will loving Him in whom rests all fruition. . . .

Good reason have the Saints to say, that Meditation operates with toil, and with fruit; Contemplation without toil, but with quiet, rest, peace, delight, and far greater fruit. Meditation sows, and Contemplation reaps; Meditation seeks, and Contemplation finds. . . .

THIRD ADMONITION

There are, moreover, two ways of Contemplation: the one imperfect, active and acquired; the other infused and passive. The active is that which may be obtained by our own diligence, the Divine Grace also assisting, and we gathering together the faculties and senses and preparing ourselves for everything that God wills.

.   .   .   .   .

Though it be said that we may with the Lord's help set ourselves to Acquired Contemplation, yet no man ought to be so bold, as to pass to it from the state of Meditation, without the counsel of an expert Director, who shall clearly know whether the Soul be called by God to this inward way. . . .

And to the end that the Soul may receive good Instruction with regard to this point, I will mention the Signs, whereby she shall know the Call to Contemplation. The first and chief is, an inability to Meditate, and if there be Meditation it will be performed with much disquiet and fatigue. . . .

The second Sign is, that though wanting in sensible Devotion, yet the Soul seeks Solitude, and avoids Conversation. The third, that the reading of Godly Books is usually tedious. . . . The fourth, that though the Soul finds her self deprived of discursive thought, yet does she firmly purpose to persevere in Prayer. The fifth is, that she will experience a great knowledge of herself, abhorring her sins, and perceiving better the holiness of God.

The other Contemplation is perfect and infused, *Wherein* (as St. Teresa says) *God speaks to a man, suspending his understanding, interrupting his thought, and taking (as they say) the word out of his*

mouth; so that if he would, he canot speak, except with great dif-
ficulty. He understands that without the noise of words, the Divine
Master is instructing him, suspending all his powers and faculties,
because if at that time they should operate, they would do more hurt
than good. They enjoy, but know not how they enjoy; the Soul is
burning with love, yet understands not how she loves; she perceives
that she enjoys what she loves, and knows not the manner of that
enjoyment; she knows that it is not an enjoyment which the under-
standing can come to desire. The Will embraces it, without knowing
how; but being unable to understand any thing, it yet perceives that
this is not a good which can be merited, even were all the labors
put together which can be suffered upon earth for the gaining thereof.
It is a gift of the Lord of the Earth and of Heaven, Who in fine gives
by His own power, to whom He pleases and as He pleases. . . .
His Majesty it is that doth all, for it is His work surpassing our nature.

FOURTH ADMONITION

The way of inner peace consists in conforming ourselves in all
things to the Divine Will. . . . O Souls! if we should submit our
own will to the Divine Will, and to all His orderings, what tranquillity
should we feel, what sweet peace, what inward serenity, what supreme
felicity and earnest of bliss! This, then, is to be the burden of this
book. . . .

THE FIRST BOOK
OF THE DARKNESS, DRYNESS, AND TEMPTATIONS WHEREWITH
GOD PURGES SOULS, AND OF INTERNAL RECOLLECTION

Thou art to know, that thy Soul is the Centre, Habitation, and
Kingdom of God. That therefore, to the end the Sovereign King may
rest on that Throne, thou oughtest to take pains to keep thy Soul
pure, quiet, void and peaceable; pure from guilt and defects; quiet
from fears; void of affections, desires and thoughts; and peaceable
in temptations and tribulations. . . .

It ought to be thy chief and continual exercise, to pacifie that
Throne of thy Heart, so that the Supreme King may rest therein. The
way to pacifie it, will be, to enter into thy self by means of internal
recollection; all thy protection is to be Prayer, and a loving recollection, in the Divine Presence.

So in the Beginning, when God intends after an extraordinary manner, to guide the Soul into the School of Divine and loving Knowledge of the internal Law, He causes her to suffer Darkness, and Dryness, that He may bring her near to Himself, because the Divine

Majestie knows very well, that it is not by the means of her own reasoning or Industry, that a Soul draws near to Him, and understands the Divine Precepts, but rather by silent and humble resignation.

What most concerns thee, O redeemed Soul, is Patience, and not to desist from Prayer, though thou can'st not enlarge in discursive thought. Walk with a firm Faith, and in a holy Silence, dying to thy self, to all thy natural efforts, because He that Is and changeth not, neither can err, intends no thing but thy good. It is clear that he who is a dying, must needs Suffer; but how well is time employed, when the Soul is dead, dumb, and resigned in the presence of God, there without trouble or perplexity, to receive the Divine Influences. . . .

Those Souls are surely infinitely to be pitied who from the beginning of their Life to the end, employ themselves in mere Meditation, constraining themselves to Reason, although God Almighty is depriving them of reasoning, that He may promote them to another State, and carry them on to a more perfect kind of Prayer. . . .

Thou shalt know that there are two sorts of Prayer, the one tender, delightful, loving, and full of emotions; the other obscure, dry, desolate, tempted and darksome. The first is that of Beginners, the second of Proficients who are in the progress to Perfection. God gives the first to gain Souls, the second to purifie them. With the first He treats them like Children and Weaklings; with the second He begins to deal with them as with strong men.

Be sure, that dryness is the Instrument of thy Good, because it is this very deprivation of sensible Pleasure, which arrests the progress of almost all pious Men, and makes them even turn back, and leave off Prayer: as may be seen in many Souls, which only persevere whil'st they taste sensible Consolation.

Know that the Lord makes use of the Veil of Dryness, to the end we may not understand what He is working in us, and so be humble; because if we felt and knew what He is working in our Souls, satisfaction and presumption would get in, we should imagine that we were doing some good thing, and reckon ourselves very near to God; which would be our undoing.

.   .   .   .   .

There are two sorts of darknesses; some unhappy, and others happy; the first are such as arise from sin, and these are unhappy, because they lead the Christian to eternal death. The second are those which the Lord suffers to be in the Soul, to establish and settle her in virtue;

and these are happy, because they illumine the Soul, fortifie her, and give her greater light. . . .

Know then that the straightest, most perfect and secure way for Proficients, is the way of darknesses; because in them the Lord placed his own Throne. *He made darkness His secret place.* By them the supernatural light, which God instills into the Soul, grows and increases. Amidst them wisdom and strong love are begotten. By them the Soul is annihilated, and the images, which hinder the right view of the Divine Truth, are consumed. By this means God leads the Soul by the Inward Way into the Prayer of Quiet, and of perfect Contemplation, experienced by so few. Finally, by them the Lord purges the senses and the sensibility which hinder the mystical progress.

So soon as thou shalt firmly resolve to mortify thy external senses, that thou mayest advance towards the high mountain of Perfection, and Union with God, His Divine Majesty will set His hand to the purging of thy evil inclinations, inordinate desires, vain complacency, self-love and pride, and other hidden vices, which thou knowest not, and which yet reign in the inner parts of thy Soul, and hinder the Divine Union.

Thou wilt never attain to this happy state, though thou tire thy self out with external acts of mortification and resignation, until the Lord purge thee inwardly, and discipline thee after His own way. . . .

God will do all this in thy Soul by means of the Cross and dry-nesses, if thou freely givest thy consent by resignation. . . . That which thou hast to do is to subject thine own will, and to give up acting by thine own choice, quietly resigning thyself to everything whereby the Lord shall think fit internally and externally to discipline thee. . . .

It concerns thee then, to make thy heart, like a white sheet of paper, whereon the Divine Wisdom may imprint characters to His own liking. . . .

In order that the Soul may be the habitation of the celestial King, it is necessary that she should be pure, and without any blemish; therefore the Lord purifies her as gold in the furnace of terrible and grievous temptations. Certain it is, that the soul never loves, nor believes more, than when she is afflicted and baited with such temptations; because these doubtings and fears that beset her, whether she believe or not, whether she consent or not, are nothing else but the refinements of love.

Thou art to know then, that temptation is thy great happiness; so that the more it besets thee, the more thou oughtest to rejoice in peace, instead of being sad; and to thank God for the favor He does thee. . . .

The Saints, in attaining to holiness, passed through this doleful valley of temptation, and the greater Saints they were the greater temptations they grappled with. . . .

Finally, thou art to know, that the greatest Temptation is to be without Temptation, wherefore thou oughtest to be glad when it shall assault thee, and with Resignation, Peace and Constancy resist it.

Internal Recollection is Faith and Silence in the Presence of God. Hence thou oughtest to be accustomed to recollect thyself in His Presence, with a loving intentness, as one that gives himself to God and is united unto Him, with Reverence, Humility and Submission. . . .

No sooner wilt thou have given thyself up to thy Lord in this inward Way, than all Hell will conspire against thee; because one single Soul wholly withdrawn into herself before Him, makes greater War against the Enemy than a thousand that walk externally; for he knows the infinite gain of a Recollected Soul.

God loves not him who does most, who feels most, nor who shows greatest affection, but him who suffers most, if he pray with faith and reverence, believing that he is in the Divine Presence. It is true that to deprive the Soul of the prayer of the Senses, and of Nature, is a rigorous martyrdom for her, but the Lord rejoices, and is glad in her peace, if she be thus quiet and resigned. Use not at that time vocal Prayer, because however good and holy it be in itself, yet to use it then, is a manifest temptation, whereby the enemy asserts that God speaks not to thy heart, because thou hast no emotional experiences, and that thus thou losest time.

God hath not regard to the multitude of words, but to the purity of the intent. His greatest content and glory at that time is to see the Soul in silence, desirous, humble, quiet and resigned. Proceed, persevere, pray, and hold thy peace; for where thou findest not emotion, thou wilt find a door whereby thou mayest enter into thine own Nothingness; knowing thyself to be nothing, that thou can'st do nothing, nay, and that thou hast not so much as a good thought.

I will conclude this Chapter by undeceiving thee of the vulgar error of those who say, that in this internal Recollection, or Prayer of Rest, the faculties operate not, and that the Soul is idle and wholly inactive. This is a manifest fallacy of those who have little experience, because although she operate not by means of the memory, nor by the second operation of the understanding, which is the judgment, nor by the third, which is reasoning, yet she operates by the first and chief operation of the understanding, which is simple apprehension, enlightened by holy Faith, and aided by the divine gifts of the Holy Spirit. And the Will is more intent on continuing one act, than on multiplying many; so that the act of the understanding, as well as that of the Will, are so simple, imperceptible, and spiritual, that hardly the Soul knows them, and far less does it reflect upon them.

When thou goest to Prayer, thou shouldest deliver thy self wholly up into the hands of God with perfect resignation, making an act of Faith, believing that thou standest in the Divine Presence, afterwards remaining in that holy repose, with quietness, silence and tranquillity; and endeavoring for a whole day, a whole year, and thy whole life to continue that first act of Contemplation, by faith and love.

Thou shouldest not endeavor to multiply these actions, nor to repeat conscious aspirations, because they hinder the purity of the spiritual and perfect act of the Will; whilst also these sweet sentiments are imperfect (because of the consciousness wherewith they are made, and the self-gratification and desire for external consolation which accompanies them, the Soul diverting herself outwardly to the exterior faculties); there is no necessity for renewing them, as the mystic Falcone has excellently explained in the following analogy:—

If a Jewel be given to a friend, and it be once committed to him, it is not necessary to repeat such a donation, by daily saying, "Sir, I give you that Jewel, Sir, I give you that Jewel," but to let him keep it, and not take it from him; because so long as thou takest it not, or desirest not to take it from him, thou hast surely given it him.

Thou oughtest then to slight all those sensibilities, to the end thy Soul may be established, and may acquire a habit of internal recollection, which is of such efficacy, that the mere resolution of going to prayer awakens a lively sense of the presence of God, which is the preparation for the Prayer that is about to be made; or rather, it is no other than a more efficacious continuation of continual Prayer, wherein the contemplative person ought to establish himself.

Oh how few are the Souls that attain to this perfect way of praying, because they penetrate not enough into this internal recollection and Mystical Silence. and because they strip not themselves of imperfect reflection and sensible pleasure! Oh that thy Soul without thoughtful attention even to herself, might give herself up to that holy and spiritual tranquility, and say with S. Augustine *Let my soul be silent and pass by herself, not thinking of herself.* Let her be silent, and desire neither to act nor to think, let her forget herself and plunge into that obscure faith. How secure and safe would she be; though it might appear to her that abiding thus in Nothingness, she is undone.

There are three kinds of Silences; the first is of Words, the second of Desires, and the third of Thoughts. The first is perfect, the second more perfect, and the third most perfect. In the first, that is of Words, Virtue is acquired; in the second, to wit of Desires, Quietness is obtained; and in the third, that of Thoughts, Internal Recollection. By not speaking, not desiring, and not thinking, the true and perfect Mystical Silence is reached, wherein God speaks with the Soul, communicates Himself to her, and in her inmost depth teaches her the most perfect and exalted Wisdom.

The perfection of the Soul consists not in speaking nor in thinking much on God, but in loving Him greatly: This love is acquired by means of perfect Resignation and inner Silence, it all consists in deeds. The love of God has but few Words. Thus does St. John the Evangelist confirm this saying: *My little Children, let us not love in Word, neither with the Tongue; but in Deed and in Truth.*

THE SECOND BOOK
OF OBEDIENCE, OF INDISCREET ZEAL; AND OF INTERNAL AND EXTERNAL PENANCE *

Thou wilt never attain to the Mountain of Perfection, nor to the high Throne of Internal Peace, if thou governest thyself according to thy own Will. This cruel and fierce Enemy of God, and of thy Soul, must be conquered, thy own Direction, thy own Judgment must be subjugated and deposed as Rebels, and reduced to Ashes in the Fire of Obedience. There thou wilt learn as by a Touch-stone, whether thou followest self love or the Divine Love, there in that Holocaust must thine own Judgment, and thine own Will be entirely Annihilated even to the last substance.

Obedience (according to St. Bonaventura) *must be ready, without delay, Devout without wearying, Voluntary without contradiction, Simple without examination, Persevering without resting, Orderly without deviation, Pleasant without trouble, Valiant without faintheartedness, and Universal without exception.* Remember, O blessed

---

* [The selections from the much shorter second book have been limited to a few passages on Obedience.—*Ed.*]

Soul, that if thou hast a mind to do the divine Will, with all diligence, thou wilt never find the way, but by the means of Obedience.   .   .   .

THE THIRD BOOK
OF SPIRITUAL MARTYRDOMS WHEREBY GOD PURGES SOULS; OF
CONTEMPLATION, INFUSED AND PASSIVE; OF PERFECT
RESIGNATION, INNER HUMILITY, DIVINE WISDOM,
TRUE ANNIHILATION, AND INTERNAL PEACE

There are two sorts of Spiritual Persons, Internal and External. The former seek God from without, by Reasonings, by the Imagination and by Considerings: they endeavor painfully to obtain Virtues, by means of many abstinences, Macerations of the Body, and Mortificaions of the Senses: they give themselves to rigorous Penances, they put on Hair-cloth, chastise the flesh by Discipline, strive after Silence. . . . they delight in continually speaking of God, very often making fervent Acts of Love; and all this is skill and Meditation. . . . This is the External Way, and the Way of Beginners, and though it be good, yet by it there is no arriving at Perfection. . . .

There are other truly Spiritual men, who have passed beyond the beginning of the Inner Way which leads to Perfection and Union with God. . . . These men, withdrawn into the inner parts of their Souls, resigning themselves wholly into the Hands of God, having forgotten and despoiled themselves of everything, even of themselves, do always go with an uplifted Spirit into the Presence of the Lord, by the means of pure Faith, without Image, Form or Figure, but with great assurance, founded in tranquillity and inner rest: in which infused Recollection the spirit gathers itself with such force, that it concentrates thereon the mind, heart, body and all the physical powers.

But know that few are the Souls which arrive at this happy State. . . . The Lord said to a Soul, "This inner Way is for the few; it is so high a Grace, that none deserves it: few walk in it, because it is no other than a Death of the senses; and few there be that are willing so to Die and be Annihilated in which disposition this so sovereign a Gift is founded."

Herewith thou wilt undeceive thy self, and perfectly know the great difference which there is between the outer and inner Way, and how different is that Presence of God which arises from Meditation, from that Infused and Supernatural Presence, which is born of inner and infused Recollection, and of passive Contemplation; and lastly, thou wilt know the great difference which exists between the outer and the inner Man.

To the end that the earthly Soul may become heavenly, and may attain to the great good of Union with God, it is necessary for it to be purified in the Fire of Tribulation and Temptation. And although it be true, and well known, that all those who serve the Lord must suffer troubles, persecutions and tribulations, yet the happy Souls which are guided by God by the secret way of the inner Path, and of purgative Contemplation, must suffer above all strong and horrible Temptations and Torments, more bitter than those wherewith the Martyrs were crowned in the Primitive Church.

The Martyrs, besides the shortness of their Torment, which hardly endured days, comforted themselves by clear light and special help in the hope of near and sure rewards. But the desolate Soul must die in her self . . . seeing her self abandoned by God, surrounded by temptations, darkness, anguish, affliction, sorrows . . . doth taste Death at every moment, in her painful Torment and tremendous Desolation; without feeling the least comfort, and with an affliction so great, that the pain of it seems nothing else but a prolonged Death, and a continual Martyrdom. . . .

Although this painful martyrdom of horrible desolation and passive purgation be so tremendous, that with reason it hath gotten the name of Hell amongst Mystics; . . . yet know, that it is necessary to endure it, in order to reach the sweet, joyous and abundant riches of high Contemplation and loving Union; and there has been no holy Soul, which has not passed through this spiritual martyrdom and painful torment.

Great is the difference which lies between doing, suffering, and dying. Doing is delightful and belongs to Beginners; suffering, with desire, belongs to those who are Proficients; dying to themselves, belongs to those who are accomplished and perfect; of which number there are very few in the world.

. . . . .

And that thou mayst be acquainted with inner and true Humility, know, that it doth not consist in external Acts in taking the lowest place, in going poorly clothed, in speaking submissively, in shutting the eyes, in affectionate sighing, nor in accusing thyself of faults, and calling thy self miserable so as to give others to understand that thou art humble. It consists only in the contempt of thyself, and in the desire to be despised, a desire proceeding from a profound knowledge, so that thou shalt not believe thyself to be humble, even though an angel reveal it to thee.

Have no Mind to be esteemed, when God incarnate was called fool, drunkard, and said to have a Devil. O the Folly of Christians! That we should desire to enjoy Happiness without desiring to imitate Him on the Cross, in Reproaches, Humility, Poverty, and in other Virtues!

.   .   .   .   .

Thou must know, that when once the Soul is accustomed to the internal Recollection, and acquired Contemplation, of which we have spoken, . . . then God is wont to withdraw her and to raise her up, without her own knowledge to a complete repose, where He sweetly and intimately infuses into her His light, His Love, and His Strength. . . .

. . . There the Soul, raised and uplifted into this passive State, finds herself united to the Highest Good, although this Union costs her no fatigue. . . .

Simple, pure, infused, and perfect Contemplation, therefore, is a known and inner manifestation which God gives of Himself, of His Goodness, of His Peace, and of His Sweetness, whose object is God, pure, ineffable, abstracted from all particular thoughts, within an inward Silence. But it is God Who delights us, God Who draws us, God Who sweetly raises us in a spiritual and pure manner; and all this is an admirable gift, which the Divine Majesty bestows on whom He wills, as He wills, and when He wills, and for what time He wills, even though the state of this Life be rather a state of the Cross, of patience, of humility, and of suffering, than of enjoyment.

Never wilt thou enjoy this Divine Nectar till thou art advanced in Virtue and inner Mortification; till thou dost heartily endeavor to possess in thy Soul a great Peace, silence, forgetfulness and internal Solitude. . . .

The steps of infused Contemplation are three. The first is Satiety, when the Soul is filled with God, and conceives a hatred for all worldly things, then she is quiet and satisfied only with Divine Love.

The second is Inebriation. And this step is a mental Excess, and an Elevation of Soul, born of Divine Love and its fullness.

The third is Security. This step casts out all fear: for the Soul is so imbued with Divine Love, and so resigned to the Divine pleasure, that she would go willingly to Hell, if she did but know this to be the will of the Most High. . . .

The Divine Wisdom is an intellectual and infused knowledge of the Divine Perfections and of the things Eternal which ought rather to be called Contemplation than Speculation. Science is acquired, and begets the knowledge of Nature. Wisdom is infused and begets the knowledge of the Divine Goodness. The former desires to know what is not to be attained unto without pains and effort: the latter desires not even to know what it doth know, although it understands everything. In a word, scientific men entertain themselves with the knowledge of the things of the world; and the wise live absorbed in God Himself.

. . . . .

The way to attain to that high state of a Mind reformed, whereby we may attain to the Highest Good, to the First Cause, and to perfect Peace, is Nothingness. Endeavor, O Soul, to be always buried in that abasement. This Nothingness, and this acknowledged abasement, is the means by which the Lord works wonders in thy Soul. . . .

O what a strong Bulwark wilt thou find in that Nothingness. Who can ever afflict thee, if once thou dost retire into that Fortress? . . .

. . . Keeping thyself in Nothingness, thou wilt bar the door against everything that is not God; thou wilt retire also from thine own self, and journey towards that internal Solitude, where the Divine Bridegroom speaks in the Heart of His Bride, teaching her high and divine Wisdom. Drown thyself in this Nothingness and there shalt thou find a holy Sanctuary against any Tempest whatsoever. . . . Lastly, consider Nothing, desire Nothing, will Nothing, endeavor after Nothing, and then in every thing thy Soul will live reposed, with quiet and enjoyment.

This is the way to obtain purity of Soul, perfect Contemplation and Inner Peace; walk therefore in this safe path, and endeavor to be overwhelmed in this Nothingness, to lose thy self, to sink deep into it, if thou hast a mind to be annihilated, united and transformed.

25

GEORGE FOX

The Inner Light *

Fox's early religious experiences reveal all the essential features of his mysticism. Significant were his deeply religious childhood and his adolescent years when doubts, temptations, and despair culminated in the first of many "openings" in 1646, in which God revealed to him that all true believers are born of God. The *Autobiography* then describes the occurrence of successive revelations or "openings" concerning the qualifications for the ministry, Fox's belief that God lives in people's hearts rather than in churches, and his belief that the Book of Revelations has been explained to him. Though he received many "openings" in this way, Fox relates that he was still somewhat troubled in mind, not knowing what to believe and losing all hope and confidence in priests and preachers. At this point there occurs the decisive "opening" that "There is one, even Christ Jesus, that can speak to thy condition"; here was the revelation, known to him experimentally, as he says, that it is Christ who enlightens, who gives grace and faith and power. Following this insight he begins preaching to the people; his religious travail is ended and he has, as he says: "been brought through the very ocean of darkness and death . . . by the eternal and glorious power of Christ." The first years of his ministry now begin and new and more abundant "openings" are received. Of these the most significant is the revelation that all men are "enlightened by the Light of Christ"—that we all possess the inner light. The concluding pages of this selection summarize the purposes and achievements of his religious career.

BOYHOOD—A SEEKER
(1624–1648)

IN MY very young years I had a gravity and stayedness of mind and spirit not usual in children. . . .

* From *Autobiography,* edited by Rufus Jones (Philadelphia: Ferris and Leach, 1919), pp. 66-108.

George Fox (1624-91) was born at Drayton, England. Of his later career (beyond that covered by the chapters in our selection) we note merely his numerous imprisonments, his marriage to Margaret Fell in 1669, his visits to Jamaica and America 1671-73, his visits to Holland in 1677 and 1684, and his retirement until his death in London. These were all years of intense proseletyzing

When I came to eleven years of age I knew pureness and righteousness; for while a child I was taught how to walk to be kept pure. The Lord taught me to be faithful in all things, and to act faithfully two ways, viz. inwardly, to God, and outwardly, to man; and to keep to Yea and Nay in all things. . . .

As I grew up, my relations thought to have made me a priest,* but others persuaded to the contrary. Whereupon I was put to a man who was a shoe maker by trade, and dealt in wool. . . . While I was with him he was blessed, but after I left him he broke and came to nothing.

I never wronged man or woman in all that time; for the Lord's power was with me and over me, to preserve me. While I was in that service I used in my dealings the word Verily, and it was a common saying among those that knew me, "If George says verily, there is no altering him." When boys and rude persons would laugh at me, I let them alone and went my way; but people had generally a love to me for my innocency and honesty.

Then, at the command of God, the ninth of the Seventh month, 1643, I left my relations, and broke off all familiarity or fellowship with young or old. . . . As I traveled through the country, professors ** took notice of me, and sought to be acquainted with me; but I was afraid of them, for I was sensible they did not possess what they professed.

During the time I was at Barnet a strong temptation to despair came upon me. I then saw how Christ was tempted, and mighty troubles I was in. Sometimes I kept myself retired to my chamber, and often walked solitary in the Chase to wait upon the Lord. I wondered why these things should come to me. I looked upon myself, and said, "Was I ever so before?" Then I thought, because I had forsaken my relations I had done amiss against them.

So I was brought to call to mind all my time that I had spent, and to consider whether I had wronged any; but temptations grew more and more, and I was tempted almost to despair; and when Satan could not effect his design upon me that way, he laid snares and baits to draw me to commit some sin, whereof he might take advantage to bring me to despair.

---

activity and organizational work for the Society of Friends, which he founded.

* The word is usually employed for any minister who receives pay for preaching. [This and later footnotes to this selection from Fox are editorial comments by Rufus Jones.—*Ed.*]

** "Professor" means here and everywhere through this book, a nominal Christian.

I was about twenty years of age when these exercises came upon me; and some years I continued in that condition, in great trouble; and fain I would have put it from me. I went to many a priest to look for comfort, but found no comfort from them.

From Barnet I went to London, where I took a lodging, and was under great misery and trouble there; for I looked upon the great professors of the city of London, and saw all was dark and under the chain of darkness. . . .

Being returned into Leicestershire, my relations would have had me married; but I told them I was but a lad, and must get wisdom. . . . Then I went to Coventry, where I took a chamber for a while at a professor's house, till people began to be acquainted with me, for there were many tender * people in that town. After some time I went into my own country again, and continued about a year, in great sorrow and trouble, and walked many nights by myself.

Then the priest of Drayton, the town of my birth, whose name was Nathaniel Stephens, came often to me, and I went often to him; and another priest sometimes came with him; and they would give place to me, to hear me; and I would ask them questions, and reason with them. This priest, Stephens, asked me why Christ cried out upon the cross, "My God, my God, why hast thou forsaken me?" and why He said, "If it be possible, let this cup pass from me; yet not my will, but thine, be done"? I told him that at that time the sins of all mankind were upon Him, and their iniquities and transgressions, with which He was wounded; which He was to bear, and to be an offering for, as He was man; but died not, as He was God; so, in that He died for all men, tasting death for every man, He was an offering for the sins of the whole world.

This I spoke, being at that time in a measure sensible of Christ's sufferings. The priest said it was a very good, full answer, and such a one as he had not heard. . . .

After this I went to another, one Macham, a priest in high account. He would needs give me some physic, and I was to have been let blood; but they could not get one drop of blood from me, either in arms or head (though they endeavored to do so), my body being, as it were, dried up with sorrows, grief and troubles, which were so great upon me that I could have wished I had never been born, or that I had been born blind, that I might never have seen wickedness or vanity: and deaf, that I might never have heard vain and wicked words, or the Lord's name blasphemed.

* Persons religiously inclined, serious, and earnest in their search for spiritual realities.

About the beginning of the year 1646, as I was going to Coventry, and approaching towards the gate, a consideration arose in me, how it was said that "All Christians are believers, both Protestants and Papists;" and the Lord opened * to me that if all were believers, then they were all born of God, and passed from death to life; and that none were true believers but such; and, though others said they were believers, yet they were not. At another time, as I was walking in a field on a First-day morning, the Lord opened unto me that being bred at Oxford or Cambridge was not enough to fit and qualify men to be ministers of Christ; and I wondered at it, because it was the common belief of people. But I saw it clearly as the Lord opened it unto me, and I was satisfied, and admired the goodness of the Lord, who had opened this thing unto me that morning. So that which opened in me I saw struck at the priest's ministry.

But my relations were much troubled that I would not go with them to hear the priest; for I would go into the orchard or the fields, with my Bible, by myself. I asked them, "Did not the Apostle say to believers that they needed no man to teach them, but as the anointing teacheth them?". . . . So neither them, nor any of the dissenting people, could I join with; but was as a stranger to all, relying wholly upon the Lord Jesus Christ.

At another time it was opened in me that God, who made the world, did not dwell in temples made with hands. This at first seemed a strange word, because both priests and people used to call their temples, or churches, dreadful places, holy ground, and the temples of God. But the Lord showed me clearly that He did not dwell in these temples which men had commanded and set up, but in people's hearts. . . .

I had also great openings concerning the things written in the Revelations; and when I spoke of them the priests and professors would say that was a sealed book, and would have kept me out of it. But I told them Christ could open the seals, and that they were the nearest things to us, for the epistles were written to the saints that lived in former ages, but the Revelations were written of things to come.

.   .   .   .   .

* The expression "opened" has a mystical import, and will be of frequent occurrence. He means to say that it was directly revealed in his soul so that he assuredly knew it to be true. Often he uses the expression in reference to some truth which he might easily have discovered in the Scriptures or have learned from contemporary sources. But in this solemn way he announces that this truth has now at length come to be a *living truth for him*. It is no longer a mere statement of fact—it is a principle, the truth of which he *sees*.

. . . I fasted much, walked abroad in solitary places many days, and often took my Bible, and sat in hollow trees and lonesome places till night came on; and frequently in the night walked mournfully about by myself; for I was a man of sorrow in the time of the first workings of the Lord in me.

During all this time I was never joined in profession of religion with any, but gave myself up to the Lord, having forsaken all evil company, taken leave of father and mother, and all other relations, and travelled up and down as a stranger in the earth, which way the Lord inclined my heart; taking a chamber to myself in the town where I came, and tarrying, sometimes more, sometimes less, in a place. For I durst not stay long in a place, being afraid both of professor and profane, lest, being a tender young man, I should be hurt by conversing much with either. For this reason I kept much as a stranger, seeking heavenly wisdom and getting knowledge from the Lord, and was brought off from outward things to rely on the Lord alone.

Though my exercises and troubles were very great, yet they were not so continual but that I had some intermissions, and I was sometimes brought into such an heavenly joy that I thought I had been in Abraham's bosom.

As I cannot declare the misery I was in, it was so great and heavy upon me, so neither can I set forth the mercies of God unto me in all my misery. O the everlasting love of God to my soul, when I was in great distress! When my troubles and torments were great, then was His love exceeding great. Thou, Lord, makest a fruitful field a barren wilderness, and a barren wilderness a fruitful field! Thou bringest down and settest up! Thou killest and makest alive! all honor and glory be to thee, O Lord of Glory! The knowledge of Thee in the Spirit is life; but that knowledge which is fleshly works death.

.   .   .   .   .

. . . Now, after I had received that opening from the Lord, that to be bred at Oxford or Cambridge was not sufficient to fit a man to be a minister of Christ, I regarded the priests less, and looked more after the Dissenting people. Among them I saw there was some tenderness; and many of them came afterwards to be convinced, for they had some openings.

But as I had forsaken the priests, so I left the separate preachers also, and those esteemed the most experienced people; for I saw there was none among them all that could speak to my condition. When all my hopes in them and in all men were gone, so that I had nothing outwardly to help me, nor could I tell what to do, then, oh, then, I heard a voice which said, "There is one, even Christ Jesus, that can speak to thy condition"; and when I heard it, my heart did leap for joy.

Then the Lord let me see why there was none upon the earth that could speak to my condition, namely, that I might give Him all the glory. For all are concluded under sin, and shut up in unbelief, as I had been; that Jesus Christ might have the preeminence, who enlightens, and gives grace, and faith, and power. Thus when God doth work, who shall hinder it? and *this I knew experimentally.*

My desire after the Lord grew stronger, and zeal in the pure knowledge of God, and of Christ alone, without the help of any man, book, or writing. For though I read the Scriptures that spoke of Christ and of God, yet I knew Him not, but by revelation, as He who hath the key did open, and as the Father of Life drew me to His Son by His Spirit. Then the Lord gently led me along, and let me see His love, which was endless and eternal, surpassing all the knowledge that men have in the natural state, or can obtain from history or books and that love let me see myself, as I was without Him.

. . . When I myself was in the deep, shut up under all, I could not believe that I should ever overcome; my troubles, my sorrows, and my temptations were so great that I thought many times I should have despaired, I was so tempted. But when Christ opened to me how He was tempted by the same devil, and overcame him and bruised his head, and that through Him and His power, light, grace, and Spirit, I should overcome also, I had confidence in Him; so He it was that opened to me when I was shut up and had no hope nor faith. Christ, who had enlightened me, gave me His light to believe in; He gave me hope, which He Himself revealed in me, and He gave me His Spirit and grace, which I found sufficient in the deeps and in weakness.

Thus, in the deepest miseries, and in the greatest sorrows and temptations, that many times beset me, the Lord in His mercy did keep me.

I found that there were two thirsts in me—the one after the creatures,° to get help and strength there, and the other after the Lord, the Creator, and His Son Jesus Christ. I saw all the world could do me no good; if I had had a king's diet, palace, and attendance, all would have been as nothing; for nothing gave me comfort but the Lord by His power. At another time I saw the great love of God, and was filled with admiration at the infiniteness of it.

One day, when I had been walking solitarily abroad, and was come home, I was taken up in the love of God, so that I could not but

---

° "creatures" here and frequently means "created things."

admire the greatness of His love; and while I was in that condition, it was opened unto me by the eternal light and power, and I therein clearly saw that all was done and to be done in and by Christ, and how He conquers and destroys this tempter the devil, and all his works, and is atop of him; and that all these troubles were good for me, and temptations for the trial of my faith, which Christ had given me.

The Lord opened me, that I saw all through these troubles and temptations. My living faith was raised, that I saw all was done by Christ the life, and my belief was in Him.

. . . About this time there was a great meeting of the Baptists, at Broughton, in Leicestershire, with some that had separated from them, and people of other notions went thither, and I went also. Not many of the Baptists came, but many others were there. The Lord opened my mouth, and the everlasting truth was declared amongst them, and the power of the Lord was over them all. For in that day the Lord's power began to spring, and I had great openings in the Scriptures. Several were convinced in those parts and were turned from darkness to light, from the power of Satan unto God, and many were raised up to praise God. . . .

. . . . .

Then came people from far and near to see me; but I was fearful of being drawn out by them; yet I was made to speak, and open things to them. There was one Brown, who had great prophecies and sights upon his death-bed of me. He spoke only of what I should be instrumental by the Lord to bring forth. And of others he spoke, that they should come to nothing, which was fulfilled on some, who then were something in show.

When this man was buried a great work of the Lord fell upon me, to the admiration of many, who thought I had been dead, and many came to see me for about fourteen days. I was very much altered in countenance and person, as if my body had been new moulded or changed. My sorrows and troubles began to wear off, and tears of joy dropped from me, so that I could have wept night and day with tears of joy to the Lord, in humility and brokenness of heart.

I saw into that which was without end, things which cannot be uttered, and of the greatness and infinitude of the love of God, which cannot be expressed by words. For I had been brought through the very ocean of darkness and death, and through and over the power of Satan, by the eternal, glorious power of Christ; even through that darkness was I brought, which covered over all the world, and which chained down all and shut up all in death. The same eternal power of God, which brought me through these things, was that which afterwards shook the nations, priests, professors and people.

Then could I say I had been in spiritual Babylon, Sodom, Egypt, and the grave; but by the eternal power of God I was come out of it, and was brought over it, and the power of it, into the power of Christ. I saw the harvest white, and the seed of God lying thick in the ground, as ever did wheat that was sown outwardly, and none to gather it; for this I mourned with tears.

A report went abroad of me, that I was a young man that had a discerning spirit; whereupon many came to me, from far and near, professors, priests, and people. The Lord's power broke forth, and I had great openings and prophecies, and spoke unto them of the things of God, which they heard with attention and silence, and went away and spread the fame thereof.

THE FIRST YEARS OF MINISTRY
(1648–1649)

After this I went to Mansfield, where was a great meeting of professors and people. Here I was moved to pray; and the Lord's power was so great that the house seemed to be shaken. When I had done, some of the professors said it was now as in the days of the apostles, when the house was shaken where they were. . . .

Soon after there was another great meeting of professors, and a captain, whose name was Amor Stoddard, came in. They were discoursing of the blood of Christ; and as they were discoursing of it, I saw, through the immediate opening of the invisible Spirit, the blood of Christ. And I cried out among them, and said, "Do ye not see the blood of Christ? See it in your hearts, to sprinkle your hearts and consciences from dead works, to serve the living God"; for I saw it, the blood of the New Covenant, how it came into the heart.° . . . This startled the professors, who would have the blood only without them, and not in them. . . .

Now, after I had some service in these parts, I went through Derbyshire into my own county, Leicestershire, again, and several tender people were convinced.

.   .   .   .   .

After this I returned into Nottinghamshire again, and went into the Vale of Beavor. As I went, I preached repentance to the people. . . .

° This is a characteristic illustration of the way Fox passed beyond theories and doctrines, and demanded practical *life-results*.

One morning, as I was sitting by the fire, a great cloud came over me, and a temptation beset me; and I sat still. It was said, "All things come by nature"; and the elements and stars came over me, so that I was in a manner quite clouded with it. But as I sat still and said nothing, the people of the house perceived nothing. And as I sat still under it and let it alone, a living hope and a true voice arose in me, which said, "There is a living God who made all things." Immediately the cloud and temptation vanished away, and life rose over it all; my heart was glad, and I praised the living God.

After some time I met with some people who had a notion that there was no God, but that all things come by nature. I had a great dispute with them, and overturned them, and made some of them confess that there is a living God. Then I saw that it was good that I had gone through that exercise. We had great meetings in those parts; for the power of the Lord broke through in that side of the country.

Thus the work of the Lord went forward, and many were turned from darkness to the light, within the compass of these three years, 1646, 1647, and 1648. Divers meetings of Friends, in several places were then gathered to God's teaching, by his light, Spirit, and power; for the Lord's power broke forth more and more wonderfully.

Now I was come up in spirit through the flaming sword, into the paradise of God. All things were new; and all the creation gave unto me another smell than before, beyond what words can utter. I knew nothing but pureness, and innocency, and righteousness; being renewed into the image of God by Christ Jesus, to the state of Adam, which he was in before he fell. The creation was opened to me; and it was showed me how all things had their names given to them according to their nature and virtue.

. . . And the Lord showed me that such as were faithful to Him, in the power and light of Christ, should come up into that state in which Adam was before he fell; in which the admirable works of the creation, and the virtues thereof, may be known, through the openings of that divine Word of wisdom and power by which they were made.

Great things did the Lord lead me into, and wonderful depths were opened unto me, beyond what can by words be declared; but as people come into subjection to the Spirit of God, and grow up in the image and power of the Almighty, they may receive the word of wisdom that opens all things, and come to know the hidden unity in the Eternal Being.

. . . the Lord opened to me three things relating to those three great professions in the world,—law, physic, and divinity (so called). He showed me that the physicians were out of the wisdom of God, by which the creatures were made; and knew not the virtues of the creatures, because they were out of the Word of wisdom, by which they were made. He showed me that the priests were out of the true faith, of which Christ is the author; . . . the mystery of which faith is held in a pure conscience. He showed me also that the lawyers were out of the equity, out of the true justice, and out of the law of God, which went over the first transgression, and over all sin, and answered the Spirit of God that was grieved and transgressed in man; and that these three . . . ruled the world out of the wisdom, out of the faith, and out of the equity and law of God; one pretending the cure of the body, another the cure of the soul, and the third the protection of the property of the people. But I saw they were all out of the wisdom, out of the faith, out of the equity and perfect law of God.

And as the Lord opened these things unto me I felt that His power went forth over all, by which all might be reformed if they would receive and bow unto it. The priests might be reformed and brought into the true faith, which is the gift of God. The lawyers might be reformed and brought into the law of God, which answers that in-dwelling Spirit of God which is in every one transgressed and which yet, if heeded, brings one to love his neighbor as himself. This lets man see that if he wrongs his neighbor, he wrongs himself; and teaches him to do unto others as he would they should do unto him. The physicians might be reformed and brought into the wisdom of God, by which all things were made and created; that they might receive a right knowledge of the creatures, and understand their virtues, which the Word of wisdom, by which they were made and are upheld, hath given them.

Abundance was opened concerning these things; how all lay out of the wisdom of God, and out of the righteousness and holiness that man at the first was made in. But as all believe in the Light, and walk in the Light,—that Light with which Christ hath enlightened every man that cometh into the world,—and become children of the Light, and of the day of Christ, all things, visible and invisible, are seen, by the divine Light of Christ, the spiritual heavenly man, by whom all things were created.

. . . Now the Lord God opened to me by His invisible power that every man was enlightened by the divine Light of Christ,* and

---

* This is the central teaching of George Fox. Everything else comes out of this elemental truth. It is, as he says, clearly enough taught in the Scriptures, but he now saw the truth as an immediate revelation—as a primary fact of experience.

I saw it shine through all; and that they that believed in it came out of condemnation to the Light of life, and became the children of it; but they that hated it, and did not believe in it, were condemned by it, though they made a profession of Christ. This I saw in the pure openings of the Light without the help of any man; neither did I then know where to find it in the Scriptures; though afterwards, searching the Scriptures, I found it. For I saw, in that Light and Spirit which was before the Scriptures were given forth, and which led the holy men of God to give them forth, that all, if they would know God or Christ, or the Scriptures aright, must come to that Spirit by which they that gave them forth were led and taught.

On a certain time, as I was walking in the fields, the Lord said unto me, "Thy name is written in the Lamb's book of life, which was before the foundation of the world": and as the Lord spoke it, I believed, and saw in it the new birth. Some time after the Lord commanded me to go abroad into the world, which was like a briery, thorny wilderness. When I came in the Lord's mighty power with the Word of life into world, the world swelled, and made a noise like the great raging waves of the sea. Priests and professors, magistrates and people, were all like a sea when I came to proclaim the day of the Lord amongst them, and to preach repentance to them.

I was sent to turn people from darkness to the Light, that they might receive Christ Jesus; for to as many as should receive Him in His Light, I saw He would give power to become the sons of God; which power I had obtained by receiving Christ. I was to direct people to the Spirit that gave forth the Scriptures, by which they might be led into all truth, and up to Christ and God, as those had been who gave them forth.

Yet I had no slight esteem of the holy Scriptures. They were very precious to me; for I was in that Spirit by which they were given forth; and what the Lord opened in me I afterwards found was agreeable to them. . . .

When the Lord God and His Son Jesus Christ sent me forth into the world to preach His everlasting gospel and kingdom, I was glad that I was commanded to turn people to that inward Light, Spirit, and Grace, by which all might know their salvation and their way to God; even that Divine Spirit which would lead them into all truth, and which I infallibly knew would never deceive any.

But with and by this divine power and Spirit of God, and the Light of Jesus, I was to bring people off from all their own ways to Christ, the new and living way. . . . And I was to bring them off from the world's teachers, made by men, to learn of Christ, who is the

Way, the Truth, and the Life, of whom the Father said, "This is my beloved Son, hear ye Him"; and off from all the world's worships, to know the spirit of Truth in the inward parts, and to be led thereby; that in it they might worship the Father of spirits, who seeks such to worship Him. And I saw that they that worshipped not in the Spirit of Truth, knew not what they worshipped.

And I was to bring people off from all the world's religions, which are vain, that they might know the pure religion; might visit the fatherless, the widows, and the strangers, and keep themselves from the spots of the world. Then there would not be so many beggars, the sight of whom often grieved my heart, as it denoted so much hard-heartedness amongst them that professed the name of Christ.

I was to bring people off from Jewish ceremonies, and from heathenish fables, and from men's inventions and worldly doctrines . . . ; and from all their beggarly rudiments, with their schools and colleges for making ministers of Christ,—who are indeed ministers of their own making, but not of Christ's; and from all their images, and crosses, and sprinkling of infants, with all their holy-days (so-called), and all their vain traditions. . . .

Moreover, when the Lord sent me forth into the world, He forbade me to put off my hat to any, high or low; and I was required to Thee and Thou all men and women, without any respect to rich or poor, great or small. . . .

About this time I was sorely exercised in going to their courts to cry for justice, in speaking and writing to judges and justices to do justly; in warning such as kept public houses for entertainment that they should not let people have more drink than would do them good; in testifying against wakes, feasts, May-games, sports, plays, and shows, which trained up people to vanity and looseness, and led them from the fear of God. . . .

I was moved, also, to cry against all sorts of music, and against the mountebanks playing tricks on their stages; for they burthened the pure life, and stirred up people's minds to vanity. . . .

The earthly spirit of the priests wounded my life; and when I heard the bell toll to call people together to the steeple-house, it struck at my life; for it was just like a market-bell, to gather people together, that the priest might set forth his ware for sale. Oh, the vast sums of money that are gotten by the trade they make of selling the Scriptures, and by their preaching, from the highest bishop to the lowest priest! What one trade else in the world is comparable to it? Notwithstanding the Scriptures were given forth freely, and Christ commanded His ministers to preach freely, and the prophets and apostles denounced judgments against all covetous hirelings and diviners for money.

But in this free Spirit of the Lord Jesus was I sent forth to declare the word of life and reconciliation freely, that all might come to Christ, who gives freely, and who renews up into the image of God, which man and woman were in before they fell, that they might sit down in heavenly places in Christ Jesus.

Part Three

FAITH

THE RATHER WIDE diversity of authors and material that we have brought together under the heading "Faith" is owing more to the complexity of the subject than to any aim to be eclectic merely for the sake of eclecticism or to represent every possible point of view. At first glance the student may see little or no order in the material in Part Three; however, he will, as he reads these introductory comments and the explanations which precede the selections, become aware of relationships between the individual selections and of their organization for an understanding of the nature of faith.

Faith admits of application to both the natural order and the supernatural order. As applied to a natural order, faith may be equated with opinion or belief and, on this level, it is natural both in character and in origin as distinct from a faith that derives from the higher level of a supernatural order, both in its origin and in its nature. Obviously, one may deny that there is such a supernatural order, and if the reader has no faith in such an order he can at least assume it for the purpose of the discussion that follows.

We often attest to our faith in an individual or declare our belief that what he says is true. The cause of this faith or belief that we have in him and his statements is entirely natural in origin. Perhaps we accept as true his statements (on the subject of relativity, for example) because we are aware of his achievements and learning, of his reputation and authority. Or it may be that our friends have told us that what he says is true, and, having confidence and trust in our friends, we then place that confidence and trust in him. On these grounds, then, we have faith in him and believe that what he says is true. Now if we were asked whether the truth of his statements was absolute and beyond all possible doubt, we should have to reply in the negative. Our belief or faith in natural truth can at best be only highly probable for such truth is limited in that it is based upon and derived from human authority—and we know from experience that men have erred in the past.

On the other hand, religious or supernatural faith, although in some ways it may parallel natural faith, nonetheless moves on an entirely different plane. Faith here is transcendent because it is divine in origin and based on the grace of God and God's authority rather than on the authority of man. Such faith is religious in the strict sense of that word and in keeping with our definition of religion. Supernatural faith excludes all doubt, for its truth is absolute as being the Word of God Himself.

We may also speak of faith in the sense of a creed by which men live, but which has no supernatural origin or cause. A man may place his faith in a set of moral ideals or doctrines taught by a great teacher and revered master—Plato or Confucius, for example. The individual who follows the doctrines of one of these two teachers is called a Platonist or a Confucianist, indicating that he believes in or is faithful to the principles they advanced.* Our selection from Confucius illustrates this non-supernatural type of faith. All that is proposed in it is a simple set of moral rules representing the wisdom and the intuitions of a great teacher. The doctrine does express briefly in a few passages the faith of the author in the moral order of the universe but there is little more of the religious touch than this. For this reason his doctrine of the golden mean presents none of the problems which arise from the doctrine of religious faith as it is encountered in Western thought. Millions of people have found his sayings inspirational in nature and have accepted them as an adequate guide to life and the pursuit of happiness—their faith resting solely in the wisdom and authority of a great teacher and the tradition of his greatness. Confucianism, then, is more strictly a philosophy than a religion.

The teachings of Buddha are a little closer to the Christian conception of religious faith only because of certain parallels that have been drawn between the life and teachings of Buddha and the life and teachings of Christ. However, the faith of Buddhists is not a faith in God but a faith in Buddha as the Enlightened One, and therefore it is not a supernatural faith but wholly natural in character and origin. There is no relation between Buddha and God, for God apparently has no existence in Buddhism. Buddha's "conversion" is really only his awakening to what he intuited as true not merely

---

* "Christian" admits of two interpretations, depending upon whether the individual so called places his faith (natural) in Christ as merely a man and a great moral teacher, or whether he accepts Him as God on the basis of a supernatural faith and revelation.

of a moral doctrine but of a whole philosophy of life and the world. The reader will note that no question is raised in the teachings of Buddha concerning the relation of faith and reason, a question which dominates Western thought, nor is there any conception in Buddhism of an act of faith as a means of justification or salvation. Acceptance of the creed of Buddha is a way of escaping the evils of the world, and what beatitude or bliss is achieved (depending upon the interpretation that is made of Nirvana) comes not from a deity but solely through man's own efforts.

In the development of religious thought in the Western world the concept of faith as supernatural has occupied the attention of many of our thinkers and it is this meaning of faith that will be explored in the selections that follow. In a few instances we have chosen material that is almost wholly theological or religious in nature, but there is adequate justification for this procedure. The major problems that follow from this conception of faith are: the relation between faith and reason, the function of faith in relation to man's salvation, and the nature of religious truth in relation to faith.

In the attainment of such truths as the existence of God or the immortality of the soul, some thinkers have held that such truths are wholly religious and accessible only through faith. Reason, they declare, is utterly inadequate or so corrupted by sin that it cannot possibly attain such truths—or indeed any truth. Others have rejected religious truths completely; they exclude faith and the supernatural order and hold that whatever reason can prove is true, and that there is no other source of truth. Some thinkers have endeavored to mediate between these extreme positions; they hold that faith and reason are complementary, although they agree that faith is always the higher court of appeal in the event of any conflict between the two. This last position is taken by the great majority of Christian thinkers and our selections from Augustine and Aquinas represent it most faithfully. There are, however, differences between individuals who share this particular perspective. The principal difference consists in the measure of independence given to reason and the emphasis that is placed on the priority of faith. The selections from Augustine illustrate that viewpoint which emphasizes the place and the importance of faith and conceives of man's quest for wisdom in the famous formula of "faith seeking understanding." Yet the Augustinian position, and the position of many who follow him (for example, Bonaventure and Scotus, to name the greatest), never deprecates human reason. For what we accept on faith often needs explication by reason; a rational faith is always preferable to a blind faith. That Augustine accepts the value of human reason may also be seen in his earlier philosophical essays in his arguments for the existence of God and the immortality of the soul, and his theology always reveals the close union that exists between faith and reason in his thinking.

Enlarge the sphere of reason, emphasize a little more the independence of reason and the faith in reason, but without denying the supremacy of faith and theology over philosophy, and you have the Thomistic viewpoint. The selections that we have chosen from the works of St. Thomas Aquinas bring out with considerable precision the relation that exists between faith and reason, the need each has of the other, the transcendence of faith over reason, and the resolution of conflicts between the two. The selection concludes with a very close analysis of the nature of faith and its cause in God.

Luther's essay "Concerning Christian Liberty" presents us with an inspiring and idealistic account of what religious faith can accomplish for man. Luther constantly insists, throughout the essay, on the need of faith—and faith only—for salvation. Faith is regarded as liberating man from sin and from the need for law; faith makes possible the Christian life in relation both to ourselves and to our neighbors. This author's treatment of faith is entirely religious in nature. Luther is not concerned with the relation between faith and reason, nor with any intellectual analysis of faith, for, as he sees it, where faith can accomplish so much what need is there for philosophy? Faith comes from God, whereas reason and philosophy embody man's self-sufficiency; but we know from Scripture, Luther would say, that no man is sufficient unto himself.

The selection from the writings of Spinoza is next in order for two reasons: chronologically it belongs here, and the contrast it offers to the selections immediately preceding and following may be helpful in understanding those different points of view. Spinoza is completely the rationalist and it is not surprising therefore that he should differ so markedly with Luther on the function of faith. For Spinoza, the function of faith lies in action rather than in a passive acceptance of grace from God which will enable us to believe and to fulfill the law of God. He declares that we are to be judged primarily by our works and by our obedience to God. Between the two spheres of faith and philosophy there can be no conflict, he says, because faith is concerned with piety and obedience and philosophy with truth; hence, there can be no question of making reason subservient to faith or faith to reason. On this relationship of faith to philosophy or reason, Spinoza's view contrasts sharply with that of Aquinas and

Augustine, and, indeed, with the whole Christian tradition. Faith is evidently not supernatural for Spinoza and his remarks on truth would seem to establish the supremacy of reason.

The selection from Barth might be read with that from Kierkegaard, for they form an interesting contrast. Both men are within the Lutheran tradition, but they diverge rather sharply on the question of the objectivity or subjectivity of faith. Barth insists strongly on the objective and historical character of faith. For Barth, the object of faith is God's Word as it appeared in time and history. For Kierkegaard, the emphasis is always on the subjective aspect of faith: it is not so much *what* we believe as *how* we believe, and God is not an Object but a Subject. The full meaning of Truth as subjectivity is explained in the selection from Kierkegaard's *Concluding Unscientific Postscript*. The selection may be difficult for the student; in brief, for the purpose of the contrast we are drawing here, truth for Kierkegaard is something that must be appropriated by the individual. For Barth, on the contrary, truth is the Word of God as revealed by God to man; it is something man believes *in* (Kierkegaard would emphasize the "believe" and omit the "in"). We may note that both men regarded their teaching as directing man once more to the real truth of Christianity: Barth rebelled against the trend in Protestantism toward liberalism and modernism, and set up instead the position of Neo-Orthodoxy; Kierkegaard regarded himself as a leader in the struggle against the Church and the Christendom of his time, and complained that they had lost sight of the central teaching of Christianity—the need to appropriate the message of Christ for oneself and to live the truth of Christianity.

The next two selections, from Stace and Berdyaev, also form an interesting contrast. Stace discovers that reason or philosophy can establish nothing as true in religion. Yet religious truths do, he believes, exist, in independence of philosophical truths. Religious truth is mystical truth and applicable only to the eternal order, whereas philosophical truth (naturalism, for example), is true only of the natural order. The two spheres are maintained in rigorous exclusion from one another and there can be no conflict between them, for their frames of reference are quite different. Stace's viewpoint seems to be a kind of modern version of the old notion of a double truth. Berdyaev's *Faith and Philosophy* illustrates an apparent tendency to separate the sphere of religious truth from that of philosophical truth. Thus, religious truths for Berdyaev are not mystical,° as they are for Stace, and since they constitute a revelation from God, they

---

° Or mythical, from the temporal perspective.

cannot clash with philosophy because they possess no cognitive element. In contrast with Stace, Berdyaev is not interested in maintaining this absolute exclusion of the two spheres. He would bring the two closer together by insisting that philosophy cannot ignore religion, that the source of much of its vitality lies in religion. On the other hand, he insists that philosophy as knowledge is by no means wholly intellectual, but is affective as well, that it is essentially human and related to the whole being of man. Transcending natural knowledge, philosophical knowledge is thus brought closer to divine knowledge. From both sides, then, philosophy and religion are brought closer together.

To conclude Part Three, and especially for those who may feel somewhat bewildered by all the debate and discussion that has transpired, we append the delightful verses from that man of simple faith, Jacapone da Todi.

26

CONFUCIUS

The Doctrine of the Mean *

THE DOCTRINE OF THE MEAN forms a part of the body of the Confucianist Scripture and is said to have been composed by Tseze, a grandson of Confucius and possibly the teacher of Mencius. The selections that follow describe the nature of the mean as constituting the moral order of the world, the exemplification of this doctrine of the mean in the life of the superior man, the obligations of duty and the practise of virtue, and the attainment of wisdom and sincerity.

I. WHAT HEAVEN has conferred is called THE NATURE; an accordance with this nature is called THE PATH *of duty;* the regulation of this path is called INSTRUCTION.

° From *The Chinese Classics,* translated by James Legge (New York: Hurd and Houghton, 1870), pp. 124-46.

Confucius (King-fu-tsze) lived in the latter part of the sixth century B.C. He devoted his life to teaching and government and exerted a very great influence on the character of the Chinese constitution. He founded the religion of *li,* or religion based on the moral order.

The path may not be left for an instant. If it could be left, it would not be the path. On this account, the superior man does not wait till he sees things, to be cautious, nor till he hears things, to be apprehensive.

There is nothing more visible than what is secret, and nothing more manifest than what is minute. Therefore the superior man is watchful over himself, when he is alone.

While there are no stirrings of pleasure, anger, sorrow or joy, the mind may be said to be in the state of EQUILIBRIUM. When those feelings have been stirred, and they act in their due degree, there ensues what may be called the state of HARMONY. This EQUILIBRIUM is the great root *from which grow all the human actions* in the world, and this HARMONY is the universal path *which they all should pursue.*

Let the states of equilibrium and harmony exist in perfection, and a happy order will prevail throughout heaven and earth, and all things will be nourished and flourish.

II. The Master said, "The superior man *embodies* the course of the Mean; the mean man acts contrary to the course of the Mean.

"The superior man's embodying the course of the mean is because he is a superior man, and so always maintains the Mean. The mean man's acting contrary to the course of the Mean is because he is a mean man, and has no caution."

III. The Master said, "Perfect is the virtue which is according to the Mean! Rare have they long been among the people, who could practise it!"

IV. The Master said, "I know how it is that the path *of the Mean* is not walked in:—The knowing go beyond it, and the stupid do not come up to it. I know how it is that the path of the Mean is not understood:—The men of talents and virtue go beyond it, and the worthless do not come up to it. . . .

V. The Master said, "Alas! How is the path of the Mean untrodden!"

.   .   .   .   .

VII. The Master said, "Men all say, 'We are wise'; but being driven forward and taken in a net, a trap, or a pitfall, they know not how to escape. Men all say, 'We are wise'; but happening to choose the course of the Mean, they are not able to keep it for a round month."

.   .   .   .   .

X. Tsze-loo asked about energy.°

° [May also be rendered as "moral strength," "courage," "strength of character," depending upon the context.—*Ed.*]

The Master said, "Do you mean the energy of the South, the energy of the North, or the energy which you should cultivate yourself?

"To show forbearance and gentleness in teaching others; and not to revenge unreasonable conduct:—that is the energy of Southern regions, and the good man makes it his study.

"To lie under arms: and meet death without regret:—this is the energy of Northern regions, and the forceful make it their study.

"Therefore, the superior man cultivates a *friendly* harmony, without being weak.—How firm is he in his energy! He stands erect in the middle, without inclining to either side.—How firm is he in his energy! When good principles prevail in the government of his country, he does not change from what he was in retirement.—How firm is he in his energy! When bad principles prevail in the country, he maintains his course to death without changing.—How firm is he in his energy!"

XI. The Master said, "To live in obscurity, and yet practise wonders, in order to be mentioned with honor in future ages;—this is what I do not do.

"The good man tries to proceed according to the right path, but when he has gone halfway, he abandons it;—I am not able *so* to stop.

"The superior man accords with the course of the Mean. Though he may be all unknown, unregarded by the world, he feels no regret.— It is only the sage who is able for this."

XII. The way which the superior man pursues, reaches wide and far, and yet is secret.

Common men and women, however ignorant, may intermeddle with the knowledge of it; yet in its utmost reaches, there is that which even the sage does not know. Common men and women, however much below the ordinary standard of character, can carry it into practice: yet in its utmost reaches, there is that which even the sage is not able to carry into practice. Great as heaven and earth are, men still find some things in them with which to be dissatisfied. Thus it is, that were the superior man to speak of his way in all its greatness, nothing in the world would be found able to embrace it, and were he to speak of it in its minuteness, nothing in the world would be found able to split it.

It is said in the Book of Poetry, "The hawk flies up to heaven; the fishes leap in the deep." This expresses how this *way* is seen above and below.

XIII. The Master said, "The path is not far from man. When men try to pursue a course, which is far from the common indications of consciousness, this course cannot be considered THE PATH.

"When one cultivates to the utmost the principles of his nature, and exercises them on the principle of reciprocity, he is not far from the path. What you do not like, when done to yourself, do not do to others."

XIV. The superior man does what is proper to the station in which he is; he does not desire to go beyond this. In a position of wealth and honor, he does what is proper to a position of wealth and honor. In a poor and low position, he does what is proper to a poor and low position. . . . The superior man can find himself in no position in which he is not himself. In a high position, he does not treat with contempt his inferiors. In a low situation, he does not court the favor of his superiors. . . . He does not murmur against heaven, nor grumble against men.

Thus it is that the superior man is quiet and calm, waiting for the appointments *of Heaven*, while the mean man walks in dangerous paths, looking for lucky occurrences.

The Master said, "In archery we have something like the way of the superior man. When the archer misses the centre of the target, he turns round and seeks for the cause of his failure in himself."

·   ·   ·   ·   ·

XX. The duke Gae asked about government.

The Master said, "The governments of Wan and Woo is displayed in *the records,*—the tablets of wood and bamboo. Let there be the men and the government will flourish; but without the men, their government decays and ceases.

"With the *right* men the growth of government is rapid. . . . Therefore the administration of government lies in *getting proper* men. Such men are to be got by means of the ruler's own character. That character is to be cultivated by his treading in the ways of duty. And the treading those ways of duty is to be cultivated by the cherishing of benevolence.

"When those in inferior situations do not possess the confidence of their superiors, they cannot retain the government of the people. Hence the sovereign may not neglect the cultivation of his own character. Wishing to cultivate his character, he may not neglect to serve his parents. In order to serve his parents, he may not neglect to acquire a knowledge of men. In order to know men, he may not dispense with a knowledge of Heaven.

"The duties of universal obligation are five, and the virtues wherewith they are practised are three. The duties are those between sovereign and minister, between father and son, between husband and wife, between elder brother and younger, and those belonging to the intercourse of friends. Those five are the duties of universal obligation. Knowledge, magnanimity, and energy, these three are the virtues universally binding. And the means by which they carry *the duties* into practice is singleness.

"Some are born with the knowledge *of those duties*; some know them by study; and some acquire the knowledge after a painful feeling of their ignorance. But the knowledge being possessed, it comes to the same thing. Some practice them with natural ease; some from a desire for their advantages; and some by strenuous effort. But the achievement being made, it comes to the same thing."

The Master said, "To be fond of learning is to be near to knowledge. To practice with vigor is to be near to magnanimity. To possess the feeling of shame is to be near to energy.

"He who knows these three things, knows how to cultivate his own character. Knowing how to cultivate his own character, he knows how to govern other men. Knowing how to govern other men, he knows how to govern the empire with all its States and families.

"In all things success depends on previous preparations, and without such previous preparation, there is sure to be failure. . . . If one's actions have been previously determined, there will be no sorrow in connection with them. . . .

"When those in inferior situations do not obtain the confidence of the sovereign, they cannot succeed in governing the people. There is a way to obtain the confidence of the sovereign;—if one is not trusted by his friends, he will not get the confidence of his sovereign. There is a way to being trusted by one's friends;—if one is not obedient to his parents, he will not be true to friends. There is a way to being obedient to one's parents;—if one, on turning his thoughts in upon himself, finds a want of sincerity, he will not be obedient to his parents. There is a way to the attainment of sincerity in one's self;— if a man does not understand what is good, he will not attain sincerity in himself.

"Sincerity is the way of Heaven. The attainment of sincerity is the way of men. He who possesses sincerity, is he who, without an effort, hits what is right, and apprehends, without the exercise of thought;— he is the sage who naturally and easily embodies the *right* way. He who attains to sincerity, is he who chooses what is good, and firmly holds it fast.

"To this attainment there are requisite the extensive study of what is good, accurate inquiry about it, careful reflection on it, the clear discrimination of it, and the earnest practice of it.

"The superior man, while there is any thing he has not studied, or while in what he has studied there is any thing he cannot understand, will not intermit his labor. . . . While there is any thing which he has not reflected on, or any thing in which he does not apprehend, he will not intermit his labor. . . . If there be any thing which he has not practised, or his practice fails in earnestness, he will not intermit his labor. If another man succeed by one effort, he will use a hundred efforts. If another man succeed by ten efforts, he will use a thousand. Let a man proceed in this way, and though dull, he will surely become intelligent; though weak, he will surely become strong."

XXI. When we have intelligence resulting from sincerity, this condition is to be ascribed to nature; when we have sincerity resulting from intelligence this condition is to be ascribed to instruction. But given the sincerity, and there shall be the intelligence; given the intelligence, and there shall be sincerity.

XXII. It is only he who is possessed of the most complete sincerity that can exist under heaven, who can give its full development to his nature. Able to give its full development to his own nature, he can do the same to the nature of other men. Able to give its full development to the nature of other men, he can give their full development to the natures of animals and things. Able to give their full development to the natures of creatures and things, he can assist the transforming and nourishing powers of Heaven and Earth. Able to assist the transforming and nourishing powers of Heaven and Earth, he may with Heaven and Earth form a ternion.

.   .   .   .   .

XXV. Sincerity is that whereby self-completion is effected, and *its* way is that by which man must direct himself. Sincerity is the end and beginning of things; without sincerity there would be nothing. The possessor of sincerity does not merely accomplish the self-completion of himself. With this quality he completes *other men* and things *also*. The completing himself *shows his* perfect virtue. The completing *other men and* things *shows his* knowledge. *Both these are* virtues belonging to the nature, and *this is* the way by which a union is effected of the external and internal. Therefore, whenever he—*the entirely sincere man*—employs them,—*that is, these virtues,—their action will be right.*

.   .   .   .   .

XXXI. It is only he, possessed of all sagely qualities that can exist under heaven, who shows himself quick in apprehension, clear in discernment, of far-reaching intelligence, and all-embracing knowledge, fitted to exercise rule; magnanimous, generous, benign, and mild, fitted to exercise forbearance; impulsive; energetic, firm, and enduring, fitted to maintain a firm hold; self-adjusted, grave, never swerving from the Mean, and correct, fitted to command reverence; accomplished, distinctive, concentrative, and searching, fitted to exercise discrimination.

All-embracing is he and vast, deep and active as a fountain, sending forth in their due seasons his virtues. All-embracing and vast, he is like heaven. Deep and active as a fountain, he is like the abyss. He is seen, and the people all reverence him; he speaks, and the people all believe him; he acts, and the people all are pleased with him. Therefore his fame overspreads the Middle Kingdom, and extends to all barbarous tribes. Wherever ships and carriages reach; wherever the strength of man penetrates; wherever the heavens overshadow and the earth sustains; wherever the sun and moon shine; wherever frosts and dews fall:—all who have blood and breath unfeignedly honor and love him. Hence it is said,—"He is the equal of Heaven."

XXXII. It is only the individual possessed of the most entire sincerity that can exist under heaven, who can adjust the great invariable relations of mankind, establish the great fundamental virtues of humanity, and know the transforming and nurturing operations of Heaven and Earth;—shall this individual have any being or anything beyond himself on which he depends?

Call him man in his ideal, how earnest is he! Call him an abyss, how deep is he! Call him Heaven, how vast is he! Who can know him, but he who is indeed quick in apprehension, clear in discernment, of far-reaching intelligence, and all-embracing knowledge, possessing all heavenly virtue?

27

GAUTAMA BUDDHA

The Gospel of Buddha *

THE TEACHINGS of the Buddha are to be found in many sources, written at different times and in different languages, although mostly in Sanscrit or Chinese. Even in the best translations this material presents varying degrees of difficulty and value for the reader. Under these circumstances the problem of selection has been determined more by the needs and interests of the general reader than by the interests of the scholar and philosopher. The selections that follow may, perhaps, lack the metaphysical profundity of the *Surangama Sutra,* but they do have the very great merit of presenting in simple, clear, and vivid language the essential teachings of the Buddha. The first two selections deal with that period in the Buddha's life when he attained Enlightenment and summarize in brief detail the four noble truths and the eightfold path that leads to Buddhahood. The third selection is taken from one of the Buddha's sermons and touches upon his doctrine of the middle path. The fourth selection contains a series of aphorisms, largely ethical in character and attributed to the Buddha, although the exact author is unknown. The last two selections bring out the notion of the Buddha as the Truth and the mirroring and possession of that Truth in the minds of his disciples and followers.

XII. ENLIGHTENMENT

BÔDHISATTVA having put to flight Mâra, gave himself up to meditation. All the miseries of the world, the evils produced by evil deeds and the sufferings arising therefrom passed before his mental eye, and he thought:

* As told by Paul Carus in *The Gospel of Buddha* (Open Court, 1895), pp. 30-36, 38-43, 111-17, 140-41, 199-201.

Gautama Buddha (563-483 B.C.) was born in the district of Glorakpur, India, of an aristocratic family. At the age of twenty-nine he gave up all family ties and became a seeker after Bôdhi (wisdom). After several years of wandering, in which he rejected the teachings of the Brahmans and tried and abandoned ascetic practices, he turned to meditation, discovered and propounded the basic truths of his doctrine, and henceforth became the Enlightened One or Buddha. His life from this point on was devoted to travelling, teaching, and converting others to his doctrine or *dharma.* He died at the age of eighty and was cremated with the highest honors.

"Surely if living creatures saw the results of all their evil deeds, they would turn away from them in disgust. But selfhood blinds them, and they cling to their obnoxious desires.

"They crave for pleasure and they cause pain; when death destroys their individuality, they find no peace; their thirst for existence abides and their selfhood reappears in new births.

"Thus they continue to move in the coil, and can find no escape from the hell of their own making. And how empty are their pleasures, how vain are their endeavors! Hollow like the plantain-tree and without contents like the bubble.

"The world is full of sin and sorrow, because it is full of error. Men go astray because they think that delusion is better than truth. Rather than truth they follow error, which is pleasant to look at in the beginning but causes anxiety, tribulation, and misery."

And Bôdhisattva began to expound the dharma. The dharma is the truth. The dharma is the sacred law. The dharma is religion. The dharma alone can deliver us from error, sin, and sorrow.

Pondering on the origin of birth and death, the Enlightened One recognized that ignorance was the root of all evil; and these are the links in the development of life, called the twelve nidânas:

"In the beginning there is existence blind and without knowledge; and in this sea of ignorance there are appetences formative and organising. From appetences, formative and organising, rises awareness or feelings. Feelings beget organisms that live as individual beings. These organisms develop the six fields, that is, the five senses and the mind. The six fields come in contact with things. Contact begets sensation. Sensation creates the thirst of individualised being. The thirst of being creates a cleaving to things. The cleaving produces the growth and continuation of selfhood. Selfhood continues in renewed births. The renewed births of selfhood are the cause of suffering, old age, sickness, and death. They produce lamentation, anxiety, and despair.

"The cause of all sorrow lies at the very beginning; it is hidden in the ignorance from which life grows. Remove ignorance and you will destroy the wrong appetences that rise from ignorance; destroy these appetences and you will wipe out the wrong perception that rises from them. Destroy wrong perception and there is an end of errors in individualised beings. Destroy errors in individualised beings and the illusions of the six fields will disappear. Destroy illusions and the contact with things will cease to beget misconception. Destroy misconception and you will do away with thirst. Destroy thirst and you will be free of all morbid cleaving. Remove the cleaving and you destroy the selfishness of selfhood. If the selfishness of selfhood is destroyed you will be above birth, old age, disease, and death, and you escape all suffering."

The Enlightened One saw the four noble truths which point out the path that leads to Nirvâna or the extinction of self:

"The first noble truth is the existence of sorrow. Birth is sorrowful, growth is sorrowful, illness is sorrowful, and death is sorrowful. Sad it is to be joined with that which we do not like. Sadder still is the separation from that which we love, and painful is the craving for that which cannot be obtained.

"The second noble truth is the cause of suffering. The cause of suffering is lust. The surrounding world affects sensation and begets a craving thirst, which clamors for immediate satisfaction. The illusion of self originates and manifests itself in a cleaving to things. The desire to live for the enjoyment of self entangles us in the net of sorrow. Pleasures are the bait and the result is pain.

"The third noble truth is the cessation of sorrow. He who conquers self will be free from lust. He no longer craves, and the flame of desire finds no material to feed upon. Thus it will be extinguished.

"The fourth noble truth is the eightfold path that leads to the cessation of sorrow. There is salvation for him whose self disappears before Truth, whose will is bent upon what he ought to do, whose sole desire is the performance of his duty. He who is wise will enter this path and make an end of sorrow.

"The eightfold path is (1) right comprehension; (2) right resolutions; (3) right speech; (4) right acts; (5) right way of earning a livelihood; (6) right efforts; (7) right thoughts; and (8) the right state of a peaceful mind."

This is the dharma. This is the truth. This is religion. And the Enlightened One uttered this stanza:

> Long have I wandered! Long!
> Bound by the chain of desire
> Through many births,
> Seeking thus long in vain,
> Whence comes this restlessness in man?
> Whence his egotism, his anguish?
> And hard to bear is samsâra
> When pain and death encompass us.
> Found! it is found!
> The cause of selfhood.
> No longer shalt thou build a house for me.
> Broken are the beams of sin;
> The ridge-pole of care is shattered,
> Into Nirvâna my mind has passed,
> The end of cravings has been reached at last.

There is self and there is truth. Where self is, truth is not. Where truth is, self is not. Self is the fleeting error of samsâra;* it is individual separateness and that egotism which begets envy and hatred. Self is the yearning for pleasure and the lust after vanity. Truth is the correct comprehension of things; it is the permanent and everlasting, the real in all existence, the bliss of righteousness.

The existence of self is an illusion, and there is no wrong in this world, no vice, no sin, except what flows from the assertion of self.

The attainment of truth is possible only when self is recognized as an illusion. Righteousness can be practised only when we have freed our mind from the passions of egotism. Perfect peace can dwell only where all vanity has disappeared.

Blessed is he who has understood the dharma. Blessed is he who does no harm to his fellow-beings. Blessed is he who overcomes sin and is free from passion. To the highest bliss has he attained who has conquered all selfishness and vanity. He has become Buddha, the Perfect One, the Blessed One, the Holy One.

.   .   .   .   .

XIV. BRAHMA'S REQUEST

The Blessed One having attained Buddhahood pronounced this solemn utterance:

"Blissful is freedom from malice. Blissful is absence of lust and the loss of pride that comes from the thought 'I am.'

"I have recognized the deepest truth, which is sublime and peace-giving, but difficult to understand. For most men move in a sphere of worldly interests and find their delight in worldly desires.

"The worldling will not understand the doctrine, for to him there is happiness in selfhood only, and the bliss that lies in a complete surrender to truth is unintelligible to him.

"He will call resignation what to the Enlightened One is the purest joy. He will see annihilation where the perfected one finds immortality. He will regard as death what the conqueror of self knows to be life everlasting.

"The truth remains hidden from him who is in the bondage of hate and desire. Nirvâna remains incomprehensible and mysterious to the vulgar mind that worldly interests surround as with clouds.

"Should I preach the doctrine and mankind not comprehend it, it would bring me only fatigue and trouble."

* [Worldliness.—*Ed.*]

Then Brahma Sahampati * descended from the heaven and, having worshipped the Blessed One, said:

"Alas! the world must perish, should the Holy One, the Tathâgata, decide not to teach the dharma.

"Be merciful to those that struggle; have compassion upon the sufferers; pity the creatures who are hopelessly entangled in the snares of sorrow.

"There are some beings that are almost pure from the dust of worldliness. If they hear not the doctrine preached, they will be lost. But if they hear it, they will believe and be saved."

The Blessed One, full of compassion, looked with the eye of a Buddha upon all sentient creatures, and he saw among them beings whose minds were but scarcely covered by the dust of worldliness, who were of good disposition and easy to instruct. He saw some who were conscious of the dangers of lust and sin.

And the Blessed One said: "Wide open be the door of immortality to all who have ears to hear. May they receive the dharma with faith."

Then, Brahmâ Sahampati understood that the Blessed One had granted the request and would preach the doctrine.

. . . . .

XVI. THE SERMON AT BENARES

The five bhikshus ** saw their old teacher approach and agreed among themselves not to salute him, nor to address him as a master, but by his name only. "For," so they said, "he has broken his vow and has abandoned holiness. He is no bhikshu but Gautama, and Gautama has become a man who lives in abundance and indulges in the pleasures of worldliness."

But when the Blessed One approached in a dignified manner, they involuntarily rose from their seats and greeted him in spite of their resolution. Still they called him by his name and addressed him as "friend."

When they had thus received the Blessed One, he said: "Do not call the Tathâgata by his name nor address him 'friend,' for he is Buddha, the Holy One. Buddha looks equally with a kind heart on all living beings and they therefore call him 'Father.' To disrespect a father is wrong; to despise him, is sin."

"The Tathâgata," Buddha continued, "does not seek salvation in austerities, but for that reason you must not think that he indulges

---

* [Carus notes (p. 225) that although this name occurs frequently in Buddhist scriptures the meaning of it is obscure.—*Ed.*]

** [Defined by Carus (p. 245) as mendicant, monk, friar.—*Ed.*]

in worldly pleasures, nor does he live in abundance. The Tathâgata has found the middle path.

"Neither abstinence from fish or flesh, nor going naked, nor shaving the head, nor wearing matted hair, nor dressing in a rough garment, nor covering oneself with dirt, nor sacrificing to Agni, will cleanse a man who is not free from delusions.

"Reading the Vedas, making offerings to priests, or sacrifices to the gods, self-mortification by heat or cold, and many such penances performed for the sake of immortality, these do not cleanse the man who is not free from delusions.

"Anger, drunkenness, obstinacy, bigotry, deception, envy, self-praise, disparaging others, superciliousness, and evil intentions constitute uncleanness; not verily the eating of flesh.

"Let me teach you, O bhikshus, the middle path, which keeps aloof from both extremes. By suffering, the emaciated devotee produces confusion and sickly thoughts in his mind. Mortification is not conducive even to worldly knowledge; how much less to a triumph over the senses!

"He who fills his lamp with water will not dispel the darkness, and he who tries to light a fire with rotten wood will fail.

"Mortifications are painful, vain, and profitless. And how can any one be free from self by leading a wretched life if he does not succeed in quenching the fires of lust.

"All mortification is vain so long as self remains, so long as self continues to lust after either worldly or heavenly pleasures. But he in whom self has become extinct is free from lust; he will desire neither worldly nor heavenly pleasures, and the satisfaction of his natural wants will not defile him. Let him eat and drink according to the needs of the body.

"Water surrounds the lotus-flower, but does not wet its petals.

"On the other hand, sensuality of all kind is enervating. The sensual man is a slave of his passions, and pleasure-seeking is degrading and vulgar.

"But to satisfy the necessities of life is not evil. To keep the body in good health is a duty, for otherwise we shall not be able to trim the lamp of wisdom, and keep our mind strong and clear.

"This is the middle path, O bhikshus, that keeps aloof from both extremes."

And the Blessed One spoke kindly to his disciples, pitying them for their errors, and pointing out the uselessness of their endeavors, and the ice of ill-will that chilled their hearts melted away under the gentle warmth of the Master's persuasion.

Now the Blessed One set the wheel of the most excellent law a-rolling, and he began to preach to the five bhikshus, opening to them the gate of immortality, and showing them the bliss of Nirvâna.

And when the Blessed One began his sermon, a rapture thrilled through all the universes.

The dêvas * left their heavenly abodes to listen to the sweetness of the truth; the saints that had parted from life crowded around the great teacher to receive the glad tidings; even the animals of the earth felt the bliss that rested upon the words of the Tathâgata: and all the creatures of the host of sentient beings, gods, men, and beasts, hearing the message of deliverance, received and understood it in their own language.

Buddha said:

"The spokes of the wheel are the rules of pure conduct; justice is the uniformity of their length; wisdom is the tire; modesty and thoughtfulness are the hub in which the immovable axle of truth is fixed.

"He who recognizes the existence of suffering, its cause, its remedy, and its cessation has fathomed the four noble truths. He will walk in the right path.

"Right views will be the torch to light his way. Right aims will be his guide. Right words will be his dwelling-place on the road. His gait will be straight, for it is right behavior. His refreshments will be the right way of earning his livelihood. Right efforts will be his steps: right thoughts his breath; and peace will follow in his footprints."

And the Blessed One explained the instability of the ego.

"Whatsoever is originated will be dissolved again. All worry about the self is vain; the ego is like a mirage, and all the tribulations that touch it will pass away. They will vanish like a nightmare when the sleeper awakes.

"He who has awakened is freed from fear; he has become Buddha; he knows the vanity of all his cares, his ambitions, and also of his pains.

"There was a man who, having taken a bath, stepped upon a wet rope, and he thought it was a snake. Horror overcame him, and he shook from fear, anticipating in his mind all the agonies caused by its venomous bite. What a relief does this man experience when he sees that it is no snake. The cause of his fright lies in his error, his ignorance, his illusion. If the true nature of the rope is recognised, his tranquillity of mind will come back to him; he will feel relieved; he will be joyful and happy.

* [Defined by Carus (p. 247) as celestial spirits, angels.—*Ed.*]

"This is the state of mind of one who has recognised that there is no self, that the cause of all his troubles, cares, and vanities is a mirage, a shadow, a dream.

"Happy is he who has overcome all selfishness; happy is he who has attained peace; happy is he who has found the truth.

"The truth is noble and sweet; the truth can deliver you from evil. There is no saviour in the world except the truth.

"Have confidence in the truth, although you may not be able to comprehend it, although you may suppose its sweetness to be bitter, although you may shrink from it at first. Trust in the truth.

"The truth is best as it is. No one can alter it; neither can any one improve it. Have faith in the truth and live it.

"Errors lead astray; illusions beget miseries. They intoxicate like strong drinks; but they fade away soon and leave you sick and disgusted.

"Self is a fever; self is a transient vision, a dream; but truth is wholesome, truth is sublime, truth is everlasting. There is no immortality except in truth. For truth alone abideth forever."

And when the doctrine was propounded, the venerable Kaundinya, the oldest one among the five bhikshus, discerned the truth with his mental eye, and he said: "Truly, O Buddha, our Lord, thou hast found the truth."

And the dêvas and saints and all the good spirits of the departed generations that had listened to the sermon of the Tathâgata, joyfully received the doctrine and shouted: "Truly, the Blessed One has founded the kingdom of righteousness. The Blessed One has moved the earth; he has set the wheel of Truth rolling, which by no one in the universe, be he god or man, can ever be turned back. The kingdom of Truth will be preached upon earth; it will spread; and righteousness, good-will, and peace will reign among mankind."

.   .   .   .   .

XLVIII. THE DHARMAPADA

This is the Dharmapada, the path of religion pursued by those who are Buddha's followers:

All that we are is the result of what we have thought: it is founded on our thoughts, it is made up of our thoughts.

By oneself evil is done; by oneself one suffers; by oneself evil is left undone; by oneself one is purified. Purity and impurity belong to oneself, no one can purify another.

You yourself must make an effort. The Tathâgatas are only preachers. The thoughtful who enter the way are free from the bondage of Mâra.

He who does not rouse himself when it is time to rise, who, though young and strong, is full of sloth, whose will and thoughts are weak, that lazy and idle man will never find the way to enlightenment.

If a man hold himself dear, let him watch himself carefully; the truth guards him who guards his self.

If a man makes himself as he teaches others to be, then, being himself subdued, he may subdue others; one's own self is indeed difficult to subdue.

If one man conquers in battle a thousand times a thousand men, and if another conquer himself, he is the greatest of conquerors.

It is the habit of fools, be they laymen or members of the clergy, to think, "This is done by *me*. May others be subject to *me*. In this or that transaction a prominent part should be played by *me*." Fools do not care for the duty to be performed or the aim to be reached, but think of their self alone. Everything is but a pedestal of their vanity.

Bad deeds, and deeds hurtful to ourselves, are easy to do; what is beneficial and good, that is very difficult to do.

If anything is to be done, let a man do it, let him attack it vigorously!

Before long, alas! this body will lie on the earth, despised, without understanding, like a useless log; yet our thoughts will endure. They will be thought again, and will produce action. Good thoughts will produce good actions, and bad thoughts will produce bad actions.

Earnestness is the path of immortality, thoughtlessness the path of death. Those who are in earnest do not die; those who are thoughtless are as if dead already.

Those who imagine truth in untruth, and see untruth in truth, never arrive at truth, but follow vain desires. They who know truth in truth, and untruth in untruth, arrive at truth, and follow true desires.

As rain breaks through an ill-thatched house, passion will break through an unreflecting mind. As rain does not break through a well-thatched house, passion will not break through a well-reflecting mind.

Well-makers lead the water wherever they like; fletchers bend the arrow; carpenters bend a log of wood; wise people fashion themselves; wise people falter not amidst blame and praise. Having listened to the law, they become serene, like a deep, smooth, and still lake.

If a man speaks or acts with an evil thought, pain follows him as the wheel follows the foot of the ox that draws the carriage.

An evil deed is better left undone, for a man will repent of it afterwards; a good deed is better done, for having done it one will not repent.

If a man commits a sin let him not do it again; let him not delight in sin; pain is the outcome of evil. If a man does what is good, let him do it again; let him delight in it; happiness is the outcome of good.

Let no man think lightly of evil, saying in his heart, "It will not come nigh unto me." As by the falling of water-drops a water-pot is filled, so the fool becomes full of evil, though he gather it little by little.

Let no man think lightly of good, saying in his heart, "It will not come nigh unto me." As by the falling of water-drops a water-pot is filled, so the wise man becomes full of good, though he gather it little by little.

He who lives for pleasure only, his senses uncontrolled, immoderate in his food, idle, and weak, him Mâra, the tempter, will certainly overthrow, as the wind throws down a weak tree. He who lives without looking for pleasures, his senses well-controlled, moderate in his food, faithful and strong, him Mâra will certainly not overthrow, any more than the wind throws down a rocky mountain.

The fool who knows his foolishness, is wise at least so far. But a fool who thinks himself wise, he is a fool indeed.

To the sinful man sin appears sweet as honey; he looks upon it as pleasant so long as it bears no fruit; but when its fruit ripens, then he looks upon it as sin. And so the good man looks upon the goodness of the dharma as a burden and an evil so long as it bears no fruit; but when its fruit ripens, then he sees its goodness.

A hater may do great harm to a hater, or an enemy to an enemy; but a wrongly-directed mind will do greater mischief unto himself. A mother, a father, or any other relative will do much good; but a well-directed mind will do greater service unto himself.

He whose wickedness is very great brings himself down to that state where his enemy wishes him to be. He himself is his greatest enemy. Thus a creeper destroys the life of a tree on which it finds support.

Do not direct thy thought to what gives pleasure, that thou mayest not cry out when burning, "This is pain." The wicked man burns by his own deeds, as if burnt by fire.

Pleasures destroy the foolish; the foolish man by his thirst for pleasures destroys himself as if he were his own enemy. The fields are damaged by hurricanes and weeds; mankind is damaged by passion, by hatred, by vanity, and by lust.

Let no man ever take into consideration whether a thing is pleasant or unpleasant. The love of pleasure begets grief and the dread of pain causes fear; he who is free from the love of pleasure and the dread of pain knows neither grief nor fear.

He who gives himself to vanity, and does not give himself to meditation, forgetting the real aim of life and grasping at pleasure, will in time envy him who has exerted himself in meditation.

The fault of others is easily perceived, but that of oneself is difficult to perceive. A man winnows his neighbor's faults like chaff, but his own fault he hides, as a cheat hides the false die from the gambler.

If a man looks after the faults of others, and is always inclined to take offence, his own passions will grow, and he is far from the destruction of passions.

Not about the perversities of others, not about their sins of commission or omission, but about his own misdeeds and negligences alone should a sage be worried.

Good people shine from afar, like the snowy mountains; bad people are not seen, like arrows shot by night.

If a man by causing pain to others, wishes to obtain pleasure for himself, he, entangled in the bonds of selffishness, will never be free from hatred.

Let a man overcome anger by love, let him overcome evil by good; let him overcome the greedy by liberality, the liar by truth.

For hatred does not cease by hatred at any time; hatred ceases by love, this is an old rule.

Speak the truth, do not yield to anger; give, if thou art asked; by these three steps thou wilt become divine.

Let a wise man blow off the impurities of his self, as a smith blows off the impurities of silver, one by one, little by little, and from time to time.

Lead others, not by violence, but by law and equity.

He who possesses virtue and intelligence, who is just, speaks the truth, and does what is his own business, him the world will hold dear.

As the bee collects nectar and departs without injuring the flower, or its color or scent, so let a sage dwell in the village.

If a traveller does not meet with one who is his better, or his equal, let him firmly keep to his solitary journey; there is no companionship with a fool.

Long is the night to him who is awake; long is a mile to him who is tired; long is life to the foolish who do not know the true religion.

Better than living a hundred years, not seeing the highest religion, is one day in the life of a man who sees the highest religion.

Some form their dharma arbitrarily and fabricate it artificially; they advance complex speculations and imagine that good results are attainable only by the acceptance of their theories; yet the truth is but one; there are not many different truths in the world. Having reflected on the various theories, we have gone into the yoke with him who has shaken off all sin. But shall we be able to proceed together with him?

The best of ways is the eightfold. This is the way, there is no other that leads to the purifying of intelligence. Go on this way! Everything else is the deceit of Mâra, the tempter. If you go on this way, you will make an end of pain! Says the Tathâgata, The way was preached by me, when I had understood the removal of the thorn in the flesh.

Not only by discipline and vows, not only by much learning, do I earn the happiness of release which no worldling can know. Bhikshu, be not confident as long as thou hast not attained the extinction of thirst. The extinction of sinful desire is the highest religion.

The gift of religion exceeds all gifts; the sweetness of religion exceeds all sweetness; the delight in religion exceeds all delights; the extinction of thirst overcomes all pain.

Few are there among men who cross the river and reach the goal. The great multitudes are running up and down the shore; but there is no suffering for him who has finished his journey.

As the lily will grow full of sweet perfume and delight upon a heap of rubbish, thus the disciple of the truly enlightened Buddha shines forth by his wisdom among those who are like rubbish, among the people that walk in darkness.

Let us live happily then, not hating those who hate us! among men who hate us let us dwell free from hatred!

Let us live happily then, free from all ailments among the ailing! among men who are ailing let us dwell free from ailments!

Let us live happily, then, free from greed among the greedy! among men who are greedy let us dwell free from greed!

The sun is bright by day, the moon shines by night, the warrior is bright in his armor, thinkers are bright in their meditation; but among all the brightest with splendor day and night is Buddha, the Awakened, the Holy, the Blessed.

•   •   •   •   •   •

LIV. BUDDHA, NOT GAUTAMA

And the Blessed One said:

"Those only who do not believe, call me Gautama Siddhârtha, but you call me Buddha, the Blessed One, and Teacher. And this is right, for I have even in this life entered Nirvâna, and the life of Gautama Siddhârtha has been extinguished.

"Self has disappeared, and the truth has taken its abode in me. This body of mine is Gautama's body and it will be dissolved in due time, and after its dissolution no one, neither God nor man, will see Gautama Siddhârtha again. But Buddha will not die; Buddha will continue to live in the holy body of the law.

"The extinction of the Blessed One will be by that passing away in which nothing remains that could tend to the formation of another self. Nor will it be possible to point out the Blessed One as being here or there. But it will be like a flame in a great body of blazing fire. That flame has ceased; it has vanished and it cannot be said that it is here or there. In the body of the dharma, however, the Blessed One can be pointed out; for the dharma has been preached by the Blessed One.

"Ye are my children, I am your father; through me ye have been released from your sufferings.

"I myself having reached the other shore, help others to cross the stream; I myself having attained salvation, am a saviour of others; being comforted, I comfort others and lead them to the place of refuge.

"I shall fill with joy all the beings whose limbs languish; I shall give happiness to those who are dying from distress; I shall extend to them succor and deliverance.

"I was born into the world as the king of truth for the salvation of the world.

"The subject on which I meditate is truth. The practice to which I devote myself is truth. The topic of my conversation is truth. My thoughts are always in the truth. For lo! my self has become the truth. I am the truth.

"Whosoever comprehendeth the truth, he will see the Blessed One, for the truth has been preached by the Blessed One."

.   .   .   .   .

XCI. THE MIRROR OF TRUTH

The Blessed One proceeded to the village of Nâdika with a great company of brethren and there he stayed at the Brick Hall. And the venerable Ânanda went to the Blessed One and mentioning to him the names of the brethren and sisters that had died, anxiously inquired about their fate after death, whether they had been reborn in animals or in hell, or as ghosts, or in any place of woe.

And the Blessed One replied to Ânanda and said:

"Those who have died after the complete destruction of the three bonds of lust, of covetousness and of the egotistical cleaving to existence, need not fear the state after death. They will not be reborn in a state of suffering; their minds will not continue as a karma of evil deeds or sin, but are assured of final salvation.

"When they die, nothing will remain of them but their good thoughts, their righteous acts, and the bliss that proceeds from truth and righteousness. As rivers must at last reach the distant main, so their minds will be reborn in higher states of existence and continue to be pressing on to their ultimate goal which is the ocean of truth, the eternal peace of Nirvâna.

"Men are anxious about death and their fate after death; but there is nothing strange in this, Ânanda, that a human being should die. However, that you should inquire about them, and having heard the truth still be anxious about the dead, this is wearisome to the Blessed One. I will, therefore, teach you the mirror of truth:

"'Hell is destroyed for me, and rebirth as an animal, or a ghost, or in any place of woe. I am converted; I am no longer liable to be reborn in a state of suffering, and am assured of final salvation.'

"What, then, Ânanda, is this mirror of truth? It is the consciousness that the elect disciple is in this world possessed of faith in the Buddha, believing the Blessed One to be the Holy One, the Fully-enlightened One, wise, upright, happy, world-knowing, supreme, the Bridler of men's wayward hearts, the Teacher of gods and men, the blessed Buddha.

"It is further the consciousness that the disciple is possessed of faith in the truth, believing the truth to have been proclaimed by the Blessed One, for the benefit of the world, passing not away, welcoming all, leading to salvation, to which through truth the wise will attain, each one by his own efforts.

"And, finally, it is the consciousness that the disciple is possessed of faith in the order, believing in the efficacy of a union among those men and women who are anxious to walk in the noble eightfold path, believing the church of the Buddha, of the righteous, the upright, the just, the law-abiding, to be worthy of honor, of hospitality, of gifts, and of reverence; to be the supreme sowing-ground of merit for the world; to be possessed of the virtues beloved by the good, virtues

unbroken, intact, unspotted, unblemished, virtues which make men
truly free, virtues which are praised by the wise, are untarnished by
the desire of selfish aims, either now or in a future life, or by the
belief in the efficacy of outward acts, and are conducive to high and
holy thought.

"This is the mirror of truth which teaches the straightest way to
enlightenment which is the common goal of all living creatures. He
who possesses the mirror of truth is free from fear, will find comfort
in the tribulations of life, and his life will be a blessing to all his
fellow-creatures."

28

ST. AUGUSTINE

Faith Seeking Understanding *

THE HISTORICAL SIGNIFICANCE of St. Augustine's contribution on
the subject of faith lies in his insistence upon the priority of faith
over reason and the need for faith if we are to have understanding.
Yet, according to St. Augustine, faith is not blind, but requires the
aid of reason. "Faith seeking understanding" is his classic statement of the quest for religious wisdom and we find this, as well
as other aspects of faith, brought out in the selections that follow.
"Sermon CXVII" is a plea for humility and for belief in God's com-

* "Sermon CXVII" and "Sermon CXXVI" are from *A Library of Fathers of the
Holy Catholic Church,* translated by Members of the English Church, Oxford,
edited by John Henry Parker (London: J. G. F. and J. Rivington, 1845), II,
499-502, 540-43.
      The "Tractate on the Gospel according to St. John," is from vol. X in *Works
of Aurelius Augustine,* translated by Rev. John Gib, edited by Marcus Dods
(Edinburgh: T. and T. Clark, 1887), 405-6.
      "On the Profit of Believing" and "On the Predestination of the Saints" are
from *A Select Library of the Nicene and Post-Nicene Fathers,* translated by C. L.
Cornish, edited by Philip Schaff (Buffalo: The Christian Literature Co., 1887),
III, 360-61, 501.

St. Augustine (354-430 A.D.) was born at Tagaste in Africa. He studied rhetoric
at Carthage and taught there and in Rome until 384. At that time he received
an appointment in the government at Milan and was joined there by his mother,
St. Monica. While at Milan, he was converted to Christianity and was baptized
Easter Sunday, 387. Shortly thereafter, he returned to Africa and in 395 was
made the bishop of Hippo. The remainder of his life was devoted to writing and
to his episcopal duties.

mandments if we would have strength of understanding. "Sermon CXXVI" is a commentary on the words of the prophet: "Unless ye believe ye shall not understand," and a brief explication of the oft-quoted definition of faith taken from Hebrews xi. 1. That God bestows faith on man and that the reward of faith is understanding is noted in the "Tractate on the Gospel according to St. John." The need for man of God's help is further developed in the selection "On the Profit of Believing" in which St. Augustine is concerned to show that, just as a fool cannot follow the way of the wise man unless he is first wise enough to know a wise man, so we need the grace of God to attain wisdom and to be persuaded of religious truth. The last selection again emphasizes the need man has of God but also notes that faith is not mere blind assent, devoid of all rational activity, but that rather, as he says, "to believe is to think with assent."

SERMON CXVII

.   .   .   .   .

5. IT IS SAID, *And the Word was God.* We are speaking of God; what marvel if thou do not comprehend? For if thou comprehend, He is not God. Be there a pious confession of ignorance, rather than a rash profession of knowledge. To reach God in any measure by the mind, is a great blessedness; but to comprehend Him is altogether impossible. God is an object for the mind. He is to be understood, a body is for the eyes, it is to be seen. . . . Lo, of the bodies which are before our eyes we say they cannot comprehend them by a glance; what eye of the heart then comprehendeth God? Enough that it reach to Him if the eye be pure. . . .

.   .   .   .   .

15. Yet above all things remember this, that the Creator transcends indescribably whatever we could gather from the creature, whether by the bodily senses, or the thought of the mind. But wouldest thou with the mind reach Him? Purify thy mind, purify thy heart. Make clean the eye whereby That, whatever It may be, may be reached. For, *blessed are the clean in heart, for they shall see God.* But whilst the heart was not cleansed, what could be provided and granted more mercifully by Him, than That Word of Whom we have spoken so great and so many things, and yet have spoken nothing worthy of Him; that That Word, *by Whom all things were made,* should become that which we are, that we might be able to attain to That Which we are not? For we are not God; but with the mind or the interior eye of the heart we can see God. Our eyes dulled by sins, blinded, en-

feebled by infirmity, desire to see; but we are in hope, not yet in possession. We are the children of God. . . .

. . . . .

17. We are making our way to great things, let us receive the little things, and we shall be great. Wouldest thou comprehend the height of God? First comprehend the lowliness of God. Condescend to be humble for thine own sake, seeing that God condescended to be humble for thy sake too; for it was not for His own. Comprehend then the lowliness of Christ, learn to be humble, be loth to be proud. Confess thine infirmity, lie patiently before the Physician; when thou shalt have comprehended His lowliness, thou risest with Him; not as though He should rise Himself in that He is the Word; but thou rather, that He may be more and more comprehended by thee. At first thou didst understand falteringly and hesitatingly; afterwards thou wilt understand more surely and more clearly. He doth not increase, but thou makest progress, and He seemeth as it were to rise with thee. So it is, brethren. Believe the commandments of God, and do them, and He will give you the strength of understanding. Do not put the last first, and, as it were, prefer knowledge to the commandments of God; lest ye be only the lower, and none the more firmly rooted. Consider a tree; first it strikes downwards, that it may grow up on high; fixes its root low in the ground, that it may extend its top to heaven. Does it make an effort to grow except from humiliation. And wouldest thou without charity comprehend these transcendent matters, shoot toward the heaven without a root? This were a ruin, not a growing. With *Christ* then *dwelling in your hearts by faith, be ye rooted and grounded in charity, that ye may be filled with all the fulness of God.*

SERMON CXXVI

1. The mysteries and secrets of the kingdom of God first seek for believing men, that they may make them understanding. For faith is understanding's step; and understanding faith's attainment. This the prophet expressly says to all who prematurely and in undue order look for understanding and neglect faith. For he says, *Unless ye believe, ye shall not understand.* Faith itself then also hath a certain light of its own in the Scriptures, in Prophecy, in the Gospel, in the Lessons of the Apostles. For all these things which are read to us in this present time, are lights in a dark place, that we may be nourished up unto the day. . . .

2. Ye see then, brethren, how exceedingly unregulated and disordered in their haste are they who like immature conceptions seek an untimely birth before the birth; who say to us, "Why dost thou bid me believe what I do not see? Let me see something that I may believe. Thou biddest me believe whilst yet I see not; I wish to see, and by seeing to believe not by hearing." Let the Prophet speak. *Unless ye believe ye shall not understand.* Thou wishest to ascend, and dost forget the steps. Surely, out of all order. O man, if I could show thee already what thou mightest see, I should not exhort thee to believe.

3. Faith then, as it has been elsewhere defined, is the *firm support of those who hope, the evidence of things which are not seen.* If they are not seen, how are they evidenced to be? What! Whence are those things which thou seest, but from That which thou seest not? To be sure thou dost see somewhat that thou mayest believe somewhat, and from that thou seest, mayest believe what thou seest not. Be not ungrateful to Him Who hath made thee see, whereby thou mayest be able to believe what as yet thou canst not see. God hath given thee eyes in the body, reason in the heart, wake up the interior inhabitant of thine interior eyes, let it take to its windows, examine the creature of God. For there is one within who sees by the eyes. For when thy thoughts within thee are on any other subject, and the inhabitant within is turned away, the things which are before thine eyes thou seest not. For to no purpose are the windows open, when he who looks through them is away. It is not then the eyes that see, but some one sees by the eyes; awake him, arouse him. For this hath not been denied thee; God hath made thee a rational animal, set thee over the cattle, formed thee after His Own image. Oughtest thou to use them as the cattle do; only to see what to add to thy belly, not to thy soul? Stir up, I say, the eyes of reason, use thine eyes as a man should, consider the heaven and earth, the ornaments of the heaven, the fruitfulness of the earth, the flight of the birds, the swimming of the fish, the virtue of the seeds, the order of the seasons, consider the works, and seek for the Author; take a view of what thou seest, and seek Him Whom thou seest not. Believe on Him Whom thou seest not, because of these things which thou seest. And lest thou think it is with mine own words that I have exhorted thee; hear the Apostle saying, *For the invisible things of God from the creation of the world are clearly seen by those things which are made.*

4. These things thou disregardest, nor didst look upon them as a man, but as an irrational animal. . . . God's daily miracles were disesteemed, not for their easiness, but their constant repetition. For

what is more difficult to understand than a man's birth, that one who was in existence should by dying depart into darkness, and that one who was not, by being born should come forth to light? What so marvellous, what so difficult to comprehend? But with God easy to be done. Men wondered that our Lord God Jesus Christ filled so many thousands with five loaves; and yet they do not wonder that through a few grains the whole earth is filled with crops. When the water was made wine, men saw it, and were amazed; what else takes place with the rain along the root of the vine? He did the one, He does the other; the one that thou mayest be fed, the other that thou mayest wonder. . . .

5. . . . Attend, I say, to what thou seest, believe what thou seest not. He hath not abandoned thee, Who hath called thee to believe; though He enjoin thee to believe that which thou canst not see; yet hath He not given thee up to see nothing whereby thou mayest be able to believe what thou dost not see. Is the creation itself a small sign, a small indication of the Creator? He also came, He did miracles. Thou couldest not see God, a man thou couldest; so God was made Man, that in One thou mightest have both what to see, and what to believe. . . .

TRACTATE ON THE GOSPEL ACCORDING TO ST. JOHN

"My doctrine," saith He, "is not mine, but His that sent me." Let him who says he has not yet understood hear counsel. For since it was a great and profound matter that had been spoken, the Lord Christ Himself did certainly see that all would not understand this so profound a matter, and He gave counsel in the sequel. Dost thou wish to understand? Believe. For God has said by the prophet: "Except ye believe, ye shall not understand." To the same purpose what the Lord here also added as He went on—"If any man is willing to do His will, he shall know concerning the doctrine, whether it be of God, or whether I speak from myself." What is the meaning of this, "If any man be willing to do His will"? But I had said, if any man believe; and I gave this counsel: If thou hast not understood, said I, believe. For understanding is the reward of faith. Therefore do not seek to understand in order to believe, but believe that thou mayest understand; since, "except ye believe, ye shall not understand." Therefore when I would counsel the obedience of believing toward the possibility of understanding, and say that our Lord Jesus Christ had added this very thing in the following sentence, we find Him to have said, "If any man be willing to do His will, he shall know of the doctrine." What is "he shall know"? It is the same thing as "He shall understand." But what is "If any man be willing to do His will"? It is the same thing as to believe. All men indeed perceive that "shall know" is the same thing as "shall understand": but that the saying, "If any man be willing to do His will," refers to believing, all do not perceive; to perceive this more accurately, we need the Lord Himself for expounder, to show us whether the doing of the Father's will does in reality refer to believing. But who does not know that this is to do the will of God, to work the work of God; that is, to work that work which is pleasing to Him? But the Lord Himself says openly in another place: "This is the work of God, that ye believe on Him whom He has sent." "That ye believe *on* Him," not, that "ye believe Him." But if ye believe *on* Him, ye believe Him; yet he that believes Him does not necessarily believe on Him. For even the devils believed Him, but they did not believe on Him. Again, moreover, of his apostles we can say, we believe Paul; but not, we believe on Paul: we believe Peter; but not we believe on Peter. For, "to him that believeth on Him that justifieth the ungodly, his faith is counted unto Him for righteousness." What then is "to believe on Him?" By believing to love Him, by believing to esteem highly, by believing to go unto Him and to be incorporated in His members. It is faith itself then that God exacts from us: and He finds not that which He exacts, unless He has bestowed what He may find. What faith, but that which the apostle has most amply defined in another place, saying "Neither circumcision availeth anything, nor uncircumcision, but faith that worketh by love"? Not any faith of any kind whatsoever, but "faith that worketh by love": let this faith be in thee, and thou shalt understand concerning the doctrine. What indeed shalt thou understand? That "this doctrine is not mine, but His that sent me"; that is, thou shall understand that Christ the Son of God, who is the doctrine of the Father, is not from Himself, but is the Son of the Father.

ON THE PROFIT OF BELIEVING

· · · · ·

27. But now hear, what I trust I shall by this time more easily persuade you of. In a matter of religion, that is, of the worship and knowledge of God, they are less to be followed, who forbid us to believe, making most ready professions of reason. For no one doubts that all men are either fools or wise. But now I call wise, not clever and gifted men, but those, in whom there is, so much as may be in man, the knowledge of man himself and of God most surely received, and a life and manners suitable to that knowledge; but all others,

whatever be their skill or want of skill, whatever their manner of life, whether to be approved or disapproved, I would account in the number of fools. And, this being so, who of moderate understanding but will clearly see, that it is more useful and more healthful for fools to obey the precepts of the wise, than to live by their own judgment?

. . . . .

28. Here again arises a very difficult question. For in what way shall we fools be able to find a wise man, whereas this name, although hardly any one dare openly, yet most men lay claim to indirectly: so disagreeing one with another in the very matters, in the knowledge of which wisdom consists, as that it must be that either none of them, or but some certain one be wise? But when the fool inquires, who is that wise man? I do not at all see, in what way he can be distinguished and perceived. For by no signs whatever can one recognize any thing, unless he shall have known that thing, whereof these are signs. But the fool is ignorant of wisdom. For not, as, in the case of gold and silver and other things of that kind, it is allowed both to know them when you see them, and not to have them, thus may wisdom be seen by the mind's eye of him who has it not. For whatever things we come into contact with by bodily sense, are presented to us from without; and therefore we may perceive by the eyes what belong to others, when we ourselves possess not any of them or of that kind. But what is perceived by the understanding is within in the mind, and to have it is nothing else than to see. But the fool is void of wisdom, therefore he knows not wisdom. For he could not see it with the eyes: but he cannot see it and not have it, nor have it and be a fool. Therefore he knows it not, and, so long as he knows it not, he cannot recognize it in another place. No one, so long as he is a fool, can by most sure knowledge find out a wise man, by obeying whom he may be set free from so great evil of folly.

29. Therefore this so vast difficulty, since our inquiry is about religion, God alone can remedy: nor indeed, unless we believe both that He is, and that He helps men's minds, ought we even to inquire after true religion itself. For what I ask do we with so great endeavor desire to search out? What do we wish to attain to? Whither do we long to arrive? Is it at that which we believe not exists or pertains to us? Nothing is more perverse than such a state of mind. Then, when you would not dare to ask of me a kindness, or at any rate would be shameless in daring, come you to demand the discovery of religion, when you think that God neither exists, nor, if He exist, has any care for us? What, if it be so great a matter, as that it cannot be found out, unless it be sought carefully and with all our might? What, if the

very extreme difficulty of discovery be an exercise for the mind of the inquirer, in order to receive what shall be discovered? For what more pleasant and familiar to our eyes than this light? And yet men are unable after long darkness to bear and endure it. What more suited to the body exhausted by sickness than meat and drink? And yet we see that persons who are recovering are restrained and checked, lest they dare to commit themselves to the fullness of persons in health, and so bring to pass by means of their very food their return to that disease which used to reject it. I speak of persons who are recovering. What, the very sick, do we not urge them to take something? Wherein assuredly they would not with so great discomfort obey us, if they believed not that they would recover from that disease. When then will you give yourself up to a search very full of pains and labor? When will you have the heart to impose upon yourself so great care and trouble as the matter deserves, when you believe not in the existence of that which you are in search of? Rightly therefore has it been ordained by the majesty of the Catholic system of teaching, that they who approach unto religion be before all things persuaded to have faith.

ON THE PREDESTINATION OF THE SAINTS

TO BELIEVE IS TO THINK WITH ASSENT

And, therefore, commending that grace which is not given according to any merits, but is the cause of all good merits, he says, "Not that we are sufficient to think anything as of ourselves, but our sufficiency is of God." Let them give attention to this, and well weigh these words, who think that the beginning of faith is of ourselves, and the supplement of faith is of God. For who cannot see that that thinking is prior to believing? For no one believes anything unless he has first thought that it is to be believed. For however suddenly, however rapidly, some thoughts fly before the will to believe, and this presently follows in such wise as to attend them, as it were, in closest conjunction, it is yet necessary that everything which is believed should be believed after thought has preceded; although even belief itself is nothing else than to think with assent. For it is not every one who thinks that believes, since many think in order that they may not believe; but everybody who believes, thinks—both thinks in believing, and believes in thinking. Therefore in what pertains to religion and piety if we are not capable of thinking anything as of ourselves, but our sufficiency is of God, we are certainly not capable of believing anything of ourselves, since we cannot do this without thinking; but our sufficiency, by which we begin to believe, is of God. Wherefore, as no one is sufficient for himself, for the beginning or the completion of any good work whatsoever . . . so no one is sufficient for himself, either to begin or to perfect faith; but our sufficiency is of God. Because if faith is not a matter of thought, it is of no account; and we are not sufficient to think anything as of ourselves, but our sufficiency is of God.

29

ST. THOMAS AQUINAS

Faith and Reason *

IN THE following selections from the *Summa Contra Gentiles,* St. Thomas shows that man can attain to truth about God in two ways: through faith and through reason. Some truths about God surpass the ability of our natural reason and these belong to the sphere of faith. Both kinds of truth, however, can be the object of faith, for otherwise serious disadvantages to man would result. Next, St. Thomas notes that there can be no real conflict between the truths of reason and the truths of faith; where an apparent conflict exists it is owing to sophistical demonstration, for the truth of faith is given by God and cannot be false though error is possible to the reason of man.

IN WHAT WAY IT IS POSSIBLE TO MAKE KNOWN THE DIVINE TRUTH

. . . . . .

Now IN THOSE THINGS which we hold about God there is truth in two ways. For certain things that are true about God wholly surpass the capability of human reason, for instance that God is three and one: while there are certain things to which even natural reason can attain, for instance that God is, that God is one, and others like these, which

---

* From the *Summa Contra Gentiles,* translated by the Fathers of the English Dominican Province (Burns, Oates and Washbourne, Ltd., 1920), I, 3, 4, 7, 8. For a brief biographical sketch of St. Thomas, see selection 3 on page 14.

even the philosophers proved demonstratively of God, being guided
by the light of natural reason.

That certain divine truths wholly surpass the capability of human
reason, is most clearly evident. For since the principle of all the
knowledge which the reason acquires about a thing, is the understanding of that thing's essence, because according to the Philosopher's teaching (2 *Anal. Post.* iii. 9) the principle of a demonstration
is *what a thing is,* it follows that our knowledge about a thing will
be in proportion to our understanding of its essence. Wherefore, if
the human intellect comprehends the essence of a particular thing,
for instance a stone or a triangle, no truth about that thing will surpass the capability of human reason. But this does not happen to us
in relation to God, because the human intellect is incapable by its
natural power of attaining to the comprehension of His essence: since
our intellect's knowledge, according to the mode of the present life,
originates from the senses: so that things which are not objects of
sense cannot be comprehended by the human intellect, except in so
far as knowledge of them is gathered from sensibles. Now sensibles
cannot lead our intellect to see in them what God is, because they are
effects unequal to the power of their cause. And yet our intellect is
led by sensibles to the divine knowledge so as to know about God
that He is, and other such truths, which need to be ascribed to the
first principle. Accordingly some divine truths are attainable by
human reason, while others altogether surpass the power of human
reason. . . .

THAT THE TRUTH ABOUT DIVINE THINGS WHICH IS ATTAINABLE
BY REASON IS FITTINGLY PROPOSED TO MAN AS AN OBJECT
OF BELIEF

While then the truth of the intelligible things of God is twofold, one
to which the inquiry of reason can attain, the other which surpasses
the whole range of human reason, both are fittingly proposed by
God to man as an object of belief. We must first show this with
regard to that truth which is attainable by the inquiry of reason, lest
it appears to some, that since it can be attained by reason, it was
useless to make it an object of faith by supernatural inspiration. Now
three disadvantages would result if this truth were left solely to the
inquiry of reason. One is that few men would have knowledge of
God; because very many are hindered from gathering the fruit of
diligent inquiry, which is the discovery of truth, for three reasons.
Some indeed on account of an indisposition of temperament, by rea-

son of which many are naturally indisposed to knowledge: so that no efforts of theirs would enable them to reach to the attainment of the highest degree of human knowledge, which consists in knowing God. Some are hindered by the needs of household affairs. For there must needs be among men some that devote themselves to the conduct of temporal affairs, who would be unable to devote so much time to the leisure of contemplative research as to reach the summit of human inquiry, namely the knowledge of God. And some are hindered by laziness. For in order to acquire the knowledge of God in those things which reason is able to investigate, it is necessary to have a previous knowledge of many things: since almost the entire consideration of philosophy is directed to the knowledge of God: for which reason metaphysics, which is about divine things, is the last of the parts of philosophy to be studied. Wherefore it is not possible to arrive at the inquiry about the aforesaid truth except after a most laborious study: and few are willing to take upon themselves this labor for the love of a knowledge, the natural desire for which has nevertheless been instilled into the mind of man by God.

The second disadvantage is that those who would arrive at the discovery of the aforesaid truth would scarcely succeed in doing so after a long time. First, because this truth is so profound, that it is only after long practice that the human intellect is enabled to grasp it by means of reason. Secondly, because many things are required beforehand, as stated above. Thirdly, because at the time of youth, the mind, when tossed about by the various movements of the passions, is not fit for the knowledge of so sublime a truth, whereas *calm gives prudence and knowledge,* as stated in 7 *Phys.* (iii. 7) Hence mankind would remain in the deepest darkness of ignorance, if the path of reason were the only available way to the knowledge of God: because the knowledge of God which especially makes men perfect and good, would be acquired only by the few, and by these only after a long time.

The third disadvantage is that much falsehood is mingled with the investigations of human reason, on account of the weakness of our intellect in forming its judgments, and by reason of the admixture of phantasms. Consequently many would remain in doubt about those things even which are most truly demonstrated, through ignoring the force of the demonstration: especially when they perceive that different things are taught by the various men who are called wise. Moreover among the many demonstrated truths, there is sometimes a mixture of falsehood that is not demonstrated, but assumed for some probable or sophistical reason which at times is mistaken for a demonstration. Therefore it was necessary that definite certainty and pure truth about divine things should be offered to man by the way of faith.

Accordingly the divine clemency has made this salutary commandment, that even some things which reason is able to investigate must be held by faith: so that all may share in the knowledge of God easily, and without doubt or error.

THAT THE TRUTH OF REASON IS NOT IN OPPOSITION TO THE TRUTH OF THE CHRISTIAN FAITH

Now though the aforesaid truth of the Christian faith surpasses the ability of human reason, nevertheless those things which are naturally instilled in human reason cannot be opposed to this truth. For it is clear that those things which are implanted in reason by nature, are most true, so much so that it is impossible to think them to be false. Nor is it lawful to deem false that which is held by faith, since it is so evidently confirmed by God. Seeing then that the false alone is opposed to the true, as evidently appears if we examine their definitions, it is impossible for the aforesaid truth of faith to be contrary to those principles which reason knows naturally.

Again. The same thing which the disciple's mind receives from its teacher is contained in the knowledge of the teacher, unless he teach insincerely, which it were wicked to say of God. Now the knowledge of naturally known principles is instilled into us by God, since God Himself is the author of our nature. Therefore the divine Wisdom also contains these principles. Consequently whatever is contrary to these principles, is contrary to the divine Wisdom; wherefore it cannot be from God. Therefore those things which are received by faith from divine revelation cannot be contrary to our natural knowledge.

Moreover. Our intellect is stayed by contrary arguments, so that it cannot advance to the knowledge of truth. Wherefore if conflicting knowledges were instilled into us by God, our intellect would thereby be hindered from knowing the truth. And this cannot be ascribed to God. . . .

From this we may evidently conclude that whatever arguments are alleged against the teachings of faith, they do not rightly proceed from first self-evident principles instilled by nature. Wherefore they lack the force of demonstration, and are either probable or sophistical arguments, and consequently it is possible to solve them.

IN WHAT RELATION HUMAN REASON STANDS TO THE TRUTH OF FAITH

It would also seem well to observe that sensible things from which human reason derives the source of its knowledge, retain a certain trace of likeness to God, but so imperfect that it proves altogether inadequate to manifest the substance itself of God. For effects resemble their causes according to their own mode, since like action proceeds from like agent; and yet the effect does not always reach to a perfect likeness to the agent. Accordingly human reason is adapted to the knowledge of the truth of faith, which can be known in the highest degree only by those who see the divine substance, in so far as it is able to put together certain probable arguments in support thereof, which nevertheless are insufficient to enable us to understand the aforesaid truth as though it were demonstrated to us or understood by us in itself. And yet however weak these arguments may be, it is useful for the human mind to be practised therein, so long as it does not pride itself on having comprehended or demonstrated: since although our view of the sublimest things is limited and weak, it is most pleasant to be able to catch but a glimpse of them. . . .

The authority of Hilary is in agreement with this statement: for he says (*De Trin.* ii. 10, 11) while speaking of this same truth: *Begin by believing these things, advance and persevere; and though I know thou wilt not arrive, I shall rejoice at thy advance. For he who devoutly follows in pursuit of the infinite, though he never come up with it, will always advance by setting forth. Yet pry not into that secret, and meddle not in the mystery of the birth of the infinite, nor presume to grasp that which is the summit of understanding: but understand that there are things thou canst not grasp.*

30

ST. THOMAS AQUINAS

On the Nature of Faith *

THIS MATERIAL from the *Summa Theologica* considers God as both the formal and the material aspect of the object of faith, and then proceeds to define more exactly the nature of faith and to distinguish it from opinion and science. The author demonstrates that one and the same thing cannot be an object of faith and knowledge. The final question points out how God is the cause of faith in man.

WHETHER THE OBJECT OF FAITH IS THE FIRST TRUTH? **

I ANSWER THAT The object of every cognitive habit includes two things: first, that which is known materially, and is the material object, so to speak, and secondly, that whereby it is known, which is the formal aspect of the object. Thus, in the science of geometry, the conclusions are what is known materially, while the formal aspect of the science consists in the means of demonstration, through which the conclusions are known.

Accordingly, if in faith we consider the formal aspect of the object, it is nothing else than the First Truth. For the faith of which we are speaking does not assent to anything, except because it is revealed by God. Hence faith bases itself on the divine Truth as on its means. If, however, we consider materially the things to which faith assents, they include not only God, but also many other things, which, nevertheless, do not come under the assent of faith except as bearing some relation to God, inasmuch as, namely, through certain effects of the divine operation man is helped on his journey towards the enjoyment of God. Consequently, from this point of view also the object of faith is, in a way, the First Truth, inasmuch as nothing comes under faith except in relation to God; even as the object of the medical art is health, for it considers nothing save in relation to health.

---

* Reprinted from the *Summa Theologica* with the permission of Benziger Brothers, Inc., publishers, II-II. Question 1, Articles 1, 4, and 5; Question 6, Article 1.

For a brief biographical sketch of St. Thomas, see selection 3 on page 14.

** Question 1, Article 1.

WHETHER THE OBJECT OF FAITH CAN BE SOMETHING SEEN? *

Objection 1. It would seem that the object of faith is something seen. For our Lord said to Thomas (*Job* xx. 29): *Because thou hast seen Me, Thomas, thou hast believed.* Therefore vision and faith regard the same object.

Obj. 2. Further, the Apostle, while speaking of the knowledge of faith, says (*1 Cor.* xiii. 12): *We see now through a glass in a dark manner.* Therefore what is believed is seen. . . .

. . . . .

On the contrary, The Apostle says (*Heb.* xi. 1) that *faith is the evidence of things that appear not.*

I answer that, Faith signifies the assent of the intellect to that which is believed. Now the intellect assents to a thing in two ways. First, through being moved to assent by its very object, which is known either by itself (as in the case of first principles, which are held by the habit of understanding), or through something else already known (as in the case of conclusions which are held by the habit of science). Secondly, the intellect assents to something, not through being sufficiently moved to this assent by its proper object, but through an act of choice, whereby it turns voluntarily to one side rather than to the other. Now if this be accompanied by doubt and fear of the opposite side, there will be opinion; while, if there be certainty and no fear of the other side, there will be faith.

Now those things are said to be seen which, of themselves, move the intellect or the senses to knowledge of them. Therefore it is evident that neither faith nor opinion can be of things seen either by the senses or by the intellect.

Reply Obj. 1. Thomas *saw one thing, and believed another.* He saw the Man and, believing Him to be God, he made profession of his faith, saying: *My Lord and my God.*

Reply Obj. 2. Those things which come under faith can be considered in two ways. First, in particular, and in this way they cannot be seen and believed at the same time, as was shown above. Secondly, in general, that is, under the common aspect of credibility; and in this way they are seen by the believer. For he would not believe unless, on the evidence of signs, or of something similar, he saw that they ought to be believed.

* Question 1, Article 4.

WHETHER THOSE THINGS THAT ARE OF FAITH CAN BE AN OBJECT OF SCIENCE? *

. . . . .

Obj. 4. Further, Opinion is further from science than faith is, since faith is said to stand between opinion and science. Now opinion and science can, in a way, be about the same object, as is stated in *Posterior Analytics* i. (89a25). Therefore faith and science can be about the same object also.

On the contrary, Gregory says that *when a thing is manifest, it is the object, not of faith, but of perception.* Therefore things that are of faith are not the object of perception, whereas what is an object of science is the object of perception. Therefore there can be no faith about things which are an object of science.

I answer that, All science is derived from self-evident and therefore *seen* principles; and so all objects of science must needs be, in a fashion, seen.

Now, as was stated above, it is impossible that one and the same thing should be believed and seen by the same person. Hence it is equally impossible for one and the same thing to be an object of science and of belief for the same person. It may happen, however, that a thing which is an object of vision or science for one, is believed by another; for we hope to see some day what we now believe about the Trinity, according to *1 Cor.* xiii. 12: *We see now through a glass in a dark manner; but then face to face.* And this vision the angels possess already, so that what we believe, they see. In like manner, it may also happen that what is an object of vision or scientific knowledge for one man, even in the state of a wayfarer, is, for another man, an object of faith, because he does not know it by demon-stration.

Nevertheless, that which is proposed to be believed equally by all is equally unknown by all as an object of science. Such are the things which are of faith absolutely. Consequently, faith and science are not about the same things.

. . . . .

Reply Obj. 4. As the Philosopher says, *science and opinion about the same object can certainly be in different men,* as we have stated above about science and faith; yet it is possible for one and the same man to have science and faith about the same thing rela-

* Question 1, Article 5.

tively, i. e. in relation to the object, but not in the same respect. For it is possible for the same person, about one and the same object, to know one thing and to have an opinion about another; and, in like manner, one may know by demonstration the unity of God, and believe that there are three Persons in God. On the other hand, in one and the same man, about the same object, and in the same respect, science is incompatible with either opinion or faith, but for different reasons. For science is incompatible with opinion about the same object absolutely, for the reason that science demands that its object should be deemed impossible to be otherwise, whereas it is essential to opinion that its object should be deemed possible to be otherwise. But that which is the object of faith, because of the certainty of faith, is also deemed impossible to be otherwise; and the reason why science and faith cannot be about the same object, and in the same respect, is because the object of science is something seen, whereas the object of faith is the unseen, as was stated above.

WHETHER FAITH IS INFUSED INTO MAN BY GOD? *

. . . . .

Obj. 3. Further, That which depends on a man's will can be acquired by him. But *faith depends on the believer's will,* according to Augustine. (*De Praedest. Sanct.,* V (PL 44, 968)) Therefore faith can be acquired by man.

On the contrary, It is written (*Ephes.* ii.8,9): *By grace you are saved through faith, and that not of yourselves* . . . *that no man may glory* . . . *for it is the gift of God.*

I answer that, Two things are requisite for faith. First, that the things which are of faith should be proposed to man; and this is necessary in order that man believe something explicitly. The second thing requisite for faith is the assent of the believer to the things which are proposed to him. Accordingly, as regards the first of these, faith must needs be from God. For the things which are of faith surpass human reason, and hence they do not come to man's knowledge, unless God reveal them. To some, indeed, they are revealed by God immediately, as those things which were revealed to the Apostles and prophets, while to some they are proposed by God in sending preachers of the faith, according to *Rom.* x. 15: *How shall they preach, unless they be sent?*

As regards the second, viz., man's assent to the things which are of faith, we may observe a twofold cause, one of external inducement,

* Question 6, Article 1.

such as seeing a miracle, or being persuaded by someone to embrace the faith; neither of which is a sufficient cause, since of those who see the same miracle, or who hear the same sermon, some believe, and some do not. Hence we must assert another and internal cause, which moves man inwardly to assent to what belongs to faith.

The Pelagians held that this cause was nothing else than man's free choice, and consequently they said that the beginning of faith is from ourselves, inasmuch as, namely, it is in our power to be ready to assent to the things which are of faith, but that the consummation of faith is from God, Who proposes to us the things we have to believe. But this is false, for since, by assenting to what belongs to faith, man is raised above his nature, this must needs come to him from some supernatural principle moving him inwardly; and this is God. Therefore faith, as regards the assent which is the chief act of faith, is from God moving man inwardly by grace.

. . . . .

Reply Obj. 3. To believe does indeed depend on the will of the believer; but man's will needs to be prepared by God with grace, in order that he may be raised to things which are above his nature. . . .

❧❧❧❧

31

MARTIN LUTHER

Faith and Works *

THE ESSAY that follows has always enjoyed a very high regard, not merely for the able manner in which it presents the Lutheran position on the meaning and the place of faith in the Christian life, but also for its literary quality, its conciliatory tone, and its popular appeal. It is not an abstruse theological tractate and is

---

* From *Concerning Christian Liberty*, translated by R. S. Grignon in *Harvard Classics* (P. F. Collier and Son, 1910), XXXVI, 362-91. Reprinted with the permission of the publisher.

Martin Luther (1483-1546) was born at Eisleben, Germany. He studied at the University of Erfurt and, in 1505, entered the Augustinian monastery at

free from some of the controversy and bitterness that has marked other essays of Luther.

The principal thesis of Luther is that the Christian faith serves to emancipate the individual from the bondage of sin, and that by faith alone, and not works, will man achieve his salvation. Through faith, God will impute righteousness to us and raise us to fellowship with Him. Faith unites the soul to Christ in a spiritual marriage and enables every individual to share in the spiritual power of God and to become a priest in Christ. Luther does not deny the value of works so long as they proceed from faith which gives them their goodness, and so long as they are not done for the purpose of justifying oneself in the eyes of God. The essay concludes by emphasing the obligations men have to their neighbors and the nature of their duties as Christians.

CHRISTIAN FAITH has appeared to many an easy thing; nay, not a few even reckon it among the social virtues, as it were; and this they do because they have not made proof of it experimentally, and have never tasted of what efficacy it is. . . .

A Christian man is the most free lord of all, and subject to none; a Christian man is the most dutiful servant of all, and subject to every one.

.　　.　　.　　.　　.

Let us examine the subject on a deeper and less simple principle. Man is composed of a twofold nature, a spiritual and a bodily. As regards the spiritual nature, which they name the soul, he is called the spiritual, inward, new man; as regards the bodily nature, which they name the flesh, he is called the fleshly, outward, old man. . . .

We first approach the subject of the inward man, that we may see by what means a man becomes justified, free, and a true Christian; that is, a spiritual, new, and inward man. It is certain that absolutely none among outward things, under whatever name they may be reckoned, has any influence in producing Christian righteousness or liberty, nor, on the other hand, unrighteousness or slavery. This can be shown by an easy argument.

Erfurt. He was later ordained and, in 1508, became professor of philosophy at the University of Wittenberg. Through personal experiences and doubts, he came to rebel against the Church and expressed his rebellion in the publication of his famous ninety-five theses in 1517. From this time on he was the leader of the Protestant Reformation in Germany. He was excommunicated in 1521. His doctrines were formulated in the Augsburg Confession of 1530, with which the Lutheran Church came into being. The remainder of Luther's life was devoted to writing and to the organization of the Lutheran Church.

What can it profit the soul that the body should be in good condition, free, and full of life; that it should eat, drink, and act according to its pleasure; when even the most impious slaves of every kind of vice are prosperous in these matters? Again, what harm can ill-health, bondage, hunger, thirst, or any other outward evil, do to the soul, when even the most pious of men and the freest in the purity of their conscience, are harassed by these things? Neither of these states of things has to do with the liberty or the slavery of the soul.

.   .   .   .   .

. . . One thing, and one alone, is necessary for life, justification and Christian liberty; and that is the most holy word of God, the Gospel of Christ, as He says, "I am the resurrection and the life; he that believeth in Me shall not die eternally" (John xi. 25), and also, "If the Son shall make you free, ye shall be free indeed" (John viii. 36), and "Man shall not live by bread alone, but by every word that proceedeth out of the mouth of God." (Matt. iv. 4.)

Let us therefore hold it for certain and firmly established that the soul can do without everything except the word of God, without which none at all of its wants are provided for. But, having the word, it is rich and wants for nothing. . . .

But you will ask, What is this word, and by what means is it to be used, since there are so many words of God? I answer, The Apostle Paul (Rom. i.) explains what it is, namely the Gospel of God, concerning His Son, incarnate, suffering, risen, and glorified, through the Spirit, the Sanctifier. To preach Christ is to feed the soul, to justify it, to set it free, and to save it, if it believes the preaching. For faith alone and the efficacious use of the word of God, bring salvation. . . . For the word of God cannot be received and honored by any works, but by faith alone. Hence it is clear that as the soul needs the word alone for life and justification, so it is justified by faith alone, and not by any works. For if it could be justified by any other means, it would have no need of the word, nor consequently of faith.

Since then this faith can reign only in the inward man, as it is said, "With the heart man believeth unto righteousness" (Rom. x. 10); and since it alone justifies, it is evident that by no outward work or labor can the inward man be at all justified, made free, and saved; and that no works whatever have any relation to him. And so, on the other hand, it is solely by impiety and incredulity of heart that he becomes guilty and a slave of sin, deserving condemnation, not by any outward sin or work. . . .

Hence a right faith in Christ is an incomparable treasure, carrying with it universal salvation and preserving from all evil, as it is said, "He that believeth and is baptised shall be saved; but he that believeth not shall be damned." (Mark xvi. 16.)

But you ask how it can be the fact that faith alone justifies, and affords without works so great a treasure of good things, when so many works, ceremonies, and laws are prescribed to us in the Scriptures? I answer, Before all things bear in mind what I have said: that faith alone without works justifies, sets free, and saves, as I shall show more clearly below.

Meanwhile it is to be noted that the whole Scripture of God is divided into two parts: precepts and promises. The precepts certainly teach us what is good, but what they teach is not forthwith done. For they show us what we ought to do, but do not give us the power to do it. They were ordained, however, for the purpose of showing man to himself, that through them he may learn his own impotence for good and may despair of his own strength. For this reason they are called the Old Testament, and are so.

Now when a man has through the precepts been taught his own impotence, and become anxious by what means he may satisfy the law—for the law must be satisfied, so that no jot or tittle of it may pass away, otherwise he must be hopelessly condemned—then, being truly humbled and brought to nothing in his own eyes, he finds in himself no resource for justification and salvation.

Then comes in that other part of Scripture, the promises of God, which declare the glory of God, and say, "If you wish to fulfil the law, and, as the law requires, not to covet, lo! believe in Christ, in whom are promised to you grace, justification, peace, and liberty." All these things you shall have, if you believe, and shall be without them if you do not believe. . . . Thus the promises of God give that which the precepts exact, and fulfil what the law commands; so that all is of God alone, both the precepts and their fulfilment. He alone commands; He alone also fulfils. . . .

From all this it is easy to understand why faith has such great power, and why no good works, nor even all good works put together, can compare with it, since no work can cleave to the word of God or be in the soul. Faith alone and the word reign in it. . . . It is clear then that to a Christian man his faith suffices for everything, and that he has no need of works for justification. But if he has no need of works, neither has he need of the law; and if he has no need of the law, he is certainly free from the law, and the saying is true, "The law is not made for a righteous man." (I Tim.

i. 9). This is that Christian liberty, our faith, the effect of which is, not that we should be careless or lead a bad life, but that no one should need the law or works for justification and salvation.

Let us consider this as the first virtue of faith; and let us look also to the second. This also is an office of faith: that it honors with the utmost veneration and the highest reputation Him in whom it believes, inasmuch as it holds Him to be truthful and worthy of belief. For there is no honor like that reputation of truth and righteousness with which we honor Him in whom we believe. . . .

. . . In doing this the soul shows itself prepared to do His whole will; in doing this it hallows His name, and gives itself up to be dealt with as it may please God. For it cleaves to His promises, and never doubts that He is true, just, and wise, and will do, dispose, and provide for all things in the best way. Is not such a soul, in this its faith, most obedient to God in all things? What commandment does there remain which has not been amply fulfilled by such an obedience? What fulfilment can be more full than universal obedience? Now this is not accomplished by works, but by faith alone.

But when God sees that truth is ascribed to Him, and that in the faith of our hearts He is honored . . . then in return He honors us on account of that faith, attributing to us truth and righteousness. . . .

The third incomparable grace of faith is this: that it unites the soul to Christ, as the wife to the husband, by which mystery, as the Apostle teaches, Christ and the soul are made one flesh. Now if . . . a true marriage . . . is accomplished between them . . . then it follows that all they have becomes theirs in common, as well good things as evil things; so that whatsoever Christ possesses, that the believing soul may take to itself and boast of as its own, and whatever belongs to the soul, that Christ claims as His.

If we compare these possessions, we shall see how inestimable is the gain. Christ is full of grace, life, and salvation; the soul is full of sin, death, and condemnation. Let faith step in, and then sin, death, and hell will belong to Christ, and grace, life, and salvation to the soul. For if He is a Husband, He must needs take to Himself that which is His wife's, and at the same time, impart to His wife that which is His. . . .

Who then can value highly enough these royal nuptials? Who can comprehend the riches of the glory of this grace? . . .

From all this you will again understand why so much importance is attributed to faith, so that it alone can fulfil the law and justify without any works. For you see that the First Commandment, which says, "Thou shalt worship one God only," is fulfilled by faith alone. If you were nothing but good works from the soles of your feet to the crown of your head, you would not be worshipping God, nor fulfilling the First Commandment, since it is impossible to worship God without ascribing to Him the glory of truth and of universal goodness. . . . Now this is not done by works, but only by faith of heart. It is not by working, but by believing, that we glorify God, and confess Him to be true. On this ground faith alone is the righteousness of a Christian man, and the fulfilling of all the commandments. For to him who fulfils the first the task of fulfilling all the rest is easy.

But, that we may have a wider view of that grace which our inner man has in Christ, we must know that in the Old Testament God sanctified to Himself every first-born male. The birthright was of great value, giving a superiority over the rest by the double honor of priesthood and kingship. For the first-born brother was priest and lord of all the rest.

Under this figure was foreshown Christ, the true and only First-born of God the Father and of the Virgin Mary, and a true King and Priest, not in a fleshly and earthly sense. For His kingdom is not of this world. . . .

So, too, His priesthood does not consist in the outward display of vestments and gestures . . . but in spiritual things, wherein, in His invisible office, He intercedes for us with God in heaven, and there offers Himself, and performs all the duties of a priest. . . . Nor does He only pray and intercede for us; He also teaches us inwardly in the spirit with the living teachings of His Spirit. Now these are the two special offices of a priest. . . .

As Christ by His birthright has obtained these two dignities, so He imparts and communicates them to every believer in Him, under that law of matrimony of which we have spoken above, by which all that is the husband's is also the wife's. Hence all we who believe on Christ are kings and priests in Christ. . . .

These two things stand thus. First, as regards kingship, every Christian is by faith so exalted above all things that, in spiritual power, he is completely lord of all things, so that nothing whatever can do him any hurt; yea, all things are subject to him, and are compelled to be subservient to his salvation. . . .

This is a spiritual power, which rules in the midst of enemies, and is powerful in the midst of distresses. And this is nothing else than that strength is made perfect in my weakness, and that I can turn all things to the profit of my salvation; so that even the cross and death are compelled to serve me and to work together for my salvation. This is a lofty and eminent dignity, a true and almighty dominion, a spiritual empire, in which there is nothing so good, nothing so bad, as not to work together for my good, if only I believe. And yet there is nothing of which I have need—for faith alone suffices for my salvation—unless that in it faith may exercise the power and empire of its liberty. This is the inestimable power and liberty of Christians.

Nor are we only kings and the freest of all men, but also priests for ever, a dignity far higher than kingship, because by that priesthood we are worthy to appear before God, to pray for others, and to teach one another mutually the things which are of God. . . .

Who then can comprehend the loftiness of that Christian dignity which, by its royal power, rules over all things, even over death, life, and sin, and by its priestly glory, is all-powerful with God. . . . This glory certainly cannot be attained by any works, but by faith only.

And now let us turn to the other part: to the outward man. Here we shall give an answer to all those who, taking offence at the word of faith and at what I have asserted, say, "If faith does everything, and by itself suffices for justification, why then are good works commanded? Are we then to take our ease and do no works, content with faith?" Not so, impious men, I reply; not so. That would indeed really be the case, if we were thoroughly and completely inner and spiritual persons; but that will not happen until the last day, when the dead shall be raised. As long as we live in the flesh, we are but beginning and making advances in that which shall be completed in a future life. . . . To this part belongs the fact I have stated before: that the Christian is the servant of all and subject to all. For in that part in which he is free he does no works, but in that in which he is a servant he does all works. Let us see on what principle this is so.

Although . . . inwardly, and according to the spirit, a man is amply enough justified by faith . . . still he remains in this mortal life upon earth, in which it is necessary that he should rule his own body and have intercourse with men. Here then works begin; here he must not take his ease; here he must give heed to exercise his body by fastings, watchings, labor, and other regular discipline, so that it may be subdued to the spirit, and obey and conform itself to the inner man and faith. . . .

These works, however, must not be done with any notion that by them a man can be justified before God—for faith, which alone is righteousness before God, will not bear with this false notion—but solely with this purpose: that the body may be brought into subjection, and be purified from its evil lusts. . . .

. . . Thus a Christian, being consecrated by his faith, does good works; but he is not by these works made a more sacred person, or more a Christian. That is the effect of faith alone; nay, unless, he were previously a believer and a Christian, none of his works would have any value at all; they would really be impious and damnable sins.

True, then, are these two sayings: "Good works do not make a good man, but a good man does good works"; "Bad works do not make a bad man, but a bad man does bad works." . . . As Christ says, "A good tree cannot bring forth evil fruit, neither can a corrupt tree bring forth good fruit." (Matt. vii. 18.)

Since then works justify no man, but a man must be justified before he can do any good work, it is most evident that it is faith alone which, by the mere mercy of God through Christ, and by means of His word can worthily and sufficiently justify and save the person; and that a Christian man needs no work, no law, for his salvation; for by faith he is free from all law, and in perfect freedom does gratuitously all that he does, seeking nothing either of profit or of salvation—since by the grace of God he is already saved and rich in all things through his faith—but solely that which is well-pleasing to God.

We do not then reject good works; nay, we embrace them and teach them in the highest degree. It is not on their own account that we condemn them, but on account of this impious addition to them and the perverse notion of seeking justification by them. These things cause them to be only good in outward show, but in reality not good, since by them men are deceived and deceive others, like ravening wolves in sheep's clothing.

·   ·   ·   ·   ·

Lastly, we will speak also of those works which he performs towards his neighbor. For man does not live for himself alone in this mortal body, in order to work on its account, but also for all men on earth; nay, he lives only for others, and not for himself. For it is to this end that he brings his own body into subjection, that he may be able to serve others more sincerely and freely, as Paul says, "None of us liveth to himself, and no man dieth to himself. For whether we live, we live unto the Lord; and whether we die, we die unto the Lord." (Rom. xiv. 7, 8.) Thus it is impossible that he should take his ease in this life, and not work for the good of his neighbors, since he must needs speak, act, and converse among men, just as Christ was made in the likeness of men and found in fashion as a man, and had His conversation among men.

Yet a Christian has need of none of these things for justification and salvation, but in all his works he ought to entertain this view and look only to this object—that he may serve and be useful to others in all that he does; having nothing before his eyes but the necessities and the advantage of his neighbor. . . .

Here is the truly Christian life, here is faith really working by love, when a man applies himself with joy and love to the works of that freest servitude in which he serves others voluntarily and for nought, himself abundantly satisfied in the fulness and riches of his own faith.

Thus a Christian, like Christ his Head, being full and in abundance through his faith, ought to be content with this form of God, obtained by faith; except that, as I have said, he ought to increase this faith till it be perfected. For this faith is his life, justification, and salvation, preserving his person itself and making it pleasing to God, and bestowing on him all that Christ has. . . . Though he is thus free from all works, yet he ought to empty himself of this liberty, take on him the form of a servant, be made in the likeness of men, be found in fashion as a man, serve, help, and in every way act towards his neighbor as he sees that God through Christ has acted and is acting towards him. . . .

Thus from faith flows forth love and joy in the Lord, and from love a cheerful, willing, free spirit, disposed to serve our neighbor voluntarily, without taking any account of gratitude or ingratitude, praise or blame, gain or loss. Its object is not to lay men under obligations nor does it distinguish between friends and enemies, or look to gratitude or ingratitude, but most freely and willingly spends itself and its goods, whether it loses them through ingratitude, or gains goodwill.

Who then can comprehend the riches and glory of the Christian life? It can do all things, has all things, and is in want of nothing; is lord over sin, death, and hell, and at the same time is the obedient and useful servant of all. But alas! it is at this day unknown throughout the world; it is neither preached nor sought after, so that we are

quite ignorant about our own name, why we are and are called
Christians. We are certainly called so from Christ, who is not absent,
but dwells among us—provided, that is, that we believe in Him and
are reciprocally and mutually one the Christ of the other, doing to
our neighbor as Christ does to us. . . .

We conclude therefore that a Christian man does not live in himself, but in Christ and in his neighbor, or else is no Christian: in
Christ by faith; in his neighbor by love. By faith he is carried upwards above himself to God, and by love he sinks back below himself
to his neighbor, still always abiding in God and His love, as Christ
says, "Verily I say unto you, Hereafter ye shall see heaven open, and
the angels of God ascending and descending upon the Son of man."
(John i. 51.)

Thus much concerning liberty, which, as you see, is a true and
spiritual liberty, making our hearts free from all sins, laws, and
commandments, as Paul says, "The law is not made for a righteous
man" (I Tim. i. 9), and one which surpasses all other external liber-
ties, as far as heaven is above earth. May Christ make us to understand and preserve this liberty. Amen.

❦❦❦❦

32

BENEDICT DE SPINOZA

Faith as Obedience *

IN THIS SELECTION, Spinoza is concerned to show that faith is a
matter of obedience and piety and that this is the basic teaching
of Scripture. He holds that we can only judge a man to be faithful
or unfaithful by his works. Religious dogmas should be pious rather
than true, so that they will provoke us to obedience. He urges that
in a universal religion there must be no dogmas or doctrines that
cause controversy among men. The nature of a universal religion is
outlined by the enumeration of the fundamental dogmas necessary
for obedience to God and his proper worship. The best faith is
possessed not by him who "displays the best reason, but by him

* From A *Theologico-Political Treatise,* translated by R. H. M. Elwes (London:
George Bell and Sons, 1913), pp. 183-99.
For a brief biographical sketch of Spinoza, see selection 10, page 74.

who displays the best fruits of justice and charity." Finally, the
author states that there is no essential connection between faith
and philosophy, for the former is concerned only with obedience
and piety, the latter with truth. Hence he finds it strange that some
should urge that reason be subservient to faith and to Scripture
and he notes the difficulty of accepting Scriptural passages that
contradict both reason and one another. Therefore, faith, or theology, and reason must be kept distinct and "we may draw the
absolute conclusion that the Bible must not be accomodated to
reason, nor reason to the Bible." The selection concludes with an
exposition of the nature of the certainty we attach to our belief in
Scripture and the need we have for Scripture.

DEFINITIONS OF FAITH, THE FAITH, AND THE FOUNDATIONS
OF FAITH, WHICH IS ONCE FOR ALL SEPARATED
FROM PHILOSOPHY

.   .   .   .   .

WE HAVE SAID . . . that the aim and object of Scripture is only
to teach obedience. Thus much, I think, no one can question. Who
does not see that both Testaments are nothing else but schools for
this object, and have neither of them any aim beyond inspiring
mankind with a voluntary obedience? For . . . I will remark
that Moses did not seek to convince the Jews by reason, but bound
them by a covenant, by oaths, and by conferring benefits; further,
he threatened the people with punishment if they should infringe
the law, and promised rewards if they should obey it. All these are
not means for teaching knowledge, but for inspiring obedience. The
doctrine of the Gospels enjoins nothing but simple faith, namely, to
believe in God and to honor Him, which is the same thing as to
obey Him. There is no occasion for me to throw further light on a
question so plain by citing Scriptural texts commending obedience,
such as may be found in great numbers in both Testaments. Moreover, the Bible teaches very clearly in a great many passages what
everyone ought to do in order to obey God; the whole duty is
summed up in love to one's neighbor. It cannot, therefore, be denied
that he who by God's command loves his neighbor as himself is
truly obedient and blessed according to the law, whereas he who
hates his neighbor or neglects him is rebellious and obstinate.

Lastly, it is plain to everyone that the Bible was not written and
disseminated only for the learned, but for men of every age and
race; wherefore we may rest assured that we are not bound by

Scriptural command to believe anything beyond what is absolutely necessary for fulfilling its main precept. . . .

.   .   .   .   .   .

Faith consists in a knowledge of God, without which obedience to Him would be impossible, and which the mere fact of obedience to him implies. This definition is so clear, and follows so plainly from what we have already proved, that it needs no explanation. The consequences involved therein I will now briefly show. (I) Faith is not salutary in itself, but only in respect to the obedience it implies, or as James puts it in his Epistle, ii. 17, "Faith without works is dead." (II) He who is truly obedient necessarily possesses true and saving faith; for if obedience be granted, faith must be granted also, as the same Apostle expressly says in these words (ii. 18): "Show me thy faith without thy works, and I will show thee my faith by my works." So also John, I iv. 7: "Everyone that loveth is born of God, and knoweth God: he that loveth not, knoweth not God; for God is love." From these texts, I repeat, it follows that we can only judge a man faithful or unfaithful by his works. If his works be good, he is faithful, however much his doctrines may differ from those of the rest of the faithful: if his works be evil, though he may verbally conform, he is unfaithful. For obedience implies faith, and faith without works is dead. . . .

From all this, I repeat, it follows that they are the true enemies of Christ who persecute honorable and justice-loving men because they differ from them, and do not uphold the same religious dogmas as themselves: for whosoever loves justice and charity we know, by that very fact, to be faithful: whosoever persecutes the faithful, is an enemy to Christ.

Lastly, it follows that faith does not demand that dogmas should be true as that they should be pious—that is, such as will stir up the heart to obey; though there be many such which contain not a shadow of truth, so long as they be held in good faith, otherwise their adherents are disobedient, for how can anyone, desirous of loving justice and obeying God, adore as Divine what he knows to be alien from the Divine nature? However, men may err from simplicity of mind, and Scripture, as we have seen, does not condemn ignorance, but obstinacy. This is the necessary result of our definition of faith, and all its branches should spring from the universal rule above given, and from the evident aim and object of the Bible, unless we choose to mix our own inventions therewith. Thus it is not true doctrines which are expressly required by the Bible, so much as doctrines necessary for obedience, and to confirm in our hearts the love of our neighbor, wherein (to adopt the words of John) we are in God and God in us.

As, then, each man's faith must be judged pious or impious only in respect of its producing obedience or obstinacy, and not in respect of its truth; and as no one will dispute that men's dispositions are exceedingly varied, that all do not acquiesce in the same things, but are ruled some by one opinion, some by another, so that what moves one to devotion moves another to laughter and contempt, it follows that there can be no doctrines in the Catholic, or universal, religion, which can give rise to controversy among good men. Such doctrines might be pious to some and impious to others, whereas they should be judged solely by their fruits.

To the universal religion, then, belong only such dogmas as are absolutely required in order to attain obedience to God, and without which such obedience would be impossible; as for the rest, each man—seeing that he is the best judge of his own character—should adopt whatever he thinks best adapted to strengthen his love of justice. If this were so, I think there would be no further occasion for controversies in the Church.

I have now no further fear in enumerating the dogmas of universal faith or the fundamental dogmas of the whole of Scripture, inasmuch as they all tend (as may be seen from what has been said) to this one doctrine, namely, that there exists a God, that is, a Supreme Being, Who loves justice and charity, and Who must be obeyed by whosoever would be saved; that the worship of this Being consists in the practice of justice and love towards one's neighbor, and that they contain nothing beyond the following doctrines:—

I. That God or a Supreme Being exists, sovereignly just and merciful, the Exemplar of the true life; that whosoever is ignorant of or disbelieves in His existence cannot obey Him or know Him as a Judge.

II. That He is One. Nobody will dispute that this doctrine is absolutely necessary for entire devotion, admiration, and love towards God. For devotion, admiration, and love spring from the superiority of one over all else.

III. That He is omnipresent, or that all things are open to him, for if anything could be supposed to be concealed from Him, or to be unnoticed by Him, we might doubt or be ignorant of the equity of His judgment as directing all things.

IV. That He has supreme right and dominion over all things, and that He does nothing under compulsion, but by His absolute fiat and grace. All things are bound to obey Him, He is not bound to obey any.

V. That the worship of God consists only in justice and charity, or love towards one's neighbor.

VI. That all those, and those only, who obey God by their manner of life are saved; the rest of mankind, who live under the sway of their pleasures, are lost. If we did not believe this, there would be no reason for obeying God rather than pleasure.

VII. Lastly, that God forgives the sins of those who repent. No one is free from sin, so that without this belief all would despair of salvation, and there would be no reason for believing in the mercy of God. He who firmly believes that God, out of the mercy and grace with which He directs all things, forgives the sins of men, and who feels his love of God kindled thereby, he, I say, does really know Christ according to the Spirit, and Christ is in him.

No one can deny that all these doctrines are before all things necessary to be believed, in order that every man, without exception, may be able to obey God according to the bidding of the Law above explained, for if one of these precepts be disregarded obedience is destroyed. But as to what God, or the Exemplar of the true life, may be, whether fire, or spirit, or light, or thought, or what not, this I say, has nothing to do with faith any more than has the question how He comes to be the Exemplar of the true life, whether it be because He has a just and merciful mind, or because all things exist and act through Him and consequently that we understand through Him, and through Him see what is truly just and good. Everyone may think on such questions as he likes.

Furthermore, faith is not affected, whether we hold that God is omnipresent essentially or potentially; that He directs all things by absolute fiat, or by the necessity of His nature; that He dictates laws like a prince, or that He sets them forth as eternal truths; that man obeys Him by virtue of free will, or by virtue of the necessity of the Divine decree; lastly, that the reward of the good and the punishment of the wicked is natural or supernatural: these and such like questions have no bearing on faith, except in so far as they are used as means to give us license to sin more, or to obey God less. I will go further, and maintain that every man is bound to adapt these dogmas to his own way of thinking, and to interpret them according as he feels that he can give them his fullest and most unhesitating assent, so that he may the more easily obey God with his whole heart.

Such was the manner, as we have already pointed out, in which the faith was in old time revealed and written, in accordance with the understanding and opinions of the prophets and people of the period; so, in like fashion, every man is bound to adapt it to his own opinions, so that he may accept it without any hesitation or mental repugnance. We have shown that faith does not so much require truth as piety, and that it is only quickening and pious through obedience, consequently no one is faithful save by obedience alone. The best faith is not necessarily possessed by him who displays the best reasons, but by him who displays the best fruits of justice and charity. . . .

It remains for me to show that between faith or theology, and philosophy, there is no connection, nor affinity. I think no one will dispute the fact who has knowledge of the aim and foundations of the two subjects, for they are as wide apart as the poles.

Philosophy has no end in view save truth: faith, as we have abundantly proved, looks for nothing but obedience and piety. Again, philosophy is based on axioms which must be sought from nature alone: faith is based on history and language, and must be sought for only in Scripture and revelation. Faith, therefore, allows the greatest latitude in philosophic speculation, allowing us without blame to think what we like about anything, and only condemning, as heretics and schismatics, those who teach opinions which tend to produce obstinacy, hatred, strife, and anger; while, on the other hand, only considering as faithful those who persuade us, as far as their reason and faculties will permit, to follow justice and charity. . . .

THEOLOGY IS SHOWN NOT TO BE SUBSERVIENT TO REASON, NOR REASON TO THEOLOGY; A DEFINITION OF THE REASON WHICH ENABLES US TO ACCEPT THE AUTHORITY OF THE BIBLE

Those who know not that philosophy and reason are distinct, dispute whether Scripture should be made subservient to reason, or reason to Scripture: that is, whether the meaning of Scripture should be made to agree with reason; or whether reason should be made to agree with Scripture: the latter position is assumed by the sceptics who deny the certitude of reason, the former by the dogmatists. Both parties are, as I have shown, utterly in the wrong, for either doctrine would require us to tamper with reason or with Scripture.

We have shown that Scripture does not teach philosophy, but merely obedience, and that all it contains has been adapted to the understanding and established opinions of the multitude. Those, therefore, who wish to adapt it to philosophy, must needs ascribe to the prophets many ideas which they never even dreamed of, and give an extremely forced interpretation to their words: those on the other hand, who would make reason and philosophy subservient to theology, will be forced to accept as Divine utterances the prejudices of the ancient Jews, and to fill and confuse their mind therewith. In short, one party will run wild with the aid of reason, and the other will run wild without the aid of reason.

The first among the Pharisees who openly maintained that Scripture should be made to agree with reason, was Maimonides. . . . Now, although this writer had much authority among his contemporaries, he was deserted on this question by almost all, and the majority went straight over to the opinion of a certain R. Jehuda Alpakhar, who, in his anxiety to avoid the error of Maimonides, fell into another, which was its exact contrary. He held that reason should be made subservient, and entirely give way to Scripture. He thought that a passage should not be interpreted metaphorically, simply because it was repugnant to reason, but only in the cases when it is inconsistent with Scripture itself—that is, with its clear doctrines. Therefore he laid down the universal rule, that whatsoever Scripture teaches dogmatically, and affirms expressly, must on its own sole authority be admitted as absolutely true: that there is no doctrine in the Bible which directly contradicts the general tenor of the whole: but only some which appear to involve a difference, for the phrases of Scripture often seem to imply something contrary to what has been expressly taught. Such phrases, and such phrases only, we may interpret metaphorically.

For instance, Scripture clearly teaches the unity of God, nor is there any text distinctly asserting a plurality of gods; but in several passages God speaks of Himself, and the prophets speak of Him, in the plural number; such phrases are simply a manner of speaking, and do not mean that there actually are several gods: they are to be explained metaphorically, not because a plurality of gods is repugnant to reason, but because Scripture distinctly asserts that there is only one.

So, again, as Scripture asserts (as Alpakhar thinks) in Deut. iv. 15, that God is incorporeal, we are bound, solely by the authority of this text, and not by reason, to believe that God has no body: consequently we must explain metaphorically, on the sole authority of Scripture, all those passages which attribute to God hands, feet, etc., and take them merely as figures of speech. Such is the opinion of Alpakhar. In so far as he seeks to explain Scripture by Scripture, I praise him, but I marvel that a man gifted with reason should wish to debase that faculty. It is true that Scripture should be explained by Scripture, so long as we are in difficulties about the meaning and intention of the prophets, but when we have elicited the true meaning, we must of necessity make use of our judgment and reason in order to assent thereto. If reason, however, much as she rebels, is to be entirely subject to Scripture, I ask, are we to effect her submission by her own aid, or without her, and blindly? If the latter, we shall surely act foolishly and injudiciously; if the former, we assent to Scripture under the dominion of reason, and should not assent to it without her. Moreover, I may ask now, is a man to assent to anything against his reason? What is denial if it be not reason's refusal to assent? In short, I am astonished that anyone should wish to subject reason, the greatest of gifts and a light from on high, to the dead letter which may have been corrupted by human malice; that it should be thought no crime to speak with contempt of mind, the true handwriting of God's Word, calling it corrupt, blind, and lost, while it is considered the greatest of crimes to say the same of the letter, which is merely the reflection and image of God's Word. Men think it pious to trust nothing to reason and their own judgment, and impious to doubt the faith of those who have transmitted to us the sacred books. Such conduct is not piety, but mere folly. And, after all, why are they so anxious? What are they afraid of? Do they think that faith and religion cannot be upheld unless men purposely keep themselves in ignorance, and turn their backs on reason? If this be so, they have but a timid trust in Scripture. . . .

. . . Perhaps it will be answered that Scripture contains nothing repugnant to reason. But I insist that it expressly affirms and teaches that God is jealous . . . and I assert that such a doctrine is repugnant to reason. It must, I suppose, in spite of all be accepted as true. If there are any passages in Scripture which imply that God is not jealous, they must be taken metaphorically as meaning nothing of the kind. . . . So also we must believe that the sky is the habitation and throne of God, for Scripture expressly says so; and similarly many passages expressing the opinions of the prophets or the multitude, which reason and philosophy, but not Scripture, tell us to be false, must be taken as true if we are to follow the guidance of our author, for according to him reason has nothing to do with the matter. Further, it is untrue that Scripture never contradicts itself directly, but only by implication. . . .

Samuel expressly denies that God ever repents, "for he is not a man that he should repent." (1 Sam. xv. 29.) Jeremiah, on the other hand, asserts that God does repent, both of the evil and of the good which He had intended to do. (Jer. xviii. 8-10.) What? Are not these two texts directly contradictory? Which of the two, then, would our author want to explain metaphorically? Both statements are general, and each is the opposite of the other—what one flatly affirms, the other flatly denies. So, by his own rule, he would be obliged at once to reject them as false, and to accept them as true. . . .

. . . . .

We may, therefore, put this theory, as well as that of Maimonides, entirely out of court; and we may take it for indisputable that theology is not bound to serve reason, nor reason theology, but that each has her own domain.

The sphere of reason is, as we have said, truth and wisdom; the sphere of theology is piety and obedience. The power of reason does not extend so far as to determine for us that men may be blessed through simple obedience, without understanding. Theology tells us nothing else, enjoins on us no command save obedience, and has neither the will nor the power to oppose reason: she defines the dogmas of faith only in so far as they may be necessary for obedience, and leaves reason to determine their precise truth: for reason is the light of the mind, and without her all things are dreams and phantoms.

By theology, I here mean, strictly speaking revelation, in so far as it indicates the object aimed at by Scripture—namely, the scheme and manner of obedience, or the true dogmas of piety and faith. This may truly be called the Word of God, which does not consist in a certain number of books. Theology thus understood, if we regard its precepts or rules of life, will be found in accordance with reason; and, if we look to its aim and object, will be seen to be in nowise repugnant thereto, wherefore it is universal to all men. . . .

To sum up, we may draw the absolute conclusion that the Bible must not be accommodated to reason, nor reason to the Bible.

Now, inasmuch as the basis of theology—the doctrine that man may be saved by obedience alone—cannot be proved by reason whether it be true or false, we may be asked, Why, then, should we believe it? If we do so without the aid of reason, we accept it blindly, and act foolishly and injudiciously; if, on the other hand, we settle that it can be proved by reason, theology becomes a part of philosophy, and inseparable therefrom. But I make answer that I have absolutely established that this basis of theology cannot be investigated by the natural light of reason, or, at any rate, that no one ever has proved it by such means, and therefore revelation was necessary. We should, however, make use of our reason in order to grasp with moral certainty what is revealed—I say, with moral certainty, for we cannot hope to attain greater certainty than the prophets: yet their certainty was only moral. . . .

Those, therefore, who attempt to set forth the authority of Scripture with mathematical demonstrations are wholly in error: for the authority of the Bible is dependent on the authority of the prophets, and can be supported by no stronger arguments that those employed in old time by the prophets for convincing the people of their own authority. Our certainty on the same subject can be founded on no other basis than that which served as foundation for the certainty of the prophets.

Now the certainty of the prophets consisted in these three elements:—(I). A distinct and vivid imagination. (II). A sign. (III). Lastly, and chiefly, a mind turned to what is just and good. It was based on no other reasons than these, and consequently they cannot prove their authority by any other reasons, either to the multitude whom they addressed orally, nor to us whom they address in writing.

The first of these reasons, namely, the vivid imagination, could be valid only for the prophets; therefore, our certainty concerning revelation must, and ought to be based on the remaining two—namely, the sign and the teaching. . . .

The only reason, then, which we have for belief in Scripture or the writings of the prophets, is the doctrine we find therein, and the signs by which it is confirmed. For as we see that the prophets extol charity and justice above all things, and have no other object, we conclude that they did not write from unworthy motives, but because they really thought that men might become blessed through obedience and faith: further, as we see that they confirmed their teaching with signs and wonders, we become persuaded that they did not speak at random, nor run riot in their prophecies. We are further strengthened in our conclusion by the fact that the morality they teach is in evident agreement with reason, for it is no accidental coincidence that the Word of God which we find in the prophets coincides with the Word of God written in our hearts. . . .

Therefore this whole basis of theology and Scripture, though it does not admit of mathematical proof, may yet be accepted with the approval of our judgment. It would be folly to refuse to accept what is confirmed by such ample prophetic testimony, and what has proved such a comfort to those whose reason is comparatively weak, and such a benefit to the state; a doctrine, moreover, which we may believe in without the slightest peril or hurt, and should reject simply because it cannot be mathematically proved: it is as though we should admit nothing as true, or as a wise rule of life, which could ever, in any possible way, be called in question; or as though most of our actions were not full of uncertainty and hazard.

I admit that those who believe that theology and philosophy are mutually contradictory, and that therefore either one or the other must be thrust from its throne—I admit, I say, that such persons are not unreasonable in attempting to put theology on a firm basis, and to demonstrate its truth mathematically. Who, unless he were desperate or mad, would wish to bid an incontinent farewell to reason, or to despise the arts and sciences, or to deny reason's certitude? But, in the meanwhile, we cannot wholly absolve them from blame, inasmuch as they invoke the aid of reason for her own defeat, and attempt infallibly to prove her fallible. While they are trying to prove mathematically the authority and truth of theology, and to take away the authority of natural reason, they are in reality only bringing theology under reason's dominion, and proving that her authority has no weight unless natural reason be at the back of it.

If they boast that they themselves assent because of the inward testimony of the Holy Spirit, and that they only invoke the aid of reason because of unbelievers, in order to convince them, not even so can this meet with our approval, for we can easily show that they have spoken either from emotion or vain-glory. . . . No spirit gives testimony concerning the certitude of matters within the sphere of speculation, save only reason, who is mistress, as we have shown, of the whole realm of truth. If then they assert that they possess this Spirit which makes them certain of truth, they speak falsely, and according to the prejudices of the emotions, or else they are in great dread lest they should be vanquished by philosophers and exposed to public ridicule, and therefore they flee, as it were to the altar; but their refuge is vain, for what altar will shelter a man who has outraged reason? However, I pass such persons over, for I think I have fulfilled my purpose, and shown how philosophy should be separated from theology, and wherein each consists; that neither should be subservient to the other, but that each should keep her unopposed dominion. Lastly, as occasion offered, I have pointed out the absurdities, the inconveniences, and the evils following from the extraordinary confusion which has hitherto prevailed between the two subjects, owing to their not being properly distinguished and separated. Before I go further I would expressly state that I consider the utility and the need for Holy Scripture or Revelation to be very great. For as we cannot perceive by the natural light of reason that simple obedience is the path of salvation, and are taught by revelation only that it is so by the special grace of God, which our reason cannot attain, it follows that the Bible has brought a very great consolation to mankind. All are able to obey, whereas there are but very few, compared with the aggregate of humanity, who can acquire the habit of virtue under the unaided guidance of reason. Thus if we had not the testimony of Scripture, we should doubt of the salvation of nearly all men.

❧❧❧

33

KARL BARTH

On Christian Faith *

IN THIS COMMENTARY on the first words of the Apostle's Creed, Barth states his concern, not with subjective faith, with the fact *that* a person believes, but rather with God as the object of faith, with our belief *in* God and His Word, with *what* we believe. Faith, he further declares, is a gift of God whereby He has freed us (from ourselves) so that we may trust in Him, know Him, and acknowledge Him. By faith we trust in God and His promises; we rely on Him for our guidance and salvation, and not on ourselves or on lesser gods or authorities. Furthermore, Christian faith is not irrational, antirational, or suprarational; it is rational. Christian faith constitutes a fullness of knowledge that merges into wisdom—it is a knowledge that embodies living with the Truth, with Christ as the ultimate absolute Truth. In conclusion, Barth emphasizes that the Christian faith is historical in character and, in addition, to being characterized as trust and knowledge, it involves a public responsibility on our part—to confess and make known our faith, for the "word and work of the believer cannot remain neutral and uncommitted."

* From *Dogmatics in Outline*, translated by G. T. Thomson (Philosophical Library, 1949), pp. 15-21, 22-27, 28-34. Reprinted by permission of the publishers.

Karl Barth (1886-) was born in Switzerland and educated at the Universities of Berne, Berlin, Tubingen and Marburg. He was a Professor of Theology at Bonn from 1930 to 1934. He was retired for his opposition to the policy of "Nazification" and was appointed Professor of Theology at the University of Basel, a post he has held since 1935. He is one of the leading Protestant theologians and is noted for his leadership of the Neo-Orthodox movement.

FAITH AS TRUST

THE CONFESSION begins with the significant words, 'I believe.' This indicates that we link up all that is to be said as fundamental to our task with this simple introduction to the Confession. We start with three leading propositions, which describe the nature of faith.

Christian faith is the gift of the meeting in which men become free to hear the word of grace which God has spoken in Jesus Christ in such a way that, in spite of all that contradicts it, they may once for all, exclusively and entirely, hold to His promise and guidance.

Christian faith, Church proclamation, which as we stated is the cause and basic reason for dogmatics, deals—well, what does it deal with? With the fact that Christians believe? And the way in which Christians believe? Actually, this fact, the subjective form of faith, the *fides qua creditur,* cannot possibly be quite excluded from proclamation. Where the gospel is proclaimed, there too of necessity the fact will be proclaimed along with it that there are men who have heard and accepted the gospel. But the fact that we believe can only be, *a priori,* a secondary matter, becoming small and unimportant in face of the outstanding and real thing involved in the Christian proclamation—*what* the Christian believes, that is, what must be confirmed as the content and object of his faith, and *what* we have to preach, that is, the object with which the Apostles' Creed deals: I believe in God, the Father, the Son and the Holy Spirit. More popularly the Confession is called the 'Belief'; and by this 'Belief' we are at the very least to realise the fact that we believe. In Christian faith we are concerned quite decisively with a meeting. 'I believe in'—so the Confession says; and everything depends on this 'in,' this *eis,* this *in* (Latin). The Creed explains this 'in,' this object of faith, by which our subjective faith lives. It is noteworthy that, apart from this first expression 'I believe,' the Confession is silent upon the subjective fact of faith. Nor was it a good time when this relationship was reversed, when Christians grew eloquent over their action, over the uplift and emotion of the experience of this thing, which took place in man, and when they became speechless as to *what* we may believe. By the silence of the Confession on the subjective side, by its speaking only of the objective Creed, it also speaks at its best, deepest and completest about what happens to us men, about what we may be, do, and experience. Here too it is true that whoso would keep his life shall lose it; but whoso shall lose it for My sake shall gain his life. Whoso means to rescue and preserve the subjective element shall lose it; but whoso gives it up for the sake of the objective, shall save it. I believe—of course! It is my, it is a human, experience and action, that is, a human form of existence.

But this 'I believe' is consummated in a meeting with One who is not man, but God, the Father, Son, and Holy Spirit, and by my believing I see myself completely filled and determined by this object of my faith. And what interests me is not myself with my faith, but He in whom I believe. And then I learn that by thinking of Him and looking to Him, my interests are also best provided for. I believe in, *credo in,* means that I am not alone. In our glory and in our misery we men are not alone. God comes to meet us and as our Lord and Master He comes to our aid. We live and act and suffer, in good and in bad days, in our perversity and in our rightness, in this confrontation with God. I am not alone, but God meets me; one way or other, I am in all circumstances in company with Him. That is, I believe in God, the Father, the Son and the Holy Spirit. This meeting with God is the meeting with the word of grace which He has spoken in Jesus Christ. Faith speaks of God, the Father, the Son and the Holy Spirit, as Him who meets us, as the object of faith, and says of this God that He is one in Himself, has become single in Himself for us and has become single once more in the eternal decree, explicated in time, of His free, unowed, unconditional love for man, for all men, in the counsel of His grace. God is gracious to us—this is what the Confession of the Father, Son and Holy Spirit, says. This includes the fact that of ourselves we cannot achieve, have not achieved, and shall not achieve a togetherness with Him; that we have not deserved that He should be our God, have no power of disposal and no rights over Him, but that with unowed kindness, in the freedom of His majesty, He resolved of His own self to be man's God, our God. He *tells* us that this is so. God's telling us, 'I am gracious to you,' is the Word of God, the central concept of all Christian thinking. The Word of God is the word of His grace. And if you ask me where we hear this Word of God, I can only point to Himself, who enables us to hear it, and reply with the mighty centre of the Confession, with the second article, that the word of God's grace in which He meets us is called Jesus Christ, the Son of God and Son of man, true God and true Man, Immanuel, God with us in this One. Christian faith is the meeting with this 'Immanuel,' the meeting with Jesus Christ and in Him with the living Word of God. In calling Holy Scripture the Word of God (and we do so call it, because it is so), we mean by it Holy Scripture as the witness of the prophets and the apostles to this one Word of God, to Jesus, the man out of Israel, who is God's Christ, our Lord and King in eternity. And in confessing this, in venturing to call the Church's proclamation God's Word, we must be understood to mean the proclamation of Jesus Christ, of Him who is true God and true Man for our good. In Him God meets us. And when we say, I believe *in* God, the concrete meaning is that I believe in the Lord Jesus Christ.

I have described this meeting as a gift. It is a meeting in which men become free to hear God's Word. The gift and the becoming free belong to each other. The gift is the gift of freedom, of the great freedom in which all other freedoms are included. . . . Freedom is God's great gift, the gift of meeting with Him. Why a gift, and why a gift of freedom? What it means is that this meeting of which the Creed speaks does not take place in vain. It rests not upon a human possibility and human initiative, nor on the fact that we men bear in us a capacity to meet God, to hear His Word. Were we to reckon up for ourselves what we men are capable of, we should strive in vain to discover anything which might be termed a disposition towards the Word of God. Without any possibility on our side God's great possibility comes into view, making possibile what is impossible from our side. It is God's gift, God's free gift, not prepared for by anything on our side, *if* we meet Him and in meeting with Him hear His Word. The Creed of the Father, Son and Holy Spirit speaks in all three articles of a nature and work absolutely new to us men, inaccessible and inconceivable to us. And as this nature and work of God the Father, the Son and the Holy Spirit is His free grace towards us, it is grace all over again if our eyes and ears are opened to this grace. As it is the mystery of God of which the Creed speaks, we are set in its midst when it is disclosed to us, when we become free to know it and to live in it. 'I believe that not of my own reason and power do I believe in my Lord or am able to come to Him, says Luther. I believe; so then, it is itself a recognition of faith, to recognize that God is to be known only through God Himself. And if we can repeat this in faith, it means that I give praise and thanks for the fact that God the Father, the Son and the Holy Spirit is what He is and does what He does, and has disclosed and revealed Himself to me, has determined Himself for me and not for Himself. I give praise and thanks for the fact that I am elect, that I am called, that my Lord has made me free for Himself. In that confidence I believe. That which I do in believing is the only thing left me, to which I have been invited, to which I have been made free by Him who can do what I can neither begin nor accomplish of myself. I make use of the gift in which God has given me Himself. I breathe, and now I breathe joyfully and freely in the freedom which I have not taken to myself, which I have not sought nor found by myself, but in which God has come to me and adopted me. It is a matter of freedom to hear the word of grace in such a way that man may hold to this word. To hold to a word means that this word is credible to me. The world is full of words, and nowadays we realize what it means when an inflation of words is reached—that is, when all old words lose their value, when they cease to have any currency. Where there is faith in the gospel, there the Word has found confidence, there the Word has so let itself be heard that the hearer cannot withdraw from it. There the Word has acquired its meaning as the Word and been established.

This remarkable Word in which faith believes is the Word of God, Jesus Christ, in whom God has spoken His Word to man once for all. So faith means trust. Trust is the act in which a man may rely on the faithfulness of Another, that His promise holds and that what He demands He demands of necessity. 'I believe' means 'I trust.' No more must I dream of trusting in myself, I no longer require to justify myself, to excuse myself, to attempt to save and preserve myself. This most profound effort of man to trust to believe, to see himself as in the right, has become pointless. I believe—not in my-self—I believe in God the Father, the Son and the Holy Ghost. So also trust in any sort of authorities, who might offer themselves to me as trustworthy, as an anchor which I ought to hold on to, has become frail and superfluous. Trust in any sort of gods has become frail and superfluous. These are the gods set up, honored and wor-shipped by men in ancient and recent times: the authorities on whom man relies, no matter whether they have the form of ideas or of any sort of powers of destiny, no matter what they are called. Faith delivers us from trust in such gods, and therefore also from fear of them, from the disillusionments which they inevitably prepare for us again and again. We are given freedom to trust in Him who de-serves our trust: freedom by holding to Him who in distinction from all other authorities is and will remain faithful. We ourselves shall never be true to ourselves. Our human path is, as such, a path from one disloyalty to another; and it is the same with the ways of the gods of this world. They do not keep what they promise. So with them there is never any real peace and clarity. In God alone is there faithfulness, and faith is the trust that we may hold to Him, to His promise and to His guidance. To hold to God is to rely on the fact that God is there for me, and to live in this certainty. This is the promise God gives us: I am there for you. But this promise at once means guidance too. I am not left to my waywardness and my own ideas; but I have His commandment, to which I may hold in everything, in my entire earthly existence. The Creed is always at the same time the gospel, God's glad tidings to man, the message of Immanuel, God with us, to us; and as such it is necessarily also the law. Gospel and law are not to be separated; they are one, in such a way that the gospel is the primary thing, that the glad tidings are first in the field and, as such, include the law. Because God is for us, we may also be for Him. Because He has given Himself to us, we may also in gratitude give Him the trifle which we have to give. To hold to God thus always means that we receive everything wholly from God and so are wholly active for Him.

And this 'in spite of all that contradicts it, once for all, exclusively and entirely.' In these four categories faith is once more described as trust. When we say that faith involves *in spite of*, once for all, exclusively and entirely, we are to hold to the fact that in faith is involved a 'may,' not a 'must.' The moment the thing becomes an ideal instance we have again dropped out of the glory of faith. The glory of faith does not consist in our being challenged to do something, in having something laid upon us which is beyond our strength. Faith is rather a freedom, a permission. It is permitted to be so—that the believer in God's Word may hold on to this Word in everything, in spite of all that contradicts it. It is so: we never believe 'on account of,' never 'because of'; we awake to faith in spite of everything. Think of the men in the Bible. They did not come to faith by reason of any kind of proofs, but one day they were so placed that they might believe and then had to believe in spite of everything. God is hidden from us outside His Word. But He is manifest to us in Jesus Christ. If we look past Him, we must not be surprised if we fail to find God and experience errors and disillusionments, if the world seems dark to us. When we believe, we must believe in spite of God's hiddenness. This hiddenness of God necessarily reminds us of our human limitation. We do not believe out of our personal reason and power. Anyone who really believes knows that. The greatest hindrance to faith is again and again just the pride and anxiety of our human hearts. We would rather not live by grace. Something within us energetically rebels against it. We do not wish to receive grace; at best we prefer to give ourselves grace. This swing to and fro between pride and anxiety is man's life. Faith bursts through them both. Of his own strength a man cannot do it. We cannot deliver ourselves from pride and anxiety about life; but there will always be a movement of defiance, not last against ourselves. If we summarize all that opposes as the power of contradiction, one has an inkling of what Scripture means by the devil. 'Has God really said. . . ?' Is God's Word true? If one believes, one will snap one's fingers at the devil. But it is no human act of heroism to believe. Beware of wanting to make a hero of Luther. Luther himself never felt like one; but he realised that if we may defy, it is really a 'may,' a permission, a freedom which we can only receive in deepest humility.

And faith is concerned with a decision *once for all*. Faith is not an opinion replaceable by another opinion. A temporary believer does not know what faith is. Faith means a final relationship. Faith is concerned with God, with what He has done for us once for all. That does not exclude the fact that there are fluctuations in faith. But seen with regard to its object, faith is a final thing. A man who believes once believes once for all. Don't be afraid; regard even that as an invitation. One may, of course, be confused and one may doubt; but whoever once believes has something like a *character indelibilis*. He may take comfort of the fact that he is being upheld. Everyone who has to contend with unbelief should be advised that he ought not to take his own unbelief too seriously. Only faith is to be taken seriously; and if we have faith as a grain of mustard seed, that suffices for the devil to have lost his game.

And thirdly, faith is concerned with our holding to God *exclusively*, because God is the One who is faithful. There is also human faithfulness, a faithfulness of God, which may look at us out of His creatures and rejoice and strengthen us; but where such faithfulness exists, its basis will always be the faithfulness of God. To believe is the freedom to trust in Him quite alone, *sola gratia* and *sola fide*. This signifies not an impoverishment of human life, but rather that the riches of God are assigned to us.

And, in conclusion, we may hold *entirely* to God's Word. Faith is not concerned with a special realm, that of religion, say, but with real life in its totality, the outward as well as the inward questions, that which is bodily as well as that which is spiritual, the brightness as well as the gloom in our life. Faith is concerned with our being permitted to rely on God as regards ourselves and also as regards what moves us on behalf of others, of the whole of humanity; it is concerned with the whole of living and the whole of dying. The freedom to have this trust (understood in this comprehensive way) is faith.

FAITH AS KNOWLEDGE

Possibly you may be struck by the emergence of the concept of *reason*. I use it deliberately. The saying, 'Despise only reason and science, man's supremest power of all,' was uttered not by a prophet, but by Goethe's Mephisto. Christendom and the theological world were always ill-advised in thinking it their duty for some reason or other, either of enthusiasm or of theological conception, to betake themselves to the camp of an opposition to reason. Over the Christian Church, as the essence of revelation and of the work of God which constitutes its basis, stands the Word: 'The Word was made flesh.' The Logos became man. Church proclamation is language, and language not of an accidental, arbitrary, chaotic and incomprehensible kind, but language which comes forward with the claim to be true and to uphold itself as the truth against the lie. Do not let us be forced from the clarity of this position. In the Word which the Church has to proclaim the truth is involved, not in a provisional, secondary sense, but in the primary sense of the Word itself—the Logos is involved, and is demonstrated and revealed in the human reason, the human *nous*, as the Logos, that is, as meaning, as truth to be learned. In the word of Christian proclamation we are concerned with *ratio*, reason, in which human *ratio* may also be reflected and reproduced. Church proclamation, theology, is no talk or babbling; it is not propaganda unable to withstand the claim, Is it then true as well, this that is said? Is it really so? . . . The Creed of Christian faith rests upon knowledge. And where the Creed is uttered and confessed knowledge should be, is meant to be, created. Christian faith is not irrational, not anti-rational, not supra-rational, but rational in the proper sense. The Church which utters the Creed, which comes forward with the tremendous claim to preach and to proclaim the glad tidings, derives from the fact that it has apprehended something—*Vernunft* comes from *vernehmen*—and it wishes to let what it has apprehended be apprehended again. These were always unpropitious periods in the Christian Church, when Christian histories of dogmatics and theology separated *gnosis* and *pistis*. *Pistis* rightly understood is *gnosis*; rightly understood the act of faith is also an act of knowledge. Faith means knowledge.

But once this is established, it must also be said that Christian faith is concerned with an illumination of the reason. Christian faith has to do with the object, with God the Father, the Son, and the Holy Spirit, of which the Creed speaks. Of course it is of the nature and being of this object, of God the Father, the Son, and the Holy Spirit, that He cannot be known by the powers of human knowledge, but is apprehensible and apprehended solely because of His own freedom, decision and action. What man can know by his own power according to the measure of his natural powers, his understanding his feeling, will be at most something like a supreme being, an absolute nature, the idea of an utterly free power, of a being towering over everything. This absolute and supreme being, the ultimate and most profound, this 'thing in itself,' has nothing to do with God. It is part of the intuitions and marginal possibilities of man's thinking, man's contrivance. Man is able to think this being; but he has not thereby thought God. God is thought and known when in His own freedom God makes Himself apprehensible. . . . God is always the One who has made Himself known to man in His own revelation, and not the one man thinks out for himself and describes as God. There is a perfectly clear division there already, epistemologically, between the true God and the false gods. Knowledge of God is not a possibility which is open for discussion. God is the essence of all reality, of that reality which reveals itself to us. Knowledge of God takes place where there is actual experience that God speaks, that He so represents Himself to man that he cannot fail to see and hear Him, where, in a situation which he has not brought about, in which he becomes incomprehensible to himself, man sees himself faced with the fact that he lives with God and God with him, because so it has pleased God. Knowledge of God takes place where divine revelation takes place, illumination of man by God, transmission of human knowledge, instruction of man by this incomparable Teacher.

We started from the point that Christian faith is a meeting. Christian faith and knowledge of Christian faith takes place at the point where the divine reason, the divine Logos, sets up His law in the region of man's understanding, to which law human, creaturely reason must accommodate itself. When that happens, man comes to knowledge; for when God sets up His law in man's thought, in his seeing and hearing and feeling, the revelation of the truth is also reached about man and his reason, the revelation of man is reached, who cannot bring about of himself what is brought about simply by God Himself.

Can God be known? Yes, God can be known, since it is actually true and real that He is knowable through Himself. When that happens, man becomes free, he becomes empowered, he becomes capable—a mystery to himself—of knowing God. Knowledge of God is a knowledge completely effected and determined from the side of its object, from the side of God. But for that very reason it is genuine knowledge; for that very reason it is in the deepest sense free knowledge. Of course it remains a relative knowledge, a knowledge imprisoned within the limits of the creaturely. Of course it is especially true here that we are carrying heavenly treasures in earthen vessels. Our concepts are not adequate to grasp this treasure. Precisely where this genuine knowledge of God takes place it will also be clear that there is no occasion for any pride. There always remains powerless man, creaturely reason with its limitations. But in this area of the creaturely, of the inadequate, it has pleased God to reveal Himself. And since man is foolish in this respect too, He will be wise; since man is petty, He will be great; since man is inadequate, God is adequate. 'Let my grace suffice for thee. For my strength is mighty in the weak' holds good also for the question of knowledge.

In the opening statement we said that Christian faith has to do with the illumination of the reason, in which men become free to live in the truth of Jesus Christ. For the understanding of Christian knowledge of faith it is essential to understand that the truth of Jesus Christ is living truth and the knowledge of it living knowledge. This does not mean that we are to revert once more to the idea that here knowledge is not basically involved at all. It is not that Christian faith is a dim sensation, an a-logical feeling, experiencing and learning. Faith is knowledge; it is related to God's Logos, and is therefore a thoroughly logical matter. The truth of Jesus Christ is also in the simplest sense a truth of facts. Its starting-point, the Resurrection of Jesus Christ from the dead, is a fact which occurred in space and time, as the New Testament describes it. The apostles were not satisfied to hold on to an inward fact; they spoke of what they saw and heard and what they touched with their hands. And the truth of Jesus Christ is also a matter of thoroughly clear and, in itself, ordered human thinking; free, precisely in its being bound. But—and the things must not be separated—what is involved is living truth. The concept of knowledge, of *scientia,* is insufficient to describe what Christian knowledge is. We must rather go back to what in the Old Testament is called wisdom, what the Greeks called *sophia* and the Latins *sapientia,* in order to grasp the knowledge of theology in its fullness. *Sapientia* is distinguished from the narrower concept of *scientia,* wisdom is distinguished from knowing, in that it not only contains knowledge in itself, but also that this concept speaks of a knowledge which is practical knowledge, embracing the entire existence of man. Wisdom is the knowledge by which we may actually and practically live; it is empiricism and it is the theory which is powerful in being directly practical, in being the knowledge which dominates our life, which is really a light upon our path. Not a light to wonder at and to observe, not a light to kindle all manner of fireworks at—not even the profoundest philosophical speculations—

but the light on our road which may stand above our action and above our talk, the light on our healthy and on our sick days, in our poverty and in our wealth, the light which does not only lighten when we suppose ourselves to have moments of insight, but which accompanies us even into our folly, which is not quenched, when the goal of our life becomes visible in death. To live by this light, by this truth, is the meaning of Christian knowledge. Christian knowledge means living in the truth of Jesus Christ. In this light we live and move and have our being (Acts 17.28) in order that we may be of Him, and through Him and unto Him, as it says in Romans 11.36. So Christian knowledge, at its deepest, is one with what we termed man's trust in God's Word. Never yield when they try to teach you divisions and separations in this matter. There is no genuine trust, no really tenable, victorious trust in God's Word which is not founded in His truth; and on the other hand no knowledge, no theology, no confessing and no Scripture truth which does not at once possess the stamp of this living truth. The one must always be measured and tested and confirmed by the other.

And just because as Christians we may live in the truth of Jesus Christ and therefore in the light of the knowledge of God and therefore with an illumined reason, we shall also become sure of the meaning of our own existence and of the ground and goal of all that happens. Once more a quite tremendous extension of the field of vision is indicated by this; to know this object in its truth means in truth to know no more and no less than all things, even man, oneself, the cosmos, and the world. The truth of Jesus Christ is not one truth among others; it is *the* truth, the universal truth that creates all truth as surely as it is the truth of God, the *prima veritas* which is also the *ultima veritas*. For in Jesus Christ God has created all things, He has created all of us. We exist not apart from Him, but in Him, whether we are aware of it or not; and the whole cosmos exists not apart from Him, but in Him, borne by Him, the Almighty Word. To know Him is to know all. To be touched and gripped by the Spirit in this realm means being led into all truth. If a man believes and knows God, he can no longer ask, What is the meaning of my life? But by believing he actually lives the meaning of his life, the meaning of his creatureliness, of his individuality, in the limits of his creatureliness and individuality and in the fallibility of his existence, in the sin in which he is involved and of which daily and hourly he is guilty; yet he also lives it with the aid which is daily and hourly imparted to him through God's interceding for him, in spite of him and without his deserving it. He recognizes the task assigned to him in this whole, and the hope vouchsafed to him in and with this task, because of the grace by which he may live and the praise of the glory promised him, by which is is even here and now secretly surrounded in all lowliness. The believer confesses this meaning of his existence. The Christian Creed speaks of God as the ground and goal of all that exists. The ground and goal of the entire cosmos means Jesus Christ. And the unheard-of thing may and must be said, that where Christian faith exists, there also exists, through God's being trusted, inmost familiarity with the ground and goal of all that happens, of all things; there man lives, in spite of all that is said to the contrary, in the peace that passeth all understanding, and which for that very reason is the light that lightens our understanding.

FAITH AS CONFESSION

Christian faith is a decision. This is where we have to begin, and wish to begin. Christian faith, to be sure, is an event in the mystery between God and Man; the event of the freedom in which God acts towards this man, and of the freedom which God gives this man. But this does not exclude, but actually includes the fact that there is faith in the sense of the Christian Creed, *history* is taking place, that there something is being undertaken, completed and carried out in time by man. Faith is God's mystery breaking forth; faith is God's freedom and man's freedom in action. Where nothing occurred—in time, of course, that is, occurred visibly and audibly—there would be no faith either. For Christian faith is faith in God, and when the Christian Confession names God the Father, the Son and the Holy Spirit, it is pointing to the fact that in His inner life and nature God is not dead, not passive, not inactive, but that God the Father, the Son and the Holy Spirit exist in an inner relationship and movement, which may very well be described as a story, as an event. God Himself is not suprahistorical, but historical. And this God has in Himself made a decree, an eternal decree, upon which everything rests of which the Confession of Faith speaks. Our fathers called it the decree of creation and of the covenant and of redemption. The decree of God was carried out in time, once for all, in the work and in the word of Jesus Christ, to which Article II of the Confession bears concrete testimony, 'who suffered under Pontius Pilate, was crucified, dead and buried. . . .' Faith is man's answer to this historical existence and nature and action of God. Faith has to do with the God who is in Himself historical and has fashioned a decree whose goal is history, and has set this history going and completed it. Christian faith which was not itself history would not be Christian faith, not faith in. . . . Where there is Christian faith there arises and grows an historical form, there arises among men, among contemporaries and non-contemporaries, a *community*, a togetherness, a brotherhood. But by means of this community, we inevitably reach, at the point where faith is Christian, a human proclamation and message as well, to the *world* outside this communion and brotherhood. A light is kindled there, which lightens all them that are in the house. In other words, where Christian faith exists, there God's congregation arises and lives in the world for the world; there Israel gathers apart from the Gentiles of the world; and there the Church gathers on its own behalf, the communion of saints. Yet not for its own purposes, but as the manifestation of the Servant of God, whom God has set there for all men, as the Body of Christ. And this story happens—now we reach the human work which answers to God's work and nature in the election of His grace—in the answer of obedience. Faith is obedience, not just a passive accommodation of oneself. Where there is obedience, there is also choice on man's part; faith is chosen instead of its opposite, unbelief, trust instead of distrust, knowledge instead of ignorance. Faith means choosing between faith and unbelief, wrong belief and superstition. Faith is the act in which man relates himself to God as is appropriate to God. For this work takes place in a stepping out of neutrality towards God, out of any disavowal of obligation towards Him in our existence and attitude, out of the private sphere, into resoluteness, responsibility and public life. Faith without this tendency to public life, faith that avoids this difficulty, has become in itself unbelief, wrong belief, superstition. For faith that believes in God the Father, the Son and the Holy Spirit cannot refuse to become public.

. . . In public responsibility, too, there is a permission granted to men, an open door, and that means a freedom. To freedom of trust and freedom of knowledge we must now add freedom of responsibility. Here one freedom is inseparable from the other. If you merely want to be free to trust God and think you can then renounce knowledge, you would not in fact be trusting Him. And if you had all trust and all knowledge and did not have the freedom to answer publicly for your trust and your knowledge, you would have to be told straight that all is not well with your trust and your knowledge! In accordance with what the Christian Church confesses of Him, God Himself is He who did not wish to remain hidden, who did not and does not wish to be God for Himself alone. He is the God who in His royal majesty emerges from the mystery, from the heights of His divine existence and comes down to the humble estate of the universe created by Him. God Himself is He who is revealed as God. He who believes in this God cannot wish to hide this God's gift, this God's love, this God's comfort and light, to hide his trust in His Word and His knowledge. The word and the work of the believer cannot possibly remain a neutral, uncommitted work and word. Where there is faith, God's *doxa, gloria,* His brightness is necessarily made known on earth. And where God's glory did not shine one way or another, however overcast and broken by our ways and our degeneration, there would be no faith; the comfort and the light we receive from God would not be accepted. God's glory is hallowed in the universe, and the Name of the Holy One hallowed on earth, where men may believe, where God's people, God's congregation assembles and goes into action. Where there is faith, man in his complete limitation and helplessness, in his utter abandonment and folly, possesses the freedom, the freedom royal in all humility, to let the light shine of the *doxa,* of the *gloria,* of the glory of God. More is not required of us; but that is required of us. This public responsibility of our trust in God's Word and of our knowledge of the truth of Jesus Christ is the general concept for what in the Christian sense is called confessing and confession.

34

SÖREN KIERKEGAARD

An Existential Faith *

THE SELECTION that follows introduces the notion of an "existential" faith by the precursor of many of the modern existential philosophers. Avoiding the usual theological discussions or any intellectual analysis of the "essence" of faith, Kierkegaard resorts to

* From Sören Kierkegaard, *Concluding Unscientific Postscript,* pp. 176-210, 290-91; translated by David Swenson and Walter Lowrie (copyright 1941, © 1969 by Princeton University Press; Princeton Paperback, 1968). Reprinted by permission of Princeton University Press and the American-Scandinavian Foundation.

Sören Kierkegaard (1813-55) was born at Copenhagen, Denmark. He studied at the University of Copenhagen and received a certificate in theology in 1840. Strongly influenced by Hegel, he reacted against him and became one of his leading critics. Kierkegaard devoted his life to writing rather than preaching and may be considered as the founder of modern existentialism, particularly in its religious aspects.

an "existential" analysis and describes faith as the encounter of
the existing individual with the Paradox and the Absurd—with
the fact that God came into existence as a particular man. Faith
becomes a venture and a risk for the individual. Its object is not a
doctrine, nor an intellectual relationship with God, but an existential relationship with Him. The act of faith is an act of appro-
priation, a dynamic thing and not a mere feeling of confidence.
Through faith the individual appropriates in passionate inwardness and subjectivity the eternal truth of God's existence.

ALL ESSENTIAL KNOWLEDGE relates to existence, or only such knowledge
as has an essential relationship to existence is essential knowledge.
All knowledge which does not inwardly relate itself to existence, in
the reflection of inwardness, is, essentially viewed, accidental knowledge; its degree and scope is essentially indifferent. That essential knowledge is essentialy related to existence does not mean . . . that
knowledge corresponds to something existent as its object. But it
means that knowledge has a relationship to the knower, who is
essentially an existing individual, and that for this reason all essential
knowledge is essentially related to existence. Only ethical and ethico-
religious knowledge has an essential relationship to the existence of
the knower.

   . . . Inwardness in an existing subject culminates in passion;
corresponding to passion in the subject the truth becomes a paradox;
and the fact that the truth becomes a paradox is rooted precisely
in its having a relationship to an existing subject. Thus the one corresponds to the other. By forgetting that one is an existing subject,
passion goes by the board and the truth is no longer a paradox. . . .

*When the question of truth is raised in an objective manner, re-
flection is directed objectively to the truth, as an object to which the
knower is related. Reflection is not focused upon the relationship,
however, but upon the question of whether it is the truth to which
the knower is related. If only the object to which he is related is
the truth, the subject is accounted to be in the truth. When the question of the truth is raised subjectively, reflection is directed subjectively to the nature of the individual's relationship; if only the
mode of this relationship is in the truth, the individual is in the
truth even if he should happen to be thus related to what is not true.*
Let us take as an example the knowledge of God. Objectively, reflection is directed to the problem of whether this object is the
true God; subjectively, reflection is directed to the question whether

the individual is related to a something *in such a manner* that his relationship is in truth a God-relationship. . . .

The existing individual who chooses to pursue the objective way enters upon the entire approximation-process by which it is proposed to bring God to light objectively. But this is in all eternity impossible, because God is a subject, and therefore exists only for subjectivity in inwardness. The existing individual who chooses the subjective way apprehends instantly the entire dialectical difficulty involved in having to use some time, perhaps a long time, in finding God objectively; and he feels this dialectical difficulty in all its painfulness, because every moment is wasted in which he does not have God.° . . .

Now when the problem is to reckon up on which side there is most truth, whether on the side of one who seeks the true God objectively, and pursues the approximate truth of the God-idea; or on the side of one who, driven by the infinite passion of his need of God, feels an infinite concern for his own relationship to God in truth . . . the answer cannot be in doubt for anyone who has not been demoralized with the aid of science. If one who lives in the midst of Christendom goes up to the house of God, the house of the true God, with the true conception of God in his knowledge, and prays, but prays in a false spirit; and one who lives in an idolatrous community prays with the entire passion of the infinite, although his eyes rest upon the image of an idol: where is there most truth? The one prays in truth to God though he worships an idol; the other prays falsely to the true God, and hence worships in fact an idol. . . .

• • • • •

The objective accent falls on WHAT *is said; the subjective accent on* HOW *it is said.* . . . At its maximum this inward "how" is the passion of the infinite, and the passion of the infinite is the truth. But the passion of the infinite is precisely subjectivity, and thus subjectivity becomes the truth. . . . It is the passion of the infinite that is the decisive factor and not its content, for its content is

° In this manner God certainly becomes a postulate, but not in the otiose manner in which this word is commonly understood. It becomes clear rather that the only way in which an existing individual comes into relation with God is as the dialectical contradiction brings his passion to the point of despair and helps him to embrace God with the "category of despair" (faith). Then the postulate is so far from being arbitrary that it is precisely a life-necessity. It is then not so much that God is a postulate, as that the existing individual's postulation of God is a necessity.

precisely itself. In this manner subjectivity and the subjective "how" constitute the truth. . . .

When subjectivity is the truth, the conceptual determination of the truth must include an expression for the antithesis to objectivity . . . this expression will at the same time serve as an indication of the tension of the subjective inwardness. Here is such a definition of truth: *An objective uncertainty held fast in an appropriation-process of the most passionate inwardness is the truth,* the highest truth attainable for an *existing* individual. . . . The truth is precisely the venture which chooses an objective uncertainty with the passion of the infinite. I contemplate the order of nature in the hope of finding God, and I see omnipotence and wisdom; but I also see much else that disturbs my mind and excites anxiety. The sum of all this is an objective uncertainty. But it is for this very reason that the inwardness becomes as intense as it is, for it embraces this objective uncertainty with the entire passion of the infinite. In the case of a mathematical proposition the objectivity is given, but for this reason the truth of such a proposition is also an indifferent truth.

But the above definition of truth is an equivalent expression for faith. Without risk there is no faith. Faith is precisely the contradiction between the infinite passion of the individual's inwardness and the objective uncertainty. If I am capable of grasping God objectively, I do not believe, but precisely because I cannot do this I must believe. If I wish to preserve myself in faith I must constantly be intent upon holding fast the objective uncertainty, so as to remain out upon the deep, over seventy thousand fathoms of water, still preserving my faith.

In the principle that subjectivity, inwardness, is the truth, there is comprehended the Socratic wisdom, whose everlasting merit it was to have become aware of the essential significance of existence, of the fact that the knower is an existing individual. For this reason Socrates was in the truth by virtue of his ignorance, in the highest sense in which this was possible within paganism. . . .

. . . The Socratic ignorance gives expression to the objective uncertainty attaching to the truth, while his inwardness in existing is the truth. . . . The Socratic ignorance is an analogue to the category of the absurd, only that there is still less of objective certainty in the absurd, and in the repellent effect that the absurd exercises. It is certain only that it is absurd, and precisely on that account it incites to an infinitely greater tension in the corresponding inwardness. The Socratic inwardness in existing is an analogue to faith; only that the inwardness of faith, corresponding as it does, not to the repulsion of the Socratic ignorance, but to the repulsion exerted by the absurd, is infinitely more profound. . . .

The infinite merit of the Socratic position was precisely to accentuate the fact that the knower is an existing individual, and that the task of existing is his essential task. . . .

Subjectivity, inwardness, has been posited as the truth; can any expression for the truth be found which has a still higher degree of inwardness? Aye, there is such an expression, provided the principle that subjectivity or inwardness is the truth begins by positing the opposite principle: that subjectivity is untruth. . . . Socratically speaking, subjectivity is untruth if it refuses to understand that subjectivity is truth, but, for example, desire to become objective. Here, on the other hand, subjectivity in beginning upon the task of becoming the truth through a subjectifying process, is in the difficulty that it is already untruth. . . .

But the subject cannot be untruth eternally, or eternally be presupposed as having been untruth; it must have been brought to this condition in time, or here become untruth in time. The Socratic paradox consisted in the fact that the eternal was related to an existing individual, but now existence has stamped itself upon the existing individual a second time. There has taken place so essential an alteration in him that he cannot now possibly take himself back into the eternal by way of recollection. . . .

Let us now call the untruth of the individual *Sin*. Viewed eternally he cannot be sin, nor can he be eternally presupposed as having been in sin. By coming into existence therefore (for the beginning was that subjectivity is untruth), he becomes a sinner. He is not born as a sinner in the sense that he is presupposed as being a sinner before he is born, but he is born in sin and as a sinner. This we might call *Original Sin*. . . .

. . . Let us now go further, let us suppose that the eternal essential truth is itself a paradox. How does the paradox come into being? By putting the eternal essential truth into juxtaposition with existence. Hence when we posit such a conjunction within the truth itself, the truth becomes a paradox. The eternal truth has come into being in time: this is the paradox. If in accordance with the determinations just posited, the subject is prevented by sin from taking himself back into the eternal, now he need not trouble himself about this; for now the eternal essential truth is not behind him but in front of him, through its being in existence or having existed, so that if the individual does not existentially and in existence lay hold of the truth, he will never lay hold of it.

When the eternal truth is related to an existing individual it becomes a paradox. The paradox repels in the inwardness of the existing individual, through the objective uncertainty and the corresponding Socratic ignorance. But since the paradox is not in the first instance itself paradoxical (but only in its relationship to the existing individual), it does not repel with a sufficient intensive inwardness. For without risk there is no faith, and the greater the risk the greater the faith; the more objective security the less inwardness (for inwardness is precisely subjectivity), and the less objective security the more profound the possible inwardness. When the paradox is paradoxical in itself, it repels the individual by virtue of its absurdity, and the corresponding passion of inwardness is faith. But subjectivity, inwardness, is the truth; for otherwise we have forgotten what the merit of the Socratic position is. But there can be no stronger expression for inwardness than when the retreat out of existence into the eternal by way of recollection is impossible; and when, with truth confronting the individual as a paradox, gripped in the anguish and pain of sin, facing the tremendous risk of the objective insecurity, the individual believes. But without risk no faith, not even the Socratic form of faith, much less the form of which we here speak.

When Socrates believed that there was a God, he held fast to the objective uncertainty with the whole passion of his inwardness, and it is precisely in this contradiction and in this risk, that faith is rooted. Now it is otherwise. Instead of the objective uncertainty, there is here a certainty, namely, that objectivity is absurd; and this absurdity, held fast in the passion of inwardness, is faith. The Socratic ignorance is a witty jest in comparison with the earnestness of facing the absurd; and the Socratic existential inwardness is as Greek light-mindedness in comparison with the grave strenuosity of faith.

What now is the absurd? The absurd is—that the eternal truth has come into being in time, that God has come into being, has been born, has grown up, and so forth, precisely like any other individual human being, quite indistinguishable from other individuals. . . .

. . . The absurd is precisely by its objective repulsion the measure of the intensity of faith in inwardness. Suppose a man who wishes to acquire faith . . . but he wishes also to safeguard himself by means of an objective inquiry and its approximation-process. What happens? With the help of the approximation-process the absurd becomes something different; it becomes probable, it becomes increasingly probable, it becomes extremely and emphatically probable. Now he is ready to believe it, and he ventures to claim for himself that he does not believe as shoemakers and tailors and simple folk believe, but only after long deliberation. Now he is ready to believe it; and lo, now it has become precisely impossible to believe it. Anything that is almost probable, or probable, or extremely and emphatically probable, is something he can almost know, or as good as know, or extremely and emphatically almost *know*—but it is impossible to *believe*. For the absurd is the object of faith, and the only object that can be believed.

.   .   .   .   .

Christianity has declared itself to be the eternal essential truth which has come into being in time. It has proclaimed itself as the *Paradox*, and it has required of the individual the inwardness of faith in relation to that which stamps itself as an offense to the Jews and a folly to the Greeks—and an absurdity to the understanding. It is impossible more strongly to express the fact that subjectivity is truth, and that the objectivity is repellent, repellent even by virtue of its absurdity. And indeed it would seem very strange that Christianity should have come into the world merely to receive an explanation; as if it had been somewhat bewildered about itself, and hence entered the world to consult that wise man, the speculative philosopher, who can come to its assistance by furnishing the explanation. . . .

Has the thing of being human now become somewhat different from what it was in older times, are the conditions not still the same, namely, to be a particular existing being, for whom existing is essential as long as he continues in existence? But men have now so much more knowledge than formerly. Quite true, but supose Christianity is not a matter of knowledge, so that the increased knowledge is of no avail, except to make it easier to fall into the confusion of considering Christianity as a matter of knowledge. And if men do have more knowledge, and we are not speaking about the knowledge of railroads, machines, and kaleidoscopes, but knowledge about the religious, how have they acquired it? Surely with the aid of Christianity. So this is the way men show their gratitude. They learn something from Christianity, misunderstand it, and by way of additional misunderstanding use it against Christianity. If in olden times the fearful thing was that one might be offended, now the fearful thing is that there is nothing fearful any more, that in a trice, before the individual has time to look around, he becomes a philosopher who speculates over faith. And over what faith does he speculate? Is it over the faith that he has, and especially over whether he has it or not? Ah, no, such a subject is too trifling for an objective speculative philosopher.

What he speculates about is the objective faith. The objective faith, what does that mean? It means a sum of doctrinal propositions. But suppose Christianity were nothing of the kind; suppose on the contrary it were inwardness, and hence also the paradox, so as to thrust the individual away objectively, in order to obtain significance for the existing individual in the inwardness of his existence, in order to place him as decisively as no judge can place an accused person, between time and eternity in time, between heaven and hell in the time of salvation. . . . In the earliest days the Christian was a fool in the eyes of the world, and to Jews and pagans alike it seemed folly for anyone to seek to become one. Now we are Christians as a matter of course, but if anyone desires to be a Christian with infinite passion he is judged to be a fool, just as it is always folly to put forth an infinite passionate exertion for the sake of becoming what one already is; as if a man were to sacrifice all his wealth to buy a jewel—which he already owned. Formerly a Christian was a fool in the eyes of the world, and now that all men are Christians he nevertheless becomes a fool—in the eyes of Christians.

    . . . A believer is one who is infinitely interested in another's reality. This is a decisive criterion for faith, and the interest in question is not just a little curiosity, but an absolute dependence upon faith's object.

    The object of faith is the reality of another, and the relationship is one of infinite interest. The object of faith is not a doctrine, for then the relationship would be intellectual, and it would be of importance not to botch it, but to realize the maximum intellectual relationship. The object of faith is not a teacher with a doctrine; for when a teacher has a doctrine, the doctrine is *eo ipso* more important than the teacher, and the relationship is again intellectual, and it again becomes important not to botch it, but to realize the maximum intellectual relationship. The object of faith is the reality of the teacher, that the teacher really exists. The answer of faith is therefore unconditionally yes or no. For it does not concern a doctrine, as to whether the doctrine is true or not; it is the answer to a question concerning a fact: "Do you or do you not suppose that he has really existed?" And the answer, it must be noted, is with infinite passion. In the case of a human being, it is thoughtlessness to lay so great and infinite a stress on the question whether he has existed or not. If the object of faith is a human being, therefore, the whole proposal is the vagary of a stupid person, who has not even understood the spirit of the intellectual and the aesthetic. The object of faith is hence the reality of the God-man in the sense of his existence. But existence involves first and foremost particularity, and this is why thought must abstract from existence, because the particular cannot be thought, but only the universal. The object of faith is thus God's reality in existence as a particular individual, the fact that God has existed as an individual human being.

Christianity is no doctrine concerning the unity of the divine and the human, or concerning the identity of subject and object; nor is it any other of the logical transcriptions of Christianity. If Christianity were a doctrine, the relationship to it would not be one of faith, for only an intellectual type of relationship can correspond to a doctrine. Christianity is therefore not a doctrine, but the fact that God has existed.

The realm of faith is thus not a class for numskulls in the sphere of the intellectual, or an asylum for the feeble-minded. Faith constitutes a sphere all by itself, and every misunderstanding of Christianity may at once be recognized by its transforming it into a doctrine, transferring it to the sphere of the intellectual. The maximum of attainment within the sphere of the intellectual, namely, to realize an entire indifference as to the reality of the teacher, is in the sphere of faith at the opposite end of the scale. The maximum of attainment within the sphere of faith is to become infinitely interested in the reality of the teacher.

Faith has in fact two tasks: to take care in every moment to discover the improbable, the paradox; and then to hold it fast with the passion of inwardness. The common conception is that the improbable, the paradoxical, is something to which faith is related only passively; it must provisionally be content with this relationship, but little by little things will become better, as indeed seems probable. O miraculous creation of confusions in speaking about faith! One is to begin believing, in reliance upon the probability that things will soon become better. In this way probability is after all smuggled in, and one is prevented from believing; so that it is easy to understand that the fruit of having been for a long time a believer is, that one no longer believes, instead of, as one might think, that the fruit is a more intensive inwardness in faith. No, faith is self-active in its relation to the improbable and the paradoxical, self-active in the discovery, and self-active in every moment holding it fast—in order to believe. Merely to lay hold of the improbable requires all the passion of the infinite and its concentration in itself; for the improbable and the paradoxical are not to be reached by the understanding's quantitative calculation of the more and more difficult. Where the understanding despairs, faith is already present in order to make the despair properly decisive, in order that the movement of faith may not become a mere exchange within the bargaining sphere of the understanding. But to believe against the understanding is martyrdom; to begin to get the understanding a little in one's favor, is temptation and retrogression.

. . . What I therefore fear and shrink from, more than I fear to die and to lose my sweetheart, is to say about Christianity that it is to a certain degree true. If I lived to be seventy years old, if I shortened the night's sleep and increased the day's work from year to year, inquiring into Christianity—how insignificant such a little period of study, viewed as entitling me to judge in so lofty a fashion about Christianity! For to be so embittered against Christianity after a casual acquaintance with it, that I declared it to be false; that would be far more pardonable, far more human. But this lordly superiority seems to me the true corruption, making every saving relationship impossible—and it may possibly be the case, that Christianity is the truth.

35

W. T. STACE

The Problem of Religious Truth *

AFTER FINDING that the naturalistic, or scientific, view of the world and the religious view are in complete contradiction with one another, Professor Stace proceeds in this chapter of his book to consider whether and in what respect the religious view might be considered as true. In this way he revises, as he confesses, an earlier position in which he had discarded the religious position as wholly false. His principal thesis here is that religious dogmas and doctrines are not literally true, but that they are myths and images. He establishes this thesis to his own satisfaction by noting and accepting the various criticisms that have been made of the arguments for the existence of God. Similarly he cites the sceptic's

* From *Religion and the Modern Mind* by W. T. Stace, copyright, 1952 by W. T. Stace, published by J. B. Lippincott Company, pp. 212-47. Reprinted with the permission of the publisher.

W. T. Stace (1886–) was born in England and educated at the University of Dublin. He is now Professor of Philosophy at Princeton University.

reasons for rejecting the traditional account of the nature of such
a Being. These criticisms lead in turn to a question: if religious
truths are myths and images, then what is it that they symbolize—
what is the nature of the religious truth at which they hint? The
answer our author finds in the life of the saint, in the experience
of the mystic; religion is identified with mysticism. Regarding the
mystic's experience we are told that there seem to be two possible
views of the nature of the universe given by such an experience:
the subjective and the objective. The author argues that each may
be true, depending upon the frame of reference we use. Thus, of
the existence of God it might be argued that if the natural order
is our frame of reference, then the mystic experience is subjective
and God an illusion. From the reference of the eternal order, the
world is an illusion and God the sole reality. Hence, our author
concludes that naturalism is true of the natural order and religion
(as mysticism) is true of the eternal order, and that neither need
interfere with the order.

IN THE MODERN EPOCH the two world-pictures, that which I have
called the naturalistic or scientific view of the world and that which
I have called the religious view, face one another in unresolved contradiction. I have said that modern culture has for its essence the
conflict between them. It is not to be solved by amiable "reconcilia-
tions" between bishops and scientists. The notion that it has been
settled because ecclesiastics now agree that the question of the age
of the earth, of whether the heliocentric or the geocentric astronomy
is true, of whether man is a "special creation" or is descended from
simian ancestors, belong to the province of science and not to that of
religion, is a sheer delusion. For science   . . .   is irrelevant to the
problem. The problem is handed over to the philosophers because
it is a matter of general world-views, and not of the details of any
science. Moreover, any mere compromise, by which one part of the
territory of the world is given to science, the other part to religion,
is worthless and shallow. This was the great insight of Kant and of
the romantic movement of the nineteenth century—whatever may be
thought of the particular solutions offered by Kant and the roman-
tics. . . .

The question may perhaps be put in the form; is religion, or is
anything in religion, true? For it can hardly be the case that the religious view of the world in general is true, but that all particular
religions are wholly false. And if the question be put in this form—
is any religion true?—I should myself, until recently, have replied
with an unqualified no. Religion, I should have said, is nothing but

a mass of false ideas and superstitions of which the ultimate source is wishful thinking. We have believed a view of the world which we want to believe, namely, that it is ruled by a power which is friendly to us and to the values of beauty and goodness which we cherish. As a result of further study and reflection I have modified this opinion. To the question asked I now find the answer to be a qualified yes.

It will be helpful to begin by regarding the religious view of the world, not as a set of intellectual propositions about the nature of the world, but as importing a way of life.   .   .   .

.   .   .   .   .

In every religion there is a way or a path, and there is a destination or experience to which it leads. "I am the way, the truth and the life," says the Jesus of St. John's gospel. The Buddhist speaks of the "noble eightfold path." The destination, the experience—which is hidden—is variously described as "salvation," "heaven," "nirvana," "union with Brahma." The different religions seem to refer to different paths and different destinations. I shall maintain that always and everywhere, in all the great religions, there is in fact only one destination, one experience, even—with some qualification—one path, but that it is "hinted at" by means of different "myths and images" which constitute the differences between the religions.

The myths and images by means of which we hint at the experience and the destination are, in my view the creeds and dogmas of the different religions. These vary and contradict one another ,and herein lie the differences between the religions. The unity between them lies, in the first instance, in the path and the destination, the way of life, which is the way of the saints.   .   .   .   Thus there are three questions which we have to discuss:

(1) The conception of religious dogmas and doctrines as myths and images.

(2) The way of life, the destination, the experience.

(3) Whether the experience implies any special view of the nature of the universe.

That all religious doctrines and dogmas are myths and images means that none of them is *literally* true. To have perceived this is the contribution made to thought by the sceptics and the atheists, in fact by the scientific view of the world. But they have missed something. They have simply said that the dogmas are not true. In this they were right. What they failed to see was that the dogmas are not merely falsehoods, but that they are myths, images, allegories which hint at a way of life, a destination, an experience, and possibly also . . . some deeper truth about the universe. What we have first to show is that the dogmas are, if understood literally, false. Hence the contentions of the next few pages, which will be designed to show this, will seem like pure atheism and skepticism. But they must be understood in the light of the later parts of this chapter.

The procedure I shall adopt will be to take only one dogma, which is common to most religions, and which will be thought by most people to be *the* most fundamental doctrine of religion, and show that, if it is understood literally, there is no reason to believe that it is true, and every reason to suppose that it is false. This is the doctrine that there exists a being, known as God, who is a person, a mind, a consciousness, who formed a plan in his mind, and who, in accordance with his purpose created a world. I do not think that this can be "proved" to be false. It is conceivable that there might be such a mind who made the world as a watchmaker makes a watch. But I think it can be shown that there is no reason at all to think that there is such a being, and that the conception of him in fact involves such difficulties that we are compelled to give it up. . . .

The first thing to say is that science has absolutely nothing to do with the matter. . . . It does not make any difference to the doctrine of the existence of God whether the sun goes round the earth or the earth round the sun. . . . The transition from the teachings of early science to a diminishing belief in God was a psychological, not a logical transition. In other words, it was a mistake. . . . We have only to suppose that God's existence is necessary to the continued existence of the world, and that he acts in it, now as in the past, always through and by means of, the operation of natural laws. . . .

What reason is there to believe in the existence of such a being? There are a number of well-known so-called "proofs of the existence of God." . . .

One of the most common has been that the world must have a first cause, which must be God. But why should not the chains of causes and effects run back into an infinite past with no beginning? This may be difficult to conceive, and some philosophers have thought that the idea of infinite time involves contradictions. But the point to be made is that the idea of God as a first cause presents exactly the same difficulties and contradictions and offers no solution of them. For the existence of God, on the traditional view, runs back into an infinite past in exactly the same way as the suggested chain of causes. It is true that some theologians, seeing this, have said that

God's eternity is not an infinite extension of time, and that God created time along with the temporal world. But this leads to contradiction. For if it is true, then time had a beginning, and before it began there was no time. But the conception of time beginning *at* a time, which was not itself *in* time, i.e., had no time before it, is self-contradictory.

The main point, however, is that there is no reason to suppose that there must have been a first cause, since the chain of causes might go infinitely backwards into infinite time; and that *if* there is a difficulty in conceiving an infinite backward time containing an infinite series of causes, there will be exactly the same difficulty in conceiving an infinite backward time containing only one infinitely prolonged cause, namely, God.

Suppose, we admit, however, that there must have been a first cause. Why should this first cause have been a mind? . . . The only answer which has ever been given to this question is that the hypothesis of a mind is the only one which will explain the evidence of purpose . . . which we find in nature. . . .

. . . In the Christian tradition this mind is infinite, eternal, omnipotent, and perfectly good. Let us consider some of these attributes. The word "mind" has to be taken in its literal sense as having the same essential meaning as it has when it is applied to human beings. Of course, the conception of the mind of God may have some symbolic meaning; it may be a myth or image which stands for something else. But we are now considering religious doctrines as taken in their literal meaning. . . . But the word "mind," taken in this literal way, means a stream of psychological states, flowing, changing, succeeding one another in a time-series. . . . Hence if God has consciousness in the only sense in which the word has meaning for us, it must be a changing consciousness. But that God's consciousness flows and changes in time contradicts that unchangeableness and immutability which is also, in all religious thought attributed to God. It at once puts God in time, and contradicts the theological conception that he is above time and created it. And it also contradicts the infinity of God's mind. The infinite cannot change. For that which changes lacks at one time some state which it has at another time; and that which lacks anything is not infinite.

There are also difficulties connected with the attribute of being all-powerful which is applied to God. Does this mean that he could create a square circle? No doubt this absurd. But if so, what this means is that the laws of logic are as binding on the mind of God as they are on the mind of man. There *are* things then which he cannot do.

The reader may perhaps consider this last consideration trivial. But he cannot think this about the difficulties which arise in connection with the idea of the infinite or perfect goodness of God. For this is notoriously irreconcilable with the existence of pain and evil in the world, and has led to one of the most famous of theological problems, the problem of evil. If God is the ultimate source of everything, then he is the ultimate source of evil; and how is this consistent with his perfect goodness? Hume wrote:

Epicurus' old questions are still unanswered. Is Deity willing to prevent evil, but not able? Then he is impotent. Is he able but not willing? Then he is malevolent. Is he both able and willing? Whence then is evil?

The point to notice is that the whole force of Hume's argument depends on taking all the terms used in it literally. It is necessary perhaps to remind the reader of the fact that what we are attempting to show is only that the doctrine of the existence of God, *if taken literally,* is a myth. Hume's argument has no force unless such words as "able" and "willing" are taken in their ordinary human senses as meaning the same things as would be meant if we were to speak of a human being as able or willing to do this or that. And it has no force if God is not thought of as a person or a mind in the same sense as human beings are persons and minds. But if the terms and ideas are taken in their literal meanings, then Hume's argument is entirely unanswerable. But it does not show that the doctrine of God's infinite goodness may not be symbolic of some deeper truth. But if so, then it is what we have called a myth.

All attempts to solve this problem on the level of literal interpretation are obvious absurdities. Some have said that evil is not a positive, but only a negative fact. It is only the absence of goodness. It is therefore nothing, and God cannot be held responsible for creating a nothingness. But this is to assert that pain and evil do not really exist at all, which is absurd. . . .

Others . . . take refuge in the concept of mystery. The ways of God are a mystery to the human mind, and we must accept evil as one of these mysteries. But this is both illogical and inconsistent. For the same people will insist that the good and beautiful things in the world are evidence of God's goodness. But if so, by exactly the same logic, the evil things must be admitted to be evidence of either his badness or his impotence. . . .

In these pages I have selected, as samples, only a few of the sceptical arguments which can be used to destroy such a proposition as: "There exists an infinitely good and powerful mind which created the world and runs it." Some of them may be more convincing, some less. . . . What is the conclusion to which they point? Not, in my opinion, that all religion is false. Not even that the proposition just quoted is false; but that such beliefs are not literally true, that they are at best "myths and images" which perhaps "hint at" some deeper truth. . . .

.   .   .   .   .

What then—to turn to our second problem—is the way of life, the the destination, the experience, which these myths and images are meant to symbolize? What is the deeper truth to which they point?

There are two ways of life, that which most of us follow, and which consists in "making the best of a bad job," and the "way of the saints"—the saints of any religion. What is this second way, and what is its destination? . . . No one can describe them, not even those who follow the way and have reached the destination. But I think that nevertheless something can be said. There do exist records, written by those who have followed the second way, which can be quoted. They too will be found not to express the literal and naked truth, not to "describe" the truth, because that truth is "inexpressible" in language. This is the reason why men invent myths and images which merely "hint at it". The "experience", which is also the "destination", is 'ineffable', which is the same as saying that it cannot be described. . . .

Buddha said: "It remains a fact and the fixed and necessary constitution of being, that all its constituents are misery." Also it is said in one of the Upanishads: "In the Infinite only is bliss. In the finite there is no bliss."

If we think candidly about them, both these statements are likely to appear to us as gross exaggerations, especially the first. It may be the case, we shall perhaps piously admit, that the highest happiness is found only in God, the Infinite, but there is, after all, a great deal of genuine happiness to be found in daily life. Yet expressions which are parallel to the verse of the Upanishad can be found in the literature of all religions. There is no happiness at all, the saints keep telling us, except in God. . . .

.   .   .   .   .

I believe that what the saints say is true—not merely that there is some truth in it, but that it is wholly true.

It is correct that, as viewed from a certain level, there are plenty of pleasures and enjoyments available in the common way of life, and that many of them are perfectly innocent. The saint is not denying this. He is not denying that you can have a good time, and that having a good time is very enjoyable. But the level at which these things are said is superficial. At a deeper level we find that all this is hollowness, vacancy, and futility. Underneath the glitter of the tinsel there is darkness. . . .

The essential truth of religion, of every religion, is that from this darkness of life *there is a way out*, a way into, the light. The destination of your present way is futility. The destination of the other way is "bliss" or "blessedness." This is not merely a higher degree of what men call happiness. It is not merely an elevated "pleasure." Blessedness and happiness—at any rate as the latter word is commonly understood—do not belong in the same order of things at all. According to all religions the way out is very long and hard. But it is possible, *if you want it enough*. What is this way?

It is generally supposed that the way of the saints consists in living a good life, that is to say, in morality. . . . To this view corresponds the suggestion that the essence of religion is ethics. . . .

This whole way of thinking is a fatal blunder. . . .

Religion is not simply ethics. Nor is it just a mixture of ethics and dogma, or of ethics and emotion. There is a third something, totally different from either, which is its essence. It is true that religion always insists on a moral life. It is true that saints are usually good men. . . . For love and compassion flow necessarily out of the peculiar vision, the peculiar experience, of the mystics or saint, are indeed parts of it, so that he cannot help being also a moralist. But his morality is not his religion.

The moral way alone will never lead to blessedness, to salvation, or whatever the destination of the path may be called. It is possible that it may lead to "happiness." . . . And yet there is a peculiar kind of disappointment, or disillusionment, which attends the life which is *only* moral. A man may do his duty, and yet remain unhappy, or at least basically unsatisfied. . . . And in any case happiness, even if the moral life does ensure it, is only a superficial phenomenon, like pleasure. It is not that blessedness which religion seeks.

What then is the way, what the destination? Strictly speaking, they "cannot be described." They are ineffable. And this word "ineffable" must be understood in its strict sense as meaning that which cannot be said, cannot be uttered at all in any conceivable words, in any conceivable language, and never will be. But it is here that the records left by the saints themselves can be of some use. Not that even they can say that which cannot be said. But they can "hint at it" more clearly than the common dogmas of religion do. Of course the saints themselves believed in and repeated the dogmas, Christian saints Christian dogmas, Hindu saints Hindu dogmas, Muslim saints Muslim dogmas. They were after all human beings conditioned in their intellectual beliefs by the different cultures in which they were brought up. And in so far as they repeated the doctrines of the particular religions to which they were attached, they contradicted one another. But sometimes they transcended these different cultures, and sought to utter the pure essence of religion itself, and when they did so their utterances show a surprising measure of agreement.

The essence of religion is not morality but mysticism. And the way of the saints is the way of mysticism. Accordingly, I use the words "saint" and "mystic" interchangeably. . . . My contention is that all religion is ultimately mystical, or springs from the mystical side of human nature. All religious men are therefore mystics in greater or less degree. There is no sharp line between mystic and non-mystic. Those who are commonly recognized as mystics, and who so recognize themselves, are only those whose mysticism is explicitly realized in the full light of consciousness. In the ordinary religious man that mysticism is implicit, lies below the threshold of consciousness, only faintly stirring the surface waters of the mind and not recognized as what it is either by himself or others. The "saint" is the religious man *par excellence,* and the substance of his life is therefore mysticism whether he, or others who watch and describe him, know it or not.

. . . . .

We come to the third of the questions which we raised at the beginning of this chapter: whether the saint's experience implies any special view of the nature of the universe. There seem to be two possible views which can be taken. It may be held that the mystic's experience is real in the sense that he does have the experience, and it has the peculiarities which he asserts of it. But it is only a subjective experience in his own mind, so that it implies nothing about the real nature of the world outside him. It is, in this way, like a dream. A dream is real in the sense that it exists as a subjective state in the dreamer's mind. But it does not exist in the outside world, and implies nothing at all about that world. This may be called the subjectivist view of mysticism.

The other possible view is that the mystical experience does imply something objective. It may be held to imply that there is an objectively real being, a mind, a person, God who is the creator of the universe. This is the view taken by most religions, and by most of the mystics themselves. For instance, in Hinduism the unifying experience is believed to be identical with Brahman, and Brahman is God—although it ought to be added that Hindu thinkers often do not think of God as a personal being. This may be called the objectivist view. Thus the question which we have to ask is: does the mystic experience imply what is ordinarily called "the existence, or objectivity, of God?"

Not all religions have taken the objective view. It is unsafe to speak with great confidence about what Buddha and his earliest disciples believed. But the earliest Buddhist writings seem to show that, although he certainly had the mystic experience . . . he did not objectify it. Brought up as a Hindu, he apparently denied the reality of Brahman, the Hindu equivalent of God. What he stressed was the state of enlightenment of the saint, which is Nirvana. On the face of it this seems like a subjectivistic interpretation. It has been followed by the southern schools of Buddhism, those of Siam, Burma, and Ceylon, though not by the northern schools. This is the reason why Buddhism is sometimes called atheistic. And Buddhism is not the only Indian creed which takes a subjectivistic view of the mystic experience. The Sankhya and Yoga systems do the same. From this it seems to follow that theism is not a necessary implication of the experience of the saint. But that it is certainly a natural implication, which the majority of religious minds tend to follow, is shown by the emphatic insistence upon it of all the other great religions, Christianity, Hinduism, Judaism, and Islam.

It may appear that either the objectivist or the subjectivist view must be true, and that we are compelled to choose between them. My suggestion is that this is not the case, and that in fact neither is the truth; or, if we prefer to put it in another way, both are true, each from a different point of view. . . .

. . . from the statement that God is not objective, it does not follow that he is subjective, or merely an illusory thought, or idea, or psychological state, in somebody's mind. For what the mystic experience teaches is that he is *neither objective nor subjective.*

That God should be neither the one nor the other may seem incomprehensible, but this should not surprise us since the incomprehensibility of God is asserted in one form or another, in all the great religions.

Nevertheless something can be done to help the mind in this dilemma. We have become accustomed in science to the conception of frames of reference. For instance, suppose that two events, X and Y, occur. According to the theory of relativity, from the point of view of one space-time frame of reference, X may have occurred before Y, but from the point of view of another, Y may have occurred before X. Thus X may be both before and after Y. Until recently this would have been thought to be a contradiction. We should have said that there can be only one time order, and that, if the two events were not simultaneous, then either X occurred before Y, or Y occurred before X.

It is dangerous to press scientific and physical analogies too far in the religious sphere. No scientific analogy can properly express religious truth. But with this warning, and remembering that it is no more than an imperfect analogy, we may say that the contradiction between the naturalistic or scientific view of the world and the religious view is due to the fact that two frames of reference are being used. We may speak of the natural or temporal order, and the eternal order, as being the two frames of reference. The eternal order is revealed in the mystic experience of the saint. The natural order is the space-time world which is revealed to the intellect and to science. If we use the natural order as our frame of reference, then from that point of view the natural order is the sole reality, the mystic experience is subjective, and God is an illusion. This is the truth presented by atheism, skepticism, and naturalism. But if we use the frame of reference of the eternal order, then from that point of view God and the eternal order is the sole reality, and the world and the natural order are illusion. Looked at from outside itself, the mystic moment is a moment in time. But looked at from within itself, it is the whole of eternity. That God is an illusion is the standpoint of naturalism. That the world is an illusion is the standpoint of the eternal. . . .

It will be observed that this view conforms to the great insight of Kant that the solution of the religious problem cannot be a compromise, but that scientific naturalism must be one hundred per cent true and religion one hundred per cent true. Naturalism is the sole truth about the natural order, and religion is the sole truth about the eternal order. Neither order interferes with the other. But the two orders may be said to intersect in the mystic experience which is both eternal—from its own standpoint—and a moment in time—from the standpoint of time. Man, as Kant said, is an inhabitant of both worlds (orders). Kant's only mistake was his failure to recognize that man can have direct experience of the eternal order in the mystical vision. . . .

. . . . .

It is here that the myths of the different religions have their function and justification. No doubt, taken literally, they are false. But whether the worshipper takes them literally or recognizes them as the myths they are, they perform the function of evoking within him those religious feelings which are in fact a far-off view of the divine. . . .

This is the justification of the myths and images, and therefore of the creeds and doctrines, of the great religions of the world. No doubt they tend to degenerate on the one side into superstitions, on the other into mere intellectual abstractions spiritually dead and powerless. . . . But basically most men will always require myths and images to evoke in them the divine vision. And when one set of symbols has degenerated into mere abstractions or debasing superstitions, another set arises. Even the great mystics . . . for the most part use the symbols of the religion in which they were born and so attach themselves to this religion or that. It is in this way that what one mystic says seems to contradict what another says. For they use different symbols for the same reality. . . .

. . . if the theory of religion which I have outlined is accepted, it should at least cause those of us who cannot find a place within any institutional religion to understand the religious side of human nature, both that of themselves and of others, and the function and justification of religious creeds for those who can still hold them, creeds to which simple-minded men have clung, and which they, the more sophisticated ones, have perhaps too hastily condemned.*

* [The view of religion that is baldly sketched in this chapter is more fully worked out in Stace's book, *Time and Eternity.*—Ed.]

36

NICOLAI BERDYAEV

Faith and Philosophy *

THE PRINCIPAL THESIS of the author is the tragic situation of the philosopher in his endeavor to maintain his independence in the face of opposition from religion and science. Pure revelation, the essence of religion, contains no cognitive elements and does not clash with knowledge or philosophy; conflict occurs when religion, in this sense, develops into theology and becomes a social phenomenon. Although philosophy has always struggled to maintain its independence, it cannot ignore religion and survive; philosophical revivals always have a religious source. Interestingly, Berdyaev contends that German Idealism was more essentially Christian than Medieval Scholasticism. He then states that philosophy also encounters hostility from science, which is as jealous of its dogmas as is religion and, like religion, would subject philosophy to these dogmas. The relation of faith and philosophy is considered in the light of this conflict; the solutions of St. Thomas and St. Bonaventure are appraised; and both Thomism and Rationalism are rejected because of their insistence on the intellectual nature of knowledge. The author maintains that philosophical knowledge is not merely intellectual but affective as well, since knowledge must deal with the whole man. Concluding, he declares that philosophy is not to be identified with science or any other form of knowing, but has its own mode of knowing in intuition. The proper sphere of such philosophical knowledge is human existence, human purpose, and human destiny.

THE PHILOSOPHER'S SITUATION is truly tragic in face of the almost universal hostility directed against him. This hostility has manifested itself in various ways throughout the history of civilization. Philosophy is, indeed, the most vulnerable part of culture; even its initial premise

° From *Solitude and Society,* translated by George Reavey (London: Geoffrey Bles: The Centenary Press, 1947), pp. 3-17. Reprinted by permission of the publisher.

Nicolai Berdyaev (1874-1948) was born at Kiev in Russia. He was expelled from Russia by the Bolshevists in 1922 as an upholder of religion. He moved to Germany and then to Paris in 1934 where he directed the Academy of the Philosophy of Religion. He maintained his allegiance to the Russian Orthodox Church and devoted the remainder of his life to writing on philosophical and religious subjects.

is incessantly questioned; and every philosopher has, first of all, to justify the validity of his claim to exercise his function. Philosophy is the victim of heterogeneous attacks: both religion and science are its avowed enemies. In short, it has never enjoyed the least semblance of popular support; nor does the philosopher ever create the impression that he is satisfying any "social demand."

In his theory of the three stages of human development, Auguste Comte assigns to philosophy the middle stage wherein metaphysics helps to bridge the gulf between religion and science. Comte was a philosopher himself, even though he did call his philosophy "positivist," that is, scientific. He maintained that this scientific philosophy was a prelude to a purely scientific era as the next stage in the development of the human spirit. It was the essence of Positivism to reject the priority and the autonomy of philosophical knowledge, and to subordinate it ultimately to science. This idea of Comte's has become more firmly rooted in the general consciousness than would appear to be the case when we consider his Positivist doctrine in the narrow sense of the word. The term 'philosopher' had become popular during the age of Enlightenment, but this vulgarization had merely degraded philosophy without producing a single great philosopher.

Religion was the source of the first and most violent attack on philosophy. The battle between these two is still being waged today, for, despite Auguste Comte, religion persists as an eternal function of the human spirit. It is this conflict above all which gives rise to the philosopher's tragic situation: the debate between philosophy and science is much less virulent. The antagonism between philosophy and religion is especially acute because religion claims to possess in theology a cognitive expression, a field of knowledge. The problems posed and resolved by philosophy are invariably the same as those propounded by theology. But theologians have always tended to oppress philosophers; they have often persecuted them and sometimes have even had them burned at the stake. . . .

The philosophers' only means of defence was to expose the two aspects of the truth they were expounding. The reason for these tortures and persecutions must not be sought in the essence of religion, but rather in the fact that religion tends to objectify itself in the social structure. Revelation, which is the basis of religion, is not itself opposed to knowledge. On the contrary, there is a correspondence between them: revelation is what is *revealed to me* and knowledge is what *I discover myself*. How could there be any conflict between what I discover cognitively and what is demonstrated to me by religion? But actually this conflict can take place and put the

philosopher in a tragic dilemma, for, as a believer, he may be prepared to accept revelation. We must rather seek the explanation in
the complex nature of religion as a social phenomenon, in the fact
that Divine Revelation, which is the pure and original essence of
religion, becomes adulterated by the immediate reactions of the human community in which it takes place, and by the way in which
men make use of it to further their own interests. This fact enables
us to consider religion from the sociological standpoint.

There is no essential affinity between revelation and knowledge,
since the former contains no cognitive element. It only becomes a
part of knowledge by virtue of what man contributes to it, by virtue
of his thought; for theology, as well as philosophy, are purely human
acts of knowledge. The intellectual interpretation of revealed truth is
the expression not so much of the individual intelligence as of the
organized collective, which is invariably the source of orthodoxy.
Hence the conflict between philosophy and theology, between individual and collective thought. Revelation may therefore prove to
be of capital importance to knowledge, for it constitutes a distinct
philosophical experience, a transcendent event which philosophy can
transform into an immanent datum. Spiritual knowledge is the essence
of philosophical knowledge; the philosopher's intuition is therefore
experimental.

Every theology comprehends a philosophy sanctioned by the religious community. This is especially true of Christian theology as
expounded by the Doctors of the Church. Oriental patristic thought
was impregnated with Platonism; in fact, it could not have built up
the Christian dogma without the formal basis of Greek philosophy.
Western Scholasticism was penetrated by Aristotelian philosophy,
without whose categories, and notably the distinction between substance and accident, it would have been unable to define the Catholic
doctrine of the Eucharist. . . .

Hence the complex relations that have always existed between
philosophy and theology. On the one hand, the doctrine of free
philosophical speculation clashed with the dogmatism of determinist
philosophy. In this way, philosophy became its own enemy, the victim of its own rigidity. On the other hand, the development of
science was impeded by the immixture of all that was falsely scientific
in the Bible—of its astronomical, geological, biological, historical
teachings, which were mostly based upon the prejudices of a primitive society. The purely religious revelation contained in the Bible
could not have proved such an obstacle. But religious revelation may
be purged of those parasitical, philosophical or scientific elements,

which are the cause of incessant conflicts. The tragedy implicit in the philosopher's position is thereby diminished, but the philosopher himself is not eliminated. Philosophy, not satisfied to assign to itself religious ends, now puts forward religious claims. The aim of the great philosophers has always been to regenerate the soul through knowledge, and they have tended to regard philosophy as a means of salvation. This was true of the Hindoo philosophers as well as of Socrates and Plato, of the Stoics and Plotinus, of Spinoza, Fichte, and Hegel, and more recently of Vladimir Solovyev. Plotinus was hostile to religion because it required a mediator to effect salvation, whereas, according to him, philosophical wisdom was capable of achieving salvation without a mediator. Thus, there has always subsisted not only dissimilarity, but also conflict, between the 'God of the philosophers' and the 'God of Abraham, Isaac and Jacob.' The extreme form of this opposition is to be found in Hegel, who gave precedence to philosophy over religion in the process of spiritual development. The tradition of philosophy has been to contest popular beliefs—the myths inherent in religion and man's unquestioned submission to the authority of the past. Socrates perished a victim of this struggle. But although philosophy may start out by discrediting the myth, it ends by acknowledging it as the sum of philosophical knowledge. Plato demonstrated this fact when he passed on from *concept* to *myth* as the means of attaining true knowledge. Hegelian philosophy shows the same process at work in German Idealism.

We can trace the origin of this antagonism back to Hellenic civilization. For whereas the Greek religious consciousness subordinated life to destiny, their philosophy subordinated life to reason. But Hellenic philosophy, in acquiring its universal importance, also laid the foundation of European humanism. We must not therefore expect philosophy ever to renounce its right to consider and, if possible, to resolve the essential problems of religion which theology claims as its monopoly. Prophecy has always been an adjunct of philosophy and there is some justification in the proposed division of philosophy into the scientific and prophetic kinds. It is the prophetic type of philosophy which finds itself in perpetual conflict with religion and theology. The true philosopher is not only satisfied to apprehend the world; he also desires to modify, to improve, and to regenerate it. . . . It is true that philosophy is primarily knowledge, but it is a *totalitarian* knowledge, one that comprehends all the aspects of human existence. Its essential aim is to discover ways of realizing *Meaning*. Philosophers have sometimes been content to expound a crude empiricism or materialism. But the essential character of a true philosopher is the love of the extra-natural; in this sphere he grapples with the transcendental world and refuses to reconcile himself to any interpretation of knowledge which would restrict his activities to the inferior world. It is the aim of philosophy to investigate beyond the limits of the empirical universe, and thus to penetrate into the intelligible universe, into the transcendental world. And I am very much inclined to believe that our love of metaphysics is engendered by our discontent with the world around us and our disgust at the empirical life.

The philosopher's immersion in the depths of existence, his Being, precedes, and also comprehends, his cognitive activity. The philosopher cannot build in the void; the pursuit of philosophy cannot separate or alienate him from Being, since he can only deduce knowledge from Being. The philosopher's tragedy is enacted in the depths of his own existence. Only his original participation in the mystery of Being can enable him to apprehend Being. But is not religion man's revealed life, his life in the depths of Being? How then can philosophy afford to ignore it? That is the essence of the tragedy as it affects the philosopher. On the one hand, he is incapable of supporting, must, indeed, refuse to suffer, the authority of religion; on the other, he tends to lose all notion of Being, and the strength it imparts, as soon as he becomes detached from religious experience.

Philosophical revivals always have a religious source. The pre-Socratic doctrines were intimately connected with Greek religious life, and there was a close relationship between Platonism and the Orphic mysteries. Medieval philosophy was consciously Christian. The philosophies of Descartes, Spinoza, Leibnitz, Berkeley, as well as German Idealism, were founded on religious elements. I am even inclined to believe, however paradoxical it may sound, that modern philosophy as a whole, and German philosophy in particular, are by reason of their themes, and by the nature of their speculation, more essentially Christian than medieval Scholasticism, which was still Hellenic, Platonic and Aristotelian, in the principles of its reflection. Christianity had not yet entirely succeeded in permeating medieval thought.

With the dawn of modern times, which coincided with the birth of Cartesian philosophy, Christianity permeated the very essence of thought, and discovered a new aspect of the philosophical problem by setting up man as the centre of the universe in conformity with the revolutionary change brought about by Christianity. The preoccupation with the *object* had been the fundamental tendency of Greek philosophy. But modern philosophy is concerned with the *subject*:

that is the result of the emancipating influence of Christianity in liberating man from the power of the objective and natural world. The problem of freedom, which had played no part in Greek thought, was the direct outcome of this emancipation. I obviously do not mean to imply that the German philosophers were better Christians than Saint Thomas Aquinas and the Scholastics, or that their philosophy is wholly Christian. It need hardly be said that Saint Thomas was nearer the divine than Kant, Fichte, Schelling, or Hegel. But whereas the philosophical aspect of Thomism could have been elaborated in a non-Christian world, German Idealism is inconceivable outside Christianity. The effect of Christianity, as it penetrated more intimately into the core of thought and knowledge, was to free man from the inward authority of the Church and its theological restrictions. Philosophy acquired an increasing measure of freedom by stripping Christianity of its determinist philosophical elements. But the theologians steadily refused to acknowledge this emancipation of the Christian consciousness, the fact that Christianity has become immanent. This immanence has always been a subject of anxiety to the official Church. But philosophy, like true religion, may exercise a beneficial influence by purifying religion of its extraneous and non-revealed elements, of all purely social accessories and outworn forms of knowledge.

The philosopher's heroic struggle was to be made all the more difficult by the appearance of another enemy. Indeed, the world seems to be united in denying to the philosopher the right to speculate freely. Hardly had he shaken off the shackles of religious dogma, of theology and of ecclesiastical authority, when he was expected to subscribe to the dogmas of science. Hardly had he become emancipated from the dictates of a superior power, when he was subjected to those of an inferior one. . . .

Science is as jealous of philosophy as religion. Like religion, science has built up a doctrine by which it claims to replace philosophy. This dogmatic scientific attitude is, indeed, the principal source of the attacks directed against it. Science has not only progressively reduced the competence of philosophy, but it has also attempted to suppress it altogether and to replace it by its own claim to universality. This process is generally known as "scientism." Max Scheler defined it as a revolt of slaves, the revolt of the inferior against the superior. Indeed, why should one refuse to submit to religion if one is content to submit to science? It is Scheler's opinion that had philosophy submitted to faith, it would have dominated science. By faith, of course, he does not mean theology, the Church's exterior authority, religion become a social institution; for faith cannot enslave philosophy, it can only nourish it. But in its fight against authoritarian religion, which punished its daring researches by the stake, philosophy was led to repudiate faith as the inner light of knowledge.

These are the conditions which have conspired to make the philosopher's situation tragic. But, perhaps, the tragedy is inherent in the situation whether the philosopher is a believer or not. If the philosopher is a non-believer, his experience and horizon grow very narrow, his consciousness is shut off from all worlds but his own immediate one, his knowledge becomes impoverished, he imposes his own limitations upon Being. *The absence of tragedy is the tragic fact about the philosopher without a faith.* Whereas faith is synonomous with the consciousness of other worlds, of the significance of Being, a philosopher of this type tends to become the slave of his own freedom. When, on the other hand, the philosopher is a believer, the tragedy assumes another form. In his endeavor to exercise freely his cognitive activity, he comes into conflict with the social structure wherein faith is externalized, that is, with the authority of the ecclesiastical hierarchy and that of the theologians, who reinforce their restrictions with accusations of heresy and with persecution. This antagonism illustrates the perennial conflict between faith as a primary phenomenon, as a relationship with God, on the one hand, and faith as a secondary, purely social phenomenon, as a relationship with the religious community, on the other. But this is not yet the whole extent of the tragedy. The philosopher only experiences its full intensity when he is alone and isolated from his fellow-beings. The philosopher is unable to forget his faith or its revealed truth even when exercising freely his cognitive faculties. Here we are no longer concerned with the outward problem of his relationship with other men or the official representatives of religion, but with the inner problem of his knowledge in relation to his particular faith and spiritual experience.

Saint Thomas Aquinas solved this problem by establishing a hierarchical order in which each degree was both relatively independent and at the same time subordinate to the degree above it. Thus philosophy functioned independently of faith; in fact, the Christian philosopher apprehended in exactly the same way as Aristotle. But in this hierarchy of degree, theology dominated philosophy as the supreme arbiter of all ultimate questions. In this hierarchy the degree of mystic knowledge had an even higher place than theology. Thus Thomism was able successfully to suppress any element of tragedy by carefully eliminating any antithesis between philosophy and faith. To all appearance philosophy was independent; but in reality it was completely servile, since it merely represented the dogmatic affirmation of a particular philosophy. Saint Bonaventura, on the other hand, resolved the problem in a different way: he affirmed that faith illuminated and transformed the intellect. I am personally more inclined to agree with him despite the fact that he too had no inkling of the tragedy underlying philosophy.

It is an error to think that emotion can only be subjective, whereas thought is objective; that the knowing subject can only apprehend Being intellectually, whereas emotion confines him to the subjective world. Indeed, that is the conception of Thomism and of rationalist philosophy in general, . . . in fact, that of the majority of philosophers. It is based upon an old philosophical prejudice which we are only just beginning to discard today. Max Scheler and other exponents of Existential philosophy have contributed a great deal to this end. Indeed, the very contrary is true. Human emotion is not subjective except for a small individual residuum; it is for the most part socially objectified. And inversely, intellection may be very subjective, and often even more individual and less dependent on social objectification than emotion, although this is only partially true. Moreover, the very meaning assigned to the terms 'subjective' and 'objective' is in need of being drastically revised. It is a question of the utmost importance to determine whether the apprehension of truth is subjective or objective. Whatever the solution, we can be certain of one thing: that philosophical apprehension is a spiritual act which involves not only intellection, but also the concentration of the totality of man's spiritual forces, of both his voluntary and sentient being.

The present tendency is increasingly to admit the existence of an affective mode of apprehension as it had been imagined by Pascal, and as it has been affirmed in our day by Max Scheler and Keyserling. It is a prejudice to believe that knowledge is always rational, that there is no such thing as irrational knowledge. Actually, we apprehend a great deal more through feeling than by intellection; and it is a matter of some note, that not only love and sympathy, but also hostility and hate, may help to further our knowledge. The heart is the centre of the entire man. That is above all a Christian truth. The whole appreciative aspect of knowledge is affective, for it expresses the "reasons of the heart." Criteria of value have an important place in philosophical knowledge. Since there is no way of apprehending *Meaning* without a criterion of value, its apprehension is primarily based on the knowledge of the heart. Philosophical apprehension involves man's entire being, that is, the union of faith and knowledge. An element of faith is present in all philosophical speculation however rational; it was present in the inspiration of Descartes, Spinoza and Hegel.

This is one of the facts which demonstrates the inconsistency of the idea of a "scientific philosophy." This philosophy is the invention of thinkers devoid of any true philosophical gift or vocation, of those who had nothing to contribute to philosophy. The product of a democratic century which discredited the very idea of philosophy, 'Scientism' is not even in a position to appreciate the significance of science itself, of man's intellectual potentialities, since the very fact of propounding the problem transcends the frontiers of science. Scientism treats every thing, even the subject himself, as object.

The existence of philosophy presupposes an appropriate *philosophical* mode of cognition as distinct from a *scientific* one. A 'scientific' philosophy is the negation of essential philosophy, the denial of its primacy. To admit an affective mode of apprehension, a sensible apprehension of value, is not to deny reason. On the contrary, reason itself demands the restitution of its integrity as it was understood in the Middle Ages, when, despite the intellectualism of the Scholastics, the intellect was often assigned a spiritual significance. The task of philosophy is not to invalidate reason, but to discover its contradictions and to demonstrate its limitations while preserving its immanence. In this light, Kant's doctrine of the antinomies retains its validity. We must not seek the criteria of truth in reason or the intellect, but rather in the integral spirit. The heart and the conscience remain the supreme agents of value as well as of knowledge. Philosophy is not synonoymous with science; it is not even the science of essences; its function is to endow the spirit with a creative consciousness of the meaning of human existence. This supposes in the philosopher an inherent experience of human contradictions and of the tragedy implicit in his vocation. How could any philosopher fail to find his knowledge both impoverished and diminished if he persisted in remaining unconscious of this tragedy?

Intuition is the *sine qua non* of philosophy. Every true philosopher has an original intuition of his own. Philosophical intuition cannot be deduced from anything else; it is primary, and secretes in itself the light which will illuminate every act of knowledge. Neither religious nor scientific truths are adequate substitutes for intuition. Philosophical knowledge depends on the range of experience, and it also supposes an essentially tragic experience of all the contradictions of human existence. *Philosophy is therefore based upon the maximum experience of human existence.* This experience integrates man's intellectual, effective and volitional life. Reason is independent of all external authority, is outwardly autonomous; it is not, however, inwardly independent in relation to the whole life of the philosopher engaged in the pursuit of knowledge. It will not allow itself to be stripped of its feelings and volition, of its loves and hates, of its criteria of value. It discovers its ontological foundation in the depths of its own Being, in the intimacy of its own existence; it adapts itself to the philosopher's belief or scepticism; it varies with his belief as the consciousness expands or contracts. But revelation transforms it.

. . . We must avoid confusing the Divine Revelation and the world of invisible things with their intellectual apprehension. This latter is a human attribute; it is man who apprehends the Divine Revelation and the invisible world. But the Divine Revelation changes man's reason, which becomes inwardly transformed as a result of the shock of the revelation, and man is thus enabled to perceive clearly all its inherent contradictions and limitations. The mere acceptance of revelation is a philosophical act however elementary. Revelation provides realities and data of a mystic order; but the intellectual attitude adopted towards these realities and data has nothing to do with revelation, since it is based on some definite philosophy. No man can live without any basis of philosophy, however primitive, naïve, childish or unconscious. Every man thinks and speaks, makes use of notions, categories, symbols, myths, and gives vent to appreciations. There is always a childish philosophy at the foundation of a childish faith. Thus the uncritical acceptance of Biblical science, that of primitive mankind, involves the use of certain categories of thought such as 'Creation,' for example, envisaged as a moment in time.

Intellection is an act and not a passive reception of things; it endows the object with meaning, and establishes a similitude, a common measure between the knowing subject and the known object. . . . Knowledge, indeed, is *humanization* in the deepest ontological sense of the word. There are various degrees of humanization: the highest lies in religious knowledge. For man is the image and likeness of God; and consequently God contains in Himself the image and likeness of man, the pure essence of humanity. Next to it is the degree of philosophical knowledge, which also involves humanization, that is, the apprehension by man of the mystery of Being inherent in him, the apprehension of the meaning of existence in so far as it is commensurable with human existence and destiny. Humanization is at its lowest degree in scientific knowledge and particularly in the physico-mathematical sciences. Contemporary physics demonstrate the dehumanization of science, for their researches are leading them outside the human universe as understood by man. But physicists are blind to the fact that the very researches of dehumanized physics symbolize the power of human knowledge; and that their rapid progress only serves to demonstrate man's originality when confronted with the mysteries of nature, and above all his essential humanity. All knowledge is rooted in the depths of human existence and manifests man's efficacy as an integral being whose power extends to contradictions and conflicts, to the very heart of the tragedy inherent in the philosopher's situation.

Knowledge is based upon the action of three principles: the human, the divine and the natural. It is the outcome of the reciprocal action of human culture, Divine Grace, and natural necessity. The philosopher's tragedy has its origin in the attempt to restrict his pursuit of knowledge by the invocation of Divine Grace or by an appeal to the universal character of natural necessity. If God and nature are the objects of philosophical investigation, then its antagonism to both dogmatic religion and science is inevitable. But its true sphere is the investigation of human existence, human destiny and human purpose. Man is the real subject of the philosopher's knowledge; through man he can apprehend both God and nature; but he cannot pursue his investigations without stumbling against objectified forms of knowledge which claim to expound the ultimate truth concerning God and nature. The philosopher is ready to accept Divine Revelation and faith, but he must avoid endorsing their naturalist interpretation, just as he must refuse to accept the universalist claims put forward by natural science.

In the conflict between religion and philosophy, truth is on the side of religion when philosophy claims to replace it in the sphere of salvation and eternal life; but truth is on the side of philosophy when it claims to attain a higher degree of knowledge than that attained by the elements of naïve knowledge incorporated in religion. In this sense, indeed, philosophy can help to purify religion by protecting it against the objective and natural processes assailing religious truths. The living God to Whom men address their prayers is the God of Abraham, Isaac and Jacob, not the philosophers' God, the idea of the Absolute. But the problem is even more complex than Pascal imagined, for the God of Abraham, Isaac and Jacob was not only the God Who Is, the living and personal God, but also the God of a primitive nomad tribe, a God reduced to the intellectual and social level of that tribe. The spirit in its quest of knowledge is always bound to clash with the slumbering spirit of tradition. It is not easy for philosophy to adapt itself to the gregarious spirit. . . .

. . . The truth he discovers takes no account of other people's reasoning; it is his own reason that must furnish the revelation of the supra-human and the divine. Society does not aid him in his pursuit of knowledge. In every philosopher there is always something of Spinoza and his destiny. The philosopher's social insecurity, the personal character of his thought, and his general situation, all combine to make his vocation akin to the prophet's. The prophet's position is even more precarious; he is more liable to be persecuted when he preoccupies himself with the destinies of a people or a community. Thus the prophetic type of philosopher is the most disarmed, the least tolerated, and the most solitary. . . .

Man has a choice of two attitudes in every creative and intellectual act; he can confront the mystery of Being, the Divine mystery; or he can restrict his relationships to a purely social plane. In the first case, he attains to an authentic philosophy by means of intuition and revelation; in the second, he is forced to adapt his philosophical knowledge as well as his revealed truth to the needs of a particular society. But in return for social security thus granted, he has to falsify his conscience and help to propagate socially useful falsehoods. In society, in the company of other men, man tends to become an actor; he is one also when he becomes an author. He is obliged to play a part because of his social position; like an actor, he depends on other people, on the public, and on the police to protect him in case of need. The man who sets out in quest of truth, and who finds himself face to face with the Divine mystery, not only often cries in the wilderness, but also leaves himself open to attack by the pontiffs of both religion and science. This situation is implicit in the very nature of philosophy and constitutes its inherent tragedy.

37

JACAPONE DA TODI

A Simple Faith *

Science is a thing divine,
Where good gold we may refine,
But sorely doth God's truth pine
Neath all our sophistry.

And so away with syllogisms,
Your reasoning chains and your sophisms
Your tiring puzzles and aphorisms
And all your subtlety.

Plato and Socrates may contend
And all the breath in their bodies spend,
Arguing without an end—
What's it all to me?   . . .

Only a pure and simple mind
Straight to heaven its way doth find;
Greets the King—while, far behind,
Lags the world's philosophy.

* From the *Sons of St. Francis*, by Anne McDonnell (G. P. Putnam's Sons, 1902), p. 369. Reprinted with the permission of the publisher.

Jacapone da Todi (1228-1306) was born of a noble family at Todi in Italy. He practiced as an advocate and became quite prosperous. On the death of his wife in 1268 he became a Franciscan. He was later imprisoned for his views as a Spiritual Franciscan, and after his release from prison in 1303 lived at Collazzone until his death.

Part Four

EVIL

PHILOSOPHY IS often said to begin in wonder, but the awful impact and shock of what men call "evil" moves not merely the philosopher but the poet and the religious man as well to seek for an explanation to quiet the dread wonder that evil provokes.

The evil that man becomes aware of falls into two distinct categories. The first category of evil may be called physical or natural evil, because it represents what we regard as some deficiency, disorder, or deformity in the natural order: the lack of sight or hearing in a creature, or the appearance of the misshapen and ugly—the birth of a monster. Or it may be some failure of what we normally expect of nature—a lack of rain, for example. The second category of evil includes those things we regard as evil in the actions of man—war, crime, and perfidy, for instance. Of these two kinds of evil, the first may seem to many to be the more evident and the more disastrous in its impact, primarily because it seems to be beyond the control of man and to be more clearly the product of nature. Moral evil, on the other hand, often seems (to these people) to be less serious, perhaps because it is more clearly the responsibility of man and therefore an evil that can be avoided or eventually overcome in the assumed moral progress of man. But moral evil, at least in the history of religious thought, has always been regarded as the more serious and calls for more than a purely philosophical explanation. To overcome moral evil requires of man a faith and a trust in God and an obedience to His commandments. And even this, the religious tell us, does not resolve the problem. Hence Leibniz or Augustine may explain away the physical evil of the universe and reconcile it with the divine goodness and omnipotence, but moral evil remains for them more of a mystery than a problem—a mystery that must eventually be referred to the secret judgments of God.*

* The problem of predestination, taken up in Part Five of this book, continues, in a way, this discussion of moral evil.

Regarding the attitudes that men have taken toward the problem
evil, both in its physical and moral aspects, let us consider first what
kind of answer the poet can give us. Now, the poet is not given to
argument, philosophical or theological, but instead relies upon a kind
of intuition and speaks directly from his emotions and feelings. His
answer may be a simple statement of his faith, like Browning's "God's
in His heaven, all's right with the world," or it may be like the
frightening blasphemy and despair of James Thomson which appears
as the first selection in Part Four. The examples could be multiplied,
but in all we would find the same reliance upon inspiration or intuition, the avoidance of rational argument, and we would conclude
that the poet attempts to persuade us merely by the sheer artistry
of his words. We don't believe that the selection from the *City of
Dreadful Night* will persuade any of our readers, but it may shock
them into the realization that there does exist a problem of evil and
that some individuals have felt it so keenly that pessimism seems to
them the only logical attitude.

The answer that religion gives the problem of evil shares something of the emotional attitude of the poet, and even something of
his intuition. Like the poet, the religious man may simply state his
faith and trust in God as an answer to the problem of evil. However,
as a religious man he can hardly accept the consistent despair of a
poet like James Thomson or the distressing uncertainties of the
sceptics. Job cannot leave unanswered the challenge that evil presents
to him, and the very shock of it puts his faith and his loyalty severely
to trial. In the selection from the Bible that describes the contrived
catastrophe that engulfs Job, the problem of evil is elaborated in the
persistent questioning of the purposes of His creator by Job and
the equally persistent justification by Job's friends of the ways of
God to man. Here the religious answers share with philosophy the
method of rational inquiry, and with poetry, the emotional insights
and lyrical expressions of the inquirer. The religious answer in this
case differs from that of philosophy, in that the outcome of the inquiry
results for Job in a renewal of his obedience to God and a reaffirma-
tion of his faith in the wisdom and the power of God; the outcome
for the philosopher would be the construction of a metaphysics to
account for the nature and existence of evil, or the abandonment of
the problem and the conviction that its solution is completely beyond the limits of human knowledge. Finally, it ought to be observed of the religious answer that it need not be as close to poetry
and as simple as the explanation offered by Job. Rather than being
a simple affirmation of faith, it may be a highly profound and phil-

osophical explanation of that faith, as we shall find in the selection by Augustine, in which the religious experience moves closer to philosophy than to poetry, and then merges into theology.

One of the earliest, and also one of the simplest, solutions to the problem of evil is found in the Zoroasterian scriptures of the pre-Christian era; this same solution was later propounded by the group that Bayle refers to as the "infamous sect of the Manichees," founded by Manes in the third century. The Manichees held that all the good in the universe is to be attributed to the principle of good or light (Mazda), and that all the evil in the universe must be attributed to the principle of evil or darkness (Ahriman). In antiquity this view was vigorously attacked by Augustine and had few defenders of any note until the appearance of Pierre Bayle, the great sceptic and precursor of the Enlightenment. Although Bayle makes a great show of denouncing the Manicheans, nevertheless he finds reason strong enough to defend their position and too weak to afford any criticism. The only ground on which he rejects Manicheism seems to be that of religious faith. Bayle, in our opinion, is not very convincing, and the Manichean solution of the problem of evil has never been sufficiently adequate, we believe, to merit serious consideration from philosophers. It affords no good argument for the priority and reality of either good or evil, and makes no attempt to reconcile the two in any way or to explain the difficulties involved in maintaining their individual supremacy and independence.

Moving beyond Manicheism, we find three more advanced explanations, each based upon a solid metaphysical system and each argued for with cogency and philosophical acumen. Two of these explanations contrast the extreme positions of pessimism and optimism, the third position represents a more moderate type of optimism.

In all the history of philosophy Schopenhauer, we are convinced, presents the best case for pessimism. For despite a sybaritic existence, Schopenhauer believes strongly in the priority, the reality, and the positive character of evil. He is equally as eloquent as any philosopher in reciting the evils of human existence, but he is not concerned with a mere recital. Instead, he chooses to construct a metaphysical system which endeavors, by rational argument, to show that evil is positive and real, and good, negative and illusory. Once having demonstrated that reality is essentially evil, Schopenhauer looks toward the possibility of the salvation of man from the evils of existence. However, the way of salvation that he offers is only for the few, and he has difficulty in showing, without contradiction, that even these few can attain salvation. His philosophy remains consistently pessimistic; in it there is no happy ending for man, as there was for Job or as Christians envision in the life to come. Yet, much as we may disagree with Schopenhauer, we cannot help but appreciate his sincerity and be impressed with his effort to construct a logically coherent philosophical pessimism.

At the other extreme from Schopenhauer, we find the philosophical optimism of Leibniz. Here we have a metaphysics that emphasizes the positive character of the good to such an extent that evil tends to vanish altogether or become an illusory phenomenon that can be readily dealt with by the logic of Leibniz' theory that "this is the best of all possible worlds." The solution of Leibniz undoubtedly carries the affirmation of optimism to an extreme and was to lead to an entertaining caricature (but not a refutation) by Voltaire in *Candide*. There is a profundity in the philosophy of Leibniz that may easily escape us simply because he writes so succinctly and because we are undoubtedly taken aback at what we regard as his preposterous optimism. Yet his position is very carefully thought out, logically argued for, and not readily refuted by any means. His solution to the problem is essentially the Christian solution, although exaggerated, of reconciling the infinite goodness and omnipotence of God with the evil in a created universe. He reaches an exaggerated optimism because, unlike most Christian philosophers, he will not admit that God could have created a better world than this one. Leibniz believes that such an answer belies the infinite perfection of God. At the risk of restricting the freedom of God he maintains the thesis that God can create only the best, and, therefore, that this must be the best of all possible worlds.

In the philosophy and theology constructed by Augustine, we find an answer to the problem of evil which, though by no means definitive or final, does take on, in our opinion, a somewhat wider perspective than that to be found in any of the preceding selections. Here we find all the faith of Job, but a faith that seeks further for understanding and culminates in both a theological and a philosophical defense of God in the face of the evil that exists in the universe. Augustine's faith is a militant one and seeks to overthrow the theory of the Manicheans, who threatened the Church of his day and questioned the omnipotence of God. He is optimistic, though moderately so; living at the time that he did, of course, he needed no recital by Bayle or Schopenhauer to make him aware of the existence of evil. Although he may seem unduly pessimistic at times in treating of the nature of man, yet he does believe firmly in the grace of

God and the eternal happiness that is possible for man. His seeming
pessimism is more than balanced by his awareness of the greatness
and goodness of God. This awareness he could never doubt, for it
stemmed from the deep religious convictions that were so wholly his
from the time of his conversion. This conversion was responsible also
for his deep awareness of the existence and nature of moral evil.
Thus his solution to this problem of moral evil is not a dispassionate
one, worked out with calm logic, but issues, instead, from the depths
of his own personal experience. Physical evil for Augustine is always
the lesser problem and much more readily explained; moral evil has
its source in sin and involves the whole nature and destiny of man.
Its solution cannot be worked out by philosophy alone, but must be
founded on the Christian revelation. Thus, Augustine's attack upon
the problem of evil displays a wider perspective than those which
preceded it, for it combines both the religious and the philosophical
answers, and issues, not merely from logic, but from religious and
personal experience as well. Finally, the real significance of the
Augustinian solution lies in the fact that it forms the substance of
so many of the later philosophical and theological solutions to the
problem of evil and, even today, affords us as definitive a solution
as can be found in philosophy and theology.

❦❦❦❦

38

JAMES THOMSON

Despair and Blasphemy *

I never knew another man on earth,
    But had some joy or solace in his life,
    Some chance of triumph in the dreadful strife:
My doom has been unmitigated dearth.

* From *The City of Dreadful Night* (Methuen and Co., Ltd., 1932), pp. 39-40.
James Thomson (1834-82) was born at Port-Glasgow, in Renfrewshire, England. At the age of seven he was placed in an orphan asylum and later entered
the model school of the Military Asylum, Chelsea. While he was employed as
an assistant army schoolmaster, he fell deeply in love with a girl of exceptional
beauty and intelligence. The death of his fiancée two years later had a profound

We gaze upon the river, and we note
The various vessels large and small that float
Ignoring every wrecked and sunken boat.

And yet I asked no splendid dower, no spoil
Of sway or fame or rank or even wealth;
But homely love with common food and health,
And nightly sleep to balance daily toil.

This all-too-humble soul would arrogate
Unto itself some signalising hate
From the supreme indifference of Fate!

Who is most wretched in this dolorous place?
I think myself; yet I would rather be
My miserable self than He, than He
Who formed such creatures to His own disgrace.

The vilest thing must be less vile than Thou
From whom it had its being, God and Lord!
Creator of all woe and sin! abhorred,
Malignant and implacable! I vow

That not for all Thy power furled and unfurled,
For all the temples to Thy glory built,
Would I assume the ignominious guilt
Of having made such men in such a world.

As if a Being, God or Fiend, could reign,
At once so wicked, foolish, and insane,
As to produce men when He might refrain!

The world rolls round for ever like a mill;
It grinds out death and life and good and ill;
It has no purpose, heart or mind or will.

While air of Space and Time's full river flow
The mill must blindly whirl unresting so:
It may be wearing out, but who can know?

---

effect upon him. His life from then on was one of despair and gloom. He wrote
intermittently and lived alone and in poverty in a room in Bloomsbury until his
death.

Man might know one thing were his sight less dim;
That it whirls not to suit his petty whim,
That it is quite indifferent to him.

Nay, does it treat him harshly as he saith?
It grinds him some slow years of bitter breath,
Then grinds him back into eternal death.

39

The Book of Job *

THE THEME of the Book of Job is the suffering and misery of a
just and virtuous man, and his eventual reconciliation with God.

In the Prologue (Chapters 1 and 2), the question of disinterested
virtue is raised. Satan would try Job, by suffering and affliction, to
determine whether he is truly a virtuous man or whether he regards
virtue simply as a means to prosperity and would renounce God
in adversity. To resolve the issue, God permits all manner of evil
to fall upon Job.

In the Dialogue between Job and his friends (Chapters 3 to
32), Job pleads his innocence to any wrong-doing and questions,
often impatiently, the justice of his suffering. Job's friends are convinced that the evil that has befallen Job is a part of the Divine
providence and a just retribution for the sins which they are sure
Job must have committed. They reproach Job for his sins and
endeavor to justify the ways of God to him.

The two Discourses of God (Chapters 38 to 42) tell of the
omnipotence and omniscience of God, and are followed by Job's
confession and submission.

The Epilogue (Chapter 42) reveals the reconciliation of Job
with God and the forgiveness and the blessings that God bestows
upon him in greater measure than before. It should be noted that

* In the selections that follow, I have omitted the speeches of Job and his
friends from Chapters 15-32. Much of this material is repetitious and, at times,
obscure or confusing. The long speech of Elihu (Chapters 32-38) has been
omitted because it does not fit into the continuity of the story. For a similar
reason I have omitted Chapter 28, dealing with wisdom. On occasion, I have
presumed to make a few minor alterations or other omissions in the text, solely
for the purpose of clarity and continuity. The King James version has been used
except in a few instances where the Douay translation provided greater clarity.

among the Israelites at this time the idea of retribution beyond the grave was apparently unknown, hence the need for God to restore Job's prosperity. No final solution to the problem of evil is given, but the principle of retribution is reaffirmed and the omnipotence of God exemplified.

THERE WAS A MAN in the land of Uz, whose name was Job; and that man was perfect and upright, and one that feared God, and eschewed evil. And there were born unto him seven sons and three daughters. His substance also was seven thousand sheep, and three thousand camels, and five hundred yoke of oxen, and five hundred she-asses, and a very great household; so that this man was the greatest of all the men of the east. And his sons went and feasted in their houses, every one his day; and sent and called for their three sisters to eat and to drink with them. And it was so, when the days of their feasting were gone about, that Job sent and sanctified them, and rose up early in the morning, and offered burnt offerings according to the number of them all, for Job said, It may be that my sons have sinned, and cursed God in their hearts. Thus did Job continually.

Now there was a day when the sons of God came to present themselves before the Lord, and Satan came also among them. And the Lord said unto Satan, Whence comest thou? Then Satan answered the Lord, and said, From going to and fro in the earth, and from walking up and down in it. And the Lord said unto Satan, Hast thou considered my servant Job, that there is none like him in the earth, a perfect and an upright man, one that feareth God, and escheweth evil?

Then Satan answered the Lord, and said, Doth Job fear God for nought? Hast not thou made a hedge about him, and about his house, and about all that he hath on every side? Thou hast blessed the work of his hands, and his substance is increased in the land. But put forth thine hand now, and touch all that he hath, and he will curse thee to thy face.

And the Lord said unto Satan, Behold, all that he hath is in thy power; only upon himself put not forth thine hand.

So Satan went forth from the presence of the Lord.

And there was a day when his sons and his daughters were eating and drinking wine in their eldest brother's house; and there came a messenger unto Job, and said, The oxen were plowing, and the asses feeding beside them; and the Sabeans fell upon them, and took them away; yea, they have slain the servants with the edge of the sword; and I only am escaped alone to tell thee.

While he was yet speaking, there came also another, and said, The fire of God is fallen from heaven, and hath burned up the sheep, and the servants, and consumed them; and I only am escaped alone to tell thee.

While he was yet speaking, there came also another, and said, The Chaldeans made out three bands, and fell upon the camels, and have carried them away, yea, and slain the servants with the edge of the sword; and I only am escaped alone to tell thee.

While he was yet speaking, there came also another, and said, Thy sons and thy daughters were eating and drinking wine in their eldest brother's house; and, behold, there came a great wind from the wilderness, and smote the four corners of the house, and it fell upon the young men, and they are dead; and I only am escaped alone to tell thee.

Then Job arose, and rent his mantle, and shaved his head, and fell down upon the ground, and worshiped, and said, Naked came I out of my mother's womb, and naked shall I return thither; the Lord gave and the Lord hath taken away: blessed be the name of the Lord.

In all this Job sinned not, nor charged God foolishly.

Again there was a day when the sons of God came to present themselves before the Lord, and Satan came also among them to present himself before the Lord. And the Lord said unto Satan, From whence comest thou? And Satan answered the Lord, and said, From going to and fro in the earth, and from walking up and down in it. And the Lord said unto Satan, Hast thou considered my servant Job, that there is none like him in the earth, a perfect and an upright man, one that feareth God, and escheweth evil, And still he holdeth fast his integrity, although thou movedst me against him, to destroy him without cause.

And Satan answered the Lord, and said, Skin for skin, yea, all that a man hath will he give for his life. But put forth thine hand now, and touch his bone and his flesh, and he will curse thee to thy face.

And the Lord said unto Satan, Behold, he is in thine hand; but save his life.

So went Satan forth from the presence of the Lord, and smote Job with sore boils from the sole of his foot unto his crown. And he took him a potsherd to scrape himself withal; and he sat down among the ashes.

Then said his wife unto him, Dost thou still retain thine integrity? Curse God, and die. But he said unto her, Thou speakest as one of the foolish women speaketh. What? shall we receive good at the hand of God, and shall we not receive evil? In all this did not Job sin with his lips.

Now when Job's three friends heard of all this evil that was come upon him, they came every one from his own place: Eliphaz the Temanite, and Bildad the Shuhite, and Zophar the Naamathite; for they had made an appointment together to come to mourn with him and to comfort him. And when they lifted up their eyes afar off, and knew him not, they lifted up their voice, and wept; and they rent every one his mantle, and sprinkled dust upon their heads toward heaven. So they sat down with him upon the ground seven days and seven nights, and none spake a word unto him: for they saw that his grief was very great.

CHAPTER 3

After this Job opened his mouth, and cursed his day. And Job spake, and said: Let the day perish wherein I was born, and the night in which it was said, there is a man child conceived. Let that day be in darkness; let not God regard it from above, neither let the light shine upon it. Let darkness and the shadow of death stain it; let a cloud dwell upon it; let the blackness of the day terrify it. As for that night, let darkness seize upon it; let it not be joined unto the days of the year, let it not come into the number of the months. Lo, let that night be solitary, let no joyful voice come therein. Let them curse it that curse the day, who are ready to raise up their mourning. Let the stars of the twilight thereof be dark; let it look for light, but have none; neither let it see the dawning of the day. Because it shut not up the doors of my mother's womb, nor hid sorrow from mine eyes.

Why died I not from the womb? Why did I not give up the ghost when I came out of the belly? Why received upon the knees? why suckled at the breasts? For now should I have lain still and been quiet, I should have slept: then had I been at rest. With kings and counsellors of the earth, who built desolate places for themselves. Or with the princes that had gold, who filled their houses with silver. Or as an hidden untimely birth I had not been; as infants which never saw light. There the wicked cease from troubling; and there the weary be at rest. There the prisoners rest together; they hear not the voice of the oppressor. The small and the great are there; and the servant is free from his master.

Wherefore light is given to him that is in misery, and life unto the bitter in soul. They long for death, but it cometh not; and they dig for it more than for hidden treasures. And they rejoice exceedingly when they have found the grave. Why is light given to a man whose way is hidden, and whom God hath hedged in? For my sighing cometh before I eat, and my roarings are poured out like the waters. For the thing which I greatly feared is come upon me, and that which I was afraid of is come unto me. I was not in safety, neither had I rest, neither was I quiet; yet trouble came.

CHAPTER 4

Then Eliphaz the Temanite answered and said: If we assay to commune with thee, wilt thou be grieved? but who can withhold himself from speaking? Behold, thou hast instructed the many, and thou has strengthened the weak hands. Thy words have upholded him that was falling, and thou hast strengthened the feeble knees. But now it is come upon thee, and thou faintest; it toucheth thee, and thou art troubled. Is not this thy fear, thy confidence, thy hope, and the uprightness of thy ways? Remember, I pray thee, who ever perished, being innocent? or where were the righteous cut off? Even as I have seen, they that plow iniquity, and sow wickedness, reap the same. By the blast of God they perish, and by the breath of his nostrils are they consumed.

.   .   .   .   .

Now a thing was secretly brought to me, and mine ear received a little thereof. In thoughts from the visions of the night, when deep sleep falleth on men, Fear came upon me, and trembling, which made all my bones to shake. Then a spirit passed before my face; the hair of my flesh stood up: It stood still, but I could not discern the form thereof: an image was before mine eyes, there was silence, and I heard a voice saying: Shall mortal man be more just than God? shall a man be more pure than his maker? Behold, he put no trust in his servants; and his angels he charged with folly: How much less in them that dwell in houses of clay, whose foundation is in the dust, which are crushed before the moth? They are destroyed from morning to evening: they perish for ever without any regarding it. Doth not their excellency which is in them go away? they die, even without wisdom.

CHAPTER 5

Call now, if there be any that will answer thee; and to which of the saints wilt thou turn? For wrath killeth the foolish man, and envy slayeth the silly one. I have seen the foolish taking root, but suddenly I cursed his habitation. His children are far from safety, and they are crushed in the gate, neither is there anyone to deliver them. Whose harvest the hungry eateth up, and taketh it even out of the thorns, and the robber swalloweth up their substance. Although affliction cometh not forth of the dust, neither doth trouble spring out of the ground. Yet man is born unto trouble, as the sparks fly upward.

I would seek unto God, and unto God would I commit my cause: Who doeth great things and unsearchable; marvellous things without number: Who giveth rain upon the earth, and sendeth waters upon the fields: To set up on high those that be low; that those which mourn may be exalted to safety. He disappointeth the devices of the crafty, so that their hands cannot perform their enterprise. He taketh the wise in their own craftiness, and the counsel of the froward is carried headlong. They meet with darkness in the daytime, and grope in the noonday as in the night. But he saveth the poor from the sword, from their mouth, and from the hand of the mighty. So the poor hath hope and iniquity stoppeth her mouth.

Behold, happy is the man whom God correcteth: therefore despise not thou the chastening of the Almighty: For he maketh sore, and bindeth up: he woundeth, and his hands make whole. He shall deliver thee in six troubles: yea, in seven there shall no evil touch thee. In famine he shall redeem thee from death, and in war from the power of the sword. Thou shalt be hid from the scourge of the tongue: neither shalt thou be afraid of destruction when it cometh. At destruction and famine thou shalt laugh: neither shalt thou be afraid of the beasts of the earth. For thou shalt be in league with the stones of the field, and the beasts of the field shall be at peace with thee. And thou shalt know that thy tabernacle shall be in peace; and thou shalt visit thy habitation, and shalt not sin. Thou shalt know also that thy seed shall be great, and thine offspring as the grass of the earth. Thou shalt come to thy grave in a full age, like as a shock of corn cometh in in his season. Lo this, we have searched it, so it is; hear it, and know thou it for thy good.

CHAPTER 6

But Job answered and said: Oh that my grief were thoroughly weighed, and my calamity laid in the balances together! For now it would be heavier than the sand of the sea: therefore my words are swallowed up. For the arrows of the Almighty are within me, the poison whereof drinketh up my spirit: the terrors of God do set themselves in array against me.

Oh that I might have my request; and that God would grant me
the thing that I long for! Even that it would please God to destroy
me; that he would let loose his hand, and cut me off! Then should
I yet have comfort; yea, I would harden myself in sorrow: let him
not spare, for I have not concealed the words of the Holy One.
What is my strength, that I should hope? and what is mine end,
that I should prolong my life? Is my strength the strength of stones?
or is my flesh of brass? Is not my help in me? and is wisdom driven
quite from me? To him that is afflicted pity should be showed from
his friend; but he forsaketh the fear of the Almighty. My brethren
have dealt deceitfully as a brook, and as the stream of brooks they
pass away; Which are blackish by reason of the ice, and wherein the
snow is hid. At the time they wax warm, they vanish: when it is
hot, they are consumed out of their place. The paths of their way
are turned aside; they go to nothing, and perish. The troops of Tema
looked, the companies of Sheba waited for them. They were confounded because they had hoped; they came thither, and were
ashamed.

For now ye are nothing; ye see my casting down, and are afraid.
Did I say, Bring unto me? or, Give a reward for me of your substance? Or, Deliver me from the enemy's hand? or, Redeem me from
the hand of the mighty? Teach me, and I will hold my tongue:
and cause me to understand wherein I have erred. How forcible are
right words: but what doth your arguing reprove? Do ye imagine to
reprove words, and the speeches of one that is desperate, which are
as wind? Yea, ye overwhelm the fatherless, and yet ye dig a pit
for your friend. Now therefore be content, look upon me; for it is
evident unto you if I lie. Return, I pray you, let it not be iniquity;
yea, return again, my righteousness is in it. Is there iniquity in my
tongue? Cannot my taste discern perverse things?

CHAPTER 7

Is there not an appointed time to man upon earth? Are not his
days also like the days of an hireling? As a servant earnestly desireth
the shadow, and as an hireling looketh for the reward of his work:
So am I made to possess months of vanity, and wearisome nights
are appointed to me. When I lie down, I say, When shall I arise, and
the night be gone? and I am full of tossings to and fro unto the
dawning of the day. My flesh is clothed with worms and clods of
dust; my skin is broken and become loathesome. My days are swifter
than a weaver's shuttle, and are spent without hope.

O remember that my life is wind: mine eye shall no more see good. The eye of him that hath seen me shall see me no more: thine eyes are upon me, and I am not. As the cloud is consumed and vanisheth away; so he that goeth down to the grave shall come up no more. He shall return no more to his house, neither shall his place know him any more. Therefore I will not refrain my mouth; I will speak in the anguish of my spirit; I will complain in the bitterness of my soul. Am I a sea, or a whale, that thou settest a watch over me? When I say, My bed shall comfort me, my couch shall ease my complaint: Then thou scarest me with dreams, and terrifiest me through visions. So that my soul chooseth strangling, and death rather than my life.

I loathe it; I would not live alway: let me alone; for my days are vanity. What is man, that thou shouldest magnify him? and that thou shouldest set thine heart upon him? And that thou shouldest visit him every morning, and try him every moment? How long wilt thou not depart from me, nor let me alone till I swallow down my spittle? I have sinned; what shall I do unto thee, O thou preserver of men? why hast thou set me as a mark against thee, so that I am a burden to myself? And why dost thou not pardon my transgression, and take away mine iniquity? for now shall I sleep in the dust; and thou shalt seek me in the morning, but I shall not be.

CHAPTER 8

Then answered Bildad the Shuhite and said: How long wilt thou speak these things? and how long shall the words of thy mouth be like a strong wind? Doth God pervert judgment? or doth the Almighty pervert justice? If thy children have sinned against him, and he hath cast them away for their transgression; If thou wouldest seek unto God betimes, and make thy supplication to the Almighty; If thou were pure and upright; surely now he would awake for thee, and make the habitation of thy righteousness prosperous. Though thy beginning was small, yet thy latter end should greatly increase.

For enquire, I pray thee, of the former age, and prepare thyself to the search of their fathers: For we are but of yesterday, and know nothing, because our days upon earth are a shadow. Shall not they teach thee, and tell thee, and utter words out of their heart? Can the rush grow up without mire? Can the bush grow without water? Whilst it is yet in his greenness, and not cut down, it withereth before any other herb. So are the paths of all that forget God; and the hypocrite's hope shall perish: Whose hope shall be cut off, and whose trust shall be a spider's web. He shall lean upon his house,

but it shall not stand; he shall hold it fast, but it shall not endure.
He is green before the sun, and his branch shooteth forth in his
garden. His roots are wrapped about the heap, and seeth the place
of stones. If he destroy him from his place, then it shall deny him,
saying, I have not seen thee. For, this is the joy of his way, and
out of the earth shall others grow.

Behold, God will not cast away a perfect man, neither will he help
the evil doers: Till he fill thy mouth with laughing, and thy lips
with rejoicing. They that hate thee shall be clothed with shame; and
the dwelling place of the wicked shall come to nought.

CHAPTER 9

Then Job answered and said: I know it is so of a truth: but how
should man be just with God? If he will contend with him, he cannot answer him one of a thousand. He is wise in heart, and mighty
in strength: who hath hardened himself against him, and hath
prospered? Who removeth the mountains, and they know not. Who
overturneth them in his anger. Who shaketh the earth out of her
place, and the pillars thereof tremble. Who commandeth the sun,
and it riseth not; and sealeth up the stars. Who alone spreadeth out
the heavens, and treadeth upon the waves of the sea. Who maketh
Arcturus, Orion, and Pleiades, and the chambers of the south. Who
doeth great things past finding out; yea, and wonders without number. Lo, he goeth by me, and I see him not: he passeth on also,
but I perceive him not. Behold, he taketh away, who can hinder him?
Who will say unto him, What doest thou? If God will not withdraw
his anger, the proud helpers do stoop under him. How much less
shall I answer him, and choose out my words to reason with him?

Though I were righteous, yet would I not answer, but I would
make supplication to my judge. If I had called, and he had answered
me; yet would I not believe that he had hearkened unto my voice.
For he breaketh me with a tempest, and multiplieth my wounds without cause. He will not suffer me to take my breath, but filleth me
with bitterness. If I speak of strength, lo, he is strong: and if of
judgment, who shall set me a time to plead? If I justify myself, mine
own mouth shall condemn me: if I say, I am perfect, it shall also
prove me perverse. Though I were perfect, yet would I not know my
soul; I would despise my life. This is one thing, therefore I said it,
He destroyeth the perfect and the wicked. If the scourge slay suddenly, he will laugh at the trial of the innocent. The earth is given
into the hand of the wicked: he covereth the faces of the judges
thereof; if not, where and who is he?

Now my days are swifter than a post: they flee away, they see no good. They are passed away as the swift ships: as the eagle that hasteth to the prey. If I say, I will forget my complaint, I will leave off my heaviness, and comfort myself. I am afraid of all my sorrows, I know that thou wilt not hold me innocent. If I be wicked, why then labor I in vain? If I wash myself with snow water, and make my hands never so clean; Yet shalt thou plunge me in the ditch, and mine own clothes shall abhor me. For he is not a man, as I am, that I should answer him, and we should come together in judgment. Neither is there anyone between us, that might lay his hand upon us both. Let him take his rod away from me, and let not his fear terrify me; Then would I speak, and not fear him; but it is not so with me.

CHAPTER 10

My soul is weary of my life; I will leave my complaint upon myself; I will speak in the bitterness of my soul. I will say unto God, Do not condemn me; show me wherefore thou contendest with me. Is it good unto thee that thou shouldest oppress, that thou shouldest despise the work of thine hands, and shine upon the counsel of the wicked? Hast thou eyes of flesh? or seest thou as man seeth? Are thy days as the days of man? are thy years as man's days, That thou enquirest after mine iniquity, and searchest after my sin? Thou knowest that I am not wicked; and there is none that can deliver out of thine hand.

Thine hands have made me and fashioned me together round about; yet thou dost destroy me. Remember, I beseech thee, that thou hast made me as the clay; and wilt thou bring me into dust again? Hast thou not poured me out as milk, and curdled me like cheese? Thou hast clothed me with skin and flesh, and hast fenced me with bones and sinews. Thou hast granted me life and favor, and thy visitation hath preserved my spirit. And these things hast thou hid in thine heart: I know that this is with thee. If I sin, then thou markest me, and thou wilt not acquit me from mine iniquity. If I be wicked, woe unto me; and if I be righteous, yet will I not lift up my head. I am full of confusion; therefore see thou mine affliction. For it increaseth. Thou huntest me as a fierce lion: and again thou showest thyself marvellous upon me. Thou renewest thy witnesses against me, and increasest thine indignation upon me, and pains war against me.

Wherefore then hast thou brought me forth out of the womb? Oh that I had given up the ghost, and no eye had seen me! I should have been as though I had not been; I should have been carried from the womb to the grave. Are not my days few? cease then, and let me alone, that I may take comfort a little. Before I go whence I shall not return, even to the land of darkness and the shadow of death; A land of darkness, as darkness itself; and of the shadow of death, without any order, and where the light is as darkness.

CHAPTER 11

Then answered Zophar the Naamathite, and said: Should not the multitude of words be answered? and should a man full of talk be justified? Should thy lies make men hold their peace? and when thou mockest, shall no man make thee ashamed? For thou has said, My doctrine is pure, and I am clean in thine eyes. But oh that God would speak, and open his lips against thee; And that he would show thee the secrets of wisdom, that they are double to that which is! Know therefore that God exacteth of thee less than thine iniquity deserveth. Canst thou by searching find out God? canst thou find out the Almighty unto perfection? He is higher than heaven, and what wilt thou do? he is deeper than hell, and how wilt thou know? The measure thereof is longer than the earth, and broader than the sea. If he cut off, and shut up, or gather together, then who can hinder him? For he knoweth vain men: he seeth wickedness also; will he not then consider it? For vain man would be wise, though man be born like a wild ass's colt.

If thou prepare thine heart, and stretch out thine hands toward him; If iniquity be in thine hand, put it far away, and let not wickedness dwell in thy tabernacles. For then shalt thou lift up thy face without spot; yea, thou shalt be steadfast, and shalt not fear; Because thou shalt forget thy misery, and remember it as waters that pass away: And thine age shall be clearer than the noonday; thou shalt shine forth, thou shalt be as the morning. And thou shalt be secure, because there is hope; yea, thou shalt dig about thee, and thou shalt take thy rest in safety. Also thou shalt lie down, and none shall make thee afraid; yea, many shall make suit unto thee.

But the eyes of the wicked shall fail, and they shall not escape, and their hope shall be as the giving up of the ghost.

CHAPTER 12

And Job answered and said: No doubt but ye are the people, and wisdom shall die with you. But I have understanding as well as you; I am not inferior to you: yea, who knoweth not such things as these? I am as one mocked of his neighbor, who calleth upon God, and he answereth him: the just upright man is laughed to scorn. He that is ready to slip with his feet is as a lamp despised in the thought of him that is at ease. The tabernacles of robbers prosper, and they that provoke God are secure; into whose hand God bringeth abundantly. But ask now the beasts, and they shall teach thee; and the fowls of the air, and they shall tell thee: Or speak to the earth, and it shall teach thee: and the fishes of the sea shall declare unto thee. Who knoweth not in all these that the hand of the Lord hath wrought this? In whose hand is the soul of every living thing, and the breath of all mankind. Doth not the ear try words? and the mouth taste his meat? With the ancient is wisdom; and in length of days understanding.

With him is wisdom and strength, he hath counsel and understanding. Behold he breaketh down, and it cannot be built again: he shutteth up a man, and there can be no opening. Behold, he withholdeth the waters, and they dry up; also he sendeth them out and they overturn the earth. With him is strength and wisdom: the decived and the deceiver are his. He leadeth counsellors away spoiled and maketh the judges fools. He looseth the bond of kings, and girdeth their loins with a girdle. He leadeth princes away spoiled, and overthroweth the mighty. He removeth away the speech of the trusty, and taketh away the understanding of the aged. He poureth contempt upon princes and weakeneth the strength of the mighty. He discovereth deep things out of darkness, and bringeth out to light the shadow of death. He increaseth the nations and destroyeth them: he enlargeth the nations, and straiteneth them again. He taketh away the heart of the chief of the people of the earth, and causeth them to wander in a wilderness where there is no way. They grope in the dark without light, and he maketh them to stagger like a drunken man.

CHAPTER 13

Lo, mine eye hath seen all this, mine ear hath heard and understood it. What ye know, the same do I know also: I am not inferior unto you. Surely I would speak to the Almighty, and I desire to reason with God. But ye are forgers of lies, ye are all physicians of no value. O that ye would altogether hold your peace! and it should be your wisdom. Hear now my reasoning, and hearken to the pleadings of my lips. Will ye speak wickedly for God? and talk deceitfully for him? Will ye accept his person? will ye contend for God? Is it good that he should search you out? or as one man mocketh another, do ye so mock him? He will surely reprove you, if ye do secretly accept persons. Shall not his excellency make you afraid? and his dread fall upon you? Your remembrances are like unto ashes, your bodies of clay.

Hold your peace, let me alone, that I may speak, and let come on me what will. Wherefore do I take my flesh in my teeth, and put my life in mine hand? Though he slay me, yet will I trust in him: but I will maintain mine own ways before him. He also shall be my salvation: for an hypocrite shall not come before him. Hear diligently my speech, and my declaration with your ears. Behold now, I have ordered my cause; I know that I shall be justified. Who is he that will plead with me? for now, if I hold my tongue, I shall give up the ghost.

Only do not two things unto me: then will I not hide myself from thee. Withdraw thine hand far from me: and let not thy dread make me afraid. Then call thou, and I will answer: or let me speak, and answer thou me. How many are mine iniquities and sins? make me to know my transgression and my sin. Wherefore hidest thou thy face, and holdest me for thine enemy? Wilt thou break a leaf driven to and fro? and wilt thou pursue the dry stubble? For thou writest bitter things against me, and makest me to possess the iniquities of my youth. Thou puttest my feet also in the stocks, and lookest narrowly unto all my paths; thou settest a print upon the heels of my feet. And I, as a rotten thing, consumeth, as a garment that is moth eaten.

CHAPTER 14

Man that is born of a woman is of few days, and full of trouble. He cometh forth like a flower, and is cut down: he fleeth also as a shadow, and continueth not. And dost thou open thine eyes upon such an one, and bringest me into judgment with thee? . . . Seeing his days are determined, the number of his months are with thee, thou hast appointed his bounds that he cannot pass. Turn from him, that he may rest, till he shall accomplish, as an hireling, his day.

For there is hope of a tree, if it be cut down, that it will sprout again, and that the tender branch thereof will not cease. Though the root thereof wax old in the earth, and the stock thereof die in the ground; Yet through the scent of water it will bud, and bring forth boughs like a plant. But man dieth, and wasteth away: yea, man giveth up the ghost, and where is he? As the waters fail from the sea, and the flood decayeth and drieth up: So man lieth down, and riseth not: till the heavens be no more, they shall not awake, nor be raised out of their sleep. O that thou wouldest hide me in the grave, that thou wouldest keep me secret, until thy wrath be past, that thou wouldest appoint me a set time, and remember me! If a man die, shall he live again? all the days of my appointed time will I wait, till my change come. Thou shalt call, and I will answer thee: thou wilt have a desire to the work of thine hands.

. . . . .

And surely the mountain falling cometh to nought, and the rock is removed out of his place. The waters wear the stones: thou washest away the things which grow out of the dust of the earth; and thou destroyest the hope of man. Thou prevailest for ever against him, and he passeth: thou changest his countenance, and sendest him away. His sons come to honor, and he knoweth it not; and they are brought low, but he perceiveth it not of them. But his flesh upon him shall have pain, and his soul within him shall mourn.

. . . . .

CHAPTER 38

Then the Lord answered Job out of the whirlwind, and said: Who is this that darkeneth counsel by words without knowledge? Gird up now thy loins like a man; for I will demand of thee, and answer thou me. Where wast thou when I laid the foundations of the earth? declare, if thou hast understanding. Who hath laid the measures thereof, if thou knowest? or who hath stretched the line upon it? Whereupon are the foundations thereof fastened? or who laid the corner stone thereof? When the morning stars sang together, and all the sons of God shouted for joy? Or who shut up the sea with doors, when it brake forth, as if it had issued out of the womb? When I made the cloud the garment thereof, and thick darkness a swaddling band for it, And I set my bounds around it, and made it bars and doors, And said, Hitherto shalt thou come, but no further: and here shall thy proud waves be stayed?

Hast thou commanded the morning since thy days; and caused the dawning to know his place; That it might take hold of the ends of the earth, that the wicked might be shaken out of it? It is turned as clay to the seal; and they stand as a garment. And from the wicked their light is witholden, and the high arm shall be broken. Hast thou entered into the springs of the sea? or hast thou walked in the search of the depth? Have the gates of death been opened unto thee? or hast thou seen the doors of the shadow of death. Hast thou perceived the breadth of the earth: declare if thou knowest it all. Where is the way where light dwelleth? and as far darkness, where is the place thereof. That thou shouldest take it to the bound thereof, and that thou shouldest know the paths to the house thereof?

Knowest thou it, because thou wast then born? or because the number of thy days is great?

Hast thou entered into the treasures of the snow? or hast thou seen the treasures of the hail, Which I have reserved against the time of trouble, against the day of battle and war? By what way is the light parted, which scattereth the east wind upon the earth? Who hath divided a watercouse for the overflowing of waters, or a way for the lightning of thunder; To cause it to rain on the earth, where no man is; on the wilderness, wherein, there is no man; To satisfy the desolate and waste ground; and to cause the bud of the tender herb to spring forth? Hath the rain a father? or who hath begotten the drops of dew? Out of whose womb came the ice? and the hoary frost of heaven, who hath gendered it? The waters are hid as with a stone, and the face of the deep is frozen.

Canst thou bind the sweet influence of Pleiades, or loose the bands of Orion? Canst thou bring forth Mazzaroth in his season? or canst thou guide Arcturus with his sons? Knowest thou the ordinance of heaven? Canst thou set the dominion thereof in the earth? Canst thou lift up thy voice to the clouds, that the abundance of waters may cover thee? Canst thou send lightnings, that they may go, and say unto thee, Here we are? Who hath put wisdom in the inward parts? or who hath given understanding to the heart? Who can number the clouds in wisdom? or who can stay the music of the spheres, When the dust groweth into hardness, and the clods cleave fast together? Wilt thou hunt the prey for the lion? or fill the appetite of the young lions, When they couch in their dens, and abide in the covert to lie in wait? Who provideth for the raven his food? when his young ones cry unto God, they wander for lack of meat.

· · · · ·

CHAPTER 40

Then answered the Lord unto Job out of the whirlwind, and said: Gird up thy loins now like a man: I will demand of thee, and declare thou unto me. Wilt thou also disannul my judgment? wilt thou condemn me, that thou mayest be righteous? Hast thou an arm like God? or canst thou thunder with a voice like him? Deck thyself now with majesty and excellency; and array thyself with glory and beauty. Cast abroad the rage of thy wrath: and behold every one that is proud and abase him. Look on every one that is proud, and bring him low; and tread down the wicked in their place. Hide them in the dust together; and bind their faces in secret. Then will I also confess unto thee that thine own right hand can save thee.

Behold now behemoth, which I made with thee; he eateth grass as an ox. Lo now, his strength is in his loins, and his force is in the navel of his belly. He moveth his tail like a cedar: the sinews of his stones are wrapped together. His bones are as strong pieces of brass; his bones are like bars of iron. He is the chief of the ways of God: he that made him can make his sword to approach unto him. Surely the mountains bring him forth food, where all the beasts of the field play. He lieth under the shady trees, in the covert of the reed, and fens. The shady trees cover him with their shadow; the willows of the brook compass him about. Behold, he drinketh up a river, and hasteth not: he trusteth that he can draw up Jordan into his mouth. He taketh it with his eyes: his nose pierceth through snares.

Canst thou draw out leviathan with an hook? or his tongue with a cord which thou lettest down? Canst thou put an hook into his nose? or bore his jaw through with a thorn? Will he make many supplications unto thee? will he speak soft words unto thee? Will he make a covenant with thee? wilt thou take him for a servant forever? Wilt thou play with him as with a bird? or wilt thou bind him for thy maidens? Shall the companions make a banquet of him? shall they part him among the merchants? Canst thou fill his skin with barbed irons? or his head with fish spears? Lay thine hand upon him, remember the battle, do no more. Behold the hope of him is in vain: shall not one be cast down even at the sight of him?

CHAPTER 41

I will not stir him up, like one that is cruel: for who can resist my countenance? Who hath prevented me, that I should repay him? whatsoever is under the whole heaven is mine. I will not conceal his parts, nor his power, nor his comely proportion.

Who can discover the face of his garment? or who can come to him with his double bridle? Who can open the doors of his face? his teeth are terrible round about. His scales are his pride, shut up together as with a close seal. One is so near to another, that no air can come between them. They are joined one to another, they stick together, that they cannot be sundered. By his sneezings a light doth shine, and his eyes are like the eyelids of the morning. Out of his mouth go burning lamps, and sparks of fire leap out. Out of his nostrils goeth smoke, as out of a seething pot or caldron. His breath kindleth coals, and a flame goeth out of his mouth. In his neck remaineth strength, and sorrow is turned into joy before him. The flakes of his flesh are joined together: they are firm in themselves; they cannot be moved. His heart is as firm as a stone; yea, as hard as a piece of the nether millstone. When he raiseth up himself, the mighty are afraid: by reason of breakings they purify themselves. The sword of him that layeth at him cannot hold: the spear, the dart, nor the breastplate. He esteemeth iron as straw, and brass as rotten wood. The arrow cannot make him flee: slingstones are turned with him into stubble. Darts are counted as stubble: he laugheth at the shaking of a spear. Sharp stones are under him: he spreadeth sharp pointed things upon the mire. He maketh the deep to boil like a pot: he maketh the sea like a pot of ointment. He maketh a path to shine after him; one would think the deep to be hoary.

Upon earth there is not his like, who is made without fear. He beholdeth all high things: he is a king over all the children of pride.

CHAPTER 42

Then Job answered the Lord, and said: I know that thou canst do everything, and that no thought can be withholden from thee. Who is he that hideth counsel without knowledge? therefore have I uttered that I understood not; things too wonderful for me, which I knew not. Hear, I beseech thee, and I will speak: I will demand of thee, and declare thou unto me. I have heard of thee by the hearing of the ear: but now mine eye seeth thee. Wherefore I abhor myself, and repent in dust and ashes.

And it was so, that after the Lord had spoken these words unto Job, the Lord said to Eliphaz the Temanite; My wrath is kindled against thee, and against thy two friends: for ye have not spoken of me the thing that is right, as my servant Job hath. Therefore take unto you now seven bullocks and seven rams, and go to my servant Job, and offer up for yourselves a burnt offering; and my servant Job shall pray for you. For Him will I accept; lest I deal with you after your folly, in that ye have not spoken of me the thing which is right, like my servant Job. So Eliphaz the Temanite and Bildad the Shuhite and Zophar the Naamathite went, and did according as the Lord commanded them; the Lord also accepted Job. And the Lord turned the captivity of Job, when he prayed for his friends; also the Lord gave Job twice as much as he had before.

Then came there unto him all his brethren, and all his sisters, and all they that had been of his acquaintance before, and did eat bread with him in his house; and they bemoaned him, and comforted him over all the evil that the Lord had brought upon him; every man also gave him a piece of money, and everyone an earring of gold.

So the Lord blessed the latter end of Job more than his beginning; for he had fourteen thousand sheep, and six thousand camels, and a thousand yoke of oxen, and a thousand she-asses. He had also seven sons and three daughters. And he called the name of the first, Jemima; and the name of the second Kezia; and the name of the third, Keren-happuch. And in all the land were no women found so fair as the daughters of Job; and their father gave them inheritance among their brethren.

After this lived Job a hundred and forty years, and saw his sons, and his sons' sons, even four generations. So Job died, being old and full of days.

40

PIERRE BAYLE

Manicheism *

THOUGH APPARENTLY CRITICAL of the Manicheans and their beliefs, Bayle covertly supports and justifies on rational grounds their belief in the existence of two principles of good and evil. His defense takes the indirect form of showing how difficult it would be to refute this doctrine, especially on an *a posteriori* basis, for experience offers such clear evidence of the existence of evil. By way of an imaginary disputation between Melissus and Zoroaster he exhibits the arguments that might be made for the existence of one principle and of two principles to explain the cause of good and evil in the universe. His bias in favor of the Zoroastrian position is quite evident, particularly in his analysis of moral evil. Some account is given of the nature of the two principles of Zoroaster and their relationship, and Bayle then concludes with the rather pessimistic observations that human reason is fit only for destruction and doubt and that if we are to meet the objections of Zoroaster we must have recourse to Scripture and revelation.

* From *The Dictionary Historical and Critical of Mr. Peter Bayle*, 2nd ed. Revised, corrected and enlarged by Mr. Des Maizeaux, IV (London, 1737), 90-97.
    Pierre Bayle (1647-1706) was born in France, the son of a Calvinist minister. He was converted to Catholicism in 1669, but reverted to Calvinism and then left France for Geneva, Switzerland. Upon his return to France he became a Professor of Philosophy at the University of Sedan. Later he accepted a position as Professor of Philosophy and History at Rotterdam. In 1693 he was deprived of this position and devoted the rest of his life to the composition of his Historical Dictionary.

MANICHEES, heretics, whose infamous sect, founded by one Manes, began in the IIId century, and established itself in several provinces, and subsisted a very long time.

They taught such doctrines, as ought to inspire us with the greatest horror. Their weakness did not consist, as at first it may seem, in their doctrine of two principles, one good and the other bad, but in the particular explanations they gave of it, and in the practical consequences they drew from it.

It must be confessed, that this false tenet, which is much more ancient than Manes, and cannot be maintained by any one, who admits the Holy Scripture, either in whole or in part, would not easily be refuted, if it were maintained by Pagan Philosophers, well skilled in disputing. By reasons *a priori* they would quickly have been routed: but the reasons *a posteriori* were their strongholds: with these they might have fought a long time, and it would have been difficult to force them. You will understand me better by the explication I shall now subjoin. The most certain and most clear ideas of order we have, teach us, that a Being, which exists by itself, which is necessary and eternal, must be one, infinite, almighty, and endowed with all kind of perfection. If therefore we consult these ideas, we shall find nothing more absurd, than the hypothesis of two eternal principles, and independent of one another, one of which has no goodness, and can put a stop to the designs of the other. This is what I call reasons *a priori;* and which necessarily lead us to reject this hypothesis, and to admit only one principle of all things. If nothing but this were required to prove the goodness of a system, the cause would be determined to the confusion of Zoroaster, and all his followers. But every system requires these two things to make it good; one, that the ideas of it be distinct; the other, that it accounts for what experience teaches us. We must see therefore whether the phenomena of nature can be conveniently explained by the hypothesis of one principle alone. When the Manichees tell us, that, since we see in the world many things, that are contrary to one another, as heat and cold, black and white, light and darkness, there must necessarily be two first principles, they argue pitifully; for the opposition between those Beings, however confirmed by what we call variations, disorders, and irregularities of nature, cannot make one half an objection against the unity, simplicity, and immutability of God. All these things may be accounted for, either by the different powers God has given to bodies, or by the laws of motion, which He has established, or from the concurrence of occasional intelligent causes, by which He is pleased to act. . . . The heavens, and the rest of the universe, declare the glory, power, and the unity of God; man alone, that masterpiece of his creation among things visible, Man alone, I say, affords the greatest objection against the unity of God. The matter is thus:

Man is wicked and unhappy: every one knows it by what he feels in himself, and by the intercourse he is obliged to have with his neighbors. He, who lives only five or six years,* may be perfectly convinced of these two things; and they, who live long, and are much engaged in worldly affairs, know this still more clearly. Travel affords perpetual lessons upon this subject: they show everywhere the monuments of men's misfortunes and wickednesses. . . . History, properly speaking, is nothing but a collection of the crimes and misfortunes of mankind; but we must observe, that these two evils, the one moral, and the other physical, do not wholly fill up history, nor all the experiences of private persons. There are everywhere some things that are physically good and morally good; some examples of virtue, and some examples of happiness: and this is that, which makes the difficulty; for if there were none but evil and unhappy men, there would be no occasion to have recourse to the hypothesis of two principles; it is the mixture of happiness and virtue with misery and vice, which requires this hypothesis; and this is the stronghold of the sect of Zoroaster. . . .

In order to make it appear how difficult it would be to refute this false system, and that we may conclude, that it is necessary to have recourse to revelation to overthrow it, let us feign here a dispute between Melissus and Zoroaster, who were both Pagans and great Philosophers. Melissus, who acknowledged but one principle, would say, at first, that his system agrees admirably with the ideas of order. The necessary being is not bounded; and therefore is infinite and almighty, and consequently one; and it would be a monstrous thing, and a contradiction, if he had no goodness, but the greatest of all vices, viz. an essential malice. I confess to you, would Zoroaster answer, that your ideas are very well connected, and I am willing to grant, that, in this respect, your hypothesis surpasses mine. I will not insist upon an objection, which I might make use of; which is this, that as infinity must include everything that is real, and malice ** being no less a real Being than goodness, the universe requires, that there should be both wicked and good Beings; and that, since a sovereign goodness, and a sovereign malice, cannot subsist in one and the same subject, there must be in nature one Being essentially good, and

---

* At that age he has played and suffered malicious tricks; he has had grief and sorrow, and has pouted many times, etc.

** That is, a malicious action. I remark this, lest any one should allege, that evil is nothing but privation.

another essentially evil: I do not insist, I say, upon this objection; I
will allow, that your system is more agreeable to the notions of order
than mine: but explain to me, I pray, by your hypothesis, whence it
comes to pass, that man is wicked and so subject to pain and grief?
I defy you to find in your principles a reason of this phenomenon, as
I can in mine; and now I have regained the advantage I gave you; for
as you surpass me in the beauty of ideas, and in reasons *a priori*, so
I surpass you in the explication of phenomena, and in reasons *a
posteriori*. And since the principal character of a good system is to
account for what experience teaches us, and that the bare incapacity
of explaining it, is a proof, that a hypothesis is not good, how beautiful
soever it appears, you must grant, that I have hit the mark, by admitting two principles, and that you have not hit it, by admitting
but one.

Here, without doubt, lies the stress of the whole matter: here Melissus has a great opportunity to show his parts. . . . Let us hear
Zoroaster continuing his discourse.

If man is the creature of one principle perfectly good, most holy
and omnipotent, can he be exposed to disease, to heat and cold, hunger and thirst, pain and grief? . . . can perfect holiness produce
a criminal creature? can perfect goodness produce an unhappy creature? would not omnipotence, joined with infinite goodness, furnish
his own work plentifully with good things, and secure it from everything that might be offensive or vexatious? if Melissus consults the
notions of order, he will answer, that man was not wicked when God
made him. He will say, that man was created by God in a happy state;
but he not following the light of his conscience, which was intended
by the author of his Being to conduct him in the way of virtue, became so wicked, and deserved, that God, who is perfectly just as well
as perfectly good, should make him feel the effects of his wrath. God
therefore is not the cause of moral evil, but he is the cause of physical
evil, i.e. of the punishment of moral evil; a punishment which is so
far from being inconsistent with a principle perfectly good, that it
flows necessarily from one of his attributes, I mean from his justice,
which is no less essential to him than his goodness. This answer which
is the best that Melissus could make, is good and sound at the bottom; but it may be opposed by reasons that have something more
specious, and dazzling: for Zoroaster would not fail to represent, that,
if man were the work of a principle infinitely good and holy, he ought
to have been created not only without any actual evil, but also without any inclination to evil, since that inclination is such a defect, as
could not have such a principle for its cause. It remains, therefore,

that we say, that man, coming out of the hands of his Creator, had only the power of determining himself to evil, and that having determined himself to it, he was the sole cause of the crime, which he committed, and of the moral evil, which has introduced itself into the world. But, I. We have no distinct idea, that can make us understand, that a Being, which does not exist by itself, can nevertheless act by itself. Zoroaster therefore will say, that the free will, which was given to man, is not able actually to determine itself, since it exists continually and totally by the act of God. II. He will put this question: did God foresee, that man would make an ill use of his free will? if you answer yes, he will say, that it seems not possible, that anything can foresee that, which depends wholly upon an indeterminate cause. But I will grant you, will he say, that God did foresee the sin of his creature, and from thence I conclude, that he would have hindered him from sinning; for the ideas of order will not suffer us to believe that a cause infinitely good and holy, which can hinder the introduction of moral evil should not hinder it especially since, by permitting it, God was obliged severely to punish his own work. If God did not foresee the fall of man, yet at least he must think it possible: since therefore he saw himself obliged, in case it should happen, to depart from his paternal goodness, and to make his children very miserable, by exercising upon them the office of a severe judge, he would have determined man to moral good, as he determined him to that which is physical; he would not have left in the soul of man any power, which should incline him to sin; any more than he has left any to incline him to misery as such. . . .

If he had recourse to retortion, he would very much perplex Zoroaster; but by once granting him his two principles, he would leave him an open way to come at the explication of the origin of evil. Zoroaster would go back to the time of the chaos, which is a state, as to his two principles, very like that which Hobbes calls the state of nature, and which he supposes to have preceded the first establishment of societies. In this state of nature one man was a wolf to another, and everything belonged to the first possessor: none was master of anything, except he was the strongest. To get out of this confusion, every one agreed to quit his right to the whole, that he might have a property in something; they transacted together, and the war ceased. The two principles, weary of the chaos, wherein each confounded and overthrew what the other would do, came at last to an agreement; each of them yielded something, each had a share in the production of man, and in the laws of the union of the soul. The good principle obtained those, which procure to man a thousand pleasures, and consented to those, which expose man to a thousand sorrows; and if it be consented, that moral good should be infinitely less in mankind than moral evil, he repaired the damage in some other kind of creatures, wherein vice should be much less than virtue. If many men in this life have more misery than happiness, this is recompensed in another state: what they have not under a human shape, they shall recover under another. By means of this agreement, the chaos was disembroiled, the chaos, I say, a passive principle, which was the field of battle between these two active principles. The poets have represented this disembroiling under the image of a quarrel ended. This is what Zoroaster might allege, boasting that he does not attribute to the good principle the production of a creature at his own pleasure, which was to be so wicked and miserable; but only after he had found by experience, that he could do no better, nor better oppose the horrible designs of the evil principle. To render his hypothesis the less offensive, he might have denied, that there was a long war between the two principles, and lay aside all those fights, and prisoners, which the Manichees speak of. The whole might be reduced to the certain knowledge of the two principles, that one could never obtain from the other but such and such conditions. And thus an eternal agreement might have been made upon this foot.

A thousand great difficulties might be objected to this Philosopher; but as he would find answers, and after all desire to be furnished with a better hypothesis, pretending to have solidly refuted that of Melissus, he would never be brought back into the way of truth. Human reason is too weak for this end: it is a principle of destruction, and not of edification; it is only fit to start doubts, and to turn itself all manner of ways, to perpetuate a dispute: and I think I am not mistaken, if I say, of natural revelation, that is, of the light of reason, what divines say of the Mosaical economy. They say, that it was only fit to discover to man his weakness, and the necessity of a redeemer, and of a law of mercy. It was a schoolmaster (those are their own words) to bring men to Jesus Christ. Let us say the same of reason; it can only discover to man his ignorance and weakness, and the necessity of another revelation, which is that of Scripture. There we find what is sufficient to refute unanswerably the hypothesis of two principles, and all the objections of Zoroaster. We find there the unity of God, and his infinite perfections; the fall of man and the consequences of it. Let anyone tell us with pompous show of arguments, that it was not possible, that moral evil should introduce itself into the world by the work of a principle infinitely good and holy; we shall answer, that this was nevertheless done, and consequently that it is very possible. There is nothing more foolish than to reason against matter of fact; this maxim, *Ab actu ad potentiam valet consequentia,* is as clear as this proposition, two and two make four. The Manichees were sensible of what I have just now observed, and therefore they rejected the Old Testament; but what they retained of the Scripture supplied the orthodox with sufficient arms against them. And so it was not very difficult to confound those Heretics, who otherwise childishly entangled themselves when they came to particulars. Now since the Scripture affords us the best solutions, I cannot be blamed for saying, that it would be difficult to gain the victory over a Heathen Philosopher in this cause. . . .

It was a happy thing, that St. Augustine, who understood so well the art of controversy, abandoned the Manichean heresy; for he would have removed its grossest errors, and framed such a system, as, by his management, would have puzzled the Orthodox. . . .

41

ARTHUR SCHOPENHAUER

The Philosophy of Pessimism *

THE PESSIMISM of Schopenhauer, much as we may disagree with it, is vigorously argued for and solidly embodied in the metaphysical system which he constructs in *The World as Will and Idea.* Hence an understanding of his pessimism requires some comprehension of his metaphysical system. After a brief introductory statement of the nature of the World as Idea, Schopenhauer proceeds to argue for his conception of the World as Will, basing

° From *The World as Will and Idea*, translated by J. B. Haldane and J. Kemp (Kegan, Paul, Trench, Trübner, 1891), pp. 3-5, 128-30, 136, 144-45, 169-71, 174-75, 191-94, 253-57, 354-56, 361-62, 404-5, 411-41, 415-17, 489-94, 506.

Arthur Schopenhauer (1788-1860) was born at Danzig, Germany. Early in life he rebelled against a business career that had been forced upon him by his father. On his father's death he prevailed upon his mother to allow him to study philosophy and the classics. He studied at the universities of Göttingen and Berlin and, in 1818, published his celebrated *The World as Will and Idea*, thus virtually completing his philosophical system at the age of thirty. He travelled extensively, lived in comparative ease and luxury, and devoted his life to study and writing.

his hypothesis upon an analogy with the will of man and the objectification of that will. The World as Will leads to the heart of his pessimism and his picture of the world as one of ceaseless want, striving, pain, suffering, and ennui. Esthetic activity and contemplation provide but transient freedom for man from the cares of the world, and it is primarily the ascetic life—the life of the saint, with its denial of the will to live—that offers the only true wav of salvation for man.

THE WORLD AS IDEA

FIRST ASPECT

1. "THE WORLD IS MY IDEA"—this is a truth which holds good for everything that lives and knows, though man alone can bring it into reflective and abstract consciousness. If he really does this, he has attained to philosophical wisdom. It then becomes clear and certain to him that what he knows is not a sun and an earth, but only an eye that sees a sun, a hand that feels an earth; that the world which surrounds him is there only as idea, i.e., only in relation to something else, the consciousness, which is himself. If any truth can be asserted *a priori*, it is this: for it is the expression of the most general form of all possible and thinkable experience: a form which is more general than time, or space, or causality, for they all presuppose it; and each of these, which we have seen to be just so many modes of the principle of sufficient reason, is valid only for a particular class of ideas: whereas the antithesis of object and subject is the common form of all these classes, is that form under which alone any idea of whatever kind it may be, abstract or intuitive, pure or empirical, is possible and thinkable. No truth therefore is more certain, more independent of all others, and less in need of proof than this, that all that exists for knowledge, and therefore this whole world, is only object in relation to subject, perception of a perceiver, in a word, idea. This is obviously true of the past and the future, as well of the present, of what is farthest off, as of what is near; for it is true of time and space themselves, in which alone these distinctions arise. All that in any way belongs or can belong to the world is inevitably thus conditioned through the subject, and exists only for the subject. The world is idea. . . .

. . . . . .

. . . The inward reluctance with which any one accepts the world as merely his idea, warns him that this view of it, however true it may be, is nevertheless one-sided, adopted in consequence of some

arbitrary abstraction. And yet it is a conception from which he can
never free himself. The defectiveness of this view will be corrected in
the next book by means of a truth which is not so immediately certain
as that from which we start here. . . .   This truth, which must be
very serious and impressive if not awful to every one, is that a man
can also say and must say, "the world is my will."

THE WORLD AS WILL

FIRST ASPECT

.   .   .   .   .

18. In fact, the meaning for which we seek of that world which is
present to us only as our idea, or the transition from the world as
mere idea of the knowing subject to whatever it may be besides this,
would never be found if the investigator himself were nothing more
than the pure knowing subject (a winged cherub without a body).
But he is himself rooted in that world; he finds himself in it as an
individual, that is to say, his knowledge, which is the necessary sup-
porter of the whole world as idea, is yet always given through the
medium of a body, whose affections are, as we have shown, the starting-point for the understanding in the perception of that world. His
body is, for the pure knowing subject, an idea like every other idea,
an object among objects. Its movements and actions are so far known
to him in precisely the same way as the changes of all other perceived
objects, and would be just as strange and incomprehensible to him
if their meaning were not explained for him in an entirely different
way. Otherwise he would see his actions follow upon given motives
with the constancy of a law of nature, just as the changes of other objects follow upon causes, stimuli, or motives. But he would not understand the influence of the motives any more than the connection
between every other effect which he sees and its cause. He would
then call the inner nature of these manifestations and actions of his
body which he did not understand a force, a quality, or a character,
as he pleased, but he would have no further insight into it. But all
this is not the case; indeed the answer to the riddle is given to the
subject of knowledge who appears as an individual, and the answer
is *will.* This and this alone gives him the key to his own existence, reveals to him the significance, shows him the inner mechanisms of his
being, of his action, of his movements. The body is given in two entirely different ways to the subject of knowledge, who becomes an
individual only through his identity with it. It is given as an idea

in intelligent perception, as an object among objects and subject to the laws of objects. And it is also given in quite a different way as that which is immediately known to everyone, and is signified by the word *will*. Every true act of his will is also at once and without exception a movement of his body. The act of will and the movement of the body are not two different things objectively known, which the bond of causality unites; they do not stand in the relation of cause and effect; they are one and the same, but they are given in entirely different ways—immediately, and again in perception for the understanding. The action of the body is nothing but the act of the will objectified, i.e., passed into perception. . . .

The double knowledge which each of us has of the nature and activity of his own body, and which is given in two completely different ways, has now been clearly brought out. We shall accordingly make further use of it as a key to the nature of every phenomenon in nature, and shall judge of all objects which are not our own bodies, and are consequently not given to our consciousness in a double way but only as ideas, according to the analogy of our own bodies, and shall therefore assume that as in one aspect they are idea, just like our bodies, and in this respect are analogous to them, so in another aspect, what remains of objects when we set aside their existence as idea of the subject must in its inner nature be the same as that in us which we call *will*. For what other kind of existence or reality should we attribute to the rest of the material world. Whence should we take the elements out of which we construct such a world? Besides will and idea nothing is known to us or thinkable. If we wish to attribute the greatest known reality to the material world which exists immediately only in our idea, we give it the reality which our own body has for each of us; for that is the most real thing for every one. But if we now analyze the reality of this body and its actions, beyond the fact that it is idea, we find nothing in it except the will; with this its reality is exhausted. Therefore we can nowhere find another kind of reality which we can attribute to the material world. Thus if we hold that the material world is something more than merely our idea, we must say that besides being idea, that is, in itself and according to its inmost nature, it is that which we find immediately in ourselves as *will*. I say according to its inmost nature, but we must first come to know more accurately this real nature of the will, in order that we may be able to distinguish from it what does not belong to itself, but to its manifestation, which has many grades.

.   .   .   .   .

22. . . . . That concept of will has hitherto commonly been subordinated to that of force, but I reverse the matter entirely, and desire that every force in nature should be thought as will. . . . If, therefore, we refer the concept of *force* to that of *will*, we have in fact referred the less known to what is infinitely better known; indeed, to the one thing that is really immediately and fully known to us, and have very greatly extended our knowledge.

.　　.　　.　　.　　.

26. The lowest grades of the objectification of will are to be found in those most universal forces of nature which partly appear in all matter without exception, as gravity and impenetrability, and partly have shared the given matter among them, so that certain of them reign in one species of matter and others in another species, constituting its specific difference, as rigidity, fluidity, elasticity, electricity, magnetism, chemical properties and qualities of every kind. They are in themselves immediate manifestations of will, just as much as human action. . . .

Thus every universal, original force of nature is nothing but a low grade of the objectification of will, and we call every such grade an eternal Idea in Plato's sense.

In the higher grades of the objectivity of will we see individuality occupy a prominent position, especially in the case of man, where it appears as the great difference of individual characters, i.e., as complete personality. . . . None of the brutes have this individuality in anything like so high a degree, though the highest species of them have a trace of it. . . . The farther down we go, the more completely is every trace of the individual character lost in the common character of the species. . . . Finally, in the inorganic kingdom of nature all individuality disappears. . . .

.　　.　　.　　.　　.

. . . everywhere in nature we see strife, conflict, and alternation of victory, and in it we shall come to recognize more distinctly that variance with itself which is essential to the will. Every grade of the objectification of will fights for the matter, the space, and the time of the others. . . . This universal conflict becomes most distinctly visible in the animal kingdom. For animals have the whole of the vegetable kingdom for their food, and even with the animal kingdom every beast is the prey and the food of another; that is, the matter in which its Idea expresses itself must yield itself to the expression of another Idea, for each animal can only maintain its existence by the constant destruction of some other. Thus the will to live everywhere preys upon itself, and in different forms is its own nourishment, till finally the human race, because it subdues all the others, regards nature as a manufactory for its use. Yet even the human race, . . . reveals in itself with most terrible distinctness this conflict, this variance with itself of the will. Meanwhile we can recognize this strife . . . in the lower grades of the objectification of will. Many insects lay their eggs on the skin, and even in the body of the larvae of other insects, whose slow destruction is the first work of the newly hatched brood. . . . But the bulldog ant of Australia affords us the most extraordinary example of this kind; for if it is cut in two, a battle begins between the head and the tail. The head seizes the tail with its teeth, and the tail defends itself bravely by stinging the head; the battle may last for half an hour, until they die or are dragged away by other ants. This contest takes place every time the experiment is tried. On the banks of the Missouri one sometimes sees a mighty oak the stem and branches of which are so encircled, fettered, and interlaced by a gigantic wild vine, that it withers as if choked. The same thing shows itself in the lowest grades; for example, when water and carbon are changed into vegetable sap, or vegetables or bread into blood by organic assimilation. . . . On a large scale it shows itself in the relation between the central body and the planet, for although the planet is in absolute dependence, yet it always resists, just like the chemical forces in the organism; hence arises the constant tension between centripetal and centrifugal force, which keeps the globe in motion, and is itself an example of that universal essential conflict of the manifestation of will which we are considering. For as every body must be regarded as the manifestation of a will, and as will necessarily expresses itself as a struggle, the original condition of every world that is formed into a globe cannot be rest, but motion, a striving forward in boundless space without rest and without end.

THE WORLD AS IDEA
SECOND ASPECT

. . . . .

38. . . . All *willing* arises from want, therefore from deficiency, and therefore from suffering. The satisfaction of a wish ends it; yet for one wish that is satisfied there remain at least ten which are denied. Further, the desire lasts long, the demands are infinite; the satisfaction is short and scantily measured out. But even the final

satisfaction is itself only apparent; every satisfied wish at once makes room for a new one; both are illusions; the one is known to be so, the other not yet. No attained object of desire can give lasting satisfaction, but merely a fleeting gratification; it is like the alms thrown to the beggar, that keeps him alive today that his misery may be prolonged till the morrow. Therefore, so long as our consciousness is filled by our will, so long as we are given up to the throng of desires with their constant hopes and fears, so long as we are the subject of willing, we can never have lasting happiness nor peace. It is essentially all the same whether we pursue or flee, fear injury or seek enjoyment; the care for the constant demands of the will, in whatever form it may be, continually occupies and sways the consciousness; but without peace no true well-being is possible. The subject of willing is thus constantly stretched on the revolving wheel of Ixion, pours water into the sieve of the Danaids, is the ever-longing Tantalus.

But when some external cause or inward disposition lifts us suddenly out of the endless stream of willing, delivers knowledge from the slavery of the will, the attention is no longer directed to the motives of willing, but comprehends things free from their relation to the will, and thus observes them without personal interest, without subjectivity, purely objectively, gives itself entirely up to them so far as they are ideas, but not in so far as they are motives. Then all at once the peace which we were always seeking, but which always fled from us on the former path of the desires, comes to us of its own accord, and it is well with us. It is the painless state which Epicurus prized as the highest good and as the state of the gods; for we are for the moment set free from the miserable striving of the will; we keep the Sabbath of the penal servitude of willing; the wheel of Ixion stands still.

Inward disposition, the predominance of knowing over willing, can produce this state under any circumstances. This is shown by those admirable Dutch artists who directed this purely objective perception to the most insignificant objects, and established a lasting monument of their objectivity and spiritual peace in their pictures of *still life*, which the aesthetic beholder does not look on without emotion; for they present to him the peaceful, still, frame of mind of the artist, free from will, which was needed to contemplate such insignificant things so objectively, to observe them so attentively, and to repeat this perception so intelligently; and as the picture enables the onlooker to participate in this state, his emotion is often increased by the contrast between it and the unquiet frame of mind, disturbed by vehement willing, in which he finds himself. . . .

All this is accomplished by the inner power of an artistic nature alone; but that purely objective disposition is facilitated and assisted from without by suitable objects, by the abundance of natural beauty which invites contemplation, and even presses itself upon us. Whenever it discloses itself suddenly to our view, it almost always succeeds in delivering us, though it may be only for a moment, from subjectivity, from the slavery of the will, and in raising us to the state of pure knowing. This is why the man who is tormented by passion, or want, or care, is so suddenly revived, cheered, and restored by a single free glance into nature: the storm of passion, the pressure of desire and fear, and all the miseries of willing are then at once, and in a marvellous manner, calmed and appeased. For at the moment at which, freed from the will, we give ourselves up to pure will-less knowing, we pass into a world from which everything is absent that influenced our will and moved us so violently through it. This freeing of knowledge lifts us as wholly and entirely away from all that, as do sleep and dreams; happiness and unhappiness have disappeared; we are no longer individual; the individual is forgotten; we are only pure subject of knowledge; we are only that *one* eye of the world which looks out from all knowing creatures, but which can become perfectly free from the service of will in man alone. Thus all difference of individuality so entirely disappears, that it is all the same whether the perceiving eye belongs to a mighty king or to a wretched beggar; for neither joy nor complaining can pass that boundary with us. So near us always lies a sphere in which we escape from all our misery; but who has the strength to continue long in it? As soon as any single relation to our will, to our person, even of these objects of our pure contemplation, comes again into consciousness, the magic is at an end; we fall back into the knowledge which is governed by the principle of sufficient reason; we know no longer the Idea, but the particular thing, the link of a chain to which we also belong, and we are again abandoned to all our woe. . . .

Lastly, it is this blessedness of will-less perception which casts an enchanting glamour over the past and distant, and presents them to us in so fair a light by means of self-deception. For as we think of days long gone by, days in which we lived in a distant place, it is only the objects which our fancy recalls, not the subject of will, which bore about with it then its incurable sorrows just as it bears them now; but they are forgotten, because since then they have often given place to others. Now, objective perception acts with regard to what is remembered just as it would in what is present, if we let it have influence over us, if we surrendered ourselves to it free from will. Hence it arises that, especialy when we are more than ordinarily disturbed by some want, the remembrance of past and distant scenes suddenly flits across our minds like a lost paradise. The fancy recalls only what was objective, not what was individually subjective, and we imagine that that objective stood before us then just as pure and undisturbed by any relation to the will as its image stands in our fancy now; while in reality the relation of the objects to our will gave us pain then just as it does now. We can deliver ourselves from all suffering just as well through present objects as through distant ones whenever we raise ourselves to a purely objective contemplation of them, and so are able to bring about the illusion that only the objects are present and not we ourselves. Then, as the pure subject of knowledge, freed from the miserable self, we become entirely one with these objects, and, for the moment, our wants are as foreign to us as they are to them. The world as idea alone remains, and the world as will has disappeared.

.   .   .   .   .

THE WORLD AS WILL

SECOND ASPECT

54. The will, which, considered purely in itself, is without knowledge, and is merely a blind incessant impulse, as we see it appear in unorganized and vegetable nature and their laws, and also in the vegetative part of our own life, receives through the addition of the world as idea, which is developed in subjection to it, the knowledge of its own willing and of what it is that it wills. And this is nothing else than the world as idea, life, precisely as it exists. Therefore we called the phenomenal world the mirror of the will, its objectivity. And since what the will wills is always life, just because life is nothing but the representation of that willing for the idea, it is all one and a mere pleonism if, instead of simply saying "the will," we say "the will to live."

Will is the thing-in-itself, the inner content, the essence of the world. Life, the visible world, the phenomenon, is only the mirror of the will. Therefore life accompanies the will as inseparably as the shadow accompanies the body; and if will exists, so will life, the world, exist. Life is, therefore, assured to the will to live; and so long as we are filled with the will to live we need have no fear for our existence, even in the presence of death. It is true we see the individual come into being and pass away; but the individual is only phenomenal. . . Birth and death belong merely to the phenomenon of will, thus to life; and it is essential to this to exhibit itself in individuals which come into being and pass away, as fleeting phenomena appearing in the form of time—phenomena of that which in itself knows no time, but must exhibit itself precisely in the way we have said, in order to objectify its peculiar nature. . . . For it is not the individual, but only the species that Nature cares for, and for the preservation of which she so earnestly strives, providing for it with the utmost prodigality through the vast surplus of the seed and the great strength of the fructifying impulse. . . . Thus Nature naively expresses the great truth that only the Ideas, not the individuals, have properly speaking, reality, i.e., are complete objectivity of the will. . . .

.   .   .   .   .

. . . The present is the form essential to the objectification of the will. It cuts time, which extends infinitely in both directions, as a mathematical point, and stands immovably fixed, like an everlasting mid-day with no cool evening, as the actual sun burns without intermission, while it only seems to sink into the bosom of night. Therefore, if a man fears death as his annihilation, it is just as if he were to think that the sun cries out at evening, "Woe is me! for I go down into eternal night." And conversely, whoever is oppressed with the burden of life, whoever desires life and affirms it, but abhors its torments, and especially can no longer endure the hard lot that has fallen to himself, such a man has no deliverance to hope for from death, and cannot right himself by suicide. . . .

.   .   .   .   .

57. . . . Now it is well worth observing that, on the one hand, the suffering and misery of life may easily increase to such an extent that death itself, in the flight from which the whole of life consists, becomes desirable, and we hasten towards it voluntarily; and again, on the other hand, that as soon as want and suffering permit rest to a man, ennui is at once so near that he necessarily requires diversion. The striving after existence is what occupies all living things and maintains them in motion. But when existence is assured, then they know not what to do with it; thus the second thing that sets them in motion is the effort to get free from the burden of existence, to make it cease to be felt, "to kill time," i.e.,

to escape from ennui. . . . As want is the constant scourge of
the people, so ennui is that of the fashionable world. In middle-class
life ennui is represented by the Sunday, and want by the six week-
days.

Thus between desiring and attaining all human life flows on
throughout. The wish is, in its nature, pain; the attainment soon
begets satiety: the end was only apparent; possession takes away
the charm; the wish, the need, presents itself under a new form;
when it does not, then follows desolateness, emptiness, ennui, against
which the conflict is just as painful as against want. That wish and
satisfaction should follow each other neither too quickly nor too
slowly reduces the suffering, which both occasion to the smallest
amount, and constitutes the happiest life. . . .

58. All satisfaction, or what is commonly called happiness, is always really and essentially only *negative,* and never positive. It is
not an original gratification coming to us of itself, but must always
be the satisfaction of a wish. The wish, i.e., some want, is the condition which precedes every pleasure. But with the satisfaction the
wish and therefore the pleasure cease. Thus the satisfaction or the
pleasing can never be more than the deliverance from a pain, from
a want; for such is not only every actual, open sorrow, but every
desire, the importunity of which disturbs our peace, and, indeed, the
deadening ennui also that makes life a burden to us. It is, however,
so hard to attain or achieve anything; difficulties and troubles without end are opposed to every purpose, and at every step hindrances
accumulate. But when finally everything is overcome and attained,
nothing can ever be gained but deliverance from some sorrow or
desire, so that we find ourselves just in the same position as we
occupied before this sorrow or desire appeared. All that is even directly given us is merely the want, i.e., the pain. The satisfaction
and the pleasure we can only know indirectly through the remembrance of the preceding suffering and want, which ceases with its
appearance.

. . . It is really incredible how meaningless and void of significance when looked at from without, how dull and unenlightened
by intellect when felt from within, is the course of the life of the
great majority of men. It is a weary longing and complaining, a dream-
like staggering through the four ages of life to death, accompanied
by a series of trivial thoughts. Such men are like clockwork, which
is wound up, and goes it knows not why; and every time a man
is begotten and born, the clock of human life is wound up anew, to
repeat the same old piece it has played innumerable times before,

passage after passage, measure after measure, with insignificant variations. . . .

. . . . . .

68. . . . If that veil of Mâyâ, the principle of individuation, is
lifted from the eyes of a man to such an extent that he no longer
makes the egotistical distinction between his person and that of others,
but takes as much interest in the sufferings of other individuals as
in his own, and therefore is not only benevolent in the highest degree,
but even ready to sacrifice his own individuality whenever such a
sacrifice will save a number of other persons, then it clearly follows
that such a man, who recognizes in all beings his own inmost and
true self, must also regard the infinite suffering of all suffering beings
as his own, and take on himself the pain of the whole world.

If we compare life to a course or path through which we must
unceasingly run—a path of red-hot coals, with a few cool places here
and there; then he who is entangled in delusion is consoled by the
cool places, on which he now stands, or which he sees near him, and
sets out to run through the course. But he who sees through the
principle of individuation, and recognizes the real nature of the
thing-in-itself, and thus the whole, is no longer susceptible of such
consolation; he sees himself in all places at once, and withdraws. His
will turns round, no longer asserts its own nature, which he reflected
in the phenomenon, but denies it. The phenomenon by which this
change is marked, is the transition from virtue to asceticism. That
is to say, it no longer suffices for such a man to love others as himself, and to do as much for them as for himself; but there arises
within him a horror of the nature of which his own phenomenal
existence is an expression, the will to live, the kernel and inner nature
of that world which is recognized as full of misery. He therefore dis-
owns this nature which appears in him, and is already expressed
through his body, and his action gives the lie to his phenomenal
existence, and appears in open contradiction to it. Essentially nothing
else but a manifestation of will, he ceases to will anything, guards
against attaching his will to anything, and seeks to confirm in himself the greatest indifference to everything. His body, healthy and
strong, expresses through the genitals, the sexual impulse; but he
denies the will and gives the lie to the body; he desires no sensual
gratification under any condition. Voluntary and complete chastity
is the first step in asceticism or the denial of the will to live. It thereby
denies the assertion of the will which extends beyond the individual
life, and gives the assurance that with the life of this body, the will,

whose manifestation it is, ceases. Nature, always true and naïve, declares that if this maxim became universal, the human race would die out; and I think I may assume, in accordance with what was said . . . about the connection of all manifestations of will, that with its highest manifestation, the weaker reflection of it would also pass away, as the twilight vanishes along with the full light. With the entire abolition of knowledge, the rest of the world would of itself vanish into nothing; for without a subject there is no object.

Asceticism then shows itself further in voluntary and intentional poverty, which not only arises *per accidens,* because the possessions are given away to mitigate the sufferings of others, but is here an end in itself, is meant to serve as a constant mortification of will, so that the satisfaction of the wishes, the sweet of life, shall not again arouse the will, against which self-knowledge has conceived a horror. He who has attained to this point, still always feels, as a living body, as concrete manifestation of will, the natural disposition for every kind of volition; but he intentionally suppresses it, for he compels himself to refrain from doing all that he would like to do, and to do all that he would like not to do, even if this has no further end than that of serving as a mortification of will. Since he himself denies the will which appears in his own person, he will not resist if another does the same, i.e., inflicts wrongs upon him. Therefore every suffering coming to him from without through chance or the wickedness of others, is welcome to him, every injury, ignominy, and insult; he receives them gladly as the opportunity of learning with certainty that he no longer asserts the will, but gladly sides with every enemy of the manifestation of will which is his own person. Therefore he bears such ignominy and suffering with inexhaustible patience and meekness, returns good for evil without ostentation, and allows the fire of anger to rise within him just as little as that of the desires. And he mortifies not only the will itself, but also its visible form, its objectivity, the body. He nourishes it sparingly, lest its excessive vigour and prosperity should animate and excite more strongly the will, of which it is merely the expression and the mirror. So he practises fasting, and even resorts to chastisement and self-inflicted torture, in order that, by constant privation and suffering, he may more and more break down and destroy the will, which he recognizes and abhors as the source of his own suffering existence and that of the world. If at last death comes, which puts an end to this manifestation of that will, whose existence here has long since perished through free denial of itself, with the exception of the weak residue of it which appears as the life of this body; it is most welcome, and is gladly received as a longed-for deliverance. Here it is not, as in the case of others, merely the manifestation which ends with death; but the inner nature itself is abolished, which here existed only in the manifestation, and that in a very weak degree; this last slight bond is now broken. For him who thus ends the world has ended also.

And what I have here described with feeble tongue and only in general terms, is no philosophical fable, invented by myself, and only of to-day; no, it was the enviable life of so many saints and beautiful souls among Christians, and still more among Hindus and Buddhists, and also among the believers of other religions. However different were the dogmas impressed on their reason, the same inward, direct, intuitive knowledge, from which alone all virtue and holiness proceed, expressed itself in precisely the same way in the conduct of life.

. . . . .

42

GOTTFRIED WILHELM FREIHERR VON LEIBNIZ

The Best of All Possible Worlds *

THE OPTIMISM of Leibniz is developed briefly, precisely, and logically in the selections that follow. In the material from the *Monadology* Leibniz begins with an explanation of the meaning of the two basic principles of contradiction and sufficient reason. From these principles, in turn, he proceeds to the necessity of God's existence and to His absolutely infinite perfection. Then from God's

* From *The Philosophical Works of Leibniz,* translated by George Martin Duncan (New Haven: Tuttle, Morehouse and Taylor, 1890), pp. 194-97, 202-4, 223-26.

Gottfried Wilhelm Freiherr von Leibniz (1646-1716) was born and educated in Germany. He studied philosophy, law, and mathematics and became remarkably proficient in each field. He is noted as the co-inventor, with Newton, of the infinitesimal calculus. He carried on a very extensive correspondence, much of which, such as the letters to Arnauld and Samuel Clarke, serves to elucidate his philosophy. In the religious struggles of the times one of his greatest concerns was to effect a reconciliation between Protestantism and Catholicism. He was a very able administrator and a diplomat and after a brief service with the Elector of Mainz, he devoted the greater part of his life to the service of the Duke of Hanover.

omnipotence and omniscience as well as His infinite perfection follows Leibniz' further deduction of the celebrated theory that this is the best of all possible worlds. This theory is elaborated on in more detail in the argument from the *Theodicy* in which the author takes up in syllogistic order the possible objections to his theory: (1) that God's knowledge, power, and goodness are deficient because He did not choose the best when He created this world; (2) that there is more evil than good in the work of God; and (3) that God did not freely create this world.

THE MONADOLOGY

.   .   .   .   .

31. Our reasons are founded on *two great principles, that of contradiction,* in virtue of which we judge that to be *false* which involves contradiction, and that *true,* which is opposed or contradictory to the false.

32. And *that of sufficient reason,* in virtue of which we hold that no fact can be real or existent, no statement true, unless there be a sufficient reason why it is so and not otherwise, although most often these reasons cannot be known to us.

33. There are also two kinds of truths, those of *reasoning* and those of *fact.* Truths of reasoning are necessary and their opposite is impossible, and those of fact are contingent and their opposite is possible. When a truth is necessary its reason can be found by analysis, resolving it into more simple ideas and truths until we reach those which are primitive.   .   .   .   .   .

36. But there must also be a *sufficient reason* for *contingent truths,* or those *of* fact,—that is, for the series of things diffused through the universe of created objects—where the resolution into particular reasons might run into a detail without limits, on account of the immense variety of objects and the division of bodies *ad infinitum.*

37. And as all this *detail* only involves other contingents, anterior or more detailed, each one of which needs a like analysis for its explanation, we make no advance: and the sufficient or final reason must be outside of the sequence or *series* of this detail of contingencies, however infinite it may be.

38. And thus it is that the final reason of things must be found in a necessary substance, in which the detail of changes exists only eminently, as in their source; and this it is which we call God.

39. Now this substance, being the sufficient reason of all this detail, which also is linked together throughout, *there is but one God, and this God suffices.*

40. We may judge also that this supreme substance, which is unique, universal and necessary, having nothing outside of itself which is independent of it, and being the simple series of possible being, must be incapable of limitations and must contain as much of reality as is possible.

41. Whence it follows that God is absolutely perfect, *perfection* being only the magnitude of positive reality taken in its strictest meaning, setting aside the limits or bounds in that which is limited. And where there are no limits, that is, in God, perfection is absolutely infinite.

42. It follows also that the creatures have their perfections from the influence of God, but that their imperfections arise from their own nature incapable of existing without limits. For it is by this that they are distinguished from God.

.   .   .   .   .

48. In God is *Power*, which is the source of all; then *Knowledge,* which contains the detail of ideas; and finally *Will*, which effects changes or products according to the principle of the best. . . .

.   .   .   .   .

53. Now, as there is an infinity of possible universes in the ideas of God, and as only one of them can exist, there must be a sufficient reason for the choice of God, which determines him for one rather than for another.

54. And this reason can only be found in the *fitness,* or in the degrees of perfection, which these worlds contain, each possible world having a right to claim existence according to the measure of perfection which it possesses.

55. And this is the cause of the existence of the Best; which wisdom makes known to God, which his goodness chooses, and which his power makes him produce.

THE THEODICY

ABRIDGEMENT OF THE ARGUMENT REDUCED TO SYLLOGISTIC FORM

Some intelligent persons have desired that this supplement should be made (to the Theodicy), and I have the more readily yielded to their wishes as in this way I have an opportunity again to remove certain difficulties and to make some observations which were not sufficiently emphasized in the work itself.

I. *Objection.* Whoever does not choose the best is lacking in power, or in knowledge, or in goodness.

God did not choose the best in creating this world.

Therefore, God has been lacking in power, or in knowledge, or in goodness.

Answer. I deny the minor, that is, the second premise of this syllogism; and our opponent proves it by this

Prosyllogism. Whoever makes things in which there is evil, which could have been made without any evil, or the making of which could have been omitted, does not choose the best.

God has made a world in which there is evil; a world, I say, which could have been made without any evil, or the making of which could have been omitted altogether.

Therefore, God has not chosen the best.

Answer. I grant the minor of this prosyllogism; for it must be confessed that there is evil in this world which God has made, and that it was possible to make a world without evil, or even not to create a world at all, for its creation has depended on the free will of God; but I deny the major, that is, the first of the two premises of the prosyllogism, and I might content myself with simply demanding its proof; but in order to make the matter clearer, I have wished to justify this denial by showing that the best plan is not always that which seeks to avoid evil, since it may happen that *the evil is accompanied by a greater good.* For example, a general of an army will prefer a great victory with a slight wound to a condition without wound and without victory. We have proved this more fully in the large work by making it clear, by instances taken from mathematics and elsewhere, that an imperfection in the part may be required for a greater perfection in the whole. In this I have followed the opinion of St. Augustine, who has said a hundred times, that God has permitted evil in order to bring about good, that is, a greater good; and that of Thomas Aquinas (in libr. II. sent. dist. 32, qu. I. art. 1), that the permitting of evil tends to the good of the universe. I have shown that the ancients called Adam's fall *felix culpa,* a happy sin, because it had been retrieved with immense advantage by the incarnation of the Son of God, who has given to the universe something nobler than anything that ever would have been among creatures except for this. And in order to effect a clearer understanding, I have added, following many good authors, that it was in accordance with order and the general good that God gave to certain creatures the opportunity of exercising their liberty, even when he foresaw that they would turn to evil, but which he could so well rectify; because it was not right that, in order to hinder sin, God should always act in an extraordinary manner.

To overthrow this objection, therefore, it is sufficient to show that a world with evil might be better than a world without evil; but I have gone even farther, in the work and have even proved that this universe must be in reality better than every other possible universe.

II. *Objection.* If there is more evil than good in intelligent creatures, then there is more evil than good in the whole work of God.

Now, there is more evil than good in intelligent creatures.

Therefore, there is more evil than good in the whole work of God.

Answer. I deny the major and the minor of this conditional syllogism. As to the major, I do not admit it at all, because this pretended deduction from a part to the whole, from intelligent creatures to all creatures, supposes tacitly and without proof that creatures destitute of reason cannot enter into comparison nor into account with those which possess it. But why may it not be that the surplus of good in the non-intelligent creatures which fill the world, compensates for, and even incomparably surpasses, the surplus of evil in the rational creatures? It is true that the value of the latter is greater; but, in compensation, the others are beyond comparison the more numerous, and it may be that the proportion of number and quantity surpasses that of value and of quality.

As to the minor, that is no more to be admitted; that is, it is not at all to be admitted; that there is more evil than good in the intelligent creatures. There is no need even of granting that there is more evil than good in the human race, because it is possible, and in fact very probable, that the glory and the perfection of the blessed are incomparably greater than the misery and the imperfection of the damned, and that here the excellence of the total good in the smaller number exceeds the total evil in the greater number. The blessed approach the Divinity, by means of a Divine Mediator, as near as may suit these creatures, and make such progress in good as is impossible for the damned to make in evil, approach as nearly as they may to the nature of demons. God is infinite, and the devil is limited; good may and does advance to infinity, while evil has its bounds. It is therefore possible, and is credible, that in the comparison of the blessed and the damned, the contrary of that which I have said might happen in the comparison of intelligent and non-intelligent creatures, takes place; namely, it is possible that in the comparison of the happy and the unhappy, the proportion of degree exceeds that of number, and that in the comparison of intelligent and non-intelligent creatures, the proportion of number is greater than that of value. I have the right to suppose that a thing is possible so long as its impossibility is not proved; and indeed that which I have here advanced is more than a supposition.

But in the second place, if I should admit that there is more evil than good in the human race, I have still good grounds for not admitting that there is more evil than good in all intelligent creatures. For there is an inconceivable number of genii, and perhaps of other rational creatures. And an opponent could not prove that in all the City of God, composed as well of genii as of rational animals without number and of an infinity of kinds, evil exceeds good. And although in order to answer an objection, there is no need of proving that a thing is, when its mere possibility suffices; yet, in this work, I have not omitted to show that it is a consequence of the supreme perfection of the Sovereign of the universe, that the kingdom of God be the most perfect of all possible states or governments, and that consequently the little evil there is, is required for the consummation of the immense good which is found there.

. . . . .

VIII. *Objection.* He who cannot fail to choose the best, is not free. God cannot fail to choose the best.
Hence, God is not free.
Answer. I deny the major of this argument; it is rather true liberty, and the most perfect, to be able to use one's free will for the best, and to always exercise this power, without ever being turned from it either by external force or by internal passions, the first of which causes slavery of the body, the second, slavery of the soul. There is nothing less servile than to be always led toward the good, and always by one's own inclination, without any constraint and without any displeasure. And to object therefore that God had need of external things, is only a sophism. He created them freely; but having proposed to himself an end, which is to exercise his goodness, wisdom determined him to choose the means best fitted to attain this end. To call this a *need,* is to take that term in an unusual sense which frees it from all imperfection, just as when we speak of the wrath of God.

Seneca has somewhere said that God commanded but once but that he obeys always, because he obeys laws which he willed to prescribe to himself: *semel jussit, semper paret.* But he had better have said that God always commands and that he is always obeyed; for in willing, he always follows the inclination of his own nature, and all other things always follow his will. And as this will is always the same, it cannot be said that he obeys only that will which he formerly had. Nevertheless, although his will is always infallible and always tends towards the best, the evil, or the lesser good, which he rejects, does not cease to be possible in itself; otherwise the necessity of the good would be geometrical (so to speak), or meta-physical, and altogether absolute; the contingency of things would be destroyed, and there would be no choice. But this sort of necessity, which does not destroy the possibility of the contrary, has this name only by analogy; it becomes effective, not by the pure essence of things, but by that which is outside of them, above them, namely, by the will of God. This necessity is called moral, because, to the sage, *necessity* and *what ought to be* are equivalent things; and when it always has its effect, as it really has in the perfect sage, that is, in God, it may be said that it is a happy necessity. The nearer creatures approach to it, the nearer they approach to perfect hap-piness. Also this kind of necessity is not that which we try to avoid and which destroys morality, rewards and praise. For that which it brings, does not happen whatever we may do or will, but because we will it well. And a will to which it is natural to choose well, merits p aise so much the more; also it carries its reward with it, which is sovereign happiness. And as this constitution of the divine nature gives entire satisfaction to him who possesses it, it is also the best and the most desirable for the creatures who are all dependent on God. If the will of God did not have for a rule the principle of the best, it would either tend toward evil, which would be the worst; or it would be in some way indifferent to good and to evil, and would be guided by chance: but a will which would allow itself always to act by chance, would not be worth more for the government of the universe than the fortuitous concourse of atoms, without there being any divinity therein. And even if God should abandon himself to chance only in some cases and in a certain way (as he would do, if he did not always work entirely for the best and if he were capable of preferring a lesser good to a greater, that is, an evil to a good, since that which prevents a greater good is an evil), he would be imperfect, as well as the object of his choice; he would not merit entire confidence; he would act without reason in such a case, and government of the universe would be like certain games, equally divided between reason and chance. All this proves that this objection which is made against the choice of the best, perverts the notions of the free and of the necessary, and represents to us even the best as evil: to do which is either malicious or ridiculous.

43

ST. AUGUSTINE

Evil as Privation of the Good *

THE ENCHIRIDION, or, as St. Augustine refers to it, *Faith, Hope and Charity*, was written by him in 421 A.D. in response to the request of a certain Lawrence for a handbook and commentary on Christian doctrine. The selected material that follows is taken from a few of the chapters on evil and presents a brief and simple analysis of the problem of evil in which St. Augustine effectively emphasises his principal contention that evil is a privation of the good, a deficiency of being. His more detailed and comprehensive solution to the problem is contained in the selection from the *City of God*, which follows.

. . . IT IS ENOUGH for the Christian to believe that the only cause of all created things, whether heavenly or earthly, whether visible or invisible, is the goodness of the Creator, the one true God and that nothing exists but Himself that does not derive its existence from Him; and that He is the Trinity—to wit, the Father, and the Son begotten of the Father, and the Holy Spirit proceeding from the same Father, but one and the same Spirit of Father and Son.

By the Trinity, thus supremely and equally and unchangeably good, all things were created; and these are not supremely and equally and unchangeably good, but yet they are good, even taken separately. Taken as a whole, however, they are very good, bcause their *ensemble* constitutes the universe in all its wonderful order and beauty.

And in the universe, even that which is called evil, when it is regulated and put in its own place, only enhances our admiration of the good; for we enjoy and value the good more when we compare it with the evil. For the Almighty God, who, as even the heathen acknowledge, has supreme power over all things, being Himself supremely good, would never permit the existence of anything evil among His works, if He were not so omnipotent and good that He

* From the *Enchiridion* in *A Select Library of the Nicene and Post-Nicene Fathers of the Christian Church*, edited by Philip Schaff, translated by J. F. Shaw (Buffalo: The Christian Literature Co., 1887), III, 240-42.

For a brief biographical sketch of St. Augustine, see selection 28 on page 255.

can bring good even out of evil. For what is that which we call evil but the absence of good? In the bodies of animals, disease and wounds mean nothing but the absence of health; for when a cure is effected, that does not mean that the evils which were present—namely, the diseases and wounds—go away from the body and dwell elsewhere: they altogether cease to exist; for the wound or disease is not a substance, but a defect in the fleshly substance—the flesh itself being a substance, and therefore something good, of which those evils—that is, privations of the good which we call health—are accidents. Just in the same way, what are called vices in the soul are nothing but privations of natural good. And when they are cured, they are not transferred elsewhere: when they cease to exist in the healthy soul, they cannot exist anywhere else.

All things that exist, therefore, seeing that the Creator of them all is supremely good, are themselves good. But because they are not, like their Creator, supremely and unchangeably good, their good may be diminished and increased. But for good to be diminished is an evil, although, however much it may be diminished, it is necessary, if the being is to continue, that some good should remain to constitute the being. [For however small or of whatever kind the being may be, the good which makes it a being cannot be destroyed without destroying the being itself.] An uncorrupted nature is justly held in esteem. But if, still further, it be incorruptible, it is undoubtedly considered of still higher value. When it is corrupted, however, its corruption is an evil, because it is deprived of some sort of good. For if it be deprived of no good, it receives no injury; but it does receive injury, therefore it is deprived of good. Therefore so long as a being is in process of corruption, there is in it some good of which it is being deprived; and if a part of the being should remain which cannot be corrupted, this will certainly be an incorruptible being, and accordingly the process of corruption will result in the manifestation of this great good. But if it does not cease to be corrupted, neither can it cease to possess good of which corruption may deprive it. But if it should be thoroughly and completely consumed by corruption, there will then be no good left, because there will be no being. Wherefore corruption can consume the good only by consuming the being. Every being, therefore, is a good; a great good if it can not be corrupted; a little good, if it can; but in any case, only the foolish or ignorant will deny that it is a good. And if it be wholly consumed by corruption, then the corruption itself must cease to exist, as there is no being left in which it can dwell.

Accordingly, there is nothing of what we call evil, if there be nothing good. But a good which is wholly without evil is a perfect good. A good, on the other hand, which contains evil is a faulty or imperfect good; and there can be no evil where there is no good. From all this we arrive at the curious result: that since every being, so far as it is a being, is good, when we say that a faulty being is an evil being, we just seem to say that what is good is evil, and that nothing but what is good can be evil, seeing that every being is good, and that no evil can exist except in a being. Nothing, then, can be evil except something which is good. And although this, when stated, seems to be a contradiction, yet the strictness of reasoning leaves us no escape from the conclusion. We must, however, beware of incurring the prophetic condemnation: "Woe unto them that call evil good, and good evil: that put darkness for light, and light for darkness: that put bitter for sweet, and sweet for bitter." And yet our Lord says: "An evil man out of the evil treasure of his heart bringeth forth that which is evil." Now, what is an evil man but an evil being? for a man is a being. Now, if a man is a good thing because he is a being, what is an evil man but an evil good? Yet, when we accurately distinguish these two things, we find that it is not because he is a man that he is an evil, or because he is wicked that he is a good; but that he is a good because he is a man, and an evil because he is wicked. Whoever, then, says, "To be a man is an evil," or, "To be wicked is a good," falls under the prophetic denunciation: "Woe unto them that call evil good, and good evil!" For he condemns the work of God, which is the man, and praises the defect of man, which is the wickedness. Therefore every being, even if it be a defective one, in so far as it is a being is good, and in so far as it is defective is evil.

Accordingly, in the case of these contraries which we call good and evil, the rule of the logicians, that two contraries cannot be predicated at the same time of the same thing, does not hold. No weather is at the same time dark and bright: no food or drink is at the same time sweet and bitter: no body is at the same time and in the same place black and white: none is at the same time and in the same place deformed and beautiful. And this rule is found to hold in regard to many, indeed nearly all, contraries, that they cannot exist at the same time in any one thing. But although no one can doubt that good and evil are contraries, not only can they exist at the same time, but evil cannot exist without good, or in anything that is not good. Good, however, can exist without evil. For a man or an angel can exist without being wicked; but nothing can be wicked except a man or an angel: and so far as he is a man or an angel, he is good; so far as he is wicked, he is an evil. And these two contraries are so far co-existent, that if good did not exist in what is evil, neither could evil exist; because corruption could not have either a place to dwell in, or a source to spring from, if there were nothing that could be corrupted; and nothing can be corrupted except what is good, for corruption is nothing else but the destruction of good. From what is good, then, evils arose, and except in what is good they do not exist; nor was there any other source from which any evil nature could arise. For if there were, then, in so far as this was a being, it was certainly a good: and a being which was incorruptible would be a great good; and even one which was corruptible must be to some extent a good, for only by corrupting what was good in it could corruption do it harm.

. . . . .

Nor can we doubt that God does well even in the permission of what is evil. For He permits it only in the justice of His judgment. And surely all that is just is good. Although, therefore, evil, in so far as it is evil, is not a good; yet the fact that evil as well as good exists, is a good. For if it were not a good that evil should exist, its existence would not be permitted by the omnipotent God, who without doubt can as easily refuse to permit what He does not wish, as bring about what He does wish. And if we do not believe this, the very first sentence of our creed is endangered, wherein we profess to believe in God the Father Almighty. For He is not truly called Almighty if He cannot do whatsoever He pleases, or if the power of His almighty will is hindered by the will of any creature whatsoever.

44

ST. AUGUSTINE

The Goodness of God and the Evil of Man * '

PERHAPS THE BEST over-all account of St. Augustine's thinking on
the problem of evil is to be found in his justly famous work *The
City of God.* Here he develops in successive chapters his principal
contributions to the problems of both physical and moral evil. He
points out first, that God in His eternity foresaw and foreordained
the goodness of the universe as following from His own goodness.
He rejects vigorously the contention of heretics like the Manicheans
who believed it necessary to assume a principle of evil to account
for the evil in the universe, and he holds that what appears to be
evil to man has its proper place in the universe and, in relation to
the purposes of a good Creator, is in reality good. He takes exception to the pessimistic thesis of Origen that the world is essentially
evil and emphasizes that all beings in so far as they are, are good.
On the question of moral evil he develops in some detail his exege-
sis of the Biblical account of the fall of man, declaring that man's
act of disobedience and revolt from God originated in pride, in
the desire of man to be like God. Moral evil is the result of a
deficiency in the will of man and has its source in the nothingness
from which man was created. The creature of necessity is less
than the Creator. In conclusion, St. Augustine justifies God's
punishment of man.

OF GOD'S ETERNAL AND UNCHANGEABLE KNOWLEDGE AND WILL, WHEREBY ALL HE HAS MADE PLEASED HIM IN THE ETERNAL DESIGN AS WELL AS IN THE ACTUAL RESULT

FOR WHAT ELSE is to be understood by that invariable refrain, "And
God saw that it was good," than the approval of the work in its
design, which is the wisdom of God? For certainly God did not in the
actual achievement of the work first learn that it was good, but, on
the contrary, nothing would have been made had it not been first
known by Him. While, therefore, He sees that that is good which,
had He not seen it before it was made, would never have been made,
it is plain that He is not discovering, but teaching that it is good.

* From *The City of God,* translated by Marcus Dods (Modern Library, 1950),
pp. 363-67, 384, 456-64. Reprinted by permission of the publisher.
For a brief biographical sketch of St. Augustine, see selection 28 on page 255.

Plato, indeed, was bold enough to say that, when the universe was completed, God was, as it were, elated with joy. And Plato was not so foolish as to mean by this that God was rendered more blessed by the novelty of His creation; but he wished thus to indicate that the work now completed met with its Maker's approval, as it had while yet in design. It is not as if the knowledge of God were of various kinds, knowing in different ways things which as yet are not, things which are, and things which have been. For not in our fashion does He look forward to what is future, nor at what is present, nor back upon what is past; but in a manner quite different and far and profoundly remote from our way of thinking. For He does not pass from this to that by transition of thought, but beholds all things with absolute unchangeableness; so that of those thing which emerge in time, the future, indeed, are not yet, and the present are now, and the past no longer are; but all of these are by Him comprehended in His stable and eternal presence. . . . For as without any movement that time can measure, He Himself moves all temporal things, so He knows all times with a knowledge that time cannot measure. And therefore He saw that what He had made was good, when He saw that it was good to make it. And when He saw it made, He had not on that account a twofold nor any way increased knowledge of it; as if He had less knowledge before He made what He saw. For certainly He would not be the perfect worker He is, unless His knowledge were so perfect as to receive no addition from his finished works. . . . Neither is there any author more excellent than God, nor any skill more efficacious than the word of God, nor any cause better than that good might be created by the good God. This also Plato has assigned as the most sufficient reason for the creation of the world, that good works might be made by a good God; whether he read this passage, or perhaps, was informed of these things by those who had read them, or, by his quick-sighted genius, penetrated to things spiritual and invisible through the things that are created, or was instructed regarding them by those who had discerned them.

OF THOSE WHO DO NOT APPROVE OF CERTAIN THINGS WHICH ARE A PART OF THIS GOOD CREATION OF A GOOD CREATOR, AND WHO THINK THAT THERE IS SOME NATURAL EVIL

This cause, however, of a good creation, namely, the goodness of God—this cause, I say, so just and fit, which when piously and carefully weighed, terminates all the controversies of those who inquire into the origin of the world, has not been recognized by some heretics,* because there, are forsooth, many things, such as fire, frost, wild beasts, and so forth, which do not suit but injure this thin-blooded and frail mortality of our flesh, which is at present under just punishment. They do not consider how admirable these things are in their own places, how excellent in their own natures, how beautifully adjusted to the rest of creation, and how much grace they contribute to the universe by their own contributions as to a commonwealth; and how serviceable they are even to ourselves, if we use them with a knowledge of their fit adaptations—so that even poisons, which are destructive when used injudiciously, become wholesome and medicinal when used in conformity with their qualities and design; just as, on the other hand, those things which give us pleasure, such as food, drink, and the light of the sun, are found to be hurtful when immoderately or unseasonably used. And thus divine providence admonishes us not foolishly to vituperate things, but to investigate their utility with care; and, where our mental capacity or infirmity is at fault, to believe that there is a utility, though hidden, as we have experienced that there were other things which we all but failed to discover. For this concealment of the use of things is itself either an exercise of our humility or a levelling of our pride; for no nature at all is evil, and this is a name for nothing but the want of good. But from things earthly to things heavenly, from the visible to the invisible, there are some things better than others; and for this purpose are they unequal, in order that they might all exist. Now God is in such sort a great worker in great things, that He is not less in little things—for these little things are to be measured not by their own greatness (which does not exist), but by the wisdom of their Designer; as, in the visible appearance of a man, if one eyebrow be shaved off, how nearly nothing is taken from the body, but how much from the beauty!—for that is not constituted by bulk, but by the proportion and arrangement of the members. But we do not greatly wonder that persons, who suppose that some evil nature has been generated and propagated by a kind of opposing principle proper to it, refuse to admit that the cause of the creation was this, that the good God produced a good creation. For they believe that He was driven to this enterprise of creation by the urgent necessity of repulsing the evil that warred against Him, and that He mixed His good nature with the evil for the sake of restraining and conquering it; and that this nature of His, being thus shamefully polluted, and most cruelly oppressed and held captive, He labors to cleanse and deliver it, and with all His pains does not wholly succeed; but such part of it as could not

---

* The Manichaeans.

be cleansed from that defilement is to serve as a prison and chain of the conquered and incarcerated enemy. The Manicheans would not drivel, or rather, rave in such a style as this, if they believed the nature of God to be, as it is, unchangeable and absolutely incorruptible, and subject to no injury; and if, moreover, they held in Christian sobriety, that the soul which has shown itself capable of being altered for the worse by its own will, and of being corrupted by sin, and so, of being deprived of the light of eternal truth—that this soul, I say, is not a part of God, nor of the same nature as God, but is created by Him, and is far different from its Creator.

OF THE ERROR IN WHICH THE DOCTRINE OF ORIGEN IS INVOLVED

But it is much more surprising that some even of those who, with ourselves, believe that there is one only source of all things, and that no nature which is not divine can exist unless originated by that Creator, have yet refused to accept with a good and simple faith this so good and simple a reason of the world's creation, that a good God made it good; and that the things created, being different from God, were inferior to Him, and yet were good, being created by none other than He. But they say that souls, though not, indeed, parts of God, but created by Him, sinned by abandoning God; that, in proportion to their various sins, they merited different degrees of debasement from heaven to earth, and diverse bodies as prison-houses; and that this is the world, and this the cause of its creation, not the production of good things, but the restraining of evil. Origen is justly blamed for holding this opinion. For in the books which he entitles *Of origins*, this is his sentiment, this his utterance. And I cannot sufficiently express my astonishment, that a man so erudite and well versed in ecclesiastical literature, should not have observed, in the first place, how opposed this is to the meaning of this author-itative Scripture, which, in recounting all the works of God, regularly adds, "And God saw that it was good"; and, when all were completed, inserts the words, "And God saw everything that He had made, and, behold, it was very good." Was it not obviously meant to be under-stood that there was no other cause of the world's creation than that good creatures should be made by a good God? In this creation, had no one sinned, the world would have been filled and beautified with natures good without exception; and though there is sin, all things are not therefore full of sin, for the great majority of the heavenly inhabitants preserve their nature's integrity. And the sinful will, though it violated the order of its own nature, did not on that ac-count escape the laws of God, who justly orders all things for good.

For as the beauty of a picture is increased by well-managed shadows, so, to the eye that has skill to discern it, the universe is beautified even by sinners, though, considered by themselves, their deformity is a sad blemish. . . .

.   .   .   .   .

THAT IN ALL NATURE, OF EVERY KIND AND RANK, GOD IS GLORIFIED

All natures, then, inasmuch as they are, and have therefore a rank and species of their own, and a kind of internal harmony, are certainly good. And when they are in the places assigned to them by the order of their nature, they preserve such being as they have received. And those things which have not received everlasting being, are altered for better or for worse, so as to suit the wants and motions of those things to which the Creator's law has made them subservient; and thus they tend in the divine providence to that end which is embraced in the general scheme of the government of the universe. So that, though the corruption of transitory and perishable things brings them to utter destruction, it does not prevent their producing that which was designed to be their result. And this being so, God, who supremely is, and who therefore created every being which has not supreme existence (for that which was made of nothing could not be equal to Him, and indeed could not be at all had He not made it) is not to be found fault with on account of the creature's faults, but is to be praised in view of the natures He has made.

.   .   .   .   .

WHETHER IT IS TO BE BELIEVED THAT OUR FIRST PARENTS IN PARADISE, BEFORE THEY SINNED, WERE FREE FROM ALL PERTURBATION

But it is a fair question, whether our first parent or first parents (for there was a marriage of two), before they sinned, experienced in their animal body such emotions as we shall not experience in the spiritual body when sin has been purged and finally abolished. For if they did, then how were they blessed in that boasted place of bliss, Paradise? For who that is affected by fear or grief can be called absolutely blessed? And what could those persons fear or suffer in such affluence of blessings, where neither death nor ill-health was feared, and where nothing was wanting which a good will could desire, and nothing present which could interrupt man's mental or bodily enjoyment? Their love to God was unclouded, and their mutual affection was that of faithful and sincere marriage; and from this love flowed a wonderful delight, because they always enjoyed what was loved. Their avoidance of sin was tranquil; and, so long as it was maintained, no other ill at all could invade them and bring sorrow. Or did they perhaps desire to touch and eat the forbidden fruit, yet feared to die; and thus both fear and desire already, even in that blissful place, preyed upon those first of mankind? Away with the thought that such could be the case where there was no sin! And, indeed, this is already sin, to desire those things which the law of God forbids, and to abstain from them through fear of punishment, not through love of righteousness. Away, I say, with the thought, that before there was any sin, there should already have been committed regarding that fruit the very sin which our Lord warns us against regarding a woman: "Whosoever looketh on a woman to lust after her, hath committed adultery with her already in his heart." As happy, then, as were these our first parents who were agitated by no mental perturbations, and annoyed by no bodily discomforts, so happy should the whole human race have been had they not introduced that evil which they have transmitted to their posterity. . . .

OF THE FALL OF THE FIRST MAN, IN WHOM NATURE WAS CREATED GOOD, AND CAN BE RESTORED ONLY BY ITS AUTHOR

. . . Accordingly God, as it is written, made man upright, and consequently with a good will. For if he had not had a good will, he could not have been upright. The good will, then, is the work of God; for God created him with it. But the first evil will, which preceded all man's evil acts, was rather a kind of falling away from the work of God to its own works than any positive work. And therefore the acts resulting were evil, not having God, but the will itself for their end; so that the will or the man himself, so far as his will is bad, was as it were the evil tree bringing forth evil fruit. Moreover, the bad will, though it be not in harmony with, but opposed to nature, inasmuch as it is a vice or blemish, yet it is true of it as of all vice, that it cannot exist except in a nature, and only in a nature created out of nothing, and not in that which the Creator has begotten of Himself, as He begot the Word, by whom all things were made. For though God formed man of the dust of the earth, yet the earth itself, and every earthly material, is absolutely created out of nothing; and man's soul too, God created out of nothing, and joined to the body, when He made a man. But evils are so thoroughly overcome by good, that though they are permitted to exist, for the sake of demonstrating how the most righteous foresight of God can make a good use even of them, yet good can exist without evil, as in the true and supreme God Himself, and as in every invisible and visible celestial creature that exists above this murky atmosphere; but evil cannot exist without good, because the natures in which evil exists, in so far as they are natures, are good. And evil is removed, not by removing any nature, or part of a nature, which had been introduced by the evil, but by healing and correcting that which had been vitiated and depraved. The will, therefore, is then truly free, when it is not the slave of vices and sins. Such was it given us by God; and this being lost by its own fault, can only be restored by Him who was able at first to give it. And therefore the truth says, "If the Son shall make you free, ye shall be free indeed"; which is equivalent to saying, If the Son shall save you, ye shall be saved indeed. For He is our Liberator, inasmuch as He is our Saviour. . . .

OF THE NATURE OF MAN'S FIRST SIN

If any one finds a difficulty in understanding why other sins do not alter human nature as it was altered by the transgression of those first human beings . . . he ought not to think that that sin was a small and light one because it was committed about food, and that not bad nor noxious, except because it was forbidden; for in that spot of singular felicity God could not have created and planted any evil thing. But by the precept He gave, God commanded obedience, which is, in a sort, the mother and guardian of all the virtues in the reasonable creature, which was so created that submission is advantageous to it, while the fulfilment of its own will in preference to the Creator's is destruction. And as this commandment enjoining abstinence from one kind of food in the midst of great abundance of other kinds was so easy to keep—so light a burden to the memory— and, above all, found no resistance to its observance in lust, which only afterwards sprung up as the penal consequence of sin, the iniquity of violating it was all the greater in proportion to the ease with which it might have been kept.

THAT IN ADAM'S SIN AN EVIL WILL PRECEDED THE EVIL ACT

Our first parents fell into open disobedience because already they were secretly corrupted; for the evil act had never been done had not an evil will preceded it. And what is the origin of our evil will but pride? For "pride is the beginning of sin." And what is pride but

the craving for undue exaltation? And this is undue exaltation, when
the soul abandons Him to whom it ought to cleave as its end, and
becomes a kind of end to itself. This happens when it becomes
its own satisfaction. And it does so when it falls away from that
unchangeable good which ought to satisfy it more than itself. This
falling away is spontaneous; for if the will had remained stedfast
in the love of that higher and changeless good by which it was
illumined to intelligence and kindled into love, it would not have
turned away to find satisfaction in itself, and so become frigid and
benighted; the woman would not have believed the serpent spoke
the truth, nor would the man have preferred the request of his
wife to the command of God, nor have supposed that it was a venial
transgression to cleave to the partner of his life even in a partnership of sin. The wicked deed, then—that is to say, the transgression
of eating the forbidden fruit—was committed by persons who were
already wicked. That "evil fruit" could be brought forth only by a
"corrupt tree." But that the tree was evil was not the result of nature; for certainly it could become so only by the vice of the will,
and vice is contrary to nature. Now, nature could not have been
depraved by vice had it not been made out of nothing. Consequently,
that it is a nature, this is because it is made by God; but that it
falls away from Him, this is because it is made out of nothing. But
man did not so fall away as to become absolutely nothing; but being
turned towards himself, his being became more contracted than it
was when he clave to Him who supremely is. Accordingly, to exist
in himself, that is, to be his own satisfaction after abandoning God,
is not quite to become a nonentity, but to approximate to that. And
therefore the holy Scriptures designate the proud by another name,
"self-pleasers." For it is good to have the heart lifted up, yet not
to one's self, for this is proud, but to the Lord, for this is obedient,
and can be the act only of the humble. There is, therefore, something
in humility which, strangely enough, exalts the heart, and something
in pride which debases it. This seems, indeed, to be contradictory,
that loftiness should debase and lowliness exalt. But pious humility
enables us to submit to what is above us; and nothing is more exalted
and above us than God; and therefore humility, by making us subject
to God, exalts us. But pride, being a defect of nature, by the very
act of refusing subjection and revolting from Him who is supreme,
falls to a low condition; and then comes to pass what is written:
"Thou castedst them down when they lifted up themselves." . . .

The devil, then, would not have ensnared man in the open and
manifest sin of doing what God had forbidden, had man not already

begun to live for himself. It was this that made him listen with pleasure to the words, "Ye shall be as gods," which they would much more readily have accomplished by obediently adhering to their supreme and true end than by proudly living to themselves. For created gods are gods not by virtue of what is in themselves, but by a participation of the true God. By craving to be more, man becomes less; and by aspiring to be self-sufficing, he fell away from Him who truly suffices him. Accordingly, this wicked desire which prompts man to please himself . . . already secretly existed in him, and the open sin was but its consequence. For that is true which is written, "Pride goeth before destruction, and before honor is humility"; that is to say, secret ruin precedes open ruin, while the former is not counted ruin. . . .

OF THE PRIDE IN THE SIN, WHICH WAS WORSE THAN THE SIN ITSELF

But it is a worse and more damnable pride which casts about for the shelter of an excuse even in manifest sins, as these our first parents did, of whom the woman said, "The serpent beguiled me, and I did eat"; and the man said, "the woman whom Thou gavest to be with me, she gave me of the tree, and I did eat." Here there is no word of begging pardon, no word of entreaty for healing. For though they do not, like Cain, deny that they have perpetrated the deed, yet their pride seeks to refer its wickedness to another—the woman's pride to the serpent, the man's to the woman. But where there is a plain transgression of a divine commandment, this is rather to accuse than to excuse oneself. For the fact that the woman sinned on the serpent's persuasion, and the man at the woman's offer, did not make the transgression less, as if there were any one whom we ought rather to believe or yield to than God.

OF THE JUSTICE OF THE PUNISHMENT WITH WHICH OUR FIRST PARENTS WERE VISITED FOR THEIR DISOBEDIENCE

Therefore, because the sin was a despising of the authority of God . . . it was just that condemnation followed and condemnation such that man, who by keeping the commandments should have been spiritual even in his flesh, became fleshly even in his spirit; and as in his pride he had sought to be his own satisfaction, God in His justice abandoned him to himself, not to live in the absolute independence he affected, but instead of the liberty he desired, to live dissatisfied with himself in a hard and miserable bondage to him to whom by sinning he had yielded himself, doomed in spite of himself to die in body as he had willingly become dead in spirit, condemned even to eternal death (had not the grace of God delivered him) because he had forsaken eternal life. Whoever thinks such punishment either excessive or unjust shows his inability to measure the great iniquity of sinning where sin might so easily have been avoided. For as Abraham's obedience is with justice pronounced to be great, because the thing commanded, to kill his son, was very difficult, so in Paradise the disobedience was the greater, because the difficulty of that which was commanded was imperceptible. And as the obedience of the second Man was the more laudable because He became obedient even "unto death," so the disobedience of the first man was the more detestable because he became disobedient even unto death. For where the penalty annexed to disobedience is great, and the thing commanded by the Creator is easy, who can sufficiently estimate how great a wickedness it is, in a matter so easy, not to obey the authority of so great a power, even when that power deters with so terrible a penalty?

In short, to say all in a word, what but disobedience was the punishment of disobedience in that sin? For what else is man's misery but his own disobedience to himself, so that in consequence of his not being willing to do what he could do, he now wills to do what he cannot? For though he could not do all things in Paradise before he sinned, yet he wished to do only what he could do, and therefore he could do all things he wished. But now, as we recognize in his offspring, and as divine Scripture testifies, "Man is like to vanity." For who can count how many things he wishes which he cannot do, so long as he is disobedient to himself, that is, so long as his mind and his flesh do not obey his will? For in spite of himself his mind is both frequently disturbed, and his flesh suffers, and grows old, and dies; and in spite of ourselves we suffer whatever else we suffer, and which we would not suffer if our nature absolutely and in all its parts obeyed our will. But is it not the infirmities of the flesh which hamper it in its service? Yet what does it matter *how* its service is hampered, so long as the fact remains, that by the just retribution of the sovereign God whom we refused to be subject to and serve, our flesh, which was subjected to us, now torments us by insubordination, although our disobedience brought trouble on ourselves, not upon God? . . .

Part Five

ESCHATOLOGY

ALTHOUGH THE TERM "eschatology," which means "of last things"
(death, judgment, hell, heaven, resurrection, the millennium), is more
theological than philosophical, it is sufficiently broad to cover the
variety of selections which we have brought together in Part Five.
The purpose of this introduction is to explain the order of the selections that follow, so that the reader may choose those that will best
meet his needs.

Three of the selections might better be read together if they are
read at all, for taken singly, the selections, as well as the subject with
which they deal, lose some of their significance: I refer to the subject
of predestination and to the selections from Calvin, Aquinas, and
Molina which discuss it. It matters little whether these three selections
are the first or last studied, but they should probably be studied as a
unit.

The problem of man's freedom is of perennial interest. Today the
existentialists dominate the old debate between the supporters of
freedom and the determinists, and determinism seems to be a lost
cause bequeathed to the sociologists. Partly on this account, but more
because we are concerned in this book with the common ground of
philosophy and religion, we have considered it desirable to study
the whole problem of man's freedom upon a different level and within
a different context. We shall consider it on the theological level and
within the context of man's will, God's grace, and His predestination
of man. At the risk that any parallels tend to imply, it might even
be possible to discover in the various positions taken by the dis-
putants on predestination, positions similar to those held by the
determinists or the advocates of free will. Thus the views of Calvin
approach the extremes of determinism; of Pelagius, the extremes
of freedom; the position of Molina represents an attempt at compromise; and of Aquinas, either determinism or compromise, depending on one's interpretation of his views.

We have omitted any material on Pelagianism, partly because of the difficulty of obtaining adequate source selections, and partly because this position is brought out adequately in the comments of both Molina and Aquinas. Some students may question the omission of Augustine here. The reason for his exclusion lies primarily in the variety of interpretations given to his views—as evidenced by the way in which he is frequently quoted with approval by both Calvin and Aquinas.

In the first selection in Part Five, we find the position taken by Calvin a disturbing one. If, however, we grant his initial premises, namely, his interpretation of certain scriptural passages, together with his doctrine of faith and grace, then his conclusions follow logically and rigorously. His defense of those conclusions is eloquent testimony to Calvin's literary and theological accomplishments. His position is a simple one, namely, that the Bible shows that God has predestined all men from eternity either to salvation or damnation and that there is nothing any one can do about it, for all grace and salvation comes from God alone and not from our will, our merits, or our good works. This doctrine is called "double predestination" because of its division of mankind into the saved and the damned from all eternity. Once this premise is granted, and once the other premises are admitted, a very disturbing conclusion follows—so disturbing that as much of Calvin's brief is given over to the justification and defense of his conclusions as to the formulation of his arguments.

Aquinas does not accept a doctrine of double predestination, but, instead, declares that God wills that all men be saved—by which he means that God wishes all men saved, or that He would save them by His antecedent will. Man is free to choose his actions, but if he chooses a life of evil then he will be condemned and punished through God's consequent will. Salvation, Aquinas holds, comes only from God, for no man is sufficient unto himself. If, then, we depend upon God and His grace for our salvation we are faced with the problem of whether this does not negate the freedom of man. Does grace wholly determine man to salvation, or does man contribute anything, even his co-operation with divine grace? Aquinas' position is a difficult one; he insists that man is free and yet that man can do nothing to attain his salvation without the grace of God predestining him to that end. Can these propositions be reconciled by drawing a distinction between antecedent will and consequent will, by the doctrine of God's premotion, or by declaring that God determines us to be free?

Molina attempts to resolve the difficulties in the Thomistic position through his doctrine of the *scientia media* and the co-operation of man's will with the grace of God. He also insists that the grace of God alone provides for our salvation, but whether his compromise view that God foresees our merits, arranges the circumstances of our actions, and then bestows His grace upon us, takes anything away from the power of God and is contrary to Scripture is a matter of interpretation.

In any event the whole controversy is still very much of a mystery to us and we always admired the rather judicious decision of Pope Clement VIII who, after hearing arguments by Dominicans in favor of the Thomist position, and similar weighty arguments by the Jesuits in favor of the Molinist position, decided that both opinions might be permitted, but with the condition that Molinists should no longer refer to Thomists as Calvinists, nor Thomists to Molinists as heretics and Pelagians.

Whatever we may conclude or assume about the predestination of man, there remains the equally interesting question of the nature of man's future life. One possible answer to this problem is that held by the positivists and materialists that man is wholly mortal and that his destiny is simply to suffer the disintegration of his material existence, or, as Lucretius more aptly expressed it, the dispersal of his atoms. Even if we assume that man has a spiritual as well as a bodily nature, we may hold that the immortality of man is wholly impersonal and that his spiritual nature, although it survives the death of the body, loses its personal identity in its union with the spiritual nature of God.

The selections we have chosen here are based on the assumption that man has an immortal personal existence, and they attempt to describe the temporal and ethical characteristics of that existence. Plato presents his fundamentally religious convictions about the life of the soul in the hereafter in the form of myths that picture for us the judgment of the soul and its pre-existence as well as its existence after death. He also explains the doctrine of the transmigration of the soul; his notion that the soul uses the body and is a prisoner of the body was to have a considerable influence on Christian thought. However, his idea of a cyclical universe, with its implied negation of any hope of finality, was to be sharply rejected by Christianity.

Whereas there is a certain affinity (in some areas) between the Platonic view and the Christian, the Indian view of the life of the soul, as illustrated in the selection from Zimmer, deepens the contrast we have already noted between the Christian and the Platonic views.

The Indian conception of cosmic cycles, with their seemingly endless duration, staggers the imagination and throws into insignificance the most extravagant calculations of Western astronomers. The continuing drama of the emanation and reabsorption of the universe and the relentlessly recurring cycles of the four ages of the world, dwarf the place of man and his values in the scheme of things. The Christian view, with its conception of the creation of the universe from nothing and its ultimate dissolution, its dogma of the creation of the soul and the progress of the soul with the grace of God toward its ultimate salvation is completely different. Rather than the cycles of either the Platonic or the Indian myths, Christianity offers instead the appearance of God in history—the Incarnation as a central event from which all history is dated and takes on significance, and from which all the hopes of man for his salvation and happiness in the life to come are derived. There is no such finality and no real hope for man in the Platonic or Indian myths.

Next in order, we have placed the selections from Meister Eckhart and the Lankavatara Scripture. They are comparable in profundity and mystical quality. Eckhart presents us with a definitely mystical conception of the nature of the Beatific Vision and of the soul's existence in its union with God. Although the Lankavatara Scripture gives some positive description of Nirvana, it is more concerned to tell us what Nirvana is not; the positive description serves mostly to inform us what we must do to attain Nirvana. The basic distinction between the accounts of Eckhart and the Lankavatara Scripture is that the former shows us how we see all things in God and the meaning of our happiness in God; the latter is more concerned with what Otto has called a "soul-mysticism" than a God-mysticism—or perhaps we might say that by subtracting God from the Beatific Vision and leaving only wisdom, love, and happiness, one may achieve this elusive state that is called Nirvana. The elaboration of the basic ideas of a Christian philosophy of history will be found in the selection from Brunner, who is also concerned to contrast the Christian ideal with the notion of an evolutionary or rationalistic philosophy of history.

Instead of assuming or believing in the future existence of the soul, some writers have been more interested in establishing such an existence by rational argument. The next two selections, from Maritain and Kant, illustrate two distinct types of demonstration. Maritain presents the traditional Scholastic arguments based upon the nature of the soul and its incorruptibility—arguments that are duplicated by some modern philosophers (particularly Descartes and Leibniz) and, in general, in the rationalist tradition. The arguments of Kant are quite the opposite, for he had definitely concluded in his earlier philosophy that reason can prove neither the existence of God nor the existence of the soul and its immortality. Hence he endeavors to establish these propositions as postulates derived from practical reason. He attempts to justify religion and religious concepts on the basis of their need, and more particularly, their necessity to complete his ethical system.

The selection from Berdyaev stands somewhat apart from the arguments of Kant and Maritain. He takes issue with the whole question of philosophical immortality, and especially the Scholastic and Idealistic notions of it. He assails it as out of date, declaring that it leaves quite untouched the more significant notion of death. He finds death to be a more significant notion because it is more closely related to the basic dogmas of Christianity, especially the dogma of resurrection, and because it links more closely with world destiny the destiny of man.

PREDESTINATION

45

JOHN CALVIN

Double Predestination *

ELECTION IN CHRIST is the central doctrine in Calvin's theology. Calvin is convinced that man has become so thoroughly corrupted through original sin that he has lost all freedom and has become the slave of sin. Man's salvation, then, can be attained only by the irresistible grace of God through Jesus Christ. It is Calvin's concern to maintain God's freedom to elect whom He will, that leads to his doctrine of double predestination, namely, that God has from the beginning willed some individuals to salvation and some to damnation. He justifies double predestination on the basis of God's omnipotence, speaks of it as "God's awful decree," and mistakenly

---

* From *The Institutes of the Christian Religion* by John Calvin as translated by John Allen. Published by the Presbyterian Board of Education, 1936, pp. 170-241.

to the same place. In the revolution she beholds justice, and temper-

believes that it can be supported by Scripture. Needless to say
theologians have long since abandoned the extreme position held
by Calvin.°

ETERNAL ELECTION, OR GOD'S PREDESTINATION OF SOME TO
SALVATION, AND OF OTHERS TO DESTRUCTION

THE COVENANT of life not being equally preached to all, and among
those to whom it is preached not always finding the same reception,
this diversity discovers the wonderful depth of the Divine judgment.
Nor is it to be doubted that this variety also follows, subject to
the decision of God's eternal election. If it be evidently the result
of the Divine will, that salvation is freely offered to some, and
others are prevented from attaining it,—this immediately gives rise
to important and difficult questions, which are incapable of any other
explication, than by the establishment of pious minds in what ought
to be received concerning election and predestination—a question, in
the opinion of many, full of perplexity; for they consider nothing
more unreasonable, than that, of the common mass of mankind,
some should be predestinated to salvation, and others to destruction. . . . Besides, the very obscurity which excites such dread,
not only displays the utility of this doctrine, but shows it to be pro-
ductive of the most delightful benefit. We shall never be clearly
convinced as we ought to be, that our salvation flows from the
fountain of God's free mercy, till we are acquainted with his eternal
election, which illustrates the grace of God by this comparison, that
he adopts not all promiscuously to the hope of salvation, but gives
to some what he refuses to others. . . .

. . . . .

V. Predestination, by which God adopts some to the hope of life,
and adjudges others to eternal death, no one, desirous of the credit
of piety, dares absolutely to deny. But it is involved in many cavils,
especially by those who make foreknowledge the cause of it. We
maintain, that both belong to God; but it is preposterous to represent
one as dependent on the other. When we attribute foreknowledge
to God, we mean that all things have ever been, and perpetually
remain, before his eyes, so that to his knowledge nothing is future
or past, but all things are present; and present in such a manner,
that he does not merely conceive of them from ideas formed in his

° For a brief but excellent analysis of the problem of predestination, see
H. Emil Brunner, *The Christian Doctrine of God*, translated by Olive Wyon
(Philadelphia: The Westminster Press, 1940), pp. 321-39.

mind, as things remembered by us appear present to our minds, but really beholds and sees them as if actually placed before him. And this foreknowledge extends to the whole world, and to all the creatures. Predestination we call the eternal decree of God, by which he has determined in himself, what he would have to become of every individual of mankind. For they are not all created with a similar destiny; but eternal life is foreordained for some, and eternal damnation for others. Every man, therefore, being created for one or the other of these ends, we say, he is predestinated either to life or to death. . . .

. . . . .

VII. . . . In conformity, therefore, to the clear doctrine of the Scripture, we assert, that by an eternal and immutable counsel, God has once for all determined, both whom he would admit to salvation, and whom he would condemn to destruction. We affirm that this counsel, as far as concerns the elect, is founded on his gratuitous mercy, totally irrespective of human merit; but that to those whom he devotes to condemnation, the gate of life is closed by a just and irreprehensible, but incomprehensible, judgment. In the elect, we consider calling as an evidence of election, and justification as another token of its manifestation, till they arrive in glory, which constitutes its completion. As God seals his elect by vocation and justification, so by excluding the reprobate from the knowledge of his name and the sanctification of his Spirit, he affords an indication of the judgment that awaits them. . . .

TESTIMONIES OF SCRIPTURE IN CONFIRMATION OF THIS DOCTRINE

All the positions we have advanced are controverted by many, especially the gratuitous election of believers, which nevertheless cannot be shaken. It is a notion commonly entertained, that God, foreseeing what would be the respective merits of every individual, makes a correspondent distinction between different persons; that he adopts as his children such as he foreknows will be deserving of his grace, and devotes to the damnation of death others, whose dispositions he sees will be inclined to wickedness and impiety. . . . Others, neither acquainted with the Scripture, nor deserving of any attention, oppose the sound doctrine with extreme presumption and intolerable effrontery. God's sovereign election of some, and preterition of others, they make the subject of formal accusation against him. But if this is the known fact, what will they gain by quarrelling with God? We teach nothing but what experience has proved, that God has always been at liberty to bestow his grace on whom he chooses. . . . Let them answer why they are men, and not oxen or asses: when it was in God's power to create them dogs, he formed them after his own image. . . . Now, it is of importance to attend to what the Scripture declares respecting every individual. Paul's assertion, that we were "chosen in Christ before the foundation of the world," certainly precludes any consideration of merit in us; for it is as though he had said, our heavenly Father, finding nothing worthy of his choice in all the posterity of Adam, turned his views towards his Christ, to choose members from his body whom he would admit to the fellowship of life. Let believers, then, be satisfied with this reason, that we were adopted in Christ to the heavenly inheritance, because in ourselves we were incapable of such high dignity. . . .

. . . . .

A REFUTATION OF THE CALUMNIES GENERALLY, BUT UNJUSTLY URGED AGAINST THIS DOCTRINE

. . . . .

II. . . . In the first place they inquire, by what right the Lord is angry with his creatures who had not provoked him by any previous offence; for that to devote to destruction whom he pleases, is more like the caprice of a tyrant than the lawful sentence of a judge; that men have reason, therefore, to expostulate with God, if they are predestinated to eternal death without any demerit of their own, merely by his sovereign will. If such thoughts ever enter the minds of pious men, they will be sufficiently enabled to break their violence by this one consideration, how exceedingly presumptuous it is only to inquire into the causes of the Divine will; which is in fact, and is justly entitled to be, the cause of everything that exists. For if it has any cause, then there must be something antecedent, on which it depends; which it is impious to suppose. For the will of God is the highest rule of justice; so that what he wills must be considered just, for this very reason, because he wills it. When it is inquired, therefore, why the Lord did so, the answer must be, Because he would. But if you go further, and ask why he so determined, you are in search of something greater and higher than the will of God, which can never be found. . . .

. . . . .

IV. They further object, Were they not, by the decree of God, antecedently predestinated to that corruption which is now stated as the cause of condemnation? When they perish in their corruption, therefore, they only suffer the punishment of that misery into which, in consequence of his predestination, Adam fell, and precipitated his posterity with him. Is he not unjust, therefore, in treating his creatures with such cruel mockery? I confess, indeed, that all the descendants of Adam fell by the Divine will into that miserable condition in which they are now involved; and this is what I asserted from the beginning, that we must always return at last to the sovereign determination of God's will, the cause of which is hidden in himself. . . .

·　·　·　·　·

V. . . . What wonder or absurdity is there in this? Would he have the Divine power so limited, as to be unable to execute more than his little capacity can comprehend? I say, with Augustine, that the Lord created those who, he certainly foreknew, would fall into destruction, and that this was actually so because he willed it; but of his will it belongs not to us to demand the reason, which we are incapable of comprehending; nor is it reasonable that the Divine will should be made the subject of controversy with us. . . .

VI. Impiety produces also a second objection. . . . Why should God impute as a fault to man those things which were rendered necessary by his predestination? What should they do? Should they resist his decrees? This would be vain, for it would be impossible. Therefore they are not justly punished for those things of which God's predestination is the principal cause. . . . Observe; all things being at God's disposal, and the decision of salvation or death belonging to him, he orders all things by his counsel and decree in such a manner, that some men are born devoted from the womb to certain death, that his name may be glorified in their destruction. If any one pleads, that no necessity was imposed on them by the providence of God, but rather that they were created by him in such a state in consequence of his foresight of their future depravity—it will amount to nothing. . . . I will readily grant, indeed, that mere foreknowledge lays no necessity on the creature, though this is not universally admitted; for there are some who maintain it to be the actual cause of what comes to pass. But Valla, a man otherwise not much versed in theology, appears to me to have discovered superior acuteness and judiciousness, by showing that this controversy is unnecessary, because both life and death are acts of

God's will, rather than of his foreknowledge. If God simply foresaw the fates of men, and did not also dispose and fix them by his determination, there would be room to agitate the question, whether his providence or foresight rendered them at all necessary. But since he foresees future events only in consequence of his decree that they shall happen, it is useless to contend about foreknowledge, while it is evident that all things come to pass rather by ordination and decree.

VII. They say it is nowhere declared in express terms, that God decreed Adam should perish by his defection; as though the same God, whom the Scripture represents as doing whatever he pleases, created the noblest of his creatures without any determinate end. They maintain, that he was possessed of free choice, that he might be the author of his own fate, but that God decreed nothing more than to treat him according to his desert. If so weak a scheme as this be received, what will become of God's omnipotence. . . . But whether they wish it or dread it, predestination exhibits itself in Adam's posterity. For the loss of salvation by the whole race through the guilt of one parent, was an event that did not happen by nature. What prevents their acknowledging concerning one man, what they reluctantly grant concerning the whole species? . . . I inquire again, how it came to pass that the fall of Adam, independent of any remedy, should involve so many nations with their infant children in eternal death, but because such was the will of God. Their tongues, so loquacious on every other point, must here be struck dumb. It is an awful decree, I confess; but no one can deny that God foreknew the future final fate of man before he created him, and that he did foreknow it because it was appointed by his own decree. . . .

VIII. Here they recur to the distinction between will and permission, and insist that God permits the destruction of the impious, but does not will it. But what reason shall we assign for his permitting it, but because it is his will? . . . Besides, their perdition depends on the Divine predestination in such a manner, that the cause and matter of it are found in themselves. For the first man fell because the Lord had determined it was so expedient. The reason of this determination is unknown to us. Yet it is certain that he determined thus, only because he foresaw it would tend to the just illustration of the glory of his name. Whenever you hear the glory of God mentioned, think of his justice. For what deserves praise must be just. Man falls, therefore, according to the appointment of Divine Providence; but he falls by his own fault. . . .

IX. . . . The reprobate wish to be thought excusable in sinning, because they cannot avoid a necessity of sinning; especially since this necessity is laid upon them by the ordination of God. But we deny this to be a just excuse; because the ordination of God, by which they complain that they are destined to destruction, is guided by equity, unknown indeed to us, but indubitably certain. Whence we conclude, that they sustain no misery that is not inflicted upon them by the most righteous judgment of God. In the next place, we maintain that they act preposterously, who, in seeking for the origin of their condemnation, direct their views to the secret recesses of the Divine counsel, and overlook the corruption of nature, which is its real source. The testimony God gives to his creation prevents their imputing it to him. For though, by the eternal providence of God, man was created to that misery to which he is subject, yet the ground of it he has derived from himself, not from God; since he is thus ruined solely in consequence of his having degenerated from the pure creation of God to vicious and impure depravity.

.   .   .   .   .

XII. Another argument often urged to overthrow predestination is, that its establishment would destroy all solicitude and exertion for rectitude of conduct. . . . If the object of election be holiness of life, it should rather awaken and stimulate us to a cheerful practice of it, than be used as a pretext for slothfulness. But how inconsistent is it to cease from the practise of virtue because election is sufficient to salvation, while the end proposed in election is our diligent performance of virtuous actions! Away, then, with such corrupt and sacrilegious perversions of the whole order of election. They carry their blasphemies much further, by asserting, that any one who is reprobated by God will labor to no purpose if he endeavor to approve himself to him by innocence and integrity of life; but here they are convicted of a most impudent falsehood. For whence could such exertion originate but from election? Whoever are of the number of the reprobate, being vessels made to dishonor, cease not to provoke the Divine wrath against them by continual transgressions, and to confirm by evident proofs the judgment of God already denounced against them; so that their striving with him in vain is what can never happen.

ELECTION CONFIRMED BY THE DIVINE CALL. THE DESTINED DESTRUCTION OF THE REPROBATE PROCURED BY THEMSELVES

But, in order to a further elucidation of the subject, it is necessary to treat of the calling of the elect, and of the blinding and hardening of the impious . . . the discriminating election of God, which is otherwise concealed within himself, he manifests only by his calling, which may therefore with propriety be termed the testification or evidence of it. "For whom he did foreknow, he also did predestinate to be conformed to the image of his Son. Moreover, whom he did predestinate, them he also called; and whom he called, them he also justified," in order to their eventual glorification. Though by choosing his people, the Lord has adopted them as his children, yet we see that they enter not on the possession of so great a blessing till they are called; on the other hand, as soon as they are called, they immediately enjoy some communication of his election. . . .

II. . . . Here, then, the infinite goodness of God is displayed, but not to the salvation of all; for heavier judgment awaits the reprobate, because they reject the testimony of Divine love. And God also, to manifest his glory, withdraws from them the efficacious influence of his Spirit. This internal call, therefore, is a pledge of salvation, which cannot possibly deceive. To this purpose is that passage of John—"Hereby we know that he abideth in us, by the Spirit which he hath given us." . . .

III. Here two errors are to be avoided. For some suppose man to be a cooperator with God, so that the validity of election depends on his consent; thus, according to them, the will of man is superior to the counsel of God. As though the Scripture taught, that we are only given an ability to believe, and not faith itself. Others . . . suspend election on that which is subsequent to it; as though it were doubtful and ineffectual till it is confirmed by faith. . . . But it is contrary to the truth to assert, that election has no efficacy till after we have embraced the gospel, and that this circumstance gives it all its energy. The certainty of it indeed, we are to seek here. . . . But when God has discovered it to us, we must ascend to loftier heights, that the cause may not be lost in the effect. . . .

.   .   .   .   .

VIII. The declaration of Christ, that "many are called, and few chosen," is very improperly understood. For . . . there are two kinds of calling. For there is a universal call, by which God, in the external preaching of the word, invites all, indiscriminately, to come to him, even those to whom he intends it as a savor of death, and an occasion of heavier condemnation. There is also a special call, with which he, for the most part, favors only believers, when, by the inward illumination of his Spirit, he causes the word preached to sink into their hearts. Yet sometimes he also communicates it to those whom he enlightens for a season, and afterwards forsakes on account of their ingratitude, and strikes with greater blindness.   .   .   .

.   .   .   .   .

X. Now, the elect are not gathered into the fold of Christ by calling, immediately from their birth, nor all at the same time, but according as God is pleased to dispense his grace to them. Before they are gathered to that chief Shepherd, they go astray, scattered in the common wilderness, and differing in no respect from others, except in being protected by the special mercy of God from rushing down the precipice of eternal death.   .   .   .   That they go not to the most desperate extremes of impiety, is not owing to any innate goodness of theirs, but because the eye of God watches over them, and his hand is extended for their preservation.

.   .   .   .   .

XII. As the Lord, by his effectual calling of the elect, completes the salvation to which he predestinated them in his eternal counsel, so he has his judgments against the reprobate, by which he executes his counsel respecting them. Those, therefore, whom he has created to a life of shame and a death of destruction, that they might be instruments of his wrath, and examples of his severity, he causes to reach their appointed end, sometimes depriving them of the opportunity of hearing the word, sometimes, by the preaching of it, increasing their blindness and stupidity. Of the former there are innumerable examples.   .   .   .   Of the second class.   .   .   .   The same sermon is addressed to a hundred persons; twenty receive it with the obedience of faith; the others despise, or ridicule, or reject, or condemn it. If it be replied, that the difference proceeds from their wickedness and perverseness, this will afford no satisfaction; because the minds of others would have been influenced by the same wickedness, but for the correction of Divine goodness. And thus we shall always be perplexed, unless we recur to Paul's question—"Who maketh thee to differ?" In which he signifies, that the excellence of some men beyond others, is not from their own virtue, but solely from Divine grace.

XIII. Why, then, in bestowing grace upon some, does he pass over others? Luke assigns a reason for the former, that they "were ordained to eternal life." What conclusion, then, shall we draw respecting the latter, but that they are vessels of wrath to dishonor? Wherefore let us not hesitate to say with Augustine, "God could convert to good the will of the wicked, because he is omnipotent. It is evident that he could. Why, then, does he not? Because he would not. Why he would not, remains with himself." For we ought not to aim at more wisdom than becomes us.

XIV. . . . When the impious hear these things, they loudly complain that God by a wanton exercise of power, abuses his wretched creatures for the sport of his cruelty. But we, who know that all men are liable to so many charges at the Divine tribunal, that of a thousand questions they would be unable to give a satisfactory answer to one, confess that the reprobate suffer nothing but what is consistent with the most righteous judgment of God. Though we cannot comprehend the reason of this, let us be content with some degree of ignorance where the wisdom of God soars into its own sublimity.

46

ST. THOMAS AQUINAS

Predestination, Freedom, and Grace *

AFTER SHOWING how God's knowledge is the cause of things and in what manner God knows future contingent things, St. Thomas proceeds to an explanation of the way in which the will of God is fulfilled. Here he interprets the words of the Apostle "that God will have all men to be saved" by means of his distinction between the antecedent and the consequent will of God. He continues by pointing out that all things are subject to the divine providence both in a general and in a particular way, and defines predestination as the direction of man toward his eternal life and as a part of the divine providence. The articles on predestination conclude his discussion; in them he is concerned to explain that it is not the foreseen merit of the individual which is the cause of his predestination, for God's will can have no cause, but that rather

* Reprinted from the *Summa Theologica* with the permission of Benziger Brothers, Inc., publishers, Question 14, Articles 8 and 13; Question 19, Article 6; Question 22, Article 2; Question 23, Articles 1, 4, and 5.

For a brief biographical sketch of St. Thomas, see selection 3 on page 14.

the individual who is elected for salvation is elected solely because
of the love that God has for him.

WHETHER THE KNOWLEDGE OF GOD IS THE CAUSE OF THINGS [*]

. . . . .

I answer that, The knowledge of God is the cause of things. For
the knowledge of God is to all creatures what the knowledge of the
artificer is to things made by his art. Now the knowledge of the
artificer is the cause of the things made by his art from the fact
that the artificer works by his intellect. Hence the form of the intellect must be the principle of action; as heat is the principle of
heating. Nevertheless, we must observe that a natural form, being
a form that remains in that to which it gives existence, denotes a
principle of action according only as it has an inclination to an
effect; and likewise, the intelligible form does not denote a principle
of action in so far as it resides in the one who understands unless
there is added to it the inclination to an effect, which inclination is through the will. For since the intelligible form has a relation
to opposite things (inasmuch as the same knowledge relates to opposites), it would not produce a determinate effect unless it were
determined to one thing by the appetite, as the Philosopher says
(*Metaph. ix.*) Now it is manifest that God causes things by His intellect, since His being is His act of understanding; and hence His
knowledge must be the cause of things, in so far as His will is joined
to it. Hence the knowledge of God as the cause of things is usually
called the *knowledge of approbation.*

WHETHER THE KNOWLEDGE OF GOD IS OF FUTURE CONTINGENT THINGS [**]

. . . . .

Obj. 2. Further, every conditional proposition of which the antecedent is absolutely necessary, must have an absolutely necessary
consequent. For the antecedent is to the consequent as principles are
to the conclusion: and from necessary principles only a necessary
conclusion can follow, as is proved in *Poster.* i. But this is a true
conditional proposition, *If God knew that this thing will be, it will
be,* for the knowledge of God is only of true things. Now, the ante-

[*] Question 14, Article 8.
[**] Question 14, Article 13.

cedent conditional of this is absolutely necessary, because it is eternal, and because it is signified as past. Therefore the consequent is also absolutely necessary. Therefore whatever God knows, is necessary; and so the knowledge of God is not of contingent things.

Obj. 3. Further, everything known by God must necessarily be, because even what we ourselves know, must necessarily be; and, of course, the knowledge of God is much more certain than ours. But no future contingent thing must necessarily be. Therefore no contingent future thing is known by God.

On the contrary, It is written (Ps. xxxii.15), *He Who hath made the hearts of every one of them: Who understandeth all their works,* that is, of men. Now the works of men are contingent, being subject to free will. Therefore God knows future contingent things.

I answer that, Since . . . God knows all things; not only things actual but also things possible to Him and the creature; and since some of these are future contingent to us, it follows that God knows future contingent things.

In evidence of this, we must consider that a contingent thing can be considered in two ways; first, in itself, in so far as it is now in act: and in this sense it is not considered as future, but as present; neither is it considered as contingent (as having reference) to one of two terms, but as determined to one; and on account of this it can be infallibly the object of certain knowledge, for instance to the sense of sight, as when I see that Socrates is sitting down. In another way a contingent thing can be considered as it is in its cause; and in this way it is considered as future, and as a contingent thing not yet determined to one; forasmuch as a contingent cause has relation to opposite things: and in this sense a contingent thing is not subject to any certain knowledge. Hence, whoever knows a contingent effect in its cause only, has merely a conjectural knowledge of it. Now God knows all contingent things not only as they are in their causes, but also as each one of them is actually in itself. And although contingent things become actual successively, nevertheless God knows contingent things not successively, as they are in their own being, as we do; but simultaneously. The reason is because His knowledge is measured by eternity, as is also His being; and eternity being simultaneously whole comprises all time. . . . Hence, all things that are in time are present to God from eternity, not only because He has the types of things present within Him, as some say; but because His glance is carried from eternity over all things as they are in their presentiality. Hence it is manifest that contingent things are infallibly known by God, inasmuch as they are subject to the divine sight in their presentiality; yet they are future contingent things in relation to their own causes.

*   *   *   *   *

Reply Obj. 2. . . . Therefore we must reply otherwise; that when the antecedent contains anything belonging to an act of the soul, the consequent must be taken not as it is in itself, but as it is in the soul: for the existence of a thing in itself is different from the existence of a thing in the soul. For example, when I say, *What the soul understands is immaterial*; this is to be understood that it is immaterial as it is in the intellect, not as it is in itself. Likewise if I say, *If God knew anything, it will be*, the consequent must be understood as it is subject to the divine knowledge, that is, as it is in its presentiality. And thus it is necessary, as also is the antecedent: *for everything that is, while it is, must necessarily be*, as the Philosopher says in *Periherm.* i.

Reply Obj. 3. Things reduced to act in time, are known by us successively in time, but by God are known in eternity, which is above time. Whence to us they cannot be certain, forasmuch as we know future contingent things as such; but they are certain to God alone, whose understanding is in eternity above time. Just as he who goes along the road, does not see those who come after him; whereas he who sees the whole road from a height, sees at once all travelling by the way. Hence what is known by us must be necessary, even as it is in itself; for what is future contingent in itself, cannot be known by us. Whereas what is known by God must be necessary according to the mode in which they are subject to the divine knowledge, as already stated, but not absolutely as considered in their own causes. Hence also this proposition, *Everything known by God must necessarily be*, is usually distinguished; for this may refer to the thing, or to the saying. If it refers to the thing, it is divided and false; for the sense is *Everything which God knows is necessary*. If understood of the saying it is composite and true; for the sense is, *This proposition, 'that which is known by God is' is necessary*.

WHETHER THE WILL OF GOD IS ALWAYS FULFILLED? *

Objection 1. It seems that the will of God is not always fulfilled. For the Apostle says (I Tim. ii. 4): *God will have all men to be saved, and to come to the knowledge of the truth*. But this does not happen. Therefore the will of God is not always fulfilled.

* Question 19, Article 6.

*   *   *   *   *

On the contrary, It is said (Ps. cxxx.11): *God hath done all things, whatsoever He would.*

I answer that, The will of God must needs always be fulfilled. In proof of which we must consider that since an effect is conformed to the agent according to its form, the rule is the same with active causes as with formal causes. The rule in forms is this: that although a thing may fall short of any particular form, it cannot fall short of the universal form. For though a thing may fail to be, for example, a man or a living being, yet it cannot fail to be a being. Hence the same must happen in active causes. Something may fall outside the order of any particular active cause, but not outside the order of the universal cause; under which all particular causes are included: and if any particular cause fails of its effect, this is because of the hindrance of some other particular cause, which is included in the order of the universal cause. Therefore an effect cannot possibly escape the order of the universal cause. Even in corporeal things this is clearly seen. For it may happen that a star is hindered from producing its effects; yet whatever effect does result, in corporeal things, from this hindrance of a corporeal cause, must be referred through intermediate causes to the universal influence of the first heaven. Since, then, the will of God is the universal cause of all things, it is impossible that the divine will should not produce its effect. Hence that which seems to depart from the divine will in one order, returns into it in another order; as does the sinner, who by sin falls away from the divine will as much as lies in him, yet falls back into the order of that will, when by its justice he is punished.

Reply Obj. 1. The words of the Apostle, *God will have all men to be saved,* etc., can be understood in three ways. First, by a restricted application, in which case they would mean, as Augustine says (*De praed. sanct.* 1.8: *Enchir.* 103), *God wills all men to be saved that are saved, not because there is no man whom He does not wish saved, but because there is no man saved whose salvation He does not will.* Secondly, they can be understood as applying to every class of individuals, not to every individual of each class; in which case they mean that God wills some men of every class and condition to be saved, males and females, Jews and Gentiles, great and small, but not all of every condition. Thirdly, according to Damascene (*De Fide Orth.* ii. 29), they are understood of the antecedent will of God; not of the consequent will. This distinction must not be taken as applying to the divine will itself, in which there is nothing antecedent nor consequent, but to the things willed.

To understand this we must consider that everything, in so far as it is good, is willed by God. A thing taken in its primary sense, and absolutely considered, may be good or evil, and yet when some additional circumstances are taken into account, by a consequent consideration may be changed into the contrary. Thus that a man should live is good; and that a man should be killed is evil, absolutely considered. But if in a particular case we add that a man is a murderer or dangerous to society, to kill him is a good; that he live is an evil. Hence it may be said of a just judge, that antecedently he wills all men to live; but consequently wills the murderer to be hanged. In the same way God antecedently wills all men to be saved, but consequently wills some to be damned, as His justice exacts. Nor do we will simply, what we will antecedently, but rather we will it in a qualified manner; for the will is directed to things as they are in themselves, and in themselves they exist under particular qualifications. Hence we will a thing simply inasmuch as we will it when all particular circumstances are considered; and this is what is meant by willing consequently. Thus it may be said that a just judge wills simply the hanging of a murderer, but in a qualified manner he would will him to live, to wit inasmuch as he is a man. Such a qualified will may be called a willingness rather than an absolute will. Thus it is clear that whatever God simply wills takes place; although what He wills antecedently may not take place.

WHETHER EVERYTHING IS SUBJECT TO THE PROVIDENCE OF GOD? *

. . . . .

I answer that, Certain persons totally denied the existence of providence, as Democritus and the Epicureans, maintaining that the world was made by chance. Others taught that incorruptible things only were subject to providence, and corruptible things not in their individual selves, but only according to their species; for in this respect they are incorruptible. . . .

We must say, however, that all things are subject to divine providence, not only in general, but even in their own individual selves. This is made evident thus. For since every agent acts for an end, the ordering of effects toward that end extends as far as the causality of the first agent extends. Whence it happens that in the effects of an agent something takes place which has no reference towards the end, because the effect comes from a cause other than, and outside

* Question 22, Article 2.

the intention of the agent. But the causality of God, Who is the first agent, extends to all being, not only as to the constituent principles of species, but also as to the individualizing principles; not only of things incorruptible, but also of things corruptible. Hence all things that exist in whatsoever manner are necessarily directed by God towards some end. . . .

WHETHER MEN ARE PREDESTINED BY GOD? *

. . . . . .

I answer that, It is fitting that God should predestine men. For all things are subject to His providence. . . . Now it belongs to providence to direct things towards their end. . . . The end towards which created things are directed by God is twofold; one which exceeds all proportion and faculty of created nature; and this end is life eternal. . . . The other end, however, is proportionate to created nature, to which end created being can attain according to the power of its nature. Now if a thing cannot attain to something by the power of its nature, it must be directed thereto by another; thus, an arrow is directed by the archer towards a mark. Hence, properly speaking, a rational creature, capable of eternal life, is led towards it, directed as it were, by God. The reason of that direction pre-exists in God; as in Him is the type of the order of all things towards an end, which we proved above to be providence. Now the type in the mind of the doer of something to be done, is a kind of pre-existence in him of the thing to be done. Hence the type of the aforesaid direction of a rational creature towards the end of life eternal is called predestination. For to destine, is to direct or send. Thus it is clear that predestination, as regards its objects is a part of providence.

WHETHER THE PREDESTINED ARE CHOSEN BY GOD? **

. . . . .

I answer that, Predestination presupposes election in the order of reason; and election presupposes love. The reason of this is that predestination . . . is a part of providence. Now providence, as also prudence, is the plan existing in the intellect directing the ordering of some things towards an end. . . . But nothing is directed towards an end unless the will for that end already exists. Whence

* Question 23, Article 1.
** Question 23, Article 4.

the predestination of some to eternal salvation presupposes, in the order of reason, that God wills their salvation; and to this belong both election and love:—love, inasmuch as He wills them this particular good of eternal salvation:—election, inasmuch as He wills this good to some in preference to others; since He reprobates some, . . . Election and love, however, are differently ordered in God, and in ourselves: because in us the will in loving does not cause good, but we are incited to love by the good which already exists; and therefore we choose someone to love, and so election in us precedes love. In God, however, it is the reverse. For His will, by which in loving He wishes good to someone, is the cause of that good possessed by some in preference to others. Thus it is clear that love precedes election in the order of reason, and election precedes predestination. Whence all the predestinate are objects of election and love.

WHETHER THE FOREKNOWLEDGE OF MERITS IS THE CAUSE OF PREDESTINATION? *

.   .   .   .   .

Obj. 3. Further, *There is no injustice in God* (Rom. ix. 14). Now it would seem unjust that unequal things be given to equals. But all men are equal as regards both nature and original sin; and inequality in them arises from the merits or demerits of their actions. Therefore God does not prepare unequal things for men by predestinating and reprobating, unless through the foreknowledge of their merits and demerits.

On the contrary, The Apostle says (Tit. iii. 5): *Not by the works of justice we have done, but according to His mercy He saved us.* But as He saved us, so He predestined that we should be saved. Therefore, foreknowledge of merits is not the cause or reason of predestination.

I answer that, Since predestination includes will . . . the reason of predestination must be sought for in the same way as was the reason of the will of God. Now it was shown (Q. 19., A. 5), that we cannot assign any cause of the divine will on the part of the act of willing; but a reason can be found on the part of the things willed; inasmuch as God wills one thing on account of something else. Wherefore nobody has been so insane as to say that merit is the cause of divine predestination as regards the act of the predestinator. But this is the question, whether, as regards the effect, predestination has any

* Question 23, Article 5.

cause; or what comes to the same thing, whether God pre-ordained that He would give the effect of predestination to anyone on account of any merits.

Accordingly there were some who held that the effect of predestination was pre-ordained for some on account of pre-existing merits in a former life. This was the opinion of Origen. . . .

Others said that pre-existing merits in this life are the reason and cause of the effect of predestination. For the Pelagians taught that the beginning of doing well came from us; and the consummation from God: so that it came about that the effect of predestination was granted to one, and not to another, because the one made a beginning by preparing, whereas the other did not. But against this we have the saying of the Apostle (2 Cor. iii. 5), that *we are not sufficient to think anything of ourselves as of ourselves.* . . .

And so others said that merits following the effect of predestination are the reason of predestination; giving us to understand that God gives grace to a person, and pre-ordains that He will give it, because He knows beforehand that He will make good use of that grace, as if a king were to give a horse to a soldier because he knows he will make good use of it. But these seem to have drawn a distinction between that which flows from grace, and that which flows from free will, as if the same thing cannot come from both. It is, however, manifest that what is of grace is the effect of predestination; and this cannot be considered as the reason of predestination, since it is contained in the notion of predestination. Therefore, if anything else in us be the reason of predestination, it will be outside the effect of predestination. Now there is no distinction between what flows from free will, and what is of predestination; as there is no distinction between what flows from a secondary cause and from a first cause. For the providence of God produces effects through the operation of secondary causes. . . . Wherefore, that which flows from free-will is also of predestination. . . .

.   .   .   .   .

Reply Obj. 3. The reason for the predestination of some, and reprobation of others, must be sought for in the goodness of God. Thus He is said to have made all thing through His goodness, so that the divine goodness might be represented in things. Now it is necessary that God's goodness, which in itself is one and undivided, should be manifested in many ways in His creation; because creatures in themselves cannot attain to the simplicity of God. Thus it is that for the completion of the universe there are required different grades of being. . . . That this multiformity of grades may be preserved in things, God allows some evils, lest many good things should never happen. . . . Let us then consider the whole of the human race, as we consider the whole universe. God wills to manifest His goodness in men; in respect to those whom He predestines, by means of His mercy, in sparing them; and in respect of others, whom he reprobates, by means of His justice, in punishing them. This is the reason why God elects some and rejects others. . . . Yet why He chooses some for glory, and reprobates others, has no reason except the divine will. . . . Neither on this account can there be said to be injustice in God, if He prepares unequal lots for not unequal things. This would be altogether contrary to the notion of justice, if the effect of predestination were granted as a debt, and not gratuitously. In things which are given gratuitously a person can give more or less, just as he pleases (provided he deprives nobody of his due), without any infringement of justice. . . .

47

LUIS DE MOLINA

The Scientia Media *

THE HERESY of Pelagius, that free will alone is sufficient for salvation, is contrasted by Molina with the view of Augustine that salvation is from God alone. Though some find the arguments of Augustine difficult to accept, the author notes that there has always been unanimous agreement among the faithful on the propositions that man has free will, and that no one can be justified solely through his own efforts, nor attain eternal life except through the grace of God. The most serious controversy involving the problem

° The material that follows is translated from the *Concordia Liberi Arbitrii* (Paris: Lethielleux, 1876), pp. 545-51.

Luis de Molina, S. J. (1535-1600) was born of noble parentage at Cuenca, New Castile, Spain. He entered the Society of Jesus at Alcalá and later studied philosophy and theology at Coimbra, Portugal. A few years after completing his studies he was named to the Chair of Theology at the University of Evora. For the next twenty years he expounded the *Summa Theologica* of St. Thomas Aquinas. In 1590 he retired to Cuenca.

of predestination is whether predestination occurs according to God's foreknowledge of our use of free will, or whether it is due solely to the will and pleasure of God. The author then states what he regards as an original solution to this problem in the form of four basic principles: the nature of the divine influence and its concurrence with our will; the gift of perseverance; the *scientia media*; and the principle that predestination depends upon foreseen merits.

. . . Two THINGS are necessary, as explained thus far, in order that an adult may attain eternal life and that he be predestined by God: the first, that God on his part has determined to give him those aids and means which He will have foreseen he would use of his own free will in order to attain the end of his life in grace; the second, that the adult himself of his own free will is willing to cooperate toward that end. The first depends upon God, the second upon the adult himself. Those holy fathers antedating the time of Pelagius and Augustine in commenting on this second point, were of the almost unanimous opinion that predestination took place in accordance with the foreknowledge of the proper use of free will and the merits of each individual, and in this sense they attempted to interpret holy scripture.

The heresy of Pelagius arose, because Pelagius contrary to holy scripture attributed all things to our free will and declared that that alone sufficed for salvation. Although he later admitted the gift of grace, nevertheless, he asserted that it was neither necessary nor was it conferred to begin our salvation (for he maintained that the beginning of our salvation depended upon us through our own will) but rather to complete our salvation. It was not as though we could not complete it, but simply that we could not do so as easily or as well. He added, moreover, that it was conferred upon each according to the nature of his previous good use of the will. Since, as I say, Pelagius taught these things, Augustine and the other fathers, in opposition to this heresy, demonstrated from holy scripture that the beginning of our salvation comes from God through his foresight and action, and that the beginning and the perfection of our salvation depends upon the grace of God, which is given to us through Christ; and that the gifts and means of grace are conferred, not according to the effort of our free will, but according to the pleasure of God.

Augustine believed that this was connected with those things which he had taught most correctly from scripture concerning grace against the heresy of Pelagius, namely, that eternal predestination is not according to the merits of the individual and his use of free will as foreseen by God, but solely according to His election and good pleasure. It was in this sense that he interpreted the Epistle of St. Paul to the Romans (IX) in many of his works and applied that interpretation to Timothy II.: "He will have all men to be saved." This was not to be understood universally of all men, but only of those predestined.* This doctrine seriously disturbed many of the faithful, particularly those living in Gaul, not only the uneducated but also the learned and it greatly endangered their salvation. For lest they adhere to that doctrine, they thought it necessary to assent rather in part to the heresy of Pelagius. The letters of Prosper and Hilary are a witness to this fact. . . . Hilary . . . after enumerating the objections which were brought forward against Augustine's doctrine by those who had been disturbed, affirms that they were troubled in this manner: Why was it necessary, they say, that the hearts of those less intelligent be disturbed by the uncertainty of this controversy? For none the less usefully has the catholic faith been defended without this definition, for so many years, by so many scholars, and in so many books. The opinion of Augustine was actually followed by the divine Thomas, and after him by many scholastics.

The following matters have been above controversy: there is in us freedom of will; no one, whether adult or child can attain eternal life except through grace derived from the merits of Christ; and no adult, by reason of his own powers and without the aid of supernatural grace, can be justified and attain eternal life. In God there is a foreknowledge of all future events and a predestination of the good to eternal life through grace, gifts and supernatural helps. The freedom of the will is related to all these and is little diminished or impeded by them. . . . It was not that since God foreknew what would happen from those things which depend on the created will that it would happen; but, on the contrary, it was because such things would happen through the freedom of the will, that He foreknew it; and that He would foreknow the opposite, if the opposite was to happen, as was possible by reason of the freedom of the will. Whether indeed the beginning of the salvation of adults rests in their believing, hoping, repenting and loving, and stems from the adults themselves through their own will, so that they anticipate the grace of God; or whether, indeed, it is through prevenient and excitant grace from God, was discussed before the occasion of the heresy of Pelagius, but no determinate opinion was arrived at. For which reason it is no wonder that Chrysostom, and others who wrote before those times, should have said the contrary, and the Gauls . . . contended against Augustine concerning the same thing at the beginning of the Pelagian heresy.

* [According to what St. Thomas would call the consequent will of God.—*Ed.*]

Although there was always a common opinion concerning the above, and a unanimous consent, not only among the fathers but also among all catholic men, one matter nevertheless was always considered among the most difficult by Augustine and the others: namely, to find a true method, which would remove all difficulties and would leave the human mind completely at ease concerning the relationships between the freedom of the will and divine grace, foreknowledge and predestination, so that an adult, with none of these three serving as obstacles, could work out or neglect his salvation as he chose, and that he might or might not attain eternal life. And although those heretics, who have sought to prejudice either divine grace or the freedom of the will, may have been effectively answered from sacred scripture and the principles of faith, I hardly know, nevertheless, if when finally explained and complete knowledge provided for reconciling the freedom of the will with grace, foreknowledge and predestination, that a way would be opened to the heretics whereby they might more easily return to the unity of the church and that the controversies which for a thousand years have risen among men may as far as is proper be composed. Of all the controversies, one and that the most ancient, has always existed, namely, whether the predestination of adults happened according to the foreknowledge of the use of free will; or whether, on the other hand by the sole will and pleasure of God. For some, both fathers as well as scholastics, considering the cooperation (divine grace, foreknowledge and predestination in no way impeding) which is placed in the will of each and which is necessary to salvation, and considering it unworthy of divine goodness, justice and equity, that without any direct consideration of the use of the will by each individual, chiefly that he might have some to punish, that these he predestined, and those on the other hand rejected, declared that predestination is established according to the foreknowledge of the use of free will and the merits of each individual. Others, considering the aids and gifts of grace which God without wrong to anyone, from his own pleasure and not by reason of the foreseen use of the will of the individual, has determined in his eternal providence to distribute, declared that predestination is made not according to the foreknowledge of the use of the will and of the individual's merits, but only according to the will and pleasure of God. Neither of these consider the two interpretations made previously by us, namely, first, that God predestined according to the foreknowledge of the use that would be made of free will, just as if he had decided to distribute his gifts and aids and had predestined according to and because of the nature of its use; the second, that he would have pre-destined without the foreknowledge of the use of the will.

In our humble opinion, the full explanation for reconciling the freedom of the will with divine grace, foreknowledge and predestina-tion, we judge to rest upon the following principles, and if these prin-ciples had always been given and explained, perhaps the Pelagian heresy would never have arisen, nor would the Lutherans have dared so impudently to deny the freedom of our will alleging that it could not be reconciled with divine grace, foreknowledge and predestination. . . .

The first and basic principle is the nature of the divine influence, both through its concurrence in the natural acts of our free will, as well as through particular aids to supernatural acts . . . which way we explained earlier. . . .*

The second is the legitimate, or better the orthodox, explanation concerning the measure of the gift of perseverance. For we have shown that no adult can persevere long in grace without special help from God and because of it perseverance in grace is a gift of God: but to no one does God deny that help which is sufficient to persevere.

---

* [In a more detailed analysis (Q. 14a. 13, disp. 7-25, 27) Molina had moved beyond the positions held by both Calvin and St. Thomas with his contention that the grace God extends becomes effective through the cooperation of man, i.e., through the free consent of man's will. In effect, there takes place a concurrence of the divine grace and the free cooperation of man's will. This is seen in his statement that: "The prevenient and auxiliary graces which are conferred upon us in our pilgrim state (on earth), are efficacious or inefficacious for conversion or justification, depend upon free will and the cooperation of our will with them, and are indeed in our free will, either to render them efficacious by con-senting to and cooperating with them towards those acts by which we are disposed to sanctification, or to render them inefficacious by refusing our consent and cooperation, or even by raising a contrary disagreement." (p. 231). And he observes (p. 565) that of two persons, one of whom is given greater grace than the other, the one who is given lesser grace is converted and he who is given a greater grace remains obdurate, for it is a matter of faith that it is within the power of the will of every one to consent to or to refuse the grace of God.

By contrast, St. Thomas and St. Augustine would say that the conversion of one individual rather than another is due solely to the greater love that God has for one person than another. And Calvin, accepting this, would go even further by refusing to admit that God wished all men to be saved, declaring that some have always been predestined to salvation and some to damnation. The problem for Calvin was to justify double predestination. For Thomists the problem is rather that of reconciling man's freedom with God's predestining. Molina claims to have a theory that will resolve this last problem. He does not deny the need of grace for salvation, as would a Pelagian, but does affirm that sufficient grace is of little value unless made efficacious by the cooperation of man's free will. In fact, he made no distinction between sufficient and efficacious grace, and he always remained troubled by the Thomist explanation of the divine causality operating through grace on man's will and yet not determining that will.—Ed.]

Moreover, with this help, with which one might persevere to the end
of life, he can if he wishes, not persevere; and with this help, which
God confers or is ready to give to him who does not persevere, he could
persevere and through Him to stand * although he does not persevere.
For which reason it happens that two things are necessary for the
gift of perseverance. One, on the part of God, namely, that he will
have decided to give those aids with which He foresaw that the adult
would persevere by his own free will. Second, that the free will of
the adult is a necessary condition; for without it the will to confer
such aids would not imply the will to confer the gift of perseverance,
namely, that the adult of his own free will would so cooperate with
such aids in order that he might persevere, which it is clearly within
his ability to do. Therefore, it should not be understood that the gift
of perseverance from God is of such a nature that it takes away the
power of not persevering. . . . On the basis of these two principles and our previous discussions we believe we have reconciled
clearly enough the freedom of our will with the divine grace.

The third principle is: that foreknowledge mediate between the
free and purely natural knowledge of God, by which . . . God
knew before the free act of His will what the created will would do
in all circumstance, if He, God, decided to place such created wills
(men and angels) in a particular set of circumstances. And to the
contrary, He would also foreknow if the created will should decide on
an opposite course of action. And on the basis of this principle the
freedom of the will is compatible with the divine foreknowledge.**

* [The Latin is *stare* and the sentence is somewhat obscure. Perhaps the
author is referring to "stand" as it is found in Ephesians 6: 10-20.—*Ed.*]

** [This is Molina's celebrated hypothesis of the *Scientia media*, a mediate
knowledge held by God as distinct from His natural knowledge of the necessity
of thing occuring in a certain determinate manner, and His free knowledge or
the knowledge of the absolutely contingent. Thus God knows that some things
occur in a purely necessary order and he knows that other things occur purely
by chance. But with His *scientia media* He knows what an individual person
would do under certain circumstances, and He then arranges those circumstances
and grants that person sufficient grace so that he can freely choose or reject a
certain act.

Note Molina's statement on the *scientia media:* "It is necessary to distinguish
a threefold knowledge in God . . . : one purely natural, which therefore
for no reason could have been different in God and by which He knew all those
things to which His divine power extended, whether immediately or by the
intervention of secondary causes. . . . A second, entirely free knowledge,
is that by which God knew absolutely and definitely from all the contingent
associations after the free act of His will and without any condition, what things
would happen and which would not. Finally, a third, of mediate knowledge
(or intermediate), by which from the highest and the inscrutable understanding
of his free will He contemplated in His essence what would take place in ac-

The fourth principle is: that since God chose to create this order of things rather than another and to bestow these aids rather than others, and by means of which he foresaw that some persons and not others will attain to eternal life, and that there was no cause or reason for this on the part of the adults whether predestined or damned. And under this heading we have thus far said that predestination has no cause or reason on the part of the use of the free will of the predestined and reprobate, but is to be attributed solely to the free will of God. Since indeed the will to create a certain order of things and to confer upon individuals certain aids, provides the reason for the predestination of adults, which depends upon the use that God had foreseen they would make of their free will. . . . Finally, we showed that there was no other difficulty involved in reconciling the freedom of our will with divine predestination, other than is found in reconciling it with divine foreknowledge. . . .

Nor indeed do I doubt that this our position concerning predestination would not have been unanimously approved by Augustine and other fathers and also the method for reconciling the freedom of the will with the divine grace, foreknowledge, and predestination, if it had been proposed to them.

I have remained longer in this disputation than I wished . . . yet because the matter is of great moment and exceedingly slippery, and because our explanation for reconciling the freedom of the will and divine predestination has hitherto been proposed by no one whom I know, I have for that reason preferred to discuss these matters a little more fully. . . .

cordance with man's innate freedom in no matter what circumstances it might be placed. . . .

Some may question whether mediate knowledge of this kind should be called free or natural. But such knowledge cannot for any reason be called free, both because it precedes the free act of the divine will as well as because it was not in God's power to know by this knowledge (mediate) anything else than He actually knew. Next it must not be termed natural in that sense, as if it were so innate in God that He could not know the contrary of what He knows by it. For if the created free will were to do the opposite, as in fact it could, He would have known that by means of this same knowledge, but not that which by the thing itself He knows. . . ."

Critics have charged that this makes God's knowledge depend upon the choice of the individual. See particularly here the excellent, though unsympathetic account of Fr. Garrigou-Lagrange in his *Predestination,* translated by Dom Bede Rose, O. S. B., St. Louis, B. Herder Book Co., 1950, pp. 146-150.—*Ed.*]

IMMORTALITY

48

PLATO

The Pilgrimage of the Soul *

IN THE MATERIAL that follows, the extract from the *Phaedo* is a
philosophical argument for the desirability of the separation of the
soul from the body. Although the body is held in low esteem in
this selection it should be noted that this opinion, though highly
influential on later philosophical and religious thinkers, did not
represent the whole of Plato's thought on this subject. The selections from the *Phaedrus, Gorgias,* and *Republic* are expressed in
the form of myths in order to indicate that their content is a
matter of belief rather than reason. The *Phaedrus* material embodies a description of the pre-existence of the soul and it is here,
especially, that Plato's conception of immortality differs sharply
from the traditional Christian account. The judgment of the soul
in the life to come is related in detail and very movingly in the
Republic myth of Er. Here, too, we find Plato developing the concept of the freedom of the individual in his choice of a future life
and the equation of the good life on earth with the good life in
the world to come.

PHAEDO

AND NOW, O my judges, I desire to prove to you that the real philosopher has reason to be of good cheer when he is about to die, and
that after death he may hope to obtain the greatest good in the
other world. And how this may be, Simmias and Cebes, I will endeavor to explain. For I deem that the true votary of philosophy
is likely to be misunderstood by other men; they do not perceive
that he is always pursuing death and dying; and if this be so, and
he has had the desire of death all his life long, why when his

---

* From *The Dialogues of Plato,* translated by Benjamin Jowett (London: The
Clarendon Press, 1892), 64-68, 245-49, 614-21. Reprinted with the permission
of the publisher.

Plato (427-347 B.C.) was born of an aristocratic family in Athens. He was a
student and friend of Socrates and a teacher of Aristotle. He founded the famous
Academy at Athens where he taught until his death.

time comes should he repine at that which he has been always pursuing and desiring?

.   .   .   .

'Have we not found,' they * will say, 'a path of thought which seems to bring us and our argument to the conclusion, that while we are in the body, and while the soul is infected with the evils of the body, our desire will not be satisfied? and our desire is of the truth. For the body is a source of endless trouble to us by reason of the mere requirement of food; and is liable also to diseases which overtake and impede us in the search after true being: it fills us full of loves, and lusts, and fears, and fancies of all kinds, and endless foolery, and in fact, as men say, takes away from us the power of thinking at all. Whence come wars, and fightings, and factions? Whence but from the body and the lusts of the body? Wars are occasioned by the love of money, and money has to be acquired for the sake and in the service of the body; and by reason of all these impediments we have no time to give to philosophy; and, last and worst of all, even if we are at leisure and betake ourselves to some speculation, the body is always breaking in upon us, causing turmoil and confusion in our enquiries, and so amazing us that we are prevented from seeing the truth. It has been proved to us by experience that if we would have pure knowledge of anything we must be quit of the body—the soul in herself must behold things in themselves: and then we shall attain the wisdom which we desire, and of which we say that we are lovers; not while we live, but after death; for if while in company with the body, the soul cannot have pure knowledge, one of two things follows—either knowledge is not to be attained at all, or, if at all, after death. For then, and not till then, the soul will be parted from the body and exist in herself alone. In this present life, I reckon that we make the nearest approach to knowledge when we have the least possible intercourse or communion with the body, and are not surfeited with the bodily nature, but keep ourselves pure until the hour when God himself is pleased to release us. And thus having got rid of the foolishness of the body we shall be pure and hold converse with the pure, and know of ourselves the clear light everywhere, which is no other than the light of truth.' For the impure are not permitted to approach the pure. These are the sort of words, Simmias, which the true lovers of knowledge cannot help saying to one another, and thinking. You would agree; would you not?

* [The philosophers.—*Ed.*]

Undoubtedly, Socrates.

But, O my freind, if this be true, there is great reason to hope that, going whither I go, when I have come to the end of my journey, I shall attain that which has been the pursuit of my life. And therefore I go on my way rejoicing, and not I only, but every other man who believes that his mind has been made ready and that he is in a manner purified.

Certainly, replied Simmias.

And what is purification but the separation of the soul from the body, as I was saying before; the habit of the soul gathering and collecting herself into herself from all sides out of the body; the dwelling in her own place alone, as in another life, so also in this, as far as she can;—the release of the soul from the chains of the body?

Very true, he said.

And this separation and release of the soul from the body is termed death?

To be sure, he said.

And the true philosophers, and they only are ever seeking to release the soul. Is not the separation and release of the soul from the body their especial study?

That is true.

And, as I was saying at first, there would be a ridiculous contradiction in men studying to live as nearly as they can in a state of death, and yet repining when it comes upon them.

Clearly.

And the true philosophers, Simmias, are always occupied in the practice of dying, wherefore also to them least of all men is death terrible. Look at the matter thus:—if they have been in every way the enemies of the body, and are wanting to be alone with the soul, when this desire of theirs is granted, how inconsistent would they be if they trembled and repined, instead of rejoicing at their departure to that place where, when they arrive, they hope to gain that which in life they desired—and this was wisdom—and at the same time to be rid of the company of their enemy. Many a man has been willing to go to the world below animated by the hope of seeing there an earthly love, or wife, or son, and conversing with them. And will he who is a true lover of wisdom, and is strongly persuaded in like manner that only in the world below he can worthily enjoy her, still repine at death? Will he not depart with joy? Surely he will, O my friend, if he be a true philosopher. For he will have a firm conviction that there, and there only, he can find wisdom in

her purity. And if this be true, he would be very absurd, as I was
saying, if he were afraid of death.

PHAEDRUS

The soul through all her being is immortal, for that which is ever
in motion is immortal; but that which moves another and is moved
by another, in ceasing to move ceases also to live. Only the self-
moving, never leaving self, never ceases to move, and is the fountain
and beginning of motion to all that moves besides. Now, the beginning is unbegotten, for that which is begotten has a beginning; but
the beginning is begotten of nothing, for if it were begotten of something, then the begotten would not come from a beginning. But if
unbegotten, it must also be indestructible; for if beginning were
destroyed, there could be no beginning out of anything, nor anything out of a beginning; and all things must have a beginning. And
therefore the self-moving is the beginning of motion; and this can
neither be destroyed nor begotten, else the whole heavens and all
creation would collapse and stand still, and never again have motion
or birth. But if the self-moving is proved to be immortal, he who
affirms that self-motion is the very idea and essence of the soul will
not be put to confusion. For the body which is moved from without
is soulless; but that which is moved from within has a soul, for such
is the nature of the soul. But if this be true, must not the soul be
the self-moving, and therefore of necessity unbegotten and immortal? . . .

Of the nature of the soul, though her true form be ever a theme
of large and more than mortal discourse, let me speak briefly, and
in a figure. And let the figure be composite—a pair of winged
horses and a charioteer, Now the winged horses and the charioteers
of the gods are all of them noble and of noble descent, but those
of other races are mixed; the human charioteer drives his in a pair;
and one of them is noble and of noble breed, and the other is ignoble
and of ignoble breed; and the driving of them of necessity gives a
great deal of trouble to him. I will endeavor to explain to you in
what way the mortal differs from the immortal creature. The soul
in her totality has the care of inanimate being everywhere, and
traverses the whole heaven in divers forms appearing:—when perfect and fully winged she soars upward, and orders the whole world;
whereas the imperfect soul, losing her wings and drooping in her
flight at last settles on the solid ground—there, finding a home, she
receives an earthly frame which appears to be self-moved, but is
really moved by her power; and this composition of soul and body

is called a living and mortal creature. For immortal no such union can be reasonably believed to be; although fancy, not having seen nor surely known the nature of God, may imagine an immortal creature having both a body and also a soul which are united throughout all time. Let that, however, be as God wills, and be spoken of acceptably to him. And now let us ask the reason why the soul loses her wings!

The wing is the corporeal element which is most akin to the divine, and which by nature tends to soar aloft and carry that which gravitates downwards into the upper region, which is the habitation of the gods. The divine is beauty, wisdom, goodness, and the like; and by these the wing of the soul is nourished, and grows apace; but when fed upon evil and foulness and the opposite of good, wastes and falls away. Zeus, the mighty lord, holding the reins of a winged chariot, leads the way in heaven, ordering all and taking care of all; and there follows him the array of gods and demi-gods, marshalled in eleven bands; Hestia alone abides at home in the house of heaven; of the rest they who are reckoned among the princely twelve march in their appointed order. They see many blessed sights in the inner heaven, and there are many ways to and fro, along which the blessed gods are passing, every one doing his own work; he may follow who will and can, for jealousy has no place in the celestial choir. But when they go to banquet and festival, then they move up the steep to the top of the vault of heaven. The chariots of the gods in even poise, obeying the rein, glide rapidly; but the others labor, for the vicious steed goes heavily, weighing down the charioteer to the earth when his steed has not been thoroughly trained:—and this is the hour of agony and extremest conflict for the soul. For the immortals, when they are at the end of their course, go forth and stand upon the outside of heaven, and the revolution of the spheres carries them round, and they behold the things beyond. But of the heaven which is above the heavens, what earthly poet ever did or ever will sing worthily? It is such as I will describe; for I must dare to speak the truth, when truth is my theme. There abides the very being with which true knowledge is concerned; the colorless, formless, intangible essence, visible only to mind, the pilot of the soul. The divine intelligence, being nurtured upon mind and pure knowledge, and the intelligence of every soul which is capable of receiving the food proper to it, rejoices at beholding reality, and once more gazing upon truth, is replenished and made glad, until the revolution of the worlds brings her round again

_ or a brief biographical sketch of John Calvin, see selection 1 on page 6.

ance, and knowledge absolute, not in the form of generation or of relation, which men call existence, but knowledge absolute in existence absolute; and beholding the other true existences in like manner, and feasting upon them, she passes down into the interior of the heavens and returns home; and there the charioteer putting up his horses at the stall, gives them ambrosia to eat and nectar to drink.

Such is the life of the gods; but of other souls, that which follows God best and is likest to him lifts the head of the charioteer into the outer world, and is carried round in the revolution, troubled indeed by the steeds, and with difficulty beholding true being; while another only rises and falls, and sees, and again fails to see by reason of the unruliness of the steeds. The rest of the souls are also longing after the upper world and they all follow, but not being strong enough they are carried round below the surface, plunging, treading on one another, each striving to be first; and there is confusion and perspiration and the extremity of effort; and many of them are lamed or have their wings broken through the ill-driving of the charioteers; and all of them after a fruitless toil, not having attained to the mysteries of true being, go away, and feed upon opinion. The reason why the souls exhibit this exceeding eagerness to behold the plain of truth is that pasturage is found there, which is suited to the highest part of the soul and the wing on which the soul soars is nourished with this. And there is a law of Destiny, that the soul which attains any vision of truth in company with a god is preserved from harm until the next period, and if attaining always is always unharmed. But when she is unable to follow and fails to behold the truth, and through some ill-hap sinks beneath the double load of forgetfulness and vice, and her wings fall from her and she drops to the ground, then the law ordains that this soul shall at her first birth pass, not into any other animal, but only into man; and the soul which has seen most of truth shall come to the birth as a philosopher, or artist, or some musical and loving nature; that which has seen truth in the second degree shall be some righteous king or warrior chief; the soul which is of the third class shall be a politician, or economist, or trader; the fourth shall be a lover of gymnastic toils, or a physician; the fifth shall lead the life of a prophet or heirophant; to the sixth the character of a poet or some imitative artist will be assigned; to the seventh the life of an artisan or husbandman; to the eighth that of a sophist or demagogue; to the ninth that of a tyrant;—all these are states of probation, in which he who

does righteously improves, and he who does unrighteously, deterio-
rates his lot.

Ten thousand years must elapse before the soul of each one can
return to the place from whence she came, for she cannot grow
her wings in less; only the soul of a philosopher, guileless and true,
or the soul of a lover, who is not devoid of philosophy, may acquire
wings in the third of the recurring periods of a thousand years; he
is distinguished from the ordinary good man who gains wings in three
thousand years:—and they who choose this life three times in succession have wings given them, and go away at the end of three
thousand years. But the others * receive judgment when they have
completed their first life, and after the judgment they go, some of
them to the houses of correction which are under the earth, and
are punished; others to some place in heaven whither they are lightly
borne by justice, and there they live in a manner worthy of the life
which they led here when in the form of men. And at the end of the
first thousand years the good souls and also the evil souls both come
to draw lots and choose their second life, and they may take any
which they please. The soul of a man may pass into the life of a
beast, or from the beast return again into the man. But the soul
which has never seen the truth will not pass into the human form.
For a man must have intelligence of universals, and be able to proceed from the many particulars of sense to one conception of reason;—this is the recollection of those things which our soul once saw
while following God—when regardless of that which we now call
being she raised her head up towards the true being. And therefore
the mind of the philosopher alone has wings; and this is just, for
he is always, according to the measure of his abilities, clinging in
recollection to those things in which God abides, and in beholding
which He is what He is. And he who employs aright these memories
is ever being initiated into perfect mysteries and alone becomes truly
perfect. But, as he forgets earthly interests and is rapt in the divine,
the vulgar deem him mad, and rebuke him; they do not see that
he is inspired.

THE REPUBLIC

Well, I said, I will tell you a tale; not one of the tales which
Odysseus tells to the hero Alcinous, yet this too is a tale of a hero,
Er the son of Armenius, a Pamphylian by birth. He was slain in
battle, and ten days afterwards, when the bodies of the dead were

* [The philosopher alone is not subject to judgment, for he has never lost the
vision of truth.—*Ed.*]

taken up already in a state of corruption, his body was found un-affected by decay, and carried away home to be buried. And on the twelfth day, as he was lying on the funeral pile, he returned to life and told them what he had seen in the other world. He said that when his soul left the body he went on a journey with a great company, and that they came to a mysterious place at which there were two openings in the earth; they were near together, and over against them were two other openings in the heaven above. In the intermediate space there were judges seated, who commanded the just, after they had given judgment on them and had bound their sentences in front of them, to ascend by the heavenly way on the right hand; and in like manner the unjust were bidden by them to descend by the lower way on the left hand; these also bore the symbols of their deeds, but fastened on their backs. He drew near, and they told him that he was to be the messenger who would carry the report of the other world to men, and they bade him hear and see all that was to be heard and seen in that place. Then he beheld and saw on one side the souls departing at either opening of heaven and earth when sentence had been given on them; and at the two other openings other souls, some ascending out of the earth dusty and worn with travel, some descending out of heaven clean and bright. And arriving ever and anon they seemed to have come from a long journey, and they went forth with gladness into the meadow, where they encamped as at a festival; and those who knew one another embraced and conversed, the souls which came from earth curiously enquiring about the things above, and the souls which came from heaven about the things beneath. And they told one another of what had happened by the way, those from below weeping and sorrowing at the remembrance of the things which they had endured and seen in their journey beneath the earth (now the journey lasted a thou-sand years), while those from above were describing heavenly de-lights and visions of inconceivable beauty. The story, Glaucon, would take too long to tell; but the sum was this:—He said that for every wrong which they had done to any one they suffered tenfold; or once in a hundred years—such being reckoned to be the length of man's life, and the penalty being thus paid ten times in a thou-sand years. If, for example, there were any who had been the cause of many deaths, or had betrayed or enslaved cities or armies, or been guilty of any other evil behavior, for each and all of their offences they received punishment ten times over, and the rewards of bene-ficence and justice and holiness were in the same proportion. I need hardly repeat what he said concerning young children dying almost as soon as they were born. Of piety and impiety to gods and parents, and of murderers, there were retributions other and greater far which he described. He mentioned that he was present when one of the spirits asked another, 'Where is Ardiaeus the Great?' (Now this Ardiaeus lived a thousand years before the time of Er: he had been the tyrant of some city of Pamphylia, and had murdered his aged father and his elder brother, and was said to have committed many other abominable crimes.) The answer of the other spirit was: 'He comes not hither and will never come. And this,' said he, 'was one of the dreadful sights which we ourselves witnessed. We were at the mouth of the cavern, and, having completed all our experiences, were about to reascend, when of a sudden Ardiaeus appeared and several others, most of whom were tyrants; and there were also besides the tyrants private individuals who had been great criminals: they were just, as they fancied, about to return into the upper world, but the mouth, instead of admitting them, gave a roar, whenever any of these incurable sinners or some one who had not been sufficiently punished tried to ascend; and then wild men of fiery aspect, who were standing by and heard the sound, seized and car- ried them off; and Ardiaeus and others they bound head and foot and hand, and threw them down and flayed them with scourges, and dragged them along the road at the side, carding them on thorns like wool, and declaring to the passers-by what were their crimes, and that they were being taken away to be cast into hell.' And of all the many terrors which they had endured, he said that there was none like the terror which each of them felt at that moment, lest they should hear the voice; and when there was silence, one by one they ascended with exceeding joy. These, said Er, were the penalties and retributions, and there were blessings as great.

Now when the spirits which were in the meadow had tarried seven days, on the eighth they were obliged to proceed on their journey, and, on the fourth day after, he said that they came to a place where they could see from above a line of light, straight as a column, extending right through the whole heaven and through the earth, in color resembling the rainbow, only brighter and purer; another day's journey brought them to the place, and there, in the midst of the light, they saw the ends of the chains of heaven let down from above: for this light is the belt of heaven, and holds together the circle of the universe, like the under-girders of a trireme. From these ends is extended the spindle of Necessity, on which all the revolutions turn. The shaft and hook of this spindle are made of steel, and the whorl is made partly of steel and also partly of other materials. Now the whorl is in form like the whorl used on earth; and the description of it implied that there is one large hollow whorl which is quite scooped out, and into this is fitted another lesser one, and another, and another, and four others, making eight in all, like vessels which fit into one another; the whorls show their edges on the upper side, and on their lower side all together form one continuous whorl. This is pierced by the spindle, which is driven home through the centre of the eighth. The first and outermost whorl has the rim broadest, and the seven inner whorls are narrower, in the following proportions—the sixth is next to the first in size, the fourth next to the sixth; then comes the eighth; the seventh is fifth, the fifth is sixth, the third is seventh, last and eighth comes the second. The largest (or fixed stars) is spangled, and the seventh (or sun) is brightest; the eighth (or moon) colored by the reflected light of the seventh; the second and fifth (Saturn and Mercury) are in color like one another, and yellower than the preceding; the third (Venus) has the whitest light; the fourth (Mars) is reddish; the sixth (Jupiter) is in whiteness second. Now the whole spindle has the same motion; but, as the whole revolves in one direction, the seven inner circles move slowly in the other, and of these the swiftest is the eighth; next in swiftness are the seventh, sixth, and fifth, which move together; third in swiftness appeared to move according to the law of this reversed motion the fourth; the third appeared fourth and the second fifth. The spindle turns on the knees of Necessity; and on the upper surface of each circle is a siren, who goes round with them, hymning a single tone or note. The eight together form one harmony; and round about, at equal intervals, there is another band, three in number, each sitting upon her throne: these are the Fates, daughters of Necessity, who are clothed in white robes and have chaplets upon their heads, Lachesis and Clotho and Atropos, who accompany with their voices the harmony of the sirens—Lachesis singing of the past, Clotho of the present, Atropos of the future; Clotho from time to time assisting with a touch of her right hand the revolution of the outer circle of the whorl or spindle, and Atropos with her left hand touching and guiding the inner ones, and Lachesis laying hold of either in turn, first with one hand and then with the other.

When Er and the spirits arrived, their duty was to go at once to Lachesis; but first of all there came a prophet who arranged them in order; then he took from the knees of Lachesis lots and samples of lives, and having mounted a high pulpit, spoke as follows: 'Hear the word of Lachesis, the daughter of Necessity. Mortal souls, behold a new cycle of life and mortality. Your genius will not be al-loted to you, but you will choose your genius; and let him who draws the first lot have the first choice, and the life which he chooses shall be his destiny. Virtue is free, and as a man honors or dishonors her he will have more or less of her; the responsibility is with the chooser—God is justified.' When the Interpreter had thus spoken he scattered lots indifferently among them all, and each of them took up the lot which fell near him, all but Er himself (he was not al-lowed), and each as he took his lot perceived the number which he had obtained. Then the Interpreter placed on the ground before them the samples of lives; and there were many more lives than the souls present, and they were of all sorts. There were lives of every animal and of man in every condition. And there were tyrannies among them, some lasting out the tyrant's life, others which broke off in the middle and came to an end in poverty and exile and beggary; and there were lives of famous men, some who were famous for their form and beauty as well as for their strength and success in games, or, again, for their birth and the qualities of their ancestors; and some who were the reverse of famous for the opposite qualities. And of women likewise; there was not, however, any definite char-acter in them, because the soul, when choosing a new life, must of necessity become different. But there was every other quality, and they all mingled with one another, and also with elements of wealth and poverty, and disease and health; and there were mean states also. And here, my dear Glaucon, is the supreme peril of our human state; and therefore the utmost care should be taken. Let each one of us leave every other kind of knowledge and seek and follow one thing only, if peradventure he may be able to learn and may find some one who will make him able to learn and discern between good and evil, and so to choose always and everywhere the better life as he has opportunity. He should consider the bearing of all these things which have been mentioned severally and collectively upon virtue; he should know what the effect of beauty is when combined with poverty or wealth in a particular soul, and what are the good and evil consequences of noble and humble birth, of private and public station, of strength and weakness, of cleverness and dull-ness, and of all the natural and acquired gifts of the soul, and the operation of them when conjoined; he will then look at the nature of the soul, and from the consideration of all these qualities he will be able to determine which is the better and which is the worse; and so he will choose, giving the name of evil to the life which will make his soul more unjust, and good to the life which will make his soul more just; all else he will disregard. For we have seen and know that this is the best choice both in life and after death. A man must take with him into the world below an adamantine faith in truth and right, that there too he may be undazzled by the desire of wealth or the other allurements of evil, lest, coming upon tyrannies and similar villainies, he do irremediable wrongs to others and suffer yet worse himself; but let him know how to choose the mean and avoid the extremes on either side, as far as possible, not only in this life but in all that which is to come. For this is the way of happiness.

And according to the report of the messenger from the other world this was what the prophet said at the time: 'Even for the last comer, if he chooses wisely and will live diligently, there is appointed a happy and not undesirable existence. Let not him who chooses first be careless, and let not the last despair.' And when he had spoken, he who had the first choice came forward and in a moment chose the greatest tyranny; his mind having been darkened by folly and sensuality, he had not thought out the whole matter before he chose, and did not at first sight perceive that he was fated, among other evils, to devour his own children. But when he had time to reflect, and saw what was in the lot, he began to beat his breast and lament over his choice, forgetting the proclamation of the prophet; for, instead of throwing the blame of his misfortune on himself, he accused chance and the gods, and everything rather than himself. Now he was one of those who came from heaven, and in a former life had dwelt in a well-ordered State, but his virtue was a matter of habit only, and he had no philosophy. And it was true of others who were similarly overtaken, that the greater number of them came from heaven and therefore they had never been schooled by trial, whereas the pilgrims who came from earth having themselves suffered and seen others suffer were not in a hurry to choose. And owing to this inexperience of theirs, and also because the lot was a chance, many of the souls exchanged a good destiny for an evil or an evil for a good. For if a man had always on his arrival in this world dedicated himself from the first to sound philosophy, and had been moderately fortunate in the number of the lot, he might, as the messenger reported, be happy here, and also his journey to another life and return to this, instead of being rough and underground, would be smooth and heavenly. Most curious, he said, was the spectacle—sad and laughable and strange; for the choice of the souls was in most cases based on their experience of a previous life. There he saw the soul which had once been Orpheus choosing the life of a swan out of enmity to the race of women, hating to be born of a woman because they had been his murderers; he beheld also the soul of Thamyras choosing the life of a nightingale; birds, on the other hand, like the swan and other musicians, wanting to be men. The soul which obtained the twentieth lot chose the life of a lion, and this was the soul of Ajax the son of Telamon, who would not be a man, remembering the injustice which was done him in the judgment about the arms. The next was Agamemnon, who took the life of an eagle, because, like Ajax, he hated human nature by reason of his sufferings. About the middle came the lot of Atalanta; she, seeing the great fame of an athlete, was unable to resist the temptation: and after her there followed the soul of Epeus the son of Panopeus passing into the nature of a woman cunning in the arts; and far away among the last who chose, the soul of the jester Thersites was putting on the form of a monkey. There came also the soul of Odysseus having yet to make a choice, and his lot happened to be the last of them all. Now the recollection of former toils had disenchanted him of ambition, and he went about for a considerable time in search of the life of a private man who had no cares; he had some difficulty in finding this, which was lying about and had been neglected by everybody else; and when he saw it, he said that he would have done the same had his lot been first instead of last, and that he was delighted to have it. And not only did men pass into animals, but I must also mention that there were animals tame and wild who changed into one another and into corresponding human natures—the good into the gentle and the evil into the savage, in all sorts of combinations.

All the souls had now chosen their lives, and they went in the order of their choice to Lachesis, who sent with them the genius whom they had severally chosen, to be the guardian of their lives and the fulfiller of the choice: this genius led the souls first to Clotho, and drew them within the revolution of the spindle impelled by her hand, thus ratifying the destiny of each; and then, when they were fastened to this, carried them to Atropos, who spun the threads and made them irreversible, whence without turning round they passed beneath the throne of Necessity; and when they had all passed, they marched on in a scorching heat to the plain of Forgetfulness, which was a barren waste destitute of trees and verdure; and then towards evening they encamped by the river of Unmindfulness, whose water no vessel can hold; of this they were all obliged to drink a certain quantity, and those who were not saved by wisdom drank more than was necessary; and each one as he drank forgot all things.

Now after they had gone to rest, about the middle of the night there was a thunderstorm and earthquake, and then in an instant they were driven upwards in all manner of ways to their birth, like stars shooting. He himself was hindered from drinking the water. But in what manner or by what means he returned to the body he could not say; only, in the morning, awaking suddenly, he found himself lying on the pyre.

And thus, Glaucon, the tale has been saved and has not perished, and will save us if we are obedient to the word spoken; and we shall pass safely over the river of Forgetfulness and our soul will not be defiled. Wherefore my counsel is that we hold fast ever to the heavenly way and follow after justice and virtue always, considering that the soul is immortal and able to endure every sort of good and every sort of evil. Thus we shall live dear to one another and to the gods, both while remaining here and when, like conquerors in the games who go round to gather gifts, we receive our reward. And it shall be well with us both in this life and in the pilgrimage of a thousand years which we have been describing.

49

HEINRICH ZIMMER

The Wheel of Rebirth *

THE TRADITIONAL conceptions of Western theism on the nature of God, the creation of the world, and the meaning of time and eternity are as a rule in marked contrast to similar conceptions found in Hindu myth, scripture, and philosophy. Certainly the con-

* From Heinrich Zimmer, *Myths and Symbols in Indian Art and Civilization*, edited by Joseph Campbell, pp. 11-19, Bollingen Series VI (copyright © 1946 by Bollingen Foundation), reprinted by permission of Princeton University Press.

Heinrich Zimmer (1890-1943) was born at Greifswald, Germany. He attended the universities of Munich and Berlin and received his Ph.D. from Berlin. In 1922 he became an Associate Professor of Philology at Heidelberg. He collaborated with Dr. Jung in a psychology seminar at the University of Zurich, and Jung's teachings became the basis of his own theories on Hindu symbolism. In 1939 he fled Germany and went to England where he became a lecturer on Indian philosophy at Balliol College, Oxford. In 1940 he joined the staff of Columbia University where he remained until his death.

trast is a sharp one in the selection that follows. Here the celebrated German scholar and authority on Hindu myths brings
out with remarkable precision the salient details of the Hindu
cosmology.

INDIA'S TREASURE of myths and symbols is immense. In the teeming
texts and multitudinous architectural monuments eloquent details so
abound that, though scholars since the end of the eighteenth century have been editing, translating, and interpreting, it is by no means
an infrequent experience to come across tales hitherto unnoticed or
unknown, images undeciphered, expressive features not yet understood, esthetic and philosophical values uninterpreted. From the second millenium B.C., the Indian traditions have been handed on in
unbroken continuity. . . .

This inheritance is both prodigious and fragmentary, and yet ho-
mogeneous to such a degree that it is possible to present the main
features in a simple, consistent outline. . . . It would not do to
seek to constrain the Oriental conceptions into the delimiting frames
familiar to the West. Their profound strangeness must be permitted
to expose to us the unconscious limitations of our own approach to
the enigmas of existence and of man.

. . . Notions of space and time are commonly taken for granted
within the pale of a given tradition and civilization. . . . the
time and space conceptions of India will at first seem to us of the
West unsound and bizarre. The fundamentals of the Western view
are so close to our eyes that they escape our criticism. . . .

The . . . visions of cosmic cycles—eons following each other
in the endlessness of time, eons contemporaneous in the infinitudes of
space—could hardly be said to enter into the sociological and psychological thinking of the West. In "timeless" India these extensive
diastoles give the life-rhythm of all thought. The wheel of birth and
death, the round of emanation, fruition, dissolution, and re-emanation,
is a commonplace of popular speech as well as a fundamental theme
of philosophy, myth and symbol, religion, politics and art. It is understood as applying not only to the life of the individual, but to
the history of society and the course of the cosmos. . . .

According to the mythologies of Hinduism, each world cycle is sub-
divided into four yugas or world ages. These are comparable to the
four ages of the Greco-Roman tradition, and, like the latter, decline
in moral excellence as the round proceeds. The Classical ages took
their names from the metals, Gold, Silver, Brass, and Iron, the Hindu
from the four throws of the Indian dice game, Krita, Tretā, Dvāpara,

and Kali. In both cases the appellations suggest the relative virtues of the periods, as they succeed each other in a slow, irreversible procession. *Krita* is the perfect participle of the verb kri, to do; it means, literally, "done, made, accomplished, perfect." This is the dice-throw that wins the jackpot, the total gain. According to the Indian conception, the idea of total, or totality, is associated with the number four. "Four square" signifies "totality." Anything complete and self-contained is conceived as possessing all of its four "quarters" (*pāda*). It is established firmly on its "four legs" (*catuh-pāda*). Thus, Krita Yuga, the first of the ages, is the perfect, or "four-quartered," yuga. Dharma, the moral order of the world (which is in virtual existence before the beginning, but then becomes manifest in the spheres, energies, and beings of the world), is during this period firm on its four legs, like a sacred cow; one hundred percent, or four quarters, effective as an all-pervading structural element in the organisms of the universe. During this yuga men and women are born virtuous. They devote their lives to the fulfillment of the duties and tasks divinely ordained by Dharma. The brahmins are established in saintliness. Kings and feudal chiefs act according to the ideals of truly royal conduct. The peasants and townsfolk are devoted to husbandry and the crafts. The lower, servile classes abide lawfully in submission. People even of the lowest extraction observe the holy order of life.

As the life-process of the world-organisms gains momentum, however, order loses ground. Holy Dharma vanishes quarter by quarter, while its converse gains the field. Tretā Yuga is therefore named after the dice-cast of the three. Tretā is the triad or triplet; three of the quarters. . . . During Tretā Yuga, the universal body, as well as the body of human society, is sustained by only three fourths of its total virtue. The modes of life proper to the four castes have begun to lapse into decay. Duties are no longer the spontaneous laws of human action, but have to be learned.

Dvāpara Yuga is the age of the dangerous balance between imperfection and perfection, darkness and light. Its name is derived from *dvi, dvā, dvau,* meaning "two". . . . This is the dice-cast of the duad. During Dvāpara Yuga, only two of the four quarters of Dharma are still effective in the manifest of the world; the others have been irrecoverably lost. The cow of ethical order, instead of firmly standing on four legs, or resting safely on three, now balances on two. Destroyed is the ideal, semidivine status of society. Lost is the knowledge of the revealed hierarchy of values. No longer does the perfection of the spiritual order energize human and universal life. All human beings, brahmins and kings as well as tradespeople and servants, blinded by passion and eager for earthly possessions, grow mean and acquisitive and averse to the fulfilment of such sacred duties as require self-denial. True saintliness, to be achieved only through devotional observances, vows, fasting and ascetic practices, becomes extinct.

Finally, Kali Yuga, the dark age, miserably subsists on twenty-five percent of the full strength of Dharma. Egotistic, devouring, blind and reckless elements now are triumphant and rule the day. *Kali* means the worst of anything; also, "strife, quarrel, dissension, war, battle" . . . In the dice-play, kali is the losing throw. During the Kali Yuga, man and his world are at their very worst. The moral and social degradation is characterized in a passage of the Vishnu Purana:° "When society reaches a stage, where property confers rank, wealth becomes the only source of virtue, passion the sole bond of union between husband and wife, falsehood the source of success in life, sex the only means of enjoyment, and when outer trappings are confused with inner religion . . . "—then we are in the Kali Yuga, the world of today. This age, in the present cycle, is computed as having begun, Friday, February 18, 3102 B.C.

Deficiency of Dharma accounts for the short duration of the Kali Yuga, which is, namely, 432,000 years. The preceding Dvāpara Yuga strong with double the amount of moral substance, is described as surviving twice as long, 864,000. Correspondingly, Tretā Yuga, provided with three of the four quarters of Dharma, endures the length of three Kali units, 1,296,000 years; and Krita Yuga, the period of Dharma "four square," 1,728,000. The grand total is thus 4,320,-000 years, ten times the duration of one Kali Yuga. This complete cycle is called Maha-Yuga, "The Great Yuga."

One thousand mahayugas—4,320,000,000 years of human reckoning—constitute a single day of Brahmā, a single kalpa. In terms of the reckoning of the gods (who are below Brahmā, but above men) this period comprises twelve thousand heavenly years. Such a day begins with creation or evolution, the emanation of a universe out of divine, transcendent, unmanifested Substance, and terminates with dissolution and re-absorption, mergence back into the Absolute. The world spheres together with all the beings contained in them disappear at the end of the day of Brahmā, and during the ensuing night persist only as the latent germ of a necessity for re-manifestation. The night of Brahmā is as long as the day.

° A classic source of Hindu mythology and tradition, dating from the first millennium of our era. Translated by H. H. Wilson, London, 1840. The above text is a condensation of a long descriptive passage in Book IV, Chapter 24.

Every kalpa is subdivided also into fourteen manvantaras, or Manu-intervals, each comprising seventy-one and a fraction mahayugas and terminating with a deluge. The intervals are named from Manu, the Hindu counterpart of Noah, the hero who escapes the flood. The present period is called the Interval of Manu Vaivasvasta, "Manu-the Son of the Radiating One," "Manu the Son of the Sun God Vivasvant." * This is the seventh manvantara of the present day of Brahmā, seven more being due to pass before the day comes to its close. And this present day is termed Varāha Kalpa, "The Kalpa of the Boar"; for it is during this day that Vishnu becomes incarnated in the figure of a boar. This is the first day of the fifty-first year in the lifetime of "our" Brahma. It will end—after seven deluges more—at the next dissolution.

The progress and decline of every kalpa is marked by mythological events that recur similarly, again and again, in magnificent, slowly and relentlessly rotating cycles. The victories of the gods, by which they become established in authority over their respective spheres of the universe; the interludes of defeat, downfall, and devastation, when they are overcome by the titans or antigods—who are their step-brothers, ever alert to overthrow them; the avatars or incarnations of Vishnu, the Supreme Being, when he assumes an animal or human, form, in order to appear in the world as its saviour and deliver the gods: these marvels, singular and breath-taking though they must seem when they come to pass, are but unchanging links in an ever-revolving chain. They are typical moments in an unvariable process, and this process is the continuous history of the world organism. They constitute the standard schedule of a day of Brahmā.

At the dawn of each kalpa, Brahmā re-emerges from a lotus that has stemmed and blossomed out of the navel of Vishnu. During the first Manu-interval of the present Varāha Kalpa, Vishnu des ended as a boar to rescue the freshly created Earth from the bottom of the sea, whither she had been ravished by a demon of the abyss. In the fourth interval or manvantara, he rescued a great elephant king from a sea monster. In the sixth occurred the cosmic event known as the Churning of the Milky Ocean: the gods and titans, contending for world dominion, concluded a temporary truce, in order to extract the Elixir of Immortality from the Universal Sea. During the present mahayuga of the seventh manvantara the events described in the

---

* Each manvantara is named from its special manifestation of the flood hero. Vaivasvata Manu, the progenitor of the present race of mankind, was rescued from the deluge by the fish incarnation of Vishnu. His father was the Sun God Vivasvant.

two great Indian epics are considered to have occurred. Those recounted in the *Rāmāyana* are assigned to the Tretā Age of the present cycle, those in the *Mahābhārata* to the Dvāpara.

It should be observed that the traditional texts allude only very seldom to the fact that the mythological events which they are describing and extolling take place again and again, recurring every four billion three hundred and twenty million years, i.e., once every kalpa. That is because, from the viewpoint of the short-lived human individual such a prodigious circumstance may be temporarily disregarded. But it cannot be totally and finally dismissed; for the short-lived individual, in the round of his transmigrations, remains involved, somehow, somewhere, under one mask or another, throughout the whole course of the protracted span. In one of the Puranic °account of the deeds of Vishnu in his Boar Incarnation or Avatār, occurs a casual reference to the cyclical ° recurrence of the great moments of myth. The Boar, carrying on his arm the goddess Earth whom he is in the act of rescuing from the depths of the sea, passingly remarks to her:

"Every time I carry you this way . . ."

For the Western mind, which believes in single, epoch-making, historical events (such as for instance, the coming of Christ, or the emergence of certain decisive sets of ideals, or the long development of invention during the course of man's mastery of nature) this casual comment of the ageless god has a gently minimizing, annihilating effect. It vetoes conceptions of value that are intrinsic to our estimation of man, his life, his destiny and task.

From the human standpoint the lifetime of a Brahmā seems to be very lengthy; nevertheless it is limited. It endures for only one hundred Brahmā years of Brahmā days and nights, and concludes with a great, or universal, dissolution. Then vanish not only the visible spheres of the three worlds (earth, heaven and the space between), but all spheres of being whatsoever, even those of the highest worlds. All become resolved into the divine, primeval Substance. A state of total re-absorption then prevails for another Brahmā century, after which the entire cycle of 311,040,000,000,000 human years begins anew.

° The Purānas are sacred books of mythological and epic lore supposed to have been compiled by the legendary sage and poet Vyāsa. There are eighteen Purānas (*purāna*, "ancient, legendary") and associated with each a number of Secondary Purānas. Among the latter are reckoned the great epics, *Rāmāyana* and *Mahābhārata*.

50

MEISTER ECKHART

The Beatific Vision *

No ACCOUNT OF man's last end would be complete without some
sketch, however brief, of the notion of the Beatific Vision. For
such a transcendent and ineffable notion it is only fitting to hear
again from Meister Eckhart.

Briefly, what Eckhart tells us in the selection that follows is that
by the grace of God the soul of man is raised to a supernatural
state in which it will know the divine essence through the perfected active intellect. Such knowledge constitutes the Beatific
Vision and follows upon the union of the soul with God. The life
of the soul in this union is one of happiness, for God's life is one
of happiness in the exercise of His active intellect, and the soul now
shares in the life and the activity of God.

KING DAVID SAID: "Lord in thy light shall we see light." Doctors debate as to the medium in which we shall see God. The common doctrine is that it will be in the light of glory. But this solution appears
to me to be unsound and untenable. From time to time I have explained that man has within him a light called the active intellect:
this is the light in which man will see God in bliss, so they seek to
prove. Now man according to his creaturely nature is in great imperfection and is unable by nature to discern God otherwise than as
creatures do, by images and forms, as I have elsewhere demonstrated.
The soul is unable of herself and by her own innate power to transcend this state; that must happen in some supernatural power such
as the light of grace. . . .

St. Paul says: "By God's grace I am that I am." He does not say
that he is "of grace." There is a difference between being by grace
and being grace itself. Doctors declare that form gives being to matter. Now there are various definitions of grace current among them.
But I say grace is nothing else than the flowing light proceeding direct from God's nature into the soul: a supernatural form of the soul

---

* From Franz Pfeiffer's edition of the *Works of Meister Eckhart*, translated by
C. de B. Evans (London: John M. Watkins, 1924), pp. 408-13. Reprinted with
the permission of the translator and the publisher.

For a brief biographical sketch of Meister Eckhart, see selection 20 on page 162.

which gives her a supernatural nature. This is what I had in mind when I stated that the soul was unable of herself to transcend her own natural activity; this she can do in the power of grace which endows her with a supernatural nature.

Observe, grace effects nothing by itself. Moreover it exalts the soul above activity. Grace is bestowed in the essence of the soul and is received into her powers; for if the soul is to effect anything in this matter, she must needs have grace by virtue of which to transcend her own activities such as knowing and loving. Whilst the soul is in process of taking this transcendental flight out of herself into the nothingness of herself and her own activity, she is "by grace"; she is grace when she has accomplished this transcendental passage and has overcome herself and now stands in her pure virginity alone, conscious of nothing but of behaving after the manner of God. As God lives, while the soul is still capable of knowing and acting after the manner of her creatureliness and as a child of nature, she has not become grace itself though she may well be by grace. For to be grace itself the soul must be as destitute of activity, inward and outward, as grace is, which knows no activity. St. John says: "To us is given grace for grace," for to become grace by grace is the work of grace. The supreme function of grace is to reduce the soul to what it is itself. Grace robs the soul of her own activity; grace robs the soul of her own nature. In this supernatural flight the soul transcends her natural light which is a creature and comes into immediate touch with God.

Now I would have you understand me. I am going to give an explanation I have never given before. The worthy Dionysius says: "When God exists not for the spirit there exists not for it either the eternal image, its eternal origin." I have said before and say again that God has wrought one act eternally in which act he made the soul in his own [likeness], and out of which act and by means of which act the soul issued forth into her created existence, becoming unlike God and estranged from her own prototype, and in her creation she made God, who was not before the soul was made. At various times I have declared: I am the cause that God is God. God is gotten of the soul, his Godhead of himself; before creatures were, God was not God albeit he was Godhead which he gets not from the soul. Now when God finds a naughted soul whose self and whose activity have been brought to naught by means of grace, God works his eternal work in her above grace, raising her out of her created nature. Here God naughts himself in the soul and then neither God nor soul is left. Be sure that this is God indeed. When the soul is capable of conceiving God's work she is in the state of no longer having any God at all; the soul is then the eternal image as which God has always seen her, his eternal Word. When, therefore St. Dionysius says that God no longer exists for the spirit, he means what I have just explained.

Now it may be asked whether the soul as here seen in the guise of the eternal image is the light meant by David wherein we shall see eternal light?

We answer, no. Not in this light will the soul see the eternal light that shall beatify her; for, says the worthy Dionysius, "Neither will the eternal image exist for the spirit." What he means is that when the spirit has accomplished its transcendental flight, its creaturely nature is brought to naught, whereby it loses God as I have already explained, and then the soul, in the eternal image, breaks through the eternal image into the essential image of the Father. Thus saith the Scriptures: "Everything flows back in the soul into the Father who is the beginning of the eternal Word and of all creatures."

It may be questioned whether this is the light, the Father namely, in which the spirit sees the eternal light?

I answer, no. Now mark my words. God works and has created all things; the Godhead does not work, it knows nothing of creation. In my eternal prototype the soul is God for there God works and my soul has equality with the Father, for my eternal prototype, which is the Son in the Godhead, is in all respects equal with the Father. One scripture says: "Naught is equal with God; to be equal with God, then, the soul must be naught." That interpretation is just. We would say, however: where there is equality there is no unity for *equal* is a privation of unity; and where there is unity there is no equality for equality resides in multiplicity and separation. Where there is equality there cannot be unity. I am not equal to myself. I am the same as myself. Hence the Son in the Godhead, inasmuch as he is Son, is equal with the Father but he is not one with the Father. There is no equality where Father and Son are one; that is, in the unity of the divine essence. In this unity the Father knows no Son nor does the Son know any Father, for there is neither Father nor Son nor Holy Ghost. When the soul enters into the Son, her eternal prototype wherein she is equal with the Father, then, breaking through her eternal prototype, she, with the Son, transcends equality and possesses unity with the three Persons in the unity of the essence. David says: "Lord in thy light shall we see light," that is: in the light of the impartible divine essence shall we see the divine essence and the whole perfection of the divine essence as rivaled in the variety of the Persons and the unity of their nature. . . .

St. John says: "All things live in him." In that the Father contemplates the Son all creatures take living shape in the Son, that being the real life of creatures. But in another passage St. John says· "Blessed are the dead that have died in God."—It seems passing strange that it should be possible to die in him who himself said that he is the life!—But see: the soul, breaking through her eternal prototype, is plunged in the absolute nothingness of her eternal prototype. This is the death of the spirit; for dying is nothing but deprivation of life. When the soul realizes that anything throws her eternal prototype into separation and negation of unity, the spirit puts its own self to death to its eternal prototype, and breaking through its eternal prototype remains in the unity of the divine nature. These are the blessed dead that are dead in God. No one can be buried and beatified in the Godhead who has not died to God, that is, in his eternal prototype, as I have explained.

Our creed says: *Christ rose from the dead:* Christ rose out of God into the Godhead, into the unity of the divine essence. That is to say that Christ's soul and all rational souls, being dead to their exemplar, rise from that divine death to taste the joys above it, namely the riches of the divine nature wherein the spirit is beatified.

Now consider the fact of happiness. God is happy in himself; and all creatures, which God must make happy, will be so in the same happiness that God is happy in, and after the same fashion that he is happy. Be sure that in this unity the spirit transcends every mode, even its own eternal being, and everything created as well as the equality which, in the eternal image, it has with the Father, and together with the Father soars up into the unity of the divine nature where God conceives himself in absolute simplicity. There, in that act, the spirit is no longer creature, it is the same as happiness itself, the nature and substance of the Godhead, the beatitude of its own self and of all creatures. Further, I hold that if God did what he is impotent to do, granted the soul while still a creature, the knowledge and enjoyment of actual beatitude, then, were the soul to be and to remain happy, it were impossible for God to remain God. Anyone in heaven knowing the saints according to their happiness, would not have anything to say of any saint but only of God; for happiness is God and all those who are happy are, in the act of happiness, God and the divine nature and substance of God. St. Paul says: "He who being naught, thinketh himself aught, deceiveth himself." In the act of happiness he is brought to naught and no creaturehood exists for him. As the worthy Dionysius says: "Lord lead me to where thou art a nothingness," meaning: lead me, Lord, to where thou transcendest every created intellect; for as St. Paul declares: "God dwells in a light that no man can approach unto"; that is: God is not to be discerned in any created light whatever.

St. Dionysius says: "God is nothing," and this is also implied by St. Augustine when he says: "God is everything," meaning: nothing is God's. So that by saying "God is nothing," Dionysius signifies that there is no thing in his presence. It follows that the spirit must advance beyond things and thingliness, shape and shapenness, existence and existences; then will dawn in it the actuality of happiness which is the essential possession of the actual intellect.

I have sometimes said that man sees God in this life in the same perfection and is happy in the same perfect fashion as in the life to come. Many people are astonished at this. Let us try therefore to understand what it means. Real intellect emanates from the eternal truth as intelligence and contains in itself intelligibly all that God contains. This noble divinity, the active intellect, conceives itself in itself after the manner of God in its emanation, and in its essential content it is downright God; but it is creature according to the motion of its nature. This intellect is to the full as noble in us now as in the after life.

Now the question may be asked: How then does this life differ from the life to come?

I answer that, this intellect which is happy in exactly the same way as God is, is at present latent in us. In this life we know God only according to potentiality. In the after life, when we are quit of body, our potentiality will be all transfigured into the act of happiness which belongs to the active intellect. This transfiguration will render the fact of happiness no more perfect than it is now; for active intellect has no accidents nor any capacity to receive more than it contains innately. It follows that when we are beatified we shall be completely deprived of potentiality and shall conceive happiness only actually, after the manner of the divine nature. As David says: "Lord in thy light shall we see light": with the divine nature we shall conceive the perfection of the divine nature, which alone is our entire felicity, here in grace and there in perfect happiness.

51

Nirvana *

THE IDEA of Nirvana has been variously interpreted, and there is still no complete agreement on its exact nature. Different Buddhist scriptures seem to yield different meanings and interpretations. According to the Hinâyana texts, Nirvana means primarily an extinction of the illusions rising from the self and a freeing of the individual from all selfish desires and passions. The Mahayâna texts emphasize Nirvana more as the attainment of truth and enlightenment. Whether this state of enlightenment entails the extinction of personality is a moot problem and none of the writings of Buddha seem to yield a definitive answer. The selection that follows is from the Lankavatara Scripture of Mahayâna Buddhism. Here we are told very specifically what Nirvana is not, of the errors of the philosophers in this respect and particularly of the error of all dualistic conceptions of Nirvana. The conclusion is more a method for attaining the highest enlightenment than a description of such a state.

THEN SAID MAHAMATI to the Blessed One: Pray tell us about Nirvana?

The Blessed One replied: the term, Nirvana, is used with many different meanings, by different people, but these people may be divided into four groups: There are people who are suffering, or who are afraid of suffering, and who think of Nirvana; there are the philosophers who try to discriminate Nirvana; there are the class of disciples who think of Nirvana in relation to themselves; and finally there is the Nirvana of the Buddhas.

Those who are suffering or who fear suffering, think of Nirvana as an escape and a recompense. They imagine that Nirvana consists in the future annihilation of the senses and the sense-minds; they are not aware that Universal Mind and Nirvana are One, and that this life-and-death world and Nirvana are not to be separated. These ignorant ones, instead of meditating on the imagelessness of Nirvana, talk of different ways of emancipation. Being ignorant of, or not understanding, the teachings of the Tathagatas,** they cling to the

---

* From the *Lankavatara Scripture* in the book *A Buddhist Bible* by Dwight Goddard. Copyright, 1938, by E. P. Dutton and Co., Inc., pp. 351-56. Author unknown.

** ["Buddhas," or "Enlightened Ones." See *Ibid.*, pp. 343-351.—*Ed.*]

notion of Nirvana that is outside what is seen of the mind and, thus, go on rolling themselves along with the wheel of life and death.

As to the Nirvanas discriminated by the philosophers: there really are none. Some philosophers conceive Nirvana to be found where the mind-system no more operates owing to the cessation of the elements that make up personality and its world; or is found where there is utter indifference to the objective world and its impermanency. Some conceive Nirvana to be a state where there is no recollection of the past or present, just as when a lamp is extinguished, or when a seed is burnt, or when a fire goes out; because then there is the cessation of all the substrata, which is explained by the philosophers as the non-rising of discrimination. But this is not Nirvana, because Nirvana does not consist in simple annihilation and vacuity.

Again, some philosophers explain deliverance as though it was the mere stopping of discrimination, as when the wind stops blowing, or as when one by self-effort gets rid of the dualistic view of knower and known, or gets rid of the notions of permanency and impermanency; or gets rid of the notions of good and evil; or overcomes passion by means of knowledge—to them Nirvana is deliverance. Some, seeing in "form" the bearer of pain are alarmed by the notion of "form" and look for happiness in a world of "no-form." Some conceive that in consideration of individuality and generality recognisable in all things inner and outer, that there is no destruction and that all beings maintain their being for ever and, in this eternality, see Nirvana. Others see the eternality of things in the conception of Nirvana as the absorption of the finite-soul in Supreme Atman; or who see all things as a manifestation of the vital-force of some Supreme Spirit to which all return; and some, who are especially silly, declare that there are two primary things, a primary substance and a primary soul, that react differently upon each other and thus produce all things from the transformations of qualities; some think that the world is born of action and interaction and that no other cause is necessary; others think that Ishvara ° is the free creator of all things; clinging to these foolish notions, there is no awakening, and they consider Nirvana to consist in the fact that there is no awakening.

Some imagine that Nirvana is where self-nature exists in its own right, unhampered by other self-natures, as the variegated feathers of a peacock, or various precious crystals, or the pointedness of a thorn. Some conceive being to be Nirvana, some non-being, while others conceive that all things and Nirvana are not to be distinguished from one another. Some, thinking that time is the creator and that as

° ["Lord," "Creator," "personal God."—*Ed.*]

the rise of the world depends on time, they conceive that Nirvana consists in the recognition of time as Nirvana. Some think that there will be Nirvana when the "twenty five" truths are generally accepted, or when the king observes the six virtues, and some religionists think that Nirvana is the attainment of paradise.

These views severally advanced by the philosophers with their various reasonings are not in accord with logic nor are they acceptable to the wise. They all conceive Nirvana dualistically and in some causal connection; by these discriminations philosophers imagine Nirvana, but where there is no rising and no disappearing, how can there be discrimination? Each philosopher relying on his own textbook from which he draws his understanding, sins against the truth, because truth is not where he imagines it to be. The only result is that it sets his mind to wandering about and becoming more confused as Nirvana is not to be found by mental searching, and the more his mind becomes confused the more he confuses other people.

As to the notion of Nirvana as held by disciples and masters who still cling to the notion of an ego-self, and who try to find it by going off by themselves into solitude: their notion of Nirvana is an eternity of bliss like the bliss of the Samadhis *—for themselves. They recognize that the world is only a manifestation of mind and that all discriminations are of the mind, and so they forsake social relations and practise various spiritual disciplines and in solitude seek self-realisation of Noble Wisdom by self-effort. They follow the stages to the sixth ** and attain the bliss of the Samadhis, but as they are still clinging to egoism they do not attain the "turning-about" at the deepest seat of consciousness and, therefore, they are not free from the thinking-mind and the accumulation of its habit-energy. Clinging to the bliss of the Samadhis, they pass to their Nirvana, but it is not the Nirvana of the Tathagatas. They are of those who have "entered the stream"; they must return to this world of life and death.

Then said Mahamati to the Blessed One: When the Bodhisattvas † yield up their stock of merit for the emancipation of all beings, they become spiritually one with all animate life; they themselves may be purified, but in others there yet remain unexhausted evil and unmatured karma.†† Pray tell us, Blessed One, how the Bodhisattvas are given assurance of Nirvana? and what is the Nirvana of the Bodhisattvas?

* [Those who achieve spiritual ecstasy by meditation.—Ed.]
** [An early state of Nirvana.—Ed.]
† [One whose essence is wisdom, a saint or future buddha.— Ed.]
†† [Law of retribution.— Ed.]

The Blessed One replied: Mahamati, this assurance is not an assurance of numbers nor logic; it is not the mind that is to be assured but the heart. The Bodhisattva's assurance comes with the unfolding insight that follows passion hindrances cleared away, knowledge hindrance purified, and egolessness clearly perceived and patiently accepted. As the mortal-mind ceases to discriminate, there is no more thirst for life, no more sex-lust, no more thirst for learning, no more thirst for eternal life; with the disappearance of these fourfold thirsts, there is no more accumulation of habit-energy; with no more accumulation of habit-energy the defilements on the face of Universal Mind clear away, and the Bodhisattva attains self-realisation of Noble Wisdom that is the heart's assurance of Nirvana.

There are Bodhisattvas here and in other Buddha-lands, who are sincerely devoted to the Bodhisattva's mission and yet who cannot wholly forget the bliss of the Samadhis and the peace of Nirvana—for themselves. The teaching of Nirvana in which there is no substrate left behind, is revealed according to a hidden meaning for the sake of these disciples who still cling to thoughts of Nirvana for themselves, that they may be inspired to exert themselves in the Bodhisattva's mission of emancipation for all beings. The Transformation-Buddhas ° teach a doctrine of Nirvana to meet conditions as they find them, and to give encouragement to the timid and selfish. In order to turn their thoughts away from themselves and to encourage them to a deeper compassion and more earnest zeal for others, they are given assurance as to the future by the sustaining power of the Buddhas of Transformation, but not by the Dharmata-Buddha.°°

The Dharma † which establishes the Truth of Noble Wisdom belongs to the realm of the Dharmata-Buddha. To the Bodhisattvas of the seventh and eighth stages, †† Transcendental Intelligence is revealed by the Dharmata-Buddha and the Path is pointed out to them which they are to follow. In the perfect self-realisation of Noble Wisdom that follows the inconceivable transformation death of the Bodhisattva's individualised will-control, he no longer lives unto himself, but the life that he lives thereafter is the Tathagata's universalised life as manifested in its transformations. In this perfect self-

---

° [Or Nirvana-Buddha. It "symbolizes the principles of differentiation and integration . . . it removes all obstacles, it harmonises all differences, it brings into perfect Oneness the discordant many." *Ibid.*, p. 349.—*Ed.*]

°° [Dharmata-Buddha "is Buddhahood in its self-nature of Perfect oneness in whom absolute Tranquillity prevails. . . ." *Ibid.*, p. 350.—*Ed.*]

† [The religion practised by the Buddhas.—*Ed.*]

†† [Stages of *Far-Going and No-recession, Ibid.*, pp. 339-342. These stages represent the transition from the stage of perfect tranquillity of mind to the attainment of Transcendental Intelligence and the recognition of life as a passing dream.—*Ed.*]

realisation of Noble Wisdom the Bodhisattva realises that for Buddhas there is no Nirvana.

The death of a Buddha, the great Parinirvana,* is neither destruction nor death, else would it be birth and continuation. It if were destruction, it would be an effect-producing deed, which it is not. Neither is it a vanishing nor an abandonment, neither is it attainment, nor is it of no attainment; neither is it of one significance nor of no significance, for there is no Nirvana for the Buddhas.

The Tathagata's Nirvana is where it is recognized that there is nothing but what is seen of the mind itself; is where, recognising the nature of the self-mind, one no longer cherishes the dualisms of discrimination; is where there is no more thirst nor grasping; is where there is no more attachment to external things. Nirvana is where the thinking-mind with all its discriminations, attachments, aversions and egoism is forever put away; is where logical measures, as they are seen to be inert, are no longer seized upon; is where even the notion of truth is treated with indifference because of its causing bewilderment; is where, getting rid of the four propositions, there is insight into the abode of Reality. Nirvana is where the twofold passions have subsided and the twofold egolessness is patiently accepted; is where, by the attainment of the "turning-about" in the deepest seat of consciousness, self-realization of Noble Wisdom is fully entered into,—that is the Nirvana of the Tathagatas.

Nirvana is where the Bodhisattva stages are passed one after another; is where the sustaining power of the Buddhas upholds the Bodhisattvas in the bliss of the Samadhis; is where compassion for others transcends all thoughts of self; is where the Tathagata stage is finally realized.

Nirvana is the realm of Dharmata-Buddha; it is where the manifestation of Noble Wisdom that is Buddhahood expresses itself in Perfect Love for all; it is where the manifestation of Perfect Love that is Tathagatahood expresses itself in Noble Wisdom for the enlightenment of all—there, indeed, is Nirvana!

There are two classes of those who may not enter the Nirvana of the Tathagatas: there are those who have abandoned the Bodhisattva ideals, saying, they are not in conformity with the sutras, the codes of morality, nor with emancipation. Then there are the true Bodhisattvas who, on account of their original vows made for the sake of all beings, saying, "So long as they do not attain Nirvana, I will not attain it myself," voluntarily keep themselves out of Nirvana. But no beings are left outside by the will of the Tathagatas; some day each

* [Near-Nirvana.—*Ed.*]

and every one will be influenced by the wisdom and love of the Tathagatas of Transformation to lay up a stock of merit and ascend the stages. But, if they only realized it, they are already in the Tathagata's Nirvana for, in Noble Wisdom, all things are in Nirvana from the beginning.

52

H. EMIL BRUNNER

Progress and the Kingdom of God *

IN OPPOSITION TO an uncritical doctrine of evolution and an exaggeration of the idea of progress, with its effects upon Christianity in its historical and temporal aspects, the author endeavors to show the confusions consequent upon the idea of progress and its contradiction with the idea of the Kingdom of God. The Kingdom of God, the teaching of the gospel, is not to be identified with any rationalistic, optimistic, evolutionary philosophy of history.

. . . THE IDEA OF PROGRESS is not very old. It is the child of eighteenth-century liberalism, rationalism, and optimism. This kind of mentality rests, as I pointed out in a previous lecture, on the idealistic dogma of the intrinsic goodness of man, which itself has a pantheistic background. If man is good, how are we to explain evil? An optimistic answer is possible only with the aid of evolution. Evil, in this view, is the good not yet perfect, but in process of becoming. Evil is a not-yet, therefore, a mere lack of something, not a positive will. This negation of evil will or sin, this evolutionary relativity, is the only way by which optimism can be, or seem to be, reconciled with reality. This compromise is made by virtue of a belief in progress.

What are we to think about progress? We certainly cannot deny it. It is an obvious fact in science, theoretical and applied, and in the

* Reprinted from *The Theology of Crisis* by Emil Brunner; copyright 1929 by Charles Scribner's Sons; renewal copyright © 1957 by H. Emil Brunner, pp. 98-113. Used by permission of the publisher.

H. Emil Brunner (1889–) was born at Winterthur, Switzerland. He studied theology at Zurich and Berlin and later became one of the leaders in the school of Dialectical Theology. He was appointed a Visiting Professor at Princeton Theological Seminary 1938-39. From 1942 to 1944 he served as Rector of the University of Zurich. He now holds the position of Professor of Systematic Theology at the University of Zurich.

general rationalisation of life. But two questions must be raised. First, where is progress possible? and second, what is its value? There is hardly any one who would claim that art has progressed since the time of the Greeks, the era of Gothic architecture, or the century of Michelangelo's sculpture. Likewise it is nonsense to claim that men to-day are better than they were two thousand years ago. The false generalization of the idea of progress rests on two confusions. First, the confusing of the natural basis of personal mind with the personal mind itself. The natural basis of mind-life, be it individual or racial, can of course develop by a natural process. But mental personal life is not a simple continuation of this development. It is no longer a natural, and, therefore, no longer an evolutionary, process. It is a matter of personal decision. This power of decision and its effects cannot be wrought by evolution or development. Only the natural basis of decision is subject to development; not decision itself, but only the level *upon* which, and the mental magnitude *in* which, it takes place, is subject to evolution. There is a difference between the decision of an adult and of a child; between the decision of a genius and of an average man. The amplitude of the decision is different but by no means the character of it. Evolution can never be made responsible for my choice of right or wrong, whether I am a boy, an ordinary man, or a genius. Evolution is a matter of mental quantity, not of mental quality.

The second misunderstanding is closely connected with the first. It is the confusing of personal mind itself with the impersonal product of mind. The products of mind can be stored up, and may be said to accumulate, in the course of time. Accumulation, however, may be predicated only of the products of mind and not of personal mind itself. Now this progressive accumulation saves us from repeating the doing of certain tasks. What others have done, I shall not have to do again; what others have discovered I shall not have to discover. To enter into the labor of others gone before us is an enormous advantage and privilege. But the possibility of it is limited to certain regions of life, and what they are it is not difficult to say. They are the regions on the surface, where mind-life has a natural, even material, character, where quantity plays a larger part than quality, that is, in science, technical work, organization, civilization. But we can hardly speak of progress where creative work must be done; and accumulation is not possible in the centre of personal life, in decision itself. Personal goodness cannot be inherited. Personal goodness, personal faith or devotion, must be one's own act and that at each moment.

This distinction makes possible for us an evaluation of the idea of progress. Its importance is the greater when we are dealing with the periphery of life and the smaller when we are dealing with the centre of personal life. That is why the superficiality of the idea of universal progress becomes most evident in the matter of moral evil. Moral evil, or better, sin, is not as the theory of progress must assume, a not-yet-good: it is a no-more-good. It is not an imperfection but a break; not a not-yet-rational or a not-yet-adjustment but an anti-rational; not a negative but a negation. And sin is not a dark spot somewhere but is the total character of our personal existence, the character of all our personal acts. Now if man evolves, and he certainly does evolve, the process of evolution does not affect the character of sin; it is not an evolving out of sin but within sin.

But someone asks, How do you reconcile this view with the teaching of the gospel, with the idea of the kingdom of God? Let me submit my answer. I hope it is definite enough to show that what I said about evolution not only does not contradict the teaching of the gospel but is the necessary presupposition for the understanding of it. The teaching of the gospel and the theory of progress are irreconcilable opposites. The acknowledgment of sin as the contradiction of the will of God by the will of man, as the irreparable cleavage in the being of man, as the hopeless confusion of the orders of creation, as the impotence of man to make good where he has done wrong . . .; this acknowledgment is the necessary presupposition of the gospel of the coming kingdom of God.

Let us begin with the Old Testament. In it nothing is known of an evolution of man toward the divine end; nothing of the unfolding of a divine germ in man's soul into godlikeness. The Old Testament is dominated by the idea that God, the Lord, the Creator, the sovereign King of the world and over the world, comes down in condescending mercy to his poor helpless sinful creatures in order to help and to save them. Not human evolution but the works of God are the subject matter of the Old Testament; not the development of immanent godlikeness but the incredible election of a wild and little-gifted people, which he does not elect for what they are but because of his own free will. And what did he choose them *for*? He chose Israel to be the object of his own actions, of his revelation, the receiver of his word, of his promises, and the messenger of his redemptive words and deeds to the whole world. God alone is the acting subject in the Bible; not Israel nor men of Israel. He, the Eternal, is the hero of this story. His election and revelation, his mercy and help, are always bestowed of his own free volition and not on account of, but rather in spite of, man's character and condition, his will and his deeds. Divine action is always that of incomprehensible grace; its power is always given to man, coming from beyond him, never from within him, not even from the inmost depths of his being. The movement, as we said before, is God's movement toward man, not man's movement toward God. This is the fundamental difference between the Old Testament and all religious books of the ancient Orient. The great men of God in the old covenant are not *homines religiosi,* like those of other religions; not saints, not mystics who, by their own inner life, find their way to God, who by their unique holiness rise step by step to divine heights. The men of God in the Bible are chosen for no other reason than God's will—and then only to be messengers of his will to the whole world. We do not know anything of their piety, we simply know of the service for which God uses them—in which he often consumes them! Even on this point there is no question of development or evolution; it is a matter not of *e-volutio* but of *in-gressio,* ingression, a breaking into the world of something beyond, something foreign and transcendent. It is not a continuous growth on the horizontal plane of history but a vertical disruption of the historical process by forces interposed from beneath or above; it is the miracle of revelation at the point where man of himself cannot know; it is the miracle of the covenant in which men have nothing to offer except their weakness and sin; the miracle of forgiveness for a sin-burdened people; the miracle of saving promises to a down-trodden and helpless "worm Jacob" crying out of the depths and to a whole world wandering in darkness.

. . . . . .

Truly the Old Testament is just as anti-evolutionary as Greek or modern philosophy and Indian or modern mysticism are evolutionary.

The same holds true of the New Testament; here the line of demarcation is even sharper. The basic theme of the New Testament is the eschatological concept of the Kingdom of God, that, is the expectation of the new creation which is based on faith in the Christ and the assurance that God will soon put an end to the disorder of a world which man cannot set right, for which on the contrary all men are responsible, and which grows worse day by day. God, however, has announced that he will make, yea, has secretly begun in Jesus Christ to make, an end of sin, death, and evil, an end of corruption of all kinds, by a re-creation and a re-constitution of the world. That this idea of the kingdom of God is the direct opposite of the evolutionary idea of it is evident from the fact that a main point in the eschatological hope is the expectation of judgment. That a final judgment will take place before the end and before the advent of the redemptive revolution of all things is a leading idea in all the New Testament writings. Judgment, however, means duality. The New Testament does not expect that things on earth are changing more and more for the good. The opposite is true; the last times shall be the most terrible. No slow progress is expected by which the forces of evil shall be gradually vanquished and the forces of the good gradually become victorious, by which the kingdom of God is continually growing and the kingdom of the world is slowly disappearing. No such evolution is hoped for; indeed, the directly opposite prospect is held out, namely, that the forces of evil must increase until the last day. This is the realism of the New Testament: there is an absence in it of modern illusionism or ideology. New Testament writers are not blinded by the idea of evolution because they know that the real enemy cannot be overcome step by step. . . . The victory is won not on the periphery but in the centre and in totality. They know that neither sin nor death can be overcome step by step. Death and sin are totalities, not attached parts; they are organic, not artifical, units. . . . There is only one contradiction in the universe, not many; though its manifestations are manifold. It is this conception of totality that make it impossible for the writers of the New Testament and for any one who sees this totality to believe in evolution. They do not hope that man will rise higher and higher, that he will become better and better; on the contrary they await the time when it will please God to end this world, to end sin and death, through a new creation. Then he will finally separate that which belongs to him and that which does not belong to him, and he will do so by the resurrection of the dead, by the restoration of the original orders of creation, and by their final perfection. The contrast between this idea and the idea of evolution is sharper and more definite because of the sharp contradiction between the good world of God and the present evil world. It is the contradiction that exists between death and eternal life.

Is the kingdom of God as taught in the New Testament merely eschatological, merely future? I answer: It is exclusively eschatological but it is not merely future. The kingdom of God in its eschatological, transcendent, anti-evolutionary sense is present in Jesus Christ, and therefore it is present in the Christian community or Church through faith in Christ. In Jesus Christ the breaking through into the historical process of the world has begun. In Jesus Christ the other world, which is in opposition to this world, appears. But let us beware of a serious misunderstanding which may even now pervert our insight into New

Testament teaching. The New World in Jesus Christ does not appear directly but indirectly. So far as Jesus belongs to the historical world he is the suffering servant of God, he is the Crucified One. His appearance in the world and the appearance of the Kingdom in the world are therefore as yet an *incognito* for the world. They are hidden from it. They can be seen only with the eyes of faith. The cross is the expression of the absolute contradiction between this world and the other; therefore the final expression of God's judgment on one hand and of God's grace on the other. The kingdom of God is here; yes, in this paradoxical form. One can truly share it, but only in a paradoxical way—through faith, not through sight. Such is also the character of the kingdom of God in the community of the saints, the Church. In what does it consist? In the share the believers have in the heavenly inheritance; so that they, who still belong to the world of sin and death, belong by faith, though not visibly, to the other world, the world to come. . . . They *have*, they *are*, they *live* in, the kingdom. But they live in it through faith, indirectly, not directly, invisibly not visibly, paradoxically not empirically. For empirically they are still under the sway of sin and death because they are still in the flesh. To be in the flesh means to belong empirically to the world of sin and death. To believe means to partake in the victory which Christ has won over sin and death. This is the paradox of their existence. It is all important that we keep before us the difference between the empirical relation to the world of sin and the believer's relation to the kingdom of God. Let us be warned against the confusion of the two. For faith, the real is not the empirical but the invisible world of God. The believer only has access to it.

This does not mean that faith has no effect within the empirical world or within man. On the contrary, it has most spectacular effects. It shows itself in a new life, so different from that which others live that even the pagans cannot help wondering at and admiring it. It becomes evident in the manifold gifts of the spirit. It works upon the empirical world so as to effect great changes in the historical process. But all these changes, however great, do not result in the kingdom of God. They are the reflection of it, but not the kingdom itself. . . . They are not the victory over the world, for the best Christians are sinners and become ill and die; but they are signs and anticipations of a victory won in the realm of the invisible world, a victory that some time will become, but is not now, visible. Therefore one cannot speak of an evolution of the Kingdom of God. One may speak of the extension of the Christian community or Church; one may also say that the influence of faith and the Spirit upon the empirical world is growing in an individual or in a certain group or in a certain time.

But in such expansion or growth there is not the least analogy to evolution. For evolution is continuous: this movement is not. Evolution is growth from within but this is growth from without. Evolution is always immanent; the Kingdom, from the beginning to the end, is transcendent, for faith rests alone on that which God does. Evolution is direct; the growth of one thing means the lessening of some other. But this movement of the Kingdom is indirect; the growth of the wheat is accompananied by the growth of the tares. Therefore the end of this paradoxical development is not a net gain, but a crisis-judgment.

One of the most fatal errors in the history of theology is the identification of the Biblical idea of the Kingdom with the rationalistic evolution and the optimistic theory of progress of the eighteenth century. It was Kant who started this unfortunate business; it was Schleiermacher, and after him Ritschl, who continued it. Under the strong influence of the Ritschlian school through the leadership of Hermann and Harnack, it entered the preaching and teaching of the Church and became the leading idea of modern theology, especially when combined with the social emphasis in Christian ethics. This school grievously confused the Christian faith in the will of God with anti-Christian optimism, and salvation by faith alone with a wholly anti-Biblical moralism and human self-reliance. How was this confusion possible? If I am not mistaken, it was due to a misunderstanding of the phrase in the gospel—the Kingdom of God *coming upon the earth.* In the New Testament this means that the heavenly world is coming down upon the earth, that Death is swallowed up in victory. The movement in the whole Bible is described as earthward, not heavenward. But this movement is from God, not from man; the contrast to the evolutionary process is not in any way minimized by the fact that the kingdom comes upon the earth. It is heaven that comes upon earth; God who comes to men. But modern rationalism gave the word "on earth" an absolutely un-Biblical interpretation when it identified its coming on earth with the evolutionary ethical process in history.

Thus the eschatological teaching of the New Testament was changed into a rationalistic, optimistic, evolutionary philosophy of history. The confusion was, and is, fatal. For the emphasis of the Bible is now completely inverted. In the Bible it is put upon God's doing; in modern pseudo-Christian evolutionism it is put upon man's doing. In the Bible attention is fixed upon what God has done in Christ for men and what God will do for man in the end; but in the modern view attention is fixed upon the process of historical evolution and not upon Christ. Our contemporaries do not believe Christ to be the Son of God and are not interested in an end which lies on the farther side of history.

Biblical Christianity does not deny either evolution or progress or the importance of an ethical and social application of faith. It does distinguish, however, the sphere in which relativity prevails from the sphere of the absolute, in which God both is and works his will. It is not pessimistic; in fact it is the only real and possible optimism. But it denies most vehemently any optimistic outlook upon the historical process as such. History is not the evolution of salvation, as the Hegelian idea has it; history is the evolution of a mankind needing and obtaining salvation through faith in Christ. But, while history is viewed pessimistically as the world of sin and death which must perish, an absolute optimism is to be found in the assurance of salvation, not by gradual betterment through evolution, but by God's will through Christ; an optimism which no modern theologian possesses and which is more and more disappearing where the modern gospel of the so-called kingdom of God is taught. The optimism of Christian faith is that of the fifteenth chapter of the First Epistle to the Corinthians, the certainty that the mortal shall put on immortality, that the eternal world will come, that God himself will be seen face to face, in an inconceivable but real personal presence. It is this hope which made our fathers strong not only in prayer but also in work, which enabled them to do things of which our generation only talks—real things. Our present Christianity abounds in activities but lacks action. The anti-evolutionary optimism of Christian faith is the true basis of a really active Christian life.

53

JACQUES MARITAIN

The Immortality of the Soul *

WITHIN THE TRADITION of Scholasticism and the philosophy of St. Thomas, Maritain first proceeds to show that the soul of man is a spiritual substance and the form of the body. The proof of this follows from the activity of man's intellect, which is demonstrated to be spiritual in nature. In addition, the subsisting principle, the source, from which this spiritual activity and power proceeds must be of a spiritual nature. Hence the soul, as the root or subsisting principle of the intellect, must be spiritual in nature. A corollary of the spiritual nature of the soul is its immortality. For a spiritual soul has no parts and is not subject to corruption. It is the source of all its energies and cannot die. This demonstration is not complete in itself, but implies a whole metaphysical system. However, even without philosophy there exists a kind of instinctive and natural belief in immortality. Finally, there is the life of the soul after death. Here the soul is no longer dependent on the body; its knowledge no longer needs the external senses or the images of imagination and memory. It knows itself in an intuitive manner. Reason cannot tell us much of this life of the soul, nor of the nature of its highest good, but through faith we know that our highest happiness will be the vision of God and a union of love with God through the grace of God.

III. PERSONAL IMMORTALITY

THE EXISTENCE OF THE SOUL

IT IS of this immortality, and of the way in which the Scholastics established its rational certainty, that I should now like to speak.

We must of course realize that we have a soul before we can discuss whether it is immortal. How does St. Thomas Aquinas proceed in this matter?

He observes first that man has an activity, the activity of the intellect, which is in itself immaterial. The activity of the intellect is immaterial because the proportionate or "connatural" object of the

---

* Reprinted with the permission of Charles Scribner's Sons from *The Range of Reason*, pages 54-65, by Jacques Maritain. Copyright 1952 by Jacques Maritain.

For a brief biographical sketch of Jacques Maritain, see selection 15 on page 120.

human intellect is not, like the object of the senses, a particular and limited category of things, or rather a particular and limited category of the qualitative properties of things. The proportionate or "connatural" object of the intellect is the nature of the sense-perceivable things considered in an all-embracing manner, whatever the sense concerned may be. It is not only—as for sight—color or the colored thing (which absorbs and reflects such or such rays of light) nor—as for hearing—sound or the sound source; it is the whole universe and texture of sense-perceivable reality which can be known by the intellect, because the intellect does not stop at qualities, but pierces beyond, and proceeds to look at essence (that which a thing *is*). This very fact is a proof of the spirituality, or complete immateriality of our intellect; for every activity in which matter plays an intrinsic part is limited to a given category of material objects, as is the case for the senses, which perceive only those properties which are able to act upon their physical organs.

There is already, in fact, a certain immateriality in sense-knowledge; knowledge, as such, is an immaterial activity, because when I am in the act of knowing, I become, or am, the very thing that I know, a thing other than myself, insofar as it is other than myself. And how can I be, or become, other than myself, if it is not in a supra-subjective or immaterial manner? Sense-knowledge is a very poor kind of knowledge; insofar as it is knowledge, it is immaterial, but it is an immaterial activity intrinsically conditioned by, and dependent upon, the material functioning of the sense-organs. . . .

But with intellectual knowledge we have to do with an activity which is in itself completely immaterial. The human intellect is able to know whatever participates in being and truth; the whole universe can be inscribed in it; this means that, in order to be known, the object known by the intellect has been stripped of any existential condition of materiality. This rose, which I see, has contours; but Being, of which I am thinking, is more spacious than space. The object of the intellect is universal, for instance that universal or de-individualized object which is apprehended in the idea of man, of animal, of atom; the object of the intellect is a universal which remains what it is while being identified with an infinity of individuals. And this is only possible because things, in order to become objects of the mind, have been entirely separated from their material existence. To this it must be added that the operation of our intellect does not stop at the knowledge of the nature of sense-perceivable things; it goes further; it knows by analogy the spiritual natures; it extends to the realm of merely possible things; its field has infinite magnitude.

Thus, the objects known by the human intellect, taken not as things existing in themselves, but precisely as objects determining the intellect and united with it, are purely immaterial.

Furthermore, just as the condition of the *object* is immaterial, so is the condition of the *act* which bears upon it, and is determined or specified by it. The object of the human intellect is, as such, purely immaterial; the act of the human intellect is also purely immaterial.

And, moreover, if the act of the intellectual power is purely immaterial, that *power* itself is also purely immaterial. In man, this thinking animal, the intellect is a purely spiritual power. Doubtless it depends upon the body, upon the conditions of the brain. Its activity can be disturbed or hindered by a physical disorder, by an outburst of anger, by a drink or a narcotic. But this dependence is an *extrinsic* one. It exists because our intelligence cannot act without the joint activity of the memory and the imagination, of the internal senses and external senses, all of which are organic powers residing in some material organ, in some special part of the body. As for the intellect itself, it is not *intrinsically* dependent upon the body since its activity is immaterial; the human intellect does not reside in any special part of the body. It is not contained by the body, but rather contains it. It uses the brain, since the organs of the internal senses are in the brain; yet the brain is not an organ of the intelligence; there is no part of the organism whose act is intellectual operation. The intellect has no organ.

Finally, since intellectual power is spiritual, or purely immaterial in itself, its *first substantial* root, the subsisting principle from which this power proceeds and which acts through its instrumentality, is also spiritual.

So much for the spirituality of the intellect. Now, thought or the operation of the intellect is an act and emanation of man as a unit; and when I think, it is not only my intellect which thinks: it is *I*, my own self. And my own self is a bodily self; it involves matter; it is not a spiritual or purely immaterial subject. The body is an essential part of man. The intellect is not the whole man.

That is the Scholastic notion of the human soul. The human soul, which is the root principle of the intellectual power, is the first principle of life of the human body, and the substantial form, the *entelechy*, of that body. And the human soul is not only a substantial form or entelechy, as are the souls of plants and animals according to the biological philosophy of Aristotle; the human soul is also a spirit, a spiritual substance able to exist apart from matter, since the human soul is the root principle of a spiritual power, the act of which is intrinsically independent of matter. The human soul is both a soul and a spirit, and it is its very substantiality, subsistence and existence, which are communicated to the whole human substance, in order to make human substance be what it is, and to make it subsist and exist. Each element of the human body is human, and exists as such, by virtue of the immaterial existence of the human soul. Our body, our hands, our eyes exist by virtue of the existence of our soul.

THE SPIRITUALITY OF THE HUMAN SOUL

Thus, the very way in which the Scholastics arrived at the existence of the human soul also established its spirituality. Just as the intellect is spiritual, that is to say, intrinsically independent of matter in its operation and in its nature, so also, and for the same reason, the human soul, the substantial root of the intellect, is spiritual, that is, intrinsically independent of matter in its nature and in its existence; it does not live by the body, the body lives by it. The human soul is a spiritual substance which, by its substantial union with matter, gives existence and countenance to the body.

That is my second point. As we have seen, the Scholastics demonstrated it by a metaphysical analysis of the intellect's operation, carefully distinguished from the operation of the senses. They adduced, of course, much other evidence in support of their demonstration. In their consideration of the intellect, they observed, for instance, that the latter is capable of *perfect reflection*, that is, of coming back entirely upon itself—not in the manner of a sheet of paper, half of which can be folded on the other half, but in a complete manner, so that it can grasp its whole operation and penetrate it by knowledge, and can contain itself and its own principle, the existing self, in its own knowing activity, a perfect reflection or self-containing of which any material agent, extended in space and time is essentially incapable. Here we are confronted with that phenomenon of self-knowledge, of *prise de conscience* or becoming aware of oneself, which is a privilege of the spirit, as Hegel (after St. Augustine) was to emphasize, and which plays so tremendous a part in the history of humanity and the development of its spiritual energies.

THE IMMORTALITY OF THE HUMAN SOUL

The third point follows immediately from the second. The immortality of the human soul is an immediate corollary of its spirituality. A soul which is spiritual in itself, intrinsically independent of matter in its nature and existence, cannot cease existing. A spirit—that is, a "form" which needs nothing other than itself (save the influx of the Prime Cause) to exercise existence—once existing cannot cease existing. A spiritual soul cannot be corrupted, since it possesses no matter; it cannot be disintegrated, since it has no substantial parts; it cannot lose its individual unity, since it is self-subsisting, nor its internal energy, since it contains within itself all the sources of its energies. The human soul cannot die. Once it exists, it cannot disappear; it will necessarily exist forever, endure without end.

Thus, philosophic reason, put to work by a great metaphysician like Thomas Aquinas, is able to prove the immortality of the human soul in a demonstrative manner. Of course, this demonstration implies a vast and articulate network of metaphysical insights, notions and principles (relating to essence and nature, substance, act and potency, matter and form, operation, etc.) the validity of which is necessarily presupposed. We can appreciate fully the strength of the Scholastic demonstration only if we realize the significance and full validity of the metaphysical notions involved. If modern times feel at a loss in the face of metaphysical knowledge, I fancy that it is not metaphysical knowledge which is to blame, but rather modern times and the weakening of reason they have experienced.

Primitive men did not philosophize; but, for all that, they had their own way, an instinctive, non-conceptual way, of believing in the soul's immortality. It was a belief rooted in an obscure experience of the self, and in the natural aspirations of the spirit in us to overcome death. We need not embark on an analysis of this natural and instinctive, non-philosophical belief in immortality. I should like merely to quote a passage from a book by the late scientist Pierre Lecomte du Noüy. Speaking of prehistoric man, he said: "Not only did the Neanderthal Man, who lived in Paleolithic times, bury his dead, but sometimes he buried them in a common ground. An example of this is the Grotte des Enfants near Menton. Because of this respect he had for his dead, we have reached an anatomical knowledge of the Neanderthal Man that is more perfect than that which we have of certain races which have recently become extinct, or which still exist, such as the Tasmanians. This is no longer a question of instinct. We are dealing already with the dawn of human thought, which reveals itself in a kind of revolt against death. And revolt against death implies love for those who have gone as well as the hope that their disappearance is not final. We see these *ideas*, the first perhaps, develop progressively alongside the first artistic feelings. Flat rocks in the shape of dolmens are placed so as to protect the faces and heads of those who are buried. Later, ornaments, weapons, food, and the colors which serve to ..lorn the body, are placed in the tombs. The idea of finality is unbearable. The dead man will awaken, he will be hungry, he will have to defend himself, he will want to adorn himself." . . .

THE CONDITION AND DESTINY OF THE IMMORTAL SOUL

What can philosophy tell us about the natural condition of the immortal soul after the death of its body? That is my fourth and last point. Philosophy can tell us very little indeed on this subject. Let us try to summarize the few indications there are. All the organic and sensuous powers of the human soul remain dormant in a separated soul, for they cannot be brought into play without the body. The separated soul is itself engulfed in a complete sleep with regard to the material world; the external senses and their perceptions have vanished; the images of memory and imagination, the impulses of instinct and passion have vanished. But this sleep is not like the sleep we know, obscure and filled with dreams; it is lucid and intelligent, alive to spiritual realities. For now light shines from within. The intellect and the spiritual powers are awake and active. From the very fact of its separation from the body, the soul now knows itself through itself; its very substance has become transparent to its intellect; it is intellectually penetrated to its innermost depths. The soul knows itself in an intuitive manner; it is dazzled by its own beauty, the beauty of a spiritual substance, and it knows other things through its own substance already known, in the measure in which other things resemble it. It knows God through that image of God which the soul itself is. And in accordance with its state of incorporeal existence, it receives from God, the sun of the spirits, certain ideas and inspirations which directly enlighten it, and help the natural light of the human intellect, of that intellect which is, as Saint Thomas Aquinas phrased it, the lowest in the hierarchy of spirits.

Saint Thomas teaches also that all that is of the intellect and the spirit, and especially the intellectual memory, which is but one with the intellect, keeps alive, in the separated soul, the whole treasure of knowledge acquired during our bodily life. The intellectual knowledge, the intellectual virtues acquired here below subsist in the separated soul. Whereas the images of the sense-memory, which had its seat in the brain disappear, that which has penetrated into the intellectual memory is preserved. Thus, in an intellectual and spiritual manner, the separated soul ever knows those whom it loved. And it loves them spiritually. And it is able to converse with other spirits by opening to them what abides in its inner thoughts and is taken hold of by its free will.

We may thus imagine that, at the moment when it leaves the body, the soul is suddenly immersed into itself as into a shining abyss, where all that was buried within it, all its dead, rise up again in full light, insofar as all this was encompassed in the subconscious or supraconscious depths of the spiritual life of its intellect and will. Then all that is true and good in the soul becomes a blessing for it at the touch of this all-pervading revelatory light; all that is warped and evil becomes a torment for it under the effect of the very same light.

I do not believe that natural reason can go further in its understanding of the natural condition of the separated soul. What would be the life and happiness of souls if their state after death were a purely natural state? Their supreme good would consist in wisdom, untrammeled spiritual life, mutual friendship, and first and foremost in advancing constantly in their natural knowledge and love of God, Whom they would, however, never see face to face. It would be happiness in motion, never absolutely fulfilled—what Leibniz called *un chemin par des plaisirs,* "a road amidst spiritual pleasures."

But if we wish to know more, can we not go beyond philosophy? Philosophy itself will then entrust us to the guidance of a knowledge whose sources are superior to its own. Christians know that man does not live in a state of pure nature. They know that he was created in a state of grace, and that, after the first sin which wounded our race, he has been living in a state of fallen and redeemed nature; they know that he is made for supernatural blessedness. In answer to the question of the separated soul's destiny, the Scholastic doctors spoke not as philosophers, but as theologians whose knowledge rests on the data of Revelation.

Insofar as man participates in the metaphysical privileges of spirit and personality, he has aspirations which transcend human nature and its possibilities, and which consequently may be called transnatural aspirations: the longing for a state in which he would know things completely and without error, in which he would enjoy perfect communion with spirits, in which he would be free without being able to fail or to sin, in which he would inhabit a realm of unfading justice, in which he would have the intuitive knowledge of the First Cause of being.

Such a longing cannot be fulfilled by nature. It can be fulfilled by grace. The immortal soul is involved and engaged in the great drama of the Redemption. If, at the moment of its separation from the body, at the moment when its choice is immutably fixed forever, the immortal soul prefers its own will and self-love to the will and gift of

God, if it prefers misery with pride to the blessing of grace, then it is granted what it has wished for. It has it, and it will never cease wanting and preferring it, for a free choice made in the condition of a *pure* spirit is an eternal choice. If the soul opens itself to the will and gift of God, Whom it loves more than its own existence, then it is granted what it has loved, it enters forever into the joy of the uncreated Being, it sees God face to face and knows Him as it is known by Him, intuitively. Thus, it becomes God by participation, as Saint John of the Cross phrased it, and through grace, it attains that communion in divine life, that blessedness for the sake of which all things have been created. And the degree of its blessedness itself, the degree of its vision, will correspond to the degree of the inner impetus which projects it into God, in other words, to the degree of love to which it has attained in its life on earth. In the last analysis, therefore, we must say with Saint John of the Cross: It is upon our love that we shall be judged. In its state of blessedness the immortal soul will know creation in the Creator, by that kind of knowledge which Saint Augustine called "matutinal" knowledge, because it is produced in the eternal morning of Creative Ideas; the immortal soul will be equal to the angels, and will communicate freely with the whole realm of spirits; it will love God, henceforth clearly seen, with a sovereign necessity; and it will exert free will with regard to all its actions concerning creatures, but its free will shall no longer be liable to failure and sin; the soul will inhabit the realm of unfading justice, that of the three divine Persons and of the blessed spirits; it will grasp and possess the divine Essence which, infinitely clearer and more intelligible than any of our ideas, will illumine the human intellect from within and will itself be the intelligible medium, the actuating form through which it will be known. According to a line of the Psalms which Saint Thomas loved and often quoted: "In Thy light shall we see light."

Such are the teachings of Saint Thomas, both as a philosopher and as a theologian, about the condition and destiny of the human soul. Immortality is not a more or less precarious, successful or unsuccessful survival in other men, or in the ideal waves of the universe. Immortality is a nature-given, inalienable property of the human soul as a spiritual substance. And grace makes eternal life possible to all, to the most destitute as well as to the most gifted. The eternal life of the immortal soul is its transforming union with God and His intimate life, a union which is to be accomplished inchoatively here below, by love and contemplation and, after the body's death, in a definite and perfect manner, by the beatific vision. For eternal life begins here upon earth, and the soul of man lives and breathes where it loves;

and love, in living faith, has strength enough to make the soul of
man experience unity with God—"two natures in a single spirit and
love, *dos naturalezas en un espiritu y amor de Dios."*

I do not believe that a philosopher can discuss the immortality of
the soul without taking into consideration the complementary notions
which religious thought adds to the true and inadequate answers
which reason and philosophy can furnish by themselves.

54

IMMANUEL KANT

Immortality and Happiness *

IN HIS *Critique of Pure Reason* Kant had analyzed the nature of
our knowledge and had reached the extreme conclusion that human
reason inevitably falls into error when it goes beyond the bounds
of experience. Among other things, he held that reason cannot
prove the immortality of the soul or the existence of God. However,
if pure reason fails in these attempts, practical reason, or will, can
validate in other ways these necessary principles of religious
thought. The demands and requirements of ethics can establish
such principles whereas metaphysics must fail. The arguments that
follow endeavor, therefore, to establish the immortality of the soul
and the existence of God as postulates of practical reason. Granting the existence of the moral law and the *summum bonum,* or
perfect happiness, as object of our will, it becomes necessary to
grant the existence of God to maintain the necessary causal relation between the moral law and the *summum bonum,* and the immortality of the soul, in order that man may have an endless existence in which to realize such an end. The consideration of the

* From the *Critique of Practical Reason,* translated by Thomas Kingsmill Abbot,
4th rev. ed. (London: Longmans, Green and Co., 1889), pp. 218-31.

Immanuel Kant (1724-1804) was born at Königsberg in East Prussia. His
parents were of the lower middle class. His mother was strongly religious and a
member of the Pietist sect. Kant was educated at the University of Königsberg
and taught there from 1755 to the end of his active life. He had an extraordinary
knowledge of travel and geography yet never left the city of Königsberg during
his entire lifetime. He was also said to be an extremely punctilious man, so much
so that the people of Königsberg were said to have set their clocks by his daily
appearance for his afternoon walk.

summum bonum next leads Kant to point up the deficiencies of the Epicurean and Stoic conceptions of this notion, and brings him to the conclusion that Christianity alone yields a satisfactory solution to the demands of practical reason and an adequate conception of the relation of the *summum bonum* and the moral life. Finally, he shows how this analysis of the *summum bonum* leads to the basic ideas of religion.

THE IMMORTALITY OF THE SOUL AS A POSTULATE OF PURE PRACTICAL REASON

THE REALIZATION OF the *summum bonum* in the world is the necessary object of a will determinable by the moral law. But in this will the *perfect accordance* of the mind with the moral law is the supreme condition of the *summum bonum*. This then must be possible, as well as its object, since it is contained in the command to promote the latter. Now, the perfect accordance of the will with the moral law is *holiness*, a perfection of which no rational being of the sensible world is capable at any moment of his existence. Since, nevertheless, it is required as practically necessary, it can only be found in a progress *in infinitum* towards that perfect accordance, and on the principles of pure practical reason it is necessary to assume such a practical progress as the real object of our will.

Now, this endless progress is only possible on the supposition of an *endless* duration of the *existence* and personality of the same rational being (which is called the immortality of the soul). The *summum bonum*, then, practically is only possible on the supposition of the immortality of the soul; consequently this immortality, being inseparably connected with the moral law, is a postulate of pure practical reason (by which I mean *a theoretical* proposition, not demonstrable as such, but which is an inseparable result of an unconditional *a priori practical* law).

This principle of the moral destination of our nature, namely, that it is only in an endless progress that we can attain perfect accordance with the moral law, is of the greatest use, not merely for the present purpose of supplementing the impotence of speculative reason, but also with respect to religion. In default of it, either the moral law is quite degraded from its *holiness*, being made out to be *indulgent*, and conformable to our convenience, or else men strain their notions of their vocation and their expectation to an unattainable goal, hoping to acquire complete holiness of will, and so they lose themselves in fantastical *theosophic* dreams, which wholly contradict self-knowledge. In both cases the unceasing *effort* to obey punctually and thoroughly a strict and inflexible command of reason, which yet is not ideal but real, is only hindered. For a rational but finite being, the only thing possible is an endless progress from the lower to higher degrees of moral perfection. The *Infinite Being,* to whom the condition of time is nothing, sees in this to us endless succession a whole of accordance with the moral law; and the holiness which His command inexorably requires, in order to be true to His justice in the share which He assigns to each in the *summum bonum,* is to be found in a single intellectual intuition of the whole existence of rational beings. All that can be expected of the creature in respect of the hope of this participation would be the consciousness of his tried character, by which, from the progress he has hitherto made from the worse to the morally better, and the immutability of purpose which has thus become known to him, he may hope for a further unbroken continuance of the same, however long his existence may last, even beyond this life, and thus he may hope, not indeed here, nor in any imaginable point of his future existence, but only in the endlessness of his duration (which God alone can survey) to be perfectly adequate to his will (without indulgence or excuse, which do not harmonize with justice.)

THE EXISTENCE OF GOD AS A POSTULATE OF PURE PRACTICAL REASON

In the foregoing analysis the moral law led to a practical problem which is prescribed by pure reason alone, without the aid of any sensible motives, namely, that of the necessary completeness of the first and principal element of the *summum bonum,* viz. Morality; and as this can be perfectly solved only in eternity, to the postulate of *immortality.* The same law must also lead us to affirm the possibility of the second element of the *summum bonum,* viz. Happiness proportioned to that morality, and this on grounds as disinterested as before, and solely from impartial reason; that is, it must lead to the supposition of the existence of a cause adequate to this effect; in other words, it must postulate the *existence* of God, as the necessary condition of the possibility of the *summum bonum* (an object of the will which is necessarily connected with the moral legislation of pure reason). We proceed to exhibit this connection in a convincing manner.

Happiness is the condition of a rational being in the world with whom *everything goes according to his wish and will;* it rests, therefore, on the harmony of physical nature with his whole end, and likewise with the essential determining principle of his will. Now the moral law as a law of freedom commands by determining principles, which ought to be quite independent on nature and on its harmony with our faculty of desire (as springs). But the acting rational being in the world is not the cause of the world and of nature itself. There is not the least ground, therefore, in the moral law for a necessary connexion between morality and proportionate happiness in a being that belongs to the world as part of it, and therefore dependent on it, and which for that reason cannot by his will be a cause of this nature, nor by his own power make it thoroughly harmonize, as far as his happiness is concerned, with his practical principles. Nevertheless, in the practical problem of pure reason, i.e., the necessary pursuit of the *summum bonum*, such a connection is postulated as necessary: we ought to endeavor to promote the *summum bonum*, which, therefore, must be possible. Accordingly, the existence of a cause of all nature, distinct from nature itself, and containing the principle of this connection, namely, of the exact harmony of happiness with morality, is also *postulated*. Now, this supreme cause must contain the principle of the harmony of nature, not merely with a law of the will of rational beings, but with the conception of this *law*, in so far as they make it the *supreme determining principle of the will*, and consequently not merely with the form of morals, but with their morality as their motive, that is, with their moral character. Therefore, the *summum bonum* is possible in the world only on the supposition of a Supreme Being having a causality corresponding to moral character. Now a being that is capable of acting on the conception of laws is an *intelligence* (a rational being), and the causality of such a being according to this conception of laws is his *will;* therefore the supreme cause of nature which must be presupposed as a condition of the *summum bonum* is a being which is the cause of nature by *intelligence* and *will*, consequently its author, that is God. It follows that the postulate of the possibility of the *highest derived good* (the best world) is likewise the postulate of the reality of a *highest original good*, that is to say, of the existence of God. Now it was seen to be a duty for us to promote the *summum bonum*; consequently it is not merely allowable, but it is a necessity connected with duty as a requisite, that we should presuppose the possibility of this *summum bonum*; and as this is possible only on condition of the existence of God, it inseparably connects the supposition of this with duty; that is, it is morally necessary to assume the existence of God.

It must be remarked here that this moral necessity is *subjective*, that is, it is a want, and not *objective*, that is itself a duty, for there cannot be a duty to suppose the existence of anything (since this concerns only the theoretical employment of reason). Moreover, it is not meant by this that it is necessary to suppose the existence of God *as a basis of all obligation in general* (for this rests, as has been sufficiently proved, simply on the autonomy of reason itself). What belongs to duty here is only the endeavor to realize and promote the *summum bonum* in the world, the possibility of which can therefore be postulated; and as our reason finds it not conceivable except on the supposition of a supreme intelligence, the admission of this existence is therefore connected with the consciousness of our duty, although the admission itself belongs to the domain of speculative reason. Considered in respect of this alone, as a principle of explanation, it may be called a *hypothesis,* but in reference to the intelligibility of an object given us by the moral law (the *summum bonum*), and consequently of a requirement for practical purposes, it may be called *faith,* that is to say a pure *rational faith,* since pure reason (both in its theoretical and its practical use) is the sole source from which it springs.

From this *deduction* it is now intelligible why the *Greek* schools could never attain the solution of their problem of the practical possibility of the *summum bonum,* because they made the rule of the use which the will of man makes of his freedom the sole and sufficient ground of this possibility, thinking that they had no need for that purpose of the existence of God. No doubt they were so far right that they established the principle of morals of itself independently on this postulate, from the relation of reason only to the will, and consequently made it the *supreme* practical condition of the *summum bonum*; but it was not therefore the the *whole* condition of its possibility. The *Epicureans* had indeed assumed as the supreme principle of morality a wholly false one, namely that of happiness, and had substituted for a law a maximum of arbitrary choice according to every man's inclination; they proceeded, however, *consistently* enough in this, that they degraded their *summum bonum* likewise just in proportion to the meanness of their fundamental principle, and looked for no greater happiness than can be attained by human prudence (including temperance and moderation of the inclinations), and this, as we know, would be scanty enough and would be very different according to circumstances; not to mention the exceptions that their maxims must perpetually admit and which make them incapable of being laws. The *Stoics,* on the contrary, had chosen their supreme practical principle quite rightly, making virtue the condition of the *summum bonum*; but when they represented the degree of virtue required by its pure law as fully attainable in this life, they not only strained the moral powers of the *man* whom they called the *wise* beyond all the limits of his nature, and assumed a thing that contradicts all our knowledge of men, but also and principally they would not allow the second *element* of the *summum bonum,* namely, happiness, to be properly a special object of human desire, but made their *wise man,* like a divinity in his consciousness of the excellence of his person, wholly independent of nature (as regards his own contentment); they exposed him indeed to the evils of life, but made him not subject to them (at the same time representing him also as free from moral evil). They thus, in fact, left out the second element of the *summum bonum,* namely, personal happiness, placing it solely in action and satisfaction with one's own personal worth, thus including it in the consciousness of being morally minded, in which they might have been sufficiently refuted by the voice of their own nature.

The doctrine of Christianity, even if we do not yet consider it as a religious doctrine, gives, touching this point, a conception of the *summum bonum* (the kingdom of God), which alone satisfies the strictest demand of practical reason. The moral law is holy (unyielding) and demands holiness of morals, although all the moral perfection to which man can attain is still only virtue, that is, a rightful disposition arising from *respect* for the law, implying consciousness of a constant propensity to transgression, or at least a want of purity, that is, a mixture of many spurious (not moral) motives of obedience to the law, consequently a self-esteem combined with humility. In respect, then, of the holiness which the Christian law requires, this leaves the creature nothing but a progress *in infinitum,* but for that very reason it justifies him in hoping for an endless duration of his existence. The *worth* of a character *perfectly* accordant with the moral law is infinite, since the only restriction on all possible happiness in the judgment of a wise and all-powerful distributor of it is the absence of conformity of rational beings to their duty. But the moral law of itself does not *promise* any happiness, for according to our conceptions of an order of nature in general, this is not necessarily connected with obedience to the law. Now Christian morality supplies this defect (of the second indispensable element of the *summum bonum*) by representing the world, in which rational beings devote themselves with all their soul to the moral law, as a *kingdom of God,* in which nature and morality are brought into a harmony foreign to each of itself, by a holy Author who makes the derived *summum bonum* possible. *Holiness* of life is prescribed to them as a rule even in this life, while the welfare proportioned to it, namely, *bliss,* is represented as attainable only in an eternity; because the *former* must always be the pattern of their conduct in every state, and progress towards it is already possible and necessary in this life; while the *latter,* under the name of happiness, cannot be attained at all in this world (so far as our own power is concerned), and therefore is made simply an object of hope. Nevertheless, the Christian principle of morality itself is not theological (so as to be heteronomy), but is autonomy of pure practical reason, since it does not make the knowledge of God and His will the foundation of these laws, but only of the attainment of the *summum bonum,* on condition of following these laws, and it does not even place the proper *spring* of this obedience in the desired results, but solely in the conception of duty, as that of which the faithful observance alone constitutes the worthiness to obtain those happy consequences.

In this manner the moral laws lead through the conception of the *summum bonum* as the object and final end of pure practical reason to *religion,* that is, to the *recognition of all duties as divine commands, not as sanctions, that is to say, arbitrary ordinances of a foreign will and contingent in themselves,* but as essential *laws* of every free will in itself, which, nevertheless, must be regarded as commands of the Supreme Being, because it is only from a morally perfect (holy and good) and at the same time all-powerful will, and consequently only through harmony with this will, that we can hope to attain the *summum bonum* which the moral law makes it our duty to take as the object of our endeavors. Here again, then, all remains disinterested and founded merely on duty; neither fear nor hope being made the fundamental springs, which if taken as principles would destroy the whole moral worth of actions. The moral law commands me to make the highest possible good in a world the ultimate object of all my conduct. But I cannot hope to effect this otherwise than by the harmony of my will with that of a holy and good Author of the world; and although the conception of the *summum bonum* as a whole, in which the greatest happiness is conceived as combined in the most exact proportion with the highest degree of moral perfection (possible in creatures), includes *my own happiness,* yet it is not this that is the determining principle of the will which is enjoined to promote the *summum bonum,* but the moral law, which, on the contrary, limits by strict conditions my unbounded desire of happiness.

Hence also morality is not properly the doctrine how we should *make* ourselves happy, but how we should become *worthy* of happiness. It is only when religion is added that there also comes in the hope of participating some day in happiness in proportion as we have endeavored to be not unworthy of it.

A man is *worthy* to possess a thing or a state when his possession of it is in harmony with the *summum bonum*. We can now easily see that all worthiness depends on moral conduct, since in the conception of the *summum bonum* this constitutes the condition of the rest (which belongs to one's state), namely, the participation of happiness. Now it follows from this that *morality* should never be treated as a *doctrine of happiness*, that is, an instruction how to become happy; for it has to do simply with the rational condition (*conditio sine qua non*) of happiness, not with the means of attaining it. But when morality has been completely expounded (which merely imposes duties instead of providing rules for selfish desires), then first, after the moral desire to promote the *summum bonum* (to bring the kingdom of God to us) has been awakened, a desire founded on a law, and which could not previously arise in any selfish mind, and when for the behoof of this desire the step to religion has been taken, then this ethical doctrine may be also called a doctrine of happiness because the *hope* of happiness first begins with religion only.

We can also see from this that, when we ask what is *God's ultimate end* in creating the world, we must not name the *happiness* of the rational beings in it, but the *summum bonum* which adds a further condition to that wish of such beings, namely, the condition of being worthy of happiness, that is, the *morality* of these same rational beings, a condition which alone contains the rule by which only they can hope to share in the former at the hand of a *wise* Author. For as *wisdom* theoretically considered signifies *the knowledge of the summum bonum*, and practically *the accordance of the will with the summum bonum*, we cannot attribute to a supreme independent wisdom an end based merely on *goodness*. For we cannot conceive the action of this goodness (in respect of the happiness of rational beings) as suitable to the highest original good, except under the restrictive conditions of harmony with the holiness of His will. Therefore those who placed the end of creation in the glory of God (provided that this is not conceived anthropomorphically as a desire to be praised) have perhaps hit upon the best expression. For nothing glorifies God more than that which is the most estimable thing in the world, respect for His command, the observance of the holy duty that His law imposes on us, when there is added thereto His glorious plan of crowning such a beautiful order of things with corresponding happiness. If the latter (to speak humanly) makes Him worthy of love, by the *former* He is an object of adoration. Even men can never acquire respect by benevolence alone, though they may gain love, so that the greatest beneficence only procures them honor when it is regulated by worthiness.

That in the order of ends, man (and with him every rational being) is *an end in himself*, that is, that he can never be used merely as a means by any (not even by God) without being at the same time an end also himself, that therefore *humanity* in our person must be *holy* to ourselves, this follows now of itself because he is the *subject of the moral law,* in other words, of that which is holy in itself, and on account of which and in agreement with which alone can anything be termed holy. For this moral law is founded on the autonomy of his will, as a free will which by its universal laws must necessarily be able to agree with that to which it is to submit itself.

55

NICOLAI BERDYAEV

Death and Immortality *

THE TRADITIONAL metaphysical accounts of immortality are criticized by Berdyaev for overlooking the significance of death. The philosophy of immortality does not show us how to die. Death shows us that we belong to eternal life as well as to the temporal; it holds out both horror as well as hope for man. Death is also the greatest evil; it is the denial of eternity and the result of sin, a return to non-being. To rebel against death is to rebel against God. To conquer death and obtain eternity is the teaching of Christianity. Death also has an aesthetic aspect: it is both hideous and beautiful—it leads to corruption and purification.

Returning to the philosophical idea of immortality, Berdyaev contends that it ignores the fact of death and denies the tragedy of it. German idealism, for example, affirms the immortality of the impersonal spirit, but not of the person. Materialism and positivism are superficial in their view of death. The development of the idea

* From *The Destiny of Man,* translated by Natalie Duddington (London: Geoffrey Bles: The Centenary Press, 1937), pp. 249-65. Reprinted with the permission of the publisher.

For a brief biographical sketch of Nicolai Berdyaev, see selection 36 on page 326.

of immortality is revealed in Greek rather than Jewish thought. In the Christian conception of the resurrection we have a true recognition of the tragedy of death and the means of conquering it. This doctrine also links the destiny of man with world destiny, for there is both a personal and a cosmic Apocalypse. The paradox of time and eternity is noted, and the author then proceeds to a brief consideration of eschatological ethics, for death, he argues, is central to any adequate system of ethics. In conclusion, he comments upon our attitude toward death and notes that the final test for a system of ethics is whether or not it can free us from the temporal and "eternal" torments of hell.

ORDINARY SYSTEMS of philosophical ethics do not deal with the problems of eschatology. If they treat of immortality, they do so without going deep into the question of death but discuss it chiefly in connection with man's moral responsibility, rewards and punishments, or, at best, with the need of satisfying his longing for infinity. The conception of immortality has been defended on the ground of naturalistic metaphysics and the idea of the soul as a substance. It left completely untouched the problem of death, so fundamental for the religious and especially for the Christian consciousness. Death is a problem not only for metaphysics but also for ontological ethics. Thinkers like Kierkegaard and Heidegger recognize this. It also acquires a central significance in Freud. It is the problem of death, inseverably connected with that of time, that has a primary significance; the problem of immortality is secondary, and as a rule it has been wrongly formulated. The very word "immortality" is inexact and implies a rejection of the mysterious fact of death. The question of the immortality of the soul forms part of a metaphysics that is utterly out of date. Death is the most profound and significant fact of life, raising the least of mortals above the mean commonplaces of life. The fact of death alone gives true depth to the question as to the meaning of life. Life in this world has meaning just because there is death; if there were no death in our world, life would be meaningless. The meaning is bound up with the end. If there were no end, i.e., if life in our world continued for ever, there would be no meaning in it. Meaning lies beyond the confines of this limited world, and the discovery of meaning presupposes an end here. It is remarkable that although men rightly feel the horror of death and rightly regard it as the supreme evil, they are bound to connect with it the final discovery of meaning. Death—the supreme horror and evil—proves to be the only way out of the "bad time" into eternity; immortal and eternal life prove to be attainable only through death.

Man's last hope is connected with death, which manifests so clearly the power of evil in the world. This is the greatest paradox of death. According to the Christian religion death is the result of sin and is the last enemy, the supreme evil which must be conquered. And at the same time in our sinful world death is a blessing and a value. It inspires us with terror not merely because it is an evil, but because the depth and the greatness of it shatter our everyday world and exceed the powers accumulated by us in this life to meet this world's requirements. Spiritual enlightenment and an extraordinary intensity of spiritual life are needed to give us a right attitude towards death. Plato was right in teaching that philosophy was the practice of death. The only trouble is that philosophy as such does not know how one ought to die and how to conquer death. The philosophic doctrine of immortality does not show the way.

. . . . .

Death has a positive significance, but at the same time it is the most terrible and the only evil. Every kind of evil in the last resort means death. Murder, hatred, malice, depravity, envy, vengeance are death and seeds of death. Death is at the bottom of every evil passion. Pride, greed, ambition are deadly in their results. There is no other evil in the world except death and killing. Death is the evil result of sin. A sinless life would be immortal and eternal. Death is a denial of eternity and therein lies its ontological evil, its hostility to existence, its striving to reduce creation to non-being. Death resists God's creation of the world and is a return to the original non-being. Death wants to free the creature by bringing it back to primeval freedom that preceded the creation of the world. There is but one way out for the creature which in its sin resists God's conception of it—death. Death is a negative testimony to God's power and to the Divine meaning manifested in the meaningless world. It might be said that the world would carry out its godless plan of an endless (but not eternal) life if there were no God; but since God exists, that plan is not realizable and ends in death. The Son of God, the Redeemer and Saviour, absolutely sinless and holy, had to accept death, and thereby He sanctified death. Hence the double attitude of Christianity to death. Christ has destroyed death by His death. His voluntary death, due to the evil of the world, is a blessing and a supreme value. In worshipping the cross we worship death which gives us freedom and victory. In order to rise again we must die. Through the cross death is transfigured and leads us to resurrection and to life. The

whole of this world must be made to pass through death and cruci-
fixion, else it cannot attain resurrection and eternity.

If death is accepted as a part of the mystery of life, it is not final
and has not the last word. Rebellion against death in our world is
rebellion against God. But at the same time we must wage a heroic
struggle against death, conquer it as the last evil and pluck out its
sting. The work of Christ in the world is in the first instance victory
over death and preparation for resurrection and eternity. The good
is life, power, fullness and eternity of life. Death proves to be the
greatest paradox in the world, which cannot be understood rationally.
Death is folly that has become commonplace. The consciousness that
death is an ordinary everyday occurrence has dulled our sense of its
being irrational and paradoxical. The last achievement of the rationalized herd-mind is to try to forget about death altogether, to conceal
it, to bury the dead as unobtrusively as possible. It is the very opposite of the spirit expressed in the Christian prayer "ever to remember death." In this respect modern civilized people are incomparably
inferior to the ancient Egyptians.

The paradox of death takes an aesthetic as well as a moral form.
Death is hideous, the acme of hideousness, it is dissolution, the loss
of all image and form, the triumph of the lower elements of the
material world. But at the same time death is beautiful, it ennobles
the least of mortals and raises him to the level of the greatest, it
overcomes the ugliness of the mean and the commonplace. There is
a moment when the face of the dead is more beautiful and harmoni-
ous than it had been in life. Ugly, evil feelings pass away and disappear in the presence of death. Death, the greatest of evils is more
noble than life in this world. The beauty and charm of the past depends upon the ennobling influence of death. It is death that purifies
the past and puts upon it the seal of eternity. Death bring with it
not only dissolution but purification as well. Nothing perishable,
spoiled and corruptible can stand the test of death—only the eternal
can. Terrible as it is to admit it, the significance of life is bound up
with death and is only revealed in the face of death. Man's moral
worth is manifested in the test of death, which abounds in life itself.

But at the same time struggle with death in the name of eternal
life is man's main task. The fundamental principle of ethics may be
formulated as follows: act so as to conquer death and affirm everywhere, in everything and in relation to all, eternal and immortal life.
It is base to forget the death of a single living being and to be reconciled to it. The death of the least and most miserable creature is
unendurable, and if it is irremediable, the world cannot be accepted

and justified. All and everything must be raised to eternal life. This means that the principle of eternal being must be affirmed in relation to human beings, animals, plants and even inanimate things. Man must always and in everything be a giver of life and radiate creative vital energy. Love for all that lives, for every creature, rising above the love for abstract ideas, means struggle against death in the name of eternal life. Christ's love for the world and for man is victory over the powers of death and the gift of abundant life.

Asceticism means struggle with death and with the mortal elements within oneself. Struggle with death in the name of eternal life demands such an attitude to oneself and to other people as though both I and they were on the point of death. Such is the moral significance of death in the world. Conquer the low animal fear of death, but always have a spiritual fear of it, a holy terror before its mystery. It was death that first gave man the idea of the supernatural. Enemies of religion such as Epicurus thought they disproved it by showing that it originated in the fear of death. But they will never succeed in disproving the truth that in the fear of death, in the holy terror of it, man comes into touch with the deepest mystery of being and that death contains a revelation. The moral paradox of life and death can be expressed by a moral imperative: treat the living as though they were dying and the dead as though they were alive, i.e. always remember death as the mystery of life and always affirm eternal life both in life and in death. . . .

The philosophical idea of the natural immortality of the soul deduced from its substantiality leads nowhere. It ignores the fact of death and denies the tragedy of it. From the point of view of such a doctrine there is no need to struggle against death and corruption for the sake of eternal life. It is rationalistic metaphysic without any tragic element in it. Scholastic spiritualism is not a solution of the problem of death and immortality, but is a purely abstract and academic theory. In the same way idealism does not solve the problem or indeed does not even face it. The idealism of the German metaphysics has no place for personality, regards it merely as a function of the world-spirit or idea, and therefore the tragedy of death does not exist for it. Death is a tragedy only when there is an acute awareness of personality. It is only because personality is experienced as eternal and immortal that death is felt to be a tragedy. The death of that which is eternal and immortal in its meaning and destination is alone tragic; there is nothing tragic about the death of the temporal and the transitory. The death of personality in man is tragic because personality is God's eternal idea of him. It is unendurable that a complete personality containing the unity of all human powers and possibilities should die. Personality is not born of the father and the mother, it is created by God. There is no such thing as immortality of man as a natural being, born in the generic process; there is no natural immortality of his soul and body. In this world man is a mortal being. But he is conscious of the Divine image and likeness in him and feels that he belongs not only to the natural but to the spiritual world as well. Man regards himself, therefore, as belonging to eternity, and yearns for eternity. What is eternal and immortal in man is not the psychical or the physical element as such but the spiritual element, which, acting in the other two, constitutes personality and realizes the image and likeness of God. Man is immortal and eternal as a spiritual being belonging to the incorruptible world, but his spirituality is not a naturally given fact; man is a spiritual being in so far as he manifests himself as such, in so far as the spirit in him gains possession of the natural elements. . . . Natural immortality belongs to the species or to the race but not to the individual. Immortality has to be won by the person and involves struggle for personality.

Idealism affirms the immortality of the impersonal or the superpersonal spirit, of the idea and value, but not of the person. . . . There is an element of truth in this. It is true that it is not the natural, empirical man who is immortal and eternal but the spiritual, ideal, valuable element in him. The idealists, however, fail to recognize that this spiritual, ideal and valuable element forms an eternal personality and transmutes all man's powers for eternity; they are wrong in separating it out and abstracting it into an ideal heaven as an impersonal and non-human spirit, abandoning the rest of man to death and corruption. A realized and completed personality is immortal. But in the spiritual world there are no self-contained personalities, they are united with God, with other personalities and with the cosmos.

Materialists, positivists and followers of similar theories accept death, legitimize it, and at the same time try to forget about it, building up life on the graves. Their views show a lack of "memory of death" and are therefore shallow and commonplace. The theory of progress is entirely taken up with the future of the species, of the race, of the coming generations, and has no concern with personality and its destiny. Progress, like evolution, is absolutely impersonal. For the progressing species death is an unpleasant fact, but one that has nothing deep or tragic about it. The species has an immortality of its own. It is only for the person and from the personal point of view that death is tragic and significant. . . .

. . . . .

The ancient Hebrews were not familiar with the idea of personal immortality. We do not find it in the Bible. . . . The Jewish people were conscious of the immortality of their race but not of persons. Only in the book of Job there is awareness of personal destiny and its tragedy. It was not until the Hellenistic era, just before the coming of Christ, that the spiritual element in the Jewish religion came to be to some extent disentangled from the naturalistic, or, in other words, that personality was liberated and no longer dissolved in the collective, racial life. But the idea of immortality was truly revealed in the Greek and not in the Jewish thought. The development of that idea in Greece is very instructive. At first man was recognized as mortal. Gods were immortal, but not men. Immortality was an attribute of the divine and not of the human nature. It came to be ascribed to man in so far as the divine, superhuman element was manifested in him. Not ordinary men but demigods, heroes and demons were immortal. The Greeks knew well the heartrending grief caused by death. Greek tragedy and poetry is full of it. Man was resigned to inevitable death; he was denied immortality which the gods appropriated for themselves alone. The mortal human and the immortal divine principles were dissevered and became united only in heroes and supermen. Man descended into the subterranean realm of shadows and nothing could be sadder than his destiny. The melancholy, characteristic of the Greek and alien in this form to the Hebraic feeling for life, was rooted in the fact that the Greeks were able to reveal the human principle but not to connect it with the divine. It was the humanity of the Greeks that gave rise to the melancholy. And it was from the Greeks we heard the words that it was better for man not to be born. This is not the Indian metaphysical pessimism which denies man and regards the world as an illusion. It is an expression of human sadness for which both man and the world are real. Greeks were realists. But the Greek genius could not endure for ever the hiatus between the divine and the human world that doomed men to death and reserved immortality for the gods. A struggle for human immortality began.

The religious mythological consciousness of Greece recognized that although the divine principle was immortal and the human mortal, man's thought brought him into communion with the divine and enabled him to rise up to it and acquire it. This was the teaching of the Mysteries, of the Orphics and of Plato's philosophy. The human soul contains a divine element, but it must be freed from the power of matter; only then will man become immortal. Immortality means that the divine element of the soul forsakes the lower, material world and does not transfigure it. Immortality is ideal and spiritual. It belongs only to that which is immortal in its metaphysical nature, but is not won for elements that are mortal and corruptible, i.e. death and corruption are not conquered. According to the Orphic myth the soul descends into the sinful material world, but it must be freed from it and return to its spiritual home. That myth had a great influence upon Plato, as can be seen particularly from *Phaedo,* and is one of the most profound human myths. It is connected with the ancient doctrine of reincarnation—one of the few attempts to understand the destiny of the soul in its past and future. And Orphism does contain a certain eternal truth. Christianity teaches of resurrection, of the victory over death for every life, for all the created world, and in this it is infinitely superior to the Greek conception of immortality which dooms a considerable part of the world to death and corruption. But the Christian view does not make clear the mystery of the genesis of the soul. The presence of the eternal element in the soul means eternity not only in the future but in the past as well. That which has an origin in time cannot inherit eternity. If the human soul bears the image and likeness of God, if it is God's idea, it arises in eternity and not in time, in the spiritual and not in the natural world. But Christian consciousness can interpret this dynamically and not statically as Platonism does. In eternity, in the spiritual world, there goes on a struggle for personality, for the realization of God's idea. Our natural earthly life is but a moment in the process which takes place in the spiritual world. This leads to the recognition of pre-existence in the spiritual world, which does not by any means involve reincarnation on earth.

The fact that man belongs to the eternal spiritual world does not imply a natural immortality of the spirit. Our natural world is the arena of the struggle for eternity and immortality, i.e. of the struggle for personality. In this struggle the spirit must gain possession of the natural elements of the soul and body for their eternal life and resurrection. Christianity teaches not so much of natural immortality which does not presuppose any struggle as of resurrection which presupposes the struggle of spiritual gracious forces with the powers of death. Resurrection means spiritual victory over death, it leaves nothing to death and corruption, as abstract spiritualism does. The doctrine of resurrection recognizes the tragic fact of death and means victory over it—which is not to be found in any doctrines of immortality, whether Orphic or Platonic or theosophical. Christianity alone faces death, recognizes both its tragedy and its meaning, but at the same time refuses to reconcile itself to it and conquers it. Eternal and immortal life is possible for man not because it is natural to the human soul, but because Christ rose from the dead and conquered the deadly powers of the world—because in the cosmic miracle of the Resurrection meaning has triumphed over meaningless.

.   .   .   .   .

Both individual death and the death of the world inspire horror. There is a personal and a cosmic Apocalypse. . . . The Apocalypse is the revelation about the death of the cosmos, though death is not the last word of it. Not only the individual man is mortal, but also races, civilizations, mankind as a whole, all the world and all created things. It is remarkable that the anguish of this thought is even greater than that of the anticipation of personal death. The fate of the individual and of the world are closely interconnected and intertwined by thousands of bonds. Man suffers anguish not only because he is doomed to death but because all the world is doomed to it. During historical epochs which were not marked by apocalyptic moods a man's death was softened by the thought of the race continuing for ever and preserving the results of his life and activity. But Apocalypse is the end of all perspectives of racial or cosmic immortality; in it every creature and all the world is directly faced with the judgment of eternity. There can be no comfort in the thought that we shall be immortal in our children and that our work will last for ever, for the end is coming to all consolations that are in time. Apocalypse is a paradox of time and eternity that cannot be expressed in rational terms. The end of our world will come in time, in time as we know it. But it is also the end of time as we know it and therefore lies beyond its limits. . . . When the end comes there shall be no more time. And therefore we must paradoxically think of the end of the world both as in time and in eternity. The end of the world, like the end of each individual man, is an event both immanent and transcendent. Horror and anguish are caused by this incomprehensible combination of the transcendent and the immanent, the temporal and the eternal. For every one of us and for the world as a whole there comes a catastrophe, a jump across the abyss, a mysterious escape from time which takes place in time. The death of an individual is also a deliverance from time taking place in time. If our sinful temporal world as we know it were endless, this would be an evil nightmare, just like the endless continuation of an individual life. It would be a triumph of the meaningless. And the presentiment of the coming end calls forth, together with horror and anguish, hope and expectancy of the final revelation and triumph of meaning. Judgment and valuation of all that has happened in the world is the final revelation of meaning. The Last Judgment of individuals and of the world, interpreted in an inner sense, is nothing other than the discovery of meaning and the affirmation of qualities and values.

The paradox of time and eternity exists for the destiny of both the world and of the individual. Eternal and immortal life may be objectified and naturalized, and then it is spoken of as life in the world beyond. It appears as a natural realm of being though different from ours. Man enters it after death. But eternal and immortal life regarded from within and not objectified is essentially different in quality from the natural and even the supernatural existence. It is a spiritual life, in which eternity is attained while still in time. If man's existence were wholly taken up into the spirit and transmuted into spiritual life so that the spiritual principle gained final possession of the natural elements of the body and the soul, death as a natural fact would not take place at all. The transition to eternity would be accomplished, without the event which externally appears to us as death. Eternal life is revealed in time, it may unfold itself in every instant as an eternal present. Eternal life is not a future life but life in the present, life in the depths of an instant of time. In those depths time is torn asunder. It is therefore a mistake to expect eternity in the future, in an existence beyond the grave and to look forward to death in time in order to enter in to the divine eternal life. Strictly speaking, eternity will never come in the future—in the future there can only be a bad infinity. Only hell can be thought of in this way. Eternity and eternal life come not in the future but in a moment, i.e. they are a deliverance from time, and mean ceasing to project life into time. . . .

The personal and the cosmic Apocalypse bring to light our failure to fulfil eternal righteousness in life and are a triumph of righteousness in the dark world of sin. The death of the world and of individuals, of nations, civilizations, customs, historical forms of state and society, is a catastrophic reminder on the part of truth and righteousness of the fact that they have been distorted and not fulfilled. This is the meaning, too, of all great revolutions which indicate an Apocalypse within history, and the meaning of catastrophic events in the individual life. The Revelation about the coming of the antichrist and his kingdom shows that the Christian truth has not been fulfilled and that men are incapable and unwilling to realize it. Such is the law of spiritual life. If men do not freely realize the Kingdom of Christ, the kingdom of the antichrist will be brought about with necessity. Death comes to all life which does not fulfil the divine meaning and the divine truth. The triumph of irrationality is the revelation of meaning in the darkness of sin. Hence death, both cosmic and individual, is not merely a triumph of meaningless dark forces and a result of sin but also a triumph of meaning. It reminds man of the divine truth and does not allow unrighteousness to be eternal.

. . . . .

Ethics must be eschatological. The question of death and immortality is fundamental to a personalistic ethics and confronts us in every act and every expression of life. Insensitiveness to death and forgetfulness of it, so characteristic of the nineteenth and twentieth century ethics, mean insensitiveness to personality and to its eternal destiny, as well as insensitiveness to the destiny of the world as a whole. Strictly speaking, a system of ethics which does not make death its central problem has no value and is lacking in depth and earnestness. Although it deals with judgments and valuations, it forgets about the final judgment and valuation, i.e. about the Last Judgment. Ethics must be framed not with a prospect to happiness in an unending life here, but in view of an inevitable death and victory over death, of resurrection and eternal life. Creative ethics calls us not to the creation of temporary, transitory and corruptible goods and values which help us to forget death, the end, and the Last Judgment, but to the creation of eternal, permanent, immortal goods and values which further the victory of eternity and prepare man for the end.

Eschatological ethics does not by any means imply a passive renunciation of creative activity. Passive apocalyptic moods are a thing of the past, they are a sign of decadence and an escape from life. On the contrary, eschatological ethics based upon apocalyptic experience demands an unprecedented intensity of human creativeness and activity. We must not passively await in horror and anguish the impending end and the death of human personality and the world. Man is called actively to struggle with the deadly forces of evil and creatively to prepare for the Kingdom of God. Christ's second coming presupposes intense creative activity on our part, preparing both mankind and the world for the end. The end itself depends upon man's creative activity and is determined by the positive results of the cosmic process. We must not passively wait for the Kingdom of Christ, any more than for that of antichrist, but must actively and creatively struggle against the latter and prepare for the Kingdom of God which is taken by force.

To regard apocalyptic prophecies with passive resignation means to interpret them in a naturalistic sense, to rationalize them and deny the mysterious combination of Divine Providence and human freedom. It is equally wrong to take up a passive and fatalistic attitude to one's own death, to the death of personality, and regard it as predetermined natural fact. We must accept death freely and with an enlightened mind, and not rebel against it; but this free and enlightened acceptance of death is a creative activity of the spirit. There is a false activity which rebels against death and refuses to accept it. It leads to unendurable suffering. But there is also the true activity which is the victory of eternity over death. An active spirit does not really fear death—only a passive spirit does. An active spirit experiences an infinitely greater fear and terror than that of death—the fear of hell and eternal torments. It lives through its own eternity; death exists for it not inwardly but merely as an external fact. It experiences terror at the thought of its eternal destiny and of the judgment which is in eternity.

We come here upon a psychological paradox which to many people is unknown and incomprehensible. An active spirit which has a direct inward experience of being eternal and indestructible may, so far from fearing death, actually desire it and envy those who do not believe in immortality and are convinced that death is the end. It is a mistake to imagine that the so-called faith in immortality is always comforting and that those who have it are in a privileged and enviable position. Faith in immortality is a comfort and makes life less hard, but it is also a source of terror and of an overwhelming responsibility. Those who are convinced that there is no immortality know nothing of this responsibility. It would be more correct to say that the unbelievers rather than the believers make life easy for themselves. Unbelief in immortality is suspicious just because it is so easy and comforting; the unbelievers comfort themselves with the thought that in eternity there will be no judgment of meaning over their meaningless lives. The extreme, unendurable terror is not the terror of death but of judgment and of hell. It does not exist for the unbelievers, only the believers know it. A passive spirit seldom experiences it, but an active one experiences it with particular intensity, because it is apt to connect its destiny, and consequently judgment and the possibility of hell, with its own creative efforts. The problem of death inevitably leads to that of hell. Victory over death is not the last and final victory. Victory over death is too much concerned with time. . . . The final task, which ethics is bound to set us in the end, is creative liberation of all beings from the temporal and "eternal" torments of hell. If this task is not realized, the Kingdom of God cannot be realized either.

INDEX